W9-BBC-221

Exploring Jewish Tradition

Exploring Jewish Tradition

A Transliterated Guide to Everyday Practice and Observance

Rabbi Abraham B. Witty

Rachel J. Witty

Illustrated by Sara Shapiro

DOUBLEDAY New York London Toronto Sydney Auckland

PUBLISHED BY DOUBLEDAY
a division of Random House, Inc.
1540 Broadway, New York, New York 10036

DOUBLEDAY, and the portrayal of an anchor with a dolphin are
trademarks of Doubleday, a division of Random House, Inc.

Book design by Richard Oriolo

Library of Congress Cataloging-in-Publication Data

Witty, Abraham.
Exploring Jewish tradition: a transliterated guide to
everyday practice and observance / Abraham and Rachel Witty.
p. cm.
Includes index.
1. Judaism—Customs and practices. 2. Fasts and feasts—Judaism.
I. Witty, Rachel J. (Rachel Jean), 1943– II. Title.

BM700 .W58 2000
296—dc21
00-020637

ISBN 0-385-49454-8

Printed in the United States of America
March 2001
First Edition
1 2 3 4 5 6 7 8 9 10

Dedicated

to the Memory of Our Parents

Cantor Noah and Fannie Steinmetz Witty

החזן נח ב״ר יצחק הלוי ופייגע בת ר׳ שלמה

Rabbi Ephraim and Sarah Weinstein Solomon

הרב אפרים ב״ר יעקב ושרה בת ר׳ מאיר הכהן

The Glory of Children Is Their Parents

תפארת בנים אבותם

Proverbs 17:6
Mishnah, *Avot* 6:8

Contents

Foreword

MUST ADMIT THAT when I first picked up *Exploring Jewish Tradition: A Transliterated Guide to Everyday Practice and Observance,* I was a bit doubtful about the need for yet another introductory text. Surely, I thought, anyone whose interest in traditional Judaism had been awakened already had a plethora of guidebooks from which to choose. Yet, when I started to read this book, I was drawn into it, because it was clear that Rabbi and Mrs. Witty understood a pedagogical technique missed by many other authors.

People turning—or, to use the more conventional parlance, returning—to traditional Jewish practice often stand apart from those who have grown up in an observant home and community. They may come to the synagogue, but often get lost in the details of the service, not knowing what comes next. When entering into a discussion with traditional Jews, they may find themselves at a loss to understand the many Hebrew and Yiddish terms that permeate the conversation. This practical dilemma has been anticipated by the authors, who have taken great pains to foresee what might be unfamiliar. They constantly introduce traditional vocabulary and idioms and reinforce their usage by continually repeating them throughout the book. The use of transliterated terms, blessings, and prayers enables readers to become conversant in the language of Jewish tradition so they can achieve a level of comfort that allows for greater participation in the rituals and observances of traditional Judaism.

The authors provide a consecutive presentation of the Jewish year, including a ten-year calendar for all holidays and festivals. They explain all the major observances, including the weekly Sabbath, the High Holidays (*Rosh HaShanah* and *Yom Kippur*), the Pilgrimage Festivals (*Pesach, Shavuot,* and *Sukkot*), the various fast days commemorating the destruction of the Temple, and the so-called Minor Festivals (*Purim* and *Chanukah*). Believing that the modern State of Israel plays a significant part in contemporary Jewish religious life, the authors also include *Yom HaAtzma'ut* (Israel Independence Day) and *Yom Yerushalayim* (commemorating the reunification of Jerusalem during the 1967 Six Day War) as legitimate religious observances of the Jewish People. So too does a discussion of the Holocaust and the *Yom HaShoah* observances associated with it become part of their overall study, much as *Tishah b'Av* (commemorating the destruction of the Temples) is explained.

Once again, the discussion of the holidays reflects a desire to create a literate and comfortable reader. The biblical sources for the holidays and their historical backgrounds are presented, but ample space is also given to less well-known customs that sometimes go unmentioned in other books. For example, some authors get so involved with the philosophical underpinnings of the Sabbath that they forget that the reader will probably notice that the *Shabbat* table has two *challot* at every meal and will need that explained. We all should know why candles are lit each *Chanukah,* but what is the reason for eating fried foods like potato *latkes* and doughnuts on the holiday? Rabbi and Mrs. Witty have not only provided a broad overview of the various ceremonies and traditions, but have also woven together the specific details into a comprehensive presentation.

Indeed, the reader is slowly but assuredly introduced not only to traditional terms and observances, but to the classic texts of Judaism as well. An important strength of *Exploring Jewish Tradition* lies in its abundant use of displayed primary sources within the narrative. Any introduction to "the People of the Book" must include at least a sampling of the major Jewish texts, and these are amply represented in this volume. Frequent citations are drawn from the Torah, the Mishnah, the Talmud, the *Midrash,* and the commentaries of renowned rabbis and scholars.

But as important as all this is, even more important is the up-front way the authors spell out a proud, uncompromised, modern expression of Torah Judaism, one that incorporates traditional values and teachings and makes them relevant in today's world. They write in a friendly narrative style that reflects Rabbi Witty's expertise as a Jewish educator and Mrs. Witty's talent as a writer and wordsmith. Valuable for Jews exploring their own traditions, this volume also gives non-Jews the opportunity to gain insight into Jewish customs and ceremonies. The authors have also included pertinent personal recollections and warm, humorous reminiscences of Jewish life.

In doing all this, Rabbi and Mrs. Witty have created a work that is authentic and authoritative, one that teaches rather than preaches, and serves as a catalyst for further study and exploration of Jewish tradition.

JOEL B. WOLOWELSKY

Dr. Joel B. Wolowelsky is the associate editor of *Tradition,* a journal of Jewish thought published by the Rabbinical Council of America. He is also the author of *Women, Jewish Law, and Modernity,* published by KTAV Publishing House, Inc. Most recently, Dr. Wolowelsky served as coeditor of *Family Redeemed,* written by the late renowned Torah scholar, Rabbi Joseph B. Soloveitchik, and published by the Toras HoRav Foundation.

Preface

UR PRIMARY OBJECTIVE in writing *Exploring Jewish Tradition: A Transliterated Guide to Everyday Practice and Observance* was to fill the need for a *comprehensive introductory text* that would serve as a basic guide to the precepts and practices of Judaism. Readers will find an abundant source of knowledge—meticulously drawn from primary Jewish texts—from which they can distill the essence of Jewish tradition and learn how to live as Jews. We have attempted to blend the divine teachings of the Torah and the wisdom of the sages into easy-to-understand explanations and descriptions of everyday Jewish living.

Judaism is both a religious faith and a legally mandated lifestyle that was prescribed for the Jewish people by God in the Torah. From the perspective of decades of experience in the rabbinate and Jewish education, we are keenly aware that not every Jew knows how to "be Jewish," and we realize that many Jews simply never have had the opportunity to learn the essential teachings of Judaism.

Exploring Jewish Tradition provides a thorough review of the concepts and conventions of Judaism as it has been observed by Jewish men, women, and children for thousands of years. Recognizing that Jewish rites and celebrations are intricately bound up with the requirements of Jewish law, we discuss the many ceremonies, rituals, and customs within the context of the Jewish laws that prompted their observance.

Accordingly, we have presented the sources for Jewish practice—from the conduct of prayer to the observance of the Sabbath and festivals to the countless traditions associated with the life cycle of the Jewish people. (*Note:* Various editions of the Mishnah differ in the way individual paragraphs are numbered.) In an easy-to-follow narrative style, *Exploring Jewish Tradition* explains *how to live a Jewish life,* and includes concise directions and informative, captioned illustrations that enhance the text.

We are also aware that many misconceptions about Judaism continue to exist in the community at large. As society leans toward pluralism and a multiethnic culture, it is our secondary aim to provide clear, accurate information to non-Jews as well. We believe it is important for those of other faiths to gain a better understanding of the Jewish experience in order to foster improved relationships among people of every faith. It is our hope that this book will help accomplish that as well.

About the Book

In ten chapters, hundreds of transliterated terms are linked together in a friendly narrative. Each chapter builds on the one before, providing continuity throughout the text. Readers do not need to know what words to look up, because the words that "go together" are presented together in the appropriate chapter context.

Chapter 1 begins with the definition of Torah; successive chapters continue with an extensive discussion of synagogue ritual, prayer, the Jewish calendar, the Sabbath, the High Holidays, the Pilgrimage Festivals, the minor festivals, the Jewish life cycle, and special words and phrases used in the day-to-day Jewish experience.

Chapters are divided into numbered sections, which provide easy-to-find cross-references throughout the text. At the end of each chapter, Word Works, a cross-referenced alphabetical listing of all the new words in the chapter, is provided. The book concludes with a complete vocabulary index (all the Word Works) and a subject index, called Sum and Substance.

Judaism is the heritage of all Jews. Accordingly, we have assiduously attempted to avoid gender-specific language and awkward constructions like he/she or him/her, even though certain precepts in Judaism pertain more to one gender than the other. We have indicated in the text where such distinctions occur. Our book reflects the Ashkenazic tradition almost exclusively.

About Hebrew, Aramaic, and Yiddish Words

No knowledge of Hebrew, Aramaic, or Yiddish is required to use this book successfully. We have attempted to use the pronunciation of modern Hebrew throughout the book. A guideline to the pronunciation of transliterated words is presented below to assist readers. In the Hebrew alphabet, which is also used in Aramaic and Yiddish, there are no capital or lowercase letters. However, we have retained the usual capitalization rules of English for the Hebrew/Aramaic/Yiddish equivalents; for example, books of the Bible, tractates of the Mishnah and Talmud, months, book and song titles, names of major prayers, and the like.

When a vocabulary word appears in the book for the first time, it is highlighted in boldface. Some words, however, are highlighted this way in more than one chapter. For example, the names of all the holidays appear in boldface when they are first introduced in Chapter 4, "The Jewish Calendar." The name of each holiday is again highlighted in boldface when it appears for the first time in its respective chapter. Thereafter, it is presented in lightface.

Most transliterated words appear in italics, indicating their foreign origin. However, several Hebrew, Aramaic, and Yiddish words appear in standard English dictionaries, and we have not italicized such words: for example, Torah, Mishnah, Talmud, Gemara, kosher. We have not italicized names or acronyms for people, even when they are obviously from the Hebrew. We have also retained the conventional English spelling for the names of Ruth and Esther, rather than transliterating them (as *Root* and *Ester*), even when used in association with another Hebrew word—for example, *Megillat Ruth,* Book of Ruth; *Megillat Esther,* Scroll of Esther.

Judaism, like other faiths, uses anthropomorphisms to describe the indescribable: God. We have used capitalization whenever we refer to Him specifically; for all Names of God and pronouns that refer to God; and in some cases, for humanlike characteristics that we attribute to God because of our inability to truly describe Him.

About Transliteration

Transliteration is an attempt to represent the sounds of one language in the symbols of another. We have not used the scholarly style found in many works. Rather, we tried to keep it simple. We offer the following guidelines:

a	as in f**a**ther: e.g., *shalom, Haggadah*
ai	as in Haw**ai**i: e.g., *Drai Vochen* also, as in s**ai**l: e.g., *Aishet Chayil, aish, B'nai Yisrael* (conventional transliteration)
aw	as in l**aw**ful: Used only for the word *kawdosh*
e	as in d**e**but: e.g., *seder, Kohen* also, frequently as in t**e**ll: e.g., *etrog, lechem mishneh* also, frequently as short vocalization between consonants, as in t**e**rrific: e.g., *tzedakah, megillah*
ei	as in n**ei**ghbor; often at the end of a transliterated word: e.g., *borei, Sifrei Torah*
i	as in s**i**ng: e.g., *mitzvah, Yom Kippur, Midrash* also, occasionally as in m**i**racle: e.g., *nisht, kittel*
o	as in h**o**me: e.g., Torah, *Kol Nidrei, shofar* also, occasionally as in f**o**r: e.g., *Drai Vochen, Kodashim*
u	as in r**u**le: e.g., Talmud, *Luchot, tikkun olam* also, as in p**u**t: e.g., *musmach, Gut Voch* (Yiddish) also, as in **u**s: e.g., *lukshen* (Yiddish)
ch	as in Ba**ch** (guttural sound): e.g., *Chanukah, halachah* Exception: in Yiddish, as in **ch**oice: e.g., *cholent, bencher, bench, benchen* but also, in Yiddish as a guttural sound: e.g., *licht, duchen*
'	indicates a pause or break between two adjacent sounds: vowel and vowel: e.g., *Yom HaAtzma'ut;* consonant and consonant: e.g., *Sh'nat Shemittah;* vowel followed by consonant: e.g., *she'hecheyanu;* consonant followed by vowel: e.g., *Tishah b'Av*
h	used at the end of transliterated term when the Hebrew word ends in the letter *hei*

Acknowledgments

Writing this book and seeing it through to publication has been an adventure, not unlike that of bringing a child into the world. Just as parents-to-be anticipate the birth of their baby, we looked forward eagerly to the arrival of this book. There are so many people to thank for sharing our joy and pride.

Gareth Esersky, our agent at the Carol Mann Agency, whose professional insights guided us from the very beginning.

At Doubleday: Eric Major, Vice-President, Director of Religious Publishing, and Michael Palgon, Deputy Publisher Doubleday Broadway, whose initial enthusiasm for our project carried us forward; Trace Murphy, Senior Editor for Religious Publishing, whose steady hand and calm, reassuring manner helped us over several major hurdles; Siobhan Dunn, Trace's assistant, who took care of so many of the small details for us; Rebecca Holland, Publishing Manager; Maria Carella, Design Director; Dana Treglia, Design Supervisor; and Richard Oriolo, Interior Designer, who all worked with us to create a design we love; Lorraine Hyland, Senior Production Manager, who navigated the book through editing and proofreading; Dean Curtis and Maureen Cullen, Copy Editors, who gently fine tuned our manuscript. We are also proud of the outstanding job done by our compositor, Folio Graphics, who handled thousands of transliterated words with near perfection.

We are grateful to our extraordinarily talented illustrator, Sara Shapiro, whose work truly illuminates our text. Her fervent appreciation of Jewish tradition can be seen in every stroke of her pen and brush. We can honestly say that every minute we spent with her was a joy. We note with appreciation the efforts of Rabbi Benjamin Yudin and Rabbi Shmuel Schneid for their contributions to the preparation of the text. We thank Tuvia Rotberg of Tuvia's Seforim Judaica and Gifts in Monsey, New York, David Sternfeld of Judaica Place in Brooklyn, New York, and Meyer Knobloch of M.K. Antiquarian Books in New Square, New York, for their assistance. We are deeply indebted to Dr. Joel B. Wolowelsky for his professional review of our manuscript. A respected editor, writer, and educator, he honors us with his kind words in the Foreword.

On a personal note, we are grateful to many of our friends, but especially to Dr. David and Ilene Jacobowitz, whose love, loyalty, and sense of humor have sustained us for many years; Raphael and Natalie Schain, whose affection we shall always cherish; Rabbi Shmuel and Pessie Rosen, for their interest and encouragement, and Yitta Halberstam Mandelbaum and the members of EMUNAH Women, Division of Writers and Editors, for their inspiration.

We also acknowledge the unwavering support of our family, including our sister, Gail A. Kalter, whose "detective work" helped make this book possible; our brother, Rabbi Yitzchak Witty, and our nephew, Rabbi Noach Witty, Esq., who consulted with us on many questions of Jewish law and custom. Finally, we sincerely thank our children whose love, devotion, and excitement have always kept us going; Elaine, who made many cogent suggestions about the development of the book proposal; her organizational skills are reflected in the structure of the text; Emily, who read the entire first draft of the manuscript—often correcting it on the subway as she commuted to work; her reflections, based in large measure on her love of and commitment to Jewish tradition and learning, provided us with a young educator's perspective; and Allison, whose love of life, keen appreciation for the funny side of things, and genuine wit (to say nothing of her proofreading skills) have nourished our souls. May they all be as proud of us as we are of them.

A Final Word

Three times we find in the Talmud:

> **The study of Torah brings one to the performance of the commandments.**
>
> **—*Megillah* 27a**
>
> **—*Bava Kamma* 17a**
>
> **—*Kiddushin* 40b**

There is no more important endeavor for the Jewish people. It is our hope that *Exploring Jewish Tradition* will help all Jews discover their heritage and observe the sacred teachings and traditions of Judaism.

RABBI ABRAHAM B. WITTY

RACHEL J. WITTY

October 2000

Tishrei 5761

Exploring Jewish Tradition

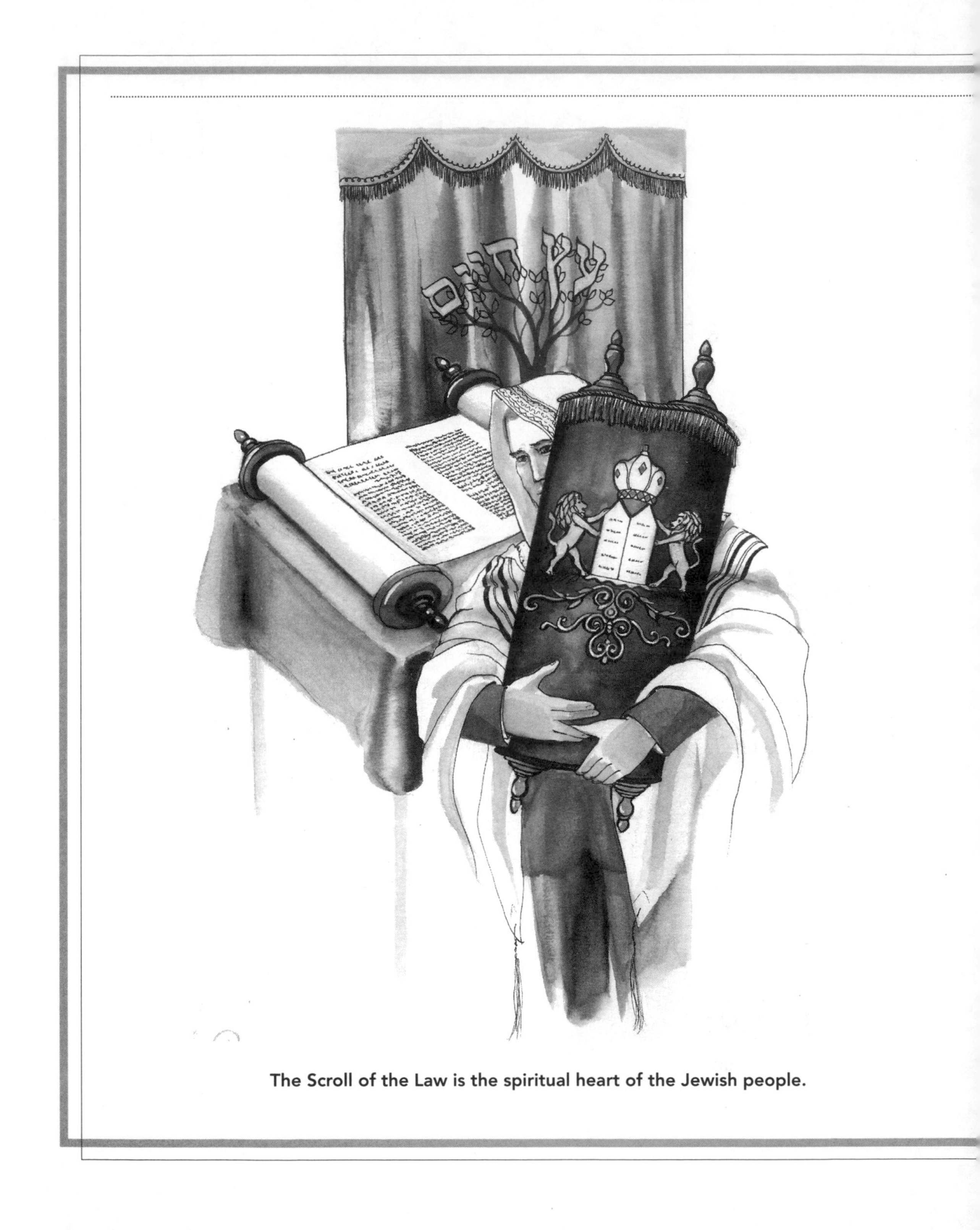

The Scroll of the Law is the spiritual heart of the Jewish people.

1

What Is Torah?

UDAISM DATES BACK almost four thousand years to the time of the patriarch Abraham and his wife, Sarah. By virtue of their recognition and belief in the existence of the One God—in contrast to the polytheism that surrounded them—they are recognized as the first Jews.

Judaism is more than a faith. It encompasses religious laws; sacred rituals and age-old customs; thousands of years of uninterrupted history; a spiritual, physical, and political attachment to the Jewish homeland; a commitment to social justice and righteousness; a deep love of learning; a dedication to the perpetuation of the Hebrew language; and varied cultural expressions in art, music, dance, and the theater.

While other faiths can be characterized in similar terms, Judaism is unique in combining: (1) the belief in the One God; (2) the notion of a people, both chosen and privileged to serve God; and (3) the acceptance of the Torah as the divine and eternal master plan for Jewish life.

Jewish history began when God made a covenant with Abraham, promising him that he would be the father of multitudes.

> **And I will make your seed like the dust of the earth;**
> **that if a man can count the dust of the earth,**
> **[so] shall your seed also be numbered.**
>
> **—Genesis 13:16**

and

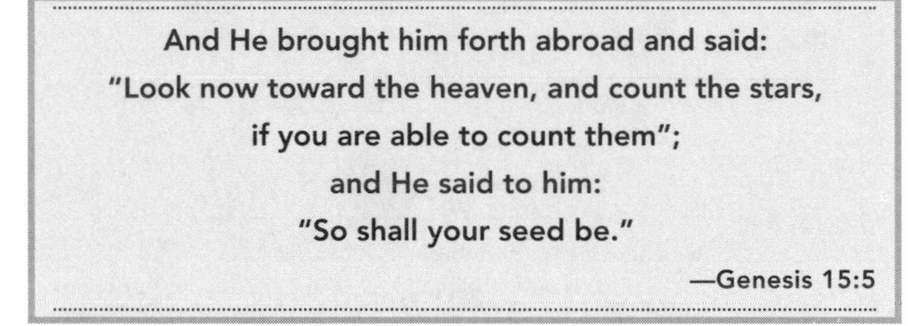

> **And He brought him forth abroad and said:**
> **"Look now toward the heaven, and count the stars,**
> **if you are able to count them";**
> **and He said to him:**
> **"So shall your seed be."**
>
> **—Genesis 15:5**

God changed Abraham and Sarah's names, reflecting His blessing.

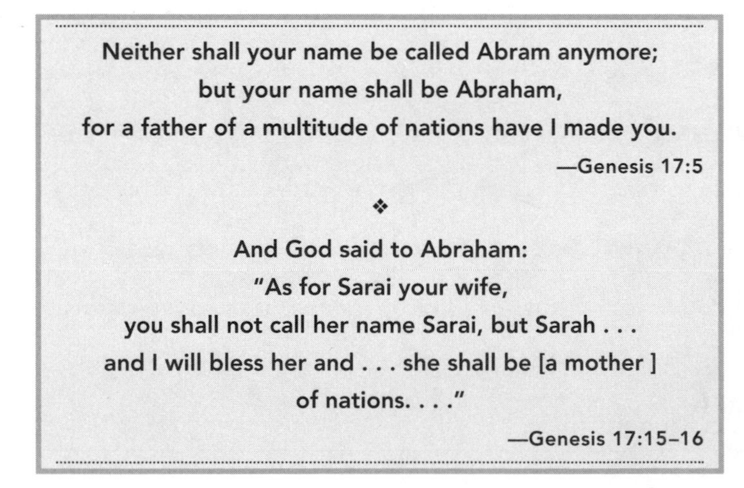

> **Neither shall your name be called Abram anymore;**
> **but your name shall be Abraham,**
> **for a father of a multitude of nations have I made you.**
>
> **—Genesis 17:5**
>
> ❖
>
> **And God said to Abraham:**
> **"As for Sarai your wife,**
> **you shall not call her name Sarai, but Sarah . . .**
> **and I will bless her and . . . she shall be [a mother]**
> **of nations. . . ."**
>
> **—Genesis 17:15–16**

It would be almost five hundred years later before the Torah was given to Moses and, in turn, to the Jewish people; but Abraham was taught the Torah by God Himself, and he observed all its precepts. That was the beginning of the Jewish faith.

In this book, we will attempt to set down in a meaningful order, and within the context of the major concepts of Judaism, a basic vocabulary of the Jewish people. We begin with the focal point of Jewish life: Torah.

1.1 Defining Torah

The word **Torah** embodies all the teachings of Judaism. It is a legal and an ethical system and a narrative account that begins with the Creation of the world and ends with the death of Moses almost three thousand years later. The Torah records only what is important for the Jewish people to know in perpetuity.

The Torah was divinely revealed by God to Moses in the wilderness on Mount Sinai. Thus, ***Hitgalut HaBorei,*** Divine Revelation of the Creator, is the everlasting bedrock of Judaism.

> **Moses received the Torah at Sinai,**
> **and handed it down to Joshua,**
> **and from Joshua to the Elders,**
> **and from the Elders to the Prophets,**
> **and the Prophets handed it down**
> **to the Men of the Great Assembly.**
>
> **—Ethics of the Fathers 1:1**

The Torah was given to the Israelites in the wilderness, as they traveled from Egypt to the Promised Land. According to the Torah, all Jewish souls, born and yet unborn, were present at Mount Sinai for the Divine Revelation, thereby obligating every generation to observe it. Moses spoke to the people of Israel and reminded them of God's words.

> **Not with you alone do I make this oath and this covenant;**
> **but with those that stand here with us this day . . .**
> **and also with those that are not here with us this day.**
>
> **—Deuteronomy 29:14**

Judaism teaches that other nations were offered the Torah, but each, in turn, refused it, because they could not accept certain of its precepts. Only the Jewish people accepted the Torah without hesitation.

In a state of great exaltation before God, the Jewish people stood in awe at the foot of Mount Sinai, afraid to approach.

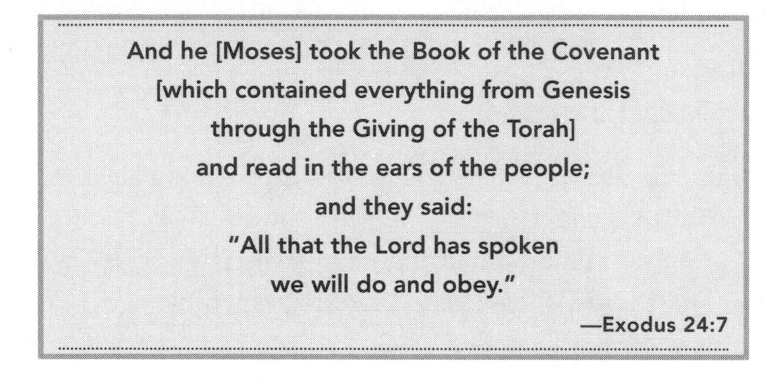

And he [Moses] took the Book of the Covenant
[which contained everything from Genesis
through the Giving of the Torah]
and read in the ears of the people;
and they said:
"All that the Lord has spoken
we will do and obey."

—Exodus 24:7

The word Torah encompasses both the Written Law, the ***Torah she'biChtav,*** and the Oral Law, the ***Torah she'b'al Peh.*** Knowledge of the Oral Law is required for understanding the Written Law, and both are essential for the proper observance of Judaism. In English, the Written Law is also called the masoretic text, meaning *transmitted* from one generation to the next. In Hebrew this never-ending process is called ***masorah,*** and it applies to both the Written and Oral Laws.

1.2 The Written Law

By itself, *the Torah* refers to the Written Law, that is, the Five Books of Moses, which comprise the first part of the ***Tanach,*** an acronym for **Torah,** the Five Books; ***Nevi'im,*** the Prophets; and ***Ketuvim,*** the Writings (see Section 1.2.2). The word *Torah,* used without the definite article, is much broader in scope. However, common English grammar often requires the use of the definite article, even when the broader term is intended.

1.2.1 The Septuagint

The Torah is also referred to as the Pentateuch, from the Greek, *penta-* plus *-teuch(os),* meaning five books. According to some sources, about the middle of the third century B.C.E. (Before the Common Era), a group of seventy-two Jewish scholars, six selected from each of the twelve tribes of Israel, set about to translate the first part of the Hebrew Bible into Greek for the Hellenized Jews living in Egypt. This translation is called the Septuagint, from the Greek word for *seventy,* a name that alludes to the number of scholars who prepared the translation. Although numerous errors and misinterpretations ultimately seeped into the various versions of the translation, the value of the Septuagint (which also contained non-Jewish works) lies in the transliterated guide it provides to the ancient pronunciation of the Hebrew names and words. Eventually, all the books of the Hebrew Bible were translated into Greek.

The English names in common usage, some of which are also derived from the Greek, refer to the contents of the text.

- Genesis — Origin: Creation of the world
- Exodus — Going out: Departure from Egypt
- Leviticus — Pertaining to Levites: Laws of Temple worship
- Numbers — Counting: Reference to the census
- Deuteronomy — Repetition: Review and interpretation

1.2.2 The Holy Scriptures

The *Tanach* is also called ***Kitvei HaKodesh,*** literally, the holy writings. An all-encompassing term, it is comprised of the Torah, the Prophets, and the Writings. In all, twenty-four books are included in the *Kitvei HaKodesh.*

Torah/Five Books of Moses

- Genesis
- Exodus
- Leviticus
- Numbers
- Deuteronomy

Nevi'im/Prophets

Earlier Prophets

- Joshua
- Judges
- 1 Samuel and II Samuel
- I Kings and II Kings

Latter Prophets

Major Prophetic Books

- Isaiah
- Jeremiah
- Ezekiel

Minor Prophetic Books (The twelve, called *Trei Asar,* are considered one book.)

- Hosea
- Joel
- Amos
- Obadiah
- Jonah
- Micah
- Nachum
- Habakkuk
- Zephaniah
- Haggai
- Zechariah
- Malachi

Ketuvim/Writings

- Psalms
- Proverbs
- Job
- The Five Scrolls (Each is considered a separate book.)
    - Song of Songs
    - Ruth
    - Lamentations
    - Ecclesiastes
    - Esther
- Daniel
- Ezra-Nehemiah
- I Chronicles and II Chronicles

These twenty-four volumes contain what is ordinarily referred to as the Hebrew Bible. We will discuss several of them in context in later chapters. Note that of the Five Scrolls, only Esther is read in the synagogue from a parchment scroll. It is not customary to read the others from a scroll, although they are available.

1.2.3 The Hebrew Text

The *Kitvei HaKodesh* are written in Hebrew. The corresponding Hebrew names of the Five Books are:

- Genesis ***Bereshit***
- Exodus ***Shemot***
- Leviticus ***Vayikra***
- Numbers ***Bamidbar***
- Deuteronomy ***Devarim***

It is important to understand that the narrative portions of the Torah are not meant to be a precise chronological account. A rule of biblical exegesis states: *There is no before and after in the Torah.* Everything in the Torah is there for only one reason: There is something to be learned from it.

Genesis/*Bereshit* (literally, in the beginning) begins with the account of Creation, and goes on to detail the day-to-day lives of the three patriarchs of Judaism: Abraham, Isaac, and Jacob; the four matriarchs: Sarah, Rebecca, Leah, and Rachel; and their families. It concludes with the death of Joseph, Jacob's eleventh son.

Exodus/*Shemot* (names) continues the narrative from the death of Joseph. It tells of the enslavement of the Israelites in Egypt, the birth of Moses, and the subsequent liberation of the Jewish people from Egyptian bondage. This second book of the Torah goes on to recount the miraculous events as the Israelites witness the Revelation of the Torah on Mount Sinai and become a united nation. It concludes with the establishment of the ***Mishkan,*** the portable Sanctuary, which was carried throughout the wilderness.

Leviticus/*Vayikra* (and He called) deals with the laws pertaining to the *Mishkan,* and subsequently the ***Bet HaMikdash,*** the Holy Temple, and enumerates the responsibilities of the ***Kohanim,*** the Priests (singular, ***Kohen***), and the ***Levi'im,*** the Levites (singular, ***Levi***), who officiated in the *Mishkan* and the Temple. It also includes such concepts as the observance of dietary regulations and the obligation to perform acts of charity and lovingkindness (see Sections 9.7.5, 10.13.1, and 10.13.2).

Numbers/*Bamidbar* (in the wilderness) relates the continuing events that transpire during the forty-year sojourn of the Israelites as they make their way through the wilderness.

Deuteronomy/*Devarim* (the words) includes the farewell discourses of Moses, as he reviews the events from the time of the Exodus; a repetition of the Ten Commandments; and an emphasis on the obligation to remain loyal to God. This fifth book of the Torah concludes with the death of Moses and the succession of Joshua as the leader of the Jewish people.

The Five Books of the Torah are collectively known as ***Chamishah Chumshei Torah,*** from the Hebrew word ***chamesh,*** five. According to the Oral Law (*Shabbat* 116a), the Torah was given in the form of seven scrolls. Genesis, Exodus, Leviticus, and Deuteronomy were each written in one scroll, while Numbers was divided into three. Later the seven were combined into five individual scrolls, one for each of the Five Books; and finally, the Five Books were combined into one scroll. However, the Torah text may be divided into five volumes for individual study. In book form, each Torah volume is called a ***Chumash.*** The usual Hebrew word for most other books is ***sefer***, while the term ***Sefer Torah*** refers to the Scroll of the Law, which contains the Five Books.

1.2.4 The Portions of the Torah

The Five Books are divided into fifty-four weekly ***sidrot,*** portions, which are read in consecutive order in the synagogue on the Sabbath (see Chapters 2, 3, and 5). Thus, over the course of the year, the entire *Sefer Torah* is read publicly. Genesis is divided into twelve *sidrot;* Exodus, eleven; Leviticus, ten; Numbers, ten; and Deuteronomy, eleven.

Each ***sidrah*** consists of seven ***parashiyot,*** sections, but the terms *sidrah* and ***parashah*** (singular) are often used interchangeably in common usage. The names of the *sidrot* are derived from the opening words.

The text of the Five Books was divided into chapters and verses in the sixteenth century, making it easier to locate and cite the text. These divisions, originally used only in the Latin translation of the Bible (the Vulgate), were, of necessity, applied to the Hebrew text in order to use a standard reference in religious disputations of the time.

The conventional divisions are:

- ***Sefer Bereshit*** (Genesis 1:1–50:26)
- ***Sefer Shemot*** (Exodus 1:1–40:38)
- ***Sefer Vayikra*** (Leviticus 1:1–27:34)
- ***Sefer Bamidbar*** (Numbers 1:1–36:13)
- ***Sefer Devarim*** (Deuteronomy 1:1–34:12)

The fifty-four weekly *sidrot*—also called the ***parashat hashavua*** (or more commonly pronounced *parshat hashavua*), the weekly *parashah*—and their respective chapters and verses are:

Sefer Bereshit **(Genesis 1:1–50:26)**

- *Parshat Bereshit* (1:1–6:8)
- *Parshat Noach* (6:9–11:32)
- *Parshat Lech Lecha* (12:1–17:27)
- *Parshat Vayera* (18:1–22:24)
- *Parshat Chayei Sarah* (23:1–25:18)
- *Parshat Toldot* (25:19–28:9)
- *Parshat Vayetzei* (28:10–32:3)
- *Parshat Vayishlach* (32:4–36:43)
- *Parshat Vayeshev* (37:1–40:23)

- *Parshat Mikketz* (41:1–44:17)
- *Parshat Vayigash* (44:18–47:27)
- *Parshat Vaychi* (47:28–50:26)

Sefer Shemot **(Exodus 1:1–40:38)**

- *Parshat Shemot* (1:1–6:1)
- *Parshat Va'era* (6:2–9:35)
- *Parshat Bo* (10:1–13:16)
- *Parshat Beshalach* (13:17–17:16)
- *Parshat Yitro* (18:1–20:23)
- *Parshat Mishpatim* (21:1–24:18)
- *Parshat Terumah* (25:1–27:19)
- *Parshat Tetzaveh* (27:20–30:10)
- *Parshat Ki Tissa* (30:11–34:35)
- *Parshat Vayakhel* (35:1–35:20)
- *Parshat Pekudei* (35:21–40:38)

Sefer Vayikra **(Leviticus 1:1–27:34)**

- *Parshat Vayikra* (1:1–5:26)
- *Parshat Tzav* (6:1–8:36)
- *Parshat Shemini* (9:1–11:47)
- *Parshat Tazria* (12:1–13:59)
- *Parshat Metzora* (14:1–15:33)
- *Parshat Acharei Mot* (16:1–18:30)
- *Parshat Kedoshim* (19:1–20:27)
- *Parshat Emor* (21:1–24:23)
- *Parshat Behar* (25:1–26:2)
- *Parshat Bechukotai* (26:3–27:34)

Sefer Bamidbar **(Numbers 1:1–36:13)**

- *Parshat Bamidbar* (1:1–4:20)
- *Parshat Naso* (4:21–7:89)
- *Parshat Beha'alot'cha* (8:1–12:16)
- *Parshat Shelach* (13:1–15:41)
- *Parshat Korach* (16:1–18:32)
- *Parshat Chukat* (19:1–22:1)
- *Parshat Balak* (22:2–25:9)
- *Parshat Pinchas* (25:10–30:1)
- *Parshat Matot* (30:2–32:42)
- *Parshat Masei* (33:1–36:13)

Sefer Devarim **(Deuteronomy 1:1–34:12)**

- *Parshat Devarim* (1:1–3:22)
- *Parshat Va'etchanan* (3:23–7:11)
- *Parshat Eikev* (7:12–11:25)
- *Parshat Re'ei* (11:26–16:17)
- *Parshat Shoftim* (16:18–21:9)
- *Parshat Ki Tetzei* (21:10–25:19)
- *Parshat Ki Tavo* (26:1–29:8)
- *Parshat Nitzavim* (29:9–30:20)
- *Parshat Vayelech* (31:1–30)
- *Parshat Ha'azinu* (32:1–52)
- *Parshat V'zot HaBerachah* (33:1–34:12)

In order to complete the reading of fifty-four *parashiyot* in one twelve-month lunar year of the Hebrew calendar (which is shorter than the solar year; see Chapter 4), more than one *parashah* is read at various times in the cycle. The following combinations occur:

- *Vayakhel/Pekudei*
- *Tazria/Metzora*
- *Acharei Mot/Kedoshim*
- *Behar/Bechukotai*
- *Chukat/Balak*
- *Matot/Masei*
- *Nitzavim/Vayelech*

When a leap year falls in the Hebrew calendar, some combinations are required. In addition, festival days may occur on the Sabbath, thereby accounting for any other breaks in the fifty-four-week schedule.

1.3 The Oral Law

There is only one Torah, but it is comprised of two complementary parts, and both were given by God at the same time on Mount Sinai. The Written Law is fixed and will always remain so, while the Oral Law continued to evolve over many centuries. The Written Law can be understood only in conjunction with the Oral Law, which itself is comprised of both divinely revealed principles and rabbinically ordained legislation. To be sure, the part that was divinely revealed at Sinai takes precedence over the rabbinic laws, even though the sages were divinely inspired to issue such regulations. *Torah she'b'al Peh* includes all the decrees, interpretations, and commentaries about *Torah she'biChtav* that the sages transmitted orally from one generation to the next.

Only after many centuries was the Oral Law committed to written form. This written form includes the legal discussions and decisions of the sages found in the **Mishnah,** which is in Hebrew, and in the **Gemara,** in Aramaic. Together they comprise the **Talmud,** a word derived from the root of the Hebrew verb that suggests both *teaching* and *learning.*

There are, in fact, two Talmuds, which represent the scholarly debates and conclusions of the sages in the two major centers of Jewish life: Babylonia and ancient Israel. They are known respectively as ***Talmud Bavli,*** the Babylonian Talmud, and ***Talmud Yerushalmi,*** the Jerusalem Talmud. Since the sixth century C.E. (Common Era), *Talmud Bavli* has been the authoritative source of Jewish scholarship for Jews of many countries. Its skillful use of language and its clarity reflect the favorable political and economic circumstances that existed for the Jewish community during the period of redaction. It is broader in scope than *Talmud Yerushalmi* and includes a vast body of knowledge dealing with all facets of human life, both secular and religious. In its broadest usage today, the word Talmud refers to the Babylonian Talmud.

1.3.1 The Mishnah

The Mishnah, which is the first portion of the Talmud, is second only to the Pentateuch in its importance as a compilation of Jewish law and ethical teachings. Written in Hebrew, it was edited under the leadership of Rabbi Judah the Prince and other sages known as the ***Tana'im.*** These scholars interpreted the Torah and taught the Oral Law for a period of some six generations. The organization of the Mishnah was completed about the end of the second century C.E. In each generation, these sages transmitted the teachings of the Torah to the people and linked them together in the eternal tradition of the *masorah* that began with Moses.

1.3.2 The Organization of the Mishnah

The Mishnah is composed of six ***sedarim*** (singular, ***seder***), orders, which contain the collective interpretations on ***halachah,*** both revealed and rabbinic law, and form the basis of the Talmud. By constant repetition, this scholarly body of work was transmitted from teacher to pupil, from generation to generation.

These *sedarim* are divided into sixty-three ***masechtot***, tractates. The Hebrew word suggests a web-like texture, perhaps alluding to the intricacies and complexities of the text. Each tractate is called a ***masechet***. The *masechtot* are divided into 524 chapters, called ***perakim*** (singular, ***perek***), which are further divided into paragraphs called ***mishnayot*** (singular, ***mishnah***). The Talmud itself is often referred to as ***Shas,*** an acronym derived from the Hebrew words ***shishah sedarim,*** the six orders of the Mishnah.

Talmud Bavli comments on only thirty-six of the sixty-three *masechtot* of the Mishnah, although in most instances the subject matter of the omitted tractates is included in the commentary of the others. *Talmud Yerushalmi* comments on thirty-nine *masechtot* of the Mishnah.

1.3.3 The Orders of the Mishnah

The six *sedarim* of the Mishnah are:

- ***Seder Zera'im***
- ***Seder Mo'ed***
- ***Seder Nashim***
- ***Seder Nezikin***
- ***Seder Kodashim***
- ***Seder Taharot***

Zera'im (seeds), which deals with laws pertaining to agriculture and includes discussions on the requirements of blessings, is comprised of eleven *masechtot.*

Mo'ed (festivals) discusses laws of observance of the Sabbath and festivals and is comprised of twelve *masechtot.*

Nashim (women) includes halachic requirements for marriage and divorce and is comprised of seven *masechtot.*

Nezikin (damages), which focuses on civil and penal laws governing such topics as property damage, personal injury, business practices, real estate transactions, and estate and inheritance matters, is comprised of ten *masechtot.*

Kodashim (sacred matters), deals with laws pertaining to Temple sacrifices, among other sacred rituals, and is comprised of eleven *masechtot.*

Taharot (purity) covers the requirements for ritual cleanliness and is comprised of twelve *masechtot.*

The six *sedarim* are sometimes referred to by the acronym ***Z'man Nakat,*** derived from the first letter of the names of each *seder:* ZMN NKT. It is a mnemonic device for remembering the names of the six orders.

1.3.4 The Tractates of the Mishnah

The sixty-three tractates are:

Seder Zera'im

- *Masechet Berachot*
- *Masechet Pe'ah*
- *Masechet Demai*
- *Masechet Kilayim*
- *Masechet Shevi'it*
- *Masechet Terumot*
- *Masechet Ma'aserot*
- *Masechet Ma'aser Sheni*
- *Masechet Challah*
- *Masechet Orlah*
- *Masechet Bikkurim*

Seder Mo'ed

- *Masechet Shabbat*
- *Masechet Eruvin*
- *Masechet Pesachim*
- *Masechet Shekalim*
- *Masechet Yoma*
- *Masechet Sukkah*
- *Masechet Beitzah*
- *Masechet Rosh HaShanah*
- *Masechet Ta'anit*
- *Masechet Megillah*
- *Masechet Mo'ed Katan*
- *Masechet Chagigah*

Seder Nashim

- *Masechet Yevamot*
- *Masechet Ketubot*
- *Masechet Nedarim*
- *Masechet Nazir*
- *Masechet Sotah*
- *Masechet Gittin*
- *Masechet Kiddushin*

Seder Nezikin

- *Masechet Bava Kamma*
- *Masechet Bava Metzia*
- *Masechet Bava Batra*
- *Masechet Sanhedrin*
- *Masechet Makkot*
- *Masechet Shevuot*
- *Masechet Eduyot*
- *Masechet Avodah Zarah*
- *Masechet Avot*
- *Masechet Horayot*

Seder Kodashim

- *Masechet Zevachim*
- *Masechet Menachot*
- *Masechet Chullin*
- *Masechet Bechorot*
- *Masechet Arachin*
- *Masechet Temurah*
- *Masechet Keritot*
- *Masechet Me'ilah*
- *Masechet Tamid*
- *Masechet Middot*
- *Masechet Kinnim*

Seder Taharot

- *Masechet Kelim*
- *Masechet Ahalot*
- *Masechet Nega'im*
- *Masechet Parah*
- *Masechet Taharot*
- *Masechet Mikva'ot*
- *Masechet Niddah*
- *Masechet Machshirin*
- *Masechet Zavim*
- *Masechet T'vul Yom*
- *Masechet Yadayim*
- *Masechet Uktzin*

1.3.5 The Gemara

The Gemara is the second part of the Talmud and includes clarifications and discussions of the first part, the Mishnah. The word Gemara, which is often used interchangeably with the word Talmud, is from the root of the Aramaic verb meaning *to learn.*

The Gemara is the Aramaic interpretation of the ***Amora'im***, the later sages who clarified and compiled the Talmud in a three-hundred-year period from the closing of the Mishnah until the end of the fifth century C.E., when the Gemara was closed to further emendation.

1.3.6 The Tractates of the Gemara

The Aramaic word ***masechta*** is equivalent to the Hebrew word *masechet* used earlier in discussing the tractates of the Mishnah. The thirty-six tractates of the Babylonian Talmud are:

- *Masechet Berachot*
- *Masechet Shabbat*
- *Masechet Eruvin*
- *Masechet Pesachim*
- *Masechet Rosh HaShanah*
- *Masechet Yoma*
- *Masechet Sukkah*
- *Masechet Shekalim*
- *Masechet Beitzah*
- *Masechet Ta'anit*
- *Masechet Megillah*
- *Masechet Mo'ed Katan*
- *Masechet Chagigah*
- *Masechet Yevamot*
- *Masechet Ketubot*
- *Masechet Nedarim*
- *Masechet Nazir*
- *Masechet Sotah*
- *Masechet Gittin*
- *Masechet Kiddushin*
- *Masechet Bava Kamma*
- *Masechet Bava Metzia*
- *Masechet Bava Batra*
- *Masechet Sanhedrin*
- *Masechet Shevuot*
- *Masechet Makkot*
- *Masechet Avodah Zarah*
- *Masechet Eduyot*
- *Masechet Horayot*
- *Masechet Zevachim*
- *Masechet Menachot*
- *Masechet Chullin*
- *Masechet Arachin*
- *Masechet Temurah*
- *Masechet Me'ilah*
- *Masechet Niddah*

Each tractate is divided into pages or leaves. Each leaf, called a ***daf,*** has two sides. Each side is called an ***amud.*** Sides are identified as (a) or (b), using the letters of the Hebrew alphabet (see Section 2.4.1). Each *daf* begins on a left-hand page and ends on a right-hand page.

The format of the Talmud is much larger than that of the Mishnah, because so many commentaries appear on the page with the talmudic text. The name of every *masechet* and the *daf* number appear in Hebrew letters at the top of every *amud,* and the talmudic text (in Aramaic) appears in a column of print in the center of the page. The mishnaic text (in Hebrew) is interwoven with the talmudic text that comments on it. Additional commentaries appear in outside columns, and footnotes, indicated by superior Hebrew letters in the talmudic text, and provide other cross-references.

1.3.7 How Mishnah and Gemara Differ

While the Mishnah comments only on *halachah,* the collective body of Jewish law, the Gemara includes discussions of *halachah* and ***aggadah***, narrations that deal with nonlegal issues. These narrative sections include proverbs and maxims that reflect moral and ethical situations, and even contain references to the sciences.

Thus, in the Gemara, *halachah* and *aggadah* are intertwined in the text. However, the preponderance of the text is concerned with *halachah.* The *aggadah* is meant to clarify the halachic discussions and inspire the faithful to greater observance of the precepts.

The linguistic style of the Talmud is distinguished by its brevity and precision of language. A single word often stands for a whole sentence. Without punctuation or other grammatical characteristics to indicate structure or enhance clarity, the talmudic text is challenging and requires diligence and concentration.

1.4 Jewish Law

The word *halachah* is derived from the root of the Hebrew verb meaning *to go.* In its most literal sense, *halachah* is the Torah's *way to go.* Jewish law is derived from the 613 precepts set forth in the Torah. However, in its broadest sense, *halachah* includes all biblical law, as well as the mishnaic and talmudic commentary, which rabbinic scholars added throughout the ages.

1.4.1 Biblical Law and Rabbinic Law

Biblical law, ***d'oraita,*** is from the Pentateuch; talmudic law, ***d'rabbanan,*** was set down by the sages according to the principles God gave to Moses. *Halachah* deals with every aspect of human behavior. It is a guide for ethical conduct and instructs the Jew to sanctify all actions, whether in public or in private, in interactions with other individuals, or in relationship with God.

The 613 biblical precepts, which are the basis for *halachah,* are known as the ***Taryag Mitzvot.*** *Taryag* is an acronym derived from the Hebrew letters *tav,* equivalent to 400; followed by *resh,* 200; followed by *yud,* 10; followed by *gimel,* 3, for a total of 613 (see Sections 2.4.2 and 2.4.3 for a discussion about the numerical values of the Hebrew alphabet).

1.4.2 What Is a *Mitzvah*?

A ***mitzvah*** (plural, ***mitzvot***) is more than a good deed. It is a divine imperative, an obligation incumbent upon every Jew. The *mitzvot* are contained in the Torah and are the essence of the *halachah.*

There are 248 positive commandments one is obligated to perform and 365 negative commandments, that is, prohibitions. Some of the commandments relate to sacrifices and Temple ritual and have not been practiced since the destruction of the Second Temple in 70 C.E. Other *mitzvot,* pertaining to certain laws of agriculture, can be performed only in the Land of Israel.

As we mentioned at the outset of this book, Torah is a legal system that sets forth the rules of conduct for every facet of Jewish life. This system provides a structure and discipline that is binding on every Jew, and performance of the *mitzvot* gives rise to a

Jew's spiritual unity with God. The *mitzvot* are the basis of the *halachah,* biblical and talmudic, as expounded upon by the ***meforshim,*** the scholarly commentators, whose interpretations make it possible for us to better grasp the meaning of the text.

1.4.3 Further Delineations of Jewish Law

Halachah, also called ***dinim*** (singular, ***din***), is comprised of ***chukim*** and ***mishpatim.*** A ***chok*** (singular) is a law for which we do not know the rationale. In the Torah, God instructed the Jewish people to observe the *chukim.* Many biblical passages begin with the words, "And God spoke." Thus, it is a matter of faith in a divine plan, even when our limited capacity makes it impossible to understand the intent of His directives. A ***mishpat,*** on the other hand, is a law that human beings can understand and fulfill as a purposeful obligation. Many *meforshim* do not try to explain the reasons for any of the *mitzvot,* although others do advocate defining their purpose in order to preclude mere mechanical observance.

1.4.4 The Code of Jewish Law

In the sixteenth century, Rabbi Joseph Karo (1488–1575) organized a comprehensive and orderly compilation of Jewish law called the ***Shulchan Aruch,*** literally, the *Prepared Table.* This work brought together the divergent opinions of the great sages into a unified code that set the standard for religious observance for Jews of Eastern European descent. A masterpiece of authoritative rulings, the *Shulchan Aruch* is to this day a practical guide to the observance of Jewish law and tradition.

The *Shulchan Aruch* is comprised of four parts: (1) ***Orach Chayim,*** which explains matters of religious conduct at home and in the synagogue; (2) ***Yoreh De'ah,*** which deals in part with permitted and forbidden things; (3) ***Even HaEzer,*** which discusses marriage and laws of family life; and (4) ***Choshen Mishpat,*** which covers matters of civil law.

Most editions of the *Shulchan Aruch* are printed with the compelling analyses and emendations of ten rabbinic commentators from the sixteenth, seventeenth, eighteenth, and nineteenth centuries.

1.5 The *Midrash*

The moral and ethical content of the biblical texts is examined in the ***Midrash.*** The two major divisions are ***Midrash Aggadah*** and ***Midrash Halachah.*** Some ***midrashim*** (interpretations) date back to the period of the *Tana'im*. Many more, however, were written in the third century C.E. The ***Midrash Rabbah,*** the *Large Midrash,* covers all Five Books of the Torah and the Five Scrolls found in the Writings, and originated at a variety of places and times. The biblical *midrashim* that are part of this collection are:

- *Bereshit Rabbah*
- *Shemot Rabbah*
- *Vayikra Rabbah*
- *Bamidbar Rabbah*
- *Devarim Rabbah*

A significant body of literature, the *Midrash* provides an additional source of ethical instruction, drawing on the biblical and talmudic texts.

1.6 The Essence of Being a Jew

What is the purpose of a Jew's life? This is an age-old question with two basic answers: (1) to get closer to God, and (2) to attain spiritual perfection. How is this done? By serving Him—which means observing the *mitzvot,* including the study of Torah, the recitation of prayers, and the performance of acts of lovingkindness.

1.6.1 The Study of Torah

The study of Torah is a daily requirement for all Jews. Its importance is paramount, as we learn from the Mishnah:

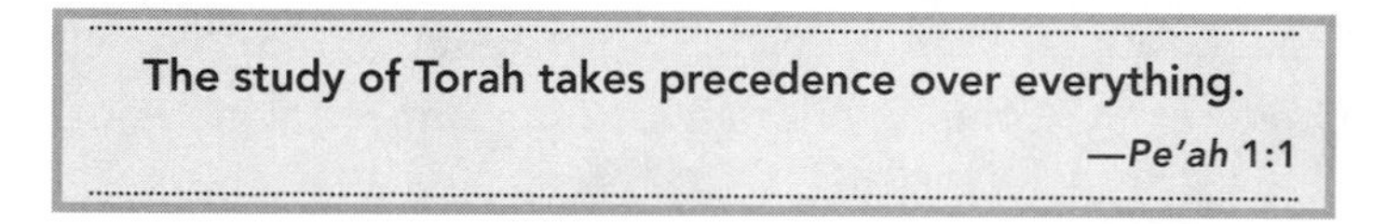
The study of Torah takes precedence over everything.

—*Pe'ah* 1:1

Torah, also referred to as the *tree of life,* is the very source of Jewish life. Again the Mishnah emphasizes this:

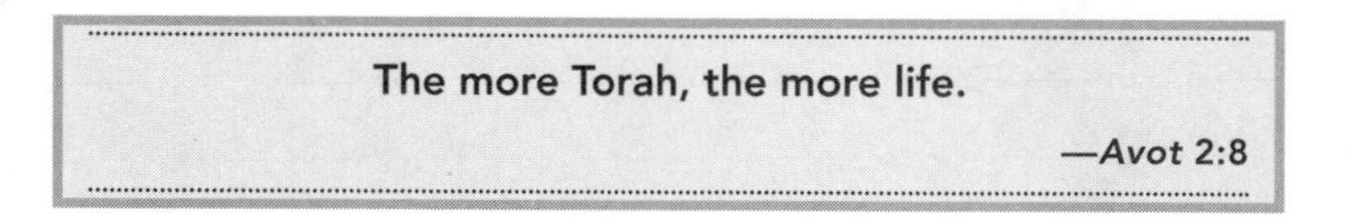
The more Torah, the more life.

—*Avot* 2:8

Many *meforshim,* on both the Torah and the Talmud, offer insight to the ***halachot*** (plural) and the duties inherent within them. To be sure, it can be daunting to commit ourselves to the study of Torah in order to learn how to observe the *mitzvot*. However, it is a duty a Jew cannot shirk. Although we are not commanded to learn everything, we are obligated to try.

In the Mishnah, Rabbi Tarfon teaches:

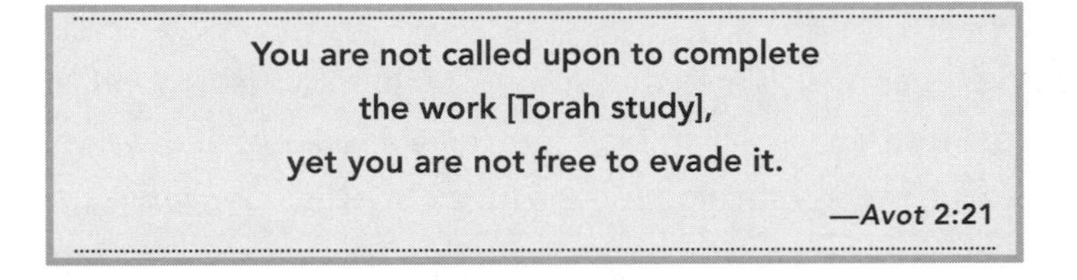
You are not called upon to complete
the work [Torah study],
yet you are not free to evade it.
***—Avot* 2:21**

In addition, the Mishnah often speaks of various personality types and encourages the fulfillment of ***midot***, characteristics of ethical conduct (*Avot* 5: 10–15, 19). Unless we study Torah, we cannot know how to perform *mitzvot*, and it is the observance of the precepts that brings us closer to God and to spiritual perfection.

1.6.2 Prayer

Torah study and prayer are often considered one and the same, in that they acknowledge a connection and a commitment to divine teachings. To whom do we pray? That answer is easy. Only to God, and without an intermediary. Other questions must also be explored.

- Why do we pray?
- What do we pray?
- How do we pray?
- When do we pray?
- Where do we pray?
- Who should pray?

We will discuss prayer in Chapter 3.

1.6.3 Acts of Lovingkindness

In the Mishnah, Simon the Just highlighted the three characteristics that distinguish the Jewish people in just a few words. He teaches:

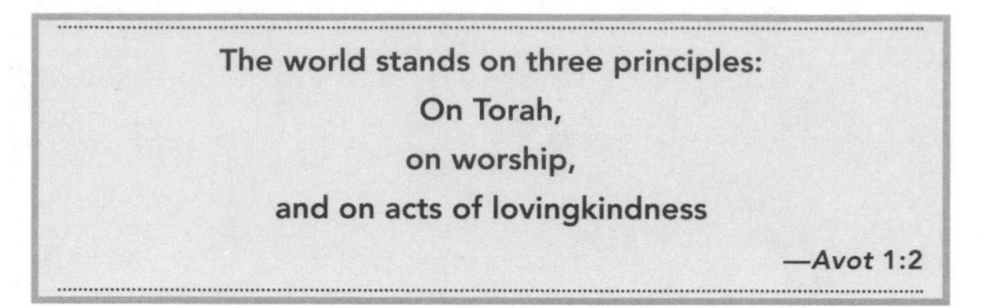

The world stands on three principles:
On Torah,
on worship,
and on acts of lovingkindness
—Avot 1:2

The Jewish people are obligated to study Torah, to worship God, and to take care of others, not just to draw closer to God, but for the sake of the world. ***Tikkun olam,*** perfecting the world, is a significant tenet of Judaism, which we will explore in Sections 3.12 and 10.13.

1.6.4 Accessibility to Torah

In ancient times, it was the responsibility of the sages to teach the people, because copies of the Torah, and later of the Mishnah and Gemara, were difficult and time-consuming to produce. However, with the advent of printing, this began to change.

Today, all of the *Kitvei HaKodesh* and the Talmud, along with numerous other texts that have become part of Jewish tradition, are available not only in printed form, but also on audiocassettes, videotapes, CDs, and on the Internet. They are available in English (among other languages), so no knowledge of Hebrew or Aramaic is required. You can decide whether to delve deeply or just take a shallow dip, and you can do it at your convenience.

Audiotapes and CDs make it possible to travel anywhere and learn Torah en route. Go online and subscribe to the *parashat hashavua,* and you will find it waiting for you every week in your e-mail, complete with interpretations and explanations. Jewish booksellers, ***mochrei sefarim,*** and Jewish book clubs provide the words of the sages and of contemporary scholars alike in easy-to-read, inexpensive formats. Most certainly, the publication of Judaica titles is also an important part of mainstream publishing. Whether you browse in the bookstores, order from catalogs, or surf the Net, you can find what you want and need.

1.7 Jewish Customs

The Hebrew word for custom is ***minhag.*** Many traditional practices are directly associated with the observance of the *mitzvot* themselves. Among the Jewish people, in all the lands of their dispersion, many customs grew up in connection with the fulfillment of these observances. Their significance is rooted in the affectionate link they provide to long-held traditions within families, even for Jews who are unfamiliar with the precepts.

According to tradition, Jews should follow the ***minhagim*** of the local Jewish community. We find several sources for this. In the *Midrash,* we note:

> **[If you come into a city,] guide yourself by its customs.**
>
> —*Bereshit Rabbah* 48:16

and in the Talmud,

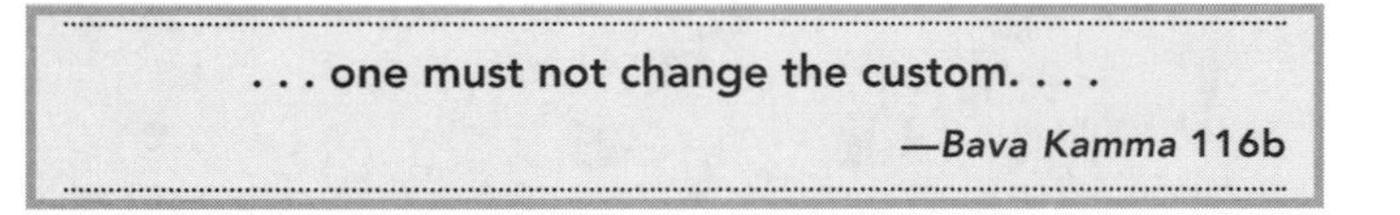

> **. . . one must not change the custom. . . .**
>
> —*Bava Kamma* 116b

In many instances, the observance of a *minhag* overrides that of a *halachah*; this is expressed by the phrase

> **A custom of Israel cancels a law.**
>
> —*Sofrim* 14:18

The Mishnah emphasizes this:

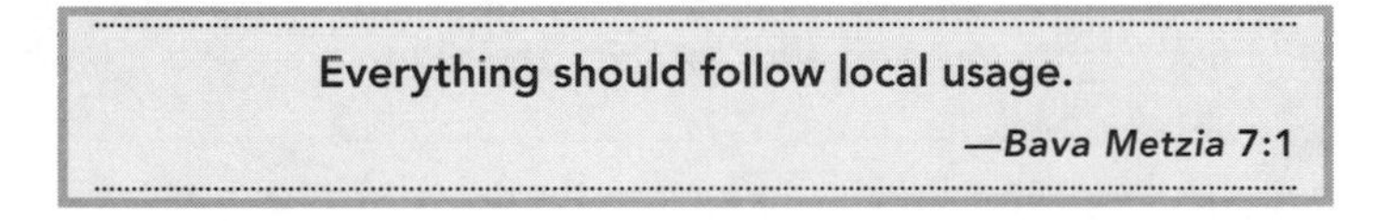

> **Everything should follow local usage.**
>
> —*Bava Metzia* 7:1

However, the Jewish community is limited by Jewish law in its ability to effect such changes in practice and must have the consent of the scholars of the time.

Specific customs observed within the context of the Sabbath, holidays and festivals, and activities of daily life will be discussed more fully in later chapters.

A Witty Remark!

... The Scriptures have inspired a variety of expression in Jewish life. Several years ago, I jotted down this recipe, which reminds us that everything can be found in the *Tanach*. Enjoy!

Scriptures Cake

INGREDIENTS	SOURCE
1/2 cup butter	Genesis 18:8
2 cups sugar	Jeremiah 6:20
2 tbs. honey	Deuteronomy 6:3
6 eggs	Deuteronomy 22:6
1 1/2 cups sifted flour	I Kings 5:2
2 tsp. baking powder	Amos 4:5
1 tbs. cinnamon	Song of Songs 4:14
1/2 tsp. cloves	Song of Songs 4:10
Pinch of salt	Leviticus 2:13
1/2 cup milk	Judges 4:19
1 cup chopped dried figs	Nachum 3:12
1 cup raisins	I Samuel 30:12
2 cups chopped almonds	Numbers 17:23

- Cream together butter, sugar, honey, and egg yolks.
- Sift dry ingredients and add alternately with milk to creamed mixture.
- Stir in fruits and nuts.
- Whip egg whites until stiff and fold into batter.
- Bake in greased 10-inch tube pan at 300 degrees for 2 hours.

LOOKING AHEAD! *In Chapter 2, we will discuss the history of the synagogue, the rituals associated with congregational observances, and the practices that characterize the observance of mitzvot in the Jewish house of learning and worship.*

The Holy Ark, which contains the *Sifrei Torah*, is the focal point of the synagogue.

2

The Synagogue

OLLOWING THE DIVINE Revelation of the Torah, God instructed Moses to speak to the Children of Israel.

> **Let them make Me a Sanctuary**
> **that I may dwell among them . . .**
> **and they shall make an Ark of acacia wood. . . .**
> —***Parshat Terumah,*** **Exodus 25:8, 10**

The *Mishkan* (also called the ***Ohel Mo'ed***), the portable Sanctuary, which housed the Ark of the Covenant, was the center of Jewish life in the wilderness. Wherever the Israelites wandered, the ***Luchot HaBrit***, Tablets of the Covenant, were carried with them in splendor. In great exactitude, God dictated the instructions for building this Sanctuary. *Sefer Shemot* contains lengthy descriptions of the sacred utensils and the vestments of the *Kohanim* that were to be used in worship.

With the establishment of the monarchy and the building of the First *Bet HaMikdash*, Jewish religious life was centered in the city of Jerusalem. It was there that the people gathered to worship God. The grandeur of the *Mishkan* was echoed in the splendor of the *Bet HaMikdash*. In time, the synagogue would fill the spiritual void left by the destruction of the two Holy Temples.

2.1 The Holy Temples

The First *Bet HaMikdash* was built in Jerusalem in 832 B.C.E., by King Solomon, the son of King David, who had succeeded Saul as the king of Israel. The requirements for building the Temple prohibited the use of any metal tools, because metal was associated with weapons of war. David had not been permitted to build the *Bet HaMikdash* because he had waged numerous battles and caused blood to be shed.

According to the Talmud, *Masechet Sotah* 48b and *Masechet Gittin* 68a, King Solomon called upon the skills of a special worm called the ***shamir***. The *shamir* was able to cut through the stones necessary for the construction of the Temple.

The Temple stood on the site where Abraham had offered his son Isaac as a sacrifice to God. The Temple included several buildings and several courts, all within the Great Court. The Temple building, also referred to as ***Bayit Rishon,*** literally, the First House, was fronted by a porch and two bronze columns at the entrance, symbolizing the two pillars—one of cloud, the other of fire—that guided the Israelites to the Promised Land.

> **And the Lord went before them—**
> **by day in a pillar of cloud to lead the way for them,**
> **and by night in a pillar of fire to light the way for them—**
> **that they might go by day and by night.**
> —*Parshat Beshalach*, Exodus 13:21

Solomon's Temple was renowned for its magnificence, some of its gold and silver acquired through commerce with distant lands and in tribute from foreign powers. Its cedar beams were brought from Lebanon, the bronze from the Jordan River valley, its massive stones from Solomon's own quarries.

The *Kohen Gadol* wore eight special garments, including a breastplate that contained twelve precious stones, one for each of the Twelve Tribes of Israel.

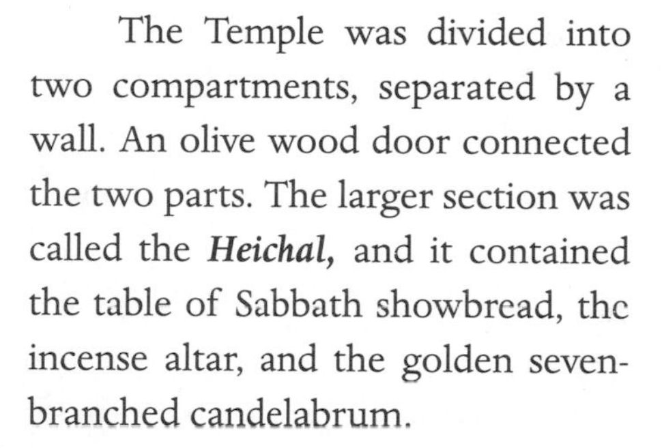

The Temple was divided into two compartments, separated by a wall. An olive wood door connected the two parts. The larger section was called the ***Heichal,*** and it contained the table of Sabbath showbread, the incense altar, and the golden seven-branched candelabrum.

The smaller section, called the ***D'vir,*** was the most sacred part of the Temple, the ***Kodesh HaKodashim,*** Holy of Holies, in which the Ark of the Covenant, adorned with golden cherubim, was placed. Throughout the structure, cedar and olive wood panels and carvings, some plated with gold, and a cypress floor glorified the setting. A Feast of Dedication was celebrated when the Ark was brought to the Temple. God's ***Shechinah,*** Holy Presence, resided in magnificence in Jerusalem.

The *Kohanim* were permitted to enter the *Heichal,* but only the High Priest, the ***Kohen Gadol,*** could enter the Holy of Holies, and then just once a year, on the Day of Atonement (see Sections 6.4 and 6.28.1). The *Kohen Gadol* wore eight special garments whenever he officiated in the Temple. Chapter 28 of *Sefer Shemot* details the vestments and the ornaments that adorned them:

1. ***ketonet*** — long shirt
2. ***michnasayim*** — short pants
3. ***mitznefet*** — hat shaped like a turban and flattened at the top
4. ***avnet*** — belt (tied over long shirt)
5. ***choshen mishpat*** — breastplate of judgment
6. ***efod*** — apron
7. ***me'il*** — coat
8. ***tzitz*** — headband

Other *Kohanim* wore the *ketonet, michnasayim,* and *avnet,* like the *Kohen Gadol.* However, they wore a pointed hat, called a ***migba'at.*** One of Judaism's greatest philosophers, Rabbi Moshe ben Maimon (1135–1204), known both as Maimonides and by the acronym Rambam, comments in the eighth book of his monumental code of Jewish law and ethics, ***Mishneh Torah*** (Book of Service, Laws of the *Bet HaMikdash* 7:14), that none of the *Kohanim* wore shoes according to God's command, so that their feet came into contact with the sacred floor of the *Mishkan,* and later, the *Bet HaMikdash.*

The implements of the Temple service were stored in other chambers of the *Bet HaMikdash.* The people brought their ***korbanot,*** sacrifices, to the Temple, where they were offered on the bronze altar by the *Kohanim* on behalf of the worshippers.

Solomon's Temple stood until 586 B.C.E., when it was destroyed by Nebuchadnezzar, king of Babylonia. ***Churban Bayit Rishon,*** the Destruction of the First Temple, marked the beginning of the Babylonian exile, a time when Jews were no longer able to bring *korbanot* to Jerusalem.

The Second *Bet HaMikdash,* ***Bayit Sheni***, was rebuilt on the same site in Jerusalem seventy years later by the exiles who returned to ***Eretz Yisrael*** under the leadership of Ezra the Scribe. It was further expanded during the reign of King Herod the Great in 20 B.C.E. The Second Temple stood until ***Churban Bayit Sheni,*** when it was burned to the ground by the Roman Empire in 70 C.E.

Part of the wall that enclosed Herod's Temple still stands today. ***HaKotel HaMa'aravi,*** the Western Wall, is considered sacred and is visited by Jews from all over the world. Prayers are often written on ***k'vitlach*** (singular, ***k'vitel***), small pieces of paper that are stuck into the crevices between the stones. *HaKotel HaMa'aravi* (or simply, the ***Kotel***), also known as the Wailing Wall, is a holy site where urgent prayers and tearful cries have been heard for centuries.

2.2 The Synagogue

Following the destruction of the First Temple, and during the subsequent exile of the Jewish people to Babylonia, the ***bet kenesset,*** house of assembly, became the focal point of the Jewish community. The synagogue, in essence, became a ***mikdash m'at,*** a miniature sanctuary, where religious and spiritual life flourished. By the time the Second Temple was destroyed by the Romans, some one thousand synagogues had been established outside *Eretz Yisrael,* and hundreds more in Jerusalem alone.

Today, as in ancient times, the synagogue serves as a ***bet tefillah,*** house of prayer, a place where Jews gather to worship. The Talmud expounds on the relative merit of praying with a congregation in contrast to praying in private. Jews are exhorted not to separate themselves from the community. As Hillel says in the Mishnah:

> **Do not distance yourself from the community.**
>
> —*Avot* 2:5

The Talmud, *Masechet Berachot* 6b, also states that God Himself inquires if a Jew, who has come to the synagogue regularly to pray, fails to come even one day.

In addition to its function as a house of assembly and a house of prayer, the synagogue is called a ***bet midrash,*** a house of learning, a place to study Torah. Jewish tradition has always made the study of Torah synonymous with worship, for Torah study takes priority over all other *mitzvot* (see Section 1.6.1).

In the ***batei midrash*** (plural) of today, whether in the synagogue or in educational institutions, this is still true. A student often joins with a ***chavruta,*** a study partner and friend, and each challenges the other, as they seek to understand the intricacies of the *Kitvei HaKodesh.*

Thus, throughout Jewish history, the synagogue has served many purposes: *bet kenesset, bet tefillah, bet midrash.* However, it is not necessary to make precise distinctions between the various aspects of the synagogue's function. As the spiritual home of the Jewish community, it was and continues to be a place for divine worship, Torah study, and communal gatherings.

2.3 Inside the Synagogue

A synagogue, which is referred to as a ***shul*** in Yiddish, may be a simple structure, or it may be an elaborate edifice. It is not so much the architecture that defines a building as a synagogue. Rather, it is the function it serves, the respect attached to it, and the religious objects found there.

2.3.1 The Holy Ark

Inside the synagogue, the ***Aron HaKodesh,*** the Holy Ark, which is the repository for the ***Sifrei Torah,*** the Scrolls of the Law, is of primary importance. Accordingly, the congregation rises whenever the Ark is opened. Symbolic of the Ark of the Covenant, the *Aron HaKodesh* is elevated on a platform and positioned against the eastern wall of the synagogue, thereby allowing worshippers to turn toward Jerusalem in prayer. (Those living east of Jerusalem face west.)

In the days of Ezra the Scribe, the ***bimah,*** pulpit, stood in the middle of the synagogue, and Torah was taught in the midst of the congregation. Even today, traditional synagogues have a raised platform where the Ark stands and a center *bimah* for ***Kriat HaTorah,*** the public Reading of the Law. In many synagogues, however, the word *bimah* refers to the platform in front of the Ark. A ***shulchan,*** table, stands in the center of the *bimah* and services are conducted from it. The *Sifrei Torah* are placed on it during *Kriat HaTorah.*

Because it is a reminder of the biblical Ark of the Covenant, which housed the *Luchot HaBrit,* the *Aron HaKodesh* is often adorned at the top with a carving or painting of the Ten Commandments. A velvet curtain, the ***parochet,*** is suspended in front of the doors of the Holy Ark. The *parochet* is customarily made of red, blue, or gold velvet. Richly embroidered with gold and silver threads, it often depicts figures of lions, an allusion to the mishnaic teaching of Yehudah ben Tema:

> **Be bold as a leopard, light as an eagle,**
> **swift as a deer, and strong as a lion**
> **to do the will of your Father in heaven.**
>
> **—Avot 5:23**

Often, the *parochet* is embroidered with the names of individuals who have donated it to the synagogue to honor or perpetuate the memory of a loved one.

2.3.2 The Eternal Light

Suspended above and in front of the *Aron HaKodesh* is the ***ner tamid,*** the eternal light. The use of a perpetual light is based on passages in Exodus and Leviticus in which the Jewish people were commanded to keep a lamp burning in the *Mishkan,* as they carried it with them in the wilderness. Twice God instructed Moses:

> **And you [Moses] shall command the Children of Israel**
> **to bring you pure olive oil . . .**
> **to make a lamp burn continually.**
>
> **—*Parshat Tetzaveh,* Exodus 27:20**

and

> **Command the Children of Israel**
> **to bring you pure olive oil . . .**
> **to make a lamp burn continually.**
>
> **—*Parshat Emor,* Leviticus 24:2**

From these passages, we can understand why the *ner tamid* is a prominent feature of the synagogue.

Originally, the *ner tamid* was an oil-burning lamp. Today, for the sake of convenience and safety, an electric light is used.

2.3.3 The *Mechitzah*

According to several sources, the *Bet HaMikdash* of King Solomon was one of several buildings within the sacred Great Court. This Court enclosed several other courts: The Court of Israel was for male worshippers, the Court of Priests for the priests. Adjoining the Court of Israel, was the Court of Women. The women's section is referred to in the Mishnah as the ***Ezrat Nashim.***

The practice of separating men and women during religious services was instituted to prevent any frivolity from taking place during sacred occasions in the Temple. In fact, the Talmud points out that mere separation is not deemed sufficient to prevent frivolous contact between men and women. Thus, the women were required to worship in a section that was physically set above that of the men, so the men could not see the women.

Even today, traditional synagogues are often built with a balcony to the rear or sides of the synagogue for the *Ezrat Nashim.* If a balcony is not built, the synagogue continues to maintain this separation of men and women during worship by the use of a physical partition called a ***mechitzah.*** The requirements for the construction and height of the *mechitzah* are delineated by the *halachah.* In all cases, a qualified rabbi should be consulted.

2.4 The Torah Scroll

The Torah is written in Hebrew, the ***lashon hakodesh,*** sacred tongue. A Semitic language, it is written and read from right to left. Scribal characters in the *Sefer Torah* are distinctly different from the written form used in other Hebrew writings.

2.4.1 The *Alef-Bet*

The ancient alphabet looked much different from the ***alef-bet*** of today, and modern technology has made it possible to print Hebrew-language materials in many typefaces. However, the *Sefer Torah* is always written by hand by a ***sofer,*** a scribe trained in the laws of writing a *Sefer Torah.*

There are twenty-two letters in the Hebrew alphabet. Five of them are doubles, distinguished by the presence, absence, or position of a dot. Each letter in the pair is pronounced differently from its mate (except in modern Hebrew where ***tav*** and ***sav*** are both pronounced like the *tav* [see below]). Five of the letters also require a special form if they appear as the final letter in a word.

There are no vowel letters in Hebrew (with the exception of ***vav*** and sometimes ***yud***). All the vowels are written as a series of symbols, which appear above, below, or alongside the consonant. There are no vowel symbols in the Torah itself.

The following basic Hebrew vowel symbols are positioned below the letter.

◌ָ	◌ַ	◌ֶ	◌ִ	◌ֵ	◌ֻ
ah/aw	**ah**	**eh**	**ee**	**ei**	**oo**

The following vowels appear within the word (between letters).

וּ	*vav* with a dot	וֹ	*vav* with a dot	◌ֹ	dot aligns with top
oo	in the middle	**oh**	above it	**oh**	of preceding consonant

The **:** symbol appears below the letter and gives voice to the consonant sound above it. Other vowels are formed by combining the **:** with basic vowels above. These sounds are somewhat shorter in duration than the basic vowel without the **:** symbol.

◌ֳ   ◌ֲ   ◌ֱ

2.4.2 The Numerical Values of the *Alef-Bet*

Each letter of the *alef-bet* also has a numerical value. The names of the letters of the *alef-bet* are listed below along with their English and numerical equivalents.

The *Alef-Bet*

Hebrew Letter	English Equivalent	Numerical Value	Printed Character	Written Character	Scribal Character
alef	silent	1	א	א	א
bet	b	2	בּ	בּ	ב
vet	v	2	ב	ב	ב
gimel	g	3	ג	ג	ג
daled	d	4	ד	ד	ד
hei	h	5	ה	ה	ה
vav	v	6	ו	ו	ו
zayin	z	7	ז	ז	ז
chet	ch	8	ח	ח	ח
tet	t	9	ט	ט	ט
yud	y	10	י	י	י
kaf	k	20	כּ	כּ	כ
chaf	ch	20	כ	כ	כ
chaf sofit	ch	20	ך	ך	ך
lamed	l	30	ל	ל	ל
mem	m	40	מ	מ	מ
mem sofit	m	40	ם	ם	ם
nun	n	50	נ	נ	נ
nun sofit	n	50	ן	ן	ן
samech	s	60	ס	ס	ס
ayin	silent	70	ע	ע	ע
pei	p	80	פּ	פּ	פ
fei	f	80	פ	פ	פ
fei sofit	f	80	ף	ף	ף
tzadi	tz	90	צ	צ	צ
tzadi sofit	tz	90	ץ	ץ	ץ
koof	k	100	ק	ק	ק
resh	r	200	ר	ר	ר
shin	sh	300	שׁ	שׁ	ש
sin	s	300	שׂ	שׂ	ש
tav	t	400	תּ	תּ	ת
sav	s	400	ת	ת	ת

Within a range of numbers, letters are combined. Note that a double apostrophe is used in numbers between the last two letters. Remember that Hebrew is written and read from right to left and, in most cases, the greater number precedes the lesser. For example,

ל = 30 + ג = 3
ל"ג = 33
ת = 400 + ר = 200 + י = 10 + ג = 3
תרי"ג = 613, *taryag*, as in *Taryag Mitzvot*

2.4.3 The Significance of Numerology

Some numerical combinations of letters are associated with specific Hebrew words. For example,

chai, life, is spelled
chet, 8 + *yud,* 10
חי = 18

koach, strength, is spelled
kaf, 20 + *chet,* 8
כח= 28

mazal, luck, is spelled
mem, 40 + *zayin,* 7 + *lamed,* 30
מזל = 77

tov, good, is spelled
tet, 9 + *vav,* 6 + *vet,* 2
טוב = 17

So, ***mazal tov,*** good luck, is spelled מזל טוב = 94.

A system of Hebrew numerology called ***gematria*** is a fascinating method of disclosing the hidden meaning of Hebrew texts by discerning their numerical equivalents. For example,

ahavah, love, is spelled
alef, 1 + *hei,* 5 + *vet,* 2 + *hei,* 5
אהבה = 13

echad, one, is spelled
alef, 1 + *chet,* 8 + *daled,* 4
אחד = 13

According to mystical teachings, these two words, which are numerically equivalent, mean that the Jewish people must always seek to attain love of God Who is One.

2.4.4 Writing a *Sefer Torah*

The last of the *Taryag Mitzvot* is:

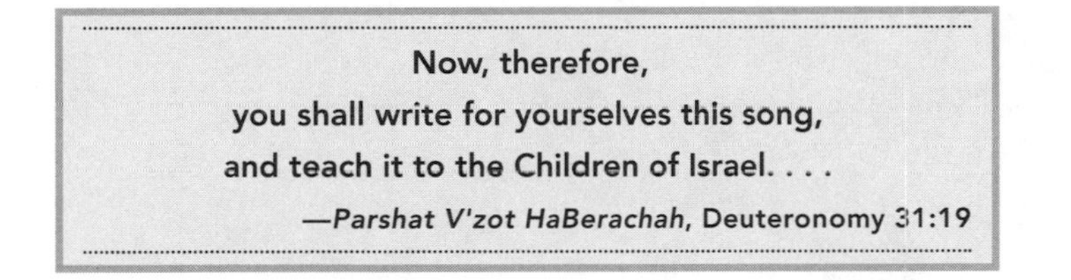

Now, therefore,
you shall write for yourselves this song,
and teach it to the Children of Israel. . . .
—*Parshat V'zot HaBerachah*, Deuteronomy 31:19

This commandment requires all Jews to either personally write a *Sefer Torah* or to have one written on their behalf. Jews who are not qualified to undertake the actual writing personally may commission a *sofer*, a scribe, to perform the *mitzvah* for them. Whenever the writing of a *Sefer Torah* is commissioned, whether by a synagogue or an individual, it is customary to invite others to share in the *mitzvah* by "purchasing" letters in the Scroll at a nominal charge. For example, participants may contribute to the cost of the preparation of the *Sefer Torah* by selecting and dedicating the letters of their Hebrew names. By personally immersing themselves in this *mitzvah*, Jews intensify their connection with the Torah that guides their lives.

Each *sofer* is an expert trained in the laws pertaining to the scribal arts, particularly the preparation of a *Sefer Torah* and other religious documents (see Chapters 3, 8, and 9). At one time, each *sofer* was required to serve as an apprentice in order to learn his craft from an experienced scribe. Today, special organizations provide the necessary training. Some courses take up to two years, although it is possible to complete the training in a matter of months.

The *sofer* must be conscientious, devout, and scrupulously careful to copy word for word, line for line, from a correct text. He begins by declaring his intention to undertake the writing of the *Sefer Torah* with the holy purpose of fulfilling the *mitzvah*. Although it is not necessary to repeat this declaration each time the *sofer* resumes the work, most scribes do so anyway. A separate assertion is made, however, every time any

The modern *sofer* continues to follow the ancient precepts for preparing a *Sefer Torah*.

of God's Names are inscribed. Each word in the *Sefer Torah* must be pronounced aloud before writing, and sufficient space must be left between letters so that they can be easily distinguished from one another.

The hand-lettering used by the scribe in the preparation of a *Sefer Torah* must meet certain religious requirements for size and shape. The *Sefer Torah* is written with a reed or quill and black iron-based ink on ***klaf***, parchment (or leather) prepared from the hides of ritually slaughtered kosher animals. Completed sheets of parchment, each called a ***yeriah***, are sewn together with sinew from ritually slaughtered kosher animals.

The sheets of parchment on which the *Sefer Torah* is written are attached to two staves. The first parchment of Genesis is attached to the right one; the last parchment of Deuteronomy to the left one. All the sheets of parchment are wound together from each end. There must be at least three columns on a *yeriah*, but not more than eight, each measuring four inches in width. Each of forty-two lines per column may contain up to thirty letters. According to some opinions, it is a long-standing custom for the *sofer* to start every column with the Hebrew letter *vav* (which means *and*), with the exception of six columns. Columns must align. No punctuation is permitted in the *Sefer Torah* itself, and only a space equivalent to four lines is permitted from one *Sefer* to the next (e.g., between *Sefer Bereshit* and *Sefer Shemot*). If a *sofer* makes a mistake, he must erase the error by scraping the dried ink from the parchment.

Every week before *Kriat HaTorah*, the ***ba'al korei*** inspects the parchment for any flaws or imperfections that would render it ***pasul***, ritually unfit for use. If any of the letters are scratched, cracked, worn, or illegible, the *Sefer Torah* must be repaired by a *sofer* before it can be used again for the public Reading of the Law.

When a *Sefer Torah* has been damaged beyond repair, it is placed in a container and buried with respect in a Jewish cemetery. In fact, all ***sheimot***, items that contain any of the Names of God, are to be buried in a similar fashion.

Often a community will collect damaged prayer books, scrolls, and the like, in the synagogue and bury all of them at the same time in a communal ceremony. They may be interred in a separate grave, perhaps near that of a pious individual; but occasionally, *sheimot* are placed in a container and buried with a deceased person at the time of a funeral. A qualified rabbi should be consulted about appropriate ritual procedures.

The objects associated directly with the *Sefer Torah* include:

- ***etz chayim***
- ***gartel***
- ***mantel***
- ***rimonim***
- ***keter Torah***
- ***choshen***
- ***yad***

We will discuss these next.

2.4.5 The *Etz Chayim*

Each of the staves on which the Torah Scroll is wound is called an *etz chayim,* a tree of life. Each of them has a handle at both ends, which is attached to a wheel-shaped disk. The disk prevents the parchment sheets from slipping off the staves. The staves may also be overlaid with silver and may be engraved to honor or memorialize a person or event.

2.4.6 The *Gartel* and the *Mantel*

When the *Sefer Torah* is wound closed, it is fastened with a *gartel,* a velvet band that keeps the Torah securely together, Once the Torah is closed and fastened, it is adorned with an embroidered velvet *mantel,* which slips over the staves of the *Sefer Torah* to cover it.

2.4.7 The *Rimonim* and the *Keter Torah*

It is customary to adorn *Sifrei Torah* with ornate silver fittings, all of which are reminiscent of the artifacts of the *Mishkan* and the vestments of the Priests. The *rimonim,* which are placed over each stave, recall the design of pomegranates and bells that adorned the vestments of the High Priest.

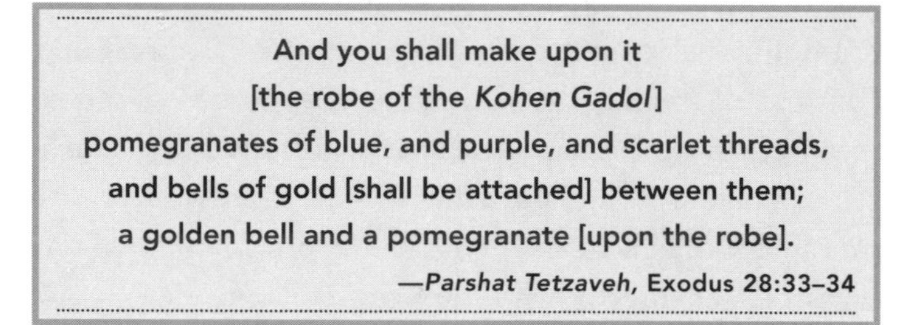
And you shall make upon it
[the robe of the *Kohen Gadol*]
pomegranates of blue, and purple, and scarlet threads,
and bells of gold [shall be attached] between them;
a golden bell and a pomegranate [upon the robe].
—*Parshat Tetzaveh,* Exodus 28:33–34

In addition to the *rimonim,* some Torah Scrolls may be adorned with a *keter Torah,* a Torah crown. In the Torah we find that a golden crown was placed above the Ark cover, a symbol of the crown of the Torah.

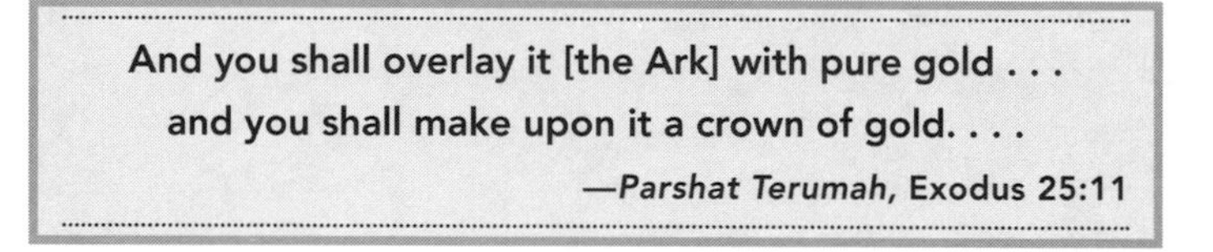
And you shall overlay it [the Ark] with pure gold . . .
and you shall make upon it a crown of gold. . . .
—*Parshat Terumah,* Exodus 25:11

Today the symbolism of the crown recalls the great esteem in which the Torah is held. The silver crown is often fitted with silver bells as well.

2.4.8 The *Choshen* and the *Yad*

Over the staves, a silver breastplate, called a *choshen,* is hung as a reminder of the Breastplate of Judgment of the *Kohen Gadol,* which he wore in the *Mishkan,* and later in the *Bet HaMikdash.* It was designed with twelve different precious stones, each representing one of the twelve Tribes of Israel, according to God's command. The Talmud (*Sotah* 48b and *Gittin* 68a) points out that the *shamir* was also used to cut the stones for the breastplate and the apron of the *Kohen Gadol.*

We find the following description of the breastplate in the Torah:

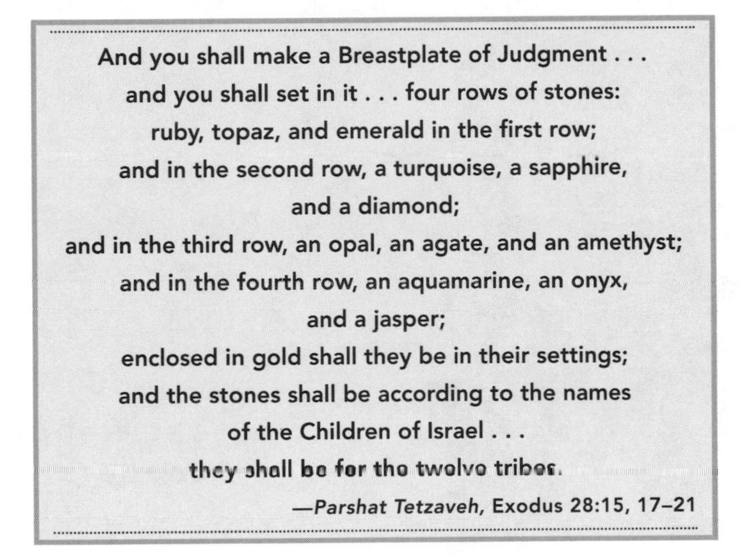

And you shall make a Breastplate of Judgment . . .
and you shall set in it . . . four rows of stones:
ruby, topaz, and emerald in the first row;
and in the second row, a turquoise, a sapphire,
and a diamond;
and in the third row, an opal, an agate, and an amethyst;
and in the fourth row, an aquamarine, an onyx,
and a jasper;
enclosed in gold shall they be in their settings;
and the stones shall be according to the names
of the Children of Israel . . .
they shall be for the twelve tribes.

—*Parshat Tetzaveh,* Exodus 28:15, 17–21

- Reuben ruby
- Simon topaz
- Levi emerald
- Judah turquoise
- Dan sapphire
- Naftali diamond
- Gad opal
- Asher agate
- Issachar amethyst
- Zevulun aquamarine
- Joseph onyx
- Benjamin jasper

On some *Sifrei Torah,* a pointer, called a *yad,* meaning *hand,* hangs over an *etz chayim* with the *choshen.* The bottom of the *yad* is configured like a hand, and the body of the pointer is usually made from silver or olive wood. The *yad* is used to follow the text in the Torah—but not touch it—because nothing must touch the sacred text.

Prior to the Reading of the Law, all the ornamental silver is removed, the *mantel* is lifted off, and the *gartel* is unfastened. The Torah Scroll is then placed on the *shulchan* and unrolled to the weekly portion.

Adorned with precious silver, the *Sifrei Torah* recall the ornamentation used in the *Mishkan* and *Bet HaMikdash*.

2.5 The Religious Leaders

Throughout Jewish history, the leaders have come from among the Elders and the Priests. Moses the Lawgiver is considered the leader and father of the prophets. Like the Torah itself, the mantle of leadership was transmitted from generation to generation.

2.5.1 The High Priest

In the days of the *Bet HaMikdash,* the *Kohen Gadol,* the High Priest, was the religious leader of the Jewish people. The *Kohen Gadol,* and all *Kohanim,* traced their ancestry to the first High Priest, Aaron, the older brother of Moses. Thus, membership in the priestly tribe was based on birth, although one had to merit worthiness within his tribe.

The primary function of the Priests in the *Bet HaMikdash* was to perform the sacrificial rites, while the *Levi'im,* the Levites, assisted the *Kohanim* and instructed the people in the Torah. Twenty-four divisions of *Kohanim* served on a weekly rotation, except on the Pilgrimage Festivals, when they officiated at the same time. Because the *Kohanim* and *Levi'im* owned no land nor had any income, they were supported by the people.

With the destruction of the Second Temple, the sacrificial responsibilities of the Priests disappeared. Today, the specific privileges and obligations of the *Kohanim* are limited to: (1) the first ***aliyah,*** Torah honor, at the Reading of the Torah; (2) leading Grace after Meals (see Sections 3.4.10 and 5.5.7); (3) the chanting of the Priestly Blessing on the High Holidays and the Pilgrimage Festivals (see Chapters 6 and 7); (4) the honor of redeeming a first-born son (see Section 9.11); and (5) the prohibition of coming in contact with the deceased (see Section 9.16.4).

2.5.2 The Rabbi

Only Moses is referred to as Moshe Rabbenu, Moses *Our Teacher.* Later religious leaders were called ***rabban,*** our master, ***rabbi,*** my master, and ***rav,*** master. These titles came into popular usage during and after the period of the Second Temple.

The most prestigious of these three titles was *rabban,* inasmuch as it applied to only three presidents of the ***Sanhedrin,*** the legislative body which interpreted biblical laws and initiated new *halachot.* The three presidents were Rabban Gamliel, Rabban Simon ben Gamliel, and Rabban Yochanan ben Zakkai.

The title *rabbi* was originally used to identify: (1) those sages who had been ordained in the academies of ancient Israel, and (2) the *Tana'im* of the Mishnah. The title *rav* was applied to the Babylonian *Amora'im.* The most renowned scholars, of course, were those known only by their names; no title was necessary to identify them or to indicate the scope of their Torah learning.

After the Talmud was compiled, the title *rabbi* was conferred upon anyone who, by virtue of his scholarship, was qualified to decide questions of Jewish law. In halachic Judaism, only men receive ***s'michah,*** rabbinical ordination.

Each candidate for ordination must undertake a rigorous course of study in the Talmud and its commentaries. In addition to attaining proficiency in biblical and talmudic sources, he must be conversant with Responsa Literature, the written responses (decisions) of eminent rabbis to questions posed to them.

When the rabbinical student completes his studies, he becomes a ***musmach,*** one who has received his *s'michah.* At that time, a special *klaf,* usually a parchment certificate, is bestowed, stating that he has successfully completed his studies, is ordained, and is worthy to be called "rabbi."

By virtue of his special training and the acquisition of Torah knowledge, the rabbi is often distinguished from the laity he serves. To be sure, anyone who possesses Torah knowledge is to be respected, and even admired (see Section 9.13.2). The rabbi's authority in Jewish law is based on the tradition that one who has received *s'michah* may confer it upon another. Thus, the chain of Torah links generations of scholars and sages with the rabbi serving the synagogue and the Jewish community of today.

A WITTY REMARK!

The story is told of the rabbinical student who studied day and night to prepare for his examinations for *s'michah*. He immersed himself in the Torah, the Talmud, and the *Shulchan Aruch*, the Code of Jewish Law. Over and over he reviewed the sacred texts. Finally, he felt ready to present himself to his rabbis and teachers.

"I have gone through all of the Torah," he proudly announced.

The rabbis looked at him and replied, "Indeed, you say you have gone through all of the Torah and are ready to receive *s'michah*, as it has been handed down from rabbi to rabbi for generations. Now, the most important question is: Has all of the Torah gone through you?"

In past generations, there have been rabbinic giants who brought spiritual illumination and exceptional Jewish scholarship to the communities of Eastern Europe. Many towns in Poland, Russia, Hungary, Lithuania, Romania, Czechoslovakia, and elsewhere were famed for the rabbis who headed their communities. Towns often competed to encourage a particular sage to settle in their midst and serve as their spiritual leader.

Several prominent rabbinic leaders today serve as talmudic authorities and provide religious guidance to the Jewish community at large. Their biblical and talmudic erudition is respected far and wide, and they truly resemble the sages of old in their commitment to Judaism and the Jewish people. These renowned Torah personalities serve as a link between the sages of ancient times and the rabbis who now serve in communities throughout the world.

2.5.3 The Cantor

The role of the cantor or ***chazan*** is different from that of the rabbi, although in smaller communities, one man often fills both positions. Facing the *Aron HaKodesh*, the *chazan* chants the liturgy in the synagogue. He is often referred to as the ***sh'liach tzibur,*** the emissary of the congregation, because he leads the service. However, it must be emphasized that the cantor is not an intermediary before God; rather, each person prays directly to Him.

Historically, the *chazan* functioned as the teacher of younger children. The Mishnah states:

> [T]he teacher
> [here the Mishnah uses the word *chazan*]
> may look in where the young children are reading. . . .
>
> —*Shabbat* 1:3

The cantor's responsibilities were further discussed in the ***Tosefta,*** tannaitic statements that were not included in the six mishnaic orders. These were, nevertheless, preserved by scholars of the second and third centuries of the Common Era. In the *Tosefta, Masechet Sukkah* 4:6, the cantor's duties also included sounding a ram's horn to announce the beginning and conclusion of the Sabbath and festivals.

The *chazan* was required to be learned in Torah and knowledgeable about the meaning and interpretation of the words he prayed. His piety and devotion to God were often more important to the congregation than his musical ability or vocal talents. However, the cantor was usually expected to be a poet, a composer, and a musician as well. He chanted the prayers, and the melodies themselves enhanced the spiritual experience for the congregation and became part of the tradition.

Jewish liturgy has several melodic modes, called ***nuscha'ot,*** each of which is associated with a particular prayer service. For example, the melodic patterns for the daily prayers is different from the ***nusach*** for the Sabbath or the festivals. The *chazan* must be familiar with all the *nuscha'ot* in order to lead the prayers.

At one time, there were many eminent cantors serving congregations throughout the world. They were gifted vocally, and their personal observance of *halachah* and *mitzvot* was never in doubt. Unfortunately, many cantors of that generation and caliber have passed away.

In many instances, the cantor is now a musician first and a Torah scholar second. The religious fervor of the *chazan* and the beauty of the liturgy as sung by the cantors of past generations will probably never be equaled. Nevertheless, to their credit, a few rabbinical seminaries are now training cantors who understand the words and can express their pathos to the congregation.

Only a man can officiate as the *chazan* in a synagogue guided by *halachah*. Similarly, the choirs are comprised of males only, in order to preclude the prohibition of ***kol ishah,*** hearing a woman's singing voice, which is considered provocative. *Halachah*-guided synagogues do not permit the use of musical instruments to accompany the cantor or the choir on the Sabbath or festivals. Similarly, the use of amplification equipment, such as a microphone or a public address system, is prohibited.

2.5.4 The Reader of the Law

The *parashat hashavua* is read publicly in the synagogue four times a week—Monday morning, Thursday morning, and Saturday morning and afternoon—by the ***ba'al korei,*** reader of the Law, a man trained to read the Hebrew text directly from the Torah Scroll, according to the melodic patterns called ***ta'amei haMikra*** or ***trop.***

The *ba'al korei* studies the vocalized text and the accompanying *trop* from a special *sefer* called a ***Tikkun laKori'im,*** because none of these symbols actually appear in the *Sefer Torah.* The biblical text with the *trop* appears on a page in the *Tikkun* in a column opposite a column of the Torah text in scribal form, which displays neither vowels nor *trop.* By constant review and practice, the *ba'al korei* familiarizes himself with the words of the *parashah* so that he can read correctly from the Torah.

The *trop* are a group of symbols or accent marks that were developed in post-talmudic times and appear above and below the biblical text, not unlike the vowels of the Hebrew *alef-bet* (which developed later). Each symbol has a distinctive melodic sound, which is imposed on a word or phrase. These musical notes also function like punctuation marks, providing grammatical structure as well as melody. They create a pattern of sensible long and short pauses in phrasing, which add to the clarity of the text. In English, these symbols are called cantillation.

Two different patterns of cantillation are applied to the twenty-four books of the *Kitvei HaKodesh.* Psalms, Proverbs, and Job use one pattern; the remaining twenty-one books use another (see Section 1.2.2). Many of the twenty-four books—or, at least, portions of them—are read publicly in the synagogue at some time during the year (see Sections 6.9, 6.26, 7.9, 7.15, 7.21.2, 8.6, and 8.8). Today the duties of the *ba'al korei* are often combined with those of the *chazan* or the rabbi.

LOOKING AHEAD! *In Chapter 3, we will discuss the role of prayer in Jewish life. As we stated earlier, we pray only to God, but there are other questions to consider:*

- *Why do we pray?*
- *What do we pray?*
- *How do we pray?*
- *When do we pray?*
- *Where do we pray?*
- *Who should pray?*

We will try to answer these questions next.

Word Works

The Western Wall of the Second Temple remains the spiritual focus of Jewish life to this day.

3

Prayer and Jewish Liturgy

RAYER IS OF primary importance in Jewish life. It is a daily obligation, a positive precept derived from the Torah, which commands us to serve God every day.

> **And you shall serve the Lord your God.**
>
> **—*Parshat Mishpatim*, Exodus 23:25**

and

> **You shall fear the Lord your God;**
> **and you shall serve Him,**
> **and by His Name you shall swear.**
>
> **—*Parshat Va'etchanan*, Deuteronomy 6:13**

The Torah does not prescribe a fixed time for prayer, a particular form, or even a specific number of prayers. In the second book of his *Mishneh Torah,* Rambam comments:

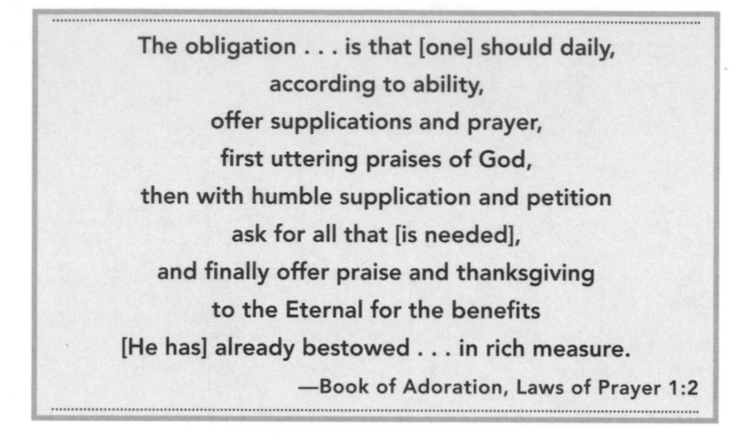

The obligation . . . is that [one] should daily,
according to ability,
offer supplications and prayer,
first uttering praises of God,
then with humble supplication and petition
ask for all that [is needed],
and finally offer praise and thanksgiving
to the Eternal for the benefits
[He has] already bestowed . . . in rich measure.

—Book of Adoration, Laws of Prayer 1:2

Thus, the three elements of prayer are: (1) praise of God; (2) supplication and petition; and (3) thanksgiving to God.

3.1 The Origin of Prayer

From the time of Moses until Ezra the Scribe, the people prayed as they saw fit: what and when and how they prayed was strictly an individual matter. During the Babylonian Exile, after the destruction of the First *Bet HaMikdash,* the people began to forget the *lashon hakodesh,* as they interacted with the Babylonian culture. In exile, Ezra the Scribe and the ***Anshei Kenesset HaGedolah,*** Men of the Great Assembly, the leaders and prophets of the time, established the content and order of the daily prayers, to provide coherence and unity in worship among the dispersed Jews.

The Babylonian Exile lasted seventy years, and those who returned to Jerusalem built the Second *Bet HaMikdash,* which stood until it was destroyed by Rome. Once again, the prayers were forgotten or revised inappropriately, and it was again necessary to empower the people with prayer and inspire them to serve God, even in the midst of the catastrophe of *Churban Bayit Sheni.*

Hebrew liturgy was formalized to replace the rituals of sacrifice, *korbanot,* which had been conducted in the *Mishkan,* and later in the *Bet HaMikdash.* The number of prayer services on a given day was to be equal in number to the sacrifices.

Sacrifices were brought twice daily, in the morning and the afternoon, and on some days an additional sacrifice was also required. Thus, the morning prayer service replaced the morning sacrifice, and the afternoon prayer service replaced the afternoon sacrifice. On those occasions when an additional offering would have been brought, an additional prayer service replaced it.

There was no evening sacrifice, but because the afternoon sacrifice continued to burn on the altar throughout the night, an evening prayer service was instituted to correspond to it, and thus, the evening service became obligatory, too.

There are textual references which suggest that prayers were, in fact, part of the sacrificial services in the *Mishkan* and *Bet HaMikdash,* not only a substitute for them. For example, we find:

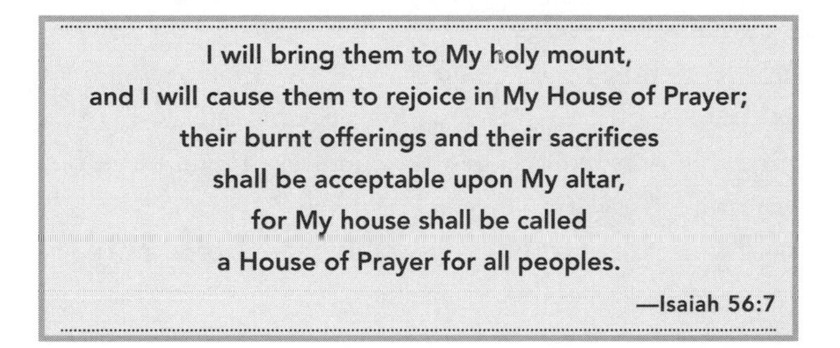

I will bring them to My holy mount,
and I will cause them to rejoice in My House of Prayer;
their burnt offerings and their sacrifices
shall be acceptable upon My altar,
for My house shall be called
a House of Prayer for all peoples.

—Isaiah 56:7

Indeed, Jewish tradition teaches that Abraham instituted the recitation of the morning prayers, Isaac, the afternoon prayers, and Jacob, the evening prayers.

After *Churban Bayit Sheni,* the synagogue became the focal point of Jewish life (see Section 2.2), and worship and Torah instruction were conducted there. From this period on, the sages endeavored to maintain uniformity in religious services.

3.2 The Names of God

All prayer is directed to God. He is the Source of all blessing, and is called by many names in the liturgy. The Third Commandment forbids the use of God's Name in vain.

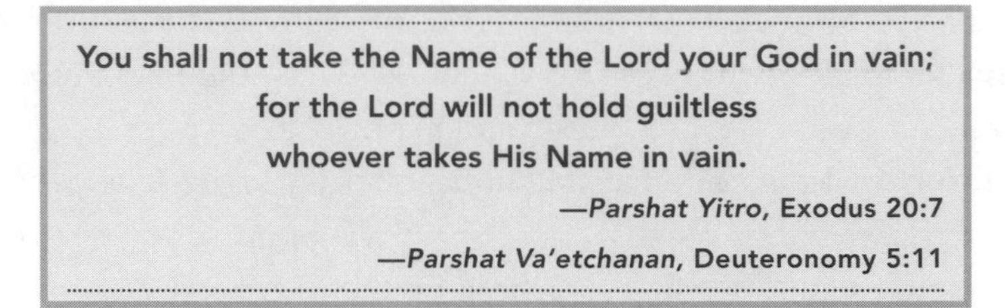
**You shall not take the Name of the Lord your God in vain;
for the Lord will not hold guiltless
whoever takes His Name in vain.**

—*Parshat Yitro,* Exodus 20:7

—*Parshat Va'etchanan,* Deuteronomy 5:11

How do we avoid taking His Name in vain? What restrictions should we put upon ourselves when we refer to God? To begin with, no English word is actually one of God's names. While it is a popular contrivance to hyphenate English words like G-d and L-rd in many religious circles, it is not a requirement that is covered under "in vain." In some cases, however, we prefer to use hyphens when writing God's Hebrew names in transliteration, as we illustrate below.

The two most commonly used Hebrew names for God are ***A-do-nai,*** which is usually translated as "Lord," and ***E-lo-him,*** usually translated as "God." We should not pronounce them, except in prayer—or when teaching them; and even then we should be cautious not to overdo it.

The English translation of some of the traditional Hebrew phrases used to refer to God are:

- The Name
- One
- King of the Universe
- Creator of the Universe
- Lord of the Universe
- Master of the Universe
- Shield of Abraham
- Healer of the Sick
- Help
- Savior
- Rock of Israel
- Redeemer of Israel
- Eternal of Israel
- Guardian of Israel
- The Almighty
- The Place
- The Great
- The Mighty
- The Awe-Inspiring

To avoid taking His Name in vain, we use "The Name," which is ***HaShem*** in Hebrew, as a substitute for *A-do-nai,* when we are not praying to Him. *HaShem* can be used whenever we speak of Him, but care should be taken not to use any divine name frivolously.

The word *A-do-nai* is actually a "stand-in" for the tetragrammaton, the four-letter Name of God, which is written in four Hebrew letters: *yud* (Y), *hei* (H), *vav* (V), and *hei* (H). It is never pronounced as written. To avoid writing out His Name in Hebrew, we replace the "h" sound (*hei*) with the "k" sound (*koof*). Also, the letter *hei* is often pronounced *kei,* substituting the "k" for the "h," when referring to God. In English, this divine Name is usually abbreviated Y'H'V'H, or even Y'K'V'K. Sometimes it is also abbreviated in English as Y'H'W'H, or Y'K'W'K, but we will use the V (*vav*) instead of the W, which is not a Hebrew sound.

Out of profound reverence and awe, *A-do-nai,* also a four-letter word in Hebrew, is substituted for Y'K'V'K in prayer, and *HaShem* is substituted for *A-do-nai* otherwise. In the prayer book, Y'K'V'K may also appear as a *yud* followed by another *yud.* In either case, it is pronounced *A-do-nai.*

Y'K'V'K, often interpreted as an abbreviation for three Hebrew words meaning "I was, I am, I will be," is also called the ***Shem HaMeforash,*** Unutterable Name, and ***Shem HaM'yuchad,*** Singular Name. In the days of the *Mishkan* and *Bet HaMikdash,* the *Kohen Gadol* uttered Y'K'V'K in its accurate pronunciation during the Day of Atonement (see Section 6.28.1), denoting the eternal nature of God's existence. However, the correct pronunciation has been lost since *Churban Bayit Sheni.*

The word *E-lo-him* connotes God's majesty, greatness, and the divine attribute of justice. We again replace the "h" sound (*hei*) with the "k" sound (*koof*)—that is, ***E-lo-kim,*** when we are not praying, but want to use this appellation or any form of it—my God, your God, our God, and the like.

The Name *E-lo-kim* also suggests God's wondrous power. In the first book of his *Mishneh Torah,* Rambam comments on God's infinite power.

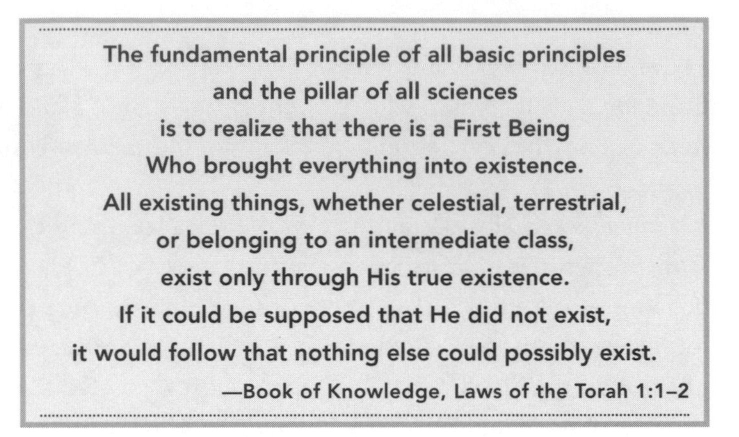

The fundamental principle of all basic principles
and the pillar of all sciences
is to realize that there is a First Being
Who brought everything into existence.
All existing things, whether celestial, terrestrial,
or belonging to an intermediate class,
exist only through His true existence.
If it could be supposed that He did not exist,
it would follow that nothing else could possibly exist.

—Book of Knowledge, Laws of the Torah 1:1–2

All names for God signify His perfection or characterize His actions in relation to human beings. His divine attributes are to be emulated by humankind in moral and ethical conduct. All of these names, among others, occur in specific prayers, but this list alone is indicative of the infinite and unlimited knowledge, presence, and power of the God of Israel. In the final analysis, God is not a being of substance, with sensory faculties. He does not move or speak, as we human beings understand those terms. It is because of our limited human capacity to comprehend the all-encompassing essence of the divine that we resort to describing Him that way.

3.3 In the Image of God

Humankind was created in God's image, ***b'tzelem E-lo-kim.***

> **And God said,**
> **"Let us make man in our image after our likeness"; . . .**
> **and God created the man in His own image,**
> **in the image of God He created him,**
> **male and female, He created them.**
>
> **—*Parshat Bereshit,* Genesis 1:26, 27**

Rabbi Shlomo ben Yitzchak (1040–1105; known as Rashi), considered the greatest of all biblical and talmudic *meforshim,* comments on the Torah's use of the plural "in our image." Rashi explains that God consulted with His heavenly court of angels, and by so doing, showed the attribute of modesty. However, only "He created them."

Because we were created in His image, we have a responsibility to strive to be like Him. What are God's attributes? In ***Moreh Nevuchim,*** *The Guide of the Perplexed*, one of the world's greatest medieval works of philosophy, the Rambam points out that just before God gave Moses the second *Luchot HaBrit* (see Section 7.13.2), Moses petitioned God:

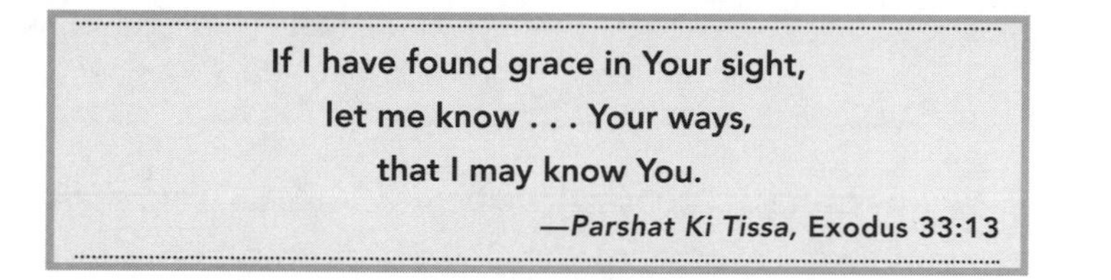

If I have found grace in Your sight,
let me know . . . Your ways,
that I may know You.

—*Parshat Ki Tissa,* Exodus 33:13

He was asking God two things: (1) to let him know His attributes; and (2) to let him know His true essence.

According to the Rambam,

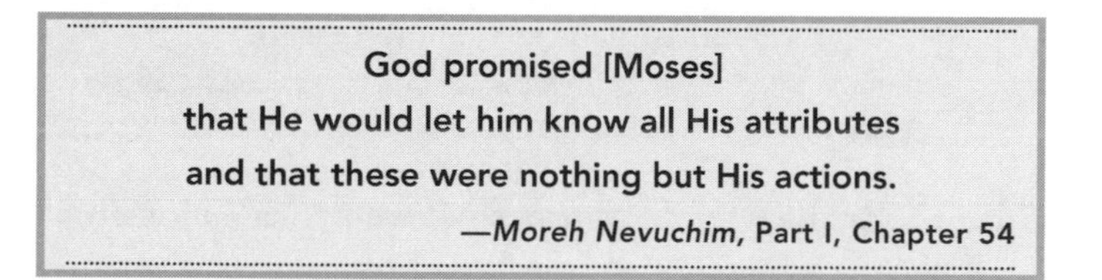

God promised [Moses]
that He would let him know all His attributes
and that these were nothing but His actions.

—*Moreh Nevuchim,* Part I, Chapter 54

Moses persisted to learn of God's essence, but even his request was denied, for God replied:

You cannot see My Face, for man shall not see Me and live.

—*Parshat Ki Tissa,* Exodus 33:20

Thus, we can know God only through His actions, but how can we emulate Him? In the Torah, we find the Thirteen Attributes of God, which have become part of the liturgy.

> **The Lord, the Lord, God,**
> **Merciful and Gracious,**
> **Long-Suffering, Abundant in Goodness and Truth;**
> **Keeping Mercy unto the thousandth generation,**
> **Forgiving Iniquity and Transgression and Sin;**
> **and Cleanses [those who repent].**
>
> **—*Parshat Ki Tissa*, Exodus 34:6–7**

So, too, shall we be merciful; so, too, shall we be gracious; so, too, shall we be patient; so, too, shall we pursue goodness; so, too, shall we be truthful; so, too, shall we be forgiving.

We also find:

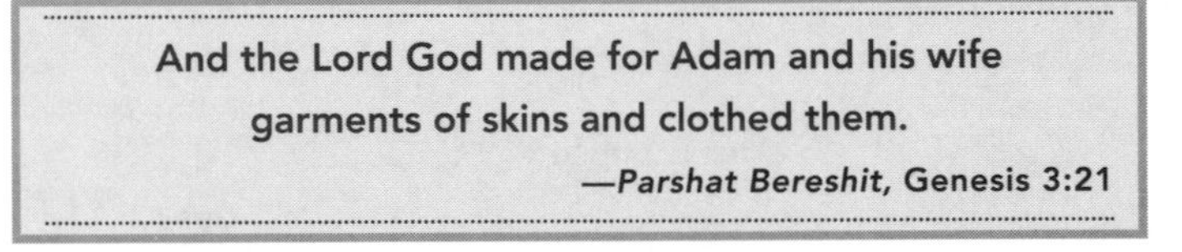

And the Lord God made for Adam and his wife garments of skins and clothed them.

—*Parshat Bereshit*, Genesis 3:21

God provided clothing for the naked; so, too, shall we provide clothing.

> **In the same day Abraham was circumcised . . .**
> **and the Lord appeared unto him**
> **[to visit the sick].**
>
> **—*Parshat Lech Lecha, Parshat Vayera*, Genesis 17:24, 18:1**

God visited the sick; so, too, shall we visit the sick,

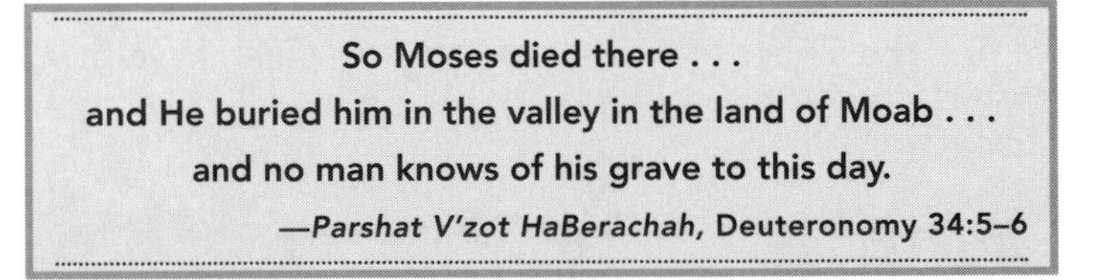

So Moses died there . . .
and He buried him in the valley in the land of Moab . . .
and no man knows of his grave to this day.

—*Parshat V'zot HaBerachah*, Deuteronomy 34:5–6

God buried the dead; so, too, shall we bury the dead.

To be sure, for most of us, it is not easy to be Godlike. We are human beings: neither wholly good, nor wholly evil. We are ***benonim,*** average people struggling to grasp the righteousness of the ***tzaddik*** and evade the evil grip of the ***rasha.*** It is by observing the *mitzvot* that we emulate God, Who created us in His image. The performance of *mitzvot* brings us closer to God, which is the ultimate purpose of our existence.

3.4 The Concept of Blessings

The laws of blessings, ***hilchot berachot,*** include hundreds of *halachot* that pertain to the recitation of ***berachot***, blessings. The *halachot* are complex, but it is essential to understand the importance and significance of *berachot* in the daily life of a Jew.

Reciting blessings is meant to be more than a mere "thank you" to God, a courteous tip of the hat, as it were, a gesture easily made or just as easily omitted. With the recitation of *berachot,* Jews fulfill the talmudic dictum of Rabbi Meir, a second-century sage:

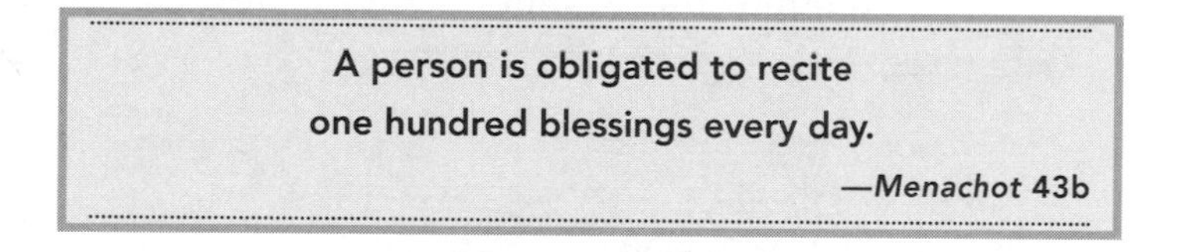

A person is obligated to recite one hundred blessings every day.

—*Menachot* 43b

Reciting *berachot* is meant to make us keenly aware of our total dependence on God. We are profoundly in His debt—for everything and forever. It is a humbling experience to realize that nothing we have in our lives comes from our own efforts alone. We require God's help at every turn, whether we recognize His beneficence or not.

3.4.1 Thanking Him for the Bad and the Good

Surprisingly, we are also obligated to thank God for the bad that befalls us in the same way that we acknowledge Him for His beneficence. In the Talmud, we find:

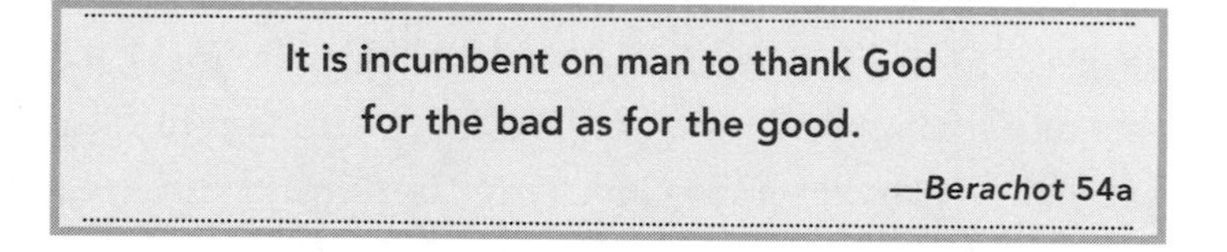

It is incumbent on man to thank God for the bad as for the good.

—*Berachot* 54a

We do not express this thanks in the same words. For good, we acknowledge God with the blessing

. . . Who is good and does good

For the tragedies of life, we recognize Him as

. . . the true Judge

The recitation of a blessing for both good news and bad affirms God's role in every aspect of life. In no way does it suggest that we rejoice over tragic events, nor do we seek to evade the reality of tragedy. Rather, by reciting a ***berachah,*** blessing, we remind ourselves that in good times and bad, we are not alone, because God is always with us. We recognize that both grief and joy are only initial responses that ultimately evoke a feeling of happiness. This gratitude for the absolute good is called ***hakarat hatov.*** In the Talmud, Rabbi Akiva states:

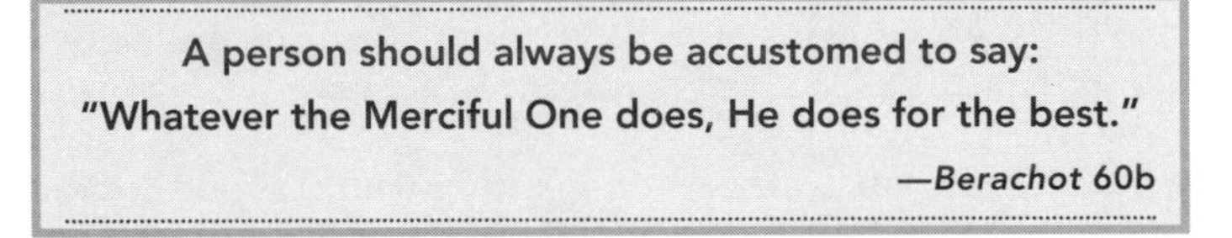

A person should always be accustomed to say: "Whatever the Merciful One does, He does for the best."

—Berachot 60b

So, too, we say that everything that God does is for the best.

3.4.2 Clinging to God

For the Jewish people, the connection with God is an all-encompassing relationship. God is not relegated to a certain place or time of day. Yet, Jews are most certainly not required to separate themselves from the world, focusing all their energies on spiritual endeavors. Instead, they are instructed to recognize the spiritual in all things and to elevate the most ordinary of life's experiences to a level of holiness. The recitation of *berachot* serves as a repeated reminder that everything we do is in fulfillment of *mitzvot,* and our participation brings us closer to God. This clinging attachment to God is called ***d'vekut.***

In the Book of Psalms, we find:

> The earth and its fullness are the Lord's,
> the entire world and all the inhabitants who dwell there.
>
> —Psalms 24:1

and

> The heavens are the heavens of God,
> but the earth He has given to man.
>
> —Psalms 115:16

How do we reconcile the seeming contradiction in the words of the psalmist? Is the earth the Lord's or did He give it to us? Both are correct. In the Talmud, *Masechet Berachot,* 35a/b, Rabbi Levi says that there is no contradiction: Before a *berachah* is recited, the earth is the Lord's; after a *berachah* has been recited, He gives it to us.

Rabbi Chaninah ben Pappa continues the talmudic discussion, saying,

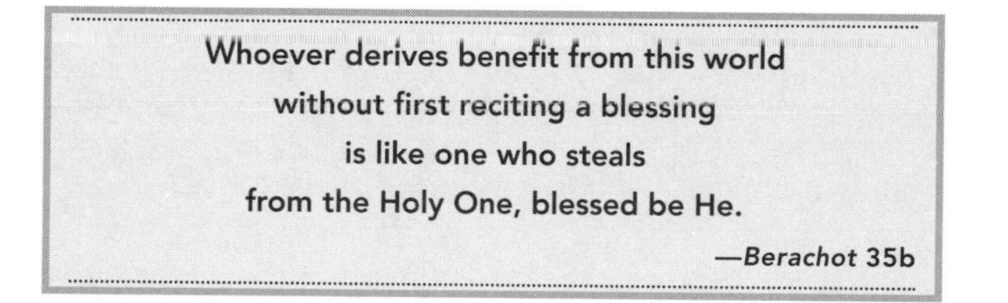

> Whoever derives benefit from this world
> without first reciting a blessing
> is like one who steals
> from the Holy One, blessed be He.
>
> —*Berachot* 35b

Thus, we learn that failure to recite a blessing represents the unauthorized use of God's possessions and is a serious sin. Why is it a sin? The purpose of all Creation is to make God's Glory manifest in the world. This is accomplished in two ways: (1) our actions indicate that it is God's world we are using; and (2) our actions reflect the use of the world as God ordained. So, failing to act accordingly precludes the possibility of fulfilling the purpose of all Creation.

3.4.3 The Derivation of *Berachot*

In the Torah, we hear the words of God; in the recitation of *berachot,* God hears our words, as we speak directly to Him. With relatively few exceptions, there is a *berachah* for virtually every human endeavor, physical and spiritual alike. The obligation to recite most *berachot* is derived from rabbinic authority. However, the obligation to recite these *berachot* is as important as the requirement to recite any specifically mentioned in the Torah. Ezra the Scribe and the *Anshei Kenesset HaGedolah* are credited with deciding on the required text for *berachot.*

3.4.4 The Categories and Structure of *Berachot*

Birchot hatefillah are blessings of praise and supplication that are part of the prayers. In addition to the *birchot hatefillah,* three categories of *berachot* are recited at other times: (1) ***birchot hanehenin,*** benedictions of enjoyment for things that give us pleasure; (2) ***birchot hoda'ah,*** blessings of thanksgiving, specific declarations for both joyous and sorrowful events in private life; and (3) ***birchot hamitzvot,*** blessings associated with the performance of a *mitzvah.*

A ***berachah rishonah*** is a preliminary blessing recited before partaking of food or drink. A ***berachah acharonah*** is recited afterward. The text of each *berachah* is infused with both simple and mystical levels of meaning. All *berachot* begin with the following expression:

Baruch Atah, HaShem E-lo-kenu, Melech HaOlam, . . .

❖

Blessed are You, Lord our God, King of the Universe, . . .

We begin by recognizing God as the Source of all blessing, and refer to Him in the second person as "You," our personal God. The structure of every blessing then switches to the third person, "Who" manifests His will in a variety of ways, all of which indicates that it is He

. . . Who creates everything with His word

or we acknowledge that it is He

. . . Who sanctified us with His commandments and commanded us . . .

to perform *mitzvot.*

This transition from the second to the third person signifies God's revealed and hidden aspects. As "You," we realize, He is nearby, revealed and easily seen, like a personal acquaintance. As the more distant "Who," we realize, He is removed from us, and

His essential nature is hidden and will remain so because of our limited human capacity to comprehend the divine.

Berachot, like all prayers, should be recited with ***kavanah,*** which is characterized by concentration and a spirit of sincere devotion. The recitation of *berachot* testifies to our dependency and makes it possible for us to receive His beneficence.

3.4.5 The Text of the Preliminary Blessings

Let us review the text of the six preliminary *berachot* for food and drink. We begin with bread and other bread products, which include all baked goods made with flour and water (even pizza and pita). If bread is eaten at the beginning of a meal, all other foods eaten during the meal do not require separate blessings. The *berachah* for bread is referred to as ***hamotzi.***

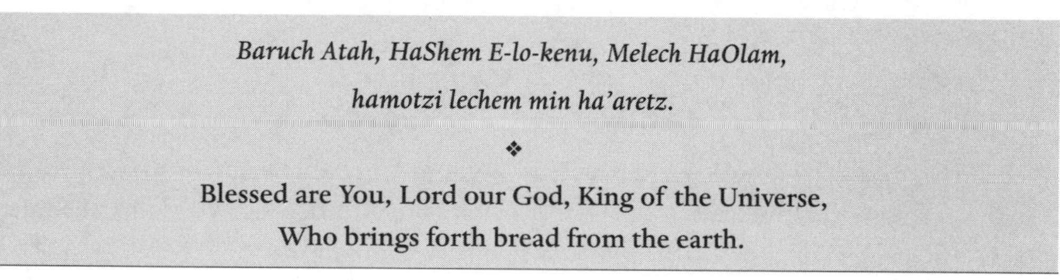

Baruch Atah, HaShem E-lo-kenu, Melech HaOlam,
hamotzi lechem min ha'aretz.

❖

Blessed are You, Lord our God, King of the Universe,
Who brings forth bread from the earth.

Other baked goods, including bread-type products made with fruit juice or other liquids instead of water, are referred to as ***mezonot*** and require the recitation of the next blessing:

Baruch Atah, HaShem E-lo-kenu, Melech HaOlam,
borei minei mezonot.

❖

Blessed are You, Lord our God, King of the Universe,
Who creates various types of food.

When bread is not served at a meal, then such baked goods (*mezonot*) also require *hamotzi,* if they are part of a meal.

The next blessing, ***borei p'ri hagafen,*** is recited before drinking wine or grape juice. It is not recited for grapes, which is considered a fruit, albeit the fruit of the vine.

Baruch Atah, HaShem E-lo-kenu, Melech HaOlam,
borei p'ri hagafen.

❖

Blessed are You, Lord our God, King of the Universe,
Who creates the fruit of the vine.

There are distinctions made between fruits that grow on trees and those that grow either on runners along the ground or on plants that are close to the ground. Most fruits require the blessing ***borei p'ri ha'etz:***

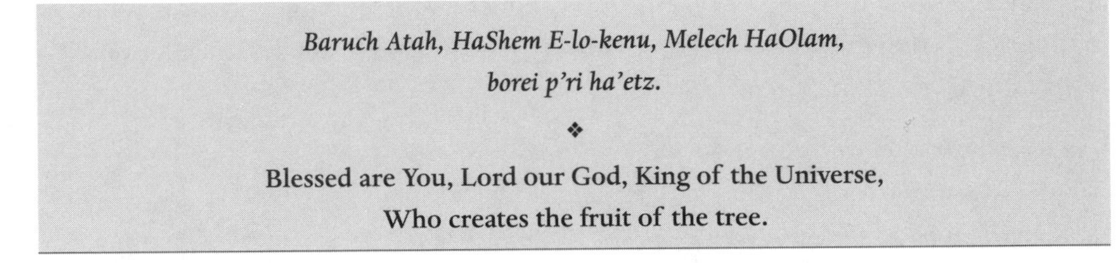

Baruch Atah, HaShem E-lo-kenu, Melech HaOlam,
borei p'ri ha'etz.

❖

Blessed are You, Lord our God, King of the Universe,
Who creates the fruit of the tree.

Virtually all vegetables—and a few fruits, including bananas, melons, strawberries, and pineapples—require the next preliminary blessing. Tomatoes, which are technically a fruit, are also covered by the blessing ***borei p'ri ha'adamah:***

Baruch Atah, HaShem E-lo-kenu, Melech HaOlam,
borei p'ri ha'adamah.

❖

Blessed are You, Lord our God, King of the Universe,
Who creates the fruit of the ground.

The respective blessings for fruits and vegetables apply regardless of whether they are fresh, frozen, dried, cooked, or raw, as long as they are recognizable as such.

The next blessing, referred to as ***she'hakol,*** is recited over water, fruit and vegetable juices, soft drinks, dairy products, candy, meat, fish, poultry, eggs, and other food products not specifically covered by another blessing:

Baruch Atah, HaShem E-lo-kenu, Melech HaOlam,
she'hakol nihi'yeh bid'varo.

❖

Blessed are You, Lord our God, King of the Universe,
Who creates everything with His word.

3.4.6 Answering "*Amen*" to *Berachot*

Only by reciting rabbinically ordained blessings (including daily prayers) can the daily required recitation of one hundred *berachot* be fulfilled. While it is preferable to recite one's own blessings, it is permissible to answer ***amen*** to another person's *berachah* to fulfill the one hundred required. The Hebrew word *amen* is linked to the word ***emunah,*** meaning faith or certainty. *Amen* is also an acronym for three Hebrew words meaning *God Who is the faithful King.*

However, in order to count the blessing as one's own, one must be mindful to hear the entire *berachah* and to wait until the recitation is completed before answering *amen* with precise clarity.

On the Sabbath and festivals, fewer blessings are recited in the daily prayers (see Sections 3.5, 3.7, and 5.3.5). Therefore, one should be sure to hear the blessings before and after the Torah Reading and the prophetic portions that are read on those days and answer *amen.* Partaking of additional food and drink during the course of these days is also encouraged to help reach the desired number.

3.4.7 Other Preliminary Blessings

Other preliminary blessings for *birchot hanehenin* are recited before smelling fragrant scents. For smelling cloves and citron (see Sections 5.10.1 and 7.19), we recite the following *berachah:*

Baruch Atah, HaShem E-lo-kenu, Melech HaOlam,
borei minei vesamim.

❖

Blessed are You, Lord our God, King of the Universe,
Who creates various kinds of fragrant spices.

For other fragrant aromas, including the scent of trees, shrubs, and flowers, the *berachah* is:

Baruch Atah, HaShem E-lo-kenu, Melech HaOlam,
borei atzei vesamim.

❖

Blessed are You, Lord our God, King of the Universe,
Who creates fragrant trees.

For fragrant herbs and grasses, we recite:

Baruch Atah, HaShem E-lo-kenu, Melech HaOlam,
borei isvei vesamim.

❖

Blessed are You, Lord our God, King of the Universe,
Who creates fragrant herbs.

On smelling the fragrance of fruits or nuts, we recite:

Baruch Atah, HaShem E-lo-kenu, Melech HaOlam,
hanoten rei'ach tov baperot.

❖

Blessed are You, Lord our God, King of the Universe,
Who gives a good scent to fruits.

3.4.8 Blessings of Thanksgiving

Birchot hoda'ah, blessings of thanksgiving, are recited for both joyous and sorrowful events in private life. As we explained above, reciting *berachot* for both good news and bad affirms God's Presence in our lives and in no way suggests that we rejoice over tragic events. Rather, we are reminded that whatever God does is for the best,

Birchot hoda'ah all begin:

> *Baruch Atah, HaShem E-lo-kenu, Melech HaOlam, . . .*
>
> ❖
>
> Blessed are You, Lord our God, King of the Universe, . . .

Then each blessing is individually worded for the particular occasion.

Blessings for events in nature include the recitation on hearing thunder:

> *Baruch Atah, HaShem E-lo-kenu, Melech HaOlam,*
> *she'kocho ugevurato malei olam.*
>
> ❖
>
> Blessed are You, Lord our God, King of the Universe,
> Whose strength and might fill the universe.

and on seeing lightning, seeing a comet, or experiencing an earthquake:

> *Baruch Atah, HaShem E-lo-kenu, Melech HaOlam,*
> *oseh ma'aseh vereshit.*
>
> ❖
>
> Blessed are You, Lord our God, King of the Universe,
> Who makes the works of Creation.

and on seeing a rainbow:

> *Baruch Atah, HaShem E-lo-kenu, Melech HaOlam,*
> *zocher habrit, v'ne'eman bivrito,*
> *v'kayam b'ma'amaro.*
>
> ❖
>
> Blessed are You, Lord our God, King of the Universe,
> Who remembers the covenant, is faithful to His covenant,
> and fulfills His word.

and on seeing the ocean:

Baruch Atah, HaShem E-lo-kenu, Melech HaOlam,
she'asah et hayam hagadol.

❖

Blessed are You, Lord our God, King of the Universe,
Who created the great sea.

Other exceptional occasions include hearing of a death:

Baruch Atah, HaShem E-lo-kenu, Melech HaOlam,
Dayan haEmet.

❖

Blessed are You, Lord our God, King of the Universe,
the True Judge.

and on escaping grave danger or illness (usually recited in the synagogue in the presence of a quorum; see Section 3.5.5):

Baruch Atah, HaShem E-lo-kenu, Melech HaOlam,
hagomel l'chayavim tovot,
she'g'malani kol tov.

❖

Blessed are You, Lord our God, King of the Universe,
Who grants favors to the unworthy,
Who has granted me everything good.

and on passing a place where only a miracle could have prevented imminent harm, such as an accident:

Baruch Atah, HaShem E-lo-kenu, Melech HaOlam,
she'asah li nes b'makom hazeh.

❖

Blessed are You, Lord our God, King of the Universe,
Who performed a miracle for me in this place.

Reciting any *berachah* is an acknowledgment of God's involvement in everyday matters. Other occasions that require a blessing include hearing good news:

Baruch Atah, HaShem E-lo-kenu, Melech HaOlam,
hatov v'hametiv.

❖

Blessed are You, Lord our God, King of the Universe,
Who is good and does good.

and putting on new garments:

Baruch Atah, HaShem E-lo-kenu, Melech HaOlam,
malbish arumim.

❖

Blessed are You, Lord our God, King of the Universe,
Who clothes the naked.

and seeing a great Torah scholar:

Baruch Atah, HaShem E-lo-kenu, Melech HaOlam,
she'chalak mechachmato lire'av.

❖

Blessed are You, Lord our God, King of the Universe,
Who has shared His knowledge with those who fear Him.

and seeing a great secular scholar:

Baruch Atah, HaShem E-lo-kenu, Melech HaOlam,
she'natan mechachmato l'vasar v'dam.

❖

Blessed are You, Lord our God, King of the Universe,
Who has given His knowledge to flesh and blood.

3.4.9 Blessings on *Mitzvot*

Birchot hamitzvot are almost always recited before performing the *mitzvah* (we will note exceptions in later chapters). They all begin with the following words:

> *Baruch Atah, HaShem E-lo-kenu, Melech HaOlam,*
> *asher kidshanu b'mitzvotav v'tzivanu . . .*
>
> ❖
>
> **Blessed are You, Lord our God, King of the Universe,**
> **Who sanctified us with His commandments and commanded us . . .**

Note the grammatical structure of this type of blessing. Like the previous preliminary blessings, this type, too, begins with the words "Blessed are You," addressing God as our personal God; but the phrase continues and concludes in the third person: "Who sanctified us . . . and commanded us . . . ," and so forth. In the third-person structure, we recognize that God is more removed from us. He is a universal Majesty, Who has commanded us to serve Him and perform His *mitzvot.* This type of blessing shows gratitude, too, but it also thanks God for His *mitzvot,* which give us both the opportunity and the privilege to serve Him.

We will discuss these in detail in later chapters within the context of the religious observances mentioned. Examples of several *mitzvot* and the phrases which conclude the recitation of the respective *birchot hamitzvot* follow. The *mitzvot* are discussed in the chapter noted in parentheses after the phrase,

- . . . to wrap ourselves in the fringed garment (3.6.3)
- . . . to wear phylacteries (3.6.5)
- . . . to kindle the lights of the Sabbath (5.2.1)
- . . . on sounding the ram's horn (6.10)
- . . . on eating unleavened bread (7.4.7)
- . . . concerning the taking of the palm branch (7.19)
- . . . to kindle the lights of the Festival of Lights (8.3)
- . . . on the reading of the Scroll [of Esther] (8.10)
- . . . concerning ritual immersion (9.6)
- . . . to separate the dough (9.7.4)
- . . . concerning circumcision (9.10.4)
- . . . to redeem the first-born son (9.11.1)

References to other *berachot* appear throughout the book as well.

3.4.10 Blessings after Eating and Drinking

We have discussed at length many of the preliminary blessings associated with *birchot hanehenin,* in particular with regard to eating and drinking. We noted earlier that it is also necessary to recite a *berachah acharonah,* a final blessing, after partaking of food and drink, recognizing God as the Source of everything.

A final blessing is required if one has eaten at least a ***k'zayit,*** an amount equivalent in volume to an olive or half an egg (a little more than one fluid ounce), or has drunk at least a ***r'vi'it,*** equivalent in volume to an egg and a half (a little more than three fluid ounces), of any liquid.

One of three different texts is recited, depending on the food or drink: (1) Grace after Meals; (2) the Abridged Text of Grace after Meals; and (3) the Blessing of the Creator of Living Things. Let us examine these briefly.

- **Grace after Meals**
  Only the obligation to bless God after eating is biblical in origin.

> **And you shall eat and be satisfied,**
> **and bless the Lord, your God,**
> **for the good land He has given you.**
> —*Parshat Eikev,* Deuteronomy 8:10

  Whenever a meal is eaten, with or without bread, it is necessary to recite the full ***Birkat HaMazon,*** Grace after Meals. Just prior to this recitation, the fingertips are washed. This is called ***mayim acharonim***, literally, final waters. Historically, the purpose was to remove salt particles which might have clung to the fingers and could harm the eyes. The four blessings in *Birkat HaMazon* (see Section 5.5.7) were composed by (1) Moses; (2) Joshua; (3) King David and King Solomon; and (4) the *Tana'im* of Yavneh (see Sections 1.3.1 and 1.3.2). There are special recitations added to Grace after Meals during a wedding feast, at a circumcision, and in a house of mourning. These occasions are all discussed in Chapter 9.

- **Abridged Text of Grace after Meals**
  A portion of a three-part *berachah* is recited after three specific groups of food/drink: (1) grain products other than bread; (2) wine; and (3) fruits, specifically, grapes, figs, pomegranates, olives, and dates. In a sense, it is a summary of the full Grace after Meals. Its recitation was authorized by the sages in special gratitude for the seven species that grow in the Land of Israel (wheat, barley, grapes, figs, pomegranates, olives, and dates).

- **Blessing of the Creator of Living Things**
  At times, neither the full Grace after Meals nor the Abridged Text is appropriate. The Blessing of the Creator of Living Things is recited after eating fruits (other than those included in the Abridged Text), vegetables, or other foodstuffs, and after drinking any beverage other than wine.

For countless generations, Jewish children have been encouraged to *"make a berachah,"* as a part of their religious and spiritual instruction. Although they may be too young to clearly understand the concept of God, they can learn to be aware of Him.

We find guidance in the words of Rashi's interpretation: Whatever we teach our children when they are young—*be it for good or for bad*—will remain with them, even in old age, as it is written:

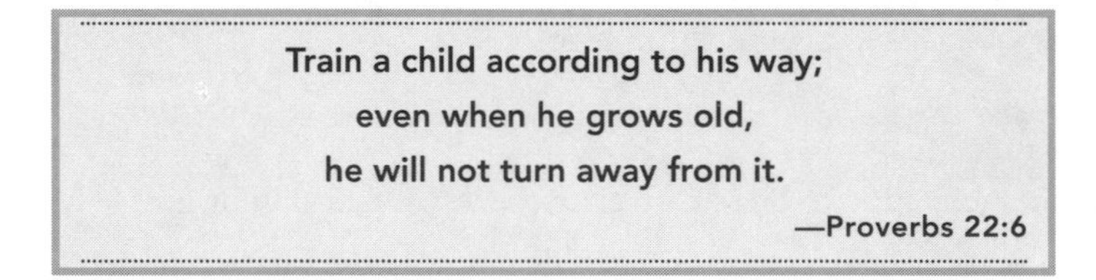

Train a child according to his way;
even when he grows old,
he will not turn away from it.
—Proverbs 22:6

3.5 The Concept of Prayer

The Hebrew word for prayer is ***tefillah,*** derived from the Hebrew verb meaning *to supplicate* or *to judge.* In Yiddish, the word for prayer is ***davenen*** (as a verb, to ***daven***). Numerous suggestions for the derivation of the Yiddish word include: (1) the Aramaic *de'avinun,* meaning *of our fathers,* referring to the patriarchs, who instituted the recitation of the three daily prayer services; (2) the Latin *divinus,* meaning *divine;* or (3) the Latin *devovere,* meaning *to exercise devotion.*

While the universal concept of prayer usually suggests God as the divine Judge, Judaism teaches that through prayer, we judge ourselves. Through introspection, we can raise our standard of moral conduct, as we strive to be like Him and fulfill our potential as human beings.

Tefillah is also more than pleading with God. It provides worshippers with an opportunity to proclaim their Jewish identity within the community and to perpetuate the *lashon hakodesh,* the holy language of Hebrew. We will now set out to answer the questions we raised in Chapter 1.

- Why do we pray?
- What do we pray?
- How do we pray?
- When do we pray?
- Where do we pray?
- Who should pray?

3.5.1 Why Do We Pray?

In the Torah, we are commanded to serve God every day.

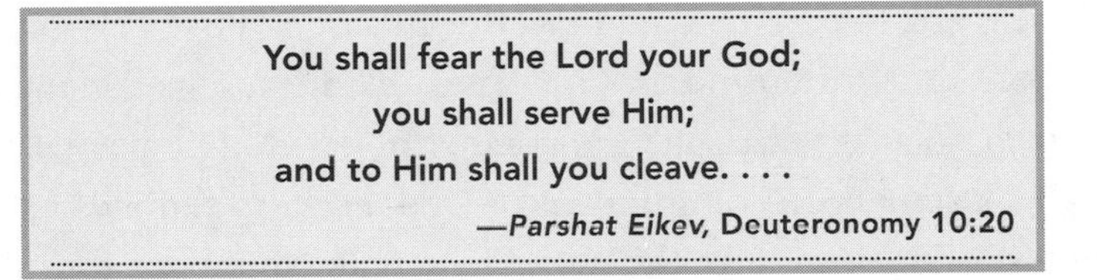

You shall fear the Lord your God;
you shall serve Him;
and to Him shall you cleave. . . .
—*Parshat Eikev*, Deuteronomy 10:20

Prayer is a positive *mitzvah* (see Section 1.4.2), and, therefore, the obligation to pray is of primary importance in the life of all Jews. According to the Talmud, *Masechet Chullin* 60b, God yearns for the prayers of the righteous. Through prayer, we are reminded of our dependence on God, and we trust that He will give us everything we need.

Surely God knows what is in our hearts and minds. Why must we put our emotions and thoughts into words? Rambam provides a succinct answer: *If we serve Him, we will be successful; if we do not, we will fail.*

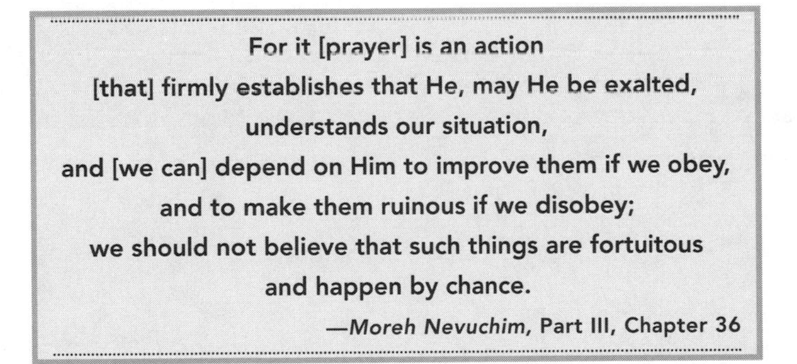

For it [prayer] is an action
[that] firmly establishes that He, may He be exalted,
understands our situation,
and [we can] depend on Him to improve them if we obey,
and to make them ruinous if we disobey;
we should not believe that such things are fortuitous
and happen by chance.
—*Moreh Nevuchim*, Part III, Chapter 36

3.5.2 What Do We Pray?

As we discussed briefly before, Hebrew prayer contains three constant elements: (1) praise of God; (2) pleas for His divine intervention on behalf of the Jewish people; and (3) gratitude for His blessings. Often, prayer also includes a fourth element: confession of sins. We praise Him because we recognize that He is the Supreme Ruler of the Universe. We plead with Him because He is our Father, and we, His children, are in need of His divine help. We thank Him because we acknowledge our obligation to Him and are cognizant of His beneficence to us. We confess to Him because He is a God of Mercy and will forgive us.

Daily prayers are, in part, derived from the *Tanach* and the Talmud. Inspirational passages from both the Written and the Oral Laws are intermingled in the daily prayers. The selection of particular verses and the manner in which they were arranged by the sages not only arouses a deep commitment to God, but also reminds us of the fundamental teachings of Judaism, from the most elementary to the most profound. Prayer instills a spiritual vitality into the souls of the worshippers and restates the basic tenets of faith in an organized pattern that becomes familiar with daily recitation.

3.5.3 How Do We Pray?

In the Torah, God commanded us to serve Him.

> **[You shall] love the Lord your God, and . . .**
> **serve Him with all your heart and with all your soul.**
>
> —***Parshat Eikev,*** **Deuteronomy 11:13**

How do we serve Him with our hearts? Service of the heart is called ***avodah she'b'lev.*** The Talmud clarifies this:

> **What is *avodah she'b'lev?***
> **It is prayer.**
>
> **—*Ta'anit 2a***

Prayer is the fundamental and spiritual expression of our souls. ***Avodah,*** which literally means "work," is an appropriate word for the difficult process we undergo in prayer: Through prayer we are *laboring* to refine our very nature. Prayer is a blend of our emotions and our thoughts, of our hearts and our minds. Thus, prayer reflects both our feelings and our beliefs.

When we *daven,* we speak directly to God, without an intermediary. Most prayers are recited in the first person plural, recognizing the shared responsibility Jews have for each other. In the Talmud, we find:

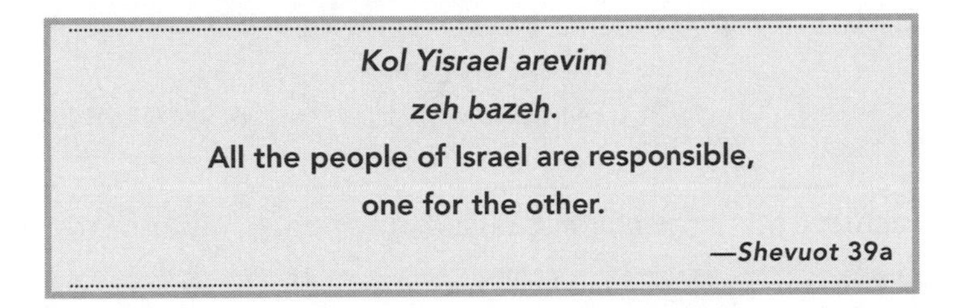
Kol Yisrael arevim
zeh bazeh.
All the people of Israel are responsible,
one for the other.
—*Shevuot* 39a

Just as there are melodic *nuscha'ot,* so, too, there are *nuscha'ot* of text style. For the most part, the main text of the prayers remains the same from style to style. However, there may be some minor alterations in the text, some variations in the order of prayers, or the addition of ***piyutim,*** prayer-poems. These *nuscha'ot* developed in many countries, including Spain, Poland, and Germany. No *nusach* is inherently more correct, only different. For this book, the text references are all based on *Nusach Ashkenaz,* which is primarily German, but refers to the style of Eastern Europe in general.

What if we don't know how to *daven* in Hebrew? While it is preferable to pray in Hebrew, the *lashon hakodesh,* it is permissible to pray in any language that is familiar.

When we pray, we are speaking to God, and must always be mindful that we are in the presence of the Lord of the Universe.

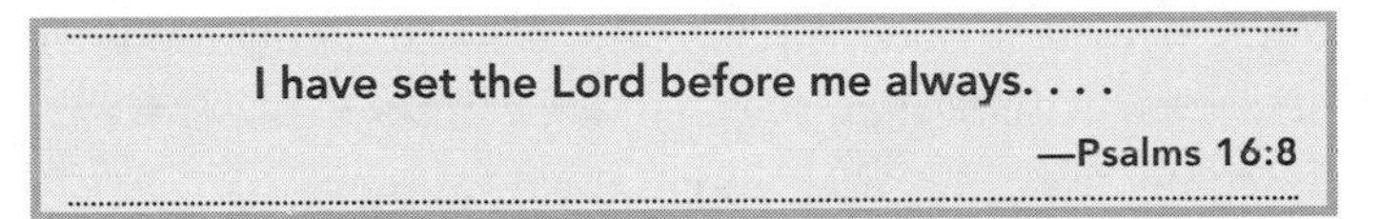
I have set the Lord before me always. . . .
—Psalms 16:8

Surely, we would address any king with respect; how much more so the King of Kings? With reverence, we should sit or stand, as required by the particular prayer. Whether we are praying at home or in the *bet kenesset,* we should be dressed appropriately, as befits one who is in the presence of the True Judge.

What else characterizes how we *daven?* In the *Mishneh Torah,* Rambam observes that:

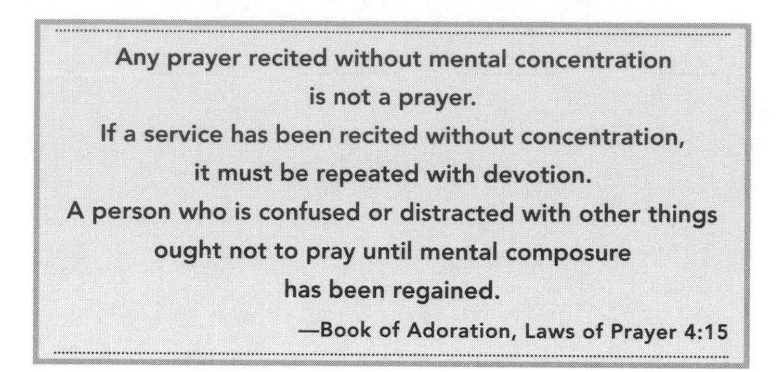

**Any prayer recited without mental concentration is not a prayer.
If a service has been recited without concentration, it must be repeated with devotion.
A person who is confused or distracted with other things ought not to pray until mental composure has been regained.**

—Book of Adoration, Laws of Prayer 4:15

How does one achieve this state of mental calm and focus? What factors make it possible to pray with devotion?

The essential ingredient in prayer is *kavanah,* or more specifically, ***kavanat halev,*** direction or intention of the heart. Attention, focus, and a spirit of sincere devotion are the characteristics of *kavanah.*

If we must recite the same prayers over and over, day after day, won't we fall into a mindless habit that minimizes our spiritual experience? Yes, we might, *at first.* Nevertheless, we should pray, if only on a superficial level. By the very act of prayer, we remain aware of God, and in time, we will come to appreciate the inner meaning of our words, thereby strengthening our *kavanah* and intensifying the personal connection we seek with the Almighty.

3.5.4 When Do We Pray?

We should not call upon God haphazardly, but with dignity and respect, and at the appropriate times. Jews recite ***tefillot,*** prayers, three times a day, at fixed time periods of the day, in the morning, the afternoon, and in the evening.

Morning	***Tefillat Shacharit***
Afternoon	***Tefillat Minchah***
Evening	***Tefillat Ma'ariv***

These scheduled prayer services provide structure in our lives and keep us mindful of the presence of God in the world. Of course, we may utter words of prayer to God at any time.

3.5.5 Where Do We Pray?

Historically, Hebrew liturgy found its primary expression in congregational worship, voicing the faith and hopes, the joys and sadness of the Jewish people. However, in time, certain prayers became part of daily activities in the home as well. Everyday life was imbued with thoughts of God, and Jews strived to do everything ***l'shem shamayim,*** for the sake of heaven. We will discuss congregational worship more fully later in the chapter.

To be sure, one may *daven* in private at home, for example, although it is preferable to pray with a ***minyan,*** a congregational quorum of ten males over the age of thirteen, because certain prayers are recited only with a *minyan.* We derive the concept of the quorum of ten from the biblical narrative of the Twelve Spies. Ten of them caused the Israelites to complain and mutter against God and Moses and Aaron.

In the Torah, God refers to the ten spies:

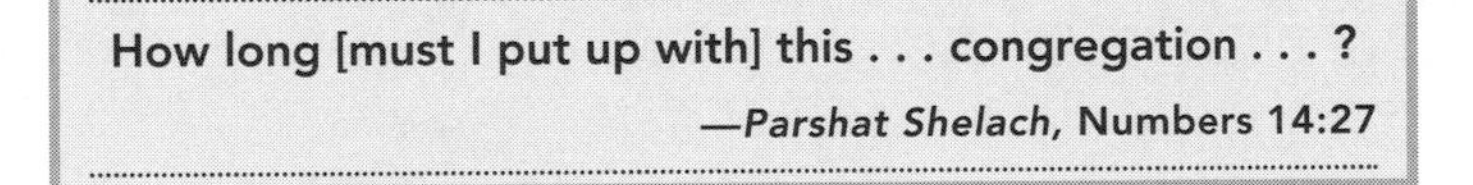

> How long [must I put up with] this . . . congregation . . . ?
>
> —*Parshat Shelach,* Numbers 14:27

From this verse, we learn that a congregation is comprised of ten men. By halachic deduction, we conclude, therefore, that a *minyan* of ten men is required for congregational worship and for public Torah Reading, among other rituals.

Does this mean women should not pray or need not, because they do not constitute a *minyan*? This brings us to the final entry in our list of questions about prayer.

3.5.6 Who Should Pray?

Let us begin with an important concept: ***mitzvah asei she'haz'man geramah.*** This phrase refers to those positive *mitzvot* which are bound by time; that is, those *mitzvot* that must be performed within a certain time period in order to be fulfilled. There are many time-bound *mitzvot,* both positive and negative; but Jewish law exempts—*not precludes*—women from performing the following seven positive commandments:

- *Tzitzit*
  Wearing the Fringed Garment
  (see Section 3.6.3 below)

- ***Tefillin***
  Phylacteries
  (see Section 3.6.5 below)
- ***Kriat Shema***
  Reciting the *Shema*
  (see Section 3.7.4 below)
- ***Shofar***
  Hearing the Sound of the Ram's Horn
  (see Sections 6.1 and 6.10)
- ***Sefirat HaOmer***
  Counting the *Omer*
  (see Section 7.4.16)
- ***Sukkah***
  Sitting in the *Sukkah*
  (see Section 7.18.2)
- ***Lulav***
  Taking the *Lulav*
  (see Sections 7.18.5 and 7.19)

While women are exempt from these *mitzvot,* it is customary for many women to observe all but *tzitzit* and *tefillin,* which some contemporary authorities forbid.

Time-bound biblical positive commandments from which women are not exempt include:

- ***Shabbat***
  Observing the Sabbath
  (see Section 5.1)
- ***Yom Kippur***
  Fasting on the Day of Atonement
  (see Section 6.4)
- ***Matzah***
  Eating Unleavened Bread
  (see Section 7.1.6)
- ***Chanukah***
  Lighting the Candles on the Festival of Lights
  (see Section 8.2)

Why were women exempt from certain time-bound *mitzvot?* A simple, albeit not untrue, answer is that in the days of the Mishnah and Gemara, the sages exempted them in order to make it possible for them to focus on the needs of their households and families. Without the necessity of performing certain *mitzvot* at a specific time, they were able to fulfill their most immediate responsibilities first.

However, this exemption applied equally to women who did not have such responsibilities, so it would be wrong to conclude that this suggests a lower spiritual status for women. In fact, women are deemed to have an enhanced sense of the inner tranquillity necessary for achieving spiritual closeness to God than do men. Therefore, men are required to perform additional *mitzvot* to actualize their spiritual potential.

So, the question arises: Is prayer a *mitzvah asei she'haz'man geramah?* The simple, but practical, answer is "No." Because no specific requirements for prayer, either in terms of content, form, or time, are to be found in the Torah itself, we can conclude that *tefillah* is a daily obligation for everyone. All Jews, men and women alike, are obligated to pray daily. The only distinction made between men and women is that most authorities feel that women must pray only twice a day—morning and afternoon—and men must pray three times, that is, in the evening as well.

Furthermore, there is little if any comment by scholars on the matter of these seven *mitzvot;* it is merely considered a fact of Jewish law, and no further clarification or comment about "why" is offered. It would seem, therefore, that its significance is not critical to the issue. In Jewish life, observant women can and do perform all of these time-bound *mitzvot,* with the possible exceptions of *tzitzit* and *tefillin.* It should be noted that a woman may undertake the commitment to fulfill any of the *mitzvot,* but she cannot forgo its observance if she does so.

So, *who should pray?* Everyone.

3.6 Getting Ready to Pray

Several religious objects are required for the proper recitation of prayer in Judaism, and all of them must meet specific religious requirements in order to be used during worship. We will discuss the basic ones: the ***siddur,*** prayer book; the ***machzor,*** holiday prayer book; the ***talit,*** prayer shawl; the ***kipah,*** skullcap; and the ***tefillin,*** phylacteries.

Other ritual objects, associated with prayers recited during specific observances, are discussed in their own context.

3.6.1 The Prayer Book

The *siddur* contains liturgical compositions that evolved over a period of some two thousand years. The daily prayer book contains all the *tefillot* for the weekday services and usually incorporates the prayers for the Sabbath and certain selections for the festivals as well (see Chapters 5, 6, and 7). The prayer book also often contains specific prayers for life-cycle events (see Chapter 9) and the *birchot hanehenin, birchot hoda'ah,* and *birchot hamitzvot,* which we discussed earlier (see Section 3.4.9).

The *siddur* is comprised of selections from *Tanach,* Mishnah, and Gemara. We find the historical narratives of the Torah blended with the religious expressions of our prophets. Talmudic passages are mingled with the inspiring hymns of praise found in the Book of Psalms. The cherished words of renowned sages and the beautiful compositions of unknown poets are equally represented within its pages.

The *siddur* is probably the book used most often in Jewish life, because it expresses the hopes and dreams, the tribulations and triumphs, the wisdom and the spirit of generations of Jews. The word *siddur* is derived from *seder,* which means *order.* The prayers are organized in a specific sequence, and in every prayer book, with minor variations, prayers are arranged in the same order.

In the synagogue, collective prayers are not intended to express personal sentiments, nor is the congregation meant to be a passive audience. Rather, each worshipper participates, and by joining voices, spirits are united in devotion, providing an unfailing sense of kinship, one Jew for another. The daily recitation of uniform prayers within a communal setting only enhances this kindred feeling. We will discuss the order of the daily prayers below.

3.6.2 The Holiday Prayer Book

The *machzor* is the prayer book used on the High Holidays and on each of the three Pilgrimage Festivals (see Chapters 6 and 7). Like the *siddur,* the *machzor* contains historical references, passages from the Torah, and portions drawn from the Talmud and the *Midrash,* among other sources. Much of the liturgy was composed by ***chazanim,*** cantors, who enriched the religious expression of the worshipper with beautiful melodies.

Special *piyutim,* prayer-poems, are an integral part of the festival *machzor.* They were written for the entire year's cycle by several thousand poets who were deeply inspired by the liturgy of the festivals. Only a small portion of the thousands of *piyutim* were later incorporated into the *machzor.* There are separate ***machzorim*** for the special prayers recited on the High Holidays and others for the three Pilgrimage Festivals. We will discuss various prayers from the *machzorim* in Chapters 6 and 7.

3.6.3 The Prayer Shawl

In the Torah, we learn about the *mitzvah* of *tzitzit,* the commandment to wear the fringed garment. Jewish men and boys, from childhood on, wear a ***talit katan,*** "small" *talit,* under their clothing. The *talit,* prayer shawl, is worn by men during *tefillah.*

The Lord spoke to Moses saying,
"Speak to the Children of Israel
and tell them to make fringes
in the corners of their garments
throughout their generations,
and to put a blue thread on the fringe of each corner;
and it shall be a fringe for you
so that you may look upon it,
and remember all the Lord's commands and do them,
and you will not follow
your heart and your eyes, which lead you astray.
It is for you to remember and do
all My commands and be holy for your God."
—*Parshat Shelach,* Numbers 15:37–41

The *talit katan* is also called ***arba kanfot,*** four corners. Worn throughout the entire day, it is usually made of cotton or wool and slips over the head. Each garment has woolen *tzitzit,* fringes, attached at the four corners. The following blessing is recited before putting on the *talit katan:*

Recite before Putting on the *Talit Katan*

Baruch Atah, HaShem E-lo-kenu, Melech HaOlam,
asher kidshanu b'mitzvotav v'tzivanu
al mitzvat tzitzit.

❖

Blessed are You, Lord our God, King of the Universe,
Who sanctified us with His commandments and commanded us
concerning the fringed garment.

The *talit katan,* which has fringes at the four corners, is worn every day by men and boys from childhood on.

Although *tzitzit* are not required to be worn at night, most men and boys do wear the *talit katan* until bedtime.

During prayer, adult Jewish males wrap themselves in the *talit,* the prayer shawl. It is worn by male worshippers, praying in private or with a congregation, during ***Shacharit,*** the Morning Service (the *talit* is worn in the evening only on the eve of the Day of Atonement; see Section 6.22). The *chazan* who leads the congregation in prayer wears a *talit* during all prayer services in the synagogue, except during ***Ma'ariv,*** the Evening Service. It is customary for young men to wear a *talit* during prayer only after marriage. A *talit* is always worn when one is honored at the Reading of the Torah, even if he is unmarried.

Traditionally, the *talit* is woven of wool, although silk and rayon are also used. It is rectangular in shape, and also has woolen *tzitzit* affixed at the corners of the garment. The fringes of both the *talit katan* and the *talit* are intended as a visual symbol to remind the Jew to remember and observe all the *mitzvot.* If a man wears a *talit,* he says the *berachah* for *tzitzit* when he puts on his *talit,* but not when he puts on his *talit katan.*

The *tzitzit* are prepared as follows: Four strings are inserted into a hole at each of the four corners of the garment; they are folded in half, making eight strings in each corner. Each string is comprised of thinner strands, and one of the thinner strands is

A Witty Remark!

My mother taught Hebrew school in our home, around the dining room table, when my father was the rabbi of a synagogue in upstate New York. She was a wonderfully gifted teacher: knowledgeable, inspiring, and in love with every student she ever met—and the kids loved her, too.

Every year at the beginning of classes, she prepared a *mitzvah* chart with the names of all the students on it. As the children learned the *berachot* for the various *mitzvot,* she gave them a shiny gold star on the chart for every *berachah* they learned and could recite by heart.

She also gave each of the boys a *talit katan* and taught them the *berachah* for *tzitzit.* Every day when the boys arrived for class, they each told her if they were wearing their *arba kanfot.* If they were, they made the *berachah,* and she gave them a star on the special *tzitzit* chart.

One day, one of her best students, who never missed class, was sick and had to stay home. Just as class was about to start, the phone rang. "Hello," a little raspy voice squeaked. "This is Daniel. I can't come to Hebrew school today, but I'm wearing my *tzitzit.* Please give me a star." Of course, she did.

longer than the others. The eight strings are tied in a knot and the longer thin strand is tightly wound seven times around the others. A double knot is made, and the long strand is wound eight times around the others. Another double knot is made, and the long strand is wound eleven times. A third double knot is made, and the long strand is wound thirteen times. The final double knot is made and the *tzitzit* is complete. This process is repeated for each of the four corners.

There is a significant symbolism attached to the four windings: 7 + 8 + 11 = 26, which is the numerical equivalent (see Section 2.4.2) of Y'K'V'K, God's Name, *HaShem;* the number 13 is equivalent to the word *Echad,* One (see Section 2.4.3). Together 26 + 13 = 39, so the symbolic equivalent of 39 is *HaShem Echad,* God is One.

Woven into the body of the *talit* are stripes of black or blue. The stripes symbolize the blue cord that was originally entwined in the fringes. A special dye was used to color the wool thread.

According to the Talmud, *Masechet Sotah* 17a and *Masechet Menachot* 43b, the color blue is a symbolic reference to the color of the sea, which resembles the color of the sky, which resembles the Chair of Glory, referring to the Almighty's throne. When the dye was no longer available, it was permitted to use white thread alone for the fringes.

How is the *talit* worn? Hold the open prayer shawl in front of you with the outer side facing you. Recite the following blessing and swing the *talit* around you, wrapping yourself in it. Adjust it on your shoulders, so the *tzitzit* do not touch the floor.

Recite before Putting on the *Talit*

Baruch Atah, HaShem E-lo-kenu, Melech HaOlam,
asher kidshanu b'mitzvotav v'tzivanu
l'hit'ateif ba'tzitzit.

❖

Blessed are You, Lord our God, King of the Universe,
Who sanctified us with His commandments and commanded us
to wrap ourselves in the fringed garment.

When prayers have been concluded, the *talit* is folded and placed in a velvet bag, which is often embroidered with religious symbols or with the worshipper's Hebrew name. It is then set aside for the next morning's prayers.

3.6.4 The Skullcap

In the days of the Temple, the *Kohanim* wore turbans during the sacrificial services. In the time of the Talmud, there were several rabbinical debates among the sages about the necessity for men and boys to cover their heads. In *Masechet Kiddushin* 31a, we find that the sage Rav Huna ben Yehoshuah did not walk more than four paces with his head uncovered, because he recognized that God's *Shechinah*, Divine Presence, was above him. Today, it is generally acknowledged as a *minhag,* but one that has attained the force of *halachah,* and going bareheaded is not acceptable in traditional Jewish circles.

Jewish men and boys wear a *kipah,* skullcap, during meals and while at prayer (the Yiddish word is ***yarmulke***). It is a sign of reverence for God and a distinguishing characteristic of the Jew, and many wear a *kipah* all the time. Because it is a constant reminder that He is always above us, the *kipah* effects a sense of humility.

Kipot come in sizes, just like men's hats, but the proper size of the *kipah* is often a topic of discussion. Ideally, it should cover the better part of the top of the head. Men and boys alike often use a hair clip or bobby pin to keep the *kipah* firmly in place.

Kipot are variously sewn from velvet, satin, and leather, among other fabrics. They may be lined or unlined, black or brightly colored, decorated or plain. Often beautiful *kipot* are hand-crocheted, sometimes with Hebrew names or with fanciful or traditional patterns and designs.

Many men opt to wear a hat outside in public, removing it when they go indoors and putting on a *kipah.* It is a familiar sight in most places and has been allowed in court, permitted in the operating room, accepted in the theater, and spotted in the halls of government.

Women and girls are not required to wear a *kipah.* The fact that some do does not make it a custom to be adopted. Many married women do cover their hair with a hat, scarf, or wig as a matter of modesty, but this has nothing to do with wearing a *kipah.*

3.6.5 The Phylacteries

Phylacteries is an English word derived from the Greek word *phylakterion,* meaning safeguard or amulet. In Hebrew the word is *tefillin,* and it refers to the small cubes of leather worn by the Jewish male during weekday *Shacharit* from the time of his ***Bar Mitzvah*** on (we will capitalize the religious ceremony).

A Jewish boy achieves religious maturity at the age of thirteen and one day. On that day he becomes a ***bar mitzvah,*** a son of the commandments, one who is fully obligated to observe all the *mitzvot* of the Torah. At the time of his *Bar Mitzvah,* a boy first puts on *tefillin* and is called up to the Reading of the Torah, an honor known as an ***aliyah la Torah*** or more commonly, just ***aliyah.*** If his *Bar Mitzvah* is celebrated on the Sabbath, when *tefillin* are not worn, he may begin to put on his *tefillin* on any weekday the Torah is read (prior to the Sabbath of his *Bar Mitzvah*), so that he can receive an *aliyah.* Many boys start wearing *tefillin* even a month before the *Bar Mitzvah.* It is these two events—putting on *tefillin* and being honored with an *aliyah*—that mark his passage into religious responsibility. We will discuss other aspects of *Bar Mitzvah,* as well as ***Bat Mitzvah*** for girls, who are not obligated to wear *tefillin,* in Section 9.14.2.

The *mitzvah* of putting on *tefillin* is found in Deuteronomy 6:8, which is one verse of the *Kriat Shema* (see below). It commands:

> And you shall bind them for a sign upon your hand;
> and they shall be for frontlets between your eyes.

There are two phylacteries: the ***tefillin shel rosh,*** the one worn on the head, and the ***tefillin shel yad,*** the one worn on the hand. The *tefillin shel rosh* contains four compartments; each holds one strip of parchment inscribed with a biblical passage. Two of

The *talit, kipah,* and *tefillin* are worn by Jewish men during daily prayer, at home or in the synagogue.

the four passages are from *Shemot*—Exodus 13:1–10 and 13:11–16—and two from *Devarim*—Deuteronomy 6:4–9 and 11:13–21. The *tefillin shel yad* contains only one compartment in which one strip of parchment is inscribed with the same four biblical passages as those found in the *tefillin shel rosh.*

The leather cube of the *shel rosh* is placed on the head from the hairline toward the back of the head. The leather cube of the *shel yad* is placed on the inside of the upper left arm muscle.

The two leather straps of the *shel rosh,* each of which is called a ***retzuah,*** are knotted at the base of the skull to form the Hebrew letter *daled.* The straps hang down the front. Attached to the *shel yad* is a single leather strap, also called a *retzuah,* which is knotted in the shape of the Hebrew letter *yud.* It is wound seven times around the left arm toward the body.

On the *shel rosh,* the Hebrew letter *shin* appears twice, once written with three strokes, once with four. The seven strokes correspond to the number of times the *retzuah* is wound on the left arm.

Together the three letters, *shin, daled,* and *yud,* spell the Hebrew word ***Shaddai***—שדי—the divine Name of the Almighty.

Tefillin are not worn on the Sabbath or on festivals. The Torah passages found in both the *shel rosh* and the *shel yad* stress the Jew's obligation to love God with his entire being, and to express that love by the strict observance of God's commandments. The Jew is to direct his mental and emotional faculties, his thoughts and feelings, to the service of God. The *shel rosh* on the head signifies the mental faculties; the *shel yad* on the left side near his heart, the emotional faculties. A man who is left-handed wears the *tefillin shel yad* on his right arm.

There is a difference of opinion between Rashi and his grandson, Rabbi Jacob ben Meir, known as Rabbenu Tam, regarding the arrangement and order of the four biblical paragraphs contained in the *tefillin*. Because of this, some Jews wear two pairs of *tefillin,* one after the other, one arranged according to the opinion of Rashi, the other according to that of his grandson. However, for most Jews, Rashi's opinion prevails.

After prayers have been concluded, the leather cubes of the *tefillin* are covered with protective cases called ***pidelach,*** the straps of the *tefillin* are wound around the edges of each of the protective covers, and the *tefillin* are placed in a velvet bag, similar to the one used for the *talit*. There they remain until the next morning service.

The *tefillin* are written on parchment by a qualified *sofer*, scribe, and may take as long as a week to prepare. The cost varies from one hundred and fifty to eight hundred dollars. When *tefillin* become *pasul,* ritually unfit for use, they should be buried with the same reverence accorded a *pasul Sefer Torah.*

3.7 The Morning Service

The Morning Service is called *Tefillat Shacharit,* from the Hebrew word ***shachar,*** dawn. It must be recited between dawn and midday. The terms *dawn* and *midday* have specifically calculated time frames. According to Jewish teaching, *Shacharit* was composed by Abraham our forefather. His life was characterized by the attribute of kindness, as he emulated the divine benevolence that was bestowed upon Him.

Tefillat Shacharit corresponds to the daily sacrifice, called ***Korban Tamid,*** which was offered in the *Bet HaMikdash* in the morning.

The *Shacharit* consists of five parts:

- ***Birchot HaShachar*** Morning Blessings
- ***Pesukei D'Zimrah*** Verses of Song
- ***Kriat Shema*** Recitation of the *Shema*
- ***Shemoneh Esrei*** Eighteen Benedictions
- ***Tachanun*** Prayers of Supplication

All the introductory prayers are a prelude to the recitation of *Kriat Shema* and *Shemoneh Esrei*.

Modeh Ani, the very first prayer of the morning, is of the first type mentioned above. It is recited immediately upon awakening, even while we are still in bed. It does not contain God's Names, and, therefore, may be said before washing.

The Talmud comments:

> **Five things are a sixtieth part of something else, [including] sleep [which] is a sixtieth of death.**
>
> **—*Berachot* 57b**

Thus, it is appropriate to acknowledge that God has once again restored our souls to us, and we thank Him for this gift of life.

Recite *Modeh Ani* When You Wake Up

I thank You, Living and Eternal King,
Who has restored my soul to me with mercy;
Your faithfulness is great.

After reciting *Modeh Ani,* we wash our hands ritually to differentiate between the "death-like" state of sleep, when impure thoughts or actions may have occurred, and the revived state of our restored spirit, when we are ready to serve God again. Just as the *Kohanim* washed their hands (and feet) before they began the service in the Temple, so, too, we begin to serve Him by washing.

1. Hold a cup in your right hand, and fill it with water.
2. Transfer the cup to your left hand, and pour some of the water over your right hand up to the wrist.
3. Transfer the cup to your right hand, and pour some of the water over your left hand up to the wrist.
4. Repeat Steps 2 and 3 twice more, so that each hand has been washed three times.

Before drying your hands, recite the following blessing.

Recite *Al N'tilat Yadayim* after Ritually Washing Your Hands

Baruch Atah, HaShem E-lo-kenu, Melech HaOlam,
asher kidshanu b'mitzvotav v'tzivanu
al n'tilat yadayim.

❖

Blessed are You, Lord our God, King of the Universe,
Who has sanctified us with His commandments and commanded us
concerning washing the hands.

It is customary to lift our hands as we say the blessing. The words ***al n'tilat yadayim*** do not literally mean "concerning washing the hands," but "lifting up the hands," indicating that we are raising our hands and ourselves to the service of *HaShem.*

3.7.1 *Birchot HaShachar*

Birchot HaShachar begin with ***Adon Olam,*** a prayer that reaffirms our belief in the all-powerful God as the Master of the World. *Adon Olam* expresses in beautiful, poetic language the ultimate trust we place in *HaShem* to care for us, to provide for us, and protect us from all harm, when we sleep and when we wake. We begin our morning prayers with confidence and faith in the Eternal God—Who was, Who is, and Who always will be.

The preliminary Morning Blessings continue with additional prayers that suggest our progression from a state of unconscious sleep to full wakefulness and readiness to serve God. These *tefillot* remind us that neither the physical body nor the spiritual soul can perform any *mitzvot* without the other. Other blessings continue the progression from sleep to wakefulness, recognizing that it is God Who provides everything from the early dawn forward.

All of the preliminary blessings mirror the daily routine. Then in complete readiness, the Jew's service of God continues with Torah study. *Birchot HaShachar* include selections from the Torah and Talmud, combined to complete the daily minimum of required Torah study.

Birchot HaShachar recount the biblical narrative of ***Akeidat Yitzchak,*** the Binding of Isaac, when *HaShem* tests Abraham's loyalty. This seminal event in Jewish history is especially significant, because it marks the tenth and final trial Abraham had to pass to prove his worthiness to be the founder of the Jewish people. This account is recalled frequently elsewhere in the liturgy, as well.

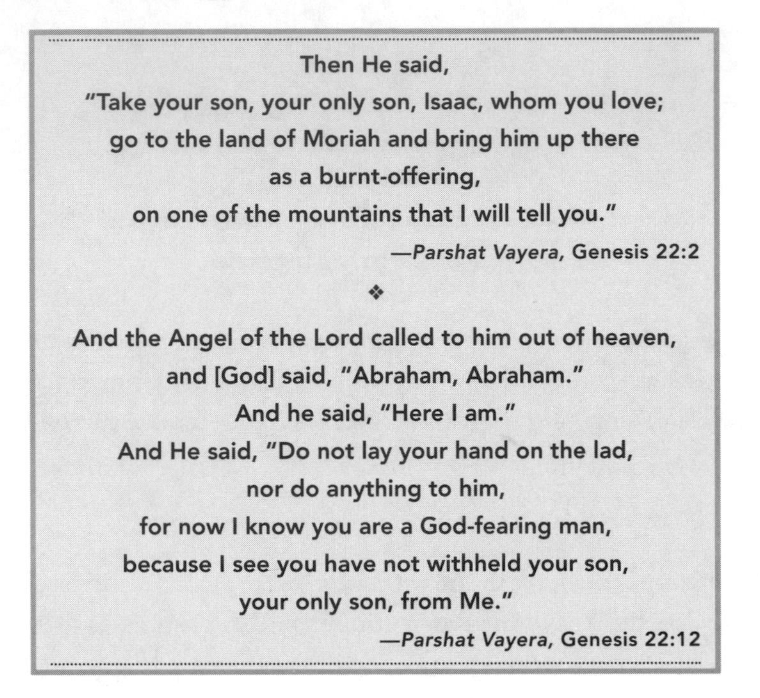
Then He said,
"Take your son, your only son, Isaac, whom you love;
go to the land of Moriah and bring him up there
as a burnt-offering,
on one of the mountains that I will tell you."
—*Parshat Vayera,* Genesis 22:2

❖

And the Angel of the Lord called to him out of heaven,
and [God] said, "Abraham, Abraham."
And he said, "Here I am."
And He said, "Do not lay your hand on the lad,
nor do anything to him,
for now I know you are a God-fearing man,
because I see you have not withheld your son,
your only son, from Me."
—*Parshat Vayera,* Genesis 22:12

Of course, it was never God's intention that Abraham really sacrifice Isaac. Rashi explains this terrifying and seemingly unreasonable request of God.

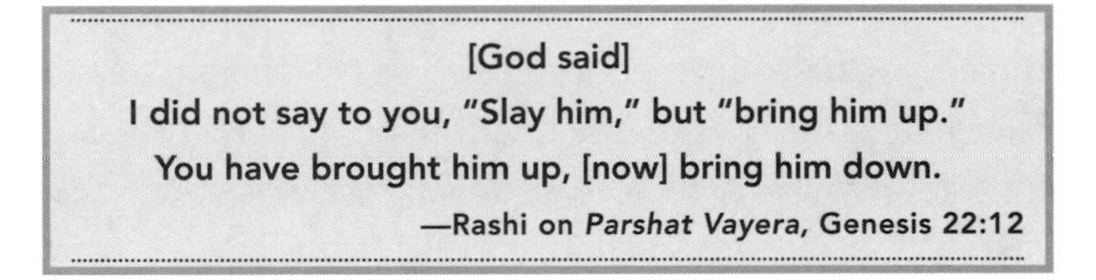
[God said]
I did not say to you, "Slay him," but "bring him up."
You have brought him up, [now] bring him down.
—Rashi on *Parshat Vayera,* Genesis 22:12

Several other passages from the Torah, the Mishnah, and the Gemara complete the *Birchot HaShachar.*

3.7.2 *Pesukei D'Zimrah*

Verses of Song, the second part of *Shacharit,* begin with the prayer ***Baruch She'Amar,*** Blessed Is He Who Spoke—that is, created the world out of nothing with His word. A prayer of thanksgiving, it is recited standing, and begins with several verses that do not contain the *Shem HaM'yuchad,* but enumerate several of God's attributes, which is how we are to come to know Him.

Pesukei D'Zimrah also incorporate passages from Chronicles, Nehemiah, various biblical verses, and several selections from Psalms, the divinely inspired poems, written in praise of God, by King David. The last six, Psalms 145–150, comprise the actual Verses of Song. These eloquent and soulful hymns express King David's fervent love of the Almighty.

Ashrei, two verses from Psalms 84:5 and 144:15, serves as a prefix to Psalm 145, which is an acrostic of the *alef-bet.*

Psalms 146–150 begin with a description of divine providence for the individual, ***hashgachah p'ratit,*** and proceed to ***hashgachah k'lalit,*** divine providence for the entire community of Israel. In Psalm 150, the praises of the individual soar and swell to the praises of the multitudes, until the entire universe joins in a crescendo of song.

Pesukei D'Zimrah continue with the prayer ***Az Yashir Moshe,*** the Song of Moses (*Parshat Beshalach,* Exodus 15:1–18), which recalls the crossing of the Red Sea. It was a time of great awe for the Jewish people, who witnessed the miracles God performed for them. As they fled from the pursuing Egyptians and saw them swallowed in the Splitting of the Red Sea, Moses and the Israelites were inspired to sing this prayer—sometimes called the Song of the Sea—in gratitude to God.

The final prayer of *Pesukei D'Zimrah,* ***Yishtabach,*** contains fifteen different expressions of praise, and completes the theme of *Baruch She'Amar* which began the section with:

Blessed is He Who spoke, and the world came into being.

Yishtabach concludes with:

Blessed are You, Lord, most glorified King,
God, deserving of thanks, Lord of wonders,
Who is pleased with hymns,
You God and King, Life of the Universe.

Thus, God is praised not only as the Creator of the World, but also as the very Life of the Universe.

3.7.3 Recitations before *Kriat Shema*

The next section begins with two verses of ***Barchu,*** which are said responsively by the cantor and then by the cantor and the congregation. These verses are omitted when praying in private.

Recite *Barchu*
Barchu et HaShem HaMevorach.
❖
Bless the Lord Who is blessed.

and

Respond to *Barchu*
Baruch HaShem HaMevorach l'olam va'ed.
❖
Blessed be the Lord Who is blessed forever and ever.

Two introductory prayers are then recited before the *Shema: **Yotzer Or*** and ***Ahavah Rabbah.*** In the first verses of *Yotzer Or,* we are not thanking God again for the new day, as in *Birchot HaShachar.* Instead, we are affirming the Unity of God. In contrast to pagan civilizations that believed in many deities, which vied for supremacy, Judaism believes in only One God, Who is responsible for both light and darkness, and in fact, for everything. *Yotzer Or* concludes by again declaring God as the Creator; thus, we realize that He renews the Creation every day.

Ahavah Rabbah, the second prayer before *Kriat Shema,* begins with our avowal of God's eternal love and mercy for the Jewish people. Dating to the early days of the Second Temple, this ancient prayer is a plea for God to enlighten us with His Torah, as He did for our ancestors.

We ask for understanding, so we not only can observe the precepts ourselves, but also teach them to our children. This foreshadows the essence of the *Shema* that follows.

3.7.4 *Kriat Shema*

Kriat Shema is a cornerstone of Jewish life and an affirmation of abiding faith in the One God. Reciting the *Shema* is tantamount to undertaking the observance of all the precepts of the Torah. It is comprised of three biblical passages: *Parshat Va'etchanan*, Deuteronomy 6:4–9; *Parshat Eikev*, Deuteronomy 11:13–21; and *Parshat Shelach*, Numbers 15:37–41.

There are very precise instructions about when, where, and how *Kriat Shema* is to be recited. In broad strokes, it is read twice a day, either in private or in the synagogue, during *Shacharit* and *Ma'ariv*. The three sections should be read in the order listed above. Words must be pronounced distinctly, taking great care not to run them together.

The first six words are found in *Parshat Va'etchanan*, Deuteronomy 6:4. The last letter of the first word, *Shema*, and the sixth word, *Echad*—that is, *ayin* and *daled*—spell the Hebrew word ***eid***, עד, witness. In the *Sefer Torah*, these two letters are written larger than the others. These words have united Jews for thousands of years, bearing witness to God's Unity. They are to be recited with great devotion and concentration. Rambam comments in the *Mishneh Torah*, as follows:

> **[Whoever] recites the *Shema* and does not concentrate . . .**
> **while reciting the first verse . . .**
> **has not fulfilled [the] obligation**
> **[to recite the *Shema*].**
> —Book of Adoration, Laws of *Kriat Shema* 2:1

It is customary to cover our eyes with our right hand when reciting these first six words, referred to as ***Shema Yisrael***, in order to enhance our *kavanah* and to focus our attention on the import of the words we are saying.

Begin the Recitation of *Kriat Shema*

Shema Yisrael, HaShem E-lo-kenu, HaShem Echad.

❖

Hear, O, Israel, the Lord is our God, the Lord is One.

The first paragraph, which continues in *Parshat Va'etchanan*, Deuteronomy 6:4–9, reminds us of God's command to love Him with all our heart, soul, and might, to educate our children in the Torah, and to be mindful of the presence of the Almighty through the observance of the *mitzvot* of *tefillin,* phylacteries (see Section 3.6.5), and ***mezuzah,*** the scroll affixed to the doorpost (see Section 9.7.1).

Continue the Recitation of *Kriat Shema*

And you shall love the Lord your God
with all your heart, and with all your soul, and with all your might;
and these shall be the words which I command you
this day upon your heart,
and you shall teach them diligently to your children;
and you shall talk of them when you sit in your house
and when you walk by the way,
and when you lie down and when you rise up;
and you shall bind them for a sign upon your hand
and they shall be for frontlets between your eyes;
and you shall write them upon the doorposts of your house
and upon your gates.

Why are we commanded to love God at all? To remind ourselves that He is the Source of everything. He is our Heavenly Father, and we love Him, and like all children, we want to please Him. We do this by obeying His commandments.

What does "with all your heart, and with all your soul, and with all your might" mean? Our hearts are often torn between the ***yetzer tov,*** our inclination to do good, and the ***yetzer hara,*** the inclination that tempts us to do bad. We must work to overcome the propensity for evil, so that our whole heart is filled with love of God. Both inclinations cannot exist in service to Him, so we must master our heart to do only good.

What about our souls? We must, in fact, be ready to give up our very souls—that is, our lives—if the choice is between serving God and a life without Him. Throughout history, Jews have chosen to die ***al kiddush HaShem,*** for the sanctification of His Name, rather than give up their love for Him. In a broader sense, every honorable act that demonstrates the Jew's faithfulness to God is a sanctification of His Name.

"With all your might" means with all our material wealth, all our possessions, our money, our property. Love of God is more precious than anything we could possibly own.

How should we interpret "and these shall be the words which I command you this day upon your heart"? We fill our hearts with the Torah's eternal teachings. Even though the Torah was given thousands of years ago, we should feel that we receive it new, like a special gift, every day.

We are commanded to "teach them diligently to your children." This phrase applies to all Jewish children, so we are obligated to support Jewish education, even if we have no children of our own.

The *Shema* may be recited sitting or standing, even en route, stopping only to recite the first verse. Rambam clarifies these phrases in the *Mishneh Torah:*

> **Everyone may read the *Shema* in the ordinary postures—**
> **standing, walking, lying down, or riding on an animal.**
> **It is forbidden to recite the *Shema* in a prone position**
> **[with one's face to the ground]**
> **or in a supine position**
> **[on one's back looking straight up].**
> **But one may read it while lying turned to one side.**
>
> —Book of Adoration, Laws of *Kriat Shema* 2:2

Why do we recite "when you lie down" before "when you rise up"? In the account of Creation, we learn

> **And God called the light Day,**
> **and the darkness He called Night,**
> **and there was evening, and there was morning, one day.**
>
> —*Parshat Bereshit,* Genesis 1:5

From this verse, we understand that the period known as a day begins with the night before. Therefore, the first reading of the *Shema* on a given day is in the evening, when we lie down, so it is mentioned first.

The correct time for the evening recitation is anytime between the appearance of the first stars and midnight. If the recitation is delayed beyond midnight but is completed before daybreak, the obligation has been fulfilled; but this is not the desirable time frame.

The daytime recitation should begin six minutes before sunrise. However, if the recitation of the *Shema* is completed by the end of the third hour after sunrise, the obligation is fulfilled.

There are many other detailed instructions about the recitation of the *Shema.* Do we interrupt our work to recite *Shema* in a timely fashion? Do we stop eating or bathing? Do we wake someone when the time to recite *Shema* has arrived? May we pause to acknowledge someone who greets us during our recitation? These and numerous other points should be studied in order to properly fulfill the *mitzvah* of *Kriat Shema.*

The first paragraph concludes "and you shall bind them for a sign upon your hand and they shall be for frontlets between your eyes; and you shall write them upon the doorposts of your house and upon your gates." These verses refer to the *mitzvot* of *tefillin*, which we discussed in Section 3.6.5 above, and *mezuzah,* which will be explained in Section 9.7.1.

The second paragraph of the *Shema* emphasizes practical religious observance as the means to attain oneness with God. In addition to reiterating the commands of the first paragraph, the second paragraph describes the reward for obeying His commandments and the punishment for failing to do so. In *Parshat Eikev,* Deuteronomy 11:13–15, we continue reading the *Shema.*

Continue the Recitation of *Kriat Shema*

And if you will carefully obey My commands . . .
I will give rain for your land at the right season . . .
that you may gather in your grain, your wine, and your oil.
And I will produce grass in your fields for your cattle,
and you will eat and be satisfied.

God's promise of reward shows His great love for the Land of Israel, but we must recognize that the blessings God bestows on the Land of Israel are dependent on our fulfillment of the *mitzvot.* Rashi interprets God's promise: "If you will do what is incumbent upon you, I [God] will do what is incumbent upon Me."

We must remember, of course, that God's promise includes the promise of His swift punishment if we fail to fulfill our obligations. We continue in *Parshat Eikev,* Deuteronomy 11:16–17:

Continue the Recitation of *Kriat Shema*

Be careful that your heart is not deceived,
[for if] you turn aside and serve other gods and worship them,
the anger of the Lord will be kindled against you,
and He will shut the heavens, and there will be no rain,
and the ground shall not yield its produce,
and you will quickly perish
from the good land that the Lord gives you.

The second paragraph also includes the repetition of the *mitzvah* of *mezuzah* (see Section 9.7.1).

The concluding paragraph of the *Shema* (1) refers to the *mitzvah* of *tzitzit*, the fringed garment; (2) warns against following the heart's evil impulses; and (3) recalls the redemption of the Jewish people from Egypt. In *Parshat Shelach*, Numbers 15:37–40, we continue:

Continue the Recitation of *Kriat Shema*

The Lord spoke to Moses saying,
"Speak to the Children of Israel
and tell them to make fringes in the corners of their garments
throughout their generations,
and to put a blue thread on the fringe of each corner;
and it shall be a fringe for you
so that you may look upon it,
and remember all the Lord's commands and do them,
and you will not follow
your heart and your eyes, which lead you astray.
It is for you to remember and do
all My commands and be holy for your God."

The third paragraph concludes with a verse from *Parshat Shelach,* Numbers 15:41:

Conclude the Recitation of *Kriat Shema*

[And God said]
"I am the Lord your God
Who brought you out of the Land of Egypt
to be your God.
I am the Lord your God."

The last verse of *Kriat Shema* recalls God's deliverance of the Jewish people from the slavery of Egypt. "I am the Lord your God" is then repeated by the cantor, and the closing words of the *Shema* and the opening word of the next prayer, ***Emet v'Yatziv,*** are recited without pausing between them, as if they were part of the same sentence:

I am the Lord your God.
True . . .

When recited together, it means "the Lord your God is true."

Emet v'Yatziv contains several themes, including: (1) sixteen expressions of "truth," which reaffirm our belief in God's Unity and confirm our acceptance of His commandments; (2) God's love for the Jewish people throughout the generations; and (3) the conviction that God will again redeem Israel.

Shacharit continues with the recitation of the *Shemoneh Esrei,* the Eighteen Benedictions, the essential daily expression of praise, petition, and benediction.

3.7.5 *Shemoneh Esrei*

The *Shema* and the *Shemoneh Esrei* are the primary components of *Shacharit.* If we are pressed for time, we should recite the *Shema* (and the blessings before and after it) and the *Shemoneh Esrei.* If we cannot recite both, then we should at least say the *Shemoneh Esrei.*

The *Shemoneh Esrei* is fourth in the order of the daily prayers. The *Birchot HaShachar, Pesukei D'Zimrah,* and *Kriat Shema* are all preliminary *tefillot* to the Eighteen Benedictions: (1) in the preliminary Morning Prayers, we thank God for granting us life, and for the privilege of serving Him as Jews; (2) in the Verses of Song, we praise Him, acknowledging Him as the Creator of the World and everything in it; and (3) in the *Kriat Shema,* we proclaim His Unity and vow to observe His commandments with all our heart and soul and might. With this spiritual preparation, we are ready to petition God directly in the *Shemoneh Esrei.*

On weekdays, the *Shemoneh Esrei* consists of nineteen blessings (on the Sabbath and festivals, it has only seven; see Chapters 5, 6, and 7). Although *Shemoneh Esrei* means eighteen in Hebrew, a nineteenth blessing was added after the destruction of the Second Temple. It became the twelfth blessing within the structure of the final nineteen.

The *Shemoneh Esrei* is divided into three groups of blessings. By the very names we use to call upon Him in each of them, we are reminded of God's presence throughout Jewish history. The *Shemoneh Esrei* is also called the ***Amidah,*** from the Hebrew word ***la'amod,*** to stand. We recite it while standing at attention, symbolic of the posture of the angels (Ezekiel 1:7). Because the words are pronounced quietly, it is often referred to as the "silent" *Shemoneh Esrei.* As we begin the *Shemoneh Esrei,* we take three steps back, as if hesitating to approach the divine King. In humility, we utter this verse:

Recite before *Shemoneh Esrei* of *Shacharit*

O, Lord,
may You open my lips
so that my mouth shall declare Your praise.

Then we take three steps forward and bend our knees and bow our heads, as we begin the first blessing.

- Blessings 1, 2, and 3 are expressions of praise, in which we approach God with reverence and awe.
  1. In Blessing (1) we call upon Him as our God and invoke His Name as the God of our patriarchs, Abraham, Isaac, and Jacob. At this point, we bend our knees and bow our heads again. The first blessing concludes: "Blessed are You, Lord, Shield of Abraham."
  2. In Blessing (2) we address Him as the Great God, as the Mighty, as the Awe-Inspiring, and as the Sublime God. We recognize Him as our Heavenly Father, Who treats His children with lovingkindness, and as the Redeemer of Israel. The second blessing concludes: "Blessed are You, Lord, Who revives the dead."
  3. In Blessing (3) we speak to Him as our Holy God. The third blessing concludes: "You are holy, and Your Name is holy, and holy beings praise You every day. Blessed are You, Lord, holy God."

- Blessings 4–16 contain all the requests we wish to bring to God's attention.
  1. Blessing (4) contains a request for knowledge. The prayer ends: "Blessed are You, Lord, Who bestows knowledge graciously."
  2. Blessing (5) is a petition that we may repent and draw closer to God in great devotion. It concludes: "Blessed are You, Lord, Who is pleased with repentance."
  3. Blessing (6) is a request for God's forgiveness, so that our souls may be healed. It ends: "Blessed are You, Lord, Who is gracious and eternally forgiving."
  4. Blessing (7) is a prayer that God will be the Advocate for the people of Israel, that they may be redeemed and spared all affliction. This *tefillah* ends: "Blessed are You, Lord, Who redeems Israel."
  5. Blessing (8) asks God to mercifully restore the sick to health. The last sentence is: "Blessed are You, Lord, Who heals the sick among His people Israel."
  6. Blessing (9) is a prayer that asks God to bless the year, especially nature's bounty that sustains us throughout the seasons. It includes requests for rain and dew, which are recited in the appropriate seasons. This beautiful blessing ends: "Blessed are You, Lord, Who blesses the years."
  7. Blessing (10) appeals to God to safeguard the people of Israel and gather them from the four corners of the earth. It concludes: "Blessed are You, Lord, Who gathers the scattered exiles among your people Israel."
  8. Blessing (11) petitions God to restore the judges and leaders of old, and it seeks God's kindness and mercy as our King and True Judge. This *tefillah* ends: "Blessed are You, Lord, Who loves righteousness and justice."
  9. Blessing (12) is the prayer that was added after the destruction of the Second Temple. It pleads for the failure of those who slander the Jewish people in their efforts to harm us. It closes with: "Blessed are You, Lord, Who shatters the enemies and humbles the haughty."
  10. Blessing (13) requests God's benediction over the righteous and saintly, over the leaders and people, and over all those who trust in God. This blessing ends: "Blessed are You, Lord, Who is the Support and Guarantor of the righteous."
  11. Blessing (14) asks that God's mercy extend over Jerusalem, that the city be rebuilt for everlasting, and that the throne of David be restored. This prayer ends: "Blessed are You, Lord, Who builds Jerusalem."
  12. Blessing (15) seeks the arrival of the ***Mashiach,*** the Messiah who will come to redeem Israel. It concludes: "Blessed are You, Lord, Who causes deliverance to prosper."
  13. Blessing (16) is the last in the second section of the *Shemoneh Esrei.* We seek God's acceptance of our prayers and ask that He fulfill them in mercy. It ends: "Blessed are You, Lord, Who hears prayers."

- Blessings 17, 18, and 19 complete the *Shemoneh Esrei.* As we prepare to withdraw from the presence of the Holy One, we offer prayers of thanksgiving and gratitude for His blessings.
    1. Blessing (17) expresses the hope that God will be pleased with our prayer and that we may worship Him in His restored Holy Sanctuary. The final words are: "May our eyes behold Your return to Zion in mercy. Blessed are You, Lord, Who restores Your divine presence to Zion."
    2. Blessing (18) is a prayer of gratitude, calling upon God as the Rock of our lives and the Shield of our salvation. We thank Him for our very lives, our souls, and for the miracles He performs for us every day. We bow our heads and bend our knees as we recite the first words, straightening up as we mention *HaShem* by His Name: "We thank You Who is *HaShem. . . .*" This blessing ends, as we again bow our heads and bend our knees: "Beneficent One, Whose mercies never waver, Merciful One, Whose benevolence has no end, You have eternally been our hope."
    3. Blessing (19) is the last blessing of the *Shemoneh Esrei.* Its theme is repeated often throughout the liturgy of the Jewish people: "Blessed are You, Lord, Who blesses Your people Israel with peace."

The *Anshei Kenesset HaGedolah* selected and organized the prayers into a coherent body that would unify Jews throughout the world and time. What one Jew prayed, all Jews prayed, and in unity they found spiritual identity, national strength, and divine inspiration to worship God as He commanded.

Although the *Shemoneh Esrei* ends with the nineteenth blessing, the worshippers remain standing in place until after reciting a concluding prayer, ***E-lo-kai Netzor,*** which is found in the Talmud, *Masechet Berachot* 17a.

Recite *E-lo-kai Netzor* Immediately after *Shemoneh Esrei*

My God, guard my tongue from evil
and my lips from speaking lies. . . .
Open my heart to Your Torah
that my soul may follow Your *mitzvot.*
Defeat . . . those who plan evil against me. . . .
Do it for the glory of Your Name;
do it for the sake of Your holiness;
do it for the sake of Your Torah. . . .
May the words of my mouth
and the meditation of my heart please You. . . .
May He Who creates peace in His high heavens
create peace for us and for all Israel.
Amen.

Then worshippers take three steps backward, bow left, right, and forward, "taking leave" of the Almighty. ***Y'hi Ratzon,*** a short concluding prayer for the rebuilding of the *Bet HaMikdash* remains.

Recite *Y'hi Ratzon* to Conclude the *Shemoneh Esrei*

May it be Your will,
Lord, our God and God of our forefathers,
that the Temple be speedily rebuilt in our days,
and grant us our share in Your Torah.
There we will serve You with reverence
as in the days of old and in former years.
Then the offering of Judah and Jerusalem
will be pleasing to the Lord,
as in the days of old and in former years.

Once the worshippers complete the so-called "silent *Shemoneh Esrei,*" it is repeated aloud by the *chazan* (or other reader—not to be confused with the *ba'al korei,* who reads the Torah) who chants the service for the congregation. During the repetition, ***Kedushah,*** a responsive prayer, is inserted into the repetition of the *Shemoneh Esrei* after Blessing (2). The congregation rises to join the *chazan* in the recitation of the *Kedushah,* which is recited only with a *minyan,* for God's holiness is proclaimed and sanctified in public worship, among the Children of Israel, as found in the following biblical source.

> **And you shall keep My commandments and do them;**
> **I am the Lord;**
> **And you shall not profane My holy Name,**
> **and I shall be sanctified among the Children of Israel;**
> **I am the Lord Who sanctified you,**
> **Who brought you out of the land of Egypt to be your God;**
> **I am the Lord.**
>
> **—*Parshat Emor,* Leviticus 22:31–33**

Kedushah, which means sanctification or holiness, is one of the most beautiful prayers in all of Jewish liturgy. There are, in fact, three prayers that are referred to as *Kedushah,* and the Talmud in *Masechet Sotah* 49a discusses their importance, commenting that it is the recitation of these prayers that sustains the world.

We are discussing only the *Kedushah* that is associated with the repetition of the *Amidah.* The words, which are said responsively by the congregation and the *chazan,* awaken intense spiritual feelings, as the *chazan* and the congregation rise to join the chorus of angels that proclaims God's holiness.

The congregation begins and the *chazan* repeats the words.

Begin the Recitation of the *Kedushah*

Congregation then Cantor:
We sanctify Your Name in this world,
as they sanctify it in the highest heavens,
as it is written by Your prophet [Isaiah 6:3]:
"The angels call out to one another; . . .

The congregation and the *chazan* continue together, rising up on their toes, as they say each of the first three words.

Continue the Recitation of the *Kedushah*

All:

. . . 'Holy, holy, holy is the Lord of multitudes;
the whole earth is filled with His glory.' "

Why is the word ***kawdosh,*** holy, used three times? We find the following explanation in the Talmud's comment on Isaiah 6:3: The angels gather in three groups each day.

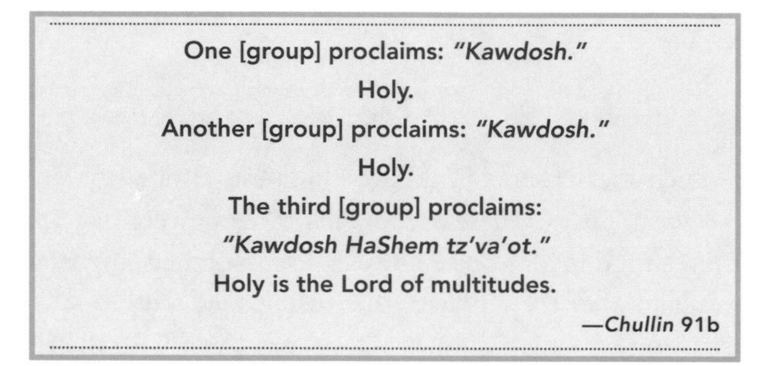

One [group] proclaims: *"Kawdosh."*
Holy.
Another [group] proclaims: *"Kawdosh."*
Holy.
The third [group] proclaims:
"Kawdosh HaShem tz'va'ot."
Holy is the Lord of multitudes.

—*Chullin* 91b

The three utterances are also an indication of His omnipresence in the spiritual world, in the physical world, and for all eternity.

The *chazan* continues.

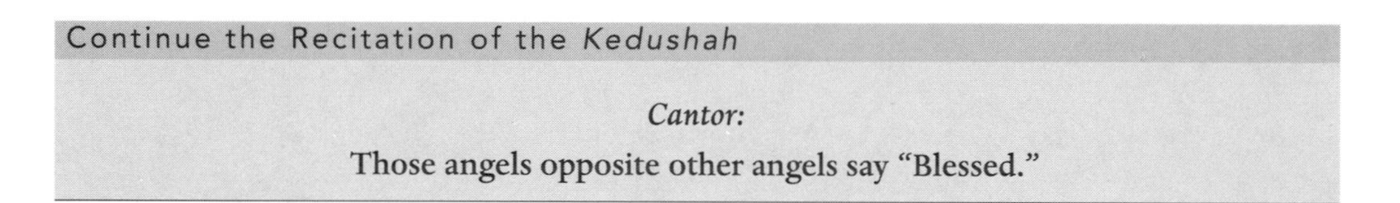

Continue the Recitation of the *Kedushah*

Cantor:

Those angels opposite other angels say "Blessed."

The *chazan* and the congregation respond, quoting from the prophet Ezekiel 3:12. They rise on their toes for the first word.

Continue the Recitation of the *Kedushah*

All:

Blessed be the glory of the Lord from His abode.
[that is, from His position of prominence]

The *chazan* continues:

Continue the Recitation of the *Kedushah*

Cantor:
And in Your holy writings it is written:

The *chazan* and the congregation respond, quoting from Psalms 146:10. They rise on their toes for the first (Hebrew) word (shall rule).

Continue the Recitation of the *Kedushah*

All:
The Lord shall rule forever.
Your God, Zion, from generation to generation.
Praise the Lord.

The *chazan* concludes:

Conclude the Recitation of the *Kedushah*

Cantor:
From generation to generation,
we shall tell of Your greatness,
and for all eternity we shall proclaim Your holiness.
Your praise, our God,
shall never leave our mouth,
for You, Lord, are the great and holy God and King.
Blessed are You, Lord, holy God.

When the *chazan* has completed the recitation of the *Kedushah,* the congregation is seated. The *chazan* continues the repetition of the *Shemoneh Esrei* with Blessing (3). While he repeats Blessing (18) aloud, the congregation recites a variation of the same prayer in an undertone. The *chazan* completes the repetition of the *Shemoneh Esrei* with Blessing (19), the prayer for peace.

Tefillat Shacharit continues with the recitation of *Tachanun,* Prayers of Supplication.

3.7.6 *Tachanun*

Tachanun, Prayers of Supplication, are special *tefillot* in which we ask for God's mercy. It is recited only on ordinary weekdays, and is omitted on the Sabbath and the festivals, and on other days when prayers of supplication are not to be offered. A longer version of *Tachanun,* in which we admit our sinful nature and ask for God's compassion and forgiveness, is recited on Mondays and Thursdays.

It is recited in a posture of supplication, that is, falling on one's face, with the head on the arm, in a modified position of prostration. This is derived from two sources: Numbers 16:22 and Joshua 7:6. Because the *tefillin* are still on the left arm, the worshipper falls on his right arm (a left-handed worshipper falls on his left arm).

The shorter form of *Tachanun* begins with David's response to the prophet Gad, who is considered David's prophet, because all his prophecies deal with David. In II Samuel 24:14, we find the opening words of *Tachanun,* in which we learn that God's mercy, even when it comes to punishment, is to be preferred over the punishment of man. We, therefore, recite *Tachanun* in a supplicant posture.

Tachanun then continues in order with Psalm 6 (except for the first verse). It concludes with a prayer comprised of verses from II Chronicles 20:12; Psalms 25:6; 33:22; 79:8; 123:3; Habbakuk 3:2; and Psalms 103:14; 79:9, in that order.

On Mondays and Thursdays, *Tachanun* begins with a very emotional recounting of the woes of the Jewish people from the time of *Churban Bayit Sheni.* It begins with Psalms 78:38 and includes verses from Psalms 40:12; 106:47; 130:3–4; 103:10; Jeremiah 14:7; Psalms 25:6; 20:2, 10; Daniel 9:15–19; Isaiah 64:7; and Joel 2:17 in that order. Before Psalm 6 is recited, we find the first verse of *Kriat Shema* from Deuteronomy 6:4, and the words from II Samuel 24:14, which are recited on other weekdays.

In all these verses, we confess our sins, recognizing that we have strayed from God, and this alone, is the cause of our suffering. We ask God to allow us to return to Him, for He opens His hand to sinners.

3.8 The Reading of the Law

The public Reading of the Law, ***Kriat HaTorah,*** is an integral part of Jewish worship. When the Torah was first given, Moses instructed the people to assemble regularly to hear the Reading of the Law, so that they would learn it thoroughly.

After the return of the Jewish people from exile in Babylonia, *Kriat HaTorah* was reinstituted by Ezra the Scribe. In order to provide instruction in Torah for the people, the weekly portion was read in the synagogue three times a week, on Monday and Thursday mornings, which were market days, and thus convenient for the people to gather, and on the morning of the Sabbath, when people had more leisure time. Thus, no more than three days would ever pass without instruction in the Law. Ezra also instituted the practice of *Kriat HaTorah* during ***Minchah*** on Sabbath afternoons. In addition, explanations and interpretations in the vernacular of the people were taught.

Today the Torah is still read at those times, as well as on all the festivals, the New Moon, and fast days. *Kriat HaTorah* requires the presence of a quorum of ten males over the age of thirteen, a *minyan*. On Monday and Thursday mornings, only three Torah honors are given; on *Shabbat* morning, seven; and at *Minchah* on *Shabbat* afternoon, three. If the New Moon (see Chapter 4) falls on a weekday, four are called; if it falls on the Sabbath, seven are called. Five or six are called on the festivals (see Chapters 6 and 7), unless they fall on the Sabbath, when seven are always called. These Torah honors are called ***aliyot,*** from the Hebrew verb meaning *to go up,* for all honorees ascend to the *bimah* for an *aliyah*.

3.8.1 Preliminary Verses before *Kriat HaTorah*

To begin, a congregant is honored with the opening of the *Aron HaKodesh*. According to mystical teachings, the heavenly gates of mercy are opened, so it is a propitious time to remove the *Sefer Torah* from the Holy Ark. The *Sefer Torah* is handed to the cantor. Taking it on his right shoulder, he turns to face the congregation and recites *Shema Yisrael* responsively with them (the following three verses are recited only on the Sabbath and festivals; on weekdays, only the third verse is recited).

Remove the Torah from the Ark and Recite *Shema Yisrael*

Shema Yisrael, HaShem E-lo-kenu, HaShem Echad.

❖

Hear, O, Israel, the Lord is our God, the Lord is One.

Still facing the congregation, the cantor raises the Torah and continues with the following verse, which is repeated by the worshippers:

Continue the Recitation

Echad E-lo-kenu, Gadol A-do-nenu, Kawdosh Shemo.

❖

One is our God, Great is our Lord, Holy is His Name.

The cantor turns back to face the *Aron HaKodesh.* He bows as he raises the *Sefer Torah* again and recites the following:

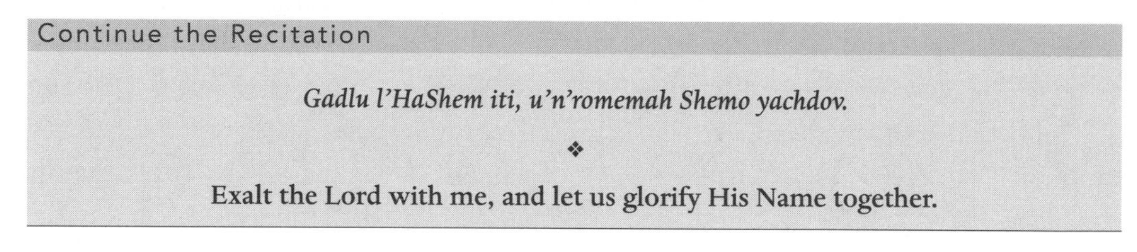
Continue the Recitation

Gadlu l'HaShem iti, u'n'romemah Shemo yachdov.

❖

Exalt the Lord with me, and let us glorify His Name together.

This verse is not repeated by the congregation.

3.8.2 The Opening Procession

The cantor then turns to his right and carries the *Sefer Torah* in procession around the synagogue. The procession usually includes the rabbi, the ***gabbai'im,*** who assist the *ba'al korei,* and other prominent leaders of the congregation. As the procession moves toward the *shulchan,* the Reader's Table, the congregation remains standing and chants with them from I Chronicles 29:11 and Psalms 99:5, 9.

As the Scroll passes by in procession, it is customary for the men of the congregation to touch the edge of the *talit* to the Torah *mantel* that covers it and then to kiss the *talit.* Similarly, women may use their ***siddurim*** to touch and kiss the Torah. It would be inappropriate to touch the Torah directly with the hand or the lips. After carrying the Torah in procession around the synagogue, the cantor places the Scroll on the Reader's Table where the *ba'al korei* will read from it, and it is unrolled to the weekly portion.

3.8.3 The Torah Honorees

The *ba'al korei* or the ***gabbai*** summons the Torah honorees to the *bimah,* one at a time, in turn, by their Hebrew names. The first *aliyah* belongs to a *Kohen,* a male descendant of the *Kohanim,* the Priests, who officiated in the *Mishkan* and in the *Bet*

HaMikdash in Jerusalem. The second *aliyah* is given to a *Levi*, a man descended from the *Levi'im,* the Levites, who assisted the Priests in the services. The third *aliyah* is given to a ***Yisrael,*** any man who is not a *Kohen* or a *Levi.* After the first three *aliyot,* all others can be given only to a *Yisrael.* Thus, a son follows his father in terms of his designation for an *aliyah.* It is a fact of birth, not of status, *per se.*

It should be noted that *aliyot* are not given successively to a father and son—nor vice versa—nor to two brothers. Specific rules also apply if there is no *Kohen* or *Levi* present. There is also a tradition that certain special occasions (like a forthcoming wedding, a *Bar Mitzvah,* or a recent birth, among others) confer the privilege of an *aliyah* on the celebrant.

A preliminary blessing is recited by each man who is called up to the Reading of the Torah. He comes to the *shulchan,* and as a sign of reverence and respect, he touches the open Torah parchment with the edge of his *talit* at the beginning of the appropriate verses, kisses the *talit,* and recites the first blessing.

The appropriate portion of the *sidrah* is then read with accurate *trop,* melodic patterns, by the *ba'al korei.* Originally, each honored person read his verses in the Torah himself, but it later became the function of the *ba'al korei,* in order not to embarrass any congregants who were unable to read the Hebrew text. When the verses have been recited, the honoree kisses the parchment with his *talit* where the *aliyah* has concluded and recites the closing blessing.

The *ba'al korei* continues to summon each of the other honorees in turn, and each kisses the Torah with his *talit* and recites the blessings. The *Kohen* remains on the *bimah* while the *Levi's* portion is read, and the *Levi* remains while the *Yisrael's* is read, and so forth.

Once the seventh (or last) has been read, the *sidrah* is concluded; but the last verses of that portion are then repeated as a separate *aliyah,* called ***Maftir.*** *Maftir* is given to the man who will recite the ***Haftarah*** (plural, ***Haftarot***), the prophetic reading associated with the weekly *sidrah.* Any man—*Kohen, Levi,* or *Yisrael*—may be honored with *Maftir.*

During any *aliyah,* it is customary for the honoree to request the recitation of special prayers, referred to collectively as a ***Mi She'Berach*** (He Who blessed), for himself and his family, or on behalf of the sick. Other *Mi She'Berach* prayers are recited when a Hebrew name is given to a newborn daughter (see Section 9.9); at the same time, it is customary to offer a prayer for the recovery of the mother. On occasion, a specific prayer to thank God for being rescued from danger is recited after the *aliyah* (see Section 3.4).

3.8.4 Elevating and Closing the *Sefer Torah*

Before the *Haftarah* is chanted, two additional Torah honors are given: ***Hagbahah,*** to the man who raises the open Torah and then turns around to show at least three columns of writing on the parchment pages to the congregation at the conclusion of the Torah Reading; and ***G'lilah,*** to the man who rewinds the Torah Scroll and dresses it.

They are summoned to the *bimah* together, and as the Torah is ceremoniously raised, the congregation stands and recites the verses from *Parshat Va'etchanan,* Deuteronomy 4:44 and *Parshat Beha'alot'cha,* Numbers 9:23.

Recite When the Torah Is Raised after *Kriat HaTorah*

V'zot HaTorah asher sam Moshe
lifnei B'nai Yisrael
al pi HaShem b'yad Moshe.

❖

And this is the Torah that Moses placed
before the Children of Israel
in accordance with the Lord's command by the hand of Moses.

The man honored with *Hagbahah* then sits in a chair on the *bimah* and holds the *Sefer Torah,* which must be kept upright. The Torah is rewound and the *gartel, mantel,* and any ornaments are replaced by the man honored with *G'lilah.* The Torah is then set in a special place of honor, usually near the Holy Ark, until it is time to return it to the *Aron HaKodesh.* The two honorees return to their seats.

3.8.5 The Prophetic Portion

The man honored with *Maftir* will recite seven blessings in all: one before the Torah Reading itself and one after—like every other Torah honoree—and one before the *Haftarah* and four after it. The *Haftarah* blessings acknowledge the righteousness of the prophets who were chosen by God.

Each Torah portion has a specific prophetic reading associated with it. The content of the *Haftarah* usually has a link to the theme of the *sidrah.* The recitation of the *Haftarah* is an honor that is also bestowed on a boy at the time of his *Bar Mitzvah* (see Section 9.14.2). Once the *Haftarah* has been chanted, the *Maftir* honoree continues with the closing blessings.

3.8.6 After the *Haftarah*

After the *Haftarah,* the Sabbath *Shacharit* service continues with prayers on behalf of the scholars and leaders of Babylonia and ancient Israel, and the congregation. An additional *Mi She'Berach* is then recited for the worshippers and for those who sustain the community and the synagogue. It is also customary to recite a prayer for the government, as well as for the State of Israel and its armed forces. On almost every Sabbath, a special memorial prayer, which dates back to the time of the Crusades, is recited on behalf of Jewish martyrs.

3.8.7 The Closing Procession

After reciting *Ashrei,* the cantor takes the Torah and begins the closing procession. The Torah is again carried around the synagogue, as Psalm 29 is chanted by the cantor and the congregation (on weekdays Psalm 24 is recited instead). As the Torah is being placed in the Ark, verses from Numbers 10:36; Psalms 132:8–10; Proverbs 4:2; 3:18, 17; and Lamentations 5:21 are recited by the cantor and the congregation.

The sacred Scroll of the Law has been returned to its holy resting place once more. The Ark is closed and the *parochet* is then drawn. *Kriat HaTorah* has been concluded.

3.8.8 Be Strong and Courageous!

Whenever the last *parashah* of one of the Five Books of Moses is completed in the synagogue, the entire congregation rises and in unison proclaims: ***Chazak! Chazak! V'nitchazek!***

Be Strong! Be Strong! And let us take courage!

These three Hebrew words are a stirring exclamation of encouragement to the Jewish people to be strong and courageous to live according to the precepts of the Torah.

3.9 The Afternoon Service

The Afternoon Service is called **Minchah.** In the Bible, the term was originally used to mean a gift or meal-offering. Another definition for *Minchah* is the "decline of the day," signifying that its recitation takes place close to the end of the day (I Kings 18:36).

Jewish tradition credits the patriarch Isaac, son of Abraham, with the authorship of the *Minchah* prayers. Unlike his father Abraham, whose life was characterized by great kindness, Isaac's life was marked by justice. *Minchah,* which is recited near the close of the day, is a time when our actions are scrutinized by the Almighty, and we are judged for our daily service to God. We may, in fact, be required to interrupt our day's routine in order to recite *Minchah* at the appropriate time.

Minchah corresponds to the *Korban Tamid* or daily sacrifice which was offered in the Holy Temple in the afternoon. *Minchah* may be recited any time between midday—which does not necessarily mean at noontime, depending on how many hours of daylight there are on a given day—and sunset when evening begins.

For the sake of convenience, *Minchah* is customarily recited just before sunset, so that only a short interval passes before the congregation can recite the Evening Service, *Ma'ariv.* It is customary to study Torah during this intervening period.

Minchah begins with the prayer of *Ashrei* and Psalm 145 (see Section 3.7.2). The *Shema* is not recited during *Minchah,* because its recitation is only obligatory "when you lie down and when you rise up," that is, in the evening and in the morning.

The *Shemoneh Esrei* is also recited at *Minchah.* Once again, as we begin to pray, we take three steps back, but in *Minchah,* we recite an additional verse:

Recite before *Shemoneh Esrei* of Minchah

When I proclaim the Name of the Lord,
attribute greatness to our God.
O, Lord,
may You open my lips
so that my mouth shall declare Your praise.

Then we take three steps forward and bend our knees and bow our heads, as we begin the first blessing. As in *Shacharit,* the nineteen blessings are recited by the worshippers, and the *chazan* repeats the *Amidah* after the congregation has recited it silently.

When a *minyan* is present, *Kedushah* is also chanted during *Minchah* in the repetition, and *Minchah* concludes with *Tachanun* on the days that it is said.

The Torah is read during the *Minchah* service on the Sabbath and on fast days after *Ashrei,* but before the *Amidah* is recited.

3.10 The Evening Service

The Evening Service, called *Ma'ariv* (derived from ***erev***, meaning *evening* or *eve of*) does not correspond to any sacrificial offering in the Holy Temple, inasmuch as sacrifices were offered only twice a day, in the morning and the afternoon. The patriarch Jacob, son of Isaac, is the author of *Ma'ariv.*

The time for *Ma'ariv* varies depending on the season of the year. It is usually recited by the congregation shortly after *Minchah* so that there is no need to inconvenience anyone to return to the synagogue. It may be recited from the time that three stars are visible in the sky. If necessary, *Ma'ariv* may be recited until the beginning of dawn, but this is not the preferred time limit.

Ma'ariv begins with verses from Psalms 78:38 and 20:10. It is followed by *Barchu,* but before *Shema* is recited during *Ma'ariv,* two blessings (different from those in *Shacharit*) are said: ***HaMa'ariv Aravim*** and ***Ahavat Olam.***

Kriat Shema is then recited. It is followed by two blessings. While the morning prayer speaks of God's love for the forefathers of the Jewish people, the evening prayer speaks of God's care and love in the present and in the future. Like the morning recitation, the evening recitation concludes with a blessing for the Redeemer of Israel.

The final prayer after *Shema* asks that the gracious and merciful God grant us peace and divine protection, for these are truly derived only from God. This prayer echoes the words from Psalms 121:4: "Behold the Guardian of Israel neither slumbers nor sleeps." We are assured that God's protection will continue through the night.

Shemoneh Esrei is recited but not repeated by the *chazan. Kedushah* is not recited.

3.11 The Additional Service

On ***Rosh Chodesh,*** the first day of the new month (see Sections 4.3 and 4.4), and on the Sabbath and festival days (see Chapters 5, 6, and 7), an Additional Service, ***Musaf,*** is recited after *Kriat HaTorah.* It commemorates the additional sacrifice which was brought to the Holy Temple on the Sabbath, festival days, and on *Rosh Chodesh.*

The structure of the *Musaf* service includes the first three and last three blessings of the *Shemoneh Esrei.* An intermediate benediction is inserted between the introductory and concluding blessings. It describes the offerings that were presented at the *Bet HaMikdash* for that day. We will discuss *Musaf* for *Rosh Chodesh* in Section 4.7, for the Sabbath in Section 5.6.3, and for the High Holidays in Sections 6.11 and 6.28, and for the Pilgrimage Festivals in Sections 7.8, 7.14, 7.21, and 7.24.

3.12 The Closing Prayers

All prayer services—daily, Sabbath, and festival—include the recitation of two prayers: ***Alenu*** and ***Kaddish***.

Alenu was composed by Joshua, the great prophet who led the Jewish people into the Promised Land. Attesting to its antiquity, it contains no references to the Holy Temple or to the longed-for return to Zion, which is so prominent in other *tefillot*. The first part of *Alenu* concludes with a quotation from Deuteronomy 4:39. At the appropriate words, we bend our knees and bow as we recite them.

Begin the Recitation of *Alenu*

It is our duty to praise the Master of all things,
to attribute greatness to the Creator,
for He has not made us like the nations of other lands,
nor placed us like other families of the earth. . . .
We bend the knee and bow in worship,
acknowledging our thanks before the King of Kings,
the Holy One, blessed is He,
for it is He who stretched out the heavens
and founded the earth. . . .
He is our God, there is no other; . . .
as it is written in His Torah:
"You shall know this day,
and reflect on it in your heart,
that it is the Lord Who is God
in the heavens above and on the earth beneath,
there is no other."

As we declare our faithfulness to *HaShem* in the second part of *Alenu,* we pray for *tikkun olam,* perfecting the world, and hope that one day all peoples of the earth will recognize the Oneness of God. *Alenu* continues, quoting from Exodus 15:18, and from the prophet Zechariah 14:9.

Continue the Recitation of *Alenu*

We hope in You, therefore, Lord our God,
that we will soon behold Your majestic splendor, . . .
to perfect the universe under the sovereignty of the Almighty. . . .
For the kingdom is Yours,
and forever and ever You shall reign in glorious honor,
as it is written in Your Torah:
"The Lord shall be King for all eternity,"
and it is said:
"The Lord shall be King over all the earth;
on that day the Lord shall be One and His Name One."

We will further explore the significance of *Alenu* in Sections 6.11.3 and 6.28.1, when we discuss the liturgy of the High Holidays.

The second of the concluding prayers is the *Kaddish*. Four versions of the *Kaddish* are recited throughout the services, for it serves as a bridge between sections of the prayer service: ***Chatzi Kaddish,*** Half *Kaddish;* ***Kaddish d'Rabbanan,*** Rabbis' *Kaddish;* ***Kaddish Yatom,*** Mourner's *Kaddish;* and ***Kaddish Shalem,*** Full *Kaddish.* ***Kaddish achar HaKevurah,*** *Kaddish* after Burial, is recited only at the cemetery on the day of burial.

We should first note that *Kaddish* is recited in Aramaic, not in Hebrew. You will recall that this is the language of the Babylonian Talmud, and this prayer was composed during the period of the Babylonian Exile by the *Anshei Kenesset HaGedolah.*

The word *Kaddish* means holy, and this prayer reflects the prophecy found in Isaiah 6:3 and Ezekiel 39:7, which stress the importance of sanctifying God's Name to assure the deliverance of the Jewish people.

Recited standing, and only in the presence of a quorum, *Kaddish* is a solemn, but not sad, prayer. It is our duty as Jews to sanctify God's Name in the world. We do this by conducting our lives according to His precepts, thereby testifying to His sovereignty. We recognize that the arrival of the Messiah and of God's redemption is closely linked with our own lives; that is, we can hasten the coming of the Redeemer by leading lives guided by the words of the Torah.

Sometimes the *Kaddish* is recited only by the *chazan,* other times, by worshippers. We will discuss the various versions briefly.

3.12.1 The Half *Kaddish*

The *Chatzi Kaddish* is recited in *Shacharit* after *Yishtabach* and before *Barchu,* after *Tachanun,* and after the Torah Reading on the Sabbath and festivals. It is also recited immediately before the *Shemoneh Esrei* of *Minchah* and *Ma'ariv.* The text is shorter than the other *Kaddish* prayers.

3.12.2 The Rabbis' *Kaddish*

At the conclusion of *Birchot HaShachar* in *Shacharit,* just before *Pesukei D'Zimrah, Kaddish d'Rabbanan,* the Rabbis' *Kaddish,* is recited. It includes words of prayer for rabbis and scholars, indeed, for all who are steeped in the study of Torah, and it is recited anytime—even when not during prayer—that a group of at least ten men complete the study of verses from the Mishnah, Talmud, *Midrash,* or *Aggadah.* The text of the *Chatzi Kaddish* forms the first part of the Rabbis' *Kaddish.*

The Reader concludes *Kaddish d'Rabbanan* with a prayer for peace. He takes three steps back and bows to the left, as he recites the first concluding phrase; then he bows to the right, as he recites the second phrase; finally, he bows forward as he recites the third and last phrase. He remains in place briefly, and then takes three steps forward, returning to his original place.

3.12.3 The Mourner's *Kaddish*

Mourners in the first eleven months after the death of a close relative and at other specified times during the year (see Section 9.16.5 for more details associated with the mourning period) recite the *Kaddish Yatom.* In some sections of the prayers—for example, at the end of *Birchot HaShachar—Kaddish d'Rabbanan* is recited by the mourners. The text of the *Kaddish Yatom* repeats the text of the *Chatzi Kaddish* and the *Kaddish d'Rabbanan,* except for the verses on behalf of our teachers and their disciples, and the words "in His mercy."

The mourner concludes the *Kaddish Yatom.* He takes three steps back and bows to the left, as he recites the first concluding phrase; then he bows to the right, as he recites the second phrase; finally, he bows forward, as he recites the third and last phrase. He then remains in place briefly, and then takes three steps forward, returning to his original place.

Kaddish Yatom is recited after Psalm 30, which introduces the *Pesukei D'Zimrah,* but before the prayer *Baruch She'Amar.* It is also recited at the end of *Shacharit, Minchah,* and *Ma'ariv* after *Alenu.*

3.12.4 The Full *Kaddish*

Kaddish Shalem is recited at the end of *Shacharit, Minchah,* and *Ma'ariv,* before *Alenu.* It includes the entire text of the *Chatzi Kaddish,* but concludes differently.

As the Reader concludes *Kaddish Shalem,* he takes three steps back and bows to the left, reciting the first concluding phrase; then he bows to the right, as he recites the second phrase; finally, he bows forward as he recites the third and last phrase. He remains in place briefly, and then takes three steps forward, returning to his original place.

3.12.5 The Burial *Kaddish*

None of the *Kaddish* prayers, not even the Mourner's *Kaddish,* deal with the concept of death or the sadness associated with the loss of a loved one. Rather, they all are an acclamation of God's greatness, and they invoke His blessings. However, a special *Kaddish* is recited at the cemetery after burial has been completed (see Section 9.16.4). It is the only *Kaddish* prayer that mentions the Redemption at the End of Days, a period of momentous spiritual beneficence, which will include the Resurrection of the Dead and the rebuilding of Jerusalem and the Temple. To be sure, these words provide comfort and solace to those who grieve, for God promises the dead will be revived. The *Kaddish achar HaKevurah* is also recited at the conclusion of a mishnaic order or a talmudic tractate.

LOOKING AHEAD! *In Chapter 4, we will take a look at the Jewish calendar and begin to put traditions and observances into a time frame.*

Word Works

The Torah is the Jewish people's guidebook, and the Jewish calendar is the timetable on which it is structured.

4

The Jewish Calendar

HE CIVIL CALENDAR in common use today throughout the world is based on the early Christians' reckoning from the time of their spiritual beginnings, which they called Year One. Divided into twelve months and four seasons, it is a solar calendar, based on the earth's rotations around the sun. The twelve-month solar year is 365 days, 5 hours, 48 minutes, and 45 seconds long. Often, a year is identified with the abbreviations B.C. or A.D., references to its Christian origins.

The Jewish calendar in use today is based on both solar and lunar cycles. The years are reckoned by the sun; the months, by the cycles of the moon. The twelve-month lunar year is shorter than the solar year: 354 days, 8 hours, 48 minutes, and 34 seconds. The use of the abbreviations B.C.E., Before the

Common Era, and C.E., Common Era, identify the Hebrew year within the framework of the Christian—or civil—year, so that modern references can be more easily identified.

4.1 The Hebrew Months and Years

The twelve Hebrew months and their equivalents are:

Hebrew Month	Civil Month
Nisan	March–April
Iyar	April–May
Sivan	May–June
Tammuz	June–July
Av	July–August
Elul	August–September
Tishrei	September–October
Cheshvan	October–November
Kislev	November–December
Tevet	December–January
Shevat	January–February
Adar	February–March

In the Torah, just prior to the Exodus from Egypt, we find that God designated the month of *Nisan* as the first of the months.

This month shall be the beginning of months for you;
the first month of the year shall it be.

—*Parshat Bo,* Exodus 12:2

All the months are designated in the Torah by number, not by name, in reference to their relationship to the Exodus from Egypt. The names that are associated with the months today developed during the period of the Babylonian Exile.

For a long time, the Exodus from Egypt (which Jewish scholars identify as 2448 years after Creation) was the reference point for calculating the Hebrew year as well. After the destruction of the Second Temple, in 70 C.E., a more universal reference point, one that applied to all peoples, rather than only to the Jewish people, was desired. Based upon biblical teachings and other records and documents available at the time, the sages proclaimed that the Hebrew year was to be reckoned from the time of Creation, and this became the accepted manner of calculation.

A simple mathematical device helps us go from the Hebrew year to the civil year, and vice versa. For example, the Hebrew year 5726 (reckoned from Creation) corresponds to 1966 in the civil calendar. We arrive at this by adding 240 to the last three digits of the Hebrew year to get the last three digits of the secular year.

$$726 + 240 = 966$$

In reverse, take the last three digits of the secular year and subtract 240 to get the last three digits of the Hebrew year.

$$966 - 240 = 726$$

Insert the first digit, 5, for the Hebrew millennium: 5 & 726 → 5726; insert 1 for the secular millennium: 1 & 966 → 1966, to find the corresponding year. There is a period of overlap to keep in mind. Whereas the secular year changes in January, the Hebrew year changes in the previous September (sometimes October). The Hebrew year 5760, which began in September 1999 and overlapped with the secular millennium, ended in September 2000. So, in computing years during the latter months of 5760 and thereafter, the secular millennium number is 2.

4.2 The Formulation of the Jewish Calendar

The Jewish calendar, or ***luach,*** was formulated according to precise mathematical and astronomical calculations during the administration of Hillel II, and it was officially adopted by Jewish communities about the middle of the fourth century of the Common Era. Its publication made it possible for Jews everywhere to know precisely when to observe the festivals and to assure that all Jews would observe them on the same days.

Prior to the development of the Jewish calendar, it was necessary to actually observe the cycles of the moon in order to calculate when the new month began. Witnesses who observed the crescent of the new moon at night reported their findings to the *Sanhedrin,* the High Court in Jerusalem, the following day. The *Sanhedrin* decided if the reports of at least two witnesses were reliable. If so, that day was proclaimed by the *Sanhedrin* as the new moon—the beginning of the month—with the words "Sanctified!

Sanctified!" Originally, bonfires were lit from mountaintop to mountaintop as beacons to signal the populace throughout Israel and beyond of the arrival of the new month. Later, it became necessary to send messengers to outlying areas to announce the new month. In this manner, the people were prepared for the arrival of the festivals that were to occur in that month according to the laws of the Torah.

The word ***Galut,*** usually translated as *Diaspora,* originally applied to the Exile of Babylonia, but has come to mean anywhere Jews settle outside the land of Israel. The word *Diaspora* is derived from the Greek for *dispersion.* Throughout history, the Jewish people have been exiled and dispersed in numerous countries, but their emotional and spiritual ties with the Jewish homeland of Israel have endured.

Because it was not always possible for messengers to reach communities outside ancient Israel in time to proclaim the new month, those communities in the *Galut* instituted the custom of adding one day to each festival to be sure that it had, in fact, been observed on the date specified in the Torah. This practice was introduced during the period of the Second Temple.

Once the calendar was in regular use, the talmudic sages debated about whether the practice of the two-day observance should be maintained (see Talmud, *Masechet Beitzah* 4b). It was decided that this custom was hallowed by previous generations, and the sages issued a rabbinic decree providing for its permanent retention.

Even today, when calendars are readily available and there is no doubt or discrepancy about the exact date a new month begins, Diaspora Jews continue to celebrate two festival days, even when the Torah requires only one. This tradition cannot be changed by any group or community of Jews.

However, in modern Israel today, festivals are observed only for the number of days decreed in the Torah. Most authorities agree that (1) Jews who live in the Diaspora must observe two days for those festivals, even when they visit in Israel; and (2) Jews who live in Israel need celebrate only one festival day, even if they are visiting in the Diaspora where two days are observed.

4.3 The Leap Year

The four seasons correspond to the relative position of the earth in relationship to the sun. At the time of the spring and autumn equinoxes, the sun appears to turn from one side of the equator to the other; in the spring, to the north side, in the autumn, to the south. At the time of the summer and winter solstices, the sun appears to be at its furthest point from the equator, to the north and to the south, respectively.

These four turning points of the sun are, of course, associated with the months of the Jewish calendar, as well:

- spring equinox *Nisan*
- summer solstice *Tammuz*
- autumn equinox *Tishrei*
- winter solstice *Tevet*

The English word *month,* of course, is derived from the word *moon*. The Torah requires that the spring festival (Passover; see Section 7.1) occur in the spring season and the autumn festival (Tabernacles; see Section 7.17) at the time of the autumn harvest. Inasmuch as the festivals are intrinsically linked to specific agricultural periods, it was necessary to find a way to combine the computations of the solar year with those of the lunar year. Otherwise, on a strictly lunar basis, the festivals would ultimately recede from their proper solar season. A special committee of the *Sanhedrin* was commissioned to devise a system that would reconcile the solar and lunar cycles. They noted that the usual gap of eleven days between the two cycles expanded to more than thirty days after a few years.

To close this gap and avoid the displacement of the agricultural festivals from their proper seasons, the committee instituted the practice of inserting a thirteenth month into the Jewish calendar, seven times in a nineteen-year cycle. To this day, that extra month, ***Adar Sheni,*** the Second *Adar,* occurs in the third, sixth, eighth, eleventh, fourteenth, seventeenth, and nineteenth years of the nineteen-year cycle. Years which contain this extra month are called leap years.

There are either twenty-nine or thirty days in a month. The number of days varies when *Adar Sheni* occurs. The time of the "birth" of the moon is the actual beginning of the month or ***Rosh Chodesh,*** but for practical purposes, we speak of the number of days in whole numbers. Sometimes there are two days called *Rosh Chodesh*.

So, we see that the Jewish calendar begins with the month of *Nisan*. The last (twelfth) month of the year is *Adar,* or in a leap year (thirteenth) ***Adar II***. However, the Jewish New Year is celebrated on the first and second days of the seventh month, *Tishrei*.

Nisan, Sivan, Av, Tishrei, and *Shevat* always have thirty days. *Iyar, Tammuz, Elul, Tevet,* and *Adar* always have twenty-nine days (note exception for ***Adar I*** below). *Cheshvan* and *Kislev* may have either twenty-nine or thirty. One of the reasons for this is that the Day of Atonement (see Chapter 6) may not fall on a Friday or a Sunday, because we do not fast into or out of the Sabbath Day (see Chapter 5). Therefore, the months of

Cheshvan or *Kislev* will vary to prevent this from happening. If a year has 355 days, then the following year will have 353. See the following chart for the possible combinations of days.

Hebrew Month	Days in a Regular Year	Days in a Leap Year	Days Following a Leap Year
Nisan	30	30	30
Iyar	29	29	29
Sivan	30	30	30
Tammuz	29	29	29
Av	30	30	30
Elul	29	29	29
Tishrei	30	30	30
Cheshvan	29 or 30	29 or 30	29 or 30
Kislev	29 or 30	29 or 30	29 or 30
Tevet	29	29	29
Shevat	30	30	30
Adar	29	—	29
Adar I	—	30	—
Adar II	—	29	—
Totals	**353–355**	**383–385**	**353–355**

When a thirtieth day occurs in a month, it is considered the first day of *Rosh Chodesh* of the next month—not the first day of the next month, but of the new moon. The following day is the first day of the new month and the second day of *Rosh Chodesh*. For example, the last or thirtieth day of *Sivan* is the first day of *Rosh Chodesh Tammuz*. The next day is the first day of *Tammuz* and the second day of *Rosh Chodesh Tammuz*.

The cycle of the months in the civil calendar has little relationship to the cycle of the moon. For example, March 21, the beginning of the spring solstice in the civil calendar, may fall as much as five weeks before the spring festival in the Jewish calendar. In the civil calendar, only one day is added to the month of February every fourth year to adjust for astronomical computations.

The Torah is the Jewish people's daily guide throughout the year, and the calendar is the timetable on which it is structured. There are special considerations when a leap year occurs. Events which took place specifically in *Adar I* or in *Adar II* are observed in the month of *Adar*, when it is not a leap year.

Let us consider two events that require this special information: ***Bar Mitzvah,*** a ceremony marking a boy's religious maturity at the age of thirteen; and ***yahrtzeit***, the annual commemoration of a person's death (see Sections 9.14.2 and 9.16.5).

If a boy is born in *Adar* of a non-leap year, and if his thirteenth birthday falls in a leap year, his *Bar Mitzvah* is celebrated in *Adar II*. If he is born in *Adar I* or *Adar II,* that is, in a leap year, his *Bar Mitzvah,* if it also occurs in a leap year would, of course, be celebrated in the same month as his birthday. However, if his thirteenth birthday occurs in a non-leap year, his *Bar Mitzvah* would be celebrated in *Adar.*

Among Ashkenazic Jews, however, if a death occurred in *Adar* (a non-leap year), then in a leap year, the anniversary of the day of death, called *yahrtzeit,* is always observed in *Adar I*. On the day of the *yahrtzeit,* the Jew comes to the synagogue and recites the special Mourner's *Kaddish* with a *minyan* (see Section 9.16.5). Note: In some congregations, it is customary to recite the *Kaddish* in both *Adar I* and *Adar II*.

There are also special rules about the months of *Cheshvan* and *Kislev,* which may have twenty-nine or thirty days. Anything that occurs on the twenty-ninth is always observed on the twenty-ninth. When a birthday occurs on the thirtieth of *Cheshvan* or *Kislev,* it is observed on the thirtieth when that day occurs in the calendar. If there is no thirtieth, then it is observed on the first of the following month, that is, *Kislev* and *Tevet,* respectively.

When a *yahrtzeit* occurs on the thirtieth of *Cheshvan* or *Kislev,* the date of the observance depends on the number of days in the month in the first year following the death. If the death occurred on the thirtieth, and if the very next year has thirty days in that month, then the *yahrtzeit* is observed on the thirtieth. In all years without a thirtieth day in the month, it is observed on the first day of the next month.

If the death occurred on the thirtieth, and if the very next year has twenty-nine days in the month, then the *yahrtzeit* is observed on the twenty-ninth day in all years without a thirtieth day.

4.4 Blessing the New Month

The advent of each new Hebrew month is announced in the synagogue on the Sabbath immediately preceding the beginning of the new month. The congregation recites the prayer ***Birkat HaChodesh,*** the Blessing of the New Month, after the Reading of the Torah has been concluded. It is derived from the Talmud, *Masechet Berachot* 16b, and was first instituted in the eighteenth century.

At that time, the cantor holds the *Sefer Torah,* which has not yet been put back in the *Aron HaKodesh* after the Reading of the Law. The congregation rises and recites the following prayer, which is then repeated by the cantor.

Recite the Blessing of the New Month

Congregation then Cantor:

**May it be Your will, Lord, our God, and God of our forefathers,
that you renew us this month for goodness and for blessing.
May you grant us long life, a life of peace, a life of goodness,
a life of blessing, a life of sustenance, a life of physical health,
a life in which there is fear of heaven and fear of sin,
a life in which there is no shame nor humiliation,
a life of wealth and honor,
a life marked by our love of Torah and fear of heaven,
a life in which our heartfelt petitions will be fulfilled for the good.
Amen Selah.**

In this monthly ritual, also called ***Mevorchim HaChodesh,*** Blessing the New Month, the cantor announces to the congregation the name of the new month and the precise day and time that the new month—that is, the new moon—will actually be "born."

In announcing the "birth" of the moon, the days of the week are identified by number: Sunday is Day 1, Monday, Day 2, and so forth. Only the seventh day is called by name: the Sabbath. For computational purposes, the day is reckoned from 6:00 P.M., Jerusalem time, which is considered Hour 0 or Hour 24.

The day is divided into twenty-four hours, so 9:00 P.M. is Hour 3, Noon is Hour 18, and so forth. The hour is divided further into parts, equal to 3.33 seconds, and the parts into moments, equal to .04 seconds. The "birth" of the moon might be announced as follows:

Rosh Chodesh Kislev
**will take place on Day 3
at 14 hours, and 30 parts, and 50 moments.**

which means

**The new month of *Kislev*
will arrive on Tuesday
at 2:00 A.M., and 1.67 minutes, and 2 seconds.**

equivalent to 2:01 A.M., and 42 seconds.

Once the cantor has announced the precise day and time, the congregation recites the following blessing and announces the name of the month and day it will arrive.

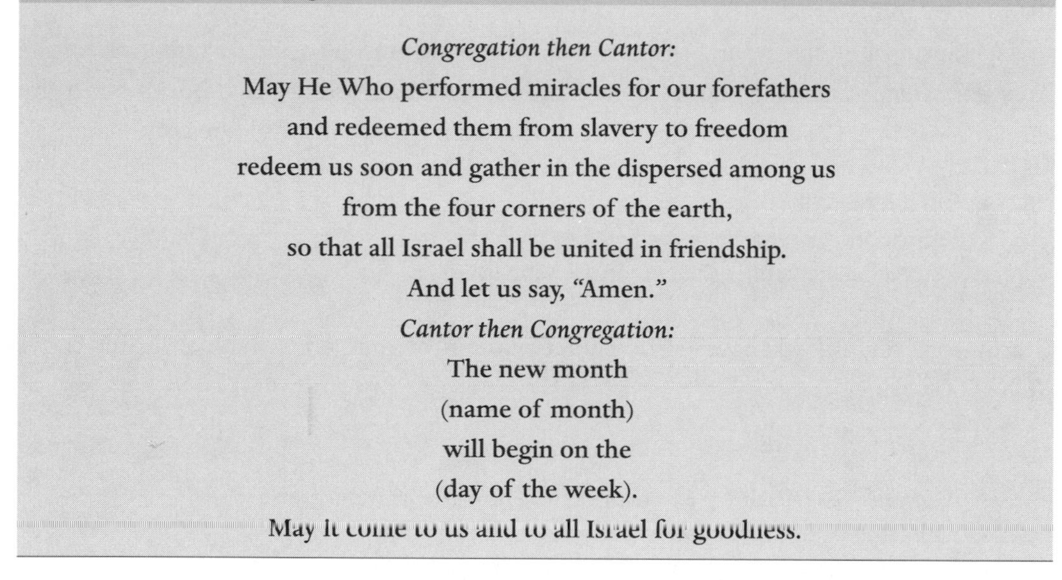
Continue the Blessing for the New Month

Congregation then Cantor:
May He Who performed miracles for our forefathers
and redeemed them from slavery to freedom
redeem us soon and gather in the dispersed among us
from the four corners of the earth,
so that all Israel shall be united in friendship.
And let us say, "Amen."
Cantor then Congregation:
The new month
(name of month)
will begin on the
(day of the week).
May it come to us and to all Israel for goodness.

The congregation followed by the cantor then concludes the blessing for the new month.

Conclude the Blessing for the New Month

Congregation then Cantor:
May the Holy One, blessed be He,
renew it for us,
and for all His people, the House of Israel,
for life and for peace,
for joy and for gladness,
for salvation and for consolation;
and let us say, "Amen."

The only exception to this practice is the Hebrew month of *Tishrei,* the month of the Jewish New Year. Jewish tradition teaches that in order to confound the heavenly adversary, Jews do not recite the *Birkat HaChodesh* on the Sabbath before the New Year.

4.5 Sanctifying the New Moon

The ritual known both as ***Kiddush Levanah,*** Sanctification of the Moon, or ***Birkat HaLevanah,*** Blessing of the Moon, is not to be confused with *Birkat HaChodesh,* Blessing of the New Month.

The ritual of sanctifying the moon has no relationship to the formulation of the calendar. *Kiddush Levanah* should be recited not less than seventy-two hours nor more than fifteen days after the "birth" of the new moon. Ideally, it should be conducted:

- in the presence of a *minyan*
- outdoors, under a clear sky
- on Saturday night at the end of the Sabbath

If any—or even all—of these circumstances cannot be met, an individual should recite *Kiddush Levanah* anyway.

The recitation includes:

- Verses 1–6 of Psalm 148, which express how the heavens praise God
- Blessing of Sanctification
- Threefold repetition of five scriptural or rabbinic verses
- Greeting of peace
- Psalm 121
- Psalm 150
- Additional scriptural verses
- Psalm 67

The Blessing of Sanctification is discussed in the Talmud, *Masechet Sanhedrin* 42a, and in the minor tractate of *Sofrim* 20:1–2. It recalls how God created the heavens and all the celestial bodies with His word alone. He established their immutable heavenly orbits, in which they rejoice, as they serve Him. So, too, the moon and the Jewish people are renewed in service to the Almighty.

Recite the Blessing of Sanctification of the Moon

Blessed are You, Lord our God, King of the Universe,
Who with His speech created the heavens,
and with the breath of His mouth, all their hosts.
A law and a fixed time did He give them,
so that they could not change their assigned task.
They are joyous and glad to perform [His] will. . . .
He told the moon to renew itself
as a crown of splendor for those [He] supported from birth,
those who are destined to renew themselves like [the moon]
and glorify their Creator for His glorious kingdom.
Blessed are You, Lord, Who renews the months.

4.6 An Outline of the Jewish Year

This section will serve as a guideline to the annual cycle of the Jewish calendar. The details of the particular observances associated with the festivals mentioned will be discussed in their respective chapters.

As we outline the Jewish year, it is important to understand that the Hebrew day and date begins with nightfall. In the biblical description of the Creation of the World, we find the following:

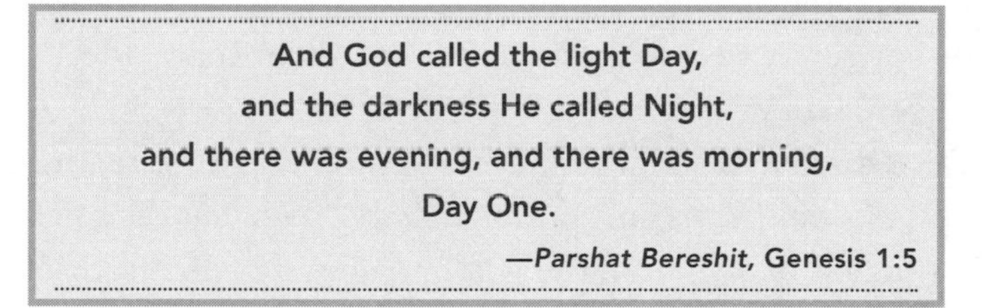

And God called the light Day,
and the darkness He called Night,
and there was evening, and there was morning,
Day One.

—*Parshat Bereshit,* Genesis 1:5

From this we learn that the day begins with the evening that precedes it.

For example, if a festival is celebrated on the tenth day of the Hebrew month, which corresponds to the eighth day of the secular month, the observance begins on the night of the seventh day of the secular month, which is the beginning of the tenth day of the Hebrew month.

This also holds true for reckoning the day of birth and the day of death. Since the time of nightfall varies with the seasons, this must be taken into consideration when calculating corresponding dates.

4.6.1 *Nisan*

Nisan is the first month of the Jewish calendar and the beginning of the spring season. *Nisan* is the month of the first Pilgrimage Festival, ***Pesach,*** Passover (see Section 7.1). The first day of Passover is on the fifteenth day of *Nisan,* and this holiday is celebrated in the Diaspora for eight days.

Yom HaShoah, Holocaust Remembrance Day, is observed on the twenty-seventh day of *Nisan.* Numerous organizations hold commemorative events, hallowing the memories of the Six Million who perished in concentration camps. Around the world, several museums dedicated to remembering the Holocaust serve as repositories of personal histories and provide final resting places for the thousands of artifacts of destroyed lives and communities.

4.6.2 *Iyar*

Iyar is the second month of the Jewish calendar. Since 1948, when the independence of the Jewish State of Israel was proclaimed, the fifth day of *Iyar* has been observed as ***Yom HaAtzma'ut,*** Israel's Independence Day. The day before *Yom HaAtzma'ut* is called ***Yom HaZikaron,*** Remembrance Day, when Israel remembers those who fell in defense of the Jewish state. If the fifth of *Iyar* falls on Friday or Saturday (the Sabbath), *Yom HaAtzma'ut* is observed on the preceding Thursday, and *Yom HaZikaron,* on Wednesday.

Beginning with the second night of Passover (evening of the sixteenth of *Nisan*), and continuing for seven weeks, Jews observe ***Sefirat HaOmer,*** the Counting of the ***Omer*** (a measure of barley).

During this ***Sefirah*** (counting) period (see Section 7.4.16), with rare exceptions, no weddings or other joyous events are permitted. Jews do not cut their hair, and many do not shave. This period of semi-mourning commemorates the death of thousands of students of Rabbi Akiva, victims of a plague during the Roman occupation.

Most communities observe this semi-mourning period from Passover until the thirty-third day of the *Omer,* which corresponds to the eighteenth day of *Iyar.* Called ***LaG baOmer*** (the numerical value of *LaG—lamed* + *gimel*—is thirty-three), it is a day of celebration because the plague stopped on that day. Other communities observe this thirty-three-day period of semi-mourning beginning with *Rosh Chodesh Iyar,* an interval that corresponds to a time of pogroms in Europe during the Crusades.

It is also customary to take field trips and light bonfires on *LaG baOmer,* recalling that Jewish students were forbidden to study Torah and went into the fields to study, where they could appear to be occupied in games.

Yom Yerushalayim, Jerusalem Day, marks the anniversary of the 1967 Reunification of Jerusalem (see Section 7.10.5). It is observed on the twenty-eighth day of *Iyar.*

4.6.3 *Sivan*

On the sixth day of *Sivan,* which is the fiftieth day after the second night of Passover, the second Pilgrimage Festival, ***Shavuot,*** called the Festival of Weeks or Pentecost, is celebrated (see Section 7.11). In the Diaspora, it is observed for two days.

4.6.4 *Tammuz*

The seventeenth day of *Tammuz* marks the beginning of a three-week period referred to in Yiddish as the ***Drai Vochen,*** the Three Weeks. The penetration of the wall around Jerusalem and the subsequent destruction of the *Bet HaMikdash* began on ***Shivah Asar b'Tammuz,*** the seventeenth day of *Tammuz.* It is observed, therefore, as a day of fasting and solemnity. The entire *Drai Vochen* is a period during which no weddings may take place. Jews refrain from listening to music, cutting their hair, shaving, or making parties.

4.6.5 *Av*

The last nine days of the *Drai Vochen* begin with *Rosh Chodesh Av,* the first day of the Hebrew month of *Av.* During these nine days, neither meat nor wine are consumed (except in honor of the Sabbath). The ninth day of *Av,* called ***Tishah b'Av,*** is the conclusion of the Three Weeks. It is a day of fasting because it marks the date of the destruction of both the First and Second Temples in Jerusalem. It is the only fast day in the Jewish calendar, except the Day of Atonement (see Chapter 6), that begins the evening before and ends after sunset the next day. If *Tishah b'Av* falls on the Sabbath, the fast is postponed until Sunday.

Special services are held in the synagogue on the eve of *Tishah b'Av.* In a somber mood, the congregation recites ***Megillat Eichah,*** the Scroll of Lamentations, which mourns the destruction of the Temples and the desolation of Jerusalem, the holy city. Additional ***kinot,*** laments, are recited in the morning.

No meat or wine may be consumed until the afternoon of the tenth of *Av*, because the flames of the Temple continued to burn and smolder throughout that day.

In talmudic times, the fifteenth day of *Av*, ***TU b'Av***, was celebrated with great merriment in Jerusalem by young men and women in search of a spouse. According to *Masechet Ta'anit* 26b, young women dressed in white and danced in the vineyards, saying: "Young man, lift your eyes and consider whom you will choose for a bride. Do not choose beauty, but look at the family." In those days, this custom also was observed on the Day of Atonement.

4.6.6 *Elul*

The month of *Elul* marks the end of the summer season and the beginning of a period of reflection and repentance in anticipation of the forthcoming High Holidays. It is customary to visit the cemetery to pay homage to the memory of departed parents and other relatives during *Elul*. Penitential prayers are recited throughout the month, and the ram's horn is sounded (see Section 6.1).

4.6.7 *Tishrei*

Tishrei is the seventh and undoubtedly the busiest of the Hebrew months. It marks the beginning of the Jewish New Year. On the first and second days of *Tishrei*, the Jewish New Year, ***Rosh HaShanah*** (literally, head of the year), is observed (see Section 6.3). The third day of *Tishrei* is ***Tzom Gedaliah,*** a fast day, observed in memory of Gedaliah, the assassinated Jewish governor, who had been appointed by Nebuchadnezzar after the destruction of Jerusalem in 586 B.C.E.

The ten-day period, from the first day of *Tishrei* until the tenth day of *Tishrei*, is called ***Aseret Y'mei T'shuvah,*** the Ten Days of Repentance. During this time, Jews reflect on their conduct during the past year, repent their misdeeds, and perform additional acts of kindness and charity, as they seek to "wipe the slate clean" and attain God's forgiveness.

The tenth day of *Tishrei* is ***Yom Kippur,*** the Day of Atonement, the holiest day in the Jewish calendar. It is a solemn day spent in penitential prayer and fasting. It is also called ***Shabbat Shabbaton,*** the Sabbath of Sabbaths (see Section 6.19).

On the fifteenth day of *Tishrei*, the third of the Pilgrimage Festivals, ***Sukkot,*** the Festival of Tabernacles, begins. It is a harvest festival, and is celebrated for seven days (see Section 7.17).

The eighth day of the festival period is called ***Shemini Atzeret,*** the Eighth Day of Holy Convocation. It is considered a separate holiday from *Sukkot,* for God asked the Jewish people to stay with Him an additional day. It is often incorrectly called the eighth day of *Sukkot* (see Section 7.23).

The next day is called ***Simchat Torah,*** the Day of Rejoicing with the Torah. It marks the *conclusion and the immediate resumption* of the Reading of the Law for the calendar year. It is also referred to as ***Atzeret,*** in the liturgy and in the Grace after Meals. In Israel, both *Shemini Atzeret* and *Simchat Torah* are observed on the eighth day (see Section 7.25).

4.6.8 Cheshvan

The month of *Cheshvan* contains no festival or fast days, and is, thus, referred to as ***Mar Cheshvan,*** Bitter *Cheshvan.* In common usage, however, the name is shortened to *Cheshvan.* It is also the time when the weather (in Jerusalem) starts to get cold.

4.6.9 Kislev

The month of *Kislev* marks the celebration of the festival of ***Chanukah,*** the Festival of Lights (see Chapter 8). The observance of *Chanukah,* which begins on the twenty-fifth day of *Kislev* and lasts eight days, was decreed by the rabbinic authorities (see Section 8.1). It recalls the miraculous discovery of one sealed cruse of sanctified oil, the rededication of the Holy Temple, and the military victory of the **Maccabees** in the second century B.C.E.

4.6.10 Tevet

The tenth day of *Tevet,* called ***Asarah b'Tevet,*** is a fast day marking the beginning of the siege against the First Temple.

4.6.11 Shevat

The month of *Shevat* is noteworthy for the observance of ***TU b'Shevat*** (also called ***Chamishah Asar b'Shevat***), the fifteenth day of *Shevat,* Jewish Arbor Day. In Hebrew, it is called ***Rosh HaShanah l'Ilanot,*** the New Year for Trees. It is customary to plant trees in Israel in observance of this day. It is also traditional to eat fruits and nuts from Israel, such as dates, figs, carob, and almonds, and others that have not yet been tasted before in that season.

4.6.12 *Adar*

The festival of ***Purim*** is celebrated on the fourteenth day of *Adar* (see Section 8.8). If it is a leap year, *Purim* is observed in *Adar II*. The Feast of Lots commemorates the victory of the Jewish people over Haman, the evil prime minister of Persia.

The day before *Purim*, the thirteenth day of *Adar*, is ***Ta'anit Esther***, the Fast of Esther, in commemoration of the fast of the Jewish queen. If it falls on the Sabbath, the fast is observed on the preceding Thursday. The day after *Purim*, the fifteenth day of *Adar*, is observed as ***Shushan Purim***, a special day of celebration that was first observed in the Persian capital of Shushan. *Purim* is observed in Jerusalem on the fifteenth of *Adar*.

A Witty Remark!

There is a Yiddish expression that always sounded so comforting to me, although I didn't really understand its profound wisdom: "God sends the cure before the blow." In my own life, this would prove to be doubly true.

My oldest daughter, my first-born and my parents' first grandchild, arrived in this world in the very early morning of November 20, which was *Cheshvan* 17 that year. My youngest daughter, my lastborn, arrived eleven years later, on November 19, which was *Cheshvan* 19 that year. To be sure, their births (and that of their middle sister, too) and their birthdays were blessed and joyful occasions for our family. Forever, these dates would be special in my life; I was certain of that.

No one adored my three children more than my father, their doting grandfather. He *rejoiced* over every milestone—every smile, every tooth, every pair of shoes, every babbled word. He carried their pictures in his pocket—all of them—from infancy on, and he showed them off like every proud grandpa. Their very existence renewed his spirit, and his face lit up whenever he saw them.

Then there came a day I had dreaded from the time I could imagine what it would mean to me. My father died on Friday, the seventeenth day of *Cheshvan*, and his funeral was held on Sunday, the nineteenth day of *Cheshvan*, two days filled with the ultimate bitterness of *Mar Cheshvan*, Bitter *Cheshvan.*

Only then did I really understand the little phrase: "God sends the cure before the blow." My oldest daughter was twenty-four years old to the day when her grandfather died, and her youngest sister was thirteen when he was laid to rest. Indeed, God had been preparing me for many years, and now I understood. My children and the joy they brought to my life over the years were meant to be the cure and the consolation that would temper the blow of my unfathomable loss.

4.6.13 The Jewish Calendar at a Glance

According to the Mishnah, *Masechet Rosh HaShanah* 1:1, there are four new years in the Jewish calendar.

***Nisan* 1**	**New Year for Kings** The reign of a Jewish monarch was reckoned from this day, even if he ascended the throne on the last day of *Adar* of that year.
***Elul* 1**	**New Year for Tithing of Animals** One-tenth of the animals born in a year had to be set aside for tithing.
***Tishrei* 1**	**New Year for Years** *Rosh HaShanah* is observed on the first and second days of the seventh month. Sabbatical Years and Jubilee Years are reckoned from this date (see Sections 4.9 and 4.10). The tithing of vegetables is reckoned from this date. The reign of non-Jewish monarchs of other countries was reckoned from this date.
***Shevat* 1**	**New Year for Trees** According to Shammai, one of the early *Tana'im*, it was to be observed on this date. According to Hillel, Shammai's contemporary and the president of the *Sanhedrin*, it was to be observed on the fifteenth of *Shevat*. Hillel's ruling prevails.

According to the Mishnah, *Masechet Rosh HaShanah* 1:2, the world is judged during four festival periods in the Jewish calendar. On these judgment days, God's verdict is rendered in four specific categories. They are:

***Nisan* 15**	***Pesach* Begins** Barley Harvest
***Sivan* 6**	***Shavuot* Begins** First Fruits

***Tishrei* 1**	***Rosh HaShanah* Begins**
	Humankind
***Tishrei* 15**	***Sukkot* Begins**
	Water

There are six days in the Jewish calendar when all Jews are obligated to fast.

***Tammuz* 17**	***Shivah Asar b'Tammuz***
	Beginning of Three Weeks
	Fast begins before dawn.
***Av* 9**	***Tishah b'Av***
	End of Three Weeks
	Fast begins with sunset on the evening before.
***Tishrei* 3**	***Tzom Gedaliah***
	Fast of Gedaliah
	Fast begins before dawn.
***Tishrei* 10**	***Yom Kippur***
	Day of Atonement
	Fast begins with sunset on the evening before.
***Tevet* 10**	***Asarah b'Tevet***
	Siege of Jerusalem
	Fast begins before dawn.
***Adar* 13**	***Ta'anit Esther***
	Fast of Esther
	Fast begins before dawn.

Special memorial prayers, referred to as ***Yizkor,*** are recited four times during the year (see Section 6.27).

***Nisan* 22**	Eighth Day of *Pesach*
***Sivan* 7**	Second Day of *Shavuot*
***Tishrei* 10**	*Yom Kippur*
***Tishrei* 22**	*Shemini Atzeret*

There are several special Sabbaths during the Jewish calendar year. Four of them are designated as the ***Arba Parashiyot,*** the Four Portions. Each of these Sabbaths is distinguished by the reading of a special additional passage during *Kriat HaTorah.* These four Sabbaths occur between the end of the month of *Shevat* and the beginning of the month of *Nisan.* They are:

- ***Shabbat Shekalim*** — The Sabbath of the *Shekalim* occurs on the Sabbath preceding the first of *Adar,* or on the first of *Adar,* if it falls on the Sabbath. When a leap year occurs in the Jewish calendar, *Shabbat Shekalim* is observed on, or just prior to, the first of *Adar Sheni,* the Second *Adar.* The additional passage read on *Shabbat Shekalim,* which serves as the *Maftir* portion, recalls that all Jewish males over the age of twenty, including *Kohanim* and *Levi'im,* were obligated to donate the sum of a half-*shekel* as an offering to the Lord. By this means, a census was taken, and funds were collected to provide for the communal sacrifices (see Section 8.9).
- ***Shabbat Zachor*** — The Sabbath of Remembrance occurs on the Sabbath preceding the Festival of Lots (*Purim*; see Chapter 8). The additional passage, which serves as the *Maftir* portion for this Sabbath, recalls the hatred of Amalek for Israel and God's command to blot out his remembrance (see Section 8.11).
- ***Shabbat Parah*** — The Sabbath of the Red Heifer occurs on the Sabbath after the Festival of Lots. The special passage, which is read as the *Maftir,* recalls the sacrifice of the red heifer, a ritual that was intended to purify.
- ***Shabbat HaChodesh*** — The Sabbath of the Month occurs on the Sabbath preceding *Rosh Chodesh Nisan.* The additional portion deals with the preparation for the Paschal sacrifice, the death of the first-born in Egypt, and the commandment to eat unleavened bread for seven days (see Section 7.1.6), beginning with the evening of the fourteenth of *Nisan.* This special Sabbath occurs between two and three weeks before the Festival of Passover begins.

In addition to the *Arba Parashiyot,* five other Sabbaths are designated by a distinctive name. They are:

- ***Shabbat HaGadol*** — The Great Sabbath occurs on the Sabbath immediately before Passover.
- ***Shabbat Chazon*** — The Sabbath of the Vision is observed on the Sabbath preceding the Fast of the Ninth of *Av.*

- ***Shabbat Nachamu*** The Sabbath of Comfort occurs on the Sabbath after the Fast of the Ninth of *Av.* If *Tisha b'Av* itself falls on Saturday, then that Sabbath is *Shabbat Chazon,* and the fast is observed on the tenth of *Av.* Accordingly, *Shabbat Nachamu* occurs on the following Sabbath.
- ***Shabbat Shuvah*** The Sabbath of Return occurs during the Ten Days of Repentance between *Rosh HaShanah* and *Yom Kippur* (see Section 6.18). *Shabbat Shuvah* is sometimes referred to as the Sabbath of Repentance as well.
- ***Shabbat Shirah*** The Sabbath of Song is always associated with *Parshat Beshalach,* Exodus 14:30–15:19 which are referred to as the Song of the Sea. It is from these Torah passages that the Sabbath of Song derives its name. It is a *minhag* to feed the birds on *Shabbat Shirah* (see Section 5.2.2).

During the year, a handful of other Sabbaths are identified by a specific name. They are:

- ***Shabbat Bereshit*** Sabbath of Genesis is especially noteworthy because it marks the beginning of the annual cycle of *Kriat HaTorah.* The cycle begins with *Parshat Bereshit* in the Book of Genesis and concludes with *Parshat V'zot HaBerachah* in the Book of Deuteronomy.
- ***Shabbat Chanukah*** Sabbath of the Festival of Lights occurs during *Chanukah,* the eight-day observance that begins on the twenty-fifth day of *Kislev* (see Chapter 8). If both the first and the eighth days of the festival fall on the Sabbath, *Parshat Vayeshev* is read on the first *Shabbat Chanukah,* and *Parshat Mikketz* is read the following week.
- ***Shabbat Chol HaMo'ed*** Sabbath of the Intermediate Days occurs during the Pilgrimage Festivals of Passover and Tabernacles, which are comprised of sacred days—***Yom Tov***—and intermediate days—***Chol HaMo'ed*** (see Sections 7.6 and 7.20). When one of the intermediate days falls on the Sabbath, the day is referred to as *Shabbat Chol HaMoed.*
- ***Shabbat Mevorchim HaChodesh*** Sabbath of Blessing the New Moon refers to the Sabbath before the beginning of a new Hebrew month, when the Blessing of the New Month is recited in the synagogue. The blessing is not recited before the month of *Tishrei.*
- ***Shabbat Rosh Chodesh*** Sabbath of the New Moon refers to the Sabbath that coincides with *Rosh Chodesh,* the beginning of a new month. Special *tefillot* are recited on *Shabbat Rosh Chodesh,* and an additional Torah portion is also read.

An overview of the year follows.

The Jewish Calendar

Nisan	
15–22	*Pesach*
	Passover
16	Begin to count *Sefirat HaOmer*
22	*Yizkor*
27	*Yom HaShoah*
	Holocaust Remembrance Day
Iyar	
4	*Yom HaZikaron*
	Remembrance Day
5	*Yom HaAtzma'ut*
	Israel Independence Day
18	*LaG baOmer*
	Thirty-third Day of the *Omer*
28	*Yom Yerushalayim*
	Reunification of Jerusalem Day
Sivan	
6 and 7	*Shavuot*
	Festival of Weeks or Pentecost
7	*Yizkor*
Tammuz	
17	*Shivah Asar b'Tammuz*
	Fast of the Seventeenth of *Tammuz*
17	The *Drai Vochen* Begin
	The Three Weeks Begin
Av	
1–9	The Last Nine Days of the *Drai Vochen*
9	*Tishah b'Av*
	Fast of the Ninth of *Av*
15	*TU b'Av*
	Day of Courtship
Elul	
1–29	Month-long period of reflection and repentance
Tishrei	
1 and 2	*Rosh HaShanah*
	Jewish New Year

3	*Tzom Gedaliah* Fast of Gedaliah
1–10	*Aseret Y'mei T'shuvah* Ten Days of Repentance
10	*Yom Kippur* or *Shabbat Shabbaton* Day of Atonement or Sabbath of Sabbaths
10	*Yizkor*
15–21	*Sukkot* Festival of Tabernacles
22	*Shemini Atzeret* Eighth Day of Holy Convocation
22	*Yizkor*
23	*Simchat Torah* Day of Rejoicing with the Torah

Cheshvan

There are no festivals or fast days in *Cheshvan,*
so it is often referred to as *Mar Cheshvan*, Bitter *Cheshvan*

Kislev

25	*Chanukah* Begins Festival of Lights Begins

Tevet

2	*Chanukah* Ends Festival of Lights Ends
10	*Asarah b'Tevet* Fast of the Tenth of *Tevet*

Shevat

15	*TU b'Shevat/Rosh HaShanah l'Ilanot* Jewish Arbor Day/New Year for Trees

Adar

13	*Ta'anit Esther* Fast of Esther
14	*Purim* Festival of Lots
15	*Shushan Purim* *Purim* observed in Jerusalem

4.7 The Liturgy of *Rosh Chodesh*

The observance of *Rosh Chodesh* requires the recitation of special *tefillot* for those days. Some are recited in addition to the usual prayers; others are substituted for the usual prayers.

In *Birchot HaShachar,* verses from *Parshat Pinchas,* Numbers 28:11–15, are recited in addition to the usual blessings. These verses explain the *korbanot* that were brought to the *Bet HaMikdash* on *Rosh Chodesh.*

If *Rosh Chodesh* falls on a weekday, the *tefillah* ***Ya'aleh v'Yavo*** is inserted within the recitation of Blessing (17) in the *Shemoneh Esrei* of *Shacharit, Minchah,* and *Ma'ariv* (see Chapter 3). A prayer for God to remember us favorably, it is derived from *Parshat Beha'alot'cha,* Numbers 10:10, which requires that special offerings be brought to the *Bet HaMikdash* in observance of the New Moon. It is appropriate that it appears within Blessing (17), which requests a return to the service in the Temple.

In some congregations, Psalm 104 is recited at the close of *Shacharit* on *Rosh Chodesh.* Following *Shacharit,* **Hallel,** a selection of hymns of praise from the Psalms, is also recited on *Rosh Chodesh.* It is comprised of Psalms 113; 114; 115:1–18; 116:1–19; 117; and 118; it concludes with a blessing not taken from Psalms, but which continues the theme of praise and concisely restates the belief that the Jewish people and the entire universe, from this world to the World to Come, will join in praise of the Almighty God.

On *Rosh Chodesh,* the Additional Service, *Musaf,* is also recited. It commemorates the additional sacrifice that was brought to the Temple on that day. In lieu of the *korbanot, Musaf* includes passages that are recited to atone for sins, including those that delay the arrival of the *Mashiach* and cause widespread illness in children.

Parshat Pinchas, Numbers 28:11, is repeated in *Musaf,* again recalling the *korbanot* that were brought to the *Bet HaMikdash* on *Rosh Chodesh.* It is followed with a final request that God favor us with all manner of beneficence in the new month, noting specifically twelve benedictions, in groups of two, one for each of the twelve months. An additional request is included during a leap year. *Musaf* continues and concludes with *Alenu* and *Kaddish* (see Section 3.12).

4.8 Blessing of the Sun

According to the Torah,

> ... God made two great lights:
> the greater light to rule the day
> and the lesser light to rule the night. ...
> And God set them in the heavens to illuminate the earth. ...
> and there was evening and there was morning,
> Day Four.
>
> —*Parshat Bereshit,* Genesis 1:16–19

According to tradition, that very moment of Creation occurred on Wednesday, the fourth day of *Nisan,* at the beginning of the spring equinox. According to calculations associated with the Jewish calendar, the precise time was equivalent to 6:00 P.M., Jerusalem time, on Tuesday evening, heading into Wednesday (see discussion about Hour 0 in Section 4.4).

In the cycle of the solar calendar, the sun returns to this position every year in the month of *Nisan*. However, the spring equinox occurs on a Tuesday evening/Wednesday only once in twenty-eight years. Only once in twenty-eight years is the sun in the exact same position it was at the time of Creation on Tuesday evening/Wednesday at 6:00 P.M.

The sages ordained that when this occurs, a special ***Birkat HaChamah,*** Blessing of the Sun, is to be recited. Because the sun cannot be seen at the same time in all places on Tuesday evening at 6:00 P.M., Jerusalem time, the blessing is to be recited everywhere on Wednesday during the day, because the light of the sun at its creation was not visible until the morning of the fourth day.

The primary source for this is found in the Talmud, which states:

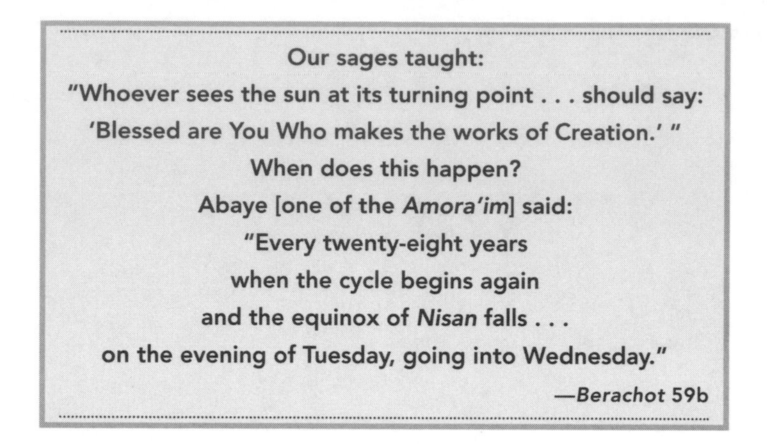

Our sages taught:
"Whoever sees the sun at its turning point . . . should say:
'Blessed are You Who makes the works of Creation.' "
When does this happen?
Abaye [one of the *Amora'im*] said:
"Every twenty-eight years
when the cycle begins again
and the equinox of *Nisan* falls . . .
on the evening of Tuesday, going into Wednesday."

—*Berachot* 59b

Birkat HaChamah was last recited on April 8, 1981. It will occur again on April 8 in 2009, 2037, 2065, and 2093. It will fall on April 9 in 2121, 2149, and 2177.

On each of those dates, Jews will revisit a moment of Creation, as they gather outside in the morning to recite the following blessing:

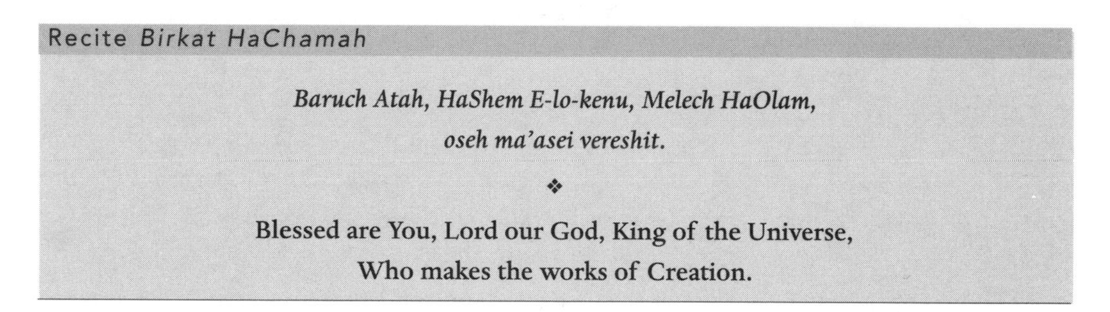

Recite *Birkat HaChamah*

Baruch Atah, HaShem E-lo-kenu, Melech HaOlam,
oseh ma'asei vereshit.

❖

Blessed are You, Lord our God, King of the Universe,
Who makes the works of Creation.

Although a *minyan* is not required for the recitation of *Birkat HaChamah,* most authorities conclude that the blessing should be recited in a large group. It may be recited early in the morning, upon first seeing the sun, or after *Shacharit,* but not later than midday. If necessary, one may recite the blessing after observing the sun through a window. In all cases, one should stand during the recitation.

If there is a likelihood that clouds will interfere with one's ability to see the sun, the blessing should be recited promptly. If the sun is completely hidden by the clouds, the full blessing is not recited. If by midday, the sun is still hidden, one should recite the blessing without God's Name:

Blessed are You Who makes the works of Creation.

Other *halachot* include:

- ***She'hecheyanu*** is not recited (see Section 6.15.1).
- A mourner should not recite the blessing before burial of the deceased. After burial, the blessing should be pronounced.
- Blind persons may ask someone else to recite the blessing on their behalf, and they should answer "Amen."
- The blessing may be recited on Passover, if the holiday coincides with the equinox.

Although there is no set order of prayers associated with *Birkat HaChamah,* several *tefillot* have been compiled for this occasion. The day's liturgy includes the recitation of biblical and prophetic verses and numerous hymns from the Psalms, leading up to the blessing itself. After the blessing has been pronounced, additional passages from the Torah and the Talmud are recited.

Mark your calendar: 2009 is not that far away.

4.9 The Sabbatical Year

The Sabbatical Year, ***Sh'nat Shemittah,*** refers to the last year of a seven-year cycle during which the Land of Israel is to remain uncultivated and, thus, unharvested. God spoke to Moses and instructed him to tell the Children of Israel:

> **When you come into the land which I give you,**
> **then the land shall observe a Sabbath unto the Lord.**
> **Six years you shall sow your field, . . .**
> **prune your vineyard, and gather in the produce thereof;**
> **but . . . the seventh year**
> **shall be a Sabbath of solemn rest for the land,**
> **a Sabbath unto the Lord. . . .**
>
> **—*Parshat Behar,* Leviticus 25:2–4**

During the Sabbatical Year, fields are not sown, nor harvests reaped. Any produce that grows untended and remains in the fields can be taken, not only by the landowner, but by all who want it, for it belongs to no one. However, one may take only an amount sufficient for a given day. Additionally, ***Shemittah*** crops may be used only for food, and edible skins and peels that are not eaten must be disposed of by wrapping them in a separate bag before placing them in the trash.

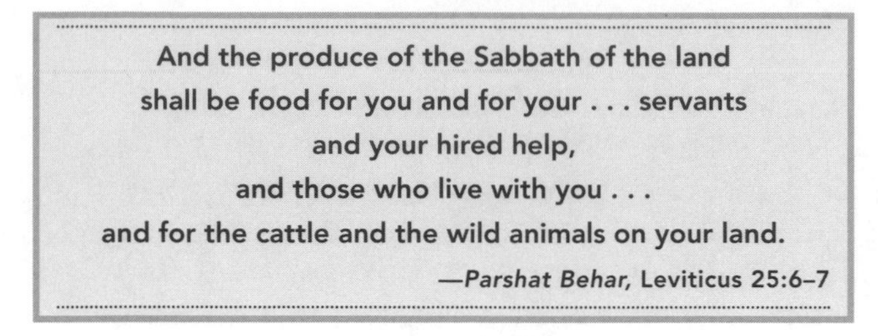

And the produce of the Sabbath of the land
shall be food for you and for your . . . servants
and your hired help,
and those who live with you . . .
and for the cattle and the wild animals on your land.

—*Parshat Behar,* Leviticus 25:6–7

The poor, too, are not to be forgotten.

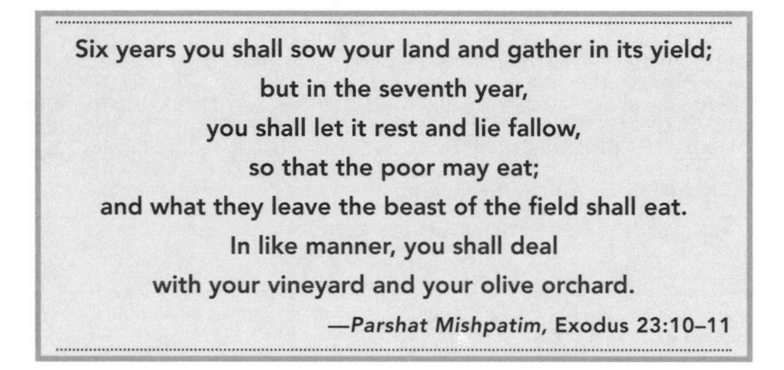

Six years you shall sow your land and gather in its yield;
but in the seventh year,
you shall let it rest and lie fallow,
so that the poor may eat;
and what they leave the beast of the field shall eat.
In like manner, you shall deal
with your vineyard and your olive orchard.

—*Parshat Mishpatim,* Exodus 23:10–11

This *mitzvah* refers to all that the land will grow, be it the produce of the earth or the fruits of the trees.

Thus, the *mitzvah* of *Shemittah* is twofold: to permit the land to rest and to leave the produce ownerless. The purpose of the laws of *Shemittah* (there are seven positive and seventeen negative precepts in all) is to firmly establish the concept that God created the world in six days *out of nothing*; and, then, on the seventh day, He rested. In order to nullify the misperception that the world existed before God created it out of nothing, Jews were required to be continually aware of the divine cycle of Creation by counting the years: six years for work and the seventh year for rest.

In addition, by the observance of *Shemittah,* the Jewish people are reminded that nothing grows year in and year out of its own power. It is the Almighty Who is the Master over the earth and over those who think they "own" it. By relinquishing their claim to the land and all it yields for a year, the Jewish people reaffirm their trust in God.

The word *Shemittah* also carries the connotation of release. During the Sabbatical Year, all debts were to be canceled, and all debtors released from their financial obligations.

> **At the end of every seven years,**
> **you shall release . . . [all debts];**
> **every creditor shall release his [claim]**
> **on what he lent to his neighbor.**
> **He shall not demand it from his neighbor and his brother;**
> **but from a foreigner he shall make his claim.**
> **—*Parshat Re'ei,* Deuteronomy 15:1–3**

Canceling a debt was considered an act of charity, for in an agricultural society, only those in need would go into debt in the first place. In later times, when business became more complicated and was not related solely to an agricultural economy, it became necessary to protect the financial interests of those who made business loans.

To encourage Jews to make interest-free loans to those in need, as prescribed by the Torah, and to preclude the creditor's obligation to cancel such debts during *Shemittah,* Hillel (first century B.C.E.) instituted the use of the ***Prozbul,*** a legal procedure that empowered the court to collect the business debt on behalf of the creditor.

The laws of *Shemittah* are observed today in modern Israel. Because of economic considerations, it is difficult, if not impossible, for Jewish farmers to observe the *mitzvot* of *Shemittah* properly. Accordingly, the Chief Rabbinate of Israel issued a Permission of Sale, allowing the Jewish farmers to sell their property to non-Jews. A contract is signed between the parties, with a rabbi acting as agent for each farmer. For the *Shemittah* period, the non-Jews assume legal ownership and may do as they see fit. The contract states that after the *Shemittah* period, the final sale price will be decided. At that time, the non-Jews may pay the full price, or they may sell it back to the Jewish farmers. During the Sabbatical Year, the Jewish farmers may work the fields for the non-Jews, because the fields no longer belong to them, and the Torah forbids cultivating "your fields." Some halachic authorities do not accept this ruling of the Chief Rabbinate, but most do allow Jewish farmers to work the fields without rendering the produce unusable. Those Israeli Jews who are uncomfortable with this procedure can buy imported produce during the *Shemittah* year.

The Sabbatical Year is reckoned from the first day of *Tishrei*, that is, from *Rosh HaShanah*.

4.10 The Jubilee Year

The Jubilee Year, ***Yovel,*** refers to the fiftieth year after seven Sabbatical Years. Although it is reckoned from the first day of *Tishrei,* the Jubilee Year is proclaimed on the tenth of the month.

> **And you shall number seven Sabbaths of years,**
> **seven years seven times . . . forty-nine years.**
> **Then you shall proclaim with the blast of the horn**
> **in the seventh month on the tenth day of the month;**
> **in the Day of Atonement, you shall make proclamation**
> **with the horn throughout all your land.**
> **And you shall hallow the fiftieth year,**
> **and proclaim liberty throughout the land**
> **unto all the inhabitants thereof;**
> **a jubilee it shall be unto you.**
>
> —*Parshat Behar,* Leviticus 25:8–10

While the laws of *Shemittah* pertain to the release of the land and the cancellation of debts, the laws of *Yovel* include the release of slaves. In some instances, an impoverished Jew might "sell" himself into slavery in order to support himself and his family. The Torah required that a slave's owner provide substantial funds (or the equivalent) to the slave at the end of his service, to help him avoid a situation that could require him to be enslaved again. In the Jubilee Year, all Jewish slaves were to be freed immediately from further service, and the sounding of the *shofar* was meant to announce their liberation.

While the term "slavery" has extreme negative connotations in today's society, it was then an acceptable social practice. A non-Jewish slave could be released from servitude if someone paid for his freedom or if the owner gave him a document of emancipation. Additionally, the Torah opposed the abuse or humiliation of any slave. If a non-Jewish slave was deliberately injured by his owner, he was freed immediately.

In addition to the laws of emancipating slaves, the observance of *Yovel* also requires the release of the land. The rules of *Shemittah* also apply during the *Yovel,* for the use of the land for cultivation and harvest is prohibited.

> A jubilee that fiftieth year shall be unto you;
> you shall not sow, nor reap . . . for it is a jubilee. . . .
> —*Parshat Behar,* Leviticus 25:11, 12

Furthermore, in keeping with Torah law, all property reverts to the original owners, who might have been forced to sell their land because of poverty during the previous forty-nine year period.

> But if he [a poor man] has no means
> to restore [his property] to himself,
> then, what he sold shall remain
> in the hands of the buyer until the year of jubilee . . .
> [when] he shall return to his possession.
> —*Parshat Behar,* Leviticus 25:28

Observance of the Jubilee Year, therefore, precludes the accumulation of vast landholdings in the hands of the more affluent. As God commanded:

> And the land shall not be sold in perpetuity;
> for the land is Mine;
> and you are [My] strangers and settlers.
> —*Parshat Behar,* Leviticus 25:23

The laws of *Yovel* were not observed during the period of the Babylonian Exile. The generally accepted meaning of the word *yovel* is *horn,* and the Jubilee Year is always marked by the sounding of the ram's horn.

While it may seem on the surface that *Shemittah* and *Yovel* are essentially agricultural considerations—resting the land being the primary focus—their *mitzvot* provide a framework for sanctification. By recognizing their dependence on God's beneficence, by relying on Him to restore the land to productivity, the Jewish people maintain an ongoing relationship of trust and faith. By observing these *mitzvot,* in spite of financial (and even physical) hardships, the Jewish people sanctify the years of the Jewish calendar.

LOOKING AHEAD! *We will fill in more details in our calendar as we delve more deeply into the observances of the Jewish year. In Chapter 5, we will begin with the weekly celebration and sanctification of the Sabbath.*

Word Works

The holy Sabbath is welcomed into the Jewish home
eighteen minutes before sundown with the lighting of candles.

5

The Sabbath

THE JEWISH PEOPLE are blessed every week with the arrival of a cherished guest. Every Friday evening at sunset, as the day turns toward night, the ***Shabbat HaMalkah,*** the Sabbath Queen, arrives, endowing the Jewish world with her gifts of sanctity and gladness. Suddenly, the frenzied pace of life is slowed; the concerns of the outside world recede; and all doubts and worries are set aside.

In Jewish tradition, the Sabbath Queen brings a day of joy, a day of rest, a day the Jewish people look forward to from the time the *Shabbat HaMalkah* departs on Saturday night until she returns again.

5.1 Remembering and Observing the Sabbath Day

God gave the Jewish people the Sabbath. In the Talmud, we find:

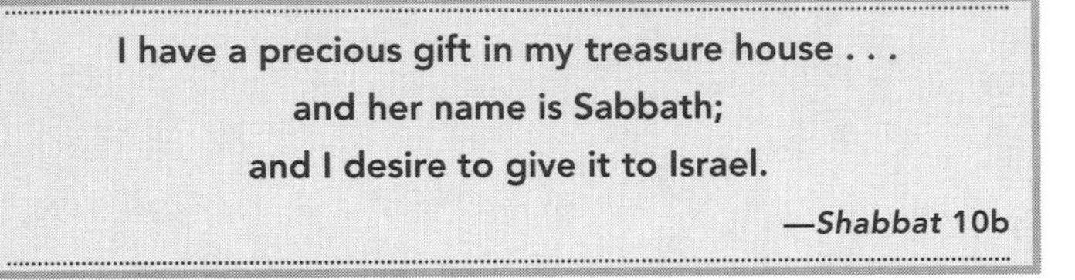
I have a precious gift in my treasure house . . .
and her name is Sabbath;
and I desire to give it to Israel.

—*Shabbat* 10b

God bestowed this gift upon the Jewish people in the ***Aseret HaDibrot,*** the Ten Commandments. The Fourth Commandment states:

> **Remember the Sabbath Day to keep it holy.**
> **Six days you shall labor, and do all your work;**
> **but the seventh day is a Sabbath to the Lord your God;**
> **you shall not do any manner of work,**
> **[not] you, nor your son, nor your daughter,**
> **nor your man-servant, nor your maid-servant,**
> **nor your cattle, nor your stranger that is within your gates.**
>
> **—*Parshat Yitro,* Exodus 20:8–10**

Why did God declare the seventh day as the Sabbath, a day of rest?

> **For in six days the Lord made heaven and earth,**
> **the seas, and all that is in them;**
> **and He rested on the seventh day;**
> **thus, the Lord blessed the Sabbath Day,**
> **and hallowed it.**
>
> **—*Parshat Yitro,* Exodus 20:11**

Because God, Himself, rested on the seventh day after Creation and sanctified it, so, too, the Jewish people were commanded.

The seventh day begins eighteen minutes before sunset on Friday and ends one hour after sunset on Saturday. This period is called ***Shabbat,*** Sabbath, from the Hebrew verb meaning *to desist from work* (in Yiddish, it is called ***Shabbos***). However, the cessation from labor not only represents the act of *remembering* the Sabbath as a day of rest. The

Shabbat is also to be hallowed and *observed* as a holy day, one that is set apart for spiritual matters.

The Sabbath is considered an everlasting covenant between the Jewish people and God, an agreement that recognizes both the responsibility to work and the obligation to rest from that work.

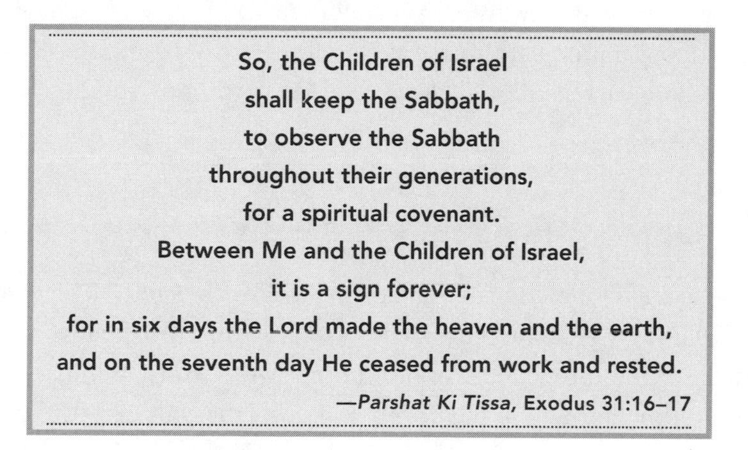

So, the Children of Israel
shall keep the Sabbath,
to observe the Sabbath
throughout their generations,
for a spiritual covenant.
Between Me and the Children of Israel,
it is a sign forever;
for in six days the Lord made the heaven and the earth,
and on the seventh day He ceased from work and rested.

—*Parshat Ki Tissa*, Exodus 31:16–17

For the Jewish people, the Sabbath provides a regular opportunity to enjoy not only a physical rest from their daily labors, but also a renewal of their souls through prayer and Torah study. By sanctifying the Sabbath, Jews bring a spirit of holiness into their homes every week of the year.

The Fourth Commandment is a twofold obligation, spoken first by God:

> **Remember the Sabbath Day to keep it holy.**
>
> **—*Parshat Yitro*, Exodus 20:8**

and restated by Moses:

> **And Moses called to all Israel and said to them: . . .**
> **"The Lord our God made a covenant with us. . . .**
> **Observe the Sabbath Day to keep it holy,**
> **as the Lord your God commanded you."**
>
> **—*Parshat Va'etchanan*, Deuteronomy 5:1, 2, 12**

Remembering the Sabbath Day and observing it are two distinct precepts. *Remembering* refers to fulfilling the positive precepts associated with the Sabbath Day. *Observing* refers to not violating the negative commandments of the Sabbath, which we discuss in Section 5.9.

5.2 Ushering in the Sabbath at Home

The Sabbath begins on Friday evening at sundown. On Friday, ***erev Shabbat,*** the eve of the Sabbath, preparations are made in the home to welcome the Sabbath Queen. Everything must be in readiness, ***lichvod Shabbat,*** in honor of the Sabbath, before candlelighting time.

5.2.1 Lighting the Sabbath Candles

The table is traditionally set with a festive white tablecloth. The Sabbath candlesticks (or candelabra), which are set aside for use only on the Sabbath (or holidays), are placed prominently on the table. A minimum of two candles are lit, symbolizing the twofold commandment found in the Torah. It is customary in many homes to add one candle upon the birth of each child. White ***nerot Shabbat,*** Sabbath candles, are most often used.

Lighting the *nerot Shabbat* is one of the *mitzvot* specifically for women. Most often candlelighting is referred to by the Yiddish expression **licht benchen,** literally, *blessing the lights.* As a verb, the phrase is *to* **bench licht.** In common usage, the verb has taken on English grammatical structure; for example, she *benches licht;* or she is *benching licht;* or she *benched licht.*

At dusk, approximately eighteen minutes before sunset, the candles are lit. The woman of the house covers her head, and with her two hands, she waves the light toward her three times, as if to draw in the spirit of holiness. She closes her eyes, covers them with her hands, and recites the *berachah* over the candles, acknowledging God's commandment. With the recitation of the blessing, she ushers in the Sabbath and takes upon herself all the *mitzvot,* both positive and negative, associated with its observance.

(You will recall from Section 3.4.9 that *birchot hamitzvot* are recited before the *mitzvah* is performed. However, in the case of the Sabbath candles, the opposite is true. We will explain why in Section 5.9.4.)

Recite the Blessing over the Sabbath Candles

Baruch Atah, HaShem E-lo-kenu, Melech HaOlam
asher kidshanu b'mitzvotav v'tzivanu
l'hadlik ner shel Shabbat.

❖

Blessed are You, Lord our God, King of the Universe,
Who has sanctified us with His commandments and commanded us
to kindle the Sabbath lights.

When she has finished the *berachah,* she recites *Y'hi Ratzon,* the prayer that is also recited at the conclusion of the *Shemoneh Esrei.*

Recite *Y'hi Ratzon* after Candlelighting

May it be Your will,
Lord, our God, and God of our forefathers,
that the Temple be speedily rebuilt in our days,
and grant us a share in Your Torah.
There we will serve You with reverence
as in the days of old and in former years.
Then the offering of Judah and Jerusalem
will be pleasing to the Lord,
as in the days of old and in former years.

Because the moment when the Sabbath candles are lit is considered an ***eit ratzon,*** a propitious hour for God to hear her *tefillot,* she may continue with a personal prayer, thanking Him for His blessings in the week just past and appealing to Him for His continued beneficence on behalf of herself and her family. She also prays that her children should grow up to follow in the ways of Torah, to be observant of the *mitzvot*. She may call upon Him to heal the sick and remember the souls of her departed relatives. She may whisper whatever is in her heart, for it is a time of mercy. She then greets those present with ***Shabbat Shalom,*** Sabbath peace, or the Yiddish ***Gut Shabbos,*** Good Sabbath.

Traditionally, a woman first lights the Sabbath candles on the first Sabbath eve after her marriage. However, an unmarried woman must also light them if she maintains her own residence. If there is no woman in the household, a man is obligated to light the candles. It is customary in some homes to allow young girls to light a single candle and recite the blessing in order to teach them the religious ritual that ushers in the Sabbath.

A WITTY REMARK!

My father was the rabbi of a congregation in northeastern Pennsylvania in the 1960s. It was a small congregation, fewer than one hundred families, in an equally small town—six blocks wide by eight blocks long, or so we joked.

In its heyday it had been a booming center of the coal mining industry; but by the time my parents took up residence in the house next door to the synagogue, the town was little more than a wisp of its former self. Only the smell of coal still lingered in the air.

Surprisingly, the Jewish community had largely stayed intact. Some of the members owned the stores that dotted Main Street, and the best dentist and the most compassionate doctor in town also belonged to the synagogue.

Every week from the end of August through November, an *erev Shabbat* visitor came to my father's door. "Rabbi," said a good-looking, tall boy, "I'm sorry to bother you before the Sabbath, but I was . . . well, I was wondering. . . ."

"What can I do for you, Larry? Just tell me," my Dad urged.

"Uh, okay, uh, sir, I was wondering if I could borrow the keys to the synagogue for a few minutes. I'll bring them right back."

"Sure, Larry, I'll get them for you."

Larry never explained why he needed the keys, and my father didn't want to pry. So, every Friday afternoon, Larry came to the door, borrowed the keys, and in a few minutes returned them to my father.

The day after Thanksgiving, as usual, Larry showed up at the door. Curiosity finally got the best of my father. "Larry," my father said, handing him the keys, "I hope you don't mind my asking, but why do you come here every Friday and borrow the keys? Why do you need to go into the synagogue every Friday afternoon?"

"Well, sir, I remember hearing you say in a sermon once that the eve of the Sabbath was an especially favorable time for prayers."

"Yes, Larry, that's true."

"Well, sir, I'm the captain of my high school football team, and . . . well . . . every Friday afternoon, just a few hours before the game, I come here, get the keys, and go into the synagogue. I say a little prayer for myself and for my team, and, sir, we haven't lost a game yet."

The team won that night, too—and finished the season as undefeated champions. Larry hadn't yet learned the true meaning of *Shabbat*, for such activities are prohibited on the Sabbath because they are not in keeping with the values and spirit of the day. However, he certainly understood about the power of prayer.

The table is bedecked for the Sabbath in anticipation of the arrival of the *Shabbat HaMalkah*.

5.2.2 The Sabbath Loaves

In addition to the *nerot Shabbat,* two unsliced loaves of ***challah,*** traditionally a specially braided bread, are placed together on the Sabbath table. They are covered with a cloth, often one that is embroidered and decorated with symbols of the Sabbath, which further enhances the beauty of the table. The two ***challot,*** called ***mishneh lechem,*** double bread, remind the Jewish people of the miracle of the double portion of manna related in the Torah.

For forty years in the wilderness, en route from the bondage of Egypt to the Promised Land of Canaan, the manna fell from heaven and provided sustenance for the Israelites. They gathered their daily bread; but on the sixth day of the week, the eve of the Sabbath, they gathered a double portion, for none fell on the Sabbath Day.

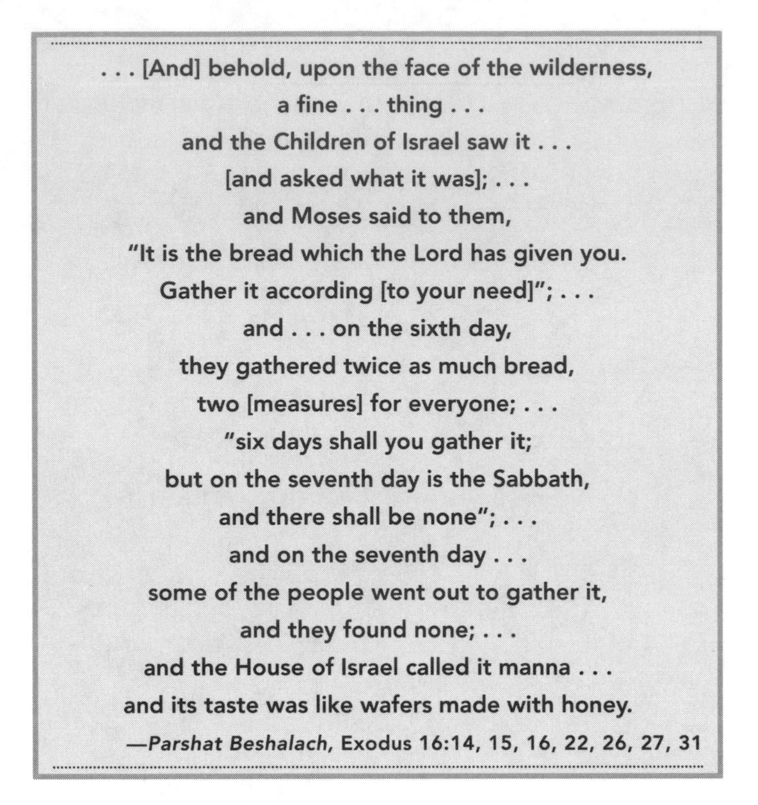
. . . [And] behold, upon the face of the wilderness,
a fine . . . thing . . .
and the Children of Israel saw it . . .
[and asked what it was]; . . .
and Moses said to them,
"It is the bread which the Lord has given you.
Gather it according [to your need]"; . . .
and . . . on the sixth day,
they gathered twice as much bread,
two [measures] for everyone; . . .
"six days shall you gather it;
but on the seventh day is the Sabbath,
and there shall be none"; . . .
and on the seventh day . . .
some of the people went out to gather it,
and they found none; . . .
and the House of Israel called it manna . . .
and its taste was like wafers made with honey.
—*Parshat Beshalach,* Exodus 16:14, 15, 16, 22, 26, 27, 31

The *Midrash* tells of two troublesome Israelites, Datan and Aviram. According to tradition, they wanted to prove that Moses had deceived the people when he told them that no manna would fall on the Sabbath. Datan and Aviram planned to collect the manna on Friday, save it, and then spread it on the ground early in the morning of the Sabbath before the people awoke. Their scheme failed because the birds ate all the manna they had prepared.

In the Hebrew month of *Shevat,* when *Parshat Beshalach* is read in the Torah, the Jewish people mark a special Sabbath (see Section 4.6.13), *Shabbat Shirah.* It is an ancient *minhag* to remember the birds by feeding them on that day.

5.3 Welcoming the Sabbath in the Synagogue

Just prior to the Sabbath, the Afternoon Service, *Minchah,* is recited. The Sabbath begins with ***Kabbalat Shabbat,*** the service of Welcoming the Sabbath. It is recited in the synagogue at sunset, about the time the candles are lit at home, and is followed by *Ma'ariv,* the Evening Service.

5.3.1 The *Kabbalat Shabbat* Service

The *Kabbalat Shabbat* service, filled with congregational melodies that usher in the Sabbath, dates back to the sixteenth-century **Kabbalists,** mystical sages, who flourished in the city of Safed, Israel. In the inspiring Sabbath ambiance of the synagogue or the home, it begins with the recitation of Psalms 95, 96, 97, 98, 99, and 29. These six psalms, symbolizing the six workdays of the week, were selected by Rabbi Moses Cordovero, the head of the school of mystics.

5.3.2 Greeting the Sabbath Bride

These hymns of praise are followed by the recitation of the religious poem ***Lecha Dodi,*** which was written by Rabbi Solomon Alkabets, a brother-in-law of Rabbi Cordovero. It consists of nine stanzas and a refrain. The author's Hebrew name, Shlomo HaLevi, is signed in a Hebrew acrostic at the beginning of each of the first eight stanzas, and the words of the hymn are derived from *Tanach.*

One of the most beautiful liturgical compositions, *Lecha Dodi* personifies the Sabbath as a bride and heralds her arrival. Just as God is often likened to a bridegroom Who rejoices over Israel, His bride, so, too, the Jewish people welcome the Sabbath Bride with the same joyous greeting accorded to a bride on her wedding day.

Recite *Lecha Dodi*

Recited Twice by the Cantor and Congregation:

Come, my friend, to meet the bride;
let us welcome the Sabbath Presence.

Congregation then Cantor:

"Observe" and "Remember" in a single utterance,
the One and Only God caused us to hear.
The Lord is One, and His Name is One,
for fame, for splendor, and for praise.
Come my friend, to meet the bride;
let us welcome the Sabbath Presence.

❖

Come, let us go to welcome the Sabbath,
for it is a source of blessing.
From the very beginning it was planned;
last in Creation, first in God's thought.
Come, my friend, to meet the bride;
let us welcome the Sabbath Presence.

The refrain is derived from the Talmud, *Masechet Shabbat* 119a, in which the sages Rabbi Chaninah and Rabbi Yannai hail the Sabbath as a bride. According to the Talmud, *Masechet Shevuot* 20b, the two words "observe" and "remember" were uttered by God at the same instant to teach the Jewish people that the two were linked forever. The second stanza points out that the Sabbath was, in fact, God's last act of Creation, but it was ordained by God before the universe was created.

The remainder of the poem focuses on Jerusalem and Israel's yearning for salvation. According to the Talmud, *Masechet Shabbat* 118b, the Messiah will come if Israel truly observes two Sabbaths according to the requirements of the *halachah*. Thus, the hope for redemption is an appropriate theme.

We learn from the words of the next two verses that the poet urges Jerusalem to wake up; to forgo her weeping; to return to her former glory; and to rise again in the certainty that the Exile will end and the City of Jerusalem will be rebuilt. The concluding two verses foretell Jerusalem's conquest of her enemies, everywhere, and hints at the sublime joy to come in the days of the Messiah, who will descend from the House of David.

The congregation then rises, turns to the sanctuary door, bows their heads, as if to welcome a guest, and chants the last stanza of *Lecha Dodi.*

Conclude the Recitation of *Lecha Dodi*

Come in peace, crown of her husband,
come in gladness and good cheer;
amid the faithful of the cherished nation,
enter, O Bride; enter, O Bride!
Come, my friend, to meet the bride;
let us welcome the Sabbath Presence.

This last verse recalls the relationship between the Sabbath and Israel. As the bride, the Sabbath is the glory of her spiritual husband, Israel; she is, in fact, its very crown. It is recited with special fervor and intense devotion, for the Sabbath Bride has now arrived.

5.3.3 Welcoming the Mourners

At the conclusion of *Lecha Dodi,* it is customary to usher in any worshippers who are in the first week of the mourning period. As they wait at the entrance to the sanctuary, the congregants greet them and offer words of consolation and condolence (see Sections 9.16.4 and 9.16.5).

Welcome Mourners to *Kabbalat Shabbat*

May the Omnipresent comfort you
among all those who mourn for Zion and Jerusalem.

The mourners are then escorted into the sanctuary to join the congregation in prayer.

5.3.4 The Significance of Psalms 92 and 93

Kabbalat Shabbat continues with the recitation of Psalms 92 and 93. While a woman takes the observance of the *mitzvot* of *Shabbat* upon herself at the time of candlelighting, a man does so formally upon the recitation of Psalm 92.

In the days of the *Bet HaMikdash,* the *Levi'im* sang this hymn of praise for God's glorious works during the sacrificial rite for the Sabbath. It reflects on God's wondrous deeds, both at the dawn of redemption and in the darkness of exile, reaffirming the belief that the happiness and prosperity of the faithful will endure in contrast to the short-lived joy of the wicked.

Psalm 93 reveals God robed in splendor as the all-powerful King whose supremacy extends over the forces of nature, a symbolic reference to the enemies of Israel. This hymn was chanted in the *Bet HaMikdash* by the *Levi'im* on Friday. It is followed by the Mourner's *Kaddish* and a selection of verses from the Mishnah, *Masechet Shabbat* 2, which describes the oil and the wicks that are appropriate to use for the Sabbath lights. A final selection from the Talmud, *Masechet Berachot* 64a, stresses the importance of peace. The Rabbis' *Kaddish* is the concluding prayer of *Kabbalat Shabbat,* which is followed by *Ma'ariv,* the Evening Service.

5.3.5 The *Ma'ariv* Service

Ma'ariv begins with *Barchu,* and includes *HaMa'ariv Aravim* and *Ahavat Olam,* as in the weekday *Ma'ariv* (see Section 3.10). *Ahavat Olam* recalls God's everlasting love for the Jewish people and foreshadows the words of the *Shema,* in which we promise to speak the words of God's Torah evening and morning, when we lie down and when we rise up, and to reflect on them day and night.

Kriat Shema is then recited. It is followed by two prayers: ***Emet v'Emunah*** and ***Hashkivenu.***

The last two words of the *Shema* and the opening word of *Emet v'Emunah* are recited without pausing, as if they were part of the same sentence.

I am the Lord your God.
True . . .

When recited together, it reads "the Lord your God is true."

Emet v'Emunah speaks of God's care and love in the present and in the future. It concludes with a blessing for God, the Redeemer of Israel. The final blessing after *Shema, Hashkivenu,* asks that the merciful God grant us peace and protection through the night.

A special prayer, ***V'Shamru,*** derived from *Parshat Ki Tissa,* Exodus 31:16–17, is then recited (see Section 5.1). It reiterates the obligation of the Jewish people to keep the Sabbath as an eternal covenant between them and God, the Creator of heaven and earth.

Recite *V'Shamru*

So, the Children of Israel
shall keep the Sabbath,
to observe the Sabbath
throughout their generations,
for a spiritual covenant.
Between Me and the Children of Israel,
it is a sign forever;
for in six days the Lord made the heaven and the earth,
and on the seventh day He ceased from work and rested.

Chatzi Kaddish is then recited and is followed by the Sabbath *Shemoneh Esrei,* which contains only seven blessings. The first three and the last three *berachot* are the same as in the Eighteen Benedictions recited at other times (see Section 3.7.5). The middle *berachah* deals with the sanctity of the Sabbath Day.

As we begin the *Shemoneh Esrei,* we take three steps backward and three steps forward, in the manner of one who approaches the Divine King. In humility, we utter this verse.

Recite before *Shemoneh Esrei* of *Ma'ariv*

O, Lord,
may You open my lips
so that my mouth shall declare Your praise.

As we begin the first blessing of the *Shemoneh Esrei,* we bend our knees and bow forward.

- Blessings (1, 2, and 3) comprise an expression in praise of God as in the weekday *Shemoneh Esrei.*
- Blessing (4) describes the sanctity of the Sabbath Day and replaces Blessings (4) to (16) of the weekday *Shemoneh Esrei.* This blessing is comprised of three paragraphs. These *tefillot* remind us that the Sabbath is a day ordained by God to serve Him. The Sabbath, which He created, provides the opportunity to come closer to His spiritual Presence. He is acknowledged as the Creator of the World, which He gave to humankind to use, according to the Torah. When His Creation was completed, He rested from His labors on the seventh day. In the final paragraph of this blessing, we ask God to accept our rest, even if we have only enjoyed the Sabbath's bounty and not made much spiritual progress. We ask Him to sanctify us through the

observance of His *mitzvot* and to purify our hearts to serve Him more devotedly. This blessing ends: "Blessed are You, Lord, Who sanctifies the Sabbath."

- Blessings 5, 6 and 7 complete the Sabbath *Shemoneh Esrei*. As we prepare to withdraw from the presence of the Holy One, we offer prayers of thanksgiving and gratitude for His blessings. If *Rosh Chodesh,* the New Moon, occurs on the Sabbath, *Ya'aleh v'Yavo* is recited within Blessing (5).

E-lo-kai Netzor is recited after Blessing (7), and *Shemoneh Esrei* ends. It is not repeated by the *chazan*.

5.3.6 The Abridged *Shemoneh Esrei*

A slightly abridged form of the *Shemoneh Esrei,* referred to as the Seven Blessings, follows the *Shemoneh Esrei*. According to Rashi's explanation on the Talmud, *Masechet Shabbat* 24b, it was originally introduced during a time when religious worship was permitted only in the outskirts of cities and towns. The addition of this prayer permitted latecomers to catch up and complete their recitation of the *Shemoneh Esrei* of *Ma'ariv* with the congregation, so they would not have to walk home alone because it was dangerous.

The cantor then concludes with the Full *Kaddish* and *Alenu*. *Ma'ariv* for the Sabbath eve is over, and the worshippers return to their homes to partake of the first Sabbath meal. It is customary even today to invite the poor among the worshippers to one's home to share the Sabbath meal.

5.4 Prelude to the First Sabbath Meal

The Talmud, *Masechet Shabbat* 119b, relates the story of two angels, one good, one evil, who accompany the Jew home from the synagogue on Friday evening. If all is in readiness for the proper observance of the Sabbath, the good angel says, "May the next Sabbath be like this one," and the evil angel is obliged to reply, "Amen." If not, the evil angel says, "May the next Sabbath be like this one," and the good angel is obliged to reply, "Amen."

5.4.1 In the Presence of the Sabbath Angels

Upon returning from the synagogue on Friday evening, the family assembles around the festive Sabbath table and sings the hymn ***Shalom Aleichem,*** greeting the Sabbath angels who have accompanied them home. In some homes, it is traditional to sing *Shalom Aleichem* three times.

Recite *Shalom Aleichem* on Friday Evening

Peace be with you, ministering angels,
angels of the Most Exalted, the Supreme King of kings,
the Holy One, blessed be He.

❖

May your coming be in peace, angels of peace,
angels of the Most Exalted, the Supreme King of kings,
the Holy One, blessed be He.

❖

Bless me with peace, angels of peace,
angels of the Most Exalted, the Supreme King of kings,
the Holy One, blessed be He.

❖

May your departure be in peace, angels of peace,
angels of the Most Exalted, the Supreme King of kings,
the Holy One, blessed be He.

5.4.2 In Praise of the Jewish Wife

Perhaps nowhere else in Jewish literature is the role of the Jewish wife so eloquently expressed as in the last twenty-two verses of Proverbs (31:10-31), which are recited following the singing of *Shalom Aleichem.* These verses in praise of the Jewish wife begin with ***Aishet Chayil,*** often translated as "A Woman of Valor," and are a moving tribute to her role as the mainstay of her home.

She is an ideal wife: dignified, respected, industrious, charitable. She is kind to the poor and gentle in her dealings with everyone. She is trusted by her husband, and is praised by him and her children who acknowledge her as the genuine source of their well-being. By caring for their physical welfare, she assures their spiritual advancement. With the sure knowledge that she has lived with honor and respect throughout her life, she will die with a good name.

These allegorical verses, which may represent the Sabbath, or the *Shechinah,* or the Torah itself, are expressed through the role of the Jewish wife, a sign of esteem and a recognition of her influence in the home. The text, which forms an alphabetical acrostic in Hebrew, is recited by her husband at the Sabbath table on Friday evening. They include:

Recite *Aishet Chayil*

A woman of valor, who can find her?
She is worth far more than pearls.
Her husband trusts in her,
And he never lacks good fortune.
She brings him good and not harm,
All the days of her life. . . .
She rises while it is still night,
And gives food to her household. . . .
She girds herself with strength,
And invigorates her arms for work. . . .
She opens her palm to the poor,
and extends her hand to the needy. . . .
Her husband is distinguished
As he sits with the elders of the land. . . .
Strength and honor are her fashion,
She smiles confidently at the future.
She opens her mouth with wisdom,
And she teaches others to be kind.
She looks after the needs of her home,
She never eats the bread of idleness.
Her children rise and laud her,
And her husband acclaims her, saying:
"Many women are worthy of praise,
But you surpass all of them."
Charm is false and beauty is vain,
Only a God-fearing woman should be praised.
Give her the fruits of her hand,
And let her deeds praise her in the gates.

5.4.3 Blessing the Children

The eve of the Sabbath is a favorable time for blessings, filled with the Sabbath spirit. Before the first Sabbath meal begins, it is also customary for parents to bless their children. The father places both his hands on the child's head. To his son he says:

Blessing a Son

May you be like Ephraim and Menasheh

the sons of Joseph and the grandsons of the patriarch Jacob. Joseph's sons were a source of great pride to Jacob, especially because they were the first Jewish children raised outside Israel, yet they were not influenced by the Egyptian culture in which they grew up.

A similar blessing is recited for a daughter.

Blessing a Daughter

May you be like Sarah, Rebecca, Rachel, and Leah

the four matriarchs, the mothers of the Jewish people, who overcame many hardships and obstacles in order to raise the children who would lead the Jewish nation.

The blessing concludes the same way for sons and daughters (*Parshat Naso*, Numbers 6:24–26).

Blessing the Children

May the Lord bless you and safeguard you.
May the Lord illuminate His Countenance for you
and be gracious to you.
May the Lord turn His Countenance toward you,
and grant you peace.

5.5 The First Sabbath Meal

Wine is represented in Jewish tradition as the essence of goodness and a symbol of joy, because it is "wine that cheers a man's heart" (Psalms 104:15). The Talmud, *Masechet Pesachim* 106a, in commenting on the commandment to "Remember the Sabbath Day," interprets it to mean "Remember it over wine." ***Kiddush,*** the prayer of sanctification over wine, is recited before the evening and morning meals on the Sabbath and festivals.

5.5.1 Reciting *Kiddush* in the Synagogue

On Friday evening, at the conclusion of the *Ma'ariv* service *Kiddush* is recited in the synagogue, and it is repeated at home. The custom of reciting the *Kiddush* in the synagogue originated in the period when visitors were given their Sabbath meal in a room adjoining the synagogue. Abudarham, a medieval scholar writing in fourteenth-century Spain, commented: "Because our predecessors set up the rule, though for a reason that no longer exists, the rule remains unshaken." (This is an example of the strength of the *minhag;* see Section 1.7).

5.5.2 Reciting *Kiddush* at Home

The *Kiddush* is recited again at the Sabbath table at home. Usually, the husband recites the *Kiddush* on behalf of his family, and he should have in mind that he is reciting on behalf of those present. Men and women alike are obligated to recite—or at least listen to the recitation of—*Kiddush.* The recitation of *Kiddush* fulfills the requirement to sanctify the Sabbath found in *Parshat Yitro,* Exodus 20:8; also, it is a reaffirmation of God's reason for Creation; in six days God created the world, so that humankind could rest on the seventh day.

It is preferable that the wine be red, although white wine or raisin wine may also be used. Even sacramental grape juice may be used by anyone who prefers not to drink wine. Traditionally, a special silver goblet or crystal glass, a ***kos shel Kiddush,*** or in Yiddish, a ***becher,*** is filled to the brim. The goblet used for *Kiddush* on the Sabbath and festivals should be large enough to hold 4.42 ounces of wine.

While there is a divergence of opinion as to whether one may stand or sit for *Kiddush,* the prevailing custom today is to stand. On Friday evening, the *Kiddush* begins with passages from *Parshat Bereshit,* Genesis 1:31 and 2:1–3, as follows.

Begin to Recite the Sabbath Eve *Kiddush*

And it was evening and it was morning, the sixth day.
Thus, the heavens and the earth
and all their multitude were finished.
By the seventh day,
God completed His work which He had made,
and He rested on the seventh day
from all His work which He had done.
God blessed the seventh day and sanctified it,
because on it He had rested
from all His work which God had created.

The blessing over the wine is then recited.

Continue to Recite the Sabbath Eve *Kiddush*

Baruch Atah, HaShem E-lo-kenu, Melech HaOlam,
borei p'ri hagafen.

❖

Blessed are You, Lord our God, King of the Universe,
Who creates the fruit of the vine.
All Respond:
Amen.

The *Kiddush* continues, as we acknowledge that God has sanctified us by giving us the Sabbath. We recall the Exodus from Egypt and remember that God chose the Jewish people from among all nations and gave us the Sabbath as an inheritance.

Conclude the Recitation of the Sabbath Eve *Kiddush*

Blessed are You, Lord our God, King of the Universe,
Who has sanctified us with His commandments,
and has been pleased with us;
With love and favor, He gave us His holy Sabbath
as a heritage, a remembrance of Creation.
For [the Sabbath] is the first among the holy festivals,
that recalls the Exodus from Egypt.
You chose us and You sanctified us from among all the nations.
You graciously gave us Your holy Sabbath as a heritage.
Blessed are You, Lord, Who sanctifies the Sabbath.

All Respond:

Amen.

If the person reciting the *Kiddush* does so with the obligation of those present in mind as well, and if the others intend for him to recite it on their behalf, then they do not have to recite the *Kiddush* themselves. In that situation, the person who recites it drinks the majority of the wine, and the remainder is then distributed to everyone else at the table. It is a *mitzvah* for everyone to taste the wine from the *kos shel Kiddush*, so, if there is not enough wine in the goblet for all, additional wine may be added to the *Kiddush* wine, so that everyone has some.

5.5.3 Ritual Washing before Eating

Ritual washing of the hands is required before eating bread. Thus, after *Kiddush*, everyone washes as follows.

1. Hold a cup in your right hand, and fill it with water.
2. Transfer the cup to your left hand, and spill some of the water twice over your right hand up to the wrist. Do not refill between spills.
3. Hold a cup in your left hand, and fill it with water.
4. Transfer the cup to your right hand, and spill some of the water twice over your left hand up to the wrist. Do not refill between spills.

Before drying your hands, lift them in front of you and recite the following blessing:

Recite *Al N'tilat Yadayim* after Ritually Washing Your Hands

Baruch Atah, HaShem E-lo-kenu, Melech HaOlam,
asher kidshanu b'mitzvotav v'tzivanu
al n'tilat yadayim.

❖

Blessed are You, Lord our God, King of the Universe,
Who sanctified us with His commandments and commanded us
concerning washing the hands.

Before the ritual washing of the hands, all rings or other impediments should be removed.

5.5.4 Reciting the *Hamotzi*

Without further talking, everyone returns to the table to recite the *hamotzi,* the blessing over the two covered *challot,* which were set on the table before the head of the household. One person, usually the head of the household, lifts the *challot* for a moment and recites the blessing; he then cuts the top *challah,* eats some, and gives *challah* to all at the table. If it was his intention to recite the blessing with their obligation in mind as well, and if they intended for him to recite it on their behalf, then they respond, *amen,* and do not have to recite the *hamotzi* themselves. If not, then they recite their own *hamotzi* and eat the *challah.*

Recite the *Hamotzi*

Baruch Atah, HaShem E-lo-kenu, Melech HaOlam,
hamotzi lechem min ha'aretz.

❖

Blessed are You, Lord our God, King of the Universe,
Who brings forth bread from the earth.

In Judaism, the table is considered symbolic of the altar where the sacrifices were brought. It is, therefore, a tradition to dip the *challah* in a bit of salt three times, a reminder of the *korbanot,* which were offered on the altar, as it is written:

> **With all your offerings, you shall offer salt.**
>
> **—*Parshat Vayikra,* Leviticus 2:13**

If wine is not available at all, *Kiddush* may be recited on the two *challot,* substituting the blessing for bread in place of the blessing for wine.

5.5.5 A Sabbath Menu

Once everyone has eaten some of the *challah,* the first Sabbath meal is served. A typical Sabbath eve menu might include:

Gefilte Fish with Chrain

Chicken Soup with K'naidlach

Mixed Green Salad

Roasted Chicken

Potato Kugel

or

Lukshen Kugel

Baked Sweet Potatoes

Assorted Desserts

Tea or Coffee

For the uninitiated, let's explain some of these delicacies.

- ***Gefilte*** fish, literally, filled fish, is usually made from ground white and pike fish. It is seasoned to taste with salt and pepper, rolled by hand into portions, and boiled in water with onions and carrots. It was originally made by wrapping the skin of the fish around the ground mixture, thus, filling it. It is customarily served with ***chrain,*** grated horseradish, which is often prepared with grated cooked beets, vinegar, and sugar. *Gefilte* fish and *chrain* are available commercially as well.
- ***K'naidlach*** are Jewish dumplings. Also called *matzah* balls, they are made from ground *matzah* meal, seasonings, eggs, and oil. The chilled batter is rolled into balls, and then they are boiled in water or chicken soup until fluffy. They are served in the soup.

The word ***kugel*** is probably derived from the Hebrew ***k'ugal,*** meaning "like a circle," so, a *kugel* is traditionally baked in a round pan. Two popular varieties are potato *kugel* and ***lukshen*** *kugel.*

- Potato *kugel* is a pudding made from finely grated potatoes, eggs, seasonings, oil, and flour. Some recipes call for grated onions as well.
- *Lukshen kugel* is a pudding made from egg noodles. It may be sweet, with sugar and raisins, or spicy, with pepper.

5.5.6 Sabbath Hymns

During the course of the meal, special Sabbath ***zemirot*** are sung. According to the Talmud, *Masechet Megillah* 12b, these hymns bring words of Torah and praise of God to the simple acts of eating and drinking. They enhance the religious experience of the Sabbath, as they express the joy of the observant Jew, the ***shomer Shabbat,*** the guardian of the Sabbath, who observes all the precepts that pertain to the commandment to "Remember the Sabbath Day to keep it holy."

Specific *zemirot* are sung Friday night at the first Sabbath meal. For example, in ***Y-ah Ribon,*** we call upon God, the Creator of the World and King of all kings, to redeem the Jewish people from exile and return us to the Temple in Jerusalem. It does not mention the *Shabbat* at all, but is one of the favorite Sabbath eve *zemirot.* ***Tzur Mishelo*** is a ***zemer,*** song, that serves to bring the first Sabbath meal to a close by introducing the ***Birkat HaMazon,*** Grace after Meals. In Yiddish, it is called ***benchen,*** and the verb form is *to* ***bench*** (see Section 5.2.1).

5.5.7 Grace after Meals

According to the Talmud, *Masechet Berachot* 48b, the tradition of blessing God after eating was instituted by Moses in response to the heavenly gift of the manna. In the Torah, we find:

> **And you shall eat and be satisfied**
> **and bless the Lord, your God,**
> **for the good land He has given you.**
> **—*Parshat Eikev,* Deuteronomy 8:10**

In accordance with this precept, *Birkat HaMazon* is recited by all at the conclusion of any meal that includes at least a minimum portion of bread (equivalent to the volume of an olive) made from any of five grains: wheat, rye, oats, barley, and spelt (see Section 3.4.10).

Birkat HaMazon consists of four distinct blessings. The first three are derived from the Torah; the fourth is rabbinic in origin.

1. The first praises God Who, in His goodness, sustains the entire universe. It begins with the words: "Blessed are You, Lord our God, King of the Universe, Who feeds the whole world." It concludes with the blessing: "Blessed are You, Lord, Who nourishes all."
2. In the second blessing, which is credited to Joshua (see Talmud, *Masechet Berachot* 48b), we express our thanks to God for giving us the Land of Israel as an inheritance. We also offer our gratitude for life, "every day, every season, every hour." This blessing concludes with "Blessed are You, Lord, for the land and for the food."
3. The third blessing, credited to King David and King Solomon (see Talmud, *Masechet Berachot* 48b), asks for God's mercy on Israel, on Jerusalem, on Zion, and on the House of David. It contains the urgent plea that we not be made dependent on the generosity of mankind, but only on the beneficence of God. "Please, Lord our God, make us not need the gifts of human hands nor their loans, but only of Your hand, which is full, open, holy, and generous, so that we will not feel inner shame nor be humiliated forever." It concludes with a blessing for the rebuilding of Jerusalem: "Rebuild Jerusalem, the holy city, soon, in our days. Blessed are You, Lord, Who rebuilds Jerusalem. Amen."

Normally, one does not recite *amen* after his/her own blessing. However, we do so at the conclusion of the first three *berachot* to mark the end of the Torah portion. The word *amen* is not actually part of the blessing, so it is said quietly, after a slight pause.

On the Sabbath, a special prayer is inserted before the prayer for the Temple and Jerusalem. We ask God to accept our observance of His Sabbath and prevent anything from disturbing or spoiling our day of rest. On *Rosh Chodesh* and the festivals, *Ya'aleh v'Yavo* is recited also (see Section 4.7).

4. The fourth blessing was introduced into the *Birkat HaMazon* by the *Sanhedrin* at Yavneh to praise God Who miraculously preserved the bodies of the victims of the Roman massacre at Betar (135 C.E.) for three years until burial was permitted by the authorities on the fifteenth of *Av*, 138 C.E. It calls upon God "Who has done good, Who does good, Who will do good," for the Jewish people. Later requests were added, including several that call upon God as the Merciful One, for example, "Who sends abundant blessing upon this house and the table upon which we have eaten." Special additions ask for God's merciful blessing for "myself, my spouse, my parents, my children, and for all who have eaten at my table." We also ask to be worthy to witness the coming of the Messiah. On the Sabbath, New Moon, and all festivals, a request for God's mercy is also added.

The text of *Birkat HaMazon* is found in the *siddur* or in a special booklet called a ***bencher*** in Yiddish. It is available in small sizes to make it handy to carry. *Birkat HaMazon* is often sung together by those assembled at the Sabbath table. This encourages participation of children, who may be too young to read the Hebrew text but "catch on" to the melody. The spirit of the Sabbath rests comfortably over the home, promising a day of joy and a day of rest to come.

5.6 The Liturgy of the Sabbath

The Sabbath is a day for ***oneg Shabbat,*** the enjoyment of the Sabbath, and for ***menuchah,*** physical rest. It is a day for worshipping God with greater *kavanah,* unhurried by the demands of the weekdays. It is a day that enhances the dignity of the soul and enables the spirit to rise above material concerns.

5.6.1 The Sabbath Morning Service

On Saturday morning, Sabbath services are held in the synagogue. Services include *Shacharit,* the Morning Service, followed by *Kriat HaTorah,* the Reading of the Torah portion, followed by *Musaf,* the Additional Service, which is recited only on the Sabbath, festivals, and *Rosh Chodesh.*

Shacharit begins with *Birchot HaShachar* and *Pesukei D'Zimrah,* as on the weekdays (see Sections 3.7.1 and 3.7.2). Psalms 92 and 93, which were also recited on Friday evening, are added to the Verses of Song. After *Az Yashir Moshe,* but before *Yishtabach,* however, additional prayers for the Sabbath are recited.

The first is ***Nishmat.*** It includes no reference to the Sabbath, but its text recalls the ***neshamah yeterah,*** the additional soul with which each Jew is blessed on the Sabbath. The *neshamah yeterah* brings an extra measure of joy and provides a heightened spiritual awareness to those who observe the Sabbath's precepts.

Shacharit for *Shabbat* continues with ***Shochen Ad.*** In this introductory paragraph that precedes *Yishtabach* and *Barchu,* we are reminded that the God of heaven dwells among us on earth through our devout observance of *mitzvot.*

In nine separate expressions of exaltation, the *tefillah* then reminds us that it is the duty of all God's creatures, in every generation, to praise Him, even beyond all the words of glorification written and sung by David, God's anointed servant.

Shacharit continues with *Yishtabach, Barchu,* and *Yotzer Or. Yotzer Or,* the first blessing before *Kriat Shema,* is supplemented with three special *tefillot* for *Shabbat,* ***HaKol Yoducha, E-l Adon***, and ***La'E-l asher Shavat***. The theme of thanksgiving to God is continued with the recitation of *HaKol Yoducha,* and *E-l Adon,* an alphabetical acrostic that dates back to the eighth century, praises God as the Creator of celestial luminaries, including the sun and moon, and hints at five of the planets: Saturn, Venus, Mercury, Jupiter, and Mars. *La'E-l asher Shavat* pays tribute to the God Who rested on the seventh day, for the Sabbath is a testament to the Creator, in and of itself, a praise of God.

The three *tefillot,* ***Titbarach Tzurenu***, ***Et Shem HaE-l***, and ***L'E-l Baruch***, all of which are found in the weekday *Shacharit,* lead up to *Ahavah Rabbah,* the final blessing before *Kriat Shema,* which is followed by *Emet v'Yatziv,* as in the weekday *Shacharit* (see Sections 3.7.3 and 3.7.4).

The *Shemoneh Esrei* for *Shabbat* morning follows. Like the *Amidah* on Friday evening, it contains only seven blessings (see Section 5.3.5). The first three and the last three are the same for *Ma'ariv* and for *Shacharit* the next morning. The middle *berachah* again deals with the holiness of the Sabbath Day. We will examine the middle *berachah* of *Shacharit,* which is somewhat different from that of *Ma'ariv.*

The first paragraph, ***Yismach Moshe,*** which is recited only in the morning, expresses Moses's joy at being selected by God to receive the Ten Commandments, which include the commandment to observe the Sabbath. Also, the *Luchot* were given on *Shabbat* morning, yet another link between Moses and the Sabbath. In *Parshat Beha'alot'cha,* Numbers 12:7, we find that Moses is called "a faithful servant." This theme is carried over to the *tefillah.* The second paragraph, *V'Shamru,* which is also recited on Friday evening (see Section 5.3.5), then follows.

The third paragraph, ***V'lo Natato,*** reminds us that the Sabbath is not merely a day of rest, but a sanctified day that God gave only to the Jewish people, as a testament to Creation. The fourth and final paragraph of the middle blessing, ***E-lo-kenu vE-lo-kei Avotenu,*** is the same as the third and final blessing in *Ma'ariv.* We ask God to accept our rest and sanctify us with His *mitzvot.* The concluding three blessings of the silent *Shemoneh Esrei* are then recited.

5.6.2 Kedushah of Shacharit

During the cantor's repetition, an expanded version of the weekday *Kedushah* is chanted. Although it does not specifically mention the Sabbath Day, the additional words inserted in the Sabbath *Kedushah* of *Shacharit* are meant to remind us of the significance of the Sabbath, in order for us to achieve sanctification and better comprehend the praises of the angels. Thereby, we become worthy of witnessing the arrival of the Messiah and the ultimate rebuilding of the Temple in Jerusalem.

After the cantor has completed the repetition of the *Shemoneh Esrei, Kriat HaTorah* follows. After *Kriat HaTorah,* the *Haftarah,* prophetic portion, is recited. *Shacharit* then continues until the *Sefer Torah* is returned to the *Aron HaKodesh.*

It is customary for the rabbi to deliver a sermon before *Musaf,* the Additional Service, begins. It may pertain to the *parashat hashavua,* or it may be an issue relevant to the community, interpreted in light of the teachings of the Torah. Occasionally, the rabbi may choose to deliver ***mussar,*** ethical teachings which are intended to inspire the congregation to greater observance of the *Taryag Mitzvot,* the 613 precepts of the Torah.

5.6.3 Musaf of Shabbat

Musaf is recited on the Sabbath, on *Rosh Chodesh,* and on the High Holidays and Pilgrimage Festivals. It recalls the additional sacrifice that was brought on those days.

The *Musaf* for *Shabbat* begins with *Shemoneh Esrei.* Once again, as we begin to pray, we take three steps backward and forward and recite:

Recite before *Shemoneh Esrei* of *Musaf*

When I proclaim the Name of the Lord,
attribute greatness to our God.
O, Lord,
may You open my lips
so that my mouth shall declare Your praise.

Then we bend our knees and bow our heads, as we begin the first blessing.

Again, there are only seven blessings in the *Shabbat Musaf.* The first three and last three are the same as in all other *Shemoneh Esrei* prayers we have discussed. The middle prayer recalls the sanctity of the Sabbath Day, the special sacrifice, and the great joy that accompanied it. It usually appears in the *siddur* in four paragraphs. The first begins with ***Tikanta Shabbat,*** the second with ***U'v'Yom HaShabbat,*** the third with ***Yis'm'chu,*** and the fourth, with *E-lo-kenu vE-lo-kei Avotenu,* as in *Ma'ariv* and *Shacharit.* We ask God to accept our rest and sanctify us with His *mitzvot.*

The first links the Sabbath and the special sacrifice that was brought to the Temple in honor of the day's holiness. It also refers to the supplementary explanations that God gave to Moses, in order to clarify the intricate Sabbath laws in the Torah. The second paragraph of the middle blessing provides the details of the sacrifice that was to be offered. The third paragraph of the middle blessing emphasizes the sense of festivity that the Sabbath imparts to those who observe it. The fourth paragraph, which completes the middle blessing of *Shemoneh Esrei* for *Musaf,* asks that God be pleased with our rest and grant us a share in His Torah. The concluding three blessings of the silent *Shemoneh Esrei* then follow.

5.6.4 *Kedushah* of *Musaf*

During the repetition of the *Shemoneh Esrei,* after the second blessing, the cantor and the congregation recite *Kedushah* (refer to Section 3.7.5 for a more detailed explanation of the order of the recitations), which is different from the *Kedushah* of *Shacharit.*

The first six words of the *Shema Yisrael,* the abiding Jewish declaration in the belief in God's Unity, appear in the *Musaf Kedushah.* This practice dates back to fifth-century Persia, when King Yezdegerd of Persia prohibited the recitation of the *Shema.* In the morning, during *Shacharit,* the king's guards were present to be sure the royal edict was obeyed. By the time of *Musaf,* they had left. In an attempt to sidestep the decree, the six words of the *Shema Yisrael* were added to the *Kedushah* of *Musaf.* To this day, it is recited by the congregation and repeated by the cantor.

5.6.5 The Concluding Prayers of *Musaf*

After the repetition of the *Musaf* is concluded, *Kaddish Shalem* is recited, and the congregation joins in the singing of ***Ein kE-lo-kenu.*** The recitation of this hymn helps to fulfill the Jew's daily obligation to recite at least one hundred blessings. The *Shemoneh Esrei* for *Shabbat* (and for the festivals and *Rosh Chodesh*) contains only seven blessings, and not nineteen as in the weekdays. *Ein kE-lo-kenu* contains a Hebrew acrostic that spells out the word *amen* four times in twelve lines. Because *amen* is the response to a blessing, adding these twelve "blessings" to the seven in *Shemoneh Esrei* brings the total in *Musaf* to nineteen.

Recite *Ein kE-lo-kenu* on *Shabbat*

There is none like our God. There is none like our Lord.
There is none like our King. There is none like our Savior.
Who is like our God? Who is like our Lord?
Who is like our King? Who is like our Savior?
Let us thank our God. Let us thank our Lord.
Let us thank our King. Let us thank our Savior.
Blessed is our God. Blessed is our Lord.
Blessed is our King. Blessed is our Savior.
You are our God. You are our Lord.
You are our King. You are our Savior.
It is You before Whom
our forefathers burned the fragrant incense.

In the first stanza, we declare our immutable belief that God is incomparable, so the questions in the second stanza are purely rhetorical.

The following paragraph continues the theme found in the last line of *Ein kE-lo-kenu.* It details the eleven spices that are combined in the preparation of the incense that was burned in the Temple during sacrificial rites. After several other passages from the Mishnah and Talmud, the *Kaddish d'Rabbanan* is recited.

Alenu and the *Kaddish Yatom* follow. Then, the congregation rises as the *Aron HaKodesh* is opened, and the Song of Glory is chanted responsively with the cantor. Psalm 92, which is the Psalm of the Day for *Shabbat,* is recited and the Mourner's *Kaddish* is repeated. *Musaf* ends with the singing of *Adon Olam.*

At the conclusion of the Sabbath services, the congregation gathers for *Kiddush,* the prayer of sanctification over wine. In some synagogues, it is customary to serve *gefilte* fish, herring, cakes, and fruits along with the wine.

5.7 The Second Sabbath Meal

After the *Kiddush* in the synagogue the family returns home to partake of the second of the Sabbath meals. *Kiddush* is repeated in the home and is comprised of Exodus 31:16–17 and 20:8–11:

Recite *Kiddush* on *Shabbat* Day

So, the Children of Israel shall keep the Sabbath,
to observe the Sabbath throughout their generations,
for a spiritual covenant.
Between Me and the Children of Israel, it is a sign forever;
for in six days the Lord made the heaven and the earth,
and on the seventh day He ceased from work and rested.
Remember the Sabbath Day to keep it holy.
Six days you shall labor, and do all your work;
but the seventh day is a Sabbath to the Lord your God;
you shall not do any manner of work,
[not] you, nor your son, nor your daughter,
nor your man-servant, nor your maid-servant,
nor your cattle, nor your stranger that is within your gates.
For in six days the Lord made heaven and earth,
the seas, and all that is in them;
and He rested on the seventh day;
thus, the Lord blessed the Sabbath Day, and hallowed it.

Each person drinks some wine and then ritually washes for the Sabbath meal. *Al n'tilat yadayim* is recited, followed by *hamotzi* over the *mishneh lechem.* Everyone eats *challah,* and traditional foods are served, including ***cholent*** (a Yiddish word), a savory dish of beans, meat, and potatoes.

Zemirot for the Sabbath Day are also sung. They include ***Baruch E-l Elyon,*** which praises the *shomer Shabbat,* literally, the one who observes the Sabbath. The refrain, which is repeated after each of seven stanzas, asks that God bestow His favor on those who keep His Sabbath.

The *zemer* ***Yom Zeh Mechubad*** urges Jews to observe the Sabbath and assures the faithful that they will lack for nothing, that God will provide everything that is needed to do so: wine for *Kiddush* and two loaves of *challah;* meat and fish; rich foods, sweet drinks, and every delight; even clothing is guaranteed to those who keep the Sabbath Day. The refrain to the six stanzas reminds us: This day is honored among all other days, because God, Who made the universe, rested on it. After lunch, *mayim acharonim* and *Birkat HaMazon* follow.

5.8 The Third Sabbath Meal

In the afternoon, Jews return to the synagogue for the *Minchah* service. The Torah is read again, although there are only three *aliyot.* These three honors are read from the *parashah* of the coming week.

After *Minchah,* ***se'udah sh'lishit,*** the third of the Sabbath meals, is served in the synagogue. It typically includes *challah* and other foods, similar to those served at *Kiddush* in the morning. (Those who are at home eat *se'udah sh'lishit* there.) *Ma'ariv* follows the *se'udah sh'lishit,* and heralds the arrival of the new week. During *se'udah sh'lishit,* additional *zemirot* are sung. Some sing Psalm 23 during the third meal, expressing their complete trust in God.

5.9 The Concept of *Work*

The Sabbath also represents a day of transformation from the activities of the weekdays. It has both a spiritual component—cessation from work—and a more tangible aspect—physical and psychological rest.

Thirty-nine categories of *work* are prohibited on the Sabbath. These are called the Thirty-nine *Melachot*. The *cessation of all work* is intended on the Sabbath, but the word *work* does not mean physical labor.

5.9.1 *Work* as an Act of Creating

Work is an act of creating, and when God completed His Creation, He gave us the Sabbath as a sign of His creative power. By refraining from *work* on the Sabbath, Jews serve as witnesses to God's role as the Ultimate Creator.

Thus, refraining from ***melachah*** is a positive spiritual act, and cessation from the performance of any of the ***melachot*** is an essential requirement for the proper observance of the Sabbath. According to the Talmud, *Masechet Shabbat* 10a, when Jews each become a "partner in the work of creation," they actively participate in God's plan for the world. Because of this, it would be very easy to consider oneself in control of the world. The *Shabbat* comes to remind us that we must set aside our human powers to create, thereby honoring the Universal Creator.

5.9.2 Physical Rest and Mental Relaxation

Physical exertion is not the criterion to be used to determine if an activity is permitted on the Sabbath or not. The blessing of physical rest can be appreciated by all of us, rich and poor alike, who, in one way or another, are enslaved by the demands of our professional lives.

The Sabbath comes to free us. It comes to soothe us, to calm us, to grant us a respite from the countless pressures that besiege us throughout the week. How does this happen? The Sabbath not only makes it possible but, in fact, encourages it, because it is a day devoted to spiritual values.

5.9.3 Privileges and Prohibitions of the Sabbath

The commandment to *"Remember the Sabbath Day to keep it holy"* is a precept that pertains to the positive acts we are privileged to observe in connection with the *Shabbat,* many of which we have already discussed. On the other hand, the commandment to *"Observe the Sabbath Day to keep it holy"* refers to the prohibitions associated with the proper observance of the Sabbath. The following examination of the Thirty-Nine *Melachot* will clarify the nature of the prohibitions.

5.9.4 The Categories of *Work*

The definition of *melachah* is found in the Torah.

> **[And God said to Moses]**
> **You [should] also speak to the Children of Israel, saying,**
> **"Unconditionally, My Sabbaths shall you keep. . . ."**
> **—*Parshat Ki Tissa,* Exodus 31:13**

Rashi, the foremost biblical commentator, explains this verse: God had previously charged Moses with commanding the Children of Israel to build the *Mishkan* in the wilderness. In this verse, God cautions Moses not to defer the laws of the Sabbath because of that command. In other words, the laws of the Sabbath were not to be suspended nor compromised, not even for building the Sanctuary.

From this our sages concluded that all the tasks associated with the construction of the Sanctuary were prohibited on the Sabbath. These tasks are the *melachot*.

They are stated in general terms—tasks of building the Sanctuary—in the Torah, but the Oral Law provides the details. According to the Mishnah, *Masechet Shabbat* 7:2, the Thirty-nine *Melachot* are:

1. Plowing
2. Sowing
3. Reaping
4. Making a sheaf
5. Threshing
6. Winnowing
7. Selecting
8. Sifting
9. Grinding
10. Kneading
11. Baking
12. Shearing sheep
13. Bleaching
14. Combing raw materials
15. Dyeing
16. Spinning
17. Weaving task 1
18. Weaving task 2
19. Weaving task 3
20. Separating into threads
21. Tying a knot
22. Untying a knot
23. Sewing
24. Tearing
25. Trapping or hunting
26. Slaughtering
27. Skinning
28. Tanning
29. Scraping pelts
30. Marking out
31. Cutting to shape
32. Writing
33. Erasing
34. Building
35. Demolishing
36. Kindling a fire
37. Extinguishing
38. Finishing off
39. Carrying from the private to the public domain and vice versa

The study of the laws of the Sabbath, ***hilchot Shabbat,*** requires constant study and review, but we will briefly examine some of these tasks. Let us begin by saying that the Oral Law provides us with the definition of the terms and shows us how to apply the *halachot* of *Shabbat* to practical contemporary situations.

As we stated earlier, *melachah* is an act of creating. Refraining from performing *melachot* is testifying that God is the Creator. What motivates human beings to create? To show human mastery over the world through their constructive use of intelligence and skill.

Each of the *melachot* listed above is actually the ***av melachah,*** the category name as it pertains to the construction of the Sanctuary. Forbidden tasks within the *av* are called ***toldot,*** derivatives that share a common purpose with the *av melachah*. In terms of practical observance, the *av* and the ***toldah*** are equal. To violate the *toldah* is as grave as violating the *av.*

Additionally, rabbinical legislation was established to safeguard the *melachot*. The purpose of such safeguards, which fully comply with the Torah, is to protect from unintentional violations of the *melachot*. In general, such protective rabbinic legislation is called a ***gezerah;*** in regard to the Sabbath, it is called a ***sh'vut.***

The *gezerot* (plural) act as restraints to prevent us from doing any activity that might cause us to perform a *melachah*. Why is such a non-*melachah* act forbidden? There are three reasons: (1) it resembles a *melachah* or can be easily confused with it; (2) it is a habit linked with the *melachah;* and (3) it usually leads to a *melachah*. Some illustrations will be helpful.

- *Av:* Cutting to shape (31)
  Gezerah: Ripping up a piece of paper
  Reason: Resemblance: ripping appears to be like shaping or can be confused with it
- *Av:* Writing (32)
  Gezerah: Agreeing to buy something
  Reason: Habit: agreement linked to writing it down
- *Av:* Reaping (3)
  Gezerah: Climbing a tree
  Reason: Leads: climbing the tree leads to breaking twigs or tearing leaves

We will define the various *melachot* in practical terms:

1. **Plowing:** any activity that makes the soil receptive for seeds or plants; also, removing anything from the soil that might prevent growth
2. **Sowing:** any activity that causes or furthers plant growth
3. **Reaping:** any activity that separates a growing plant from its place of growth
4. **Making a sheaf:** any activity in which natural products are gathered into a unit for a useful purpose
5. **Threshing:** any activity that separates a natural solid or liquid from its natural container

6–8. **Winnowing, Selecting, Sifting:** any activity that improves a mixture by removing its less desirable parts

9. **Grinding:** any activity that divides a substance (by use of an appropriate tool) into small particles to make better use of it
10. **Kneading:** any activity that combines small particles of a substance with a liquid to form a paste or dough
11. **Baking:** any activity that changes the state of a substance by heating it, thereby improving it for use
12. **Shearing sheep:** any activity that removes parts of a human or animal that serve as its outer covering
13. **Bleaching:** any activity that frees garments or cloth from dirt, dust, or stains, or which imparts a gloss to them

14. **Combing raw materials:** any activity that changes tangled or compressed materials into separate fibers
15. **Dyeing:** any activity that changes the existing color—whether natural or artificial—of an object or substance
16. **Spinning:** any activity that removes fibers from raw material by pulling, twisting, or turning it

17–19. **Weaving tasks 1, 2, and 3:** any activity that comprises the weaving operation, from inserting thread into the loom to removing the finished item

20. **Separating into threads:** any activity that separates woven material of any type into individual threads
21. **Tying a knot:** any activity that creates a lasting bond between two objects
22. **Untying a knot:** any activity that eliminates a lasting bond for some useful purpose
23. **Sewing:** any activity that joins two materials—whether same or different—by using a third substance
24. **Tearing:** any activity that eliminates sewing
25. **Trapping or hunting:** any activity that restricts the freedom of movement of a bird or animal, so as to control it
26. **Slaughtering:** any activity that shortens or ends the life of any living thing, or even causes loss of blood
27. **Skinning:** separating the skin of a dead animal from the flesh for manufacturing purposes
28. **Tanning:** any activity that involves chemical or physical processing of raw materials to render them more usable or durable for human use
29. **Scraping pelts:** any activity that smooths the surface of any material by grinding, rubbing, polishing, etc.
30. **Marking out:** any activity that involves marking or scoring lines on a surface to make it ready for cutting, writing, or other useful purpose
31. **Cutting to shape:** any activity of manufacturing that alters the size or shape of an item to make it more useful for human use
32. **Writing:** any activity that makes durable marks on a durable material
33. **Erasing:** any activity that effects a clean surface for writing
34. **Building:** any of a wide range of activities that (1) construct, repair, improve, or otherwise make suitable any structure or part thereof; (2) permanently connect two or more things to make them a usable unit; and (3) permanently change the form of any substance for a useful purpose
35. **Demolishing:** any activity that facilitates the preparation of a space for building by demolishing an existing structure or by undoing any activities in Category 34
36. **Kindling a fire:** any activity that initiates or prolongs combustion or other light- or heat-yielding processes
37. **Extinguishing:** any activity that shortens, slows, or ends any activity in Category 36

38. **Finishing off:** any activity that provides the finishing touch to a manufactured product or repairs or improves it
39. **Carrying from the private to the public domain and vice versa:** removing an object for any purpose from an enclosed private area (one's home) to a public one (the street); or moving any object within a public area a distance of about seven feet

Let's look at some of the *toldot* and *gezerot,* if any, derived from the *av melachot* a little more closely.

1.	*Av:*	Plowing
	Toldot:	Leveling the ground; fertilizing the soil; digging
	Gezerah:	Sweeping the floor with a hard broom
2.	*Av:*	Sowing
	Toldot:	Pruning trees; watering the lawn; weeding
	Gezerah:	Adding fresh water to a vase of cut flowers
3.	*Av:*	Reaping
	Toldot:	Cutting flowers; picking berries, fruit, etc.
	Gezerot:	Climbing a tree; horseback riding
4.	*Av:*	Making a sheaf
	Toldah:	Piling up fruit for storage or sale
	Gezerah:	Making a bouquet of flowers
5.	*Av:*	Threshing
	Toldot:	Shelling nuts, except for immediate use; milking animals; squeezing juice out of fruits grown expressly for juice
	Gezerah:	Squeezing juice out of other fruits as a drink
6–8.	*Av:*	Winnowing, Selecting, Sifting
	Toldot:	Sifting flour; straining liquids; removing spoiled fruit from good fruit (that is, leaving the good) to make the aggregate more suitable for human use
	Gezerah:	Removing good fruit from spoiled fruit (that is, leaving the bad) to make the aggregate more suitable for human use
9.	*Av:*	Grinding
	Toldot:	Milling or grinding corn, coffee, or pepper; crushing substances in a mortar; grating vegetables or cheese (with a grater); brushing dried mud from boots or clothes
	Gezerah:	Preparing or taking medicines or any treatment to relieve mild pain or discomfort (does not refer to acute pain or illness)

We will skip Category 10.

11.	*Av:*	Baking
	Toldot:	Cooking in any form; adding ingredients to a boiling pot; melting any solid
	Gezerah:	Adding cold milk directly to hot tea or coffee
12.	*Av:*	Shearing sheep
	Toldot:	Cutting or otherwise removing hair, nails, wool, feathers, etc., from a living organism
	Gezerot:	Tearing off nails (by hand); combing hair (the use of a soft brush is permitted)
13.	*Av:*	Bleaching
	Toldot:	Soaking, rubbing, or wringing out clothes; ironing; removing stains with water or otherwise
	Gezerot:	Brushing clothes; handling wet wash; hanging wash to dry

We will skip Category 14.

15.	*Av:*	Dyeing
	Toldot:	Painting walls; dyeing clothes; dissolving colors in water
	Gezerot:	Adding food coloring, except for immediate use; applying makeup (special cosmetics which last over the Sabbath and preclude the need to freshen one's appearance are available)

We will skip Category 16.

17–19.	*Av:*	Weaving tasks 1, 2, and 3
	Toldot:	Knitting; crocheting; darning; embroidering; basket weaving
	Gezerah:	Braiding hair

We will skip Category 20.

21–22.	*Av:*	Tying and untying a knot
	Toldot:	Tying and untying a double knot between two ends of string, thread, shoelaces, etc. (it is permissible to tie and untie a bow, because it is not considered a permanent connection)
	Gezerah:	Knotting the end of a sewing thread

We will skip Categories 23 and 24.

25.	*Av:*	Trapping or hunting
	Toldot:	Catching animals by hand, in nets, or in traps; closing a window to prevent the exit of a bird or butterfly that inadvertently flew in
26.	*Av:*	Slaughtering
	Toldot:	Killing by any means; includes animals, fish, birds, insects; drawing blood for a blood test

We will skip Categories 27 and 28.

29.	*Av:*	Scraping
	Toldot:	Using scouring powder for utensils or other surfaces; applying ointment or face cream; rubbing soap to make lather; polishing shoes

We will skip Category 30.

31. *Av:* Cutting to shape
    Toldot: Cutting out material to a pattern; sharpening a pencil; clipping a newspaper article or ad (cutting food for immediate use is permitted)
32. *Av:* Writing
    Toldot: Writing; printing; typing; drawing; painting; embroidering; making wax impressions
    Gezerot: Drawing on moist pane of glass; tracing in the sand; doing anything associated with taking notes: e.g., making appointments; buying and selling; making agreements; reading business correspondence; reading law decisions, marriage contracts, divorce documents
33. *Av:* Erasing
    Toldot: Cleaning off any writing to make space for new writing
    Gezerah: Tearing through lettering on a food label or package (unless contents are needed urgently)
34. *Av:* Building
    Toldot: Leveling or smoothing floors and walls; hammering a nail into a wall; erecting a tent
    Gezerot: Opening an umbrella; unfolding a screen

We will skip Category 35.

36. *Av:* Kindling a fire
    Toldot: Producing fire by any means, including from one flame to another; stirring the fire to increase the oxygen that feeds it; regulating a flame by turning it up or down; smoking a cigarette; producing an electric spark; starting the ignition of a car; driving a car; using the telephone; turning on electric lights or appliances
    Gezerot: Moving a lighted lamp or candle; traveling in a vehicle, even if driven by a non-Jew
37. *Av:* Extinguishing
    Toldot: Putting out a candle to fix a wick
    Gezerot: Extinguishing fire for any purpose, except in the case of danger to life; turning off the gas; switching off an electric light
38. *Av:* Finishing off
    Toldot: Removing hanging threads from a new garment; putting laces in new shoes; repairing a clock, machine, or instrument
    Gezerot: Setting or winding a clock or watch; playing a musical instrument; rowing; cycling

39.	*Av:*	Carrying from the private to the public domain and vice versa
	Toldot:	Carrying by hand, over the arm or shoulder, in the pockets, bag, or other container; pushing, throwing, pulling, or handling items from one domain to another or from one place to another within the public domain
	Gezerot:	Articles of clothing may be worn as part of one's attire; however, garments must be worn, not carried on one's arm or over the shoulders. Eyeglasses not permanently required may not be worn; children may not be carried or pushed in a carriage or stroller.

Let's take a further look at Category 11: Baking. Inasmuch as the tasks involved in the preparation of food are among the Thirty-nine *Melachot,* all food for the Sabbath must be prepared on Friday before the Sabbath commences at sunset.

This does not mean we must eat only cold food on the Sabbath. We keep cooked foods warm on the Sabbath by using a ***blech,*** a metal sheet, usually made of tin or aluminum. One burner (or more) is lit before the Sabbath, and the *blech* is placed over the range top, with an edge bent to cover the control knobs. Pots of cooked foods and water are placed on the *blech,* where they will stay warm for the Sabbath.

The *blech* precludes the further cooking of any foods, because the flame does not come into direct contact with the cooking utensils. Furthermore, we will not be able to adjust the flame, because we have taken the added precaution of covering the knobs with the edge of the *blech.* A *blech* must be used on a gas or electric range.

We mentioned *cholent* earlier in our discussion of the Sabbath Day menu. All the beans, meat, and potatoes must be thoroughly cooked before the Sabbath begins. The covered pot is placed on the *blech* before *Shabbat* and left there until lunch the next day, when the *cholent* is served. It has stayed hot all night, and the flavors and seasonings have melded into a richly satisfying meal, all in one pot.

You will recall that in Section 5.2.1, we mentioned that the Sabbath candles are lit and then the blessing is recited. From our discussion of Category 36, kindling a fire, it is clear that once the Sabbath begins, a match cannot be struck to light the candles. Thus, the candles are lit first, and then the *berachah* is recited.

5.9.5 The Blending of Domains

Let us also take a further look at Category 39: Carrying. First, a brief definition of the halachic meaning of private and public domain is in order. *Private:* an enclosed space, usually a house or a garden area, not less than fifteen inches square bounded by walls not less than three feet high. *Public:* an open-ended unroofed street or road, often used by the public, not less than (approximately) twenty-eight feet wide.

Two aspects of this *melachah* are to be considered: On the Sabbath, (1) carrying or moving an item is not permitted from the private area of one's home or garden to the public domain of the street or vice versa; (2) carrying or moving an item a distance greater than approximately seven feet is not permitted within the public domain. Additionally, one may not even walk beyond the limits of the city for more than a distance of approximately three-fourths of a mile.

It is possible to blend or intermingle the domains of several private residences by the symbolic act of creating an ***eruv.*** The *halachot* of *eruv,* which means blending, are more involved than we will present here. Suffice it to say that it is possible to blend domains so that Jews may carry on the Sabbath from public to private and vice versa, and to extend the distance one may walk outside the city limits. Many large cities have a rabbinically approved *eruv* encompassing the entire city. In Israel, virtually every city has an *eruv.*

5.9.6 Setting Things Aside

There is a *gezerah* that applies to handling and using all objects associated with the performance of any one of the Thirty-nine *Melachot.* We take this precaution lest we inadvertently perform one of the forbidden types of work and forget the sanctity of the Sabbath. These objects are referred to as ***muktzeh,*** meaning to set aside or store away. It is a complex topic, and a great deal has been written on the various categories and *halachot* of *muktzeh.*

Muktzeh includes myriad items too numerous to list; a sampling: fruit that fell from a tree on *Shabbat;* money or checks; useless items, like pieces of a broken dish; also, pencils, pens, scissors, umbrellas, flashlights, battery-operated toys, computers, telephones, fax machines, televisions, radios, VCRs, CDs, fireplace equipment, and matches. The Sabbath candlesticks themselves are *muktzeh* and are not to be touched on the Sabbath once the candles have been lit.

5.9.7 Activities of the Weekdays

Some activities are avoided, although they are not *melachot.* Rather they are considered weekday activities and are not performed because they are not in the spirit of *Shabbat.* For example, we don't rearrange the furniture, nor engage in sports; we don't pack or unpack suitcases, nor make plans for the week ahead, even in our heads; we don't discuss business, nor open the mail; we try to avoid anything that will disrupt or detract from the spirit of the Sabbath.

5.9.8 Desecration of the Sabbath

Desecration of the Sabbath, ***chilul Shabbat,*** is equivalent to idol-worship. The importance of sanctifying the Sabbath is indicated by the severity of the punishment for desecrating it.

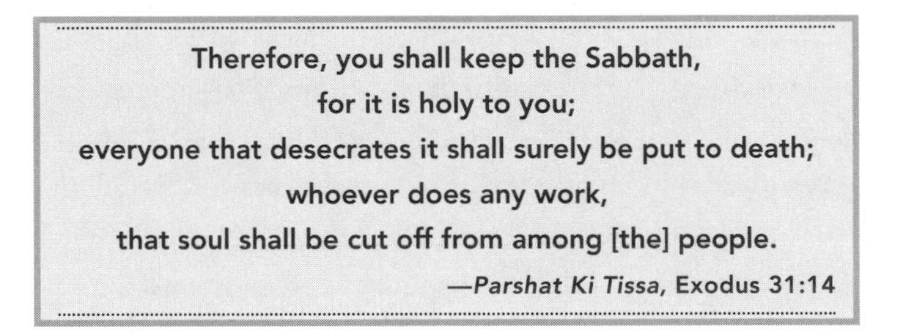

Therefore, you shall keep the Sabbath,
for it is holy to you;
everyone that desecrates it shall surely be put to death;
whoever does any work,
that soul shall be cut off from among [the] people.

—*Parshat Ki Tissa,* Exodus 31:14

There is one exception: When a person's life is in danger, it is not only permitted but required to violate the Sabbath in order to save a life. The Talmud sums it up:

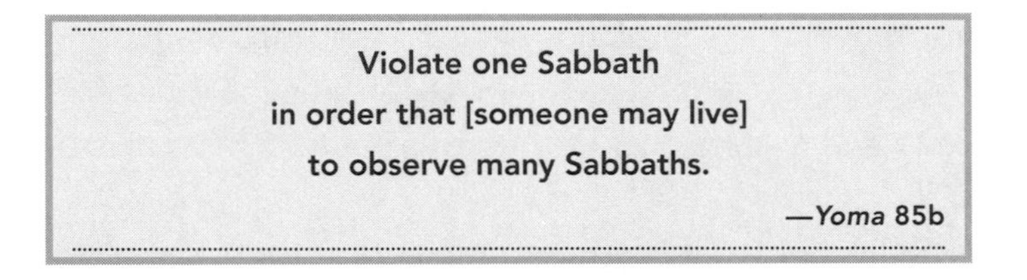

Violate one Sabbath
in order that [someone may live]
to observe many Sabbaths.

—*Yoma* 85b

The deliberate desecration is more than outweighed by the potential for future sanctification of the Sabbath and of God's Name.

5.10 The Conclusion of the Sabbath

After *Minchah* and *se'udah sh'lishit* are over, *Ma'ariv* is recited. It is followed immediately by ***Havdalah,*** the ceremony of separating the holy Sabbath from the weekdays. In the last lingering moments of the Sabbath, we recognize ever more keenly the distinction between the sacred and the ordinary.

Havdalah is recited in the synagogue and then again at home, for those who were not present at services to hear it. We speak, therefore, of God's blessing in the recitation of the introductory verses of *Havdalah.* It is followed by three *berachot:* over wine, over the light of the *Havdalah* candle, and over fragrant spices.

5.10.1 The Ceremony of *Havdalah*

Just as the Sabbath was inaugurated and remembered with wine, so, too, a *berachah* over wine is recited as the Sabbath ends. The cup is filled to overflowing, symbolizing the hope for a new week filled with blessings.

The second blessing is recited over fragrant spices. The spices, called ***besamim,*** usually cloves, are kept in a special spice box, often fanciful in design, made of silver, olive wood, or other decorative materials. When the blessing is recited, everyone inhales the fragrance of the spices, to cheer the soul, saddened as the *neshamah yeterah* withdraws from us.

The third blessing is recited over the ***ner Havdalah,*** the special candle which is lit at the beginning of the ceremony. It must contain at least two wicks, so that it will glow like a torch, and is often made in various colors. After the blessing is recited, everyone, in turn, looks at their fingers, bent inward in the glow of the candlelight. Everyone turns their hands over and extends their fingers toward the light, gazing at the illumination on their nails. According to the Talmud, *Masechet Pesachim* 54a, the recitation of this *berachah* is a reminder that fire was discovered by Adam at the end of the first Sabbath.

The wine is poured, the candle is lit, the spice box is prepared. The cup is lifted, and the *Havdalah* service begins.

Recite the *Havdalah* Service

Behold! God is my help.
I will trust and not fear;
truly the Lord is my strength and my song;
the Lord has been my salvation. . . .
Lord of Hosts, happy is the man who trusts in You.
Lord, save us.
The King will answer us on the day we call.

At this point, the *ner Havdalah* is lifted and the following verse is recited.

Continue to Recite the *Havdalah* Service

For the Jews there was
light and gladness,
joy and honor;
so may it be for us

The candle is lowered and the cup is raised.

Continue to Recite the *Havdalah* Service

I will raise the cup of deliverance
and will call upon the Name of the Lord.

The three blessings are recited, and all respond *amen* to each.

Continue to Recite the *Havdalah* Service

Baruch Atah, HaShem E-lo-kenu, Melech HaOlam,
borei p'ri hagafen.

❖

Blessed are You, Lord our God, King of the Universe,
Who creates the fruit of the vine.

❖

Baruch Atah, HaShem E-lo-kenu, Melech HaOlam,
borei minei vesamim.

❖

Blessed are You, Lord our God, King of the Universe,
Who creates various kinds of fragrant spices.

❖

Baruch Atah, HaShem E-lo-kenu, Melech HaOlam,
borei m'orei ha'aish.

❖

Blessed are You, Lord our God, King of the Universe,
Who creates the lights of fire.

The wine is poured, the candle is lit, the spice box is prepared, it is time for *Havdalah*.

The concluding verses are chanted.

Conclude the *Havdalah* Service

Blessed are You, Lord our God, King of the Universe,
Who has made a distinction
between holy and profane,
between light and darkness,
between Israel and other nations,
between the seventh day and the six days of work.
Blessed are You, Lord,
Who separates the holy from the profane.

Everyone responds, *amen,* and *Havdalah* is concluded. The candle is extinguished by pouring some of the wine over it into a dish. The remainder is drunk by the person who recited the *Havdalah*. Some observe the custom of dipping their fingertips into the wine in the dish and touching their eyelids and inner pockets, symbolizing the hope that the *mitzvah* of *Havdalah* will guide them and bring blessings in the week ahead. The Sabbath has ended (at least) one hour after sunset on Saturday evening, approximately twenty-five hours after it began. Greetings of ***Shavua Tov,*** or ***Gut Voch,*** A Good Week, are exchanged.

If one is unable to recite the *Havdalah* on Saturday evening, or forgets to recite it at the proper time, it is permissible to recite it anytime through Tuesday of the coming week. From Wednesday on, the Jew is already preparing for the advent of the next Sabbath, buying and cooking special foods, inviting guests, cleaning the house, polishing the candlesticks, and the like, all in honor of the Sabbath to come.

The Sabbath is the pivotal day of the week: From Sunday through Tuesday, we are still looking back, reflecting on the one just past; but by Wednesday we are looking ahead, anticipating the arrival of the next seventh day.

5.10.2 Farewell to the Sabbath Queen

On Saturday night, called ***motza'ei Shabbat,*** when the Sabbath has gone out, it is traditional to have a ***se'udat melaveh Malkah,*** a meal to accompany the Sabbath Queen as she departs.

Special hymns and songs bid farewell to the holy Sabbath Day. They include: ***Eliyahu HaNavi,*** a hymn in praise of the prophet Elijah, whose appearance will herald the arrival of the Messiah, and ***HaMavdil,*** a *zemer* that is a hymn for forgiveness as the new week begins.

The holy Sabbath, with its beautiful rituals and customs, departs, leaving the Jewish people with a renewed sense of spiritual vitality for the coming week. Asher Hirsch Ginsberg, a noted Hebrew author known as Ahad HaAm (1856–1927), wrote what is perhaps the definitive statement about the relationship between the Jewish people and the Sabbath:

More than Israel has preserved the Sabbath,
the Sabbath has preserved Israel.

LOOKING AHEAD! *In Chapter 6, we will discuss the High Holidays: the Jewish New Year and the Day of Atonement.*

The *shofar* summons Jews the world over to a period of spiritual contemplation and reflection.

6

The Days of Awe

HE BEGINNING OF the Jewish year (but not of the Jewish calendar; see Chapter 4) occurs in the seventh month, *Tishrei,* which falls in September and/or October. It is the busiest month of the year, marked by twelve festival days of both heartfelt solemnity and delightful celebration. We begin to focus our attention on the coming holidays a month earlier, in *Elul.* The overriding themes of this period—from *Rosh Chodesh Elul* through *Tishrei*—are a blend of deep introspection, sincere repentance, and joyous return to God; it is a period of proclaiming His Kingship and dominion and accepting Him as Master of the World.

In Chapter 6, we will examine three of those days: the two days of ***Rosh HaShanah,*** the Jewish New Year, and ***Yom Kippur,*** the Day of Atonement. The others will be explained in Chapter 7.

Let's begin with a discussion of *Elul.*

6.1 The Month of *Elul*

As we discussed in Chapter 4, *Elul* is the last month of the Jewish year. It introduces a period of reflection and repentance in anticipation of the forthcoming holidays.

As we approach the new year, we find ourselves filled with mixed feelings: we look back on the eleven months just past (twelve in a leap year), and we look ahead to the promise of the days to come. This process begins with *Rosh Chodesh Elul.* A period of contrition and spiritual refinement, *Elul* provides a month-long opportunity to ready ourselves for the Days of Awe ahead.

Several traditions are associated with *Elul.* Throughout the entire month (except on ***erev Rosh HaShanah***), the ***shofar,*** ram's horn, is sounded daily after *Shacharit.* Psalm 27 is recited every day after *Shacharit* and *Ma'ariv* from the beginning to the end of the festival period in *Tishrei.* According to the *Midrash,* this psalm was added to the daily *tefillot* because it alludes to all the festivals in this period. It is also customary to visit the cemetery to pay homage to the memory of departed parents and other relatives during *Elul.*

In some communities, special penitential prayers, ***Selichot,*** are recited throughout the month of *Elul.* According to the Ashkenazic tradition, Jews gather in the synagogue on the last Saturday night in *Elul,* after midnight—that is, early Sunday morning, to begin the recitation of *Selichot.* If there are fewer than four days until the New Year, then the recitation of *Selichot* begins one week earlier, so that *Selichot* is recited for at least four days. This tradition is derived from Psalms.

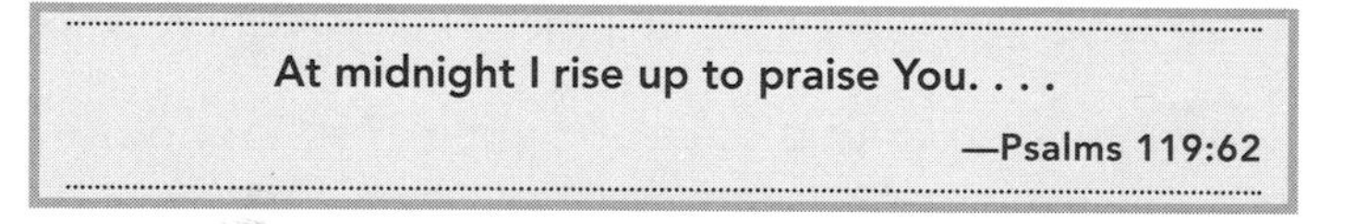
At midnight I rise up to praise You. . . .

—Psalms 119:62

The cantor ushers in the introduction to the High Holiday period with the chanting of *Selichot.* In recounting the historic tragedies of Jewish persecution in these prayers, penitents search out the root of adversity in their own failings. In humility, Jews beseech God for forgiveness and mercy.

A primary feature of the *Selichot* prayers (and also of the *tefillot* of *Rosh HaShanah* and *Yom Kippur*) is the repeated recitation of God's Thirteen Attributes of Mercy. According to the Talmud, *Masechet Rosh HaShanah* 17b, this practice is based on God's promise to heed the prayers that recount these attributes. The prayer of the Thirteen Attributes, which is derived from *Parshat Ki Tissa,* Exodus 34:6–7, requires the presence of a *minyan*. If one prays at home, then the Attributes are omitted.

Recite the Thirteen Attributes of Mercy

The Lord, the Lord, God, Merciful and Gracious,
Long-Suffering and Abundant in Goodness and Truth;
Keeping Mercy unto the thousandth generation;
Forgiving Iniquity and Transgression and Sin;
and Cleanses

How do we count this as Thirteen Attributes and what characteristics do they represent?

1.	Lord	God's mercy before a person sins
2.	Lord	God's mercy after a person sins
3.	God	God's power
4.	Merciful	God's compassion
5.	Gracious	God's kindness, even to the undeserving
6.	Long-Suffering	God's patience, giving the sinner ample time to repent
7.	Abundant in Goodness	God's forgiveness for those who have no personal merit
8.	and Truth	God's promise to reward those who fulfill His will
9.	Keeping Mercy unto the thousandth generation	God's assurance that the deeds of the righteous will accrue to the benefit of countless future generations
10.	Forgiving Iniquity	God's forgiveness of the penitent who sinned intentionally because of a personal desire to sin
11.	and Transgression	God's forgiveness of the penitent who sinned intentionally for the purpose of angering God
12.	and Sin	God's forgiveness of the penitent who sinned because of error or inattention
13.	and Cleanses	God's removal of the sins of all who repent

By appealing to God's Divine Attributes again and again, we pray for His favorable judgment throughout the High Holiday season.

6.2 Standing in Judgment

Rosh HaShanah and *Yom Kippur* are known as the ***Yamim Nora'im,*** the Days of Awe, for all humankind stands in judgment before God. The liturgy of *Rosh HaShanah* and *Yom Kippur,* which we will discuss more fully below, stresses the frailty of human life as Jews ask God to forgive their transgressions and inscribe them and seal them in the ***Sefer HaChayim,*** the Book of Life, for another year. The symbolism of God's Book is found in traditional sources. In the Mishnah we find:

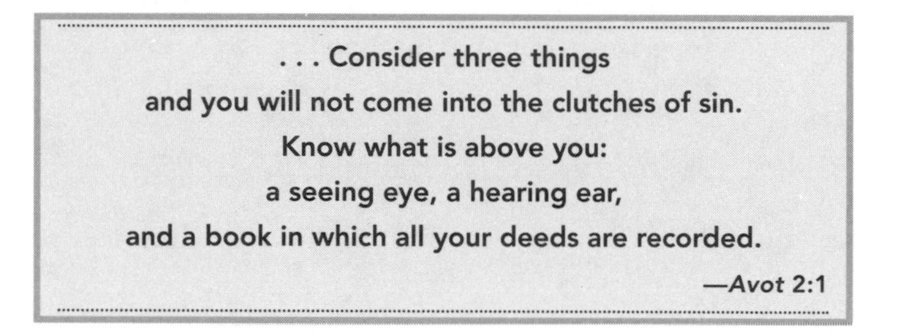
. . . Consider three things
and you will not come into the clutches of sin.
Know what is above you:
a seeing eye, a hearing ear,
and a book in which all your deeds are recorded.

—Avot 2:1

and in *Ketuvim,*

> **Let them [the wicked] be wiped away**
> **from the Book of Life,**
> **and with the righteous let them not be inscribed.**
>
> **—Psalms 69:29**

According to the Talmud, *Masechet Rosh HaShanah* 16b, there are three books: the completely wicked are immediately inscribed and sealed in the Book of Death; the completely righteous are immediately inscribed and sealed in the Book of Life; everyone else is in a third book, where their fate is suspended as they await judgment between *Rosh HaShanah* and *Yom Kippur.* When God's verdict is rendered, they are inscribed and sealed for life or death.

Of course, both the celebration of *Rosh HaShanah* and the observance of *Yom Kippur* are derived from biblical commandments.

6.3 *Rosh HaShanah*

Rosh HaShanah, literally, the head of the year, is celebrated on the first and second days of *Tishrei*. In the Torah it is referred to as ***Shabbaton,*** a day of rest, like *Shabbat,* and ***Yom Teruah,*** the Day of Sounding the *Shofar*.

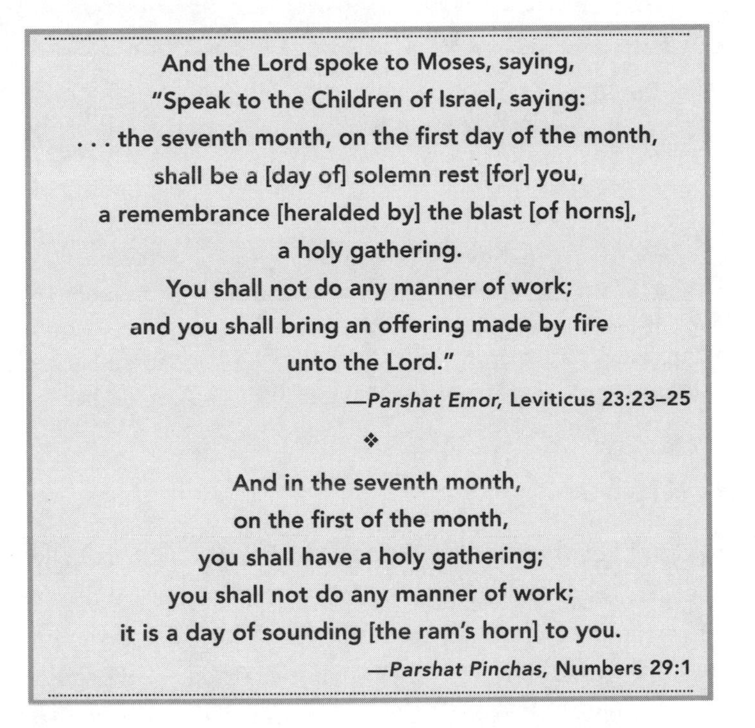

And the Lord spoke to Moses, saying,
"Speak to the Children of Israel, saying:
. . . the seventh month, on the first day of the month,
shall be a [day of] solemn rest [for] you,
a remembrance [heralded by] the blast [of horns],
a holy gathering.
You shall not do any manner of work;
and you shall bring an offering made by fire
unto the Lord."

—*Parshat Emor,* Leviticus 23:23–25

❖

And in the seventh month,
on the first of the month,
you shall have a holy gathering;
you shall not do any manner of work;
it is a day of sounding [the ram's horn] to you.

—*Parshat Pinchas,* Numbers 29:1

The Torah only requires one day, but the *Tana'im* instituted the practice of observing *Rosh HaShanah* for two days. Thus, both in Israel and in the Diaspora, *Rosh HaShanah* is observed for two days. In the Talmud, *Masechet Beitzah* 4b, Rashi refers to it as a "long day" of forty-eight hours.

The name *Rosh HaShanah* is not found in the Torah, but the tradition of marking the beginning of the new year in *Tishrei* can almost certainly be linked to the decision to reckon the calendar years from the time of Creation (see Section 4.1). It should be recalled here that we do not recite the Blessing of the New Moon on the *Shabbat* before the month of *Tishrei*.

In the liturgy, *Rosh HaShanah* is called ***Yom HaDin,*** the Day of Judgment, and ***Yom HaZikaron,*** the Day of Remembrance. These themes are repeated many times throughout the *tefillot*. *Rosh HaShanah* is also referred to as the birthday of the world. Medieval scholars noted that the letters of the Hebrew word *Bereshit*—in the beginning—which refers to the Creation of the World, can be rearranged to spell *the first of Tishrei*: בראשית or א׳ בתשרי.

Calendar for the First Day of *Rosh HaShanah*

Secular Year	Hebrew Year	Day of the Week	Secular Date
2001	5762	Tuesday	September 18
2002	5763	Saturday	September 7
2003	5764	Saturday	September 27
2004	5765	Thursday	September 16
2005	5766	Tuesday	October 4
2006	5767	Saturday	September 23
2007	5768	Thursday	September 13
2008	5769	Tuesday	September 30
2009	5770	Saturday	September 19
2010	5771	Thursday	September 9

6.4 *Yom Kippur*

The ten-day period between *Rosh HaShanah* and *Yom Kippur* is called ***Aseret Y'mei T'shuvah,*** the Ten Days of Repentance. It is a solemn period devoted to ***t'shuvah***, thoughtful contemplation and earnest remorse for the misdeeds of the past year. The meaning of *t'shuvah* is *return*. The Ten Days are not characterized by raucous parties, intoxicated revelry, or frenzied behavior. On the contrary, it is a time of subdued reflection, taking stock, and pledging ourselves to do better in the new year. Jews continue to recite *Selichot* and to examine their conduct, resolving to strengthen their commitment in the new year and rededicate themselves to observing the precepts of the Torah.

Yom Kippur is observed on the tenth of *Tishrei*.

> **[And] the tenth day of this seventh month**
> **is the day of atonement;**
> **there shall be a holy gathering [for] you;**
> **and you shall afflict your souls,**
> **and you shall bring an offering made by fire**
> **unto the Lord.**
>
> —*Parshat Emor,* Leviticus 23:27

The *Yamim Nora'im* reach their high point on *Yom Kippur,* the most sacred and solemn day in the Jewish calendar. It is a day devoted to fasting, prayer, and the repeated recitation of the ***Viduy***, the confessional prayer. We will examine this more closely when we discuss the liturgy of the Day of Atonement (see Section 6.24.1).

Yom Kippur marks the culmination of the process that began in *Elul.* Through *t'shuvah* Jews have the opportunity to cast off sin and free themselves from its burden. Resolving not to sin again makes it possible to approach life with confidence and optimism.

The central themes of the *Yamim Nora'im* are repentance and atonement. While Jewish law teaches that Jews can repent at any time during the year, the most propitious time for atonement is the period from *Rosh Chodesh Elul* to *erev Yom Kippur.*

What constitutes repentance? Jewish law prescribes several distinct actions for *t'shuvah.* According to the Rambam in his *Mishneh Torah,* Book of Knowledge, Laws of Repentance 2:2, the *halachot* of *t'shuvah* require:

- cessation of sin
- resolving not to sin in the future
- feeling genuine remorse for having sinned
- verbal confession of sin

A man or woman who repents and observes the *mitzvot* is called a ***ba'al t'shuvah*** or a ***ba'alat t'shuvah,*** respectively, one who *returns* to the faith (plural, ***ba'alei t'shuvah***).

Yom Kippur means the day of ***kaparah,*** atonement. What does *atonement* mean? Simply put: making amends. It is important to note that the Almighty can forgive only those transgressions committed ***ben adam laMakom,*** between individuals and God. In fact, the day of *Yom Kippur* itself—if it includes sincere repentance—effects atonement for all sins committed against God.

On the other hand, Jews must personally seek ***mechilah,*** forgiveness, from others if they have wronged them. This is true throughout the year, but especially on the eve of *Yom Kippur.* Surely, if we seek forgiveness, then we must be willing to extend it to others.

According to the Mishnah, *Masechet Yoma* 8:9, restitution and appeasement are required for misconduct ***ben adam lachavero,*** between one human being and another. In asking for pardon, Jews must approach their friends and family—or even more casual acquaintances, if the circumstances warrant it—as many as three times seeking forgiveness for misdeeds. If after three attempts, forgiveness is not granted, the burden of seeking exoneration is removed from the transgressor.

Calendar for *Yom Kippur*

Secular Year	Hebrew Year	Day of the Week	Secular Date
2001	5762	Thursday	September 27
2002	5763	Monday	September 16
2003	5764	Monday	October 6
2004	5765	Saturday	September 25
2005	5766	Thursday	October 13
2006	5767	Monday	October 2
2007	5768	Saturday	September 22
2008	5769	Thursday	October 9
2009	5770	Monday	September 28
2010	5771	Saturday	September 18

6.5 Getting Ready for the *Yamim Nora'im*

For *Rosh HaShanah* and *Yom Kippur,* the synagogue is transformed. The brilliantly colored Ark curtain is replaced by a white *parochet;* each *Sefer Torah* is dressed in a white *mantel;* and the *shulchan* is also covered in white. Many congregations hire a *chazan,* who is especially knowledgeable and experienced with the various *nuscha'ot* of the liturgy of the *Yamim Nora'im.* Throughout the services, the cantor, the rabbi, and many men of the congregation wear a ***kittel,*** a white robe, the color symbolic of purity and atonement. According to the Jerusalem Talmud, *Masechet Rosh HaShanah* 1:3, white also represents the hopefulness and confidence with which the Jewish people repent, anticipating God's mercy on this Day of Judgment; according to the talmudic commentary of the Levush (1535–1612) is also a reminder of the shroud, the end for all humankind.

All *tefillot* for *Rosh HaShanah* and *Yom Kippur* are to be found in the *machzor,* the prayer book used for the holidays (see Section 3.6.2). The word *machzor* suggests the concept of cycle or return; indeed, all the festivals occur in an annual cycle; we return to them yearly, renewing our acquaintance with the hallowed texts of our people.

Before the Oral Law was committed to writing in order to accommodate its burgeoning content, all prayers were recited from memory. Subsequently, early prayer books set down groups of prayers and the laws for reciting them. Later editions included interpretations and textual references. As the prayer book evolved, it became more comprehensive, providing descriptions and explanations about religious observances for the entire year. These relatively early prayer books were called *machzorim,* indicating their cyclical use.

Originally, all prayers were included in one *machzor.* In time, daily and Sabbath prayers were arranged in the *siddur,* and festival prayers were published in individual *machzorim,* one for each of the various holidays (see Sections 3.6.1 and 3.6.2).

6.6 The Liturgy of *Rosh HaShanah*

The *tefillot* of *Rosh HaShanah* are divided into four services: (1) *Ma'ariv;* (2) *Shacharit;* (3) *Musaf;* and (4) *Minchah.* These prayer services appear in the *machzor* in that order. Some prayers can be traced back to early Jewish history. Others date from the period of the First Temple, but the majority of them were compiled and edited during the time of the Second Temple.

In Chapter 3, we noted that the daily and Sabbath *tefillot* are largely derived from *Tanach* and the Talmud, with only occasional selections from *piyutim,* liturgical poems, and *Selichot,* prayers for forgiveness. In the *machzor, piyutim* and *Selichot* comprise a large portion of the holiday prayers.

The *piyutim* date back to the seventh or eighth century. Over several centuries, almost a thousand different poets were known to have written these so-called synagogue poems. By the 1500s the popularity of this form of poetry declined, and by the 1700s, *piyutim* had virtually disappeared.

Rabbinic leaders were largely opposed to the inclusion of *piyutim* in the liturgy; but many philosophical and mystical selections were inserted into the *tefillot* because their popularity among the people demanded it. These liturgical poems often start with the words

Based on the custom of our wise and enlightened teachers . . .

thereby justifying the interruption in the *tefillot,* by virtue of the great wisdom of revered scholars. Other prayers that are included in the *machzor* are derived from the *Selichot.*

We will look more closely at the *tefillot* in the next sections.

6.7 *Ma'ariv* of *Rosh HaShanah*

The opening prayers of the Evening Service of *Rosh HaShanah* are similar to those recited during ordinary weekdays (see Chapter 3). We will take a brief look at some of the *tefillot. Ma'ariv* begins with the call to worship: *Barchu.*

Barchu is followed by two blessings: *HaMa'ariv Aravim* and *Ahavat Olam. Kriat Shema* is then recited and is followed by two blessings: *Emet v'Emunah* and *Hashkivenu.* After *Hashkivenu,* the prayer *V'Shamru* is recited if it is Friday evening. In any case, the first verse that refers to the festival, ***Tiku vaChodesh,*** is then recited.

Recite *Tiku vaChodesh*

Blow the *shofar* at the new moon,
at the designated time for our festive day.
It is a statute for Israel,
a decree for the God of Jacob.

God decreed that the *shofar* be sounded on *Rosh HaShanah,* a reminder of *Akeidat Yitzchak,* the Binding of Isaac, when a ram was caught in the thicket and was sacrificed in his place.

The Half *Kaddish* is then recited. One word is repeated in all *Kaddish* prayers throughout the *Aseret Y'mei T'shuvah* to emphasize God's majesty during this period. The phrase

. . . beyond all the blessings and hymns, . . .

is modified to read

. . . beyond and [even further] beyond all the blessings and hymns, . . .

After *Chatzi Kaddish,* the *Shemoneh Esrei* is recited.

6.7.1 *Shemoneh Esrei of Ma'ariv*

The *Shemoneh Esrei* of *Ma'ariv* is structured like that of *Shabbat.* It contains seven blessings: the first three and the last three are basically the same as in all *Amidah* prayers, but four inserts are recited in the *Shemoneh Esrei* during the Ten Days of Repentance. The middle blessing also contains prayers specifically for the festival.

6.7.2 Four Special Inserts

In Blessing (1), the first special verse is inserted, for *Rosh HaShanah* is the Day of Remembrance when God remembers all His creations.

Remember us for life, King Who desires life,
and inscribe us in the Book of Life—
for Your sake, Living God.

In Blessing (2), we appeal to God Who extends His mercy to us, even though we are undeserving. The second special verse is:

Who is like You, Merciful Father?
In mercy He remembers His creatures for life!

In Blessing (3), which deals with God's holiness, five paragraphs are added to the *tefillah* (not part of the four special verses). The first paragraph asks that God imbue all His creatures with awe for Him and hints at the time to come when all peoples will worship the One God and tranquillity will fill an ethical world.

The second paragraph asks God to grant honor to those who worship and praise Him and to assure that (1) the entire universe will recognize Israel's greatness; (2) Israel and Jerusalem will be restored; and (3) the monarchy of King David will be reestablished.

The third paragraph asserts that when God grants the previous two blessings, then the righteous will rejoice and all evil will disappear from the world.

The fourth paragraph summarizes the outcome of the preceding blessings: God will reign unchallenged as the King of the universe.

The final paragraph of the third blessing refers to God's holiness and omnipotence over all things, for He created everything. During the *Aseret Y'mei T'shuvah,* this blessing concludes:

Blessed are You, Lord, the holy King.

Addressing God as the holy King is further recognition that His power is absolute and refers to His exacting judgment. At other times during the year, the blessing ends: ". . . Lord, the holy God," which suggests His mercy.

Now, let's take a closer look at Blessing (4), the middle blessing of *Ma'ariv.* This *berachah* deals with the holiness of the day. It is comprised of four paragraphs.

The first paragraph of the middle blessing reminds us that God chose the Jewish people to receive the Torah, and, therefore, we have an obligation to discharge our responsibilities.

At this point on Saturday night, an additional paragraph is inserted distinguishing between the holiness of the Sabbath and the sanctity of *Rosh HaShanah*. The three blessings associated with *Havdalah* at other times are not recited.

The second paragraph of the middle blessing continues the theme: God has chosen the Jewish people to give them *this day.* Because of the solemnity of the day, *Rosh HaShanah* is not described as a joyous festival. We add the parenthetical words on the Sabbath.

Recite in the Second Paragraph of the Middle Blessing of *Ma'ariv*

And You gave us, Lord, our God, with love . . .
(this Sabbath Day and)
this Day of Remembrance,
a day of (remembering) the sounding of the *shofar,*
(with love)
a holy gathering,
a reminder of the Exodus from Egypt.

The third paragraph of the middle blessing is *Ya'aleh v'Yavo,* which we learned in Section 4.7 in our discussion of *Rosh Chodesh.* Of course, instead of "on this day of *Rosh Chodesh,*" we insert the words "on this Day of Remembrance" on *Rosh HaShanah.*

The last paragraph provides a review of the previous three. It is a prayer for God's supremacy over the universe, over the physical world, and over all who inhabit it. Where appropriate, this prayer includes inserts for the Sabbath.

Conclude the Last Paragraph of the Middle Blessing of *Ma'ariv*

Blessed are You, Lord, King over all the earth,
Who sanctifies (the Sabbath,)
Israel and the Day of Remembrance.

Blessings (5), (6), and (7) of the *Shemoneh Esrei* for *Ma'ariv* are like those in all other *Amidah* prayers with a few modifications for *Rosh HaShanah*. In Blessing (5), we insert the third of the special verses:

And inscribe all the Children of Your covenant for a good life.

In Blessing (7), the prayer for peace, we find the fourth special insert, which refers to the book of life. Blessing (7) for *Ma'ariv* is below.

Establish bountiful peace upon your people Israel forever,
for You are King, Lord of all peace.
May it be pleasing in Your eyes
to bless Your people Israel with Your peace,
at every time and every hour.

The last of the four special inserts follows:

In the book of life,
blessing, and peace,
and good sustenance,
may we and Your entire people,
the House of Israel,
be remembered and inscribed before You
for a good life and for peace.

The Evening Service concludes as usual. On Friday night, the concluding Sabbath prayers after the *Amidah* are also recited. *Ma'ariv* is not repeated by the *chazan*, nor is *Kedushah* recited.

6.8 *Shacharit of Rosh HaShanah*

The Morning Service begins with *Birchot HaShachar* and *Pesukei D'Zimrah* (see Sections 3.7.1 and 3.7.2). The Sabbath pattern continues with the recitation of *Az Yashir Moshe* and *Nishmat* (see Sections 3.7.2 and 5.6.1).

At this point, before *Shochen Ad,* in a custom that dates back to the thirteenth century, the *chazan* ascends to the *bimah,* and in an emphatic voice proclaims God the King, and in a softer voice, Who sits in judgment.

Begin to Recite *Shacharit* for Rosh HaShanah

HaMelech!
Yoshev al kisei ram v'nisa.

❖

The King!
Who is sitting on a lofty and exalted throne.

These few words act as a transitional prayer between the preliminary benedictions and the prelude to *Shacharit.*

The service continues with *Yishtabach, Barchu,* and *Yotzer Or.* In some congregations a liturgical poem is introduced at this point. On the first day, the text refers repeatedly to God's supremacy and His ultimate victory over the forces of evil. On the second day, a different poem is recited. We reassert the belief that God will bring the redemption and recall that God extended His mercy to Adam when he sinned. So, too, we plead for mercy.

Shacharit continues with *Kriat Shema,* including the usual blessings before and after.

6.8.1 *Shemoneh Esrei* of *Shacharit*

The *Shemoneh Esrei* of *Shacharit* is identical to that of *Ma'ariv,* except for the final blessing.

Grant peace, goodness and blessing,
kindness and mercy to us and to all
Your people Israel.
Bless us . . . with the light of Your countenance,
for with [it], You gave us . . . the Torah of life,
and a love of kindness, righteousness, blessing,
mercy, life, and peace.
May it be pleasing in Your eyes
to bless . . . Israel with Your peace,
at every season and every hour.
The Rosh HaShanah Insert Follows:
In the book of life,
blessing, and peace,
and good sustenance,
may we and Your entire people,
the House of Israel,
be remembered and inscribed before You
for a good life and for peace.

During the repetition of the *Shemoneh Esrei,* within Blessing (1), the cantor, as the messenger of the congregation, begs God to accept him as an emissary and to hear his pleas on their behalf. The Ark is opened several times, and many worshippers stand throughout the entire repetition, even during the intervals when the Ark is closed.

Numerous *piyutim* specific to the holiday are woven within the *Shemoneh Esrei* text. Many of these liturgical poems contain acrostics, indicating the name of the poet. Some invoke the memory of forebears, like Abraham and Sarah. Others continue to reflect the theme of God as the King, surrounded by the light of the Torah and wrapped in the charitable acts of the Jewish people.

The added text of the first day varies somewhat from that of the second. Also, Sabbath text is included when appropriate. On both days, *Kedushah* is recited.

6.8.2 Kedushah of Shacharit

The *Kedushah* of *Shacharit* of *Rosh HaShanah* is like that of the Sabbath (see Section 5.6.2). The return to Jerusalem and the Temple and the coming of the Messiah are the dominant themes. The references to the hymns of the angels once again remind us of the omnipresence of the Almighty in the physical and spiritual realms and in the World to Come.

After *Kedushah,* the cantor continues his repetition of the *Shemoneh Esrei* with the rest of Blessing (3), the sanctification of God's Name. It is followed by Blessing (4), which contains the four paragraphs specific for the holiness of the day of *Rosh HaShanah* (see Sections 6.7.1 and 6.7.2 above). The repetition of the last three blessings of the *Shemoneh Esrei* conclude the repetition.

6.9 *Kriat HaTorah* for *Rosh HaShanah*

On *Rosh HaShanah,* there are only five *aliyot,* unlike the Sabbath, when seven are called. If one day falls on the Sabbath, then the text for the five *aliyot* is divided into seven instead. Receiving an *aliyah* on *Rosh HaShanah* is a great honor, and in many congregations, the men purchase the privilege before the holiday begins.

The Torah reading for the first day is from *Parshat Vayera,* Genesis 21:1–34, which recounts the blessing of Abraham and Sarah and the birth of Isaac. The *Maftir* portion, which follows the last *aliyah* and is read by the man (or by the *ba'al korei* on his behalf) honored with the *Haftarah,* prophetic portion, is from *Parshat Pinchas,* Numbers 29:1–6 (see Section 6.9 above). These six verses recount the commandment to observe *Rosh HaShanah,* to refrain from all work, and to bring both the festival and new moon offerings on that day to the Temple. The *Haftarah* for the first day is taken from I Samuel 1:1–2:10.

The Torah reading for the second day is from *Parshat Vayera,* Genesis 22:1–24. In this account of the *Akeidah,* the Binding of Isaac, we are reminded of the great devotion that both Abraham and Isaac showed to God in their willingness to fulfill His bidding. Here we find the biblical link to *Rosh HaShanah* as *Yom Teruah.*

And Abraham lifted up his eyes and looked,
and behold a ram [was] caught in the thicket by its horns
after [the angel spoke to Abraham].
And Abraham went and offered it up for a burnt-offering
in place of his son.

—*Parshat Vayera,* Genesis 22:13

As a reward for his incomparable obedience to God, Abraham was assured the survival of the Jewish people.

Although the *Maftir* for the second day is the same as on the first day, the *Haftarah* on the second day is from Jeremiah 31:1–19.

6.10 The Call to Repentance

Without a doubt, the most memorable and inspiring feature of the *Rosh HaShanah* liturgy is the sounding of the ram's horn, ***tekiat shofar.*** At the end of *Shacharit* on both days of *Rosh HaShanah,* after the *Haftarah* has been chanted, but before the *Sefer Torah* is returned to the Holy Ark, the *shofar* is sounded for the first time. The *shofar* is not sounded on the Sabbath.

The sounding of the *shofar* proclaims God's sovereignty and calls Jews to repent as they face the Divine Judge, to turn away from the misconduct of the past year, and to seek to live according to the divine precepts set down in the Torah. As all of God's creations pass before Him, He remembers all deeds—good and bad—and extends the promise of mercy as He recalls the merit of our ancestors at the Binding of Isaac.

The ***ba'al tekiah*** blows the *shofar* in three distinct sound patterns: ***tekiah, shevarim,*** and ***teruah,*** sounded in combinations. *Tekiah* is a single, abrupt blast; *shevarim* is comprised of three short intermittent blasts; and *teruah* is a pattern of nine quivering sounds, equivalent to three *shevarim.* The *ba'al tekiah* ascends to the *bimah* and faces the Holy Ark. He pulls his *talit* over his head and with *kavanah* recites the following two blessings before sounding the *shofar* for the first time during the services.

Blessings Before *Tekiat Shofar*

Ba'al Tekiah:

Baruch Atah, HaShem E-lo-kenu, Melech HaOlam,
asher kidshanu b'mitzvotav v'tzivanu
lish'moa kol shofar.

❖

Blessed are You, Lord our God, King of the Universe,
Who sanctified us with His commandments and commanded us
to hear the sound of the ram's horn.

Congregation:

Amen.

❖

Ba'al Tekiah:

Baruch Atah, HaShem E-lo-kenu, Melech HaOlam,
she'hecheyanu v'kiy'manu,
v'higiyanu laz'man hazeh.

❖

Blessed are You, Lord our God, King of the Universe,
Who has kept us alive, sustained us,
and brought us to this season.

Congregation:

Amen.

These *berachot* apply to all *shofar* blasts, including those yet to be sounded later in the service, and are not repeated. Note that the *mitzvah* of *shofar* is to hear the *shofar* sounds, not to blow them. Accordingly, one must clearly hear every note.

The congregation stands in awed silence as the piercing sounds of the *shofar* begin to vibrate in the air. A total of one hundred blasts will be sounded by the time *Musaf* is concluded. No conversation is permitted from the time the *shofar* first sounds until the end of *Musaf,* especially during the first series of thirty blasts, which fulfills the minimum biblical requirement for sounding the *shofar.*

A special reader, called the ***makrei,*** announces the name of each sound or combination of sounds to the *ba'al tekiah.*

Tekiah . . . Shevarim Teruah . . . Tekiah
Tekiah . . . Shevarim Teruah . . . Tekiah
Tekiah . . . Shevarim Teruah . . . Tekiah
Tekiah . . . Shevarim . . . Tekiah
Tekiah . . . Shevarim . . . Tekiah
Tekiah . . . Shevarim . . . Tekiah
Tekiah . . . Teruah . . . Tekiah
Tekiah . . . Teruah . . . Tekiah
Tekiah . . . Teruah . . . Tekiah

After hearing each note of the three groups of sounds, the congregation recites the following *Y'hi Ratzon* prayer.

Recite *Y'hi Ratzon* during *Tekiat Shofar*

May it be Your will, Lord, our God,
and God of our forefathers,
to permit the sounds that come forth from our *shofar*
to ascend and to plead before Your throne of glory
for the atonement of all our sins.
Blessed are You, Master of mercy.

If one cannot attend services in the synagogue, the obligation to hear *shofar* remains. Many communities arrange for a *ba'al tekiah* to go to the homes of shut-ins, to hospitals and nursing homes, and the like, to sound the *shofar,* so that everyone can have the opportunity to fulfill the *mitzvah* of hearing the sounds of the *shofar.*

6.11 *Musaf of Rosh HaShanah*

Some of the most moving of all *tefillot* of the *Yamim Nora'im* are recited during *Musaf.* It opens with the Cantor's Prayer, ***Hineni.*** In many synagogues, the *chazan* who chants *Musaf* stands at the back of the sanctuary and begins to chant this special *tefillah.* With trepidation, he moves slowly to the *bimah.*

The Cantor Begins to Recite *Hineni*

Here I am, poor in deeds,
trembling and frightened in dread of Him
Who is enthroned on Israel's praises.
I have come to stand and plead before You for Your people Israel
who have made me their messenger,
although I am neither deserving nor qualified to do so.
Therefore, I beg of You . . .
merciful and gracious God of Israel, . . .
grant me success [as I] plead for mercy for myself
and for those who sent me. . . .
Accept my prayer as if I were experienced . . .
with a sweet voice and pleasing to other people.
May You denounce [the accuser] Satan, that he not hinder me.
May You change all misery and evil to happiness and joy,
to life and peace, for us and for all Israel . . .
and may there be no obstacle to my prayer. . . .
May it be Your will, Lord, . . . that the angels who carry up prayers
may [they] present my prayer before Your Throne of Glory . . .
on behalf of the righteous . . . and for the sake of Your . . . Name.
Blessed are You Who hears prayer.

The words of supplication of the *sh'liach tzibur* convey the profound reverence and fear that the worshippers feel, as they begin to recite the *Shemoneh Esrei* of *Musaf.*

6.11.1 *Shemoneh Esrei* of *Musaf*

The *Shemoneh Esrei* of *Musaf* is the longest *Amidah* in Jewish liturgy. Unlike others we have discussed, it contains nine blessings. The first three and the last three are identical to those in all other *Amidah* prayers. However, instead of just one middle blessing, there are three.

During the repetition of the *Shemoneh Esrei,* many additions, mostly liturgical poems, are inserted in all nine blessings. Of course, the basic theme of the blessings is carried over in the *piyutim.*

In the repetition of the *Amidah* of *Musaf,* between Blessings (2) and (3), we find two of the most inspiring prayers in all Jewish liturgy: ***U'Netaneh Tokef*** and ***B'Rosh HaShanah.***

According to tradition, *U'Netaneh Tokef* was composed by Rabbi Amnon, a tenth-century aristocrat and scholar from Mayence. Many times he was pressured by the bishop to abandon his faith. Once, in a weak moment, he evaded the demand by asking for three days to think it over. When he returned home, he was horribly despondent, for he had given the bishop reason to think that he might consider renouncing his belief in God.

When he did not return after three days, he was arrested and sentence was pronounced: His hands and feet were cut off. A few days later, dying from his wounds, he asked to be brought to the synagogue on the first day of *Rosh HaShanah*. Just before *Kedushah*, he was carried before the Ark where he was inspired to recite *U'Netaneh Tokef.*

Recite *U'Netaneh Tokef*

Congregation then Cantor:

Let us tell of . . . this day's holiness, for it is awesome and frightening. . . .
Truly, You are the One Who judges . . . and contemplates and witnesses;
Who writes and seals; . . . Who remembers all that was forgotten;
You will open the Book of Remembrances,
and it will read itself, [for] everyone's signature is in it.
The great *shofar* will be sounded,
and a gentle, thin sound will be heard.
The angels . . . trembling [with] terror . . . will say:
"Behold this is the Day of Judgment. . . ."
All mankind will pass before You like a flock.
Like a shepherd . . . making his sheep pass under his staff,
so shall You cause the souls of all the living to pass,
[You] count, number, . . . and inscribe their verdicts.

As he uttered the last words, he died. Three days later Rabbi Amnon appeared in a dream to the renowned mystic, talmudic scholar, and poet, Rabbi Kalonymus, and taught him the prayer, which was subsequently introduced in all congregations. It is recited on both days of *Rosh HaShanah* and on *Yom Kippur.*

U'Netaneh Tokef is followed immediately by *B'Rosh HaShanah,* a prayer that describes God's judgment. This prayer declares unequivocally that both life and death are determined by God's judgment, and nothing occurs by happenstance or accident, even if it seems that way.

Recite B'Rosh HaShanah

Congregation then Cantor:
On *Rosh HaShanah,* it is inscribed,
and on *Yom Kippur,* it is sealed:
How many will pass away and how many will be born;
Who will live and who will die;
Who will have a timely end and who an untimely end;
Who by fire and who by water;
Who by sword and who by beast;
Who by hunger and who by thirst;
Who by earthquake and who by plague;
Who by strangling and who by stoning;
Who will rest and who will wander about;
Who will be safe and who will be harmed;
Who will have peace and who will be tormented;
Who will become poor and who will become rich;
Who will be humiliated and who will be ennobled

The prayer concludes with the exhortation found in the Talmud, *Masechet Rosh HaShanah* 16b, that it is possible to influence God's decision on the Day of Judgment.

Conclude B'Rosh HaShanah

Congregation then Cantor:
U't'shuvah, u'tefillah, u'tzedakah
ma'avirin et roa hagezerah.

❖

But repentance, prayer, and charity
avert the evil decree.

6.11.2 Kedushah of Musaf

Two *piyutim* precede *Kedushah.* The first encourages the sinner to repent, for

God's anger can be assuaged by sincere remorse. Because God understands the failings of humankind, He will be inclined to be merciful to lowly sinners. The second restates the theme that God has no beginning and no end. His existence is eternal, and the angels fulfill His intent in the world.

Kedushah of *Musaf* is similar to that of *Kedushah* of *Musaf* on *Shabbat* and on festival days. It is chanted within Blessing (3), which deals with the sanctification of God's Name. The congregation joins with the angels in the recitation of the *Shema Yisrael,* a noble act worthy of His grace.

After *Kedushah,* Blessing (3) of the *Amidah* is completed. A discussion of the three middle blessings of the *Shemoneh Esrei* follow.

6.11.3 The Middle Blessings of *Musaf*

Instead of saying there are three middle blessings in the *Shemoneh Esrei,* we might say that the middle blessing of *Musaf* is divided into three major sections: ***Malchuyot,*** Sovereignty, ***Zichronot***, Remembrances, and ***Shofarot,*** Sounding of the Ram's Horn. Each section also contains ten selections: three from the Torah; three from *Ketuvim,* specifically from Psalms; three from *Nevi'im,* Prophets; and a concluding verse from the Torah. The first two sections each conclude with a verse from the Torah (see exception in *Shofarot* below).

Malchuyot talks of God as the Sovereign of the Universe; *Zichronot,* God Who remembers and judges all things; and *Shofarot,* God Who reveals Himself (on Mount Sinai) amid the sounds of the *shofar.*

You will recall that during *Shacharit*, the *ba'al tekiah* sounded thirty *shofar* blasts. According to the Mishnah, ***Masechet Rosh HaShanah*** 4:5–6, ten blasts of the *shofar* are also to be sounded during the repetition of the *Musaf Amidah* at the conclusion of each of these major sections, as follows:

Tekiah . . . Shevarim Teruah . . . Tekiah
Tekiah . . . Shevarim . . . Tekiah
Tekiah . . . Teruah . . . Tekiah

In each section, after the *shofar* is sounded, a short prayer, ***HaYom Harat Olam,*** recalls that *Rosh HaShanah* is the birthday of the world. We will present this prayer in context below. Now, let's take a closer look at the text of *Malchuyot, Zichronot,* and *Shofarot.*

Malchuyot begins with the recitation of *Alenu* (see Section 3.12) which was introduced at this point in the *Rosh HaShanah* liturgy by the third-century Babylonian sage, Rav. Here, *Alenu* is not a concluding prayer. Rather it serves as a prelude to *Malchuyot* in that it speaks of God's sovereignty. *Malchuyot* verses are interwoven with the usual middle-blessing prayers that are recited on a festival day. The first verse of the ten selections that comprise *Malchuyot* occurs later in the blessing, but *Alenu* sets the tone because it deals with God's sovereignty. The Ark is opened and the congregation rises.

Begin to Recite *Alenu*

It is our duty to praise the Master of all things,
to attribute greatness to the Creator,
for He has not made us like the nations of other lands,
nor placed us like other families of the earth. . . .
Cantor and Congregation Kneel Here:
We bend the knee and bow in worship,
acknowledging our thanks before the King of Kings,
the Holy One, blessed is He,
for it is He who stretched out the heavens
and founded the earth. . . .
He is our God, there is no other; . . .
as it is written in His Torah:
"You shall know this day,
and reflect on it in your heart,
that it is the Lord Who is God
in the heavens above and on the earth beneath,
there is nothing else."

At the point that we recite

We bend the knee and bow in worship, . . .

the cantor, and in many synagogues, the entire congregation, kneels and bows, in acknowledgment of God's sovereignty. It is a custom in some congregations to touch one's face to the floor, recalling the service in the Temple; in others it is not. In any case, it is prohibited to prostrate oneself on the floor with arms and legs extended. As we declare our faithfulness to *HaShem,* we pray that one day all peoples of the earth will recognize the dominion of the One God.

Continue to Recite *Alenu*

We hope in You, therefore, Lord our God,
that we will soon behold Your majestic splendor. . . .
For the kingdom is Yours,
and forever and ever You shall reign in glorious honor,
as it is written in Your Torah:
"The Lord shall be King for all eternity,"
and it is said:
"The Lord shall be King over all the earth;
on that day the Lord shall be One and His Name One."

Alenu is followed by the cantor's prayer that God will be with the agent of His people. *Malchuyot* continues with the ten selections from *Tanach,* all of which pertain to God's majestic rule. The first three biblical verses are from *Parshat Beshalach,* Exodus 15:18; *Parshat Balak,* Numbers 23:21; and *Parshat V'zot HaBerachah,* Deuteronomy 33:5. Together they depict God as the loving King of the Jewish people, Whose coronation was commemorated when the Torah was given at Mount Sinai and, specifically, when the Jewish people accepted it.

The next three selections from *Ketuvim* are from Psalms 22:29; 93:1; and 24:7–10. These three selections combine to recall: (1) God as the Sovereign over all nations; (2) the God of Creation, Who is revealed as the dominant force in nature; and (3) the glorious Master, Who shows favor to those who worship Him.

The three prophetic verses are from Isaiah 44:6; Obadiah 1:21; and Zechariah 14:9. These verses express the belief in the One and only God Who will bring the redemption, and fulfill the promise that the oppressors of Israel will be judged, and all nations will acknowledge Him as King.

The final verse in *Malchuyot* is *Shema Yisrael,* from *Parshat Va'etchanan,* Deuteronomy 6:4. The six words are the ultimate statement of Jewish faith and are an assertion of God's sovereignty. The closing blessing for *Malchuyot* is:

Blessed are You, Lord, King of the Universe,
Who sanctifies (the Sabbath,) Israel and the Day of Remembrance.

As we noted above, the *shofar* is sounded, ten blasts in all. Then *HaYom Harat Olam* celebrates *Rosh HaShanah* as the birthday of the world.

Recite *HaYom Harat Olam*

> **Today is the birthday of the world.**
> **Today all creatures of the world stand in judgment,**
> **as children of God or as servants.**
> **If as children, be merciful with us,**
> **as a father has mercy on his children.**
> **If as servants, . . . be gracious to us**
> **and pronounce our verdict clear as light,**
> **revered and holy One.**

A final prayer concludes the first section of the middle blessing—or Blessing (4)—of *Shemoneh Esrei* for *Musaf.*

> **Accept with mercy and graciousness our recital of *Malchuyot.***

By the conclusion of *Malchuyot,* forty *shofar* blasts have been sounded.

The verses of the second section, *Zichronot,* are the heart of Blessing (5) of the *Shemoneh Esrei.* All living things—humankind and animal—and, indeed, all spiritual beings, too, stand in judgment on *Rosh HaShanah.* So, too, are verdicts rendered for countries: war or peace, bounty or famine. God remembers everything since the time of Creation. He keeps watch and sees the very end of all generations.

The ten verses from *Tanach* begin with a biblical verse from *Parshat Noach,* Genesis 8:1:

> **And God remembered Noah and every living thing. . . .**

recalling that God extended His mercy and remembered Noah and his family and the creatures of the world, at a time of extraordinary wickedness and corruption, when the Flood destroyed everything and all seemed irrevocably lost. We pray that God will likewise extend His grace and compassion to all of us.

The text of *Zichronot* continues with a verse from *Parshat Shemot,* Exodus 2:24:

> **And God heard their moaning,**
> **and God remembered His covenant**
> **with Abraham, with Isaac, and with Jacob.**

This reference to the slavery of Egypt and His promise to redeem the Jewish people then and in the future is further proof of God's enduring mercy.

The third biblical verse, from *Parshat Bechukotai,* Leviticus 26:42, also invokes the names of the three patriarchs, albeit in reverse order, as if to say that were the merit of Jacob not enough, then that of Isaac would be; and if not, then certainly the merit of Abraham would bring the fulfillment of God's covenants.

The next three verses, from Psalms 111:4, 5, and 106:45, are indicative of God's wondrous creation of the Sabbath and festivals, which serve to remind us of His marvels in Egypt and of His readiness to help in time of tyranny and oppression.

The three verses from *Nevi'im* come from Jeremiah 2:2, Ezekiel 16:60, and Jeremiah 31:19. The first is a reference to the prophet Jeremiah who appealed to the Jewish people and urged them to repent. With love, he reminded them that God would always remember the love the new Jewish nation showed to Him when they made an unconditional covenant with Him in the wilderness.

The second and third verses from the Prophets speak of Ephraim, who, among the Ten Tribes, symbolizes the Jewish people at the time of the Babylonian Exile. In spite of their errant conduct, God longs for them to return from exile and promises to take pity on them.

Zichronot continues with the prayer that God should remember the Jewish people favorably. The tenth verse, derived from *Parshat Bechukotai,* Leviticus 26:45, again recalls the covenant He made with the patriarchs, promising to redeem Israel from the bondage of Egypt. This verse is followed by the concluding blessing of *Zichronot.*

Blessed are You, Lord, Who remembers the covenant.

Ten blasts of the *shofar* are sounded again, and *HaYom Harat Olam* is chanted again. A final prayer concludes the second section of the middle blessing—or Blessing (5)—of *Shemoneh Esrei* for *Musaf.*

Accept with mercy and graciousness our recital of *Zichronot.*

By the conclusion of *Zichronot,* fifty *shofar* blasts have been sounded.

The sixth blessing of *Shemoneh Esrei* is the concluding section of the middle blessing: *Shofarot.* Like the preceding sections, it also contains ten selections from *Tanach.* The first three are all from *Parshat Yitro,* Exodus 19:16, 19, and 20:15. It begins with a powerful description of the Revelation at Mount Sinai, which culminated in the mighty sound of the *shofar.* Thus, *Shofarot* begins with the description of the sounding of the ram's horn when the Torah was given.

The verses from *Ketuvim* are comprised of Psalms 47:6, 98:6, and 81:4–5. A fourth selection from Psalms 150:1–6 follows (there is no concluding Torah verse in *Shofarot*). Again, all of them allude to the sounding of the *shofar* and its wailing sounds, which change God's anger to compassion.

The verses from the Prophets, Isaiah 18:3 and 27:13, and Zechariah 9:14–15, all tell of the final redemption, when the sound of the *shofar* will signal the ingathering of the Jewish people and the ultimate coming of the Messiah.

Shofarot concludes with the following blessing.

Blessed are You, Lord, Who hears the sound of the *shofar* of His people Israel with mercy.

Once again, the *shofar* is sounded, and *HaYom Harat Olam* is chanted. A final prayer concludes the third section of the middle blessing—or Blessing (6)—of *Shemoneh Esrei* for *Musaf.*

Accept with mercy and graciousness our recital of *Shofarot.*

By the conclusion of *Shofarot,* sixty blasts have been sounded.

6.11.4 The Conclusion of *Musaf*

The remaining three blessings of the *Shemoneh Esrei* are repeated by the cantor. Within Blessing (5), the ***Birkat Kohanim,*** Priestly Benediction, is chanted (see Section 7.8.2 for a further discussion of this ritual). The special inserts are also added for *Rosh HaShanah.*

The concluding prayer of *Musaf* is recited with the Ark open. The worshippers rise. The cantor recites each verse, and the congregation responds *amen* and recites the next verse.

Conclude the Repetition of *Musaf*

Today, strengthen us.

Amen.

Today, bless us.

Amen.

Today, exalt us.

Amen.

Today, seek us out for goodness.

Amen.

Today, hear our cry.

Amen.

Today, accept our prayers with mercy and grace.

Amen.

Today, sustain us with the righteousness of Your right hand.

Amen.

The Full *Kaddish* is then recited, followed by the closing hymns of *Ein kE-lo-kenu* and *Alenu*. The Mourner's *Kaddish* is recited, followed by forty blasts of the *shofar*. Different customs prevail about when these forty blasts are sounded. In any case, a total of one hundred blasts is sounded on each of the two days of *Rosh HaShanah*.

As before, thirty are sounded in the following sequences:

Tekiah . . . Shevarim Teruah . . . Tekiah
Tekiah . . . Shevarim Teruah . . . Tekiah
Tekiah . . . Shevarim Teruah . . . Tekiah
Tekiah . . . Shevarim . . . Tekiah
Tekiah . . . Shevarim . . . Tekiah
Tekiah . . . Shevarim . . . Tekiah
Tekiah . . . Teruah . . . Tekiah
Tekiah . . . Teruah . . . Tekiah
Tekiah . . . Teruah . . . Tekiah

Then the final ten climax in the ***tekiah gedolah***, the great *tekiah*, a long, penetrating, wailing sound.

Tekiah . . . Shevarim Teruah . . . Tekiah
Tekiah . . . Shevarim . . . Tekiah
Tekiah . . . Teruah . . . Tekiah Gedolah

Musaf is over.

6.12 Minchah of Rosh HaShanah

In the late afternoon, a propitious time for prayer, the congregation returns to the synagogue for the recitation of *Minchah.* If the Sabbath coincides with *Rosh HaShanah,* then the Torah is read at *Minchah* before the *Amidah.* The Torah portion, which is divided into three *aliyot,* is from *Parshat Ha'azinu,* Deuteronomy 32:1–12.

Minchah begins with two introductory verses: Psalms 84:5 and Psalms 144:15. It continues with Psalm 145, *Ashrei,* an alphabetical acrostic that is recited quietly. The Half *Kaddish* follows and serves as a transition to *Shemoneh Esrei,* which is identical to the *Shemoneh Esrei* of *Ma'ariv* for the night before. A short *Kedushah* is recited between Blessings (2) and (3). After *Shemoneh Esrei,* the Ark is opened, and the congregation rises to recite ***Avinu Malkenu,*** a prayer of supplication comprised of forty-three verses, each of which begins with "Our Father, Our King." The first fourteen verses are recited quietly. A selection follows.

Recite *Avinu Malkenu* to *Minchah*

Our Father, our King,
we have sinned before You.
Our Father, our King,
we have no king but You. . . .
Our Father, our King,
renew us for a good year. . . .
Our Father, our King,
forgive and pardon all our iniquities.
Our Father, our King,
blot out . . . our willful transgressions and errors . . .

The next nine verses are recited responsively by the cantor and the congregation.

Continue to Recite *Avinu Malkenu*

Our Father, our King,
return us to You in perfect repentance.
Our Father, our King,
send complete healing to the sick among Your people.
Our Father, our King,
tear up the evil judgment decreed against us.
Our Father, our King,
remember us favorably before You.
Our Father, our King,
inscribe us in the Book of Good Life.
Our Father, our King,
inscribe us in the Book of Redemption and Salvation.
Our Father, our King,
inscribe us in the Book of Maintenance and Support.
Our Father, our King,
inscribe us in the Book of Merit.
Our Father, our King,
inscribe us in the Book of Forgiveness and Pardon.

The next twenty are again recited quietly by all. A selection follows.

Continue to Recite *Avinu Malkenu*

Our Father, our King,
cause salvation to flourish for us soon. . . .
Our Father, our King,
hear our voice, pity us, and be merciful to us.
Our Father, our King,
accept our prayer with mercy and favor.
Our Father, our King,
open the gates of heaven to our prayer.
Our Father, our King,
remember that we are but dust. . . .
Our Father, our King,
take pity on us and on our children and infants.
Our Father, our King,
act for the sake of those who were murdered for Your holy Name. . . .
Our Father, our King,
act for Your sake if not for ours. . . .
Our Father, our King,
act for the sake of Your great, mighty, and awesome Name
by which we are called.

In most synagogues, the cantor and congregation chant the last verse together. In others, the cantor chants the last verse, and the congregation repeats it.

Conclude *Avinu Malkenu*

Our Father, our King,
be gracious to us and answer us,
though we have no meritorious deeds;
treat us charitably and kindly,
and save us.

Avinu Malkenu is not recited on Friday afternoon or on the Sabbath, with the exception of the concluding service of *Yom Kippur* (see Section 6.31).

6.13 Casting Away Our Sins

On the first day of *Rosh HaShanah,* after *Minchah* has been recited, it is traditional for the congregation to walk to the banks of a nearby stream for the service of ***Tashlich.*** The word *tashlich* means "you shall cast," a phrase found in Micah, one of the Minor Prophetic Books of the Latter Prophets.

> **You shall cast all their sins into the depths of the sea.**
>
> **—Micah 7:19**

The tradition of *Tashlich* dates back to the fourteenth century, according to the Maharil, Rabbi Jacob Moelin (1355–1427), a renowned scholar of Jewish customs and liturgy. *Tashlich* refers to the custom of *symbolically* casting away our sins in a body of running water—if possible, one that contains fish. It is a common *misconception* that we are supposed to throw bread crumbs to feed the fish.

The *Tashlich* service consists primarily of the recitation of two passages. The first, from Micah 7:18–20, contains thirteen phrases, and each phrase corresponds to one of God's Thirteen Attributes of Mercy, as found in the Torah. According to the Talmud, *Masechet Rosh HaShanah* 17b, we invoke the penitential Thirteen Attributes because God told Moses that He would always answer prayers when Israel transgressed and recited the Attributes.

Recite *Tashlich*

Who, God, is like You,
Who forgives iniquity,
and disregards the transgression
of the remnant of His heritage?
He does not retain His wrath forever.
for He desires kindness.
He will return and again be merciful to us.
He will suppress our iniquities;
and You shall cast all their sins into the depths of the sea.
Grant truth to Jacob, kindness to Abraham,
as You swore to our forefathers
from ancient times.

The second passage of *Tashlich,* which invokes only nine of the Thirteen Attributes, comes from Psalms 118:5–9.

Continue to Recite *Tashlich*

From the depths of despair I called upon God.
God answered me with great generosity.
The Lord is with me,
I have no fear;
what can man do [to harm] me?
The Lord is with me [and with those who] help me,
therefore, I can face my enemies.
It is better to take refuge in the Lord than to rely on man.
It is better to take refuge in the Lord than to rely on [powerful] nobles.

In addition to these passages, *Tashlich* also includes the recitation of Psalm 33, which describes God's omnipotence and reminds the Jewish people to rely only on Him and not on military power, and Psalm 130, which is a heartfelt expression of regret and a plea for divine forgiveness. Some congregations also recite a prayer for sustenance, appropriate to *Rosh HaShanah* when we are being judged. After *Tashlich,* the congregation returns to the synagogue for *Ma'ariv.*

If the first day of *Rosh HaShanah* falls on the Sabbath, *Tashlich* is recited on the second day. It is permissible to postpone *Tashlich* to the Ten Days of Repentance, if there is no stream of running water within walking distance, or in the case of inclement weather.

6.14 The Second Day of *Rosh HaShanah*

On the second day, the *Rosh HaShanah* liturgy is basically the same, with certain differences in the selection of *piyutim.* It again includes the four prayer services: *Ma'ariv, Shacharit, Musaf,* and *Minchah.*

After *Minchah* on the second day, the *Ma'ariv* service, which is the first service of the following day, is recited. It includes the nineteen-blessing *Amidah,* because *Rosh HaShanah* ended with the recitation of *Minchah,* so the weekday prayers are resumed.

If the second day of *Rosh HaShanah* is Friday, then the usual Sabbath *tefillot,* including *Ma'ariv*—but not *Kabbalat Shabbat*—are recited after *Minchah* instead.

6.15 Customs and Observances of *Rosh HaShanah*

We have spent a considerable amount of time describing the liturgy of *Rosh HaShanah*. Let us now take a short look at some of the customs and observances associated with the Days of Awe.

6.15.1 Candlelighting for *Rosh HaShanah*

In the home, *Rosh HaShanah* is ushered in with *licht benchen,* candlelighting. Approximately eighteen minutes before sunset, two candles are lit. If one cannot afford two candles, one candle may be used, but it is customary to light at least two.

The woman of the house covers her head, closes her eyes and covers them with her hands, and recites the following two blessings over the candles, acknowledging God's commandment. With the recitation of the blessings, she ushers in the ***Yom Tov,*** the festival (literally, good day). If the festival coincides with the Sabbath, the words in parentheses are added. On the second night, the candles are lit from an existing flame, such as a pilot light or a long-burning candle, because striking a match is not permitted on the festival.

Recite the First Blessing over the *Yom Tov* Candles

Baruch Atah, HaShem E-lo-kenu, Melech HaOlam
asher kidshanu b'mitzvotav v'tzivanu
l'hadlik ner shel (Shabbat v') Yom Tov.

❖

Blessed are You, Lord our God, King of the Universe,
Who has sanctified us with His commandments and commanded us
to kindle the (Sabbath and) festival lights.

A second blessing is then recited.

Recite the Second Blessing over the *Yom Tov* Candles

Baruch Atah, HaShem E-lo-kenu, Melech HaOlam,
she'hecheyanu, v'kiy'manu,
v'higiyanu laz'man hazeh.

❖

Blessed are You, Lord our God, King of the Universe,
Who has kept us alive, sustained us,
and brought us to this season.

There is some disagreement about whether the second blessing, referred to as ***she'hecheyanu,*** should be recited at candlelighting, inasmuch as it is later recited at *Kiddush*. However, it is the usual practice practically everywhere that women recite *she'hecheyanu* at candlelighting and hear it at *Kiddush* as well.

There is also some difference of opinion among the sages about whether the second blessing should be recited at all on the second night. Is *Rosh HaShanah* just one long day, and, therefore, should the *berachah* be recited just on the eve of the first day? Or is it two distinct days and requires *she'hecheyanu* for each? The prevailing opinion is that of Rashi: *Rosh HaShanah* is observed for two distinct days and requires *she'hecheyanu* for both.

However, we take note of the other ruling by eating a new fruit—one that has not yet been enjoyed in that season. Whenever a new fruit is tasted for the first time in any season, *she'hecheyanu* is recited after *borei p'ri ha'etz,* the *berachah* for the fruit itself. Therefore, we keep in mind to eat the new fruit because of the *she'hecheyanu* blessing that was recited during *Kiddush*.

6.15.2 Eating Symbolic Foods

Many other foods are eaten on the first night—and often on the second, as well—because of their symbolism as good omens. For example, it is a favorite custom, and one that is observed almost universally, to recite the *hamotzi* over round—not braided—*challot* filled with raisins. The round shape probably symbolizes the cycle of life. The first piece of *challah* is dipped in honey, a symbol of the sweet new year. Then, everyone takes a piece of apple, sweetens it with honey, which is often served in a fancifully designed dish shaped like an apple, and recites the following:

Recite before Eating an Apple with Honey

Baruch Atah, HaShem E-lo-kenu, Melech HaOlam,
borei p'ri ha'etz.

❖

Blessed are You, Lord our God, King of the Universe,
Who creates the fruit of the tree.

Everyone tastes a bit of the apple in fulfillment of the *berachah* and then recites the following *Y'hi Ratzon.*

Recite after Tasting an Apple with Honey

Y'hi ratzon milfanecha, HaShem E-lo-kenu, v'E-lo-kei avotenu,
she't'chadesh alenu shanah tovah u'metukah.

❖

May it be Your will, Lord our God, and God of our forefathers,
to renew us for a good and sweet year.

The apple is an allusion to the fragrance of the field mentioned in connection with Isaac's blessing of Jacob in *Parshat Toldot,* Genesis 27:27. In Hebrew, the word *honey* is numerically equivalent to the Hebrew phrase for *Father of Mercy,* certainly a fitting attribute associated with *Rosh HaShanah.*

One of the most popular fruits for *Rosh HaShanah* is the pomegranate because it is said to contain 613 seeds, equivalent to the *Taryag Mitzvot,* the 613 commandments found in the Torah. The pomegranate also symbolizes the hope that we will merit to perform *mitzvot* as numerous as the seeds.

It is also a custom to wish for a good and sweet year, a ***shanah tovah u'metukah.*** In keeping with this tradition, foods made with honey are included in the holiday menu. Honey cake and pastries, candied yams, carrots glazed with honey, and sweet fruits, like dates and figs, are among the most popular dishes.

Other symbolic foods include carrots, which grow in abundance and represent fertility. Also, fish is served with the head, symbolizing the hope that in the coming year we will be like the head and not the tail—that is, powerful and not weak. This custom is derived from a biblical verse.

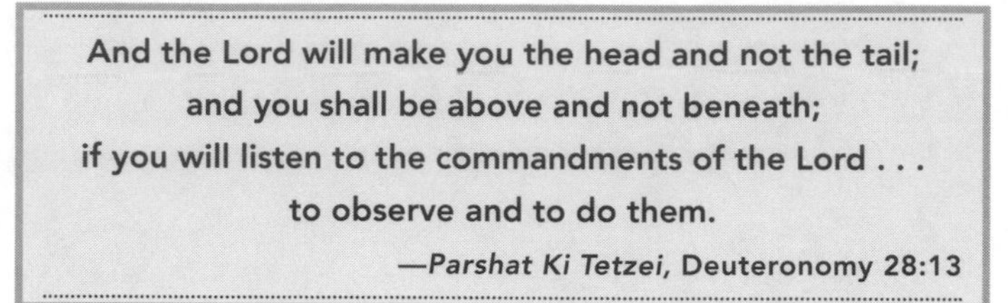
**And the Lord will make you the head and not the tail;
and you shall be above and not beneath;
if you will listen to the commandments of the Lord . . .
to observe and to do them.**
—*Parshat Ki Tetzei,* Deuteronomy 28:13

For the head of the fish, we say,

Recite before Eating the Head of the Fish

**May it be Your will, Lord our God, and God of our forefathers,
that we be like the head and not like the tail.**

Fish is also a symbol of fertility, and we recite the following *Y'hi Ratzon* before eating it.

Recite before Eating Fish

**May it be Your will, Lord our God, and God of our forefathers,
that we be fruitful and multiply like fish.**

An equivalent but opposite tradition is to refrain from eating bitter or sour foods, like pickles or horseradish.

6.15.3 Greetings for the New Year

Throughout the *Aseret Y'mei T'shuvah,* it is customary for one Jew to greet another with the words

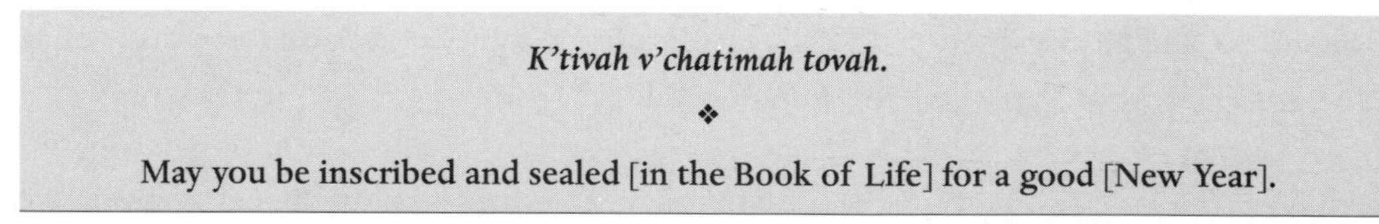
K'tivah v'chatimah tovah.
❖
May you be inscribed and sealed [in the Book of Life] for a good [New Year].

for on *Rosh HaShanah,* our names are inscribed, and on *Yom Kippur,* God's decree is sealed.

It is also a common practice to send New Year greetings, and a wide selection of cards specifically designed for this purpose, many with the text written in Hebrew and English, is readily available.

Perpetuating these traditions is as much a part of the holiday observance as repentance and prayer and hearing the *shofar.* We will conclude our discussion of *Rosh HaShanah* in the next section.

6.16 *Havdalah* after *Rosh HaShanah*

Just as we recite *Havdalah* when the Sabbath ends and we return to the weekdays (see Section 5.10), so, too, we recite *Havdalah* when *Rosh HaShanah* is over. If it is not Friday night, we recite the following:

Recite the *Havdalah* Service after *Rosh HaShanah*

Baruch Atah, HaShem E-lo-kenu, Melech HaOlam,
borei p'ri hagafen.

❖

Blessed are You, Lord our God, King of the Universe,
Who creates the fruit of the vine.

We do not make the blessings over the spices and the candle, but we do recite the concluding paragraph.

Conclude the *Havdalah* Service

Blessed are You, Lord our God, King of the Universe,
Who has made a distinction
between holy and profane,
between light and darkness,
between Israel and other nations,
between the seventh day and the six days of work.
Blessed are You, Lord,
Who separates the holy from the profane.

If it is Friday night, we do not recite *Havdalah* at all.

6.17 The Fast of Gedaliah

The third day of *Tishrei* is observed as ***Tzom Gedaliah,*** the Fast of Gedaliah (see Sections 4.6.7 and 4.6.13). After the destruction of the First Temple in 586 B.C.E., the Babylonian ruler, Nebuchadnezzar, appointed Gedaliah as governor of Jerusalem. In spite of warnings from the prophet Jeremiah, who exhorted the king of Israel, Zedekiah, and the people to submit to the rule of the Babylonian conquerors, Gedaliah was assassinated by a member of the Jewish royal family. This tragedy, which occurred on the third of *Tishrei,* marked the bitter end of the First Commonwealth of Israel.

The Fast of Gedaliah is mentioned in one of the Minor Prophetic Books of the Latter Prophets, as one of the four fast days associated with the destruction of the First Temple in Jerusalem. This prophecy indicates these four days will ultimately be observed as occasions of joy.

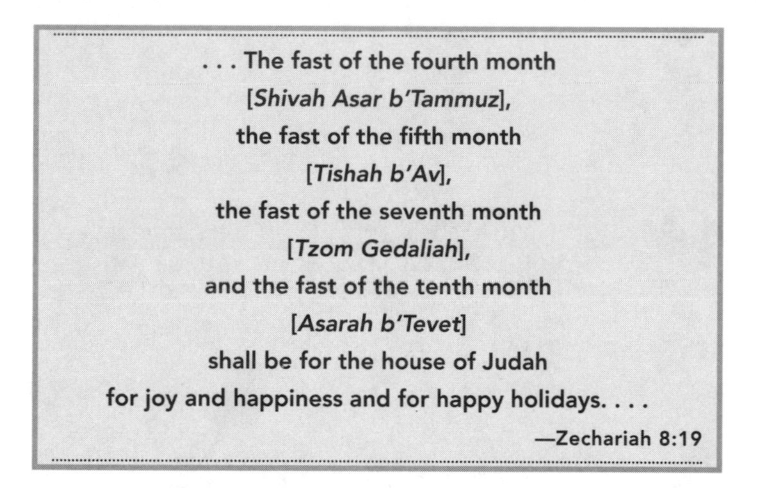

. . . The fast of the fourth month
[*Shivah Asar b'Tammuz*],
the fast of the fifth month
[*Tishah b'Av*],
the fast of the seventh month
[*Tzom Gedaliah*],
and the fast of the tenth month
[*Asarah b'Tevet*]
shall be for the house of Judah
for joy and happiness and for happy holidays. . . .

—Zechariah 8:19

The Torah is read on *Tzom Gedaliah* during *Shacharit* and *Minchah.* The Torah portion at both services is from *Parshat Ki Tissa,* Exodus 32:11–14 and 34:1–10. At both services, three *aliyot* are called, but during *Minchah,* the third *aliyah* is given to the one honored with *Maftir,* who recites the *Haftarah* from Isaiah 55:6–56:8.

If the third of *Tishrei* falls on the Sabbath, when fasting is prohibited, the fast is postponed until Sunday.

6.18 The Sabbath of Return

The Sabbath which falls during the *Aseret Y'mei T'shuvah* is called ***Shabbat Shuvah,*** the Sabbath of Return. One of several specially designated Sabbaths of the Jewish year, it is highlighted by the reading of a special *Haftarah* which begins with the word ***shuvah,*** return. The *Haftarah* is comprised of passages from three prophetic books: Hosea 14:2–10; Micah 7:18–20; and Joel 2:15–27.

It is possible for *Shabbat Shuvah* to fall on the third of *Tishrei,* the day immediately after *Rosh HaShanah,* that is, *Tzom Gedaliah.* Then the fast would be observed on Sunday (see Section 6.17).

Historically, the rabbi addressed the congregation only twice a year, on *Shabbat Shuvah* and on the Sabbath before Passover. On *Shabbat Shuvah,* in the late afternoon, just prior to the recitation of *Minchah,* it was the prevailing custom for the rabbi to deliver a specially inspiring sermon encouraging spiritual renewal and repentance. In many congregations, this practice has been retained.

We will now begin our discussion of the holiest day in the Jewish year: *Yom Kippur,* the Day of Atonement.

6.19 The Day of Atonement

The High Holidays culminate in *Yom Kippur,* the Day of Atonement. *Yom Kippur* is the most sacred and solemn day in the Jewish calendar. It is called ***Shabbat Shabbaton,*** the Sabbath of Sabbaths, indicating the sanctity that is associated with it and the faithfulness with which it must be observed. All the laws pertaining to the observance of the Sabbath apply to the observance of *Yom Kippur.* Additionally, *Yom Kippur* is marked by the observance of five restrictions: abstaining from (1) eating and drinking; (2) washing/bathing; (3) applying oils to the body; (4) sexual relations; and (5) wearing leather shoes. It is a day devoted to spiritual reflection, intense prayer, and the repeated recitation of the *Viduy,* the confessional prayer, ***Al Chet.***

6.20 Customs and Observances of *Yom Kippur*

A brief historical description is in order about *Yom Kippur.* We have already noted that its observance is ordained in the Torah (see Section 6.4). Let us take a brief look at the events that led up to that commandment.

After the Revelation at Mount Sinai, Moses received the Ten Commandments on Mount Sinai. After forty days on the mountain, he returned only to find that the newly liberated Israelites, who had witnessed the Revelation, were worshipping a golden calf. He shattered the *luchot.*

Greatly ashamed of their sin, the people prayed and repented, and finally God forgave them. Moses returned to the mountain to receive the second tablets. He returned on the tenth of *Tishrei,* and this time he found the people contrite and resolute to prove their faithfulness to God. That day became the first *Yom Kippur,* the day when God Himself accepted the pleas of the Jewish people.

Now we will look at some of the customs and observances associated with the Day of Atonement.

6.20.1 The Ceremony of Atonement

On the eve of *Yom Kippur,* it is traditional for Jews to perform the ceremony known as ***Kaparot.*** This ceremony reminds us of our mortality, that our very lives are at risk, for truly we deserve God's punishment. Today, most people observe this ritual by giving charity, which must be concomitant with repentance. We pray that our good deeds will atone for our sins, that our financial "sacrifice" will stand in our stead.

Holding the money in the right hand, we resolve it over the head, and recite the following verses three times.

Recite the Ceremony of *Kaparot*

This is my exchange, this is my substitute, this is my atonement.
This money will go to charity,
while I will enter to a good long life and to peace.

There are many variations on this custom. For example, an adult may recite it on behalf of another adult, and a pregnant woman may recite it and give charity on her own behalf and on that of her unborn child.

Historically, money was not used for *kaparot.* Instead, a live rooster (for a man) or a hen (for a woman) was held over the head and revolved while the verses were recited. The chickens were then ritually slaughtered (see Section 9.7.5) and donated to the poor, also a charitable act. In a number of communities, atonement is still made in this way, symbolic of the scapegoat that was sacrificed on the Day of Atonement during the Temple service (see Section 6.28.1). Accordingly the recitation is as follows:

Recite the Ceremony of *Kaparot*

> This is my exchange, this is my substitute, this is my atonement.
> This rooster (or hen) will go to its death,
> while I will proceed to a good and long life and to peace.

6.20.2 The Meal of Separation

Jews are obliged to eat a festive meal, called ***se'udah hamafseket,*** the meal of separation, before the fast begins. The obligation to eat before *Yom Kippur* is as important as the obligation to fast on this most holy day. Of course, salty or spicy foods should be avoided, because even water is not permitted during the fast. Again, one should consult a rabbi and physician if there is a medical concern about fasting.

6.20.3 Blessing the Children

Before going to the synagogue for the Evening Service, the parents bless their children, young and grown alike. For a son, begin:

Blessing a Son

> May you be like Ephraim and Menasheh. . . .

and for a daughter:

Blessing a Daughter

> May you be like Sarah, Rebecca, Rachel, and Leah. . . .

The blessing concludes the same way for sons and daughters.

Blessing the Children

. . . May the Lord bless you and safeguard you.
May the Lord illuminate His Countenance for you
and be gracious to you.
May the Lord turn His Countenance toward you,
and grant you peace.

A special *Y'hi Ratzon* prayer follows, asking God to bless them so that they may always love and fear Him, in order not to sin; that they may grow to be ever more learned in Torah; that their livelihood and their sustenance shall come only from God and never be dependent on the gifts of other people; and that they may be signed and sealed in the Book of Life.

6.20.4 *Yom Kippur* Attire

Throughout the Day of Atonement, men of the congregation, like the cantor and the rabbi, wear a *kittel,* a white robe, symbolizing purity and atonement (see Section 6.5). Women, too, often wear white suits or dresses. Because leather shoes are not permitted, everyone wears soft shoes, such as slippers or cloth or canvas sneakers. The soft shoes must not contain any leather, neither in the sole nor heel, nor as ornamentation. In the synagogue, some people prefer to stand in their stocking feet, which is permissible.

6.20.5 Candlelighting for *Yom Kippur*

On the eve of *Yom Kippur,* many women light candles at home and immediately walk to the synagogue. Others choose to light candles in the synagogue, usually in a room provided for that purpose. Women may bring their own candles, or may use those provided by the congregation, if that is the custom.

Two candles are lit. The woman covers her head, closes her eyes and covers them with her hands, and recites the following two blessings. If *Yom Kippur* coincides with the Sabbath, the words in parentheses are added.

Recite the First Blessing over the *Yom Tov* Candles

Baruch Atah, HaShem E-lo-kenu, Melech HaOlam,
asher kidshanu b'mitzvotav v'tzivanu
l'hadlik ner shel (Shabbat v') Yom HaKippurim.

❖

Blessed are You, Lord our God, King of the Universe,
Who has sanctified us with His commandments and commanded us
to kindle the (Sabbath and) *Yom Kippur* lights.

The *she'hecheyanu* blessing is then recited.

Recite the Second Blessing over the *Yom Tov* Candles

Baruch Atah, HaShem E-lo-kenu, Melech HaOlam,
she'hecheyanu, v'kiy'manu,
v'higiyanu laz'man hazeh.

❖

Blessed are You, Lord our God, King of the Universe,
Who has kept us alive, sustained us,
and brought us to this season.

6.21 The Liturgy of *Yom Kippur*

Unlike the liturgy of *Rosh HaShanah,* the liturgy of *Yom Kippur* is divided into five distinct services: (1) *Ma'ariv,* the Evening Service, which begins with ***Kol Nidrei,*** the declaration of nullification of vows; (2) *Shacharit,* the Morning Service, which is followed by *Kriat HaTorah* and ***Yizkor,*** the Memorial Prayer; (3) *Musaf,* the Additional Service, which contains the ***Avodah,*** recalling the worship service performed by the High Priest in the *Bet HaMikdash;* (4) *Minchah,* the Afternoon Service, when the Book of Jonah is recited as the *Haftarah;* and (5) ***Ne'ilah,*** the Concluding Service, when the Gates of Heaven begin to close.

Let us examine some of the most meaningful prayers of *Yom Kippur.* We start with *Minchah* of *Yom Kippur* eve.

6.22 Minchah of Yom Kippur Eve

It is noteworthy that the Afternoon Service before *Yom Kippur,* which is not part of the five *tefillot* of the Day of Atonement (see Section 6.21) contains certain liturgical elements recited only on *Yom Kippur* itself. The *Shemoneh Esrei* contains the usual nineteen blessings of a weekday service, and, of course, it includes the four insertions recited throughout the *Aseret Y'mei T'shuvah.*

> Remember us for life, King Who desires life,
> and inscribe us in the Book of Life—
> for Your sake, Living God.

> Who is like You, Merciful Father?
> In mercy He remembers His creatures for life!

> And inscribe all the Children of Your covenant for a good life.

> In the book of life,
> blessing, and peace,
> and good sustenance,
> may we and Your entire people,
> the House of Israel,
> be remembered and inscribed before You
> for a good life and for peace.

Throughout *Yom Kippur,* including the Afternoon Service before *Kol Nidrei,* we will continue to ask God to *inscribe* us in the Book of Life, as we did on *Rosh HaShanah.* As we discussed previously,

> On *Rosh HaShanah,* it is inscribed,
> and on *Yom Kippur,* it is sealed.

Only in the concluding service of *Ne'ilah,* do we ask to be *sealed* in the Book of Life, for when *Yom Kippur* is over, the decree is sealed.

Minchah also includes the first recitation of the *Viduy,* the confessional prayer. There are two confessional prayers: ***Ashamnu,*** a shorter version, and *Al Chet.* Suffice it to say here that we recite the confessional prayers in the afternoon before *Yom Kippur* in case sudden illness or, in the extreme, death, preclude its recitation on *Yom Kippur.* We will discuss both of these prayers in the next section. The *tefillot* of *Yom Kippur* begin with the recitation of *Kol Nidrei.* Men don a *talit* before *Kol Nidrei,* the only time a prayer shawl is worn at night by the congregation.

6.23 *Kol Nidrei*

Yom Kippur is ushered in just before sunset with the plaintive recitation of *Kol Nidrei,* All Vows. Written in Aramaic, it is a declaration made by every Jew that all vows and pledges which may be made in the coming year, between this *Yom Kippur* and the next, are to be considered null and void. It refers only to those vows and pledges that affect the individual alone, and *in no way negates* those obligations undertaken by the Jew in respect to other persons. It is not an attempt to void the promises and oaths made to other people, to abrogate contracts, or to nullify agreements, as has so often been charged by anti-Semites.

6.23.1 The Prelude to *Kol Nidrei*

The *Kol Nidrei* service begins as the Ark is opened and the congregation rises. The *Sifrei Torah,* which are dressed in white (see Section 6.5) and adorned with silver ornaments, are removed and carried in procession around the synagogue. All but two are then returned to the Ark, which remains open. Two members of the congregation, each holding a *Sefer Torah,* stand on each side of the cantor. The service begins with the following two recitations, which serve as a prelude to *Kol Nidrei* itself.

Begin the *Kol Nidrei* Service

Light is sown for the righteous and joy for the upright of heart.

❖

With the consent of the Omnipresent One,
and with the consent of this congregation,
with the approval of the [heavenly] upper court,
and with the approval of the [earthly] lower court,
we declare it lawful to pray with sinners.

The first verse promises light and happiness to the righteous who perform good deeds and to the upright of heart who retain their faith no matter the adversity. The second recitation invites all worshippers, including those who have sinned, to join in prayer with the congregation.

Historically, *Kol Nidrei,* which dates back some one thousand years, had special significance during the time of the Spanish Inquisition when Jews were forced to deny their faith and take on the rites and rituals of the church. Many practiced their Judaism in secret and used the *Kol Nidrei* prayer as a vehicle for renouncing the vows which their persecutors forced them to make. In recognition that these conversions were forced upon so many, these transgressors, who came at the time of *Kol Nidrei* to repent, even at risk to their lives, were welcomed back into the congregation.

Indeed, all sinners who come in a spirit of true repentance are to be accepted by the congregation, and, thus, it is declared lawful to worship with them.

A Witty Remark!

Some people live their entire lives oblivious to the profound significance of the Day of Atonement. The following tale is told of a simple man, but it could surely be about the most sophisticated of us.

In a European village, there once lived a foolish old man whose coat was covered with many curious patches, all of them large and unsightly. Once before *Yom Kippur,* the rabbi asked him why he had them on his coat. "Oh!" he proudly replied. "Because they represent the sins and shortcomings of my neighbors. When I wear them, I am doing a *mitzvah,* reminding them of their errors."

On the back of his coat, between his shoulders, there was one tiny patch. "And this one?" the rabbi asked. "Oh," the old man replied, "that represents my own faults, but I really can't see them."

To paraphrase Thomas Carlyle, the nineteenth-century British author, who, perhaps, said it best: "The greatest of faults . . . is to be conscious of none"—but those of other people.

6.23.2 The Nullification of Vows

The Ark is open, and the worshippers stand attentively, as *Kol Nidrei,* the transcendent supplication, is recited three times. It is recited softly at first, symbolizing the hesitant approach of a fearful penitent to the palace of the Divine King. The second time, it is chanted a little louder, with more confidence, as we approach the God of Mercy; and finally, it is chanted louder still, with great vitality, as might be expressed by one familiar with approaching the Almighty in His court.

Kol Nidrei is not really a prayer, for it never mentions God or even repentance and atonement, the major themes of the sacred day. Rather, it is a declaration of repudiation for the various categories of personal oaths and pledges. As *Kol Nidrei* is chanted by the cantor, the congregation recites along with him in a hushed undertone. The following translation is an approximation of the Aramaic text.

Recite *Kol Nidrei*

All personal vows, all prohibitions,
all personal oaths, all personal pledges,
or other such declarations that we are likely to make
from this Day of Atonement until the next Day of Atonement,
we hereby renounce them all publicly.
Let them all be canceled and abandoned,
null and void, without firmness or permanence.
Let our personal vows, pledges, and oaths
be considered neither vows nor pledges nor oaths.

Kol Nidrei is followed immediately by the following pleas for forgiveness:

Recite Immediately after *Kol Nidrei*

Cantor then Congregation (three times):
May the entire congregation of the Children of Israel be forgiven,
including the stranger who lives among them,
for all the people [have sinned] carelessly.
Cantor:
Please pardon the iniquities of this people,
according to Your abundant kindness,
as You have forgiven this people ever since they left Egypt.
Congregation and Cantor (three times):
The Lord said: "I forgive them as you have asked."

The *she'hecheyanu* blessing is then recited.

Recite *She'hecheyanu*

Cantor:

Baruch Atah, HaShem E-lo-kenu, Melech HaOlam,

she'hecheyanu, v'kiy'manu,

v'higiyanu laz'man hazeh.

❖

Blessed are You, Lord our God, King of the Universe,

Who has kept us alive, sustained us,

and brought us to this season.

Congregation:

Amen.

6.24 *Ma'ariv of Yom Kippur*

Following the recitation of *Kol Nidrei, Ma'ariv* for *Yom Kippur* begins with *Barchu* and *Kriat Shema.* After the *Chatzi Kaddish,* the "silent" *Shemoneh Esrei* is recited. It contains seven blessings, three preliminary, three concluding, and the middle blessing which pertains to the festival day itself.

The middle blessing contains four paragraphs, like that of other festivals, except *Musaf* of *Rosh HaShanah* (see Section 6.11.1). The first paragraph reminds us that God chose the Jewish people to receive the Torah, and, therefore, we have an obligation to discharge our responsibilities.

The second paragraph of the middle blessing continues the theme: God has chosen the Jewish people to give them *this day*. The solemnity of the day is highlighted in this paragraph. Add the parenthetical words on the Sabbath.

Recite in the Second Paragraph of the Middle Blessing of *Ma'ariv*

And You gave us, Lord our God, with love . . .
(this Sabbath day for holiness and rest and)
this Day of Atonement,
for pardon, forgiveness, and atonement,
wherein all our iniquities [will be] pardoned
(with love)
a holy gathering,
a reminder of the Exodus from Egypt.

The third paragraph of the middle blessing is *Ya'aleh v'Yavo.* Of course, we insert the words "on this Day of Atonement."

The last paragraph is special for the Day of Atonement. It is a prayer for God's forgiveness in which we beseech Him to wipe away our sins and grant us atonement through our repentance. Where appropriate, this prayer includes inserts for the Sabbath.

Conclude the Last Paragraph of the Middle Blessing of *Ma'ariv*

Blessed are You, Lord, King over all the earth,
Who sanctifies (the Sabbath),
Israel and the Day of Atonement.

The *Viduy* is the intense confessional prayer in the liturgy of the Day of Atonement.

6.24.1 The Confessional Prayers

After the last blessing of the *Shemoneh Esrei,* we find the confessional prayers, *Ashamnu* and *Al Chet*. When confessing, we stand in a contrite posture, with head and body bowed slightly. As we enumerate each sin, we strike the left side of the chest, near the heart, with the right fist.

It is noteworthy that the confession is recited in the plural, an indication that all Jews are responsible for one another (Talmud, *Masechet Shevuot* 39a). The *Viduy* is a collective confession in which all Jews atone for all sins committed by them as a people. It does not mean that every Jew is guilty of every specific sin, but we acknowledge that as a people we are guilty of all the sins we mention, even if we are not individually accountable for some of them.

Additionally, we confess in the past tense and admit to the sins of prior generations, for which, logically, we should not be accountable. However, we are liable for them, if we have adopted their practices or condoned, even by our silence, the unrepentant conduct of our ancestors.

Both confessional prayers are structured according to the Hebrew *alef-bet*. *Ashamnu* contains twenty-four statements, one for each of the twenty-two Hebrew letters, and two additional statements that begin with the last letter, *tav*.

Recite *Ashamnu*

We have become culpable;
we have betrayed and robbed and slandered;
we have caused corruption and wickedness;
we have willfully sinned;
we have extorted and lied;
we have sanctioned evil and practiced deception;
we have been scornful and rebellious;
we have been offensive and self-satisfied;
we have been devious and reckless;
we have tormented and been stubborn;
we have been evil and immoral;
we have been loathsome;
we have wandered away and You have let us wander away.

The *Viduy* continues, as we acknowledge that the Omniscient One knows all we have done and why. We can hide nothing from Him, because He knows all secrets.

The *Al Chet* is also structured according to the *alef-bet*, with two verses for every one of the letters. Every one of the forty-four statements of confession in the *Al Chet* begins with the same four Hebrew words, which are translated

For the sin we have sinned before You . . .

The forty-four verses are divided into three groups of twenty, twelve, and twelve. At the end of each group, we find the following verse.

For all of these [sins], God of forgiveness,
forgive us, pardon us, grant us atonement.

Let us look more closely at the text.

For the sin we have sinned before You . . .

- under duress and willingly
- by hardening the heart
- without knowing
- with the expression of our lips
- by immoral behavior
- in public and in private
- with knowledge and with deception
- with abusive speech
- by oppressing a neighbor
- with improper thoughts
- with lewd association
- by insincere confession
- by showing disdain for parents and teachers
- intentionally and unintentionally
- by the use of power
- by desecrating the Name
- with unclean lips
- with foolish speech
- by surrendering to the evil inclination
- against those who know and those who don't know

**For all of these [sins], God of forgiveness,
forgive us, pardon us, grant us atonement.**

- by denial and dishonesty
- by acceding to bribery
- by derision
- by defamation
- in business matters
- in matters of food and drink
- by usury and extortion
- by arrogance
- by a careless manner of speech
- by intrusive eyes
- by haughty looks
- by shameless conduct

For all of these [sins], God of forgiveness,
forgive us, pardon us, grant us atonement.

- by throwing off the yoke of responsibility
- by passing judgment
- by plotting against friends
- with a jealous eye
- by acting frivolously
- by being obstinate
- by running to perpetrate evil
- by gossiping
- by swearing in vain
- by baseless hatred
- by failing to extend a hand
- with a confused heart

For all of these [sins], God of forgiveness,
forgive us, pardon us, grant us atonement.

Al Chet concludes with an enumeration of the nine penalties for our sins. They include sacrificial offerings required for the least serious offenses to the death penalty for the most serious.

For the sins for which we are obligated to bring . . .

- a burnt-offering
- a sin-offering
- a variable-offering
- a guilt-offering
- corporal punishment (lashes)
- forty lashes
- premature death
- spiritual excision and childlessness
- four death penalties:
  stoning, burning, beheading, or strangling

In the absence of the *Bet HaMikdash,* penalties set forth in the Torah cannot be implemented. However, by focusing on the penalties for which we would be liable, we recognize the gravity of our offenses and are motivated to repent. Nevertheless, it is certain that God exacts the appropriate punishment, even if it appears to be an accidental or natural occurrence. Judaism does not believe in happenstance or coincidence.

After enumerating the penalties, we also confess to the sin of violating the positive and negative commandments. We have confessed to the sins we know about, and God knows the sins we do not know about.

We recognize our unworthiness, and as we approach the end of the *Viduy,* we plead for compassion and mercy once again.

Conclude the *Viduy*

My God,
before I was formed, I was worthless,
and now that I have been formed,
it is as if I were not formed.
I am dust in my life,
and [will be] even more so in my death.
In Your sight, I am an object filled with shame and humiliation.
May it be Your will, Lord, my God, and God of my forefathers,
that I sin no more.
In Your abundant mercy,
may You cleanse [away the sins]
I have committed against You—
but not by suffering or serious illness.

Both *Ashamnu* and *Al Chet* are recited in every *Shemoneh Esrei* and in every repetition of the *Amidah* by the cantor throughout *Yom Kippur,* except *Ne'ilah,* when only *Ashamnu* is recited.

After the "silent" *Shemoneh Esrei,* it is customary in many synagogues for the rabbi to deliver a sermon appropriate to the theme of the day. It is a time when the worshippers are especially receptive to a call for repentance and charity.

6.24.2 The Extended Prayers of *Ma'ariv*

Unlike other *Ma'ariv* services, the Evening Service of *Yom Kippur* continues with the recitation of numerous *Selichot,* penitential prayers. Once again, the recitation of the Thirteen Attributes of Mercy forms the focal point of these prayers, just as they do in the *Selichot* that were recited before *Rosh HaShanah* (see Section 6.1). The Ark is opened during these prayers, and the congregation rises.

In addition to *Selichot, Ma'ariv* is comprised of many *piyutim,* liturgical poems. In a poem styled after Jeremiah 18:6, God is compared to the master craftsmen who use their tools and raw material. So, too, He fashions the Jewish people in His hands.

As the service progresses, ***Shema Kolenu,*** Hear Our Voice, is recited responsively by the cantor and the congregation. One of the most heartfelt selections of the *Yom Kippur* liturgy, it awakens a profound emotional response, as we ask God not to cast us off from before His Presence. The cantor's plaintive cry fills the heart to overflowing with the tears of bygone centuries. Any translation is a poor attempt to capture the deep pathos and melancholy with which this prayer is imbued. The Ark is opened and the congregation rises.

Recite *Shema Kolenu*

Hear our voice, Lord our God, be merciful and gracious to us,
and accept our prayer with compassion and good will.

❖

Return us to You, Lord, and we shall return.
Renew our days as of old.

❖

Give ear to our words, God, and discern our thoughts.

❖

Do not cast us away from You, nor remove Your holy spirit from us.

❖

Do not cast us away in old age;
when our strength fails us, do not forsake us.

The two *Viduy* prayers, *Ashamnu* and *Al Chet,* are also repeated in the extended service of *Ma'ariv.* After numerous other prayers derived from *Tanach,* the Evening Service draws to a close with the recitation of *Avinu Malkenu* (see Section 6.12).

After the Full *Kaddish, Alenu,* and the Mourners' *Kaddish, Ma'ariv* concludes with Psalm 27 and *Adon Olam,* the hymn in which God is described as the Eternal One Who existed before the world was created and Who will exist after the world ends. It expresses in poetic language the ultimate trust we place in *HaShem* (see Section 3.7.1).

6.25 Shacharit of Yom Kippur

Shacharit includes all the preliminary Morning Blessings and Verses of Song (see Sections 3.7.1 and 3.7.2). Like the Morning Service of *Rosh HaShanah* (see Section 6.8), the *chazan* begins by proclaiming God the King, Who sits in judgment. These words serve as a transition between the preliminary benedictions and verses and the prelude to *Shacharit.* There are numerous *piyutim* inserted in the text before *Kriat Shema,* and on the Sabbath appropriate *tefillot* are also included.

6.25.1 Shemoneh Esrei of Shacharit

The "silent" *Amidah* is identical to that of *Ma'ariv,* with the exception of the final blessing for peace. This distinction occurs in the *tefillot* for the weekdays as well. After the last blessing, the Confessional Prayers are recited.

In the cantor's repetition of the *Amidah,* numerous *piyutim* specific to the Day of Atonement are woven within the text. Many of these liturgical poems contain acrostics, indicating the name of the poet. Like the ones found in the *Amidah* of *Rosh HaShanah,* their words convey the mood of the day (see Section 6.6). These amplifications of the *Amidah* enhance its significance by intensifying the mood of the day.

The repetition, once again, includes *Shema Kolenu, Ashamnu, Al Chet,* and *Avinu Malkenu. Kedushah* is also recited in the repetition.

6.25.2 Kedushah of Shacharit

On *Yom Kippur,* the *Kedushah* of *Shacharit* is identical to the one that is recited during the *Musaf* service of the Sabbath or festivals. We recite this *Kedushah* at *Shacharit,* because on *Yom Kippur,* we are considered like the angels, and are, thus, truly worthy to recite it.

6.26 Kriat HaTorah for Yom Kippur

On *Yom Kippur* morning, the Torah Reading is from *Parshat Achrei Mot,* Leviticus 16:1–34. Appropriately, it deals with the ordinances for the *Avodah,* the Temple service that was conducted by the *Kohen Gadol* in the *Bet HaMikdash* on *Yom Kippur.* The *Avodah* forms a major portion of the *Musaf* service, which we will discuss below.

Two Torahs are removed from the Ark, one for the Torah portion of the day and the other for *Maftir.* Six people are called to the Torah on *Yom Kippur* morning, one more than on other festivals. If *Yom Kippur* falls on the Sabbath, then seven *aliyot* are called.

The text describes how Aaron the High Priest was commanded to prepare himself and how he was to conduct the ritual of sacrifice on *Yom Kippur* to atone on behalf of himself, his family, and the Children of Israel. He was forbidden to enter the most sacred Holy of Holies, which was separated from the Sanctuary, except on the Day of Atonement.

After the festival portion has been read, the Torah is raised and fastened and temporarily set to the side. The second Scroll is unfastened, and the person honored with *Maftir* is called to the Torah. The *Maftir* portion is read from *Parshat Pinchas,* Numbers 29:7–11. These five verses explain the details of the additional offerings that were brought on *Yom Kippur.*

The *Haftarah* for *Yom Kippur* morning is from Isaiah 57:14–58:14. It deals with the prophet's rebuke to the Jewish people who complained that their fasting brought no material change in their lives. Isaiah chastised them, saying that true repentance required more than a pretense of fasting. He urged them to make a sincere commitment to turn their lives to the service of God by showing kindness to the poor and destitute. Such an expression of repentance would surely bring God's favor.

After the *Haftarah,* the *Sefer Torah* is not immediately returned to the Ark. At this point in the service, the rabbi usually delivers a sermon that serves as a prelude to the recitation of *Yizkor,* the memorial service.

6.27 *Yizkor:* Remembering the Souls of the Dead

The custom of reciting *Yizkor* dates back to antiquity. It is a reaffirmation of the Jewish belief in the eternity of the soul. By reflecting on the lives of departed relatives, by invoking the names of the righteous, and by pledging to donate to charitable causes in their memory, Jews preserve the spiritual link to their ancestors. As they recall the pure souls of those who died, they pray that the righteous will plead on their behalf before the Heavenly Court. They are reminded of their own mortality and are inspired to repent.

It is customary in some synagogues to read the names of the departed members of the congregation. In those synagogues that have lighted memorial tablets on the walls, the light beside each name is lit before *Kol Nidrei* and left burning throughout *Yom Kippur* day. Many congregations print special booklets that include the names of departed members and the memorial prayers that are to be recited.

During the *Yizkor* service, it is customary for children and adults whose parents are still alive to leave the synagogue. Contrary to a popular misconception, mourners who are within the first year after the death of their loved one should say *Yizkor.*

Yizkor may be recited for any deceased person, and there are appropriately worded texts for each: father, mother, spouse, brothers, sisters, grandfathers, grandmothers, aunts, uncles, as well as members of the extended family. *Yizkor* is also recited for the martyrs of the Holocaust and for Israeli soldiers killed in defense of *Eretz Yisrael.*

In many synagogues it is traditional to begin the *Yizkor* liturgy with the recitation of selected verses from the Psalms and Ecclesiastes.

Begin the *Yizkor* Liturgy

Lord, what is man that You should recognize him?
What is a mortal that You should consider him?
Man is like a breath, his days like a passing shadow.
He flourishes and is invigorated in the morning
and is felled and withers by evening.
Teach us how to reckon our days
that we may acquire a wise heart.
Guard the innocent and watch over the upright,
for peace is the future of such a man.
Surely God will free my soul from the grasp of the grave,
for He will take me, indeed.
My flesh and my heart falter, Rock of my heart,
my share is God forever.
Dust returns to the earth, as it was,
and the spirit returns to God Who gave it.

Many congregations then say Psalm 91 before beginning the *Yizkor* prayers. The text of *Yizkor* varies only in terms of the names and relationships that are inserted. Below is the text for a mother. The words in brackets are not part of the actual Hebrew text, but serve to clarify it.

Recite *Yizkor*

May God remember the soul
of my mother, my teacher
(her Hebrew name)
daughter of
(her father's Hebrew name)
who has gone to [eternal rest in] her world.
I pledge to give charity on her behalf.
As a reward for this,
may her soul be bound in the Bond of [Eternal] Life
with the souls of
Abraham, Isaac, and Jacob,
Sarah, Rebecca, Rachel, and Leah,
and with the other righteous men and women
in the Garden of Eden.
Amen.

Our pledge to give charity and our prayers on behalf of the dead bring credit to us and elevate the souls of our loved ones. The greater the merit achieved by the departed soul while on earth, together with the good deeds performed on behalf of the departed soul, the more it will rise to join together with the souls of the righteous patriarchs and matriarchs.

After *Yizkor,* an additional prayer for the soul of the departed is recited. It is a further request that God grant complete and perfect rest to the soul. Again, we pledge charity on behalf of the soul, which adds to its merit and elevates it. Of course, it is of great importance that we pay our pledges as soon after *Yom Kippur* as possible.

After *Yizkor,* the *Sifrei Torah* are returned to the Ark, and *Shacharit* is concluded. Many people think it is acceptable to leave the synagogue after *Yizkor.* It is not. For those who remain, the words and the melodies of the Additional Service that follows bring both physical and spiritual energy and historical insight.

6.28 *Musaf of Yom Kippur*

The *Musaf* service is comprised of some of the most awesome and inspiring prayers of the entire Day of Atonement. It begins with the cantor's dramatic, but humble, recitation of *Hineni* (see Section 6.11).

The *Shemoneh Esrei* contains seven blessings. Again, the first three are blessings of praise and the last three are blessings of thanksgiving. The fourth blessing deals with the holiness of the Day of Atonement. Of course, we continue to recite *Ashamnu* and *Al Chet* and to ask God to inscribe us in the Book of Life.

During the cantor's repetition of the *Amidah,* numerous *piyutim* are again included, and we invoke the wisdom of the ancient scholars whose words add poetry to the prayers. One poem recalls the image of "clay in the hands of the potter" (see Section 6.24.2). Still another pleads for the restoration of the Temple and the redemption of the Jewish people.

Again we recite Rabbi Amnon's haunting *U'Netaneh Tokef* and the vivid depiction of the Day of Judgment, *B'Rosh HaShanah* (see Section 6.11.1). Other *piyutim* lead up to and follow the *Kedushah,* which is the same as in *Shacharit* (see Section 6.25.2).

Blessing (4) of the *Shemoneh Esrei* includes the remarkable description of the *Avodah,* the Temple service that was conducted on *Yom Kippur* by the *Kohen Gadol.* We will focus most of our discussion of *Musaf* on this section of the *tefillot.*

6.28.1 The *Avodah*

The *Avodah* is one of the most majestic sections of the *Yom Kippur* prayers. It is introduced with the opening paragraph of *Alenu.* At the appropriate words, the Holy Ark is opened, and the cantor and the entire congregation, men and women, young and old, alike, to the best of their physical ability, kneel on the covered floor in worship to God. Although the daily ritual in the *Bet HaMikdash* included kneeling as a part of worship, today kneeling is permitted only on the *Yamim Nora'im* (see Section 6.11.3). It symbolizes the day's awesome solemnity, as Jews join at the same moment to kneel and accept God's sovereignty.

The description of the *Avodah,* which is sketched below, includes the preparations of the *Kohen Gadol* before *Yom Kippur,* as well as his actual *tefillot,* all of which are recited by the cantor and the congregation during *Musaf.*

Begin to Recite *Alenu*

It is our duty to praise the Master of all things,
to attribute greatness to the Creator,
for He has not made us like the nations of other lands,
nor placed us like other families of the earth. . . .
Cantor and Congregation Kneel Here:
We bend the knee and bow in worship,
Cantor and Congregation Rise Here:
acknowledging our thanks before the King of Kings,
the Holy One, blessed is He,
for it is He who stretched out the heavens
and founded the earth. . . .
He is our God, there is no other; . . .
as it is written in His Torah:
"You shall know this day,
and reflect on it in your heart,
that it is the Lord Who is God
in the heavens above and on the earth beneath,
there is nothing else."

Our understanding of the significance of the *Avodah* is enhanced when we realize that the destiny of the Jewish nation rested on the *Kohen Gadol's* ability to successfully atone before God on behalf of all the people on the Day of Atonement. Today, we have no Temple, and accordingly, our recitation of the *Avodah* replaces the ritual service itself.

According to the Mishnah, *Masechet Yoma* 1:1, and the Talmud, *Masechet Yoma* 2a, the *Kohen Gadol* left his home seven days before *Yom Kippur* and moved into a special chamber in the Temple Courtyard. The purpose of this was to preclude the possibility that he might become ritually impure and, therefore, prohibited from performing the Temple ritual. A second *Kohen* was prepared as a substitute in the event the *Kohen Gadol* became disqualified.

During that week of seclusion, the High Priest performed parts of the daily service—which were usually assigned to other *Kohanim*—so that he would become familiar with it. The *Kohen Gadol* had to be ready to conduct the *Yom Kippur* service by himself. Consequently, members of the *Sanhedrin* taught him the laws of the *Yom Kippur* ritual (*Parshat Acharei Mot,* Leviticus 16:1–33), in case he had forgotten it, or had never learned it.

On the morning of *Yom Kippur* eve, the sages escorted the *Kohen Gadol* to the Eastern Gate of the Courtyard and showed him the various animals that would be used in the sacrifices the following day.

Throughout the week, he had been permitted to eat as usual, but in the afternoon of *Yom Kippur* eve, he was permitted to eat only a little, lest overeating induce sleep, for he was not allowed to fall asleep.

The sages of the *Sanhedrin* relinquished him to the continuing vigilance of the elders of the priesthood, who exacted an oath from him to do exactly as they had instructed him. The *Kohen Gadol* swore an oath and wept because they suspected that he might not fulfill his duty properly; and they wept because they had to caution him, although they had no reason to doubt him.

By dawn of *Yom Kippur* day, the Courtyard was already filled with worshippers. The *Kohen Gadol* was then escorted to the ritual bath to immerse himself, even if he was not in a state of impurity, for no one could enter the Temple to perform the service otherwise.

During the course of the day, the *Kohen Gadol* would immerse himself and change his clothes five times and sanctify his hands and feet ten times. He wore gold embroidered vestments when he was performing those rituals not specifically associated with the sacrifices of atonement. He wore white linen when he performed the rituals associated with the sacrifices of atonement.

The *Kohen Gadol* dressed in gold embroidered vestments, prepared the lamps and the incense, and performed the daily morning sacrifice, the *Korban Tamid.* He also offered the ***Korban Musaf,*** the additional sacrifice associated with the festival day.

He then changed into white linen vestments, and with his hands on his bullock, he offered the first of three confessions for *Yom Kippur.*

The cantor and congregation chant the first confession.

Recite the Confession of the *Kohen Gadol*

And so he said:
"Lord, I beseech You,
for I have offended You,
transgressed, and willfully sinned against You,
I and my household.
Lord, I beseech You,
forgive the offenses, transgressions, and willful sins,
which I and my household
have committed before You,
as it is written in the Torah of Your servant Moses:
'On this day atonement shall be made for you,
to purify you from all your sins before the Lord.' "

The *Kohen Gadol* pronounced God's Name twice, uttering the true pronunciation of the four-letter name, the *Shem HaMeforash,* the Unutterable Name, which was said only on *Yom Kippur* (see Section 3.2). His moving and heartfelt plea resounded throughout the Courtyard, and when the *Kohanim* and worshippers who were assembled there heard him pronounce God's Unspoken Name, they fell on their knees, prostrated themselves, worshipped Him, and proclaimed:

Blessed be His Name, the Glory of His Kingdom is forever and ever.

So, too, the cantor and congregation fall on their knees and recite the very same blessing.

The *Kohen Gadol* completed the sacred utterance as they completed the blessing, and then he pronounced:

You will be cleansed.

After asking God to be merciful and forgive him, the *Kohen Gadol* continued the ritual. He prepared two goats as an atonement for the community. By drawing lots, it was determined that the first would be sacrificed as a sin-offering to *HaShem,* the second would be sent into the wilderness as a scapegoat for the sins of Israel. The *Kohen Gadol* tied a scarlet thread around the neck of the first goat and a second red string around the head of the second.

He then again placed his hands on his bullock and recited the same confession, but this time, on behalf of himself, his household, and all other *Kohanim*. Again, the priests and the people heard him pronounce the *Shem HaMeforash,* and again they all fell to their knees, prostrating themselves in worship. The *Kohen Gadol* completed the sacred utterance as they completed the blessing, and then he pronounced:

You will be cleansed.

Then the High Priest slaughtered his own bullock and then entered the Holy of Holies with an offering of incense, one of the most intricate rituals of the service. He placed the pan of incense between the staves of the Ark and left the Holy of Holies.

He then returned to the Holy of Holies where he sprinkled the blood of his bullock on the golden altar. The first goat was slaughtered as a sin-offering, and its blood was sprinkled on the altar as well. Then the altar was cleaned.

The *Kohen Gadol* recited the same confession, this time placing his hands on the head of the scapegoat. He asked for forgiveness for the intentional and unintentional sins of the people of Israel. Again the priests and the worshippers in the Courtyard heard him pronounce the Unutterable Name, and they fell on their knees, prostrated themselves, and worshipped God. The *Kohen Gadol* completed the sacred utterance as they completed the blessing, and then he pronounced:

You will be cleansed.

The *Kohen Gadol* signaled a designated man to lead the scapegoat into the wilderness, where it was sent to its death over a rocky cliff, symbolically removing the sin from the Jewish people. A messenger announced that the red thread on the head of the scapegoat had turned white, a miraculous sign that God had accepted the atonement of the people of Israel.

The *Kohen Gadol* continued the ritual sacrifice at the golden altar. He then recited aloud the Torah portion for the Day of Atonement. Afterwards, he changed into gold embroidered vestments and sacrificed one ram for himself and another for the people. He concluded the sacrifices of *Musaf* and the incense sacrifice of the bullock and the goat.

The High Priest changed into white vestments again and removed the implements of the incense offering from the Holy of Holies. Upon leaving, he offered the following prayer for his safe completion of the *Avodah* of *Yom Kippur,* for had he failed, he would have died there.

May it be Your will, Lord, our God, and God of our forefathers,
that the coming year shall be filled
with abundant prosperity for Your people Israel;
a year of grain, wine, and oil;
of attainment and success;
a year of meeting in Your Sanctuary . . .
a year of enjoyable life . . .
of dew, rain, and warmth . . .
a year in which You will bless our progeny
and the fruit of our land;
a year in which You will bless our comings and goings . . .
save our community . . . and be merciful to us . . .
a year of peace and serenity . . .
a year in which Your people Israel will not need one another's aid
nor the support of another people,
for You will bless the products of their own hands.

He changed into gold embroidered vestments again, completed the *Korban Musaf*, and offered the evening *Korban Tamid*.

He then put on his own clothes and was escorted to his home by the rejoicing throng. His face shone, for his very life and the destiny of the Jewish people had depended on his proper performance of the service of atonement. In appreciation for his safe return from the Holy of Holies, he declared a festival and made a feast for his family and friends.

6.28.2 The Ten Martyrs

Another major liturgical portion of the repetition of the *Amidah* of *Musaf* is the recitation of the Ten Martyrs. Written in the acrostic style of a liturgical poem, it is recited by the congregation and chanted by the cantor, often with great emotion and weeping, for it describes the brutal martyrdom of ten of the greatest sages and leaders of the Jewish people.

According to the liturgy and numerous midrashic sources, the evil Roman tyrant Hadrian filled his palace with shoes and summoned ten eminent sages of Israel to his palace. He asked them to render a decision on a verse in the Torah.

> **And he that kidnaps a man and sells him,**
> **and [if he is found guilty], he shall surely be put to death.**
> **—*Parshat Mishpatim,* Exodus 21:16**

The sages affirmed: "That kidnapper dies."

Because the ten sons of Jacob had sold their brother Joseph to a caravan of Ishmaelites for a sum of silver (*Parshat Vayeshev,* Genesis 37:27–28), with which they purchased shoes, and because no punishment had ever been exacted for that deed, the tyrant responded by demanding that the ten sages be condemned in their place.

The command to execute them all was given by the wicked despot. Rabbi Ishmael, the *Kohen Gadol,* and Rabban Simon ben Gamliel, the head of the *Sanhedrin,* were led to the execution site. Each wished to be the first to die, in order not to witness the other's murder. Lots were cast, and Rabban Simon was swiftly decapitated with a sword. Rabbi Ishmael wept, "Woe, that such as he, so wise in the Torah's teachings, should lick the dust."

Rabbi Ishmael was brutally whipped, and the skin of his face was ripped off while he was still alive. He endured his suffering with great courage, weeping only when the executioner reached the place of his *tefillin.*

The angels wailed, "Is this the reward for Torah?" and a heavenly voice cried out, "This is My decree."

Rabbi Akiva was martyred when they lacerated his body with combs of iron; yet he continued to pray with a peaceful smile on his face. He died as he finished the words of the *Shema:* The Lord is One.

Rabbi Chananiah ben Teradyon was wrapped in the Torah parchment from which he had been teaching and placed on a pyre of green wood, which did not burn readily. His body was repeatedly drenched with water to prolong the agony. He told his disciples, "I see the parchment burning, but the letters of the Torah soar heavenward." Despite their urging, he refused to open his mouth to allow the fire to consume him more quickly. "The one Who gives life should take it," he consoled them. The executioner was so moved that he fanned the flames to end the dying man's suffering and then immolated himself.

Six other eminent sages of Israel were also tortured to death: Rabbi Chuspit the Interpreter; Rabbi Elazar ben Shamua; Rabbi Chaninah ben Chanikai; Rabbi Yeshevav the Scribe; Rabbi Judah ben Dama; and Rabbi Judah ben Bava.

According to the Talmud, not all of these deaths occurred on the same day, so this liturgical account is presented in such a dramatic fashion in order to heighten the emotions and bring about further repentance. However, it is historically true that Rome forbade the establishment of Jewish schools and the teaching of Torah, and that all these scholars and teachers of Israel died as martyrs. The *tefillah* ends with the following supplication:

> This has befallen us; we pour it out with a grieving heart.
> From heaven, heed our plea;
> You, Lord, are a merciful and compassionate God.
> Look down from on high and see the blood of the righteous;
> remove all stains of guilt, God,
> King Who sits on the throne of mercy.

By their martyrdom, these sages of Israel sanctified the Name of God. Their sacrifice is eternally etched in the collective memory of the Jewish people.

6.28.3 The Conclusion of *Musaf*

Shema Kolenu, Ashamnu, and *Al Chet* follow soon after, as we continue to plead before the Almighty. Blessings (5) and (6) of *Shemoneh Esrei* are repeated. If *Kohanim* are present, the Priestly Blessing is then recited (see Section 7.8.2). Blessing (7) concludes the *Amidah*. Then the Ark is opened, and the concluding prayer is recited. The congregation recites *amen* after each verse.

Conclude the Repetition of *Musaf*

> Today, strengthen us.
> Today, bless us.
> Today, exalt us.
> Today, seek us out for goodness.
> Today, hear our cry.
> Today, accept our prayers with mercy and grace.
> Today, sustain us with the righteousness of Your right hand.

The Full *Kaddish* is then recited, and *Musaf* is concluded. In most synagogues, *Musaf* ends in mid afternoon. It has been an arduous day, made more intense by the repeated confessions, emotional prayers, and the continuing fast. Most congregations return for *Minchah* later in the afternoon.

6.29 Minchah of Yom Kippur

The distinguishing features of the liturgy of *Minchah* are the *Kriat HaTorah* and the recitation of the entire Book of Jonah, which we will discuss in the next section.

Throughout the day, the Jewish people have fasted and prayed, seeking God's divine forgiveness and acceptance of their atonement. In the Afternoon Service, Jews continue to ask God to *inscribe* them in the Book of Life for the new year.

The *Amidah* of *Minchah* contains seven blessings and is identical to the *Ma'ariv Amidah* recited on the eve of *Yom Kippur,* with the exception of the variation in the seventh prayer for peace. After the *Shemoneh Esrei,* the *Viduy* is again recited.

In the cantor's repetition, numerous *piyutim* and *Kedushah* are inserted. *Shema Kolenu* is followed by the *Viduy.* After Blessing (7), the Full *Kaddish* brings *Minchah* to an end.

6.30 Kriat HaTorah for Minchah

Kriat HaTorah and the recitation of the *Haftarah* from the Book of Jonah both precede the *Shemoneh Esrei.* The Torah portion is from *Parshat Acharei Mot,* Leviticus 18:1–30, and is divided into three *aliyot: Kohen, Levi,* and *Yisrael.* The third *aliyah* also serves as the *Maftir* for the *Haftarah.*

Chapter 18 of Leviticus enumerates the sexual relationships forbidden by the Torah. The concept of family purity is at the heart of Jewish life and provides a moral dimension to the most intimate of human relationships (see Section 9.6). How does this relate to the themes of *Yom Kippur?* By hearing this chapter and reflecting on it, worshippers are reminded that any of them who have sinned in the manner the Torah describes should repent.

The recitation of the Book of Jonah is considered a great honor, because its message is so central to the theme of repentance. Therefore, the *aliyah* of *Maftir* is highly prized. The connection between this prophetic reading and *Yom Kippur* is to teach us that true repentance can alter Heaven's decree. Additionally, the text teaches that no human being can take flight from the Almighty, as Jonah tried to do.

6.31 *Ne'ilah:* The Concluding Service

As twilight descends, the *Ne'ilah* service symbolizes the imminent closing of the Gates of Heaven. As the most sacred day of the Jewish year approaches its finale, the worshippers now ask that the Almighty *seal* them in the Book of Life, that He grant them the atonement for which they have prayed and fasted throughout the entire night and day.

Ne'ilah begins before sunset with the recitation of *Ashrei*. It continues into nightfall and includes the "silent" *Amidah,* which is comprised of seven blessings. The four insertions, which have been included throughout the *Yamim Nora'im* (see Sections 6.7.1 and 6.7.2), are also included; but in Blessings (1), (5), and (7), the inserts are modified. Our destiny has been determined. On *Rosh HaShanah,* it *was* inscribed, and on *Yom Kippur,* it is sealed, so we pray in Blessing (1):

Remember us for life, King Who desires life,
and *seal* us in the Book of Life—
for Your sake, Living God.

and in Blessing (5):

And *seal* all the Children of Your covenant for a good life.

and in Blessing (7):

In the book of life, blessing, and peace, and good sustenance,
may we and Your entire people,
the House of Israel,
be remembered and *sealed* before You
for a good life and for peace

Another change is that in the *Amidah,* we recite *Ashamnu,* but not the full *Viduy.* This will be the very last opportunity of *Yom Kippur* to truly repent.

As the cantor begins the repetition of *Ne'ilah,* the Ark is opened, and everyone rises and remains standing (if physically possible) throughout the entire service. Together, worshippers seem like one penitent, united in their expectation and faith that the Divine Judge will, indeed, grant their petition at this time of *Ne'ilah,* this hour of closing.

Numerous *piyutim* are again inserted into the repetition. They again recall the three patriarchs. *Kedushah* is also chanted again, as it has been in each of the previous services. Within Blessing (4), *Ya'aleh v'Yavo* is recited, and then we return to the familiar *Selichot* prayers, including the Thirteen Attributes of Mercy (see Section 6.1). This prayer is recited eight times in the repetition of *Ne'ilah*, for we recall that God promised to take heed of the prayers that included it.

So, one last time we recite *Ashamnu*.

Recite *Ashamnu* for *Ne'ilah*

We have become culpable;
we have betrayed and robbed and slandered;
we have caused corruption and wickedness;
we have willfully sinned;
we have extorted and lied;
we have sanctioned evil and practiced deception;
we have been scornful and rebellious;
we have been offensive and self-satisfied;
we have been devious and reckless;
we have tormented and been stubborn;
we have been evil and immoral;
we have been loathsome;
we have wandered away and You have let us wander away.

One of the last liturgical compositions of *Ne'ilah* is also one of the most touching.

Recite at the Conclusion of *Ne'ilah*

You reach out a hand to sinners,
and Your right hand is extended to accept the repentant.
You taught us, Lord, God, to confess our sins . . .
so You will accept us in perfect repentance, as You promised. . . .
You know that our ultimate end is the worm,
so You have graciously provided abundant pardon.
What are we? What is our life?
What is our goodness? What is our righteousness?
What is our salvation? What is our strength?
What is our might?
What can we say to You, Lord,
our God and God of our forefathers?
All heroes are like nothing in Your sight;
all the famous like they never existed;
the wise are without wisdom and the intelligent without insight;
their deeds are worthless and their lives empty.
Mankind's superiority over the beasts does not exist,
for everything is vanity.

After Blessing (7), the *Avinu Malkenu* is recited to *Ne'ilah,* even if *Yom Kippur* coincides with the Sabbath. The cantor chants the last of the forty-three verses, and the congregation repeats it.

Conclude *Avinu Malkenu*

Our Father, our King,
be gracious to us and answer us,
though we have no meritorious deeds;
treat us charitably and kindly,
and save us.

The Ark is closed, but the congregation remains standing. The moment of closing is upon us.

Ne'ilah concludes with the recitation of the *Shema Yisrael.* With fervor, the *chazan* chants and the congregation repeats the six timeless words of the Jewish faith:

Recite the Concluding *Shema Yisrael* for *Ne'ilah*

Shema Yisrael, HaShem E-lo-kenu, HaShem Echad.

❖

Hear, O Israel, the Lord is our God, the Lord is One.

Then, three times we pray:

Blessed be His Name, the Glory of His Kingdom is forever and ever!

❖

Blessed be His Name, the Glory of His Kingdom is forever and ever!

❖

Blessed be His Name, the Glory of His Kingdom is forever and ever!

Finally, seven times, with great exuberance

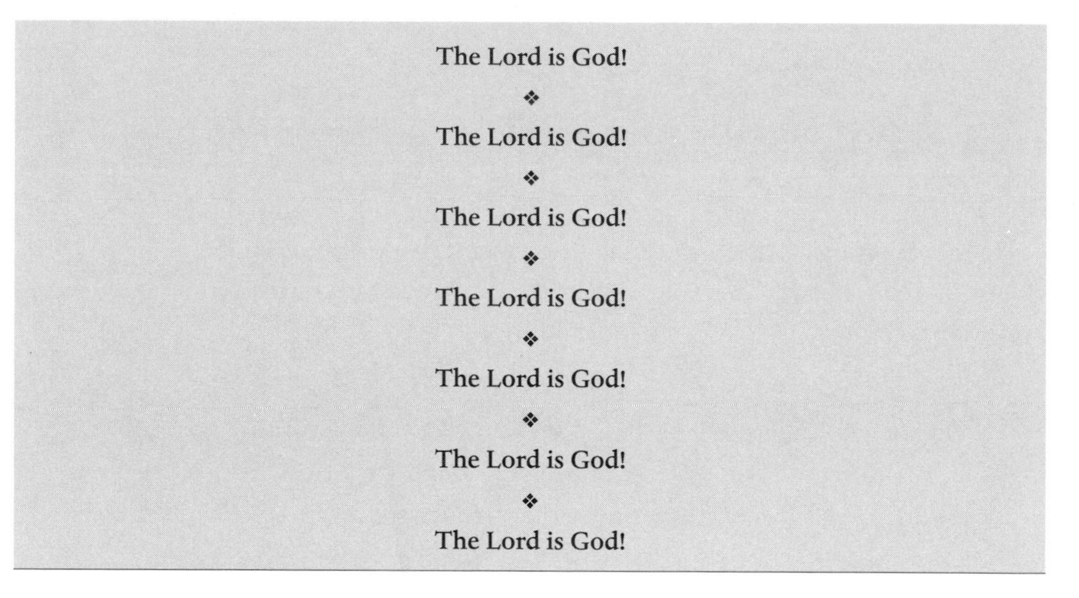

The Lord is God!

❖

The Lord is God!

❖

The Lord is God!

❖

The Lord is God!

❖

The Lord is God!

❖

The Lord is God!

❖

The Lord is God!

The piercing sound of the *shofar* follows—*tekiah gedolah*—and the eternal wish resounds throughout the synagogue.

Next year in Jerusalem!

The Day of Atonement has concluded.

LOOKING AHEAD! *In Chapter 7, we will discuss the three Pilgrimage Festivals: the Festival of Passover, the Festival of Weeks, and the Festival of Tabernacles.*

Word Works

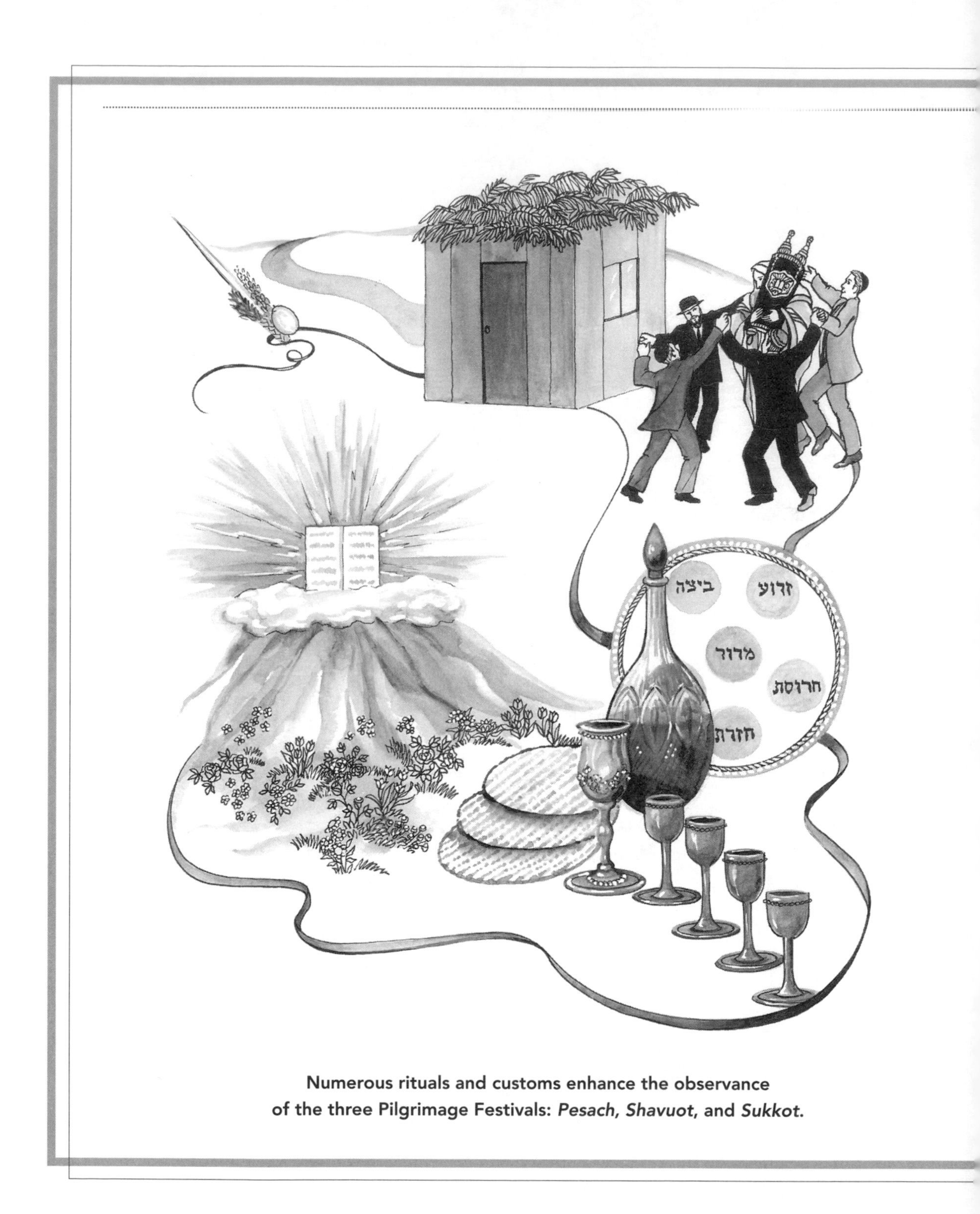

Numerous rituals and customs enhance the observance of the three Pilgrimage Festivals: *Pesach*, *Shavuot*, and *Sukkot*.

7

The Pilgrimage Festivals

HE THREE PILGRIMAGE Festivals, the ***Shalosh Regalim,*** correspond to the annual pilgrimages made by the Jewish people during the days of the Holy Temple. The word *regalim* is derived from the Hebrew word ***regel,*** meaning *foot.* Three times a year Jews came to Jerusalem to worship at the *Bet HaMikdash* and to bring special festival sacrifices as required by the Torah.

The *Shalosh Regalim* are: ***Chag HaPesach,*** the Festival of Passover, ***Chag HaShavuot,*** the Festival of Weeks, and ***Chag HaSukkot,*** the Festival of Tabernacles. They are known by several names in the Torah and the liturgy, but they are listed together as the *Shalosh Regalim* in the Torah, as follows:

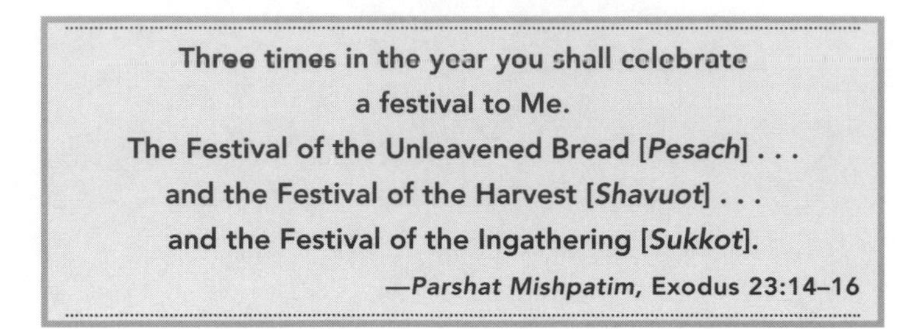
Three times in the year you shall celebrate
a festival to Me.
The Festival of the Unleavened Bread [*Pesach*] . . .
and the Festival of the Harvest [*Shavuot*] . . .
and the Festival of the Ingathering [*Sukkot*].
—*Parshat Mishpatim,* Exodus 23:14–16

As we examine each of these festivals, we will notice some similarities among them and learn the distinctive traditions, customs, and ceremonies that make their observance unique in Jewish life.

7.1 Passover

The first festival of the Jewish calendar, *Pesach,* is most often referred to in English as Passover. It celebrates and commemorates the deliverance of the Jewish people from the tyranny and slavery of the Egyptian Pharaoh more than three thousand years ago. The story of the Exodus is God's declaration of His power, as He brings His might to bear against the limited mortal power of the Egyptian Pharaoh.

7.1.1 The Jewish People in Egypt

How did the Jewish people come to be in Egypt in the first place? According to the biblical account in the Book of Genesis, there was a great famine in Canaan, and ten of Jacob's sons traveled to Egypt, hoping to purchase grain. Joseph, the patriarch's eleventh son, had been sold into slavery by his brothers. At the time of the famine in Canaan, Joseph was serving as viceroy to the Egyptian Pharaoh, whose dreams he had interpreted. As a result, the storehouses in Egypt overflowed because Joseph had foreseen the need to establish granaries. Joseph and his brothers were reunited, and they ultimately brought their father to Egypt and settled there.

In time, another Pharaoh came to the throne. Fearing that the multitude of Jews would rise up against him, he enslaved them and, in the belief that their numbers would increase, he issued a decree that all their newborn sons were to be drowned in the Nile River.

7.1.2 The Designation of Moses

The Book of Exodus goes on to relate the story of the birth of Moses, the Father of the Prophets, who was destined to lead his people out of Egypt and to the Promised Land of Canaan. Moses, the younger son of Amram and Yocheved from the tribe of Levi, was raised in the court of the Pharaoh, because he had been rescued from the waters of the Nile by Pharaoh's daughter.

As he grew up, he perceived the cruelty of the Pharaoh and killed an Egyptian taskmaster who mercilessly whipped a Jewish slave. Moses fled Egypt in fear of the wrath of Pharaoh who wanted to kill him. He traveled to Midian where he met Yitro, the priest of Midian, and married his oldest daughter, Tzipporah. As Moses tended the flocks of his father-in-law, God revealed Himself to Moses through the Burning Bush. God chose him and his brother Aaron to be the leaders of the Jewish people, and He charged Moses with leading them out of the slavery of Egypt to the Promised Land.

> **And the Lord said [to Moses],**
> **"Surely, I have seen the affliction of My people in Egypt,**
> **and I have heard their cry . . .**
> **and I have come down to deliver them**
> **from the hand of the Egyptians**
> **and to bring them out of that land**
> **into a good and broad land flowing**
> **with milk and honey; . . .**
> **and, therefore, I will send you to Pharaoh**
> **to bring My people, the Children of Israel, out of Egypt."**
>
> —*Parshat Shemot*, Exodus 3:7–8, 10

7.1.3 The Confrontation with Pharaoh

Moses returned to Egypt, and he and Aaron confronted Pharaoh with God's demand: Let all the Children of Israel, men, women, and children alike, together with their sheep and cattle, leave Egypt for three days to worship God in the wilderness.

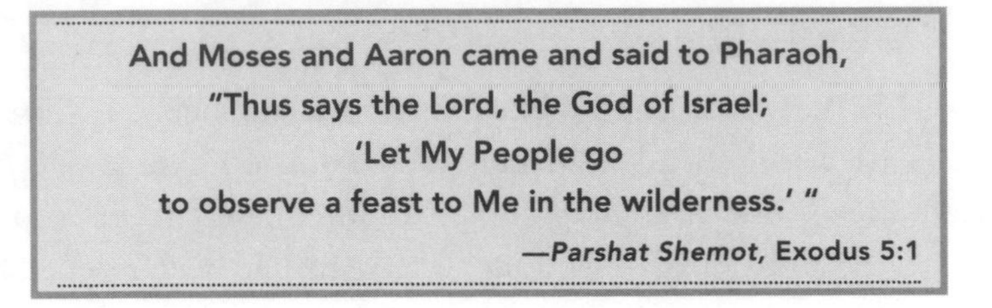

> **And Moses and Aaron came and said to Pharaoh,**
> **"Thus says the Lord, the God of Israel;**
> **'Let My People go**
> **to observe a feast to Me in the wilderness.' "**
>
> —***Parshat Shemot,*** **Exodus 5:1**

Moses and Aaron approached Pharaoh several times in the Name of the Jewish God asking him to allow the Israelites to leave Egypt to worship God, but his heart was hardened, and he repeatedly refused.

7.1.4 The Plagues

Displaying His omnipotence, God marshaled the forces of nature and brought numerous plagues down upon Egypt:

1. God turned all the water in Egypt to blood.
2. God caused the land to be overrun with frogs.
3. God caused lice to swarm over the land.
4. God sent the plague of evil beasts, serpents, and scorpions.
5. God smote the herds and the flocks with pestilence.
6. God caused the Egyptians to be covered with boils.
7. God caused thunder and hail to rain down on Egypt,
   and everyone and everything it touched died.
8. God caused locusts to swarm over Egypt, eating anything that remained after the hail.
9. God brought total darkness upon Egypt for three days.

After the ninth plague, Pharaoh threatened Moses and told him not to approach him again, and Moses assured him that Pharaoh would not see his face again.

7.1.5 The Paschal Sacrifice

Yet a tenth plague would strike the Egyptians: the death of the first-born. Before this could take place, God instructed Moses and Aaron about the festival sacrifice for *Pesach.*

> This month [*Nisan*] shall be the beginning
> of the months . . .
> the first month of the year.
> Speak to the congregation of Israel, saying,
> "On the tenth day of this month,
> every man shall take a lamb . . .
> a male yearling without blemish . . .
> and keep it until the fourteenth day of the month
> and slaughter it at dusk."
>
> —*Parshat Bo,* Exodus 12:2–3, 5–6

Moses instructed the Jewish people to slaughter the lamb—an Egyptian deity—as a sacrifice and to mark their doorposts with its blood. After marking their doorways, they roasted the lamb, called the ***Korban Pesach,*** and ate it with unleavened bread and bitter herbs.

> . . . and you shall eat it in haste—
> it is the *Pesach* of the Lord.
> For I will go through the land of Egypt in the night,
> and I will smite all the first-born in the land of Egypt,
> both man and beast.
>
> —*Parshat Bo,* Exodus 12:11–12

The following verse pinpoints why the festival is called Passover.

> And the blood [of the Paschal lamb]
> shall be a sign upon the houses where you are;
> and when I see the blood, I will pass over you;
> and there shall be no plague upon you,
> to destroy you,
> when I smite the land of Egypt.
>
> —*Parshat Bo,* Exodus 12:13

7.1.6 The Prohibition of Leaven

God further commanded:

> **For seven days you shall eat unleavened bread . . .**
> **and . . . put away leaven from your houses;**
> **whoever eats leavened bread shall be**
> **cut off from Israel. . . .**
>
> —*Parshat Bo,* Exodus 12:15

What is unleavened bread? The simple answer is: bread that contains no leavening. Unleavened bread is called ***matzah.*** Any products that cause fermentation to occur so that dough rises are prohibited on Passover. These products constitute the basic form of ***chametz,*** leavening.

On Passover, the Jewish people are forbidden to eat, or even have in their possession, any trace of *chametz,* which results when any of five types of grain—wheat, barley, spelt, rye, and oats—or their derivatives, remain in contact with water for at least eighteen minutes. At that time, the leavening process begins. Any food, drink, or other substance that contains even a minute amount of *chametz* may not be consumed or used on *Pesach.*

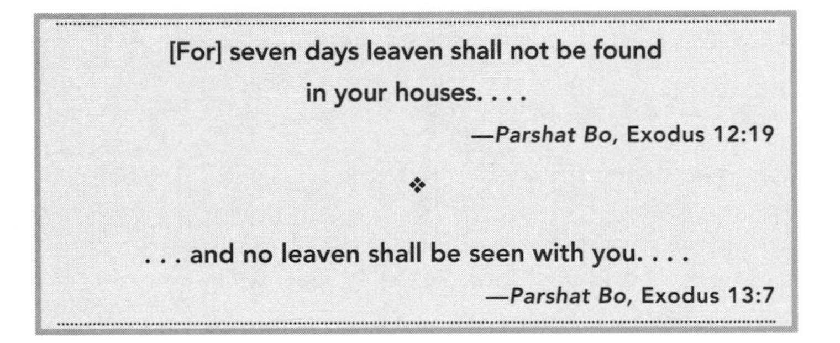
[For] seven days leaven shall not be found
in your houses. . . .

—*Parshat Bo,* Exodus 12:19

❖

. . . and no leaven shall be seen with you. . . .

—*Parshat Bo,* Exodus 13:7

According to the Mishnah, *Masechet Pesachim* 2:5, flour from any of these grains may be used on Passover for *matzah,* but it must be mixed quickly with water—which itself acts like a leavening agent in combination with the flour—formed into dough, and baked within eighteen minutes. Otherwise, it is certain that *chametz* will have formed.

Chametz can be found not only in bread, rolls, and bagels, but also in cakes, cookies, muffins, pies, all pasta products, candy and gum, juices, oils, spices, processed meats, cosmetics, cereals, toothpaste and mouthwash, baby powder, vinegar, whiskey, ice cream, medications, and myriad other products. Even the wrappers on paper towels may contain cornstarch, a form of *chametz*. Additionally, Ashkenazic (and some Sephardic) Jews do not eat rice, corn, beans, peas, lentils, and other legumes on Passover.

All products used on Passover and throughout the year must carry the symbol of a reputable kosher supervision service (see section 9.7.5) to ensure their acceptability for the Jewish home. Passover products must also bear the label "Kosher for Passover" on the packaging.

The laws of *chametz* are very intricate, so it is necessary to study these *halachot* prior to *Pesach*. Many Passover guides are also available, and if a question arises, a qualified rabbi should be consulted.

7.1.7 The Tenth Plague

At midnight God brought the tenth and final plague. The day of redemption was at hand.

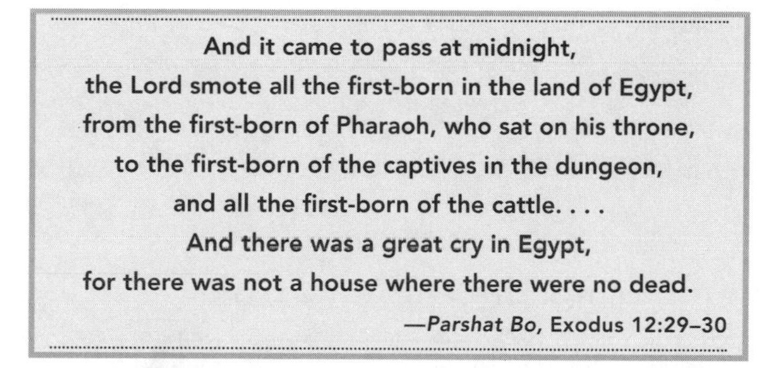

And it came to pass at midnight,
the Lord smote all the first-born in the land of Egypt,
from the first-born of Pharaoh, who sat on his throne,
to the first-born of the captives in the dungeon,
and all the first-born of the cattle. . . .
And there was a great cry in Egypt,
for there was not a house where there were no dead.

—***Parshat Bo,*** **Exodus 12:29–30**

The death of the first-born of every household in Egypt—but not among the Jewish people—forced Pharaoh to acknowledge the power of the God of Israel. His own son was dead, but Pharaoh, himself a first-born son, did not die, in order that he might bear witness to the might of the God of Israel. He called for Moses and Aaron, telling them to take all the Children of Israel out of Egypt to serve their Lord.

After hundreds of years in Egypt, including the years in slavery, a multitude of Jews—men, women, and children—left Egypt in great haste. They did not have time to let their dough rise, so they took with them the flat, unleavened bread called ***matzot,*** which symbolize both the haste with which the Israelites left Egypt and the *poor* bread they ate in slavery.

Finally, in the spring of 1312 B.C.E., Moses, the greatest of Judaism's prophets, led the Exodus from Egypt, as God commanded him.

> **And the Children of Israel**
> **journeyed . . . on foot,**
> **some six hundred thousand adults,**
> **[not including]**
> **the little ones.**
> **And also a diverse throng . . . went with them,**
> **[as did] flocks and herds and many cattle.**
>
> **—*Parshat Bo,* Exodus 12:37–38**

God proclaimed the festival as an eternal reminder of their redemption from Egypt:

> **The first and seventh days [of the festival]**
> **shall be a holy convocation . . .**
> **and you shall observe the [festival of] unleavened bread; . . .**
> **for on this day I brought you out of the land of Egypt;**
> **thus, you shall observe it throughout your generations,**
> **as an ordinance forever.**
>
> **—*Parshat Bo,* Exodus 12:16–17**

7.2 Remembering the Redemption

Passover is celebrated in the month of *Nisan,* which corresponds to March or April in the secular calendar (see Chapter 4). The Sabbath before *Rosh Chodesh Nisan,* when we bless the new month, is called *Shabbat HaChodesh,* and it is one of the four special Sabbaths in the Jewish calendar (see Section 4.6.13). *Shabbat HaChodesh* may also fall on *Rosh Chodesh* itself, that is, on the first day of *Nisan.* The following Sabbath, the one just before Passover, is called *Shabbot HaGadol,* the Great Sabbath. There is a special Torah reading for *Shabbat HaChodesh* and a special *Haftarah* for both *Shabbat HaChodesh* and *Shabbat HaGadol.*

Passover begins on the evening of the fourteenth day of *Nisan,* and lasts for eight days in the Diaspora.

Calendar for the First Day of *Pesach*

Secular Year	Hebrew Year	Day of the Week	Secular Date
2001	5761	Sunday	April 8
2002	5762	Thursday	March 28
2003	5763	Thursday	April 17
2004	5764	Tuesday	April 6
2005	5765	Sunday	April 24
2006	5766	Thursday	April 13
2007	5767	Tuesday	April 3
2008	5768	Sunday	April 20
2009	5769	Thursday	April 9
2010	5770	Tuesday	March 30

In Israel, it is observed for seven days, according to the biblical precept.

> **And in the first month,**
> **on the fourteenth day of the month is the Lord's Passover;**
> **and on the fifteenth day of this month, shall be a feast;**
> **[for] seven days unleavened bread shall be eaten.**
>
> —*Parshat Pinchas,* Numbers 28:16–17

7.2.1 Other Festival Names

The name *Chag HaPesach,* Festival of Passover, also refers to the *Korban Pesach,* the Paschal sacrifice that was prepared and eaten in Egypt on the eve of the redemption. The festival is also known by several other names:

1. ***Chag HaMatzot,*** the Festival of Unleavened Bread, commemorating the hasty departure of the Israelites from Egypt
2. ***Z'man Cherutenu,*** the Season of Our Freedom, a reminder of the miraculous liberation of the Jewish people after hundreds of years of slavery

We find these names in the Torah and in the festival liturgy.

You, Lord, our God, have given us in love
(Sabbaths for rest,)
holidays for gladness, festivals for happiness,
on this (Sabbath and this)
Festival of Unleavened Bread, the Season of Our Freedom.

3. ***Chag HaAviv***, the Festival of Spring, denoting the season of the year and hinting at its agricultural significance as a time of harvest, when a measure of barley was brought as a sacrifice to the Temple

In the Torah, several references to *Aviv* are found, including:

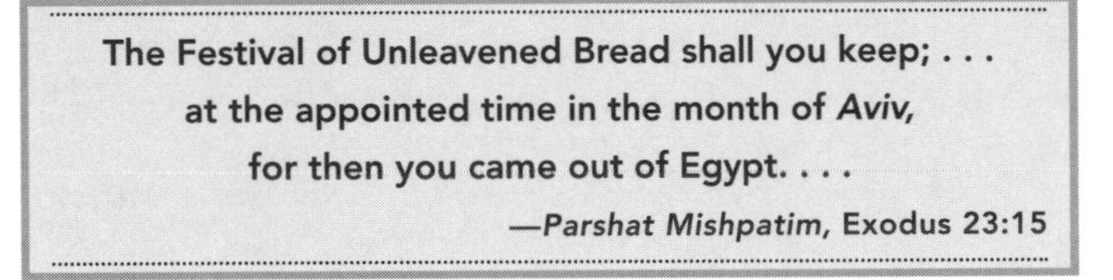
The Festival of Unleavened Bread shall you keep; . . .
at the appointed time in the month of *Aviv*,
for then you came out of Egypt. . . .
—*Parshat Mishpatim*, Exodus 23:15

7.2.2 Predominant Themes

Passover is the story of the liberation of an enslaved people and the birth of the Jewish nation. The predominant theme of the celebration is the retelling of the story of the redemption from Egyptian bondage. So crucial is this recitation, that it is a part of the first of the Ten Commandments given by God at Mount Sinai.

I am the Lord your God
Who brought you out of the land of Egypt,
out of the house of bondage.

Similarly, the *Shema*, the most important prayer in Jewish life (see Section 3.7.4), the Jew's declaration of his belief in the Unity of God, concludes with these words:

I am the Lord your God
Who brought you out of the land of Egypt to be your God;
I am the Lord your God.

It is incumbent upon every generation of Jews to tell their children the story of the liberation of the Jewish people from Egyptian bondage. Nowhere in Jewish ritual is this more evident than in the Passover ceremony called the ***seder.*** Passover is a family-oriented holiday. Often, relatives and friends from far and near gather to celebrate the Passover *seder* together. It is an ideal time for the story of the Exodus to be told.

No less important in this time of reuniting families is the *mitzvah* of ***ma'ot chitim*** (literally, money for wheat), providing funds for *matzah* and other Passover necessities for the poor. As we prepare to sit down at our *seder* table laden with God's bounty, it is incumbent upon us to remember less fortunate Jews in our own community and elsewhere. Often the synagogue collects money for this purpose, which is distributed before the holiday so people have time to shop and prepare. In addition, several Jewish organizations provide food to the poor throughout the year, and Passover is an especially important time to support these communal efforts.

7.3 Preparing for Passover

In the Jewish home, preparations for Passover begin early, often a month before. The house is cleaned from basement to attic. Closets and cabinets are emptied, drawers are tidied, pockets are turned inside out, and schoolbags are thoroughly examined. All traces of crumbs must be removed throughout the house, because on Passover, Jews are forbidden to eat, or even have in their possession, any trace of *chametz.*

There is a special quality, a difference, attached to the festival because the preparations for the holiday include the complete removal of all dishes, cooking utensils, flatware, and the like, that are used during the year with bread and other products that contain *chametz.* Special dishes and utensils, used only on Passover, are unpacked. The novelty of taking out the special dishes, which have been packed away all year long, adds to the festivities.

7.3.1 Selling the *Chametz*

All food that is not permitted during the holiday must be burned or sold to a non-Jew, as explained below. Jews must remove from their possession—that is, from their ownership—all items which have been used with or contain *chametz;* for example, dishes, glassware, pots and pans, silverware, baking utensils, plastic tablecloths, food containers, dish racks and trays, small appliances, *blech,* and bottles of liquor. This applies both to *chametz* found in their homes, vehicles, and business establishments.

It would be very difficult to dispose of all *chametz* by burning, as required by Jewish law. Accordingly, the *halachah* provides a legal alternative: Before Passover begins, arrangements are made to sell such goods to a non-Jew. The rabbi often acts as the agent (although any Jew can act on his own behalf), representing individuals in the Jewish community to the non-Jew, who takes legal possession of the *chametz* by making a down payment on the full value of the goods.

In the ***shtar harsha'ah,*** the document of authorization between the rabbi and the seller, the names and addresses of all the Jews who entered into the contract are listed. An inventory of the types of objects which contain *chametz* is included as well. A separate document, called a ***shtar mechirah,*** a bill of sale, is drawn up between the rabbi, as agent, and the non-Jew as buyer. It names the rabbi as agent on behalf of those listed in the *shtar harsha'ah.* It also indicates where these items are to be stored during the festival.

After Passover, immediately following the conclusion of the holiday, the rabbi, again acting as the agent for those he represents, meets with the non-Jew to conclude the transaction. If the non-Jew wants to buy all the property that contains *chametz,* he must pay for the goods themselves, inasmuch as it is impossible to sell just the *chametz* from the items. If the non-Jew does not want to buy the *chametz,* that is, the items that contain it, his down payment is refunded, and the right of ownership returns to the Jews named in the contract. It is common to offer the non-Jew a small profit for selling the *chametz* back to the Jew, although this cannot be a condition of the sale. This transaction is *not* a *token gesture or a legal fiction.* It is considered a binding contract which may be enforced legally, both in Jewish and civil law.

7.3.2 Searching for the *Chametz*

On the night before the eve of Passover, after the house has been scrupulously cleaned, ***Bedikat Chametz,*** Search for the *Chametz,* begins. It is customary to cut a slice of bread into ten small pieces and place them in rooms throughout the house, wherever *chametz* may have been used during the year. By doing this, the blessing recited before the search which contains God's Name, will not be recited in vain. The following *berachah* is recited as the search commences.

Recite before Searching for the *Chametz*

Baruch Atah, HaShem E-lo-kenu, Melech HaOlam,
asher kidshanu b'mitzvotav v'tzivanu
al biur chametz.

❖

Blessed are You, Lord our God, King of the Universe,
Who has sanctified us with His commandments and commanded us
concerning the burning of *chametz.*

Children, too, are eager to participate in this *mitzvah,* and in many homes, they are the ones who hide the *chametz* before the search begins. By candlelight, the family proceeds through the house, searching for the small pieces of bread, the last bits of *chametz* to be found in the house. The use of a candle is required by the Mishnah, *Masechet Pesachim* 1:1, so that the search will be carefully conducted and every nook and cranny meticulously examined.

The pieces of *chametz* are brushed with a feather into a wooden spoon. After the ten pieces have been found, the spoon, feather, and candle are wrapped and tied together and placed conspicuously by the door. Special *Bedikat Chametz* kits, containing the feather, candle, spoon, and a copy of the appropriate prayers, are usually available from Jewish bookstores or from the synagogue.

After the search has been completed, the Declaration of Nullification is pronounced stating that all *chametz* which has been seen and unseen, shall now be null, like the dust of the earth.

Recite after Searching for the *Chametz*

Any *chametz* in my possession,
which I did not see, nor remove, nor know about,
shall be considered nullified and ownerless,
like the dust of the earth.

7.3.3 The Fast of the First-Born

In gratitude to God for the deliverance of the first-born of the Israelites during the tenth plague, it is obligatory for first-born sons to fast on the day before Passover, beginning at dawn. However, it is permissible to break this fast in order to participate in a

se'udat mitzvah, a repast associated with a *mitzvah.* This is accomplished by the completion of a tractate of the Talmud, called a ***siyum.***

It has become the custom to conduct the ***Siyum B'chorim,*** *Siyum* of the First-Born, in the synagogue immediately after *Shacharit.* Someone who has been studying a talmudic *masechet* completes the tractate in the presence of those assembled. Thereafter, everyone—including the men and boys who are fasting—participates in the *se'udat mitzvah.* They are relieved, therefore, of the obligation to fast the entire day. The meal usually consists of light breakfast foods, inasmuch as it takes place early in the morning. Everyone then returns home to burn the *chametz.*

7.3.4 Burning the *Chametz*

In the morning of ***erev Pesach,*** the eve of Passover, within a specified time period, the *chametz* is burned. The wooden spoon which contains the collected crumbs, the feather, and the candle are all placed in a safe container, such as a metal can, and set afire. When it has all turned to ash, a second Declaration of Nullification is recited.

Recite after Burning the *Chametz*

Any *chametz* in my possession,
which I did or did not see, which I did or did not remove,
shall be considered nullified and ownerless,
like the dust of the earth.

No *chametz* may be eaten until after the festival, and *no matzah* may be eaten before the *seder.* When *erev Pesach* falls on the Sabbath, the *chametz* is burned on Friday.

7.3.5 Holiday Cooking

The first two days of Passover are considered sacred days of *Yom Tov*, literally, *good day,* but more significantly, holy festival days, when all the laws of Passover and of the Sabbath apply, except two. These two exceptions are the Sabbath laws pertaining to cooking and baking, and the laws pertaining to carrying outside of one's own private domain (see Sections 5.9.4 and 5.9.5).

On *Yom Tov,* it is permissible to cook, but only in an amount sufficient for the particular day on which it will be consumed. Therefore, it is preferable to do most of the cooking before the holiday starts, and in many homes, all meals for at least the first two days are prepared before Passover starts.

If the second day of *Yom Tov* falls on the Sabbath, or if the first two days are followed by the Sabbath, when cooking is forbidden, it is necessary to make an ***eruv tavshilin***, a combining of prepared foods. In order to prepare food for the Sabbath on *Yom Tov*, a special portion, comprised of a cooked food and a baked item—for example, a piece of chicken cooked before the festival and a *matzah*—is set aside to be eaten on the Sabbath.

The items are held in the right hand and the following is recited.

Recite the Blessing for *Eruv Tavshilin*

Blessed are You, Lord our God, King of the Universe,
Who has sanctified us with His commandments
and commanded us concerning the *mitzvah* of *eruv*.

❖

With this *eruv*,
may we be permitted to bake, cook, fry, insulate,
light candles, and make all necessary preparations
on *Yom Tov* for the sake of *Shabbat*—
for ourselves and for all Jews who live in this city.

By reciting this formula, it will be permissible on *Yom Tov* to cook any additional foods that are required for the Sabbath. Of course, if one of the *Yom Tov* days happens to fall on the Sabbath, all Sabbath restrictions prevail.

7.3.6 The Symbols of the *Seder*

As *erev Pesach* approaches, the holiday table is set with a festive cloth, one that is used only for the *Pesach* holiday. By now the Passover pots and pans, china, crystal, and silver have all been unpacked from the boxes in which they have been stored away all year.

The gleaming silver candlesticks are prepared and the wine is poured into decanters. The ***k'arah***, *seder* plate, is filled with the symbols of *Pesach*, the ***kos shel Eliyahu***, Elijah's cup, is prominently displayed on the table, and a ***Haggadah***, which recounts the story of the Exodus, is placed at each setting. On each chair a fluffy pillow rests, so that we may recline to left comfortably on it during the *seder*.

Symbols of *Pesach* are displayed on the *k'arah* for use in the rituals of the *seder.*

The boxes of crisp *matzot* are opened and the pungent aroma of grated horseradish melds with the sweet and savory scents of the festival meal. The anticipation builds: the *seder* will soon begin.

On the *k'arah,* the following symbols of Passover are displayed.

- ***karpas*** — vegetable
- ***maror*** — bitter herbs
- ***chazeret*** — bitter herbs
- ***charoset*** — apple-nut-wine mixture
- ***zeroa*** — shankbone
- ***beitzah*** — roasted egg

The *maror* is placed in the center of the plate, and the other five symbols are positioned in a ring around it.

Karpas refers to the eating of a vegetable that symbolizes the spring season (see Section 7.4.3). Usually a piece of celery is used, although carrots, radishes, or boiled potatoes are also acceptable.

The *maror* represents the bitterness of slavery (see Section 7.4.9). In most homes, horseradish—cut or freshly grated—or romaine lettuce stems are used for *maror.* Although horseradish is emphatically more biting, many prefer romaine lettuce because it has the distinct quality of being sweet early in the season, but more bitter the longer it stays in the ground. This is symbolic of slavery in Egypt, which became progressively more bitter as time went on. At Passover time, both horseradish root and romaine lettuce are readily available in the produce section of most supermarkets.

Chazeret is placed on the *k'arah* as an additional symbol of the bitterness of slavery. Many people use romaine lettuce for *chazeret* and horseradish for *maror.*

Charoset is typically made from a mixture of ground walnuts, grated apples, sugar, cinnamon, ginger, and red wine. Its muddy color belies its delicious taste. The *charoset* represents the mortar which was made into bricks by the Israelite slaves (see Section 7.4.10).

The *zeroa,* a roasted bone with some meat on it, represents the *Korban Pesach,* the Paschal lamb that was sacrificed by the Israelites. Although the *Korban Pesach* was eaten on the eve of the Exodus, the *zeroa* is never eaten during the *seder.*

There are at least three explanations for the *beitzah,* the roasted hard-boiled egg: (1) it represents the ***Korban Chagigah,*** the special sacrifice that was brought to the *Bet HaMikdash* on festival days; (2) it is a symbol of mourning for the destruction of the Temple; and (3) it symbolizes the character of the Jewish people in their response to oppression; just as an egg is the only food that gets harder as it is cooked, so too the Jewish people, who have become firmer in their resolve to survive in spite of many centuries of persecution.

7.3.7 Ushering in the Festival

The family has gathered, dressed in their holiday finery; the table is bedecked, as befits a momentous occasion; all is in readiness, as sunset approaches. The festival candles are lit, and *Yom Tov* is ushered into the home with *licht benchen.*

Recite the First Blessing over the *Yom Tov* Candles

Baruch Atah, HaShem E-lo-kenu, Melech HaOlam,
asher kidshanu b'mitzvotav v'tzivanu
l'hadlik ner shel (Shabbat v') Yom Tov.

❖

Blessed are You, Lord our God, King of the Universe,
Who has sanctified us with His commandments and commanded us
to kindle the (Sabbath and) festival lights.

A second blessing is then recited.

Recite the Second Blessing over the *Yom Tov* Candles

Baruch Atah, HaShem E-lo-kenu, Melech HaOlam,
she'hecheyanu, v'kiy'manu,
v'higiyanu laz'man hazeh.

❖

Blessed are You, Lord our God, King of the Universe,
Who has kept us alive, sustained us,
and brought us to this season.

In the synagogue, *Ma'ariv* is under way. Soon everyone will return home and gather round the table to retell the ancient story. We will touch on the liturgy of *Pesach* in Section 7.8.

7.4 The *Seder*

On the first two nights of Passover, after nightfall, the head of the household, customarily robed in his white *kittel,* a symbol of purity, conducts the *seder.* The word *seder* means *arrangement* or *order,* and the *seder* ritual is arranged in a specific order.

The text for the conduct of the *seder* is contained in a special book called the *Haggadah,* a term derived from the Hebrew verb *to tell.* Each person at the *seder* is given a copy of the *Haggadah* to follow along as the *seder* unfolds.

This guidebook, arranged by the sages of the *Anshei Kenesset HaGedolah,* is a compilation of prayers, midrashic literature, hymns, and the requisite chronicle of God's redemption of the Children of Israel from Egyptian bondage. The biblical text is woven together with the interpretations and commentaries of many rabbinic scholars, making it possible to learn and teach the Passover story to young and old alike.

Some ***Haggadot*** are embellished with reproductions of ancient illuminated manuscripts, depicting the history of the Jewish people. Others are prepared specifically for use by children, with large letters and fanciful drawings that spark their imagination, keeping them interested and attentive as the *seder* proceeds. The *Haggadah* has been published in many languages and is also available in a large-print format and even in Braille. To be sure, there is a *Haggadah* appropriate for everyone.

For centuries, the timeless words and the traditional melodies have combined to create memories that capture the heart and nourish the soul. The *Haggadah* is like an old friend, and each year we renew our acquaintance, finding reminders of the past in the hallowed words and on the wine-stained pages. The words of the *Haggadah* are both an affirmation of faith and an expression of hope, a reflection of miracles long past and a source of inspiration for the future.

All this comes together in the fifteen distinct rituals of the Passover *seder.* They are:

- ***Kadesh***
- ***Urchatz***
- ***Karpas***
- ***Yachatz***
- ***Magid***
- ***Rachtzah***
- ***Motzi***
- ***Matzah***
- ***Maror***
- ***Korech***
- ***Shulchan Orech***
- ***Tzafun***
- ***Barech***
- ***Hallel***
- ***Nirtzah***

We will explain each of them in turn.

7.4.1 *Kadesh*

Kadesh is the recitation of the *Kiddush* for festivals, the sanctification over wine, which includes the recitation of the phrase:

> **. . . and You have given us . . . the Festival of Unleavened Bread,**
> **the Season of Our Freedom . . .**
> **a remembrance of the Exodus from Egypt.**

During the course of the *seder,* the ***arba kosot,*** four cups of wine, are drunk, representing the four expressions used in the Torah to describe God's redemption of the Israelites.

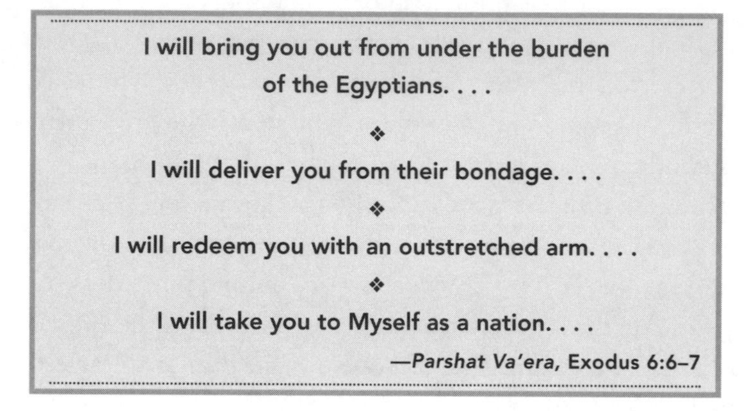
I will bring you out from under the burden of the Egyptians. . . .

❖

I will deliver you from their bondage. . . .

❖

I will redeem you with an outstretched arm. . . .

❖

I will take you to Myself as a nation. . . .

—*Parshat Va'era,* Exodus 6:6–7

These expressions of redemption range from that of the purely physical—easing the sufferings of slavery—to the ultimate spiritual goal—becoming God's Chosen People.

Each statement of redemption requires its own recitation of sanctification over wine. Throughout the following discussion, we will indicate where these expressions occur in the *seder* ritual. This *mitzvah* is not fulfilled if the four cups of wine are consumed at one time.

If possible, red wine should be used, because it symbolizes the marking of the doorposts as the homes of the Israelites were passed over on the eve of redemption. However, for those who cannot drink wine, grape juice may be substituted to fulfill the obligation for any of the four cups. The first of the four cups of wine is sanctified by the recitation of *Kiddush,* which may be recited while sitting or standing. *Kiddush* represents the first promise of redemption:

I will bring you out from under the burden of the Egyptians. . . .

The *seder* begins with *Kiddush.*

Begin to Recite *Kiddush* for *Pesach* on Friday Night

And it was evening and it was morning, the sixth day.
Thus, the heavens and the earth and all their multitude were finished.
By the seventh day God completed His work which He had made,
and He rested on the seventh day from all His work which He had done.
God blessed the seventh day and sanctified it,
because on it He had rested from all His work which God had created.

On all other nights, begin to recite *Kiddush,* as follows, adding the words in parentheses on Friday night.

Recite the *Kiddush* for *Pesach*

Baruch Atah, HaShem E-lo-kenu, Melech HaOlam,
borei p'ri hagafen.

❖

Blessed are You, Lord our God, King of the Universe,
Who creates the fruit of the vine.
All Respond:
Amen.

Continue to Recite *Kiddush* for *Pesach*

Blessed are You, Lord our God, King of the Universe,
Who has chosen us from all nations,
exalted us above all tongues,
and sanctified us with His commandments.
You, Lord, our God, have lovingly given us
(Sabbaths for rest)
holidays for gladness, festivals and seasons of joy,
(this Sabbath day and)
this Festival of Unleavened Bread,
this Season of our Freedom (in love),
a holy gathering in remembrance
of the Exodus from Egypt.
You chose and sanctified us above all peoples,
(in love and favor) You granted us as a heritage
(the Sabbath and) Your holy festivals
in gladness and joy.
Blessed are You, Lord, Who sanctifies (the Sabbath,)
Israel and the festive occasions.

If one of the *seder* nights falls on Saturday, the following *Havdalah* is inserted here:

Continue to Recite *Kiddush* for *Pesach* on Saturday Night

Baruch Atah, HaShem E-lo-kenu, Melech HaOlam,
borei m'orei ha'eish.

❖

Blessed are You, Lord our God, King of the Universe,
Who creates the lights of fire.

❖

Blessed are You, Lord our God, King of the Universe,
Who has made a distinction between holy and profane,
between light and darkness, between Israel and other nations,
between the seventh day and the six days of work.
You have distinguished between
the sanctity of the Sabbath
and the sanctity of a festival,
and have hallowed the seventh day above the six days of work.
You distinguished and sanctified
Your nation, Israel, with holiness.
Blessed are You, Lord,
Who distinguishes the holy from the holy.

The *Kiddush* concludes with the recitation of *she'hecheyanu.*

Conclude the Recitation of *Kiddush* for *Pesach*

Baruch Atah, HaShem E-lo-kenu, Melech HaOlam,
she'hecheyanu, v'kiy'manu,
v'higiyanu laz'man hazeh.

❖

Blessed are You, Lord our God, King of the Universe,
Who has kept us alive, sustained us,
and brought us to this season.

The first cup of wine should be drunk immediately. It is customary for everyone to lean to the left side, reclining on a pillow, like nobility, a symbol of our freedom.

There is a specific religious requirement to drink 3.3 fluid ounces of wine each time. On Friday night, the one reciting *Kiddush* for those assembled should drink 4.42 ounces. All others at the *seder* may drink 3.3 ounces.

7.4.2 Urchatz

Urchatz is the ritual washing of the hands (see Section 5.5.3), but without the recitation of *al n'tilat yadayim,* the *berachah* that follows ritual washing. It is simply a washing of the hands prior to the eating of the *karpas.* In many homes it is a custom to bring a cup and bowl for washing to the table, especially for the leader of the *seder.*

7.4.3 Karpas

The vegetable is a symbolic reminder of the spring season, and the salt water symbolizes the bitterness of slavery and the tears shed by the Israelite slaves in Egypt. Each person takes a piece of *karpas,* dips it in salt water, and recites the following *berachah.*

Recite the *Berachah* for *Karpas*

Baruch Atah, HaShem E-lo-kenu, Melech HaOlam,
borei p'ri ha'adamah.

❖

Blessed are You, Lord our God, King of the Universe,
Who creates the fruit of the ground.

Everyone eats a piece of the vegetable, smaller than the size of an olive.

7.4.4 Yachatz

Three *matzot,* whole pieces of unleavened bread, are set before the head of the household who conducts the *seder.* According to one explanation, each *matzah* represents one of the three groups of Jews, *Kohanim, Levi'im,* and *Yisraelim.* Another interpretation suggests they represent the three patriarchs, Abraham, Isaac, and Jacob.

The three *matzot* are often presented in a special *matzah* cover which consists of three pockets. It is usually embroidered with symbols of the festival, embellished with decorative threads and trimming. Many beautiful silver *seder* plates, which hold the various symbols of the festival, are designed with three trays beneath to hold the *matzot.* One *matzah* is placed in each pocket or tray.

Matzah shmurah, which means *matzah* that has been scrupulously *watched* since the reaping of the wheat to avoid the formation of *chametz,* is preferred for the *seder.* Both machine-made and handmade *matzah shmurah* are available. It is more expensive than non-*shmurah,* but its enhancement of the *mitzvah* is not measurable in money.

As the *seder* continues, the leader takes the middle *matzah* and breaks it into two pieces. This breaking of the *matzah* is called *Yachatz.* The larger piece is wrapped and placed in a special bag, often embroidered with Passover symbols, for the ***afikoman*** (from the Greek for *dessert*), the olive-sized portion of *matzah* that is to be eaten at the end of the festival meal. More about the *afikoman* later in Section 7.4.12.

7.4.5 *Magid*

Magid, the telling of the story of the Exodus from Egypt, begins with the following recitation, which explains the significance of the *matzah.*

> This is the bread of affliction
> that our forefathers ate in the land of Egypt.
> Whoever is hungry—let him come and eat.
> Whoever is needy—let him come and celebrate *Pesach.*
> Now we are here; next year may we be in the land of Israel.
> Now we are slaves; next year may we be free men.

The cup of wine is refilled, and *Magid* continues as the youngest present asks the Four Questions, each dealing with certain aspects of the conduct of the *seder.* The Four Questions, in fact, are really one question with four distinct parts. The Four Questions begin with a prefatory query.

Recite the Four Questions

Why is this night different from all other nights?

1. On all other nights, we may eat bread or *matzah*, unleavened bread; but on this night, we eat only *matzah*.
2. On all other nights, we may eat herbs of any kind; but on this night, we eat only *maror*, bitter herbs.
3. On all other nights, we do not dip our food even once; but on this night, we dip twice—once, *karpas* in salt water, the other, *maror* in *charoset*.
4. On all other nights, we may sit upright or we may recline [at the table]; but on this night, we all recline.

Although it is not part of the actual *Haggadah* text, it is customary to conclude the Four Questions with the following request:

Please give me the answer to my questions.

In some homes, all the children, even adult children around their father's table, recite the Four Questions. If no children are present, anyone may recite them. If no one else is present, the one conducting the *seder* recites them himself.

Then, the leader of the *seder,* and all those present, recite the text of the *Haggadah* which contains the narration of the Exodus. All the text of *Magid,* indeed, of the entire *Haggadah,* serves as a response to the child's questions. It begins with the reminder that

We were slaves unto Pharaoh in Egypt,
but God took us out of there
with a mighty hand and an outstretched arm.
Had the Holy One, blessed be He,
not taken our forefathers out of Egypt,
then we, our children, and our children's children
would still be slaves unto Pharaoh.
Even if we were all men of wisdom, understanding,
experience, and knowledge of the Torah,
we would still be obligated to tell of the Exodus from Egypt.
The more one tells about the Exodus,
the more he is praiseworthy.

Magid also includes the ritual of the Ten Plagues. Each person dips the tip of a spoon into their wine cup, spilling off a little, as they recite each of the Ten Plagues.

Recite the Ten Plagues

- blood
- frogs
- lice
- beasts
- pestilence
- boils
- hail
- locusts
- darkness
- death of the first-born of Egypt

Spilling off some wine is meant to remind us that many Egyptians died during the Ten Plagues. Although they were our enemies, the joy of our freedom is nevertheless tempered by the recognition that so many human beings met their deaths. It is inappropriate to lick off any remaining drops of wine from our spoon or finger. The dishes in which the drops have been spilled are removed from the table before the *seder* continues.

Magid continues with Torah verses, scholarly discourses, and hymns of praise. Following the *Haggadah* text, the leader recites:

Pesach . . . Matzah . . . Maror

referring to the three central rituals of the *seder:* (1) the roasted shank bone, symbol of the *Korban Pesach,* Paschal sacrifice; (2) the middle *matzah,* symbol of the bread of affliction; and (3) the *maror,* bitter herbs, a reminder of the bitterness of slavery. The corresponding verses, explaining the significance of these symbols, are recited. According to Rabban Gamliel (Mishnah, *Pesachim* 10:5), anyone who has not recited these three things has not fulfilled the *mitzvah* of *Magid.*

Lively discussions of the Exodus, an extraordinary event in Jewish history, and the focal point of the celebration itself, often last for hours. Everyone is encouraged to participate, to share the rabbinic commentaries found in many editions of the *Haggadah,* and to retell the story of the Exodus as if they had been there themselves.

Magid concludes with the second cup of wine, symbolic of the second promise of redemption.

I will deliver you from their bondage. . . .

The following *berachah* is recited before the second cup:

Recite before Drinking the Second Cup

Baruch Atah, HaShem E-lo-kenu, Melech HaOlam,
borei p'ri hagafen

❖

Blessed are You, Lord our God, King of the Universe,
Who creates the fruit of the vine.

7.4.6 *Rachtzah*

After the story of the Exodus has been told, all those present wash their hands ritually and recite the appropriate *berachah. Rachtzah,* the ritual washing of the hands, requires the removal of any rings or other impediments. Jews ritually wash before every meal at which (bread or) *matzah* is eaten (see Section 5.5.3). No talking is permitted between washing the hands and eating the *matzah.*

7.4.7 *Motzi*

In the first of the Four Questions, the child inquired about the requirement to eat only unleavened bread at the *seder.* This *mitzvah* is derived from several verses in the Torah, which require Jews to eat *matzah* on Passover. They include:

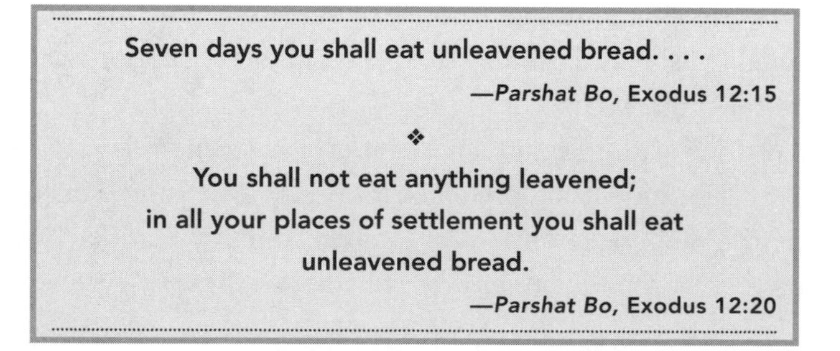

Seven days you shall eat unleavened bread. . . .

—*Parshat Bo,* Exodus 12:15

❖

You shall not eat anything leavened;
in all your places of settlement you shall eat
unleavened bread.

—*Parshat Bo,* Exodus 12:20

Motzi/Matzah are the seventh and eighth steps in the order of the *seder.* They occur one after the other without any intervening text or conversation. Two *berachot* are recited before eating *matzah.* The first *berachah, hamotzi,* is recited immediately after the ritual of washing the hands.

The *seder* leader lifts the remaining two-and-a-half *matzot* and recites the first blessing:

Recite the First *Berachah* before Eating *Matzah*

Baruch Atah, HaShem E lo kenu, Melech HaOlam,
hamotzi lechem min ha'aretz.

❖

Blessed are You, Lord our God, King of the Universe,
Who brings forth bread from the earth.

7.4.8 *Matzah*

The second blessing before eating the *matzah* at the *seder* immediately follows the first, without interruption or pause.

Recite the Second *Berachah* before Eating *Matzah*

Baruch Atah, HaShem E-lo-kenu, Melech HaOlam,
asher kidshanu b'mitzvotav v'tzivanu
al achilat matzah.

❖

Blessed are You, Lord our God, King of the Universe,
Who has sanctified us with His commandments and commanded us
concerning the eating of the *matzah*.

After the *berachot* are recited, the leader of the *seder* distributes pieces of the two-and-a-half *matzot* and any additional *matzot* that are necessary, so that all assembled receive the minimum required portion—equivalent to a piece 7 × 6.25 inches—to fulfill the *mitzvah*. Of course, additional *matzot* may be used as needed throughout the *seder*. The second blessing is recited only on the two *seder* nights, and not at any other time during the eight days of Passover, or during the rest of the year when *matzah* is served.

Egg *matzah*, which is usually made with oil and fruit juice (or other liquid) instead of water, is considered an *enriched matzah*, as contrasted with the *poor bread of affliction*, that is required (see Section 7.1.7). Therefore, it should not be used for Passover, except in cases of illness or infirmity. *Matzah* and *matzah* products that are produced during the year are not to be used for Passover, because special rabbinic supervision for Passover is required in the production process. The requirement to prevent the formation of *chametz* during the production process exists only at Passover.

7.4.9 Maror

In the Four Questions in *Magid*, the child mentions the use of bitter herbs, the *maror*. The symbolism of the *maror*, of course, is the bitterness of slavery. The minimum required portion of grated *maror* is equivalent to the volume of 1.1 fluid ounces. On the eve of the Exodus, the *maror* was eaten with the *Korban Pesach* sacrifice.

And they shall eat
the [roasted] meat [of the Paschal lamb] . . .
on that night,
and unleavened bread;
with bitter herbs they shall eat it.

—*Parshat Bo*, Exodus 12:8

Although the *Korban Pesach* is no longer eaten, the *mitzvah* of eating *maror* has been retained by rabbinic authorities. Before eating the *maror*, the following *berachah* is recited.

Recite before Eating *Maror*

Baruch Atah, HaShem E-lo-kenu, Melech HaOlam,
asher kidshanu b'mitzvotav v'tzivanu
al achilat maror.

❖

Blessed are You, Lord our God, King of the Universe,
Who has sanctified us with His commandments and commanded us
concerning the eating of *maror*.

7.4.10 *Korech*

The child has also questioned the dipping of foods on the *seder* nights. *Karpas* has already been dipped in salt water (see Section 7.4.3). *Korech*, the tenth ritual in the *seder*, is fulfilled by eating *matzah* and *maror* together. The *maror* is first dipped in *charoset*, which is largely shook off, and eaten between two pieces of *matzah*. The minimum portions for *matzah* and *maror* in *Korech* are:

- *matzah* 7 × 6.25 inches
- *maror* equivalent in volume to 0.7 fluid ounces

The following is recited before eating the sandwich.

Recite before Eating *Korech*

In remembrance of the *Bet HaMikdash,*
we do as Hillel did
in the time of the Temple:
he would combine
[the *Korban Pesach* offering with]
matzah with *maror* in a sandwich
and eat them together in fulfillment
of what is written in the Torah:
They shall eat it with *matzot* and *maror.*

After *Korech* has been eaten, the festival meal, called *Shulchan Orech,* meaning the *prepared table,* is served.

7.4.11 *Shulchan Orech*

At the *seder* table, each person is given a pillow to lean on. Reclining was a sign of freedom practiced by the nobility, and at the *seder,* it is a sign that we are free. Therefore, at the *seder,* all Jews should conduct themselves as if they were nobility, too. We recline while we drink the four cups and during the meal, in reply to the child's fourth question.

The *seder* plate and any remaining symbolic foods are cleared away, and the festival meal is served. It is appropriate to sing Passover songs, tell stories, and encourage the participation of the children. The meal should continue to be a spiritually uplifting occasion for all. One should avoid overeating so the *afikoman* may be enjoyed at the end of the meal.

7.4.12 *Tzafun*

You will recall that at the beginning of the *seder,* the middle *matzah* was broken in half and one part was put aside for the *afikoman* (see Section 7.4.4). *Tzafun* is the eating of the *afikoman,* the dessert. It symbolizes the *Korban Pesach,* which we no longer eat, and the *matzah* that was eaten with it. It is the last thing that is eaten at the *seder,* so that we may continue to savor the taste of the *matzah,* just as the taste of the *Korban Pesach* lingered on the eve of the redemption.

It is traditional to make a game of finding the *afikoman*. In many homes, during the course of the evening, the father, or someone he designates, hides the *afikoman*, thereby keeping the children alert and interested as the evening grows late. Once dinner has been served, the children try to find the *afikoman* so that the *seder* can continue. Once the *afikoman* is found, the child is rewarded with a prize in exchange for its return.

Everyone eats a piece of the dessert *matzah*—and additional *matzah* as necessary—to fulfill the minimum portion of a piece 7 × 6.25 inches. Nothing else may be eaten after the *afikoman*.

A WITTY REMARK!

In our home, it has always been the custom for one of us to hide the *afikoman* and for our children to search for it. On both *seder* nights, while dinner was being served, the dessert *matzah* was hidden.

One year, on the first night, our oldest daughter, then a young teenager, found it hidden in the front hall closet. After much debate, she finally returned it in exchange for our promise to buy her a camera after *Yom Tov*. She was delighted, but her two sisters could only hope for better luck on the following night.

The second *seder*, always a bit less hectic than the first, moved along at a more relaxed pace, but our two younger daughters, especially, could hardly wait to get to the *afikoman*. Once it had been hidden, the three of them were off on their hunt.

After a rather prolonged search, our middle daughter, then about eight, found it outside in the mailbox. Ecstatically, she demanded an extensive wardrobe—for her Barbie doll—and we had to agree.

Her little sister, a precocious four-year-old, was clearly perturbed. She came back to the table, and with the wisdom born of her "painful" experience, she placed her hands on her hips and emphatically declared: "Next year, I'm going to hide the *afikoman*, and I'm going to find it!"

7.4.13 *Barech*

After the *afikoman* has been eaten, the *seder* continues with *Barech*, the recitation of the *Birkat HaMazon*, the Grace after Meals. It is identical to the daily recitation, except for the addition of *Ya'aleh v'Yavo* (see Section 4.7) and the insertion of a special prayer asking God to grant us a day of complete goodness. If *Pesach* and *Shabbat* coincide, then both the festival and Sabbath insertions are recited.

The third cup of wine is poured just before the recitation of *Birkat HaMazon*. It recalls the third level of redemption:

I will redeem you with an outstretched arm. . . .

The blessing is then recited on the third cup.

Recite before Drinking the Third Cup

Baruch Atah, HaShem E-lo-kenu, Melech HaOlam,
borei p'ri hagafen.

❖

Blessed are You, Lord our God, King of the Universe,
Who creates the fruit of the vine.

After drinking the third cup, the Cup of Elijah is filled.

The *Kos shel Eliyahu,* the Cup of Elijah, usually a large goblet used specifically for this purpose, is filled to overflowing for the arrival of Elijah the Prophet. The Cup of Elijah is said to symbolize the fifth phase of redemption:

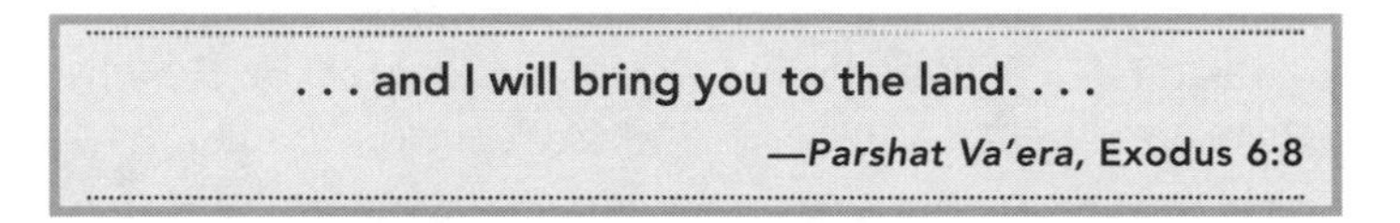

. . . and I will bring you to the land. . . .

—*Parshat Va'era,* Exodus 6:8

There is a disagreement about whether this fifth cup should be drunk, because this divine promise has not yet been fulfilled. According to tradition, Elijah will herald the arrival of the *Mashiach*, the Messiah, and at that time, the final redemption will be realized. The prevailing practice is not to drink from the Cup of Elijah, but rather to leave it on the table to await his arrival. In talmudic times, when religious matters could not be resolved among scholars, it was the custom to say that the matter would be left for the prophet Elijah to decide. No doubt, he will resolve the matter of drinking the fifth cup at the *seder* as well.

The wine is poured, and everyone at the *seder* table proceeds to the front door to open it in anticipation of the prophet's visit. As the door is opened, the welcome is proclaimed by all.

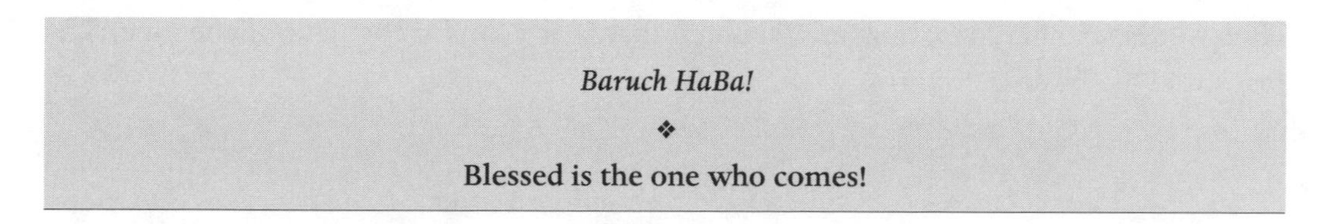
Baruch HaBa!

❖

Blessed is the one who comes!

In many homes, a prayerful hymn is sung for the speedy arrival of Elijah, the herald of the Messiah from the House of David.

Another special passage in the *Haggadah* is then recited. This prayer was instituted in the eleventh century, when numerous blood libels were brought against the Jews. Falsely accused of killing Gentile children and mixing their blood into the Passover *matzot,* they asked God to punish those who tormented them. After this recitation, the door is closed, and all return to the table to continue the *seder.*

It is also customary in some homes to recite special prayers at the second *seder* in memory of those who perished during the Holocaust, remembering especially those martyrs of the Warsaw Ghetto uprising, which began on the second night of Passover. However, these prayers are not actually part of the *Haggadah.*

7.4.14 *Hallel*

Before proceeding, the fourth cup of wine is poured, but not yet drunk. The *seder* continues with the recitation of several passages from the Book of Psalms called *Hallel,* in praise of God. The first half of *Hallel* was recited before *Shulchan Orech.* The rest is recited after the meal, as the *seder* ritual continues to draw to a close. These passages, in a longer form, are also incorporated in the synagogue services, immediately following the *Shacharit.*

At the conclusion of *Hallel,* the blessing is recited on the fourth cup of wine, representing the fourth promise of redemption:

I will take you to Myself as a nation. . . .

Recite before Drinking the Fourth Cup

Baruch Atah, HaShem E-lo-kenu, Melech HaOlam,
borei p'ri hagafen.

❖

Blessed are You, Lord our God, King of the Universe,
Who creates the fruit of the vine.

Afterwards, a concluding blessing is recited thanking God for the fruit of the vine. The last ritual of the *seder* follows.

7.4.15 *Nirtzah*

Nirtzah, the last ritual of the *seder,* begins with the following passage and brings the *seder* to a close. It expresses the hope that the *seder* was conducted in a way that was acceptable to God.

Begin *Nirtzah*

The *seder* is now ended,
in accordance with its laws, statutes, and precepts.
As we were privileged to recite its order,
so may we merit to perform it.
Pure One, Who dwells on high,
raise up the congregation of Your countless people soon.
Guide the shoots of your plants,
redeemed to Zion with joyous song.

7.4.16 *Sefirat HaOmer*

On the second night of Passover, that is, the eve of the second day, the ritual known as *Sefirat HaOmer,* the Counting of the *Omer,* begins (see Sections 4.6.1, 4.6.2, and 4.6.13). The Torah requires the Jewish people to count the days and weeks from the eve of the second day of *Pesach* until *Shavuot* seven weeks later, a total of forty-nine days.

During the time of the *Bet HaMikdash,* a communal meal-offering of barley was brought on the second day of Passover. This measure of coarsely ground barley flour, called an *omer,* was offered in the form of *matzah,* unleavened bread. The *omer* offering was the first offering brought to the *Bet HaMikdash* from the spring crop.

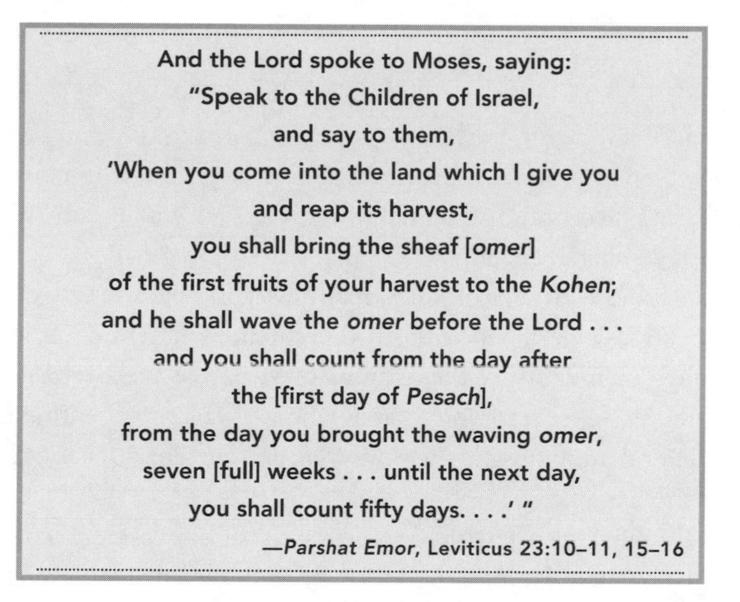
And the Lord spoke to Moses, saying:
"Speak to the Children of Israel,
and say to them,
'When you come into the land which I give you
and reap its harvest,
you shall bring the sheaf [*omer*]
of the first fruits of your harvest to the *Kohen*;
and he shall wave the *omer* before the Lord . . .
and you shall count from the day after
the [first day of *Pesach*],
from the day you brought the waving *omer*,
seven [full] weeks . . . until the next day,
you shall count fifty days. . . .' "

—*Parshat Emor*, Leviticus 23:10–11, 15–16

From this night forward for the next seven weeks, it is a religious obligation to count the days until the festival of *Shavuot*, the Festival of Weeks, which is the fiftieth day. Derived from the Torah precept, this *mitzvah* links these two pilgrimage festivals, tying the commemoration of our physical freedom to the spiritual liberation embodied in God's giving and our acceptance of the Torah at Mount Sinai.

Every night from the second night of Passover, the following blessing is recited and the day and week of the *omer* are enumerated:

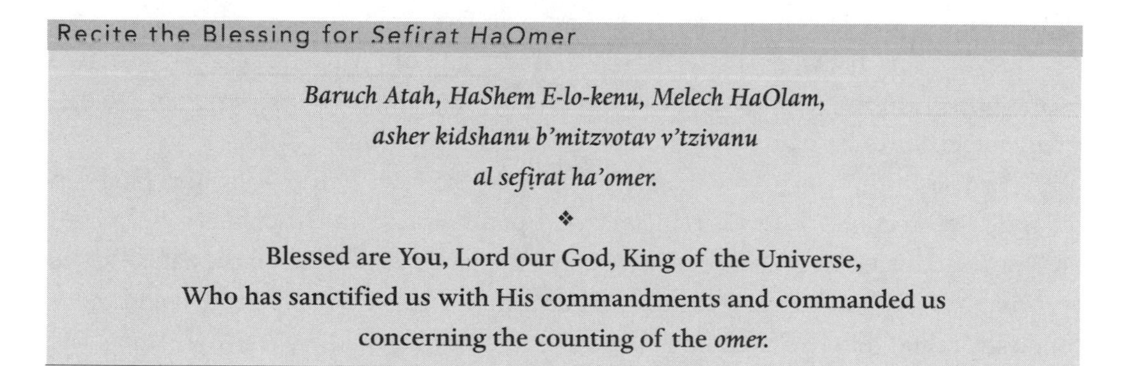
Recite the Blessing for *Sefirat HaOmer*

Baruch Atah, HaShem E-lo-kenu, Melech HaOlam,
asher kidshanu b'mitzvotav v'tzivanu
al sefirat ha'omer.

❖

Blessed are You, Lord our God, King of the Universe,
Who has sanctified us with His commandments and commanded us
concerning the counting of the *omer*.

Then the day is counted:

Today is the first day of the *omer.*

On each successive night, for seven weeks, the blessing is recited, and the day and week of the *omer* are pronounced, provided there was no break in counting the days. The festival of *Shavuot* commences on the fiftieth day. We will discuss this second festival of the *Shalosh Regalim* in Section 7.11.

Nirtzah concludes with several songs, many extolling the strength of the Almighty, others more allegorical, designed to keep the children's attention from waning. Although these songs are not part of the required recitation of the *Haggadah,* they are certainly a part of the Passover tradition. In many homes, the *seder* continues late into the night—but not later than midnight—with singing and further discussions of the miraculous events of the Exodus.

Synagogues and other Jewish organizations often conduct community-wide *sedarim,* making it possible for Jews to participate in the *seder* ritual, even if they are unable to prepare for it themselves.

The final chant of the *seder* gives voice to the age-old longing of the Jewish heart and soul:

Next year in Jerusalem!

7.5 The First Two Days of Passover

As we discussed in Section 7.3.5, the first two days of *Pesach* are considered sacred days of *Yom Tov,* when all the laws of Passover, and of the Sabbath, apply, with two exceptions: (1) those pertaining to cooking and baking; and (2) those pertaining to carrying outside of one's own private domain (see Sections 5.9.4 and 5.9.5).

On *Yom Tov,* it is permitted to cook food for the Sabbath if an *eruv tavshilin* has been set aside (see Section 7.3.5). Carrying between public and private domains is permitted on *Yom Tov,* but specific laws of *muktzeh* apply on *Yom Tov* as they do on the Sabbath (see Section 5.9.6) with a few exceptions. It is permissible, for example, to touch and move candlesticks and to wheel a carriage or stroller for a small child on *Yom Tov.* When *Yom Tov* and *Shabbat* coincide, the laws of *Shabbat* prevail.

In Israel, only the first day of Passover is a sacred day, that is, when all the laws of the Sabbath and festival apply. Diaspora Jews conduct two *sedarim;* in Israel, they conduct only one.

7.6 The Intermediate Days of Passover

Following the first days of *Yom Tov*, four intermediate days, called ***Chol HaMo'ed***, so-called weekdays of the festival, are observed. All the laws of Passover still apply, but the restrictions of the Sabbath do not apply, except, of course, if one of the days of *Chol HaMo'ed* is the Sabbath. There are many laws associated with the proper observance of *Chol HaMo'ed*. They are still days of *Yom Tov*, and some people do not go to work during these intermediate days.

7.7 The Last Two Days of Passover

The last two days of *Pesach* are also considered *Yom Tov*, when all the laws of the Passover festival and of the Sabbath, except the two aforementioned, are observed.

On the eighth day of Passover, *Yizkor* is recited in the synagogue in memory of departed relatives and Jewish martyrs (see Section 6.27).

Passover ends one hour after sunset at the conclusion of the eighth day of the festival. The rabbi concludes the transaction with the non-Jew, and buys back the *chametz* for those listed in the *shtar harsha'ah*.

Jews refrain from eating bread or leavened products at least until the rabbi has had sufficient time to buy back the *chametz*. Many wait until the next day, in order to avoid eating any *chametz* products which may have been made on the holiday. In the case of a Jewish bakery, where there is a doubt as to whether the Jewish owner sold the *chametz* and was closed during Passover, Jewish law requires that Jews refrain from purchasing products there for at least thirty days, thereby allowing sufficient turnover of flour and other *chametz* stock, which should have been sold prior to the festival.

Havdalah is recited over the wine, but not over the candle or the spices. At home, the special dishes and utensils for Passover are packed up once again and stored away for another year. So ends *Pesach*, the first of the *Shalosh Regalim*, the Pilgrimage Festivals.

7.8 The Liturgy of Passover

The *tefillot* of Passover are similar in structure and content to those of the Sabbath. *Shemoneh Esrei* is identical for *Ma'ariv*, *Shacharit*, and *Minchah*, except for the variation in Blessing (7) for peace, which we encountered before in Chapter 6.

The *Shemoneh Esrei* for the first two and last two days, for all four services—*Ma'ariv*, *Shacharit*, *Musaf*, and *Minchah*—contains seven blessings, the first three and the last three identical to those of the Sabbath. Blessing (4), the middle blessing, reflects the holiness of the day, and verses specific to the festival are recited.

Blessing (4) reminds us that God chose the Jewish people to receive the Torah. We also recall that God has given the Jewish people the festival days as a time of gladness and joyous celebration. *Ya'aleh v'Yavo* is also recited. Blessing (4) concludes with the prayer that God will bestow the blessings of His festival on us, as He promised; that He will sanctify us with His commandments and grant us a share in His Torah.

(On *Shabbat,* specific Sabbath inserts are added to Blessing (4), and on Saturday night, a paragraph is inserted distinguishing between the holiness of the Sabbath and the sanctity of the festival.)

After the *Amidah* of *Shacharit,* we recite *Hallel,* hymns of praise. Part of *Hallel* was recited during the *seder,* but the complete *Hallel* is recited on the *Shalosh Regalim,* among other times, Except for the *berachah* recited before *Hallel* and the closing paragraph, it is comprised entirely of selections from Psalms. When the festival falls on a weekday, the Thirteen Attributes of Mercy is recited when the Ark is opened before *Kriat HaTorah.*

7.8.1 The Prayer for Dew

Musaf is recited on all eight days of *Pesach.* During the repetition of the *Shemoneh Esrei,* ***Tefillat Tal,*** the Prayer for Dew, is recited on the first day of Passover. This prayer is a liturgical poem asking that the plants be regularly refreshed by dew during the warm season and that the earth be fertile and restored in the Land of Israel. This prayer, too, is an indication of the agricultural significance of the Passover festival in the time of the Temple (see Section 7.2.1).

Specific prayers dealing with the festival sacrifices are also inserted each day of *Pesach. Kedushah* is also recited (the *Kedushah* for *Minchah* is shorter than that of *Shacharit*), and if *Kohanim* are present, the Priestly Blessing is also chanted during *Musaf.*

7.8.2 The Priestly Blessing

In the days of the *Bet HaMikdash,* the *Korban Tamid,* daily sacrifice, was offered in the morning and at dusk. Immediately after the morning offering, the *Kohanim* recited the ***Birkat Kohanim,*** the Priestly Blessing, invoking God's beneficence on the Jewish people, according to the biblical precept.

> **And the Lord spoke unto Moses, saying,**
> **"Speak unto Aaron and unto his sons, saying,**
> **'So shall you bless the Children of Israel. . . .' "**
>
> **—*Parshat Naso,* Numbers 6:22–23**

The ritual was conducted from a platform, called a ***duchan,*** and, therefore, the ritual is also known as ***duchenen,*** (as a verb, *to* ***duchen***). *Duchenen* continues to this day, both in Israel and the Diaspora, with certain variations.

We no longer have the Holy Temple, and prayer has replaced the rituals of sacrifice, but in the Diaspora, *Birkat Kohanim* is still chanted during the repetition of the *Amidah of Musaf* on *Rosh HaShanah* and *Yom Kippur* (see Chapter 6) and on the Pilgrimage Festivals, *Pesach, Shavuot,* and *Sukkot.* On those days, just prior to the recitation of Blessing (5) of the repeitition of the *Shemoneh Esrei,* the *Kohanim* ascend to the *bimah* to bless the congregation.

In early biblical times, God blessed the people directly, but this divine right passed first to the patriarchs, and then to the Priests by His command when the Torah was given. It remains their sacred duty to this day. It is of *utmost importance* that the *Kohanim* and the worshippers of today understand that the Priests cannot bless the people—only God can. The *Kohanim* were selected by God to be His instrument of blessing and to serve as His representatives.

Before the *Kohanim* go up to the *bimah,* the *Levi'im* wash the hands of the *Kohanim,* as it was done during the days of the Temple. The *Kohanim* dry their hands, but do not recite any *berachah.*

Once the *Kohanim* ascend to the *bimah,* they remain facing the Ark until summoned by the cantor. They draw their prayer shawls over their heads to avoid any distractions, and keep their faces hidden. At the appropriate time, they turn toward the congregation.

With their arms raised to shoulder height—with the right hand slightly above the left and thumbs touching—they turn their hands palms down, extend their arms toward the worshippers, and spread out their fingers according to the traditional practice.

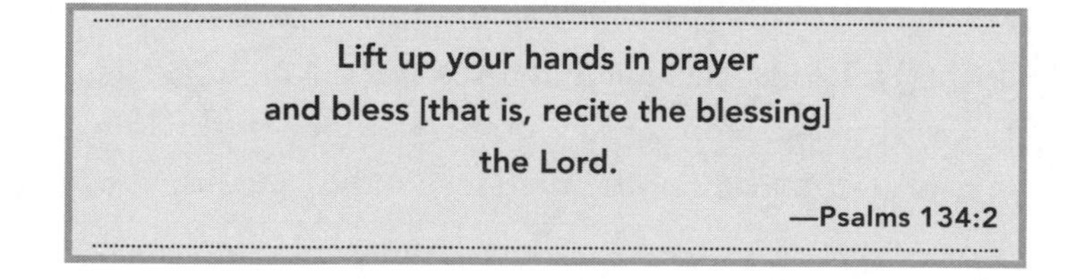

Lift up your hands in prayer
and bless [that is, recite the blessing]
the Lord.

—Psalms 134:2

The *Kohanim* ascend to the *bimah* to recite the *Birkat Kohanim*, invoking God's blessing on the Jewish people.

This lifting of the hands is called ***Nesiat Kapayim,*** a term which more correctly identifies what the *Kohanim* do as they recite the *Birkat Kohanim*. By raising their hands, which they enfold within the prayer shawl, they become a vehicle from which God's blessings flow, and they pronounce the blessing with great joy.

During *Nesiat Kapayim,* the congregation stands attentively facing the *Kohanim.* Neither the *Kohanim* themselves nor the worshippers may look at the raised hands of the Priests. However, the congregation should not turn their backs to the *Kohanim,* but should merely bow their heads, keeping their eyes averted.

Repetition of the *Amidah* continues with the cantor's hushed recitation followed by the resounding call to the Priests, who then respond by reciting the *berachah.*

Summon the *Kohanim*

Cantor:
Our God and God of our forefathers,
bless us with the three-verse blessing in the Torah
that was written by the hand of Moses, Your servant,
that was said by Aaron and his sons, the
KOHANIM
Cantor and Congregation:
Your holy people—as it is said
Kohanim:
Blessed Are You, Lord our God, King of the Universe,
Who has sanctified us with the holiness of Aaron,
and has commanded us to bless His people Israel with love.
Congregation:
Amen.

The Priestly Blessing consists of three verses, comprised of a total of fifteen words, from *Parshat Naso,* Numbers 6:24–26. Each word is first pronounced by the cantor and then repeated by the *Kohanim.* Some congregations recite ancillary verses as each word is said by the *Kohanim,* but this is not a universally accepted practice.

The pattern of the three-fold blessing suggests a sense of ascendancy from the material to the spiritual. The first blessing contains three Hebrew words; the second, five; and the third, seven. The first blessing, according to the commentators, is for material necessities. The second is for needs of a spiritual nature. The third combines the material and the spiritual, culminating in a blessing for peace.

Recite the First Blessing of *Birkat Kohanim*

Cantor followed by Kohanim:
May [the Lord] bless you . . .
Cantor followed by Kohanim:
the Lord . . .
Cantor followed by Kohanim:
and safeguard you.
Congregation:
Amen.

After the first blessing, the *Kohanim* sing a prolonged wordless chant, as the congregation recites a second supplication in an undertone. Then the *Kohanim* continue with the recitation of the second verse.

Recite the Second Blessing of *Birkat Kohanim*

Cantor followed by Kohanim:

May [the Lord] illuminate . . .

Cantor followed by Kohanim:

the Lord . . .

Cantor followed by Kohanim:

His Countenance . . .

Cantor followed by Kohanim:

for you . . .

Cantor followed by Kohanim:

and be gracious to you.

Congregation:

Amen.

Before the last word of the second blessing, the chant is again intoned by the *Kohanim,* and the congregation recites the same supplication in an undertone. Then the *Kohanim* continue with the recitation of the third verse of the Priestly Blessing.

Recite the Third Blessing of *Birkat Kohanim*

Cantor followed by Kohanim:

May [the Lord] turn . . .

Cantor followed by Kohanim:

the Lord . . .

Cantor followed by Kohanim:

His Countenance . . .

Cantor followed by Kohanim:

toward you . . .

Cantor followed by Kohanim:

and grant . . .

Cantor followed by Kohanim:

you . . .

Cantor followed by Kohanim:

peace.

Congregation:

Amen.

Again, the chant is intoned by the *Kohanim* before the last word of the third blessing, as the congregation again repeats a different supplication in a hushed voice.

After completing the third verse of the blessing, the *Kohanim* turn back to the Ark and lower their hands. The cantor immediately continues with the repetition of Blessing (7) for peace. The *Kohanim* remain on the *bimah,* and the cantor, the *Kohanim,* and the congregation recite the following verses simultaneously.

Cantor:	*Kohanim:*	*Congregation:*
Grant peace,	Master of the World	Supreme One,
goodness	we have	You are
and blessing	performed	on high,
kindness and mercy	what You	[You] Who dwells
to us and to all	have decreed	in might!
Your people Israel.	upon us;	You
Bless us . . .	now may You	are
with the light of	also fulfill	Peace
Your Countenance,	what You have	and
for with [it],	promised us.	Your
You gave us . . .	Look down	Name
the Torah of life,	from heaven,	is
and a love	Your sacred	Peace!
of kindness,	dwelling,	May it be
righteousness,	and bless Your	Your will
blessing, mercy,	people Israel	that You
life and peace.	and the land	grant us
May it be pleasing	You have	and all
in Your eyes	given us—	of Your people,
to bless	as You swore	the House
your people Israel	to our forefathers—	of Israel,
with Your peace.	a land flowing	life and blessing
at every season	with milk	to safeguard
and every hour.	and honey.	peace.

The *Kohanim* remain on the *bimah* until the cantor has completed the repetition of Blessing (7) of the *Amidah* and recited the Full *Kaddish*. Then, they return to their seats.

No *Kohen* should attempt to shirk his responsibility to *duchen* for the congregation by leaving the sanctuary. However, if he feels inadequate to the task or otherwise reluctant to serve, then he must leave the sanctuary before the cantor begins Blessing (5) and should stay out of the sanctuary until the Priestly Blessing is completed.

The recitation of *Birkat Kohanim* is an especially moving and significant occasion, and all Jews should try to be present in the synagogue to receive God's blessing on those days when it is chanted.

7.9 *Kriat HaTorah* for Passover

The Torah is read in the synagogue on all eight days of Passover. On the first two and last two days, there are five *aliyot,* except if the festival day coincides with the Sabbath, when there are seven *aliyot.* During *Chol HaMo'ed,* there are four *aliyot,* except on *Shabbat Chol HaMo'ed,* when there are seven. Below is a summary of the Torah portion, which is read from the first *Sefer Torah;* the *Maftir,* which is read from the second *Sefer Torah;* and the *Haftarah,* the prophetic portion, for the first two and last two days. Note that the *Maftir* portion is the same on the first two days, referring to the commandment to observe the Festival of Unleavened Bread and bring the festival sacrifices, and on the last two days, referring only to the festival sacrifices.

First Day
Parshat Bo, Exodus 12:21–51
Maftir: Parshat Pinchas, Numbers 28:16–25
Haftarah: Joshua 3:5–7; 5:2–6: 1; 6:27

Second Day
Parshat Emor, Leviticus 22:26–23:44
Maftir: Parshat Pinchas, Numbers 28:16–25
Haftarah: II Kings 23:1–9, 21–25

The Torah portions for *Chol HaMo'ed* vary, depending on whether or not a *Shabbat* intervenes.

Seventh Day
Parshat Beshalach, Exodus 13:17–15:26
Maftir: Parshat Pinchas, Numbers 28:19-25
Haftarah: II Samuel 22: 1–51

Eighth Day
Parshat Re'ei, Deuteronomy 14:22–16:17 (Sabbath); 15:19–16:17 (weekday)
Maftir: Parshat Pinchas, Numbers 28:19–25
Haftarah: Isaiah: 10:32–12:6

The Exodus is more than a historical event. It marked the turning point in the life of the Jewish people, because its purpose was the Divine Revelation of the Torah at Mount Sinai. Thus, *Pesach* is eternally linked with the most important event in Jewish history. We will explore that in our discussion of *Shavuot*, the Festival of Weeks (see Section 7.11).

7.10 Between *Pesach* and *Shavuot*

According to the Talmud, *Masechet Yevamot* 62b, in the second century C.E., twenty-four thousand students, all disciples of Rabbi Akiva, died between *Pesach* and *Shavuot*. In remembrance of this, a period of solemnity and mourning is observed throughout *Sefirah*. No marriages take place, music and other forms of entertainment are avoided, new clothes are not purchased, and cutting of the hair is restricted.

However, as the days of *Sefirah* approach the Festival of Weeks, several noteworthy days occur in the Jewish calendar. They include ***Yom HaShoah, Yom HaZikaron, Yom HaAtzma'ut, LaG baOmer,*** and ***Yom Yerushalayim.*** We will discuss each of these briefly.

7.10.1 *Yom HaShoah*

On the twenty-seventh day of *Nisan,* we observe *Yom HaShoah,* Holocaust Remembrance Day. Since the end of World War II, the systematic atrocities perpetrated by the Nazis against six million Jews have become part of the consciousness of the world. The horror and the insanity of that period in history must never be forgotten, for to forget history is to repeat it.

In recent years, several local and national organizations, both public and private, as well as ordinary people around the world, have supported efforts to make the Holocaust part of the moral conscience of all people. Museums in Washington, DC, Los Angeles, and New York have attracted visitors to their displays of thousands of artifacts and pages of personal testimony. In Jerusalem, Yad VaShem, Israel's national memorial to the martyrs of the Holocaust, draws thousands of visitors annually.

Synagogues, schools, and other Jewish organizations schedule special programs for *Yom HaShoah.* Candles are lit, prayers are recited, and an ever-dwindling number of survivors continue to bear witness, so that future generations will remember.

As we are enjoined to remember the Exodus from Egypt, we should feel the same obligation to remember those who perished *al kiddush HaShem,* for the sanctification of God's Name.

7.10.2 *Yom HaZikaron*

On the fourth day of *Iyar,* the State of Israel stops to mourn her war dead. On *Yom HaZikaron,* Remembrance Day, the entire country stops to acknowledge the sacrifice of the young men and women who have died in defense of their homeland. Only after paying homage to her heroes can Israel proudly celebrate her independence.

7.10.3 *Yom HaAtzma'ut*

As *Yom HaZikaron* ends, Israelis rejoice as they mark *Yom HaAtzma'ut,* Independence Day. Since May 14, 1948, when the State of Israel, ***Medinat Yisrael,*** was declared by Israel's first prime minister, David Ben-Gurion, the fifth day of *Iyar* has been celebrated in Israel and in Jewish communities worldwide. In the Diaspora, schoolchildren, like their Israeli counterparts, dress in blue and white, the colors of Israel's flag. Israeli foods, such as hummus and falafel, are served, and Israeli songs and dances are performed. In Israel, military parades, fireworks, and concerts add to the spirited festivities. If the fifth of *Iyar* falls on *Shabbat, Yom HaAtzma'ut* is celebrated on the previous Thursday, and *Yom HaZikaron* is observed on Wednesday.

7.10.4 *LaG baOmer*

The thirty-third day of the *Omer,* which corresponds to the eighteenth day of *Iyar,* is called *LaG baOmer* (the numberical value of *LaG—lamed + gimel—*is thirty-three). It is considered a minor holiday and is observed as a day of celebration because the deaths of Rabbi Akiva's students stopped on that day. In recognition of this, the restrictions that apply to the *Omer* period are suspended for that day (see Section 4.6.2).

7.10.5 *Yom Yerushalayim*

On the twenty-eighth day of *Iyar,* we celebrate *Yom Yerushalayim,* Jerusalem Day, marking the anniversary of the 1967 Reunification of Jerusalem during the Six Day War. Jerusalem, the eternal capital of the ancient Land of Israel, *Eretz Yisrael,* and the modern State of Israel, *Medinat Yisrael.*

7.11 The Festival of Weeks

Chag HaShavuot, the Festival of Weeks, is celebrated on the sixth and seventh days of the month of *Sivan.* The second of the Pilgrimage Festivals, it derives its name from the Hebrew word ***shavua,*** meaning *week.* The name *Chag Shavuot* is found in the Torah.

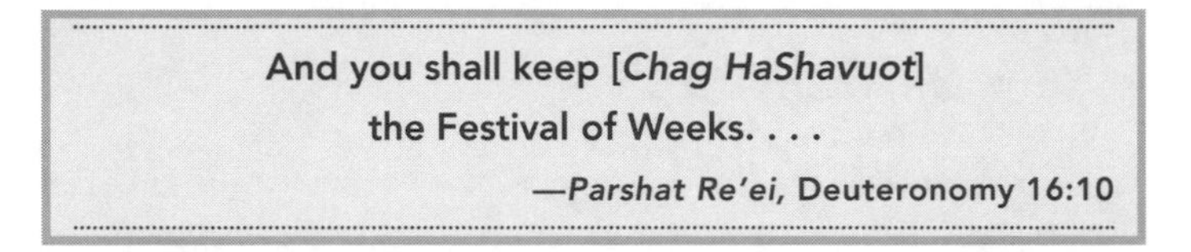
And you shall keep [*Chag HaShavuot*]
the Festival of Weeks. . . .
—*Parshat Re'ei,* Deuteronomy 16:10

In the discussion of *Sefirat HaOmer* (see Section 7.4.16), it was noted that we count seven weeks from the second night of *Pesach* until *Shavuot.* In the Diaspora, *Shavuot* is observed for two days, in Israel, for one.

Calendar for the First Day of *Shavuot*

Secular Year	Hebrew Year	Day of the Week	Secular Date
2001	5761	Monday	May 28
2002	5762	Friday	May 17
2003	5763	Friday	June 6
2004	5764	Wednesday	May 26
2005	5765	Monday	June 13
2006	5766	Friday	June 2
2007	5767	Wednesday	May 23
2008	5768	Monday	June 9
2009	5769	Friday	May 29
2010	5770	Wednesday	May 19

7.11.1 Other Festival Names

Shavuot is also known by several other names, including: (1) ***Yom HaBikkurim,*** the Day of the First Fruits, commemorating the time when the Jewish people joyfully brought the best of the first yield of the wheat harvest to the Temple as a sacrifice. This name is found in the Torah.

> **On the Day of the First Fruits [*Yom HaBikkurim*],**
> **when you bring a new meal-offering to the Lord,**
> **in your Festival of Weeks [*Chag HaShavuot*],**
> **you shall have a holy convocation;**
> **you shall not do any manner of servile work.**
> **—*Parshat Pinchas*, Numbers 28:26**

Other names are: (2) ***Chag HaKatzir,*** Festival of the Harvest, because the wheat harvest, from which the *bikkurim* offering was taken, was brought in from the fields.

> **. . . and the Festival of the Harvest [*Chag HaKatzir*]. . . .**
> **—*Parshat Mishpatim*, Exodus 23:16**

Another name is: (3) ***Z'man Matan Toratenu,*** the Season of the Giving of Our Torah, because it is the day on which the Torah, the moral foundation of the Jewish people, was given at Mount Sinai. This name is not found in the Torah, but is used in the liturgy, in the middle blessing of the *Shemoneh Esrei.*

> You, Lord, our God, have given us in love
> (Sabbaths for rest,)
> holidays for gladness, festivals for happiness,
> on this (Sabbath and this)
> Festival of Weeks . . . the Season of the Giving of Our Torah.

It is noteworthy that the festival is called the Season of the *Giving* of Our Torah, not of *receiving* it. According to the Talmud, *Masechet Eruvin* 54a, the Torah is considered a gift from God to the Jewish people. Those who humbly undertake to study it will be able to remember what they have learned; otherwise, they will not. In *Masechet Avodah Zarah* 19a, the Talmud further comments that even those who don't have the innate intellectual ability to learn Torah will be granted it as a gift provided they strive earnestly to acquire it.

The other names for *Shavuot* also include: (4) ***Atzeret,*** a term that refers to a "concluding festival," because *Shavuot* serves as a conclusion to Passover, when *Sefirat HaOmer,* the period of counting days to *Shavuot,* started (Talmud, *Masechet Yevamot* 62b; *Midrash, Vayikra Rabbah* 28:3); and occasionally, (5) ***Chag HaYerek,*** the Festival of Greenery, in recognition of its setting in the wilderness. Although this name does not appear in the Torah or the Talmud, we do find reference to the grassy lands around the mountain in *Parshat Ki Tissa,* Exodus 34:3.

7.11.2 The Covenant with God

Z'man Matan Toratenu represents the spiritual essence of the festival of *Shavuot*. It puts the crowning touch on the seven-week period that began on *Pesach,* linking the two festivals and fulfilling the divine purpose of the Exodus.

In the biblical account of the Exodus, the Israelites left Egypt in haste, heading into the wilderness en route to *Eretz Yisrael.* On the sixth day of *Sivan,* seven weeks after the Exodus, they encamped at Mount Sinai. On that day, they received the Ten Commandments at Mount Sinai directly from God, marking the first time that the Jewish people as a nation affirmed their covenant with God and pledged themselves to the observance of the precepts of the Torah. Not only was the covenant made with the Jews at Mount Sinai, but even with those yet to be born.

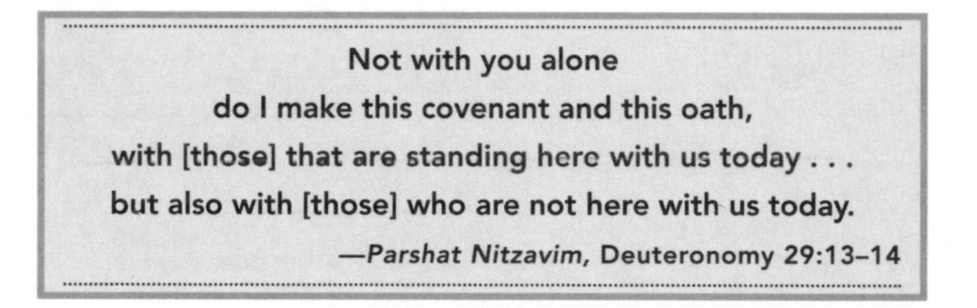

Not with you alone
do I make this covenant and this oath,
with [those] that are standing here with us today . . .
but also with [those] who are not here with us today.
—*Parshat Nitzavim,* Deuteronomy 29:13–14

According to the *Midrash Aseret HaDibrot* and the Talmud, *Masechet Avodah Zarah* 2b, God also offered the Torah to other nations. Each refused to accept it because they would not observe certain commandments. When God offered the Torah to the Jewish people, they accepted unconditionally.

And he [Moses] took the Book of the Covenant
and read in the ears of the people;
and they said:
"All that the Lord has spoken,
we will do and obey."
—*Parshat Mishpatim,* Exodus 24:7

The Revelation is the culminating event that joins *Pesach* and *Shavuot,* for physical freedom from slavery without the spiritual guidelines set forth in the Torah would have been meaningless.

7.12 Customs and Observances of *Shavuot*

There are no *mitzvot* associated *specifically* with the observance of *Shavuot.* Of course, the kindling of festival lights, the recitation of *Kiddush,* the obligation to pray, and the observance of all the laws of the festival, including *eruv tavshilin* (when appropriate), apply to *Shavuot,* as to all other festivals. There are, however, a few special customs and observances that mark the Festival of Weeks: (1) eating dairy foods; (2) decorating with greenery; and (3) studying Torah throughout the first night of the *Yom Tov.*

7.12.1 Eating Dairy Foods

Once the Torah was given, the Jewish people were required to immediately observe the dietary laws (see Section 9.7.5), which require the separation of meat and dairy foods and utensils. Because they did not have the proper utensils for preparing both dairy and meat, and were not able to fully comply with these laws, they were instructed to eat only dairy foods. Therefore, it is a traditional practice to eat special foods, such as ***blintzes,*** thin pancakes (crepes) filled with sweetened cheese, cheesecakes, and other dairy delights, for at least one festival meal. This practice also may suggest the "land flowing with milk and honey," the land of Canaan, the Promised Land.

7.12.2 Decorating with Greenery

On *Chag HaYerek,* it is customary to decorate both the synagogue and the home with greenery and flowers, recalling the mountain foliage that surrounded Mount Sinai. It is also symbolic of the reeds in which the infant Moses was hidden in Egypt and from which he was rescued on the sixth of *Sivan.*

Some communities adorn the Torah scrolls themselves with roses, a reference to Israel, who, according to a midrashic interpretation of Song of Songs, is likened to the one fragrant rose among the thorns in the world willing to accept the Torah.

Because of the laws of *muktzeh* (see Section 5.9.6), all decorating must be completed before *Yom Tov,* but may not be done on the Sabbath in preparation for the coming festival.

7.12.3 Studying Torah on the First Night

It is also traditional to stay awake all night on the first night of *Shavuot* to study Torah. Often synagogues hold special study sessions where scholars and beginners alike can gather in the late evening to study together until dawn.

7.13 The Revelation

The Revelation at Sinai stands as the seminal event in Jewish history. Encamped at the foot of the mountain, six hundred thousand Jewish men, together with their wives and children, were summoned to hear the word of God directly from Him. The translation that follows is based on Rashi's commentary.

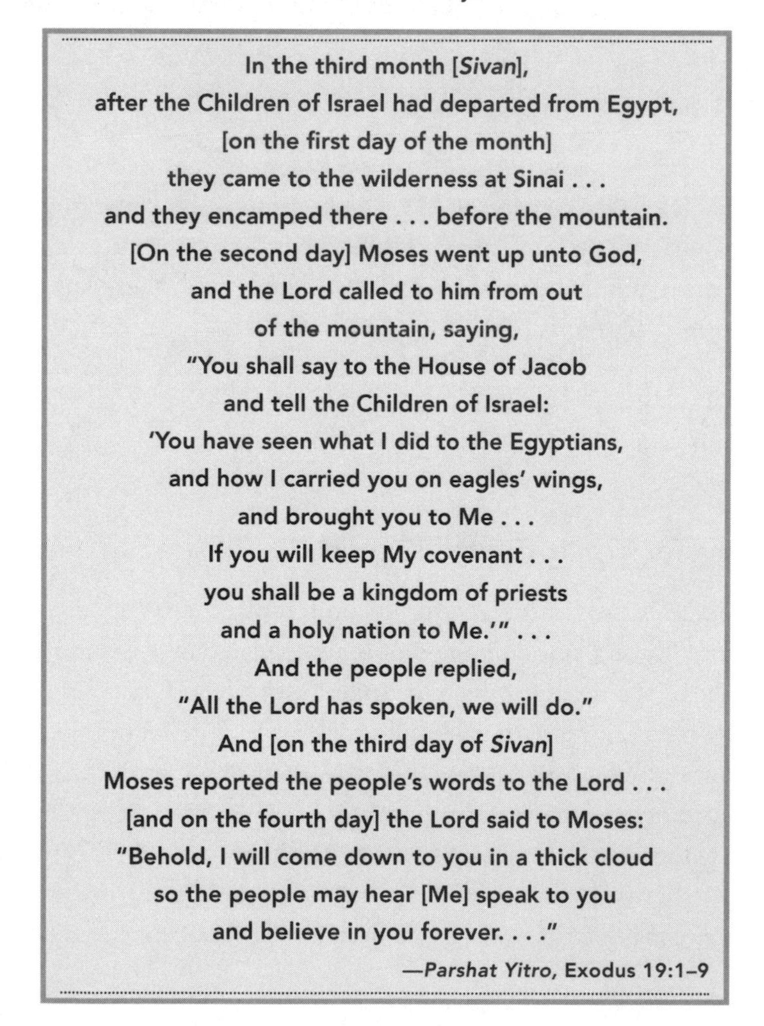

In the third month [*Sivan*],
after the Children of Israel had departed from Egypt,
[on the first day of the month]
they came to the wilderness at Sinai . . .
and they encamped there . . . before the mountain.
[On the second day] Moses went up unto God,
and the Lord called to him from out
of the mountain, saying,
"You shall say to the House of Jacob
and tell the Children of Israel:
'You have seen what I did to the Egyptians,
and how I carried you on eagles' wings,
and brought you to Me . . .
If you will keep My covenant . . .
you shall be a kingdom of priests
and a holy nation to Me.'" . . .
And the people replied,
"All the Lord has spoken, we will do."
And [on the third day of *Sivan*]
Moses reported the people's words to the Lord . . .
[and on the fourth day] the Lord said to Moses:
"Behold, I will come down to you in a thick cloud
so the people may hear [Me] speak to you
and believe in you forever. . . ."

—*Parshat Yitro*, Exodus 19:1–9

God then told Moses to instruct the people to sanctify themselves and wash their garments on the fourth and fifth days of *Sivan*, preparing themselves for what would transpire on the sixth day.

> **. . . For on the third day**
> **[after the preparation, that is, the sixth day of *Sivan*],**
> **the Lord will come down**
> **before the eyes of all the people on Mount Sinai.**
> **And you [Moses] shall set up boundaries**
> **around [the mountain], saying**
> **"Take heed [not] to go up into the mountain**
> **or to touch its borders. . . ."**
>
> —*Parshat Yitro,* Exodus 19:11–12

The people sanctified themselves and washed their garments in preparation for the Revelation.

> **And it came to pass**
> **on the morning of [the sixth day of *Sivan*],**
> **there was thunder, lightning,**
> **and a thick cloud upon the mountain. . . .**
>
> —*Parshat Yitro,* Exodus 19:16

The people stood in the camp below the mountain, and they trembled, as they heard the sound of an extraordinarily loud *shofar.*

> **And Moses brought the people forward to meet God. . . .**
> **Now Mount Sinai [burned and] smoked,**
> **because the Lord descended upon it in fire . . .**
> **and the whole mountain quaked mightily.**
> **And when the sound of the *shofar* grew louder and louder,**
> **Moses spoke and God answered him. . . .**
> **And the Lord came down upon Mount Sinai**
> **to the top of the mountain.**
>
> —*Parshat Yitro,* Exodus 19:17–20

God commanded Moses to warn the people to stay back, lest they die in their zealous attempt to see Him. He instructed Moses to come up with Aaron and the Priests, and Moses went and told them what God had said.

7.13.1 The Ten Commandments

We find in *Parshat Yitro,* Exodus 20:2-14, that God spoke the words of the ***Aseret HaDibrot,*** the Ten Commandments, in one utterance.

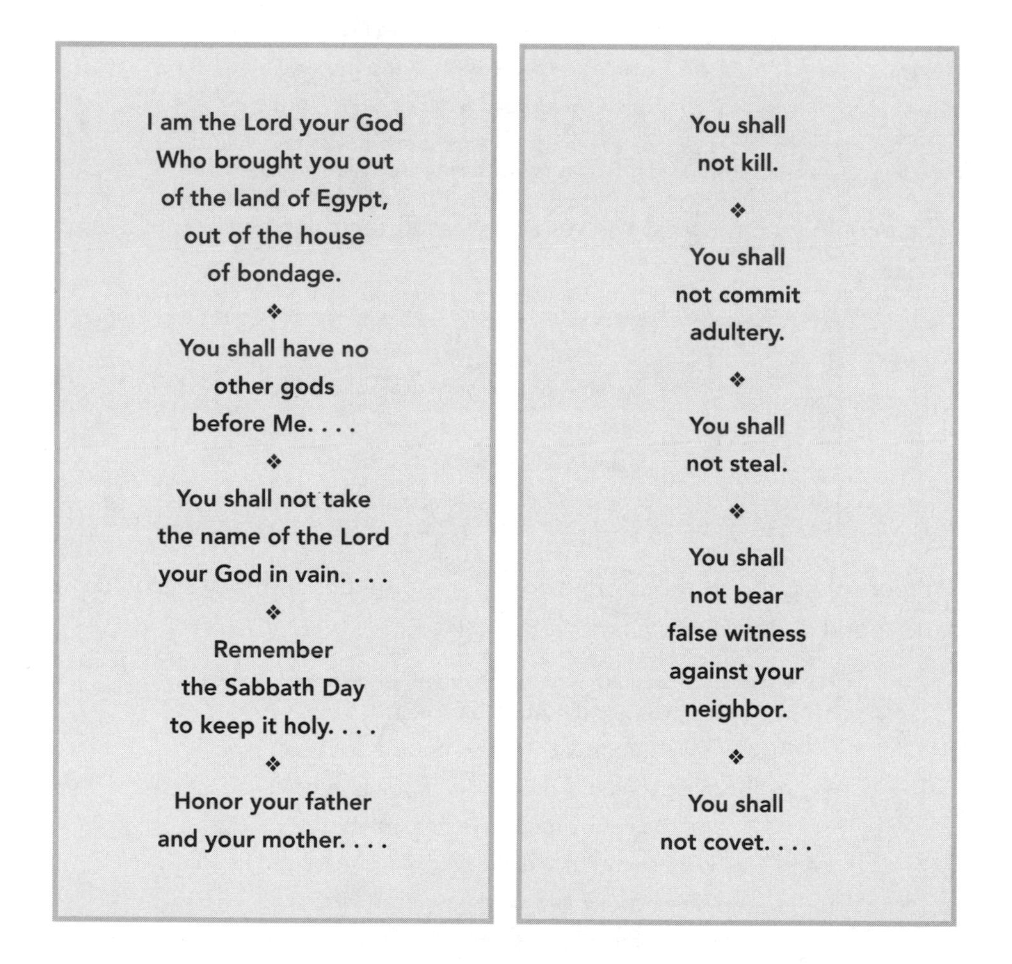

I am the Lord your God Who brought you out of the land of Egypt, out of the house of bondage.
You shall have no other gods before Me. . . .
You shall not take the name of the Lord your God in vain. . . .
Remember the Sabbath Day to keep it holy. . . .
Honor your father and your mother. . . .
You shall not kill.
You shall not commit adultery.
You shall not steal.
You shall not bear false witness against your neighbor.
You shall not covet. . . .

All the people witnessed the thunder and lightning, the sound of the *shofar,* and the smoking mountain, and they trembled and moved far off. Because the people heard God speak to Moses directly, he was forever established as the true prophet of Israel.

From generation to generation, the Jewish people continue to bear witness to the Revelation every day, to fulfill the *mitzvah* of remembering the events at Sinai, not just on *Shavuot,* but always.

In *Parshat Yitro,* Exodus 19:3, above, we read:

> You shall say to the House of Jacob and tell the Children of Israel. . . .

From Rashi, we learn that "House of Jacob" refers to the women and "Children of Israel" to the men. Thus, the Torah was given to both women and men—but to the women first.

In the midrashic commentary on Exodus, we find a description of the awesome moments before the Revelation. Rabbi Avahu says in the name of Rabbi Yochanan:

> **When the Holy One, blessed be He, revealed the Torah,**
> **not a bird twittered, not a fowl took flight,**
> **not an ox bellowed,**
> **not an angel ascended nor a seraph proclaimed *Kedushah.***
> **The sea did not surge, and not a creature uttered a sound.**
> **The limitless universe was silent and still.**
> **Then the voice went forth and proclaimed,**
> **"I am the Lord, your God."**
>
> ***—Shemot Rabbah* 29:9**

Motivated by pure love of God, the Jewish people had promised to "do and obey" all that God told them, even before He revealed the Torah at Sinai. They trembled at the enormity of the Revelation, which, with its tremendous noise and fire, kindled a feeling of utter terror and a heightened sense of reverence. Thus, we recognize that both boundless love and fear—that is, awe—are required in relationship to God and His Torah. We rejoice in the wisdom of its eternal truth and pray that God will grant us a portion in His Torah, so that we can attain a measure of knowledge of God and draw closer to Him, which is the ultimate purpose of the Jewish people.

All 613 *mitzvot* are subsumed in the words of the *Aseret HaDibrot.* The Ten Commandments were inscribed on the two *Luchot HaBrit,* Tablets of the Covenant, five on each. Moses ascended Mount Sinai to receive the *Luchot* from God. For forty days and nights, He taught him the entire Torah, commanding him to teach it to the Children of Israel.

And He gave to Moses—
when He finished speaking with him on Mount Sinai—
the two Tablets of the testimony,
tablets of stone written with the finger of God.

—*Parshat Ki Tissa*, Exodus 31:18

And the Tablets were the work of God,
and the writing was the writing of God,
engraved upon the Tablets.

—*Parshat Ki Tissa*, Exodus 32:16

The two Tablets, which were identical in size and shape, are of equal religious signficance, and are to be considered as one tablet. The first five commandments refer to *mitzvot* between the individual and God. The remaining five represent obligations between individuals. These two constituent parts form an inseparable whole, for only by observing them in their entirety can we serve God properly.

According to some commentaries, the two *Luchot* symbolize the Written and Oral Laws, which were both transmitted to Moses by God at Mount Sinai. As we discussed in Chapter 1, everything in the Oral Law is found in the Written Law; so, they, too, are eternally linked.

According to the Talmud, *Masechet Makkot* 23b, the *Taryag Mitzvot,* as perceived on a human level, are derived from the Ten Commandments. On a more profound level, the Ten Commandments all echo and evolve from the First Commandment.

Each *mitzvah* can be identified in one of the Ten Commandments, according to the teachings of Rabbi Sa'adiah Gaon (880–942), a philosopher, scholar, and biblical commentator of Egyptian heritage. The sainted Gaon of Vilna, Elijah ben Solomon (1720–1797), also draws an analogy between the words of the Ten Commandments and the words of the *Kriat Shema,* which we recite twice daily.

The Ten Commandments are the guiding principles of ethical behavior and constitute the moral foundation for all civilization. For the Jewish people, they encompass all 613 *mitzvot,* and, thus, embody the code of righteous conduct in a single divine utterance.

7.13.2 The Second *Luchot*

When Moses descended from Mount Sinai on the seventeenth day of *Tammuz* with the *Luchot,* he was horrified to see that, in his absence, the people had created a golden calf. He smashed the Tablets, and the people, who only days before had been proclaimed a holy nation, were reduced to a level of sinfulness.

After repenting, the people were forgiven by God, and again Moses ascended the mountain to receive new *Luchot.* On the tenth of *Tishrei,* which was *Yom Kippur,* he returned with the second set. This set was different from the first in that God had engraved them, but they had been formed into tablets by Moses. According to Rashi, the *Luchot,* both the first and the second, were carved from sapphires.

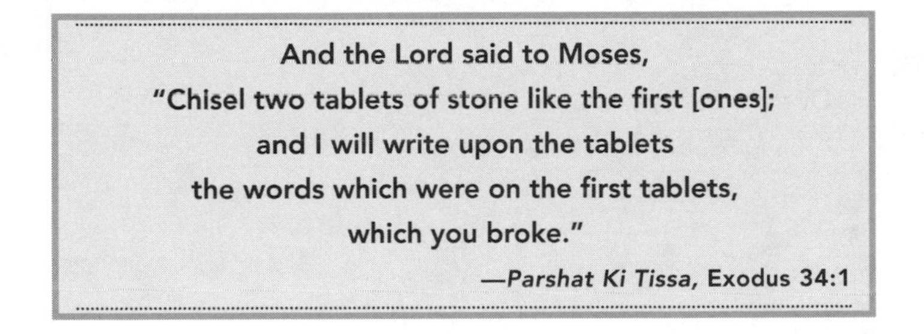

And the Lord said to Moses,
"Chisel two tablets of stone like the first [ones];
and I will write upon the tablets
the words which were on the first tablets,
which you broke."

—*Parshat Ki Tissa,* Exodus 34:1

According to the Talmud, *Masechet Bava Batra* 14b, God instructed Moses to place both the new *Luchot* and the shattered pieces of the first Tablets in the Holy Ark.

7.14 The Liturgy of *Shavuot*

The liturgy of *Shavuot* parallels that of *Pesach.* The *Shemoneh Esrei* contains seven blessings, and the middle blessing expresses the holiness of the festival day. The words "Festival of Weeks" and "Season of the Giving of Our Torah" replace "Festival of Unleavened Bread" and "Season of Our Freedom."

After *Shacharit, Hallel* is recited on both days, and during *Musaf,* prayers specific to the holiday are inserted. *Yizkor* is recited on the second day.

7.15 *Kriat HaTorah* for *Shavuot*

The Torah is read in the synagogue on both days of *Shavuot.* There are five *aliyot,* except if the festival day coincides with the Sabbath, when there are seven *aliyot.* Below is a listing of the Torah portion, the *Maftir,* and the *Haftarah* for the two days. Note that the *Maftir* portion is the same on both days, inasmuch as the text refers to the commandment to observe the Festival of Weeks.

First Day
Parshat Yitro, Exodus 19:1–20:23

When the Ten Commandments, Exodus 20:2–14, are read during the fourth *aliyah,* it is customary in some synagogues for the congregation to rise and remain standing until the *aliyah* is concluded.

Maftir: Parshat Pinchas, Numbers 28:26–31
Haftarah: Ezekiel 1:1–28; 3:12

Second Day
Parshat Re'ei, Deuteronomy 14:22–16:17
Maftir: Parshat Pinchas, Numbers 28:26–31
Haftarah: Habakkuk 2:20–3:19

7.16 Special Readings for *Shavuot*

Two special readings are associated with *Shavuot:* ***Akdamut*** and ***Megillat Ruth.***

7.16.1 *Akdamut*

On the first day of *Shavuot,* just before *Kriat HaTorah,* it is customary to recite a liturgical poem, *Akdamut,* a mystical depiction of the Creation of the World, the greatness of the Creator, the excellence of the Torah, and the joys of the World to Come.

The Torah is removed from the Ark, and the *Kohen* is summoned; but before he recites the first blessing on the Torah, *Akdamut* is chanted. Written in Aramaic, *Akdamut* begins with the poet's request for permission, both from God and the worshippers, to offer his interpretation of the words of the Torah, that is, the Ten Commandments.

In ninety verses, comprised of two main themes, Rabbi Meir ben Yitzchak, an eleventh-century poet, describes: (1) the angels' praise of God in the heavens; and (2) the greatness of the Jewish people on earth, who remain faithful to God in spite of their tribulation.

When *Akdamut* has been concluded, the *Kohen* recites the blessings on the Torah, and *Kriat HaTorah* begins.

7.16.2 *Megillat Ruth*

On the second day of *Shavuot* after *Hallel,* but before the Torah is removed from the Ark, the Book (literally, Scroll) of Ruth, is read in the synagogue.

The Book of Ruth is set during the period of the Judges in ancient Israel, about three thousand years ago. It was a time of famine, and Elimelech, a wealthy leader of the Jewish community, his wife Naomi, and their two sons, Machlon and Killion, fled from *Eretz Yisrael* to the land of Moab, where he sought to escape his responsibilities to help the Jewish community. He died in Moab, leaving his widow to raise her two sons.

In time, Machlon and Killion married Ruth and Orpah, daughters of the king of Moab. Instead of returning to their homeland to help, they, too, met untimely deaths, and the three widows were left destitute.

Eventually, Naomi heard that the famine was over, and she longed to return to *Eretz Yisrael.* She encouraged her daughters-in-law to stay in Moab. Orpah wept, but, in time, she bid her mother-in-law farewell; Ruth wept also, but she pleaded with Naomi to allow her to come along with her. In the famous passage, Ruth professed her loyalty and affirmed her desire to become a Jew and adopt the ways of her mother-in-law.

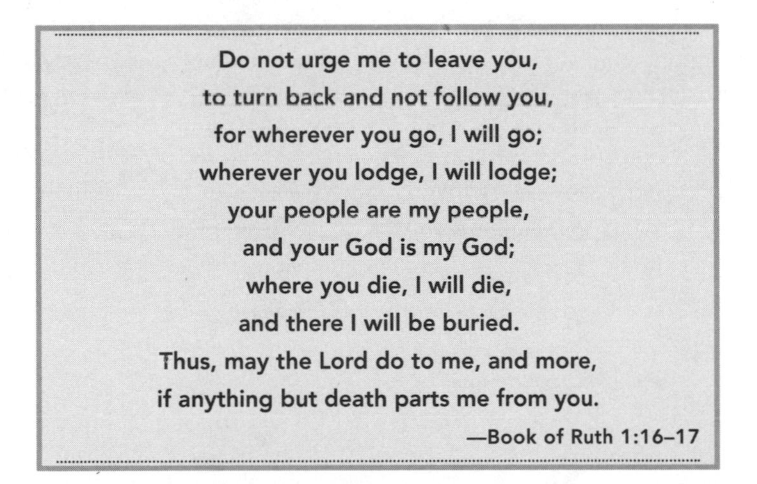

Do not urge me to leave you,
to turn back and not follow you,
for wherever you go, I will go;
wherever you lodge, I will lodge;
your people are my people,
and your God is my God;
where you die, I will die,
and there I will be buried.
Thus, may the Lord do to me, and more,
if anything but death parts me from you.
—Book of Ruth 1:16–17

The two impoverished women returned to *Eretz Yisrael,* where the prosperous Boaz, a relative of Elimelech, was the judge and leader of the Jewish community. Boaz admired Ruth's devotion to Naomi, and he watched as she gathered the overlooked sheaves in his fields.

With Naomi's encouragement, Ruth and Boaz met and were married. Ruth gave birth to Oved, the father of Jesse, whose son David would rise to become the King of Judah and Israel. Ruth's decision to convert to the faith of her mother-in-law and her subsequent marriage to Boaz, the spiritual leader of his generation, marked the beginning of the House of David, from which the Messiah will come to bring the ultimate redemption.

On *Shavuot,* the story of Ruth inspires us to fulfill our spiritual potential, as Ruth fulfilled hers and became the Mother of Royalty.

7.17 The Festival of Tabernacles

The third of the *Shalosh Regalim* is *Chag HaSukkot,* the Festival of Tabernacles. *Sukkot* begins on the fifteenth day of *Tishrei,* just five days after *Yom Kippur* (see Chapter 6). In the Diaspora, it is observed for seven days: two days of *Yom Tov* followed by five days of *Chol HaMo'ed.* In Israel, only the first day is observed as *Yom Tov,* and the remaining six are *Chol HaMo'ed.*

> **And the Lord spoke to Moses, saying,**
> **"Speak to the Children of Israel, saying,**
> **'On the fifteenth day of this seventh month**
> **is the Festival of Tabernacles, seven days for the Lord.' "**
>
> **—*Parshat Emor,* Leviticus 23:34**

Calendar for the First Day of *Sukkot*

Secular Year	Hebrew Year	Day of the Week	Secular Date
2001	5762	Tuesday	October 2
2002	5763	Saturday	September 21
2003	5764	Saturday	October 11
2004	5765	Thursday	September 30
2005	5766	Tuesday	October 18
2006	5767	Saturday	October 7
2007	5768	Thursday	September 27
2008	5769	Tuesday	October 14
2009	5770	Saturday	October 3
2010	5771	Thursday	September 23

Two additional holy days (one in Israel), which are really separate festivals, follow *Chol HaMo'ed.* We will discuss these later.

Sukkot commemorates the time in the wilderness when the Jewish people lived in huts or tabernacles, as they journeyed from Egypt to the Promised Land. The hut is called a ***sukkah,*** from which the festival derives its most familiar name.

As we noted at the beginning of the chapter, *Sukkot* is also referred to in the Torah as ***Chag HaAsif,*** Festival of the Ingathering of the autumn harvest, at the end of the growing season (*Parshat Mishpatim,* Exodus 23:16). Rashi explains that this is the Festival of Tabernacles.

In the liturgy, it is referred to as ***Z'man Simchatenu,*** Season of Rejoicing, a reference to the biblical commandment:

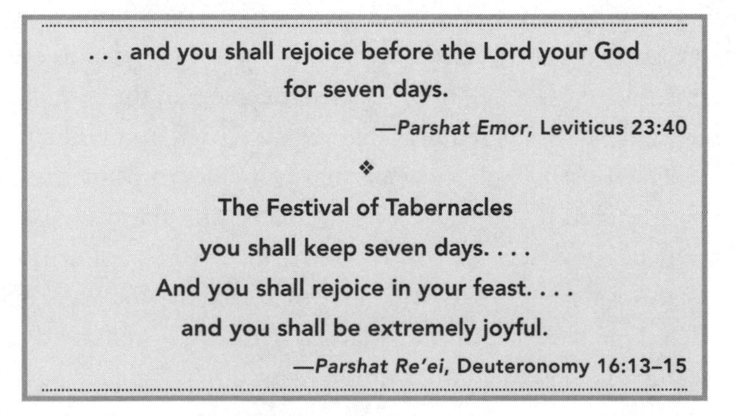
. . . and you shall rejoice before the Lord your God for seven days.

—*Parshat Emor,* Leviticus 23:40

❖

The Festival of Tabernacles
you shall keep seven days. . . .
And you shall rejoice in your feast. . . .
and you shall be extremely joyful.

—*Parshat Re'ei,* Deuteronomy 16:13–15

The Festival of Tabernacles is the culminating observance of the *Yamim Nora'im,* the Days of Awe, which precede it. While the other two festivals of the *Shalosh Regalim* are certainly intended to be occasions to rejoice, it is specifically mentioned three times in the Torah in connection with *Sukkot.*

7.18 Customs and Observances of *Sukkot*

There are several rituals and customs associated with the observance of *Sukkot,* including: (1) building the *sukkah;* (2) decorating the *sukkah;* (3) taking the Four Species; and (4) the Feast of Drawing Water. Let's take a look at these more closely.

7.18.1 Building the *Sukkah*

In observance of the biblical precept to dwell in booths, Jews build a *sukkah,* a fragile hut, outside their homes.

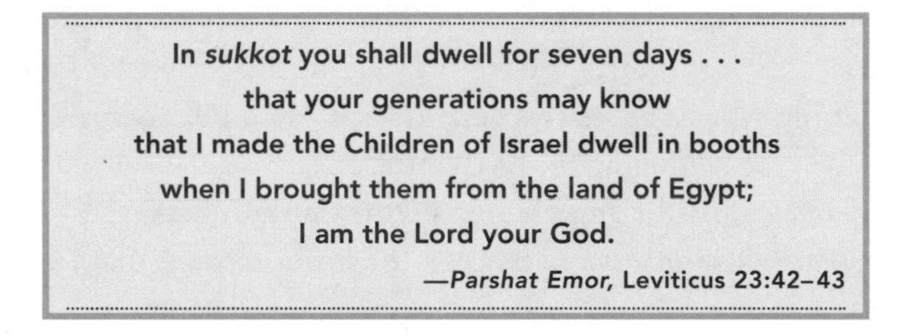

In *sukkot* you shall dwell for seven days . . .
that your generations may know
that I made the Children of Israel dwell in booths
when I brought them from the land of Egypt;
I am the Lord your God.

—*Parshat Emor,* Leviticus 23:42–43

The *sukkah* must be a temporary structure, only strong enough to withstand normal wind gusts. The construction of the *sukkah* should begin as soon after *Yom Kippur* as possible. It is permissible, however, to erect it before *Yom Kippur,* if there will be insufficient time to finish it before *Sukkot* begins. If it is not possible to erect a *sukkah* at home, it is permissible to use a neighbor's *sukkah* or to eat in the *sukkah* erected by the synagogue, because the *halachah* requires that we dwell in it, not build it.

How is a *sukkah* constructed? The walls may be made from any material—wooden boards, canvas suspended on a metal frame (available commercially in various sizes), even stones. It may be professionally constructed, for example, out of fiberglass panels, so that it is easy to reassemble year after year; or it may be the work of an amateur, hastily designed and put together. It must have at least three walls, and each wall must be at least thirty-eight inches high but not more than thirty-five feet.

The roof, called ***s'chach,*** must be made from a material which comes from a living plant, such as branches of pine or willow, bamboo poles or mats, or even cornstalks. No metal may be used in the construction of the roof, and the *sukkah* must not be built under overhanging trees or under a balcony or other projection. The stars should be visible at night, but the *s'chach* must be thick enough so that there is more shade than sunlight inside the *sukkah* during the day.

7.18.2 Decorating the *Sukkah*

In keeping with the spirit of joy that is the dominant theme of the festival, it is customary to decorate the *sukkah* with ***noi sukkah,*** including real or artificial fruits, gourds, glittery garlands and ornamental objects (available in Jewish bookstores and craft shops), and so forth. According to the Talmud, *Masechet Sukkah* 28b, the *mitzvah* is further beautified by using a festive tablecloth, fine dishes, and the like, in the *sukkah.*

It is also traditional to symbolically invite seven ancestors as honored guests. These unseen visitors, who are said to visit the *sukkah* during the holiday, are called ***Ushpizin.*** According to tradition, all seven visit the *sukkah* every day of the festival, but one, in turn, is the special guest of honor each day, and a specific verse is recited in his honor. They are:

- Day 1 Abraham
- Day 2 Isaac
- Day 3 Jacob
- Day 4 Joseph
- Day 5 Moses
- Day 6 Aaron
- Day 7 King David

During the week of *Sukkot,* Jews are obligated to live in the *sukkah,* to eat meals there, and even sleep there, if possible. If rain is heavy and interferes with the ordinary use of the *sukkah,* it is permissible to eat in the house. On the first two days of the festival, which are called *Yom Tov,* and on the Sabbath, the following *berachah* is recited at the beginning of the festival meal after *Kiddush*. On the other days of *Sukkot*, it is recited after *hamotzi*. Of course, it is not recited if one eats indoors.

Recite the *Berachah* in the *Sukkah*

Baruch Atah, HaShem E-lo-kenu, Melech HaOlam,
asher kidshanu b'mitzvotav v'tzivanu
leishev basukkah.

❖

Blessed are You, Lord our God, King of the Universe,
Who has sanctified us with His commandments and commanded us
to dwell in the *sukkah*.

It is customary to invite guests for festival meals, especially if they do not have a *sukkah* of their own.

7.18.3 *Sukkot* in the Synagogue

In the synagogue, a committee of members, usually volunteers, is appointed to erect and decorate the congregation's *sukkah*. Often of sizable proportions, the *sukkah* is set up to the side or back of the synagogue building. Some synagogues plan for the *sukkah* in their architectural design, allowing sufficient space to accommodate the membership.

Following services, in the evening and in the morning, the worshippers gather in the *sukkah* to partake of the festival *Kiddush*. At a minimum, wine and cakes are served, and everyone recites the appropriate blessings.

In some communities, a festival meal, usually arranged by reservation, is served during the holiday week. Elsewhere, congregants and their guests may simply bring their own food to the synagogue *sukkah*, where they can fulfill the *mitzvah* and rejoice in celebrating the festival together.

In some locales, kosher hotels and restaurants erect a *sukkah* for the convenience of their patrons during the holiday as well.

7.18.4 The Feast of Drawing Water

According to the sages, each year, there are four judgment days for the world.

- *Pesach* grain
- *Shavuot* first fruits
- *Rosh HaShanah* humankind
- *Sukkot* water

We have discussed the first three previously. What is the meaning of a judgment day for water? Just as God judges the crops in their seasons, so, too, does He judge the Jewish people. In the autumn, we petition Him for abundant water, and God renders His judgment at *Sukkot,* the time of the rainy season in Israel.

Simchat Bet HaSho'evah, the Feast of Drawing Water, refers to the water ceremony conducted on the first day of *Sukkot* at nightfall in the *Bet HaMikdash.* This celebration lasted throughout the night and into the next day.

According to the Mishnah, *Sukkah* 5:1-4, only those who have been fortunate enough to have witnessed *Simchat Bet HaSho'evah* have experienced true rejoicing. With the outer court of the Temple brilliantly illuminated by golden candelabra, the people gathered, singing and dancing in torchlight processions.

In the morning at daybreak, one of the *Kohanim,* who was selected especially for the task of drawing the water for the ceremony, was escorted by the procession to the Siloam pool in Jerusalem. He filled a golden vessel with water and brought it back to the Temple, where the water offering was poured on the sacrificial altar (with a libation of wine, as well), marking the beginning of the rainy season in *Eretz Yisrael.*

Today, many synagogues hold a special celebration on the first day of *Sukkot* at nightfall in commemoration of the *Simchat Bet HaSho'evah.*

7.18.5 Taking the Four Species

In addition to dwelling in the *sukkah,* Jews are obligated to take the Four Species, called the ***Arba Minim,*** on *Sukkot.* They are: (1) the ***lulav,*** palm branch; (2) the ***hadassim,*** myrtle; (3) the ***aravot,*** willow; and (4) the ***etrog,*** citron. All must meet specific requirements as set forth in the *Shulchan Aruch,* the Code of Jewish Law.

The ritual of the Four Species is based on the following biblical commandment.

> **And you shall take for yourselves on the first day**
> **the fruit of the goodly trees [*etrog*],**
> **branches of palm trees [*lulav*],**
> **boughs of thick-leafed trees [*hadassim*],**
> **and willows of the brook [*aravot*],**
> **and you shall rejoice before the Lord your God**
> **for seven days.**
>
> —*Parshat Emor,* Leviticus 23:40

The *etrog* is a lemon-colored—or sometimes green—citron with a fragrant scent, like that of a lemon. It is the most important of the Four Species. In order to be considered fit for ritual use, it must have a bumpy skin (unlike a lemon which is smooth) that is free of blemishes, and the flowering tip of the fruit, the ***pittum,*** and the stem at the base, the ***oketz,*** must be intact. (Some species grow without a *pittum* and are ritually fit for use.)

The *lulav* is a small branch of the date palm. The leaves overlap one another along a straight spine, coming to a point at the top. The front of the leaves are white, the backs are light green.

The *hadassim* are from the myrtle tree. A minimum of three twigs, covered from top to bottom with dark green leaves, in clusters of three, are required for fulfilling the obligation of the Four Species.

The *aravot* come from the willow tree that grows by the water. Two reddish twigs, covered with long, slender green leaves, are required for the *Arba Minim.* The edges of the leaves should be smooth.

The *lulav, hadassim,* and *aravot* are bound together by a band of palm leaves. The myrtle is positioned to the right of the palm, the willow to the left. The *lulav* is held in the right hand, the *etrog* in the left.

Selecting the perfect *etrog,* the straightest *lulav,* and the most beautifully shaped *hadassim* and *aravot* is often a time consuming process, but it is a tradition not to be missed. As Jews converge on Jewish bookstores, or cluster around sidewalk vendors who temporarily set up shop on street corners, the atmosphere is filled with palpable excitement as everyone checks and chooses, trying to buy the finest *Arba Minim* in honor of the festival. ***Etrogim*** (plural) are usually imported from Israel, but other crops are harvested in Morocco and Greece. The *Arba Minim* are available in all price ranges.

7.19 The Ritual of the Four Species

The ritual of the *Arba Minim* is performed during the day every day of the *Yom Tov,* except the Sabbath. Often, family members gather in the *sukkah* to perform the *mitzvah* before going to *shul.* The *lulav,* which is bound together with the *hadassim* and *aravot,* is picked up with the right hand, and the *etrog* with the left hand, *pittum* down. Then the following blessings are recited while standing.

The *Arba Minim,* which are used every day of *Sukkot* except the Sabbath, symbolize the many types of Jews.

Recite the *Berachot* on First Taking the *Arba Minim*

Baruch Atah, HaShem E-lo-kenu, Melech HaOlam,
asher kidshanu b'mitzvotav v'tzivanu
al n'tilat lulav.

❖

Blessed are You, Lord our God, King of the Universe,
Who has sanctified us with His commandments and commanded us
concerning the taking of the *lulav.*

❖

Baruch Atah, HaShem E-lo-kenu, Melech HaOlam,
she'hecheyanu, v'kiy'manu,
v'higiyanu laz'man hazeh.

❖

Blessed are You, Lord our God, King of the Universe,
Who has kept us alive, sustained us,
and brought us to this season.

On the first day, the *she'hecheyanu* blessing is added, expressing our gratitude for being permitted to reach this season again. It is not recited on the remaining days of the festival.

After reciting the blessings, the *etrog* is turned upright, and the Four Species are held together and waved in all six directions: first to the east, then south, then west, then north, then up, and then down. Originally, the individual's obligation to take the Four Species pertained only to the first day of the festival, as prescribed in the Torah (see above).

According to the Rambam (*Mishneh Torah,* Book of Seasons, Laws of Taking the *Lulav,* 7:13–17), in the days of the Holy Temple, the ritual was performed on all seven days except the Sabbath, unless the first day of *Sukkot* was on the Sabbath. After the Temple was destroyed, the sages decreed that the ritual should continue to be performed as it was during the days of the Temple; but today if the first day falls on the Sabbath, the Four Species are not used until the second day.

There are several symbolic interpretations of the Four Species. Just as the *etrog* tastes good and has a pleasant aroma, so too there are righteous individuals who are learned in Torah and perform good deeds. The *lulav* bears sweet fruit—dates—but has no fragrance; it is likened to those who are learned, but perform no good deeds. The *hadassim* bear no fruit, but have a pleasant fragrance; they are likened to those who are not knowledgeable in Torah, but perform good deeds; and finally, the *aravot,* which have neither fragrance nor fruit, are likened to those who are neither knowledgeable in the ways of Torah nor perform good deeds (*Midrash, Vayikra Rabbah* 30:11).

By combining the Four Species, all Jews are symbolically united, the pious and the indifferent, the learned and the untutored, bound together by their common heritage and their destiny to serve God.

Another interpretation of the Four Species compares them to four parts of the body. The *lulav* represents the spine; the *hadassim* are shaped like the eyes; the *aravot* are thin and tapered like the lips; and the *etrog* represents the heart. All these parts of the body join to work together to fulfill God's precepts.

7.20 The Seven Days of *Sukkot*

The first two days of *Sukkot* are called *Yom Tov,* and all the laws pertaining to the festival and to the Sabbath apply to these days with the exception of two: the preparation of food, and carrying between the private and the public domains. The same principles explained for *Pesach* and *Shavuot* apply to *Sukkot* as well (see Section 7.5).

The next five days are called *Chol HaMo'ed,* the Intermediate Days, so-called weekdays of the festival (see Section 7.6). Special restrictions of work, that is, *melachah,* apply to *Chol HaMo'ed,* but the full restrictions of the Sabbath do not, unless, of course, one of the days of *Chol HaMo'ed* falls on the Sabbath. The last day of *Chol HaMo'ed Sukkot* is called ***Hoshanah Rabbah,*** the Great ***Hoshanah,*** which we will discuss below.

7.21 The Liturgy of *Sukkot*

The basic *tefillot* of *Sukkot* are virtually identical to those of *Pesach* and *Shavuot,* except that the appropriate names of the festival are substituted as necessary. *Ya'aleh v'Yavo* is inserted in every *Amidah,* and *Hallel* is again recited every day after *Shacharit.* However, there are certain additions that are special to *Sukkot.*

7.21.1 Prayers for Salvation

In the synagogue, after the repetition of the *Shemoneh Esrei* of *Musaf,* special prayers called ***Hoshanot,*** meaning "please save," are recited on the first six days. These six prayers for deliverance, which are derived from biblical and midrashic sources, are recited in a particular order, depending on the day of the week.

The *Hoshanot* describe the destructive forces of nature and include prayers for God's protection of both animal and plant life. They allude to the patriarchs, matriarchs, Twelve Tribes of Israel, prophets, and kings.

One Torah Scroll is removed from the Ark, and the cantor leads the male members of the congregation, each holding his *Arba Minim,* in a counterclockwise procession once around the sanctuary, as the *Hoshanot* are recited.

7.21.2 *Hoshanah Rabbah*

On *Hoshanah Rabbah,* the fifth day of *Chol HaMo'ed,* which is the last day of *Sukkot,* all the *Sifrei Torah* are removed from the Ark as the congregational procession, led by the *chazan,* circles the sanctuary seven times with the *Arba Minim. Hoshanot* for that day are recited as the procession makes its way around the synagogue.

Hoshanah Rabbah is called the "day of striking twigs," according to the Mishnah in *Masechet Sukkah* 4:6. When the *Hoshanot* prayers are concluded, a bundle of five willow twigs, which are also referred to as ***hoshanot***, are struck against the floor five times. This symbolic casting off of sins on the last day of *Sukkot* is a ritual that links *Sukkot* with *Rosh HaShanah* and *Yom Kippur.*

Hoshanah Rabbah is also considered the last opportunity to recite *Tashlich,* a traditional service of *Rosh HaShanah* afternoon in which we *symbolically* cast away our sins (see Section 6.13). It is the final moment to pray to the Almighty to grant us a favorable decree. Until *Hoshanah Rabbah,* therefore, it is customary to wish our family and friends ***g'mar chatimah tovah,*** expressing our profound hope that they be *completely and irrevocably sealed* in the Book of Life for the coming year.

As the *Hoshanot* conclude, we loudly chant:

Conclude the Recitation of *Hoshanot*

The messenger heralds and proclaims.
The messenger heralds and proclaims.
The messenger heralds and proclaims.

We strike the floor five times with the *hoshanot* and recite:

. . . Accept with mercy and favor our processions . . .
hear our pleas and grant us the favorable seal . . .
seal us in the Book of Good Life. . . .
Amen.

7.22 *Kriat HaTorah* for *Sukkot*

The Torah is read every day of *Sukkot,* including *Chol HaMo'ed.* There are five *aliyot* on the days of *Yom Tov* and four on *Chol HaMo'ed,* except if any of those days fall on the Sabbath when seven honorees are called. The Torah reading and the *Maftir* are the same for the first two days, but different *Haftarot* are recited. A brief listing follows.

First Day
Parshat Emor, Leviticus 22:26–23:44
Maftir: Parshat Pinchas, Numbers 29:12–16
Haftarah: Zechariah 14:1–21

Second Day
Parshat Emor, Leviticus 22:26–23:44
Maftir: Parshat Pinchas, Numbers 29:12–16
Haftarah: I Kings 8:2–21

The Torah portions for *Chol HaMo'ed* vary, depending on whether or not there is a *Shabbat Chol HaMo'ed.*

7.23 The Eighth Day of Holy Convocation

The often-called eighth day of *Sukkot* is really a separate holiday called ***Shemini Atzeret,*** the Eighth Day of Holy Convocation. It commemorates God's desire to spend another day with the Jewish people, to have them stay with Him just a little longer, now that *Sukkot* has ended.

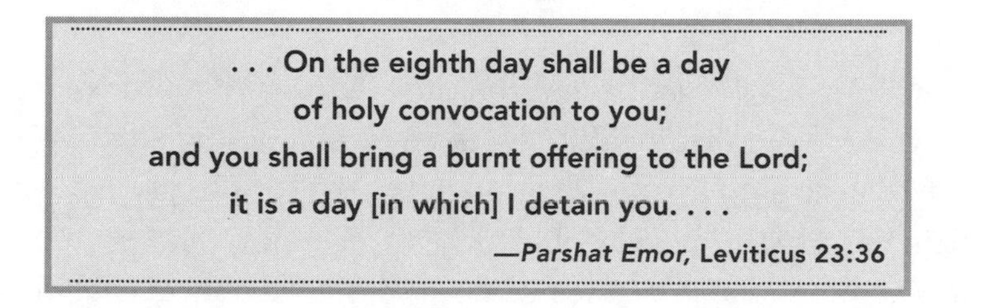

. . . On the eighth day shall be a day
of holy convocation to you;
and you shall bring a burnt offering to the Lord;
it is a day [in which] I detain you. . . .

—*Parshat Emor,* Leviticus 23:36

On this day, also called *Yom Tov,* all the laws of the festivals and the Sabbath apply in the same way as for the first two days of *Sukkot.*

Calendar for *Shemini Atzeret*

Secular Year	Hebrew Year	Day of the Week	Secular Date
2001	5762	Tuesday	October 9
2002	5763	Saturday	September 28
2003	5764	Saturday	October 18
2004	5765	Thursday	October 7
2005	5766	Tuesday	October 25
2006	5767	Saturday	October 14
2007	5768	Thursday	October 4
2008	5769	Tuesday	October 21
2009	5770	Saturday	October 10
2010	5771	Thursday	September 30

7.24 The Liturgy of *Shemini Atzeret*

In the liturgy, *Shemini Atzeret* like *Sukkot* (see Section 7.17), is also called *Z'man Simchatenu,* a Season of Rejoicing. The structure of the prayer services remains the same as for *Sukkot,* with the appropriate substitutions. In addition to *Hallel,* prayers in praise of God, *Yizkor* is recited. There are certain additions to the service that are specific to *Shemini Atzeret:* ***Tefillat Geshem***, the Prayer for Rain, and the reading of the Book of ***Kohelet,*** Ecclesiastes.

7.24.1 The Prayer for Rain

On *Shemini Atzeret, Tefillat Geshem* is recited during the cantor's repetition of the *Musaf.* The sages decreed that *Tefillat Geshem* be recited during *Sukkot,* the Pilgrimage Festival that falls nearest to the rainy season in Israel. However, because of the obligation to dwell in the *sukkah,* rainfall would make it uncomfortable or impossible to fulfill this *mitzvah.* Therefore, the Prayer for Rain was designated for recitation immediately after the *Sukkot* festival.

7.24.2 The Book of Ecclesiastes

Kohelet, which is attributed to King Solomon, is recited on *Shemini Atzeret* before *Kriat HaTorah.* It is one of the Five Scrolls that make up part of *Ketuvim.* Written in twelve chapters, it contains numerous fundamental truths and witty remarks about the sometimes-futile struggles of life and the cycles that seem to repeat throughout history. Although it seems to be written in a pessimistic tone, its wisdom rings true and provides illumination for the spirit.

7.25 *Kriat HaTorah* for *Shemini Atzeret*

The Torah portion of *Shemini Atzeret* is the same as that read on the eighth day of *Pesach* and the second day of *Shavuot.* The *Maftir* and *Haftarah* portions are specific to the festival.

Parshat Re'ei, Deuteronomy 14:22–16:17 (Sabbath); 15:19–16:17 (weekday)
Maftir: Parshat Pinchas, Numbers 29:35–30:1
Haftarah: I Kings 8:54–9:1

7.26 Bidding Farewell to the *Sukkah*

As we noted above, *Shemini Atzeret* is the day that God added to the *Sukkot* festival—to keep the Jewish people with Him just one more day. In keeping with that sentiment, we eat in the *sukkah* both on *Shemini Atzeret* eve and during the day, but without reciting the blessing:

> **. . . Who has . . . commanded us to dwell in the *sukkah*.**

On *Shemini Atzeret* day, after the festival meal, we bid farewell to the fragile, little hut.

7.27 The Day of Rejoicing with the Law

In the Diaspora, *Shemini Atzeret* is followed by ***Simchat Torah,*** the day of Rejoicing with the Law. In Israel, *Simchat Torah* and *Shemini Atzeret* are the same. In the Diaspora, *Simchat Torah,* like *Shemini Atzeret,* is observed as a day of *Yom Tov.* We rejoice because on this day, the annual cycle of the Reading of the Law is concluded and immediately begins again. The *Simchat Torah* festivities begin in the synagogue in the evening with ***Hakafot.***

During *Ma'ariv* on *Simchat Torah* eve, all the *Sifrei Torah* are removed from the *Aron HaKodesh.* All the men in the synagogue are honored with carrying a Torah in a gala procession called *Hakafot.* Often led by the rabbi and cantor, the congregation exuberantly parades around the sanctuary seven times carrying the Torah Scrolls, a tradition that dates back many centuries. (We can find a parallel to this in the days of the *Bet HaMikdash,* when the altar was encircled seven times, a recollection of the seven times Joshua circled Jericho before the walls of the city collapsed.) Singing joyful hymns of gratitude and praise, and dancing to express their great happiness, they circle around the synagogue—and sometimes into the street—with the *Sifrei Torah.* Their enthusiasm often continues for hours, or at least until every man in the synagogue has had an opportunity to carry the *Sefer Torah.*

It is customary in many synagogues for members to bid for the honor of reciting one of the special verses that are chanted prior to each procession. Sometimes a member purchases the honor on behalf of the rabbi, cantor, another congregant, or even the entire congregation.

Even young boys are honored in the procession, and children of all ages march with special flags, decorated with biblical themes and passages in celebration of the completion of the cycle of the Reading of the Torah. Women often form their own dance circles, joining in the celebration and sharing in the *mitzvah* to rejoice with the Torah.

After the evening *Hakafot,* a portion of the last *sidrah* of Deuteronomy *(Parshat V'zot HaBerachah)* is read. Depending on the *minhag* of the synagogue, either three or five men are called to the Reading of the Torah.

7.28 *Kriat HaTorah* for *Simchat Torah*

On *Simchat Torah* morning after *Hakafot,* all but three of the Torah Scrolls are returned to the Ark, and the Torah portion is divided among those *Sifrei Torah.* The entire *sidrah* of *V'zot HaBerachah* (Deuteronomy 33:1–34:12) is read in the synagogue amidst great celebration. The first five *aliyot* are read from the first Torah. Then, one man is honored as the ***Chatan Torah,*** the Bridegroom of the Torah. He recites the blessing before the concluding verses of *V'zot HaBerachah* are also read from the first Torah.

During the *aliyah* of *Chatan Torah,* all the young children present in the synagogue come up to the *shulchan* where the Torah is being read for ***Kol HaN'arim,*** literally, "all the youngsters." Several men hold the edges of a large *talit* and spread it like a canopy above the heads of the *ba'al korei,* the *Chatan Torah,* and the children. The children join in the recitation of the *berachot* before the Torah Reading. Then the final portion in Deuteronomy is read.

The annual cycle of *Kriat HaTorah* begins again, as another man is honored with the *aliyah* of ***Chatan Bereshit,*** the Bridegroom of Genesis. His portion is read from the second *Sefer Torah.* The *Maftir* portion is then read from the third *Sefer Torah.* The Torah readings are as follows:

First Torah

Parshat V'zot HaBerachah, Deuteronomy 33:1–26

Chatan Torah

Parshat V'zot HaBerachah, Deuteronomy 33:27–34:12

Second Torah

Chatan Bereshit

Parshat Bereshit, Genesis 1:1–2:3

Third Torah

Maftir: Pinchas, Numbers 29:35–30:1

Haftarah: Joshua 1:1–18

The rejoicing continues as Deuteronomy is completed and Genesis is begun again once more. By ending and immediately starting the cycle of Torah Reading again, the Jewish people reaffirm the belief that the study of Torah never ends, for the sages teach that the study of Torah must be a part of Jewish life every day.

Simchat Torah marks the end of a month of festivals. The *machzorim* are returned to the bookshelf, the honey dish is tucked safely away in the breakfront. The *sukkah* is dismantled, to be built again next year. The *lulav* and *etrog* are beginning to dry out. In past generations, it was a custom to save the *lulav*, setting it aside to use for lighting the fire to bake *matzot* before the next Passover. The *etrog* is often made into jelly, or saved and studded with cloves, its fragrant aroma mixing with the sweet spices, to be used during the *Havdalah* service, perhaps, a delightful reminder of the incense in the Temple.

LOOKING AHEAD! *The autumn months have begun, and Jews the world over begin to look forward to the rabbinically ordained celebrations of the Festival of Lights and the Festival of Lots. We will discuss these cherished holidays in Chapter 8.*

Word Works

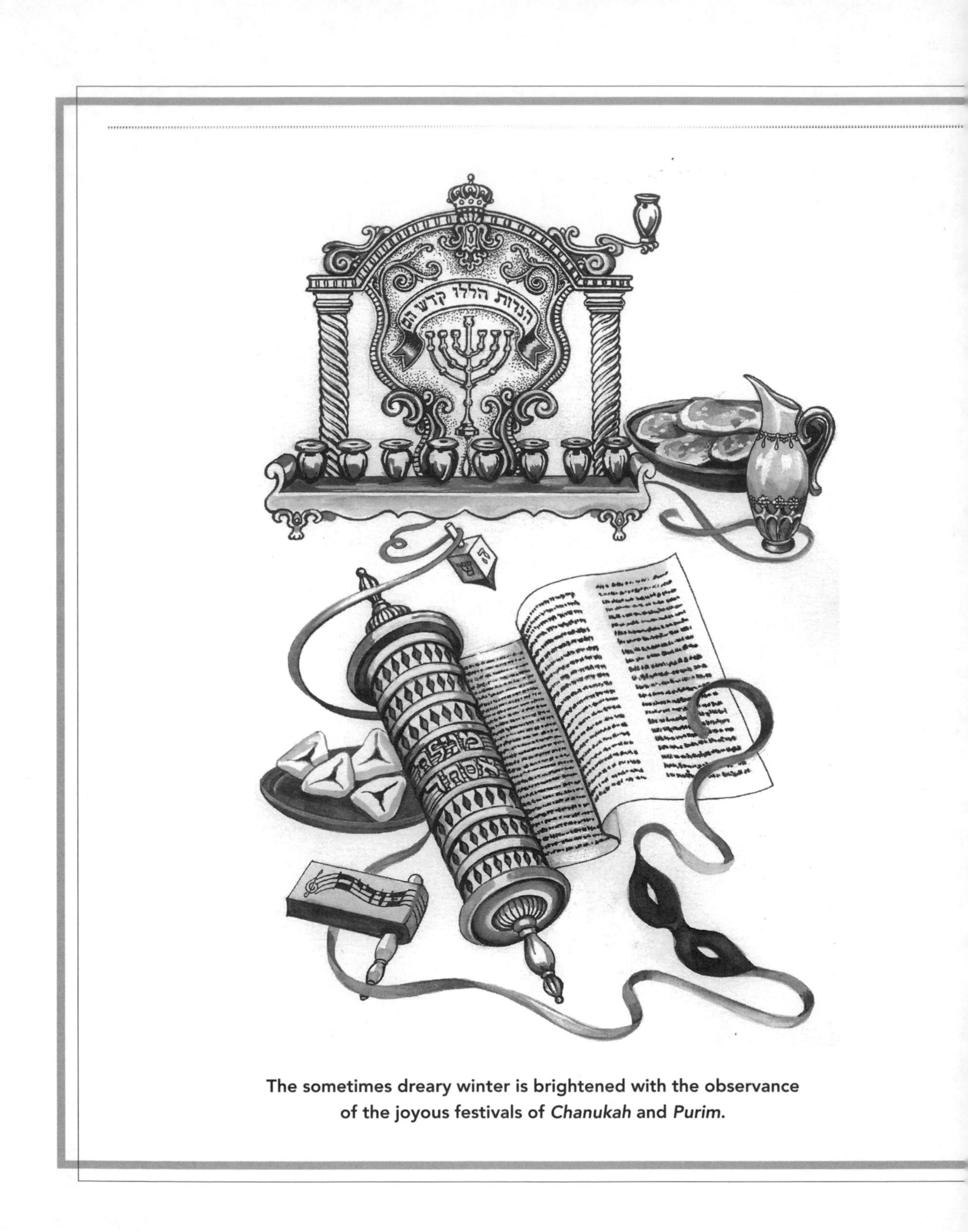

The sometimes dreary winter is brightened with the observance of the joyous festivals of *Chanukah* and *Purim*.

8

The Minor Festivals

HE FESTIVAL OF Lights, ***Chanukah***, and the Festival of Lots, ***Purim***, are both observed as minor festivals of the Jewish calendar. The use of the word *minor* in no way means to detract from the importance of the festivals. It merely expresses the fact that the obligation to observe them is not derived from the Torah. Rather, they were ordained by rabbinic authority.

Although they are not mentioned in the Torah, and there are no biblical commandments associated with their celebration, their significance in Jewish history and the prominence attached to their rituals and customs in Jewish life tend to propel them to the forefront of Jewish consciousness. Moreover, they commemorate God's deliverance of the Jewish people from spiritual and physical annihilation.

Both *Chanukah* and *Purim* reveal the heroism of Jewish men and women who acted as God's agents. The events of *Chanukah* took place in the middle of the second century before the Common Era; *Purim,* some two hundred years earlier. We will discuss *Chanukah* first, however, because it is celebrated before *Purim* in the Jewish calendar.

8.1 The Festival of Lights

Chanukah commemorates both the spiritual and military victories of the Jewish people over the tyranny of the Greco-Syrian Empire in a three-year struggle that took place between 168 and 165 B.C.E., during the reign of the Greek tyrant, Antiochus Epiphanes.

In 516 B.C.E., seventy years after the Babylonian Exile, thousands of Jews returned to *Eretz Yisrael* and rebuilt the *Bet HaMikdash.* Jewish life was reestablished on a strong foundation of Torah and religious autonomy. In time, however, Judea was conquered by the Greeks under Alexander the Great. For many years the Jewish community continued to flourish under Alexander, and their religious life was undisturbed.

By the middle of the second century B.C.E., however, the classical culture of Greek civilization was replaced by the immoral conduct of a corrupt new Hellenism that lauded the decadent. Antiochus Epiphanes then ruled over the Jewish people. He forced them to adopt immoral Hellenistic practices. The observance of religious traditions, such as the Sabbath, festivals, and other sacred rituals, was forbidden under the threat of death, and Antiochus tested the loyalty of the Jews by setting up altars throughout Judea.

In the Holy Temple in Jerusalem, *Sifrei Torah* and sacred books were destroyed. The Temple was grossly defiled, converted to the worship of Zeus, and given over to harlots who plied their heathen ways within its walls.

Many Jews chose to die a martyr's death rather than surrender to idol worship and paganism. Others, however, chose to rise up in revolt. Under the leadership of a small band of **Hasmoneans,** also known as the Maccabees, they rallied Jewish forces to victory over their Hellenic oppressors.

Mi l'HaShem elai!

❖

Whoever is for the Lord follow me!

Led first by Mattathias, the High Priest, and then by Judah the Maccabee, his third son, the pagans were defeated, and the Temple was restored and rededicated on the twenty-fifth day of *Kislev,* three years to the day that it had first been defiled.

However, it is not the military victory that is paramount in the commemoration marked by the Festival of Lights. Rather, it is the miracle which occurred in the *Bet HaMikdash,* the Holy Temple.

In 165 B.C.E., when the Maccabees restored the Temple, only one vessel of sanctified olive oil was found intact with the seal of the *Kohen Gadol.* Only one, enough to burn for only one day in the ***menorah,*** the seven-branch candelabra in the Temple, was not defiled.

The golden *menorah* was kindled. Miraculously, this tiny amount of oil continued to burn for eight days, enough time for additional fresh oil to be obtained. The following year, the Hasmoneans designated the observance of those eight days as days of thanks in praise of God. This practice was adopted by the sages who ordained its observance from that time forward.

The emphasis on the miracle of the oil, rather than on the Maccabees' success in the military struggle, highlights God's role, reminding us that He alone was responsible for their victory.

8.2 The *Chanukah* Candles

The Festival of Lights, also called ***Chag HaUrim,*** (from the Hebrew word ***or,*** light), begins on the twenty-fifth day of the Hebrew month of *Kislev* and is observed for eight days.

Calendar for the First Day of *Chanukah*

Secular Year	Hebrew Year	Day of the Week	Secular Date
2001	5762	Monday	December 10
2002	5763	Saturday	November 30
2003	5764	Saturday	December 20
2004	5765	Wednesday	December 8
2005	5766	Monday	December 26
2006	5767	Saturday	December 16
2007	5768	Wednesday	December 5
2008	5769	Monday	December 22
2009	5770	Saturday	December 12
2010	5771	Thursday	December 2

The name *Chanukah* can be interpreted as two Hebrew words—*chanu* and *kah*—meaning

They rested [from their battle on the] twenty-fifth [day]

with *kah,* the two Hebrew letters *kaf* and *hei,* כה, equivalent to twenty-five.

The focal point of the celebration in modern times is the kindling of the *Chanukah* candles. Inasmuch as there no longer is a Holy Temple, the *menorah* is no longer in use, except as a symbol of the modern State of Israel.

Instead of a seven-branch *menorah,* an eight-branch candelabra, more correctly called a ***chanukiah*** (although in common usage, *chanukiah* and *menorah* are used interchangeably), is used. The branches are in a straight line so that no candle is higher than any other. On the first night of *Chanukah,* one candle is lit. On the second night, two candles are lit. On each successive night, one candle is added until the eighth night when eight candles are lit in the *chanukiah.*

The candles are *positioned* in the *chanukiah* from right to left; that is, the first candle is placed at the extreme right, and the new candle is added to its left. However, the candles are *lit* from left to right; thus, the new candle is lit first each night.

The candles must be lit after sundown. It is customary to light them as early as is permissible. In addition to the eight candles, there is a ***shammash,*** a servant candle, which is used to light all the other candles in the *chanukiah.* Most candelabras which are designed for use on *Chanukah* include an additional branch to hold the *shammash* candle.

It is usually set apart from or positioned slightly above the eight branches to differentiate it.

Some families provide a separate *chanukiah* for each member of the family. This is preferable. Other families have one *chanukiah,* and each member takes a turn in lighting the candles.

Many shops sell miniature candelabra, designed to be used with small birthday candles, which do not fulfill the religious requirement of burning at least thirty minutes. A so-called electric *menorah* does not fulfill the halachic requirement for lighting *Chanukah* candles either.

In some homes, the *chanukiah* is designed to burn with olive oil rather than candles. The oil cups are filled, and a wick is placed in each cup. The oil wicks are kindled in exactly the same way as candles.

On Friday, the *Chanukah* lights are to be lit before the Sabbath candles, and must burn at least thirty minutes past sundown. For this reason, larger candles, or a greater quantity of oil, must be used on Friday to be sure that the *Chanukah* lights burn into the darkness.

8.3 The *Chanukah* Blessings

When the appropriate number of candles (or oil wicks) have been placed in the *chanukiah,* the *shammash* is lit and the following blessings are recited:

Recite before Lighting the *Chanukah* Candles

Baruch Atah, HaShem E-lo-kenu, Melech HaOlam,
asher kidshanu b'mitzvotav v'tzivanu
l'hadlik ner shel Chanukah.

❖

Blessed are You, Lord our God, King of the Universe,
Who has sanctified us with His commandments and commanded us
to kindle the *Chanukah* light.

❖

Baruch Atah, HaShem E-lo-kenu, Melech HaOlam,
she'asah nisim la'avotenu,
bayamim haheim baz'man hazeh.

❖

Blessed are You, Lord our God, King of the Universe,
Who has made miracles for our forefathers
in those days at this season.

❖

On the First Night, Recite She'hecheyanu:
Baruch Atah, HaShem E-lo-kenu, Melech HaOlam,
she'hecheyanu, v'kiy'manu,
v'higiyanu laz'man hazeh.

❖

Blessed are You, Lord our God, King of the Universe,
Who has kept us alive, sustained us,
and brought us to this season.

Once the blessings have been recited, the candles are lit as the *Chanukah* prayer ***HaNerot Halalu*** is chanted. It is then customary to sing several songs including ***Ma'oz Tzur,*** which tells of the deliverance of the Jewish people from the bondage of Egypt, the exile of Babylonia, and the oppression and persecution of the Persians and the Greco-Syrians.

Other songs, such as ***Mi Y'malel,*** which heralds the military victory of the Maccabees in their courageous struggle against the might of Antiochus, and the ever-popular Yiddish melody, ***Oy Chanukah,*** which emphasizes the delights of the holiday, are also traditional.

8.4 The Delights of *Chanukah*

Chanukah is a festival to be enjoyed by all. Many families customarily gather on one day of *Chanukah* to celebrate the miracle and enjoy the holiday together. There are special customs associated with the observance of *Chanukah*. Every family has its own favorites.

8.4.1 *Chanukah* Games

In addition to the religious rituals which are part of the observance of *Chanukah*, many customs have been handed down from generation to generation. Because the *halachah* forbids any utilitarian use of the lights of *Chanukah* (such as to read by), it is customary to play games, tell stories, and eat while the candles are burning. No work is permitted while the candles still burn.

The traditional *Chanukah* game is *Dreidel*. The ***dreidel*** (from the Yiddish meaning *to turn*), a small spinning top, made from wood, plastic, or metal, is called a ***s'vivon*** in Hebrew. There are four sides to the top. In the game, each player spins the *dreidel*, and it whirls until it lands with one side facing up. On each of the sides, a Hebrew letter appears: *nun, gimel, hei,* or *shin:* נ ג ה ש. These four letters stand for the following Hebrew words:

Nes gadol hayah sham.

❖

A great miracle happened there.

This, of course, refers to the miracle of the oil in the Holy Temple in Jerusalem. It is interesting to note that in Israel today, the fourth letter on the *dreidel* is not *shin* for *sham* (there), but rather *pei* for ***po***, meaning *here*, that is, in Israel: נ ג ה פ.

The game begins when each player puts a coin into the "pot." The *dreidel* is spun by each player in turn. If the *dreidel* lands on *nun*, then nothing is done because *nun* stands for ***nisht***, meaning *none* or *not*. If it lands on *gimel*, then the player wins all the coins, because *gimel* stands for ***gantz***, meaning *all*. Each player then contributes another coin to begin again. If the *dreidel* lands on *hei*, the player takes half of the coins because *hei* stands for ***halb***, meaning *half*. If the *dreidel* lands on *shin*, the player must add a coin to the pot because *shin* stands for ***shtel***, meaning *to put in*. The game ends when one player has won all the coins.

While the candles burn, the family gathers around the table for a lively game of *Dreidel*.

Another variation of the *dreidel* game is to score points according to the numerical value of the letter which turns up.

נ	*nun*	=	50
ג	*gimel*	=	3
ה	*hei*	=	5
שׁ	*shin*	=	300

The game continues until a player reaches a predetermined score, perhaps, three thousand points. As the *dreidel* whirls and spins about, every Jewish child sings the popular "I Have a Little *Dreidel*," hoping to win the game.

Sing "I Have a Little *Dreidel*"

I have a little *dreidel,* I made it out of clay;
and when it's dry and ready, oh, *dreidel* I shall play!
Refrain:
Oh, *dreidel, dreidel, dreidel,* I made it out of clay;
and when it's dry and ready, oh, *dreidel* I shall play!

❖

It has a lovely body, with leg so short and thin;
and when it is all tired, it stops and then I win!
Refrain

❖

My *dreidel* is always playful, it loves to dance and spin;
a happy game of *dreidel,* come play, now let's begin!
Refrain

8.4.2 *Chanukah* Gelt

Once the Maccabees had restored the Jewish people to political autonomy, they minted coins for use as currency. Because of this, it has become traditional to give gifts of money, especially coins, called ***gelt,*** on each evening of the festival.

There are many storybooks available in Jewish bookstores that relate the events of *Chanukah,* and some are designed with special slots to hold a coin on each page. Candy manufacturers wrap round pieces of chocolate in gold and silver foil, decorated with symbols of the holiday, to represent the coins minted by the Maccabees.

8.4.3 *Chanukah* Foods

One of the special delights of *Chanukah* is culinary. In commemoration of the miracle of the cruse of oil, it is traditional to eat foods prepared with oil. The two most popular foods are ***latkes*** and ***sufganiyot.***

Latkes, made from grated potatoes, eggs, seasoning, and a bit of flour, are fried into delicious potato pancakes. They are served with sour cream or applesauce, depending on personal preference.

Sufganiyot, another holiday favorite, are doughnuts, usually filled with jelly or custard, and deep-fried to a golden brown. Often they are sprinkled with powdered sugar.

There are even a few *Chanukah* songs that extol the pleasures of eating *Chanukah latkes* and *sufganiyot*.

8.5 The Liturgy of *Chanukah*

During *Chanukah,* several liturgical portions relevant to the festival are added to the daily prayer services. A brief historical account of the events of *Chanukah,* contained in the prayer ***Al HaNisim,*** is inserted during the *Amidah* and the *Birkat HaMazon.*

Recite *Al HaNisim* for Chanukah

For the miracles
and the salvation and the mighty deeds,
and the victories and the wonders,
and the consolations and the battles
that You performed
for our forefathers in those days and at this season.
In the days of Mattathias, the Hasmonean, and his sons,
when a wicked Greek Empire rose up against Your people Israel
to make them forget Your Torah . . .
You mercifully championed their cause,
defended their rights, and avenged the wrongs they suffered.
You delivered the strong into hands of the weak,
the many into the hands of the few, . . .
the wicked into the hands of the righteous,
and the arrogant into the hands
of those who were faithful to Your Torah. . . .
Your children . . . purified Your Sanctuary
and kindled lights in the courtyards . . .
and established these eight days of *Chanukah*
to express thanks and praise Your great Name.

In addition, *Hallel,* the prayers in praise of God, which are recited on the three Pilgrimage Festivals (see Chapter 7) among other occasions, are also recited on each of the eight days of *Chanukah.*

8.6 *Kriat HaTorah* for *Chanukah*

Special Torah portions are read for *Chanukah,* even though the holiday is not mentioned in the Torah. Instead, we read about the dedication of the *Mishkan* in the wilderness and about the lighting of the golden *menorah.* The Torah portions during the weekdays of *Chanukah* are from *Parshat Naso,* Numbers 7:1–89 through *Parshat Beha'alot'cha,* Numbers 8:1–4.

Each day, there are three *aliyot,* except on *Rosh Chodesh Tevet*—which falls during the eight-day period—when there are four, and the reading is from two *Sifrei Torah.* On the Sabbath, seven are called, and two *Sifrei Torah* are used. If *Rosh Chodesh Tevet* falls on the Sabbath, then seven are called, and the reading is from three *Sifrei Torah.*

Most often, the Torah portions for ***Shabbat Chanukah,*** the Sabbath which falls during the eight days (see Section 4.6.13), is from *Parshat Mikketz,* Genesis 41:1–44:17. The *Haftarah* is from Zechariah 2:14–4:7, and contains the following verse:

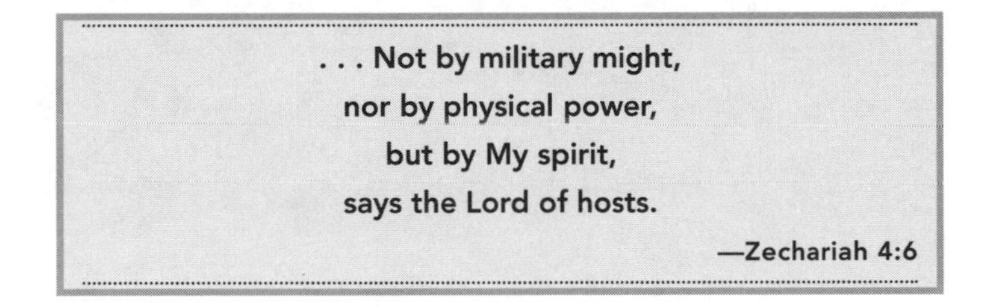
. . . Not by military might,
nor by physical power,
but by My spirit,
says the Lord of hosts.

—Zechariah 4:6

a prophecy of the spiritual victory of God in every generation.

Occasionally, both the first and eighth days of *Chanukah* fall on the Sabbath. The portion for the first Sabbath is *Parshat Vayeshev,* Genesis 37:1–40:23, and the *Haftarah* is from Zechariah 2:14–4:7. In that instance, *Parshat Mikketz* is read on the second Sabbath, and its *Haftarah* is I Kings 7:40 50.

8.7 Publicizing the Miracle

Maimonides, perhaps, offers the definitive word on the significance of the celebration of *Chanukah.* In his *Mishneh Torah,* he writes:

Lighting the Chanukah candles in the window publicizes the miracle of the oil in the *Bet HaMikdash*.

> Even if one has no food to eat
> except what he begs from charity,
> he should beg or sell some of his clothing
> to purchase the oil and lamps to light. . . .
> If one . . . needs wine for *Kiddush*
> and oil to light the *Chanukah* lamp,
> he should give preference to the purchase of the oil . . .
> since it serves as a memorial to the miracle of *Chanukah*.
>
> —Book of Seasons, Laws of *Chanukah* 4:12, 13

The miracle of the oil is so integral a part of the *Chanukah* celebration that the kindling of the *Chanukah* lights must be visible from the public domain. Publicizing the miracle is called ***pirsumei nisah.*** To fulfill this obligation, the *chanukiah* is placed conspicuously near a window or in the open doorway so that all who pass by become aware of the miracle. In some cities, *Chanukah* candles are lit in public places in order to publicize the miracle.

Candles are lit in the synagogue as well as in the home to further publicize the miracle and thus sanctify God's Name among the multitudes. Inasmuch as the miracle took place in the *Bet HaMikdash,* the synagogue, which is considered a *mikdash m'at,* a small sanctuary, is an appropriate place to light them as well. On Saturday night, the *Chanukah* lights are lit in the synagogue before *Havdalah.* At home, they are kindled before or after, according to the custom of the family.

A Witty Remark!

Chanukah has always had special significance in our house. On my twenty-second birthday, which was four days before the first night of *Chanukah* that year, I met my husband for the first time. Needless to say, I was not thunderstruck. In fact, I was furious!

He had called me for a date the night before; my friend's husband had given him my name and number, and, although I was not thrilled about going on another blind date, I agreed to go out on Saturday night, the first night of *Chanukah.*

Instead, he came to my office the next day—my birthday. I was working in the Hebrew library at Yeshiva University—my first job out of college—and he was studying for ordination there. So, after class that day, he decided to come over and "meet me." Ha! He wanted to see what I looked like!

When he introduced himself, I was livid. "How dare he come to look me over!" I fumed to myself. I walked off in a huff.

That night I went out for a birthday dinner with my friend. "I am going to stand him up on Saturday night," I concluded, after telling her the whole sorry saga. She agreed that he deserved a rude brush-off for his abominable behavior.

Later that night, after eleven, my phone rang: It was HIM!

"Did I startle you?" he asked, meaning it was rather late.

"You certainly did!" I retorted. "Do you always check out a girl before a blind date? If you don't trust the friends who fixed us up, I don't trust them either—and besides, you ruined my birthday!"

He was flabbergasted—struggling for words. "I just thought that . . . uh . . . since I was at YU, and . . . uh . . . you worked there, we could maybe meet before our date . . . you know . . . get to know each other."

I was chagrined. "Oh? Really?" I mumbled.

He apologized profusely and invited me to lunch the next day—albeit at the greasy spoon across from the library. I agreed.

We met outside the library doors. "A little something for you," he said. "A peace offering and a belated birthday present." He handed me a box that held a crystal bottle of perfume.

We went to lunch that day, and the next, and finally it was Saturday night, the first light of *Chanukah,* the night of our first date. We went to the Yiddish theater on Second Avenue, and during the intermission, he said, "I think you need a husband to take care of you. Shall I volunteer for the position?" I just smiled.

P.S. We got engaged on the first night of *Chanukah,* and in Hebrew, our monogram spells *"or,"* the word for *light.*

8.8 The Jolly Feast of *Purim*

The sages teach that if all the festivals in the Jewish calendar were to be nullified, *Purim,* the Festival of Lots, would still be observed.

Both the Rambam (in the *Mishneh Torah*) and the midrashic literature comment:

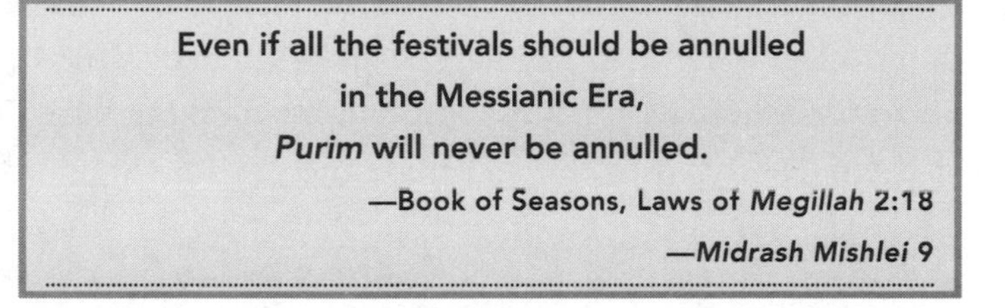

Even if all the festivals should be annulled in the Messianic Era, *Purim* will never be annulled.

—Book of Seasons, Laws of *Megillah* 2:18

—*Midrash Mishlei* 9

Purim is a clear example of *hashgachah k'lalit,* divine providence for the entire community of Israel (see Section 3.7.2).

In Persia, during the reign of Achashverosh, in 365 B.C.E., his viceroy, Haman, plotted to destroy the Jewish people. The story of Haman's thwarted attempt, and the subsequent proclamation of the Festival of *Purim,* are set down in the Scroll of Esther, ***Megillat Esther.*** It is a story of intrigue in the court of one of the Persian Empire's most wicked kings.

King Achashverosh had invited the princes from 127 outlying provinces to a feast in Shushan, the capital city of the Persian Empire. He summoned his wife, Queen Vashti, to appear before the assembled guests wearing only her crown, because he wished to show off her great beauty. When she refused to appear—because of God's providence, Vashti was suddenly stricken with leprosy, setting the stage for the downfall of Haman—the king set about to replace her, to find a new queen to join him on the throne.

In the meantime, Haman, the vain and powerful member of the royal court, had persuaded King Achashverosh to sign a decree requiring all subjects of the realm to bow down to the sinister viceroy as a sign of homage and respect.

At that time, there was a sizable Jewish population living in the Persian Empire.

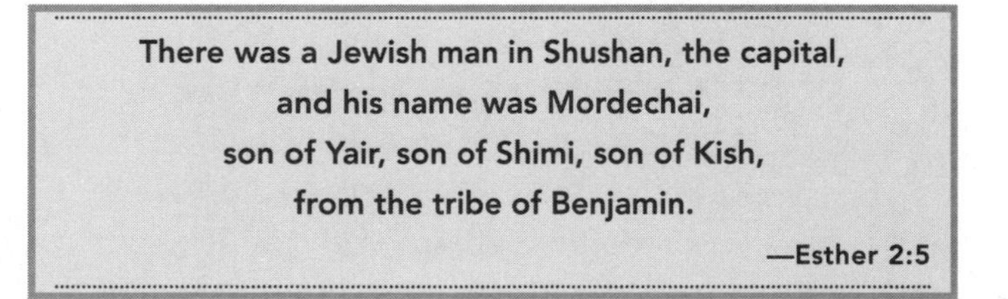

There was a Jewish man in Shushan, the capital, and his name was Mordechai, son of Yair, son of Shimi, son of Kish, from the tribe of Benjamin.

—Esther 2:5

Mordechai and his niece Esther, whom he had raised after the death of her parents, were descendants of the royal house of Saul, the first anointed king of Israel. According to the midrashic literature, *Esther Rabbah* 7:6, Haman had fastened an idol to his clothes, forcing all who paid him homage, as required by royal decree, to bow before the idol as well.

In keeping with his beliefs, Mordechai, of course, had refused to obey this decree. Haman hated Mordechai, and when he realized that Mordechai was a Jew, Haman turned his wrath toward the Jewish people throughout the kingdom, deciding to do away with all of them. He drew lots to determine the day he would exterminate the Jews.

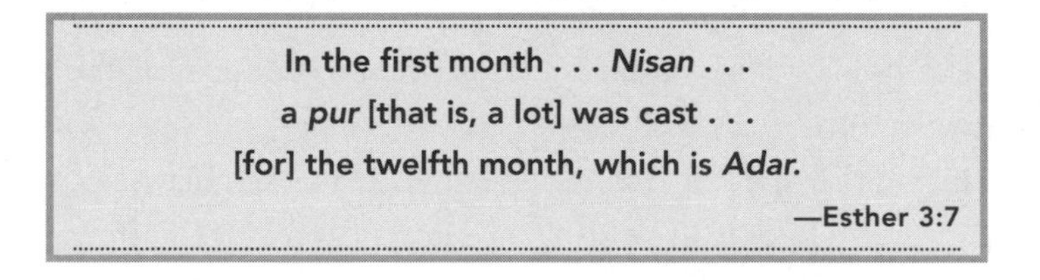

In the first month . . . *Nisan* . . .
a *pur* [that is, a lot] was cast . . .
[for] the twelfth month, which is *Adar.*

—Esther 3:7

He drew ***pur*** after *pur* for the day and month: the thirteenth of *Adar.*

Haman then went to King Achashverosh and complained about the Jews, misrepresenting them to the king as a dangerous and disloyal faction in his midst.

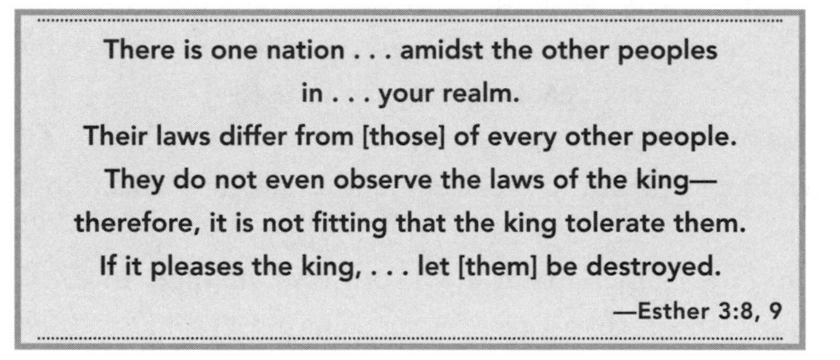

There is one nation . . . amidst the other peoples
in . . . your realm.
Their laws differ from [those] of every other people.
They do not even observe the laws of the king—
therefore, it is not fitting that the king tolerate them.
If it pleases the king, . . . let [them] be destroyed.

—Esther 3:8, 9

King Achashverosh granted Haman permission to deal with the Jews in his own way.

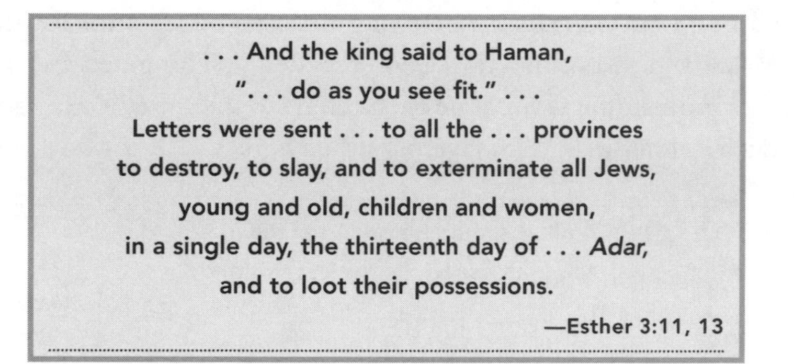
. . . And the king said to Haman,
". . . do as you see fit." . . .
Letters were sent . . . to all the . . . provinces
to destroy, to slay, and to exterminate all Jews,
young and old, children and women,
in a single day, the thirteenth day of . . . *Adar,*
and to loot their possessions.

—Esther 3:11, 13

Haman dictated the letters himself. Sealed with the king's signet ring, the letters were carried by couriers to all the provinces: Massacre all the Jews on the thirteenth day of *Adar.*

8.8.1 The Plot Thickens

In the meantime, King Achashverosh had selected Esther as his new queen. He did not know she was a Jew, nor did she tell him. Mordechai learned of a plot to murder Achashverosh, and he reported it to Esther. The plot and Mordechai's role in uncovering it came to the king's attention, and the matter was recorded in the king's annals.

When Mordechai learned of Haman's evil designs, he dressed in sackcloth and came to the King's Gate. When Esther learned how he was dressed, she sent garments so he could remove his sackcloth; but Mordechai refused. Esther sent a messenger to learn what was happening. Mordechai sent a message in return informing her of Haman's plot, and urged her to appeal to the king, to plead for her people.

For three days Esther fasted as she sought God's help in her mission. She knew that it was forbidden for anyone, even the queen, to come to the king without being summoned. Nevertheless, Esther persevered. She appeared before King Achashverosh and invited him and Haman to a banquet that day. She did not reveal her purpose to the king then, but invited him and Haman to return the next day.

Hurrying home to his family and friends to boast that only he had accompanied King Achashverosh to the queen's banquet, Haman looked forward to the next day's banquet as well. Haman's wife, Zeresh, and his friends encouraged him to build a gallows for Mordechai so that he could attend the second banquet in good spirits. Haman liked this idea and ordered the erection of the gallows.

That night when he was unable to sleep, Achashverosh called for the court chronicles and read of Mordechai's valor in saving the king's life. After learning from his chamberlains that Mordechai had not been rewarded, the king decided to honor him.

Just at that moment, Haman came to the court to speak to the king about hanging Mordechai. Seeing him there, Achashverosh asked him:

> **What should be done for the man**
> **the king especially desires to honor?**
>
> **—Esther 6:6**

Thinking that the king referred to him, Haman suggested that the man be dressed in the king's robes, seated on the king's horse, and led through the streets by a noble officer proclaiming:

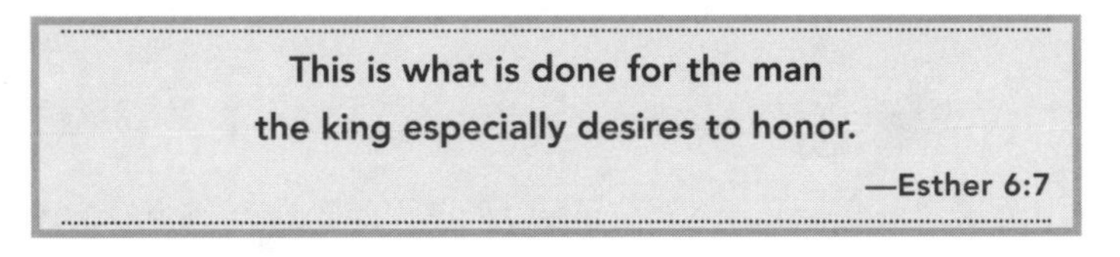

> **This is what is done for the man**
> **the king especially desires to honor.**
>
> **—Esther 6:7**

Achashverosh approved of Haman's suggestion and ordered him to dress Mordechai in royal robes and lead him through the streets on horseback, proclaiming Mordechai as the man the king wished to honor. Thus was Haman required to do.

8.8.2 The Plot Unravels

Returning home despondent, Haman told his wife and friends what had happened. His wife replied:

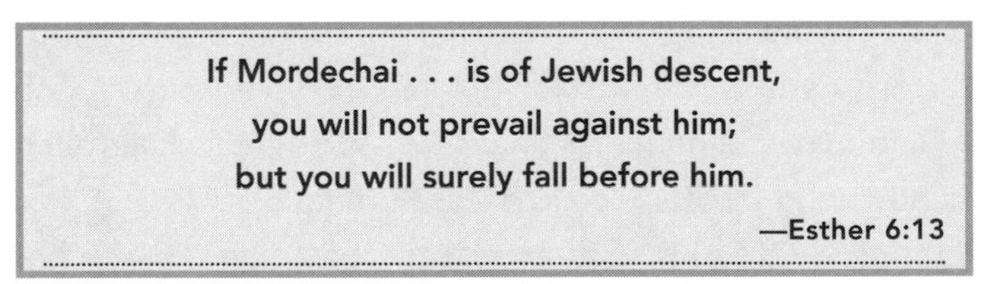

> **If Mordechai . . . is of Jewish descent,**
> **you will not prevail against him;**
> **but you will surely fall before him.**
>
> **—Esther 6:13**

The chamberlains arrived to escort Haman to the queen's second banquet. When Haman appeared, Esther revealed his plot to destroy the Jews, explaining to King Achashverosh that if he permitted Haman to carry out his plan, she too would be killed for she was a Jew.

The king condemned Haman to hang on the gallows he had prepared for Mordechai. He issued another decree permitting the Jews to organize and arm themselves against all who threatened them. On the thirteenth day of *Adar,* the Jews defended themselves and were victorious. Haman and his ten sons were hanged.

Mordechai became the viceroy to King Achashverosh.

> **And Mordechai left the king's presence**
> **attired in royal garb of blue and white,**
> **a large gold crown on his head,**
> **and a robe of fine purple linen.**
> **Then the city of Shushan was cheerful and glad.**
> **The Jews had light and gladness and joy and honor.**
> **—Esther 8:15–16**

Mordechai sent letters instructing Jews in every province to observe the fourteenth and fifteenth days of *Adar* annually. He was a distinguished leader among the Jewish people. *Megillat Esther* concludes by reminding us that

> **Mordechai the Jew was viceroy to King Achashverosh.**
> **A great man among the Jews,**
> **he was well liked by . . . his brethren.**
> **He continued to seek the good of his people**
> **and was concerned for the well-being of his posterity.**
> **—Esther 10:3**

The Festival of *Purim* is observed on the fourteenth day of *Adar* to this day. The fifteenth of *Adar* is called ***Shushan Purim,*** because the war ended in the capital city on that day. In Jerusalem, an ancient walled city like Shushan, *Purim* is observed on *Shushan Purim.*

Calendar for *Purim*

Secular Year	Hebrew Year	Day of the Week	Secular Date
2001	5761	Friday	March 9
2002	5762	Tuesday	February 26
2003	5763	Tuesday	March 18
2004	5764	Sunday	March 7
2005	5765	Friday	March 25
2006	5766	Tuesday	March 14
2007	5767	Sunday	March 4
2008	5768	Friday	March 21
2009	5769	Tuesday	March 10
2010	5770	Sunday	February 28

8.9 The *Mitzvot* of *Purim*

There are several religious requirements associated with the Festival of *Purim.* They include:

- ***Ta'anit Esther***
  The Fast of Esther is observed on *Adar* 13 to commemorate Queen Esther's three-day fast. If the thirteenth falls on the Sabbath when fasting is prohibited (except for *Yom Kippur* when one must fast even on the Sabbath, see Chapter 6), the Fast of Esther is observed on the preceding Thursday.

There are seven *mitzvot* of *Purim:*

- ***Mikra Megillah***
  Mikra Megillah, Reading the Scroll of Esther, takes place in the evening immediately following the Fast of Esther, and on the following morning, which is *Purim* Day. *Megillat Esther* is read publicly in the synagogue. The *ba'al korei* folds it back like a letter, because the decree to celebrate *Purim* was sent in a letter in scroll (***megillah***) form to all the Jews after the victory.

> **And Mordechai . . . sent letters to all the Jews**
> **in all the provinces of King Achashverosh . . .**
> **instructing them to observe**
> **the fourteenth and fifteenth days of *Adar* every year. . . .**
> **And the Jews took it upon themselves to do**
> **what Mordechai had asked of them.**
>
> **—Esther 9:20, 23**

Thus, the *Megillah* is not read by unwinding it from parchment page to parchment page, the way a *Sefer Torah* is read. For those who are unable to go to the synagogue, it may be read at home.

- ***Machtzit HaShekel***
  In the evening, just before the Reading of the *Megillah,* it is customary to donate three half-dollars to charity. This recalls the biblical commandment to donate *machtzit hashekel,* a half-*shekel,* during the month of *Adar,* in order to pay for the twice-daily sacrifices that were offered by the *Kohanim* in the Temple on behalf of all the Jewish people. The three half-dollars are symbolic of the three times *machtzit hashekel* is mentioned in the Torah (*Parshat Ki Tissa,* Exodus 30:13, 15).
- ***Mishloach Manot***
  Sending gifts of food to friends is also derived from the *Megillah* (Esther 9:19, 22). In order to fulfill this *mitzvah,* each person must send at least two different kinds of ready-to-eat foods, such as cake and fruit, to at least one person. The phrase *different kinds* means that the two foods each require the recitation of a different blessing before eating.
- ***Se'udat Purim***
  It is a *mitzvah* to have an especially festive meal on *Purim* Day, in keeping with the words of the *Megillah.*

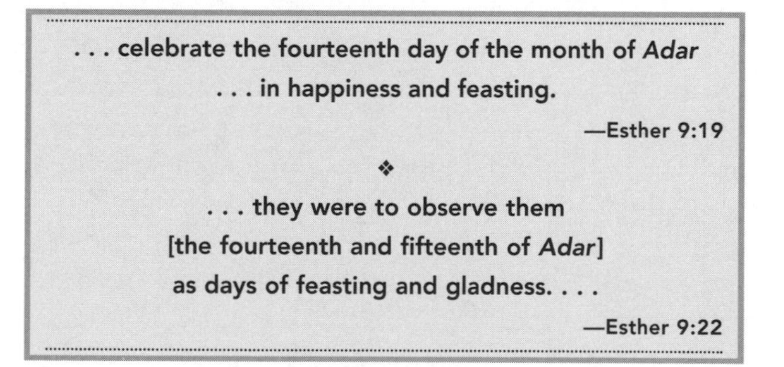

. . . celebrate the fourteenth day of the month of *Adar*
. . . in happiness and feasting.

—Esther 9:19

❖

. . . they were to observe them
[the fourteenth and fifteenth of *Adar*]
as days of feasting and gladness. . . .

—Esther 9:22

The *se'udah* should start in the late afternoon and continue into the nighttime. It is customary to drink wine or other alcoholic beverages on *Purim, **ad lo yada,*** until one does not know the difference between

Blessed is Mordechai!
and
Cursed is Haman!

- ***Matanot L'Evyonim***
  Giving gifts to the poor is a *mitzvah* of *Purim*. Ready-to-eat food, or money to buy food, must be given to at least two poor people. This *mitzvah,* also found in Esther 9:22, is more important than *mishloach manot* or *se'udat Purim,* for the Rambam teaches that there is nothing more joyful than gladdening the poor, the orphaned, the widowed, and the strangers among us (*Mishneh Torah,* Book of Seasons, Laws of *Megillah* 2:17).
- ***Kriat HaTorah***
  The Torah is read in the synagogue on *Purim* Day before *Megillat Esther* is read. The Torah portion is from *Parshat Beshalach,* Exodus 17:8–16, which describes the attack of Amalek upon the Israelites in the wilderness (see Sections 8:11 and 8.12 below).
- ***Al HaNisim***
  The additional prayer *Al HaNisim* (concerning the miracles) is recited during the prayer services on *Purim* and in the Grace after Meals. Similar to the *Al HaNisim* prayer recited on *Chanukah,* this prayer is a brief account of the miraculous events of *Purim*. It begins with the following opening passage:

Recite *Al HaNisim* for *Purim*

For the miracles
and the salvation and the mighty deeds,
and the victories and the wonders,
and the consolations and the battles
that You performed
for our forefathers in those days and at this season.
In the days of Mordechai and Esther,
in Shushan, the capital,
Haman, the evil one, rose up against them,
seeking to destroy, slay, and annihilate all the Jews,
young and old, infants and women . . .
on the thirteenth day . . . of *Adar*,
and to loot their possessions.
But, You in Your abundant mercy,
canceled his advice, foiled his intentions,
and made his plan backfire on his own head;
and they hanged him and his sons on the gallows.
You performed miracles and wonders for them,
and we give thanks to Your great Name.

8.10 Reading the *Megillah*

Megillat Esther is written on parchment and is read by the *ba'al korei* in the evening and again in the morning; he first recites the following three blessings:

Recite the Blessings before *Megillat Esther*

**Blessed are You, Lord our God, King of the Universe,
Who has sanctified us with His commandments and commanded us
concerning the reading of the Scroll [of Esther].**

❖

**Blessed are You, Lord our God, King of the Universe,
Who made miracles for our forefathers
in those days at this season.**

❖

**Blessed are You, Lord our God, King of the Universe,
Who has kept us alive, sustained us,
and brought us to this season.**

The congregation must hear *every word* in order to be able to fulfill the biblical commandment to *blot out the remembrance of Amalek.*

When the Israelites left Egypt, they were attacked in the wilderness by the Amalekites, descendants of Esau, the twin brother of the patriarch, Jacob. The Israelites bore no animosity toward the Amalekites, who came from afar with but one purpose in mind: to destroy the people of Israel.

The Amalekites were the first adversaries to force the Israelites to defend themselves. They belittled God's divine intervention in Jewish destiny, and they believed that their superior might could destroy the Israelites.

The Jewish people were commanded:

> Remember what Amalek did to you . . .
> as you came forth out of Egypt.
> How he met you by the way, . . .
> and attacked you . . . from the rear,
> when you were faint and weary; and he did not fear God.
> Therefore, . . . when the Lord your God has given you rest
> from all your enemies around you,
> in the land which the Lord your God gives you
> for an inheritance to possess it,
> you shall blot out
> the memory of Amalek from under heaven;
> you shall not forget.
>
> —*Parshat Ki Tetzei,* Deuteronomy 25:17–19

8.11 Blotting Out the Name of Haman

Based on this verse, to blot out the memory of Amalek and what he did, the Festival of *Purim* requires that during the reading of *Megillat Esther,* the name of Haman, too, is to be blotted out, for Haman was a direct descendant of Amalek.

Haman's name appears fifty-four times in the ten chapters of the *Megillah.* When the *ba'al korei* reads the name, the congregation blots it out with noisemakers, called ***groggers,*** or by stamping their feet. Some people even write the name of Haman on the soles of their shoes, and literally blot out the name as they stamp their feet.

During the reading, four verses are enthusiastically recited aloud by the congregation and then repeated from the *Megillah* by the *ba'al korei.* These verses are Esther 2:5; 8:15; 8:16; and 10:3.

8.12 *Purim* Day

On *Purim* Day, after returning home from *Shacharit* and the morning reading of *Megillat Esther,* Jews busy themselves with preparing and delivering *mishloach manot* to their friends and neighbors. At least two items of ready-to-eat food must be given to at least one person. Beautifully decorated boxes are available in Jewish bookstores to hold the cakes, cookies, candies, fruits, nuts, and other assorted items. Many families set up virtual assembly lines, trying to prepare all the packages of *mishloach manot* for friends and neighbors. It is also customary to give a small gratuity to the messenger who delivers the *mishloach manot* to your door.

In the afternoon, the *se'udat Purim* begins. The table is set for a feast. In many homes, a large *challah,* called a ***koiletch,*** is prominently placed on the table. After ritually washing, the blessing of *hamotzi* is recited, and the feasting begins.

There is *no religious requirement* to kindle festival candles, but it is customary to light candles to add a glow to the festivities, recalling the phrase in *Megillat Esther,*

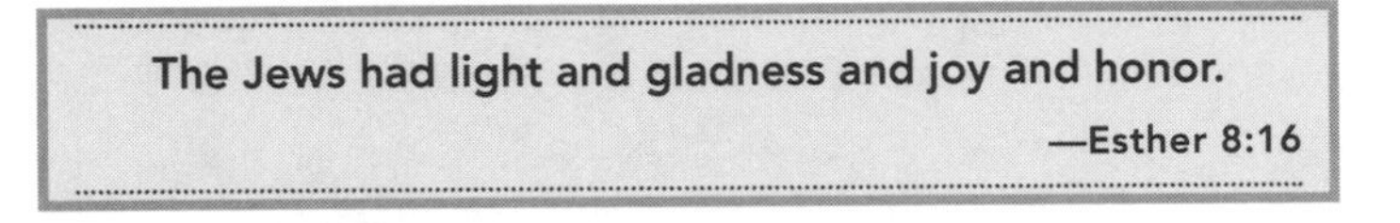

The Jews had light and gladness and joy and honor.

—Esther 8:16

when they were victorious over their enemies.

It is traditional to eat ***hamantashen,*** a three-cornered cake filled with poppy seeds or jelly. The dough may be flaky like pastry, or it may be firm like a cookie. The shape is said to represent the three-cornered hat worn by the infamous Haman.

Kiddush is not recited on *Purim,* but, as always, before drinking wine, the following blessing is recited:

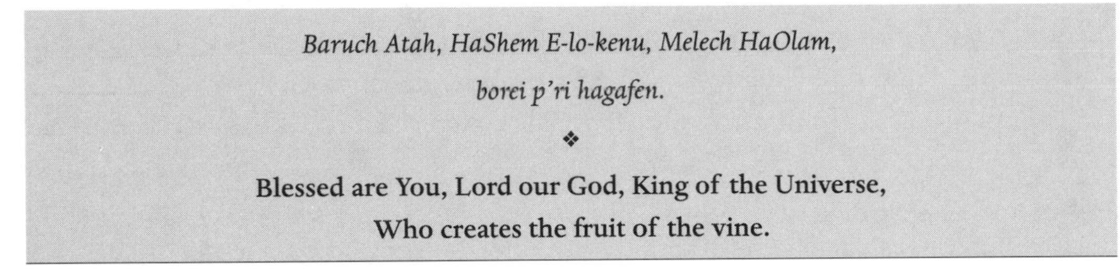

Baruch Atah, HaShem E-lo-kenu, Melech HaOlam,
borei p'ri hagafen.

❖

Blessed are You, Lord our God, King of the Universe,
Who creates the fruit of the vine.

Purim is a day given over completely to merrymaking and fun, a day to celebrate and rejoice in the defeat of the enemy and the victory of the spirit.

It is also traditional on *Purim* Day to dress up in masquerade, often as characters in the *Purim* story. Masquerading is a custom that reminds us that the Face of God was hidden from the Jewish people during this period in Jewish history, although surely His presence is hinted at numerous times in the text. Thus, masquerading, in which our faces are hidden from each other, reminds us that although we cannot see or hear God directly, He is always there.

A Witty Remark!

It was three days before *Purim.* Our Hebrew Day School was holding a Masquerade Party, and I was in charge. Why I ever agreed to chair that event, I don't know. After all, I was nine months pregnant, due, in fact, on *Purim* Day, with our second child.

My husband dressed up as King Achashverosh; but what could I be—after all, I was so-o-o-o pregnant. I decided: no costume for me, and off we went to the Masquerade.

It was a great evening. Everyone enjoyed the music, the food, the *Mishloach Manot* Mystery Raffle, and especially the Masquerade Parade.

Afterwards, we sat down with the other couples at our table. One of the women, a good friend of mine, had come dressed in an old granny frock and shawl, her hair styled in a gray granny bun. She had black patent leather high-button shoes on her feet (I don't know where she found them or how she could walk in them), and she had tucked a pillow under her dress. A pregnant granny! How shocking! She had won a well-deserved prize for her clever costume.

As we were chatting, a woman, whom I did not know, came over to our table. Standing between me and my friend, she laughed, "Isn't that great! You both dressed up as pregnant grannies!"

I gulped and exploded in laughter. My friend had tears running down her cheeks. "She thought I was wearing a costume," I gasped hysterically. Every time I thought about it that night, I burst out laughing, and the next morning I was still laughing.

I went into labor that afternoon, and I laughed all the way to the hospital. I wasn't due for two more days, but I was going to laugh my child into this world that night!

As the eve of *Ta'anit Esther,* the Fast of Esther, arrived, so did our daughter. Every year, we celebrate her birthday twice—in February and on *Purim* Day. No parties on a fast day!

We named her Chavah Orah, which means "life and light"; Chavah for my aunt, and Orah, because we learn in *Megillat Esther* that on *Purim,* "the Jews had light and gladness and joy and honor," and so do we!

8.13 The Minor Festivals Are Major

Chanukah and *Purim* are the only festivals that are not mentioned in the Torah at all. The observance of *Chanukah* was instituted by the Hasmoneans, and the observance of *Purim* is based on the decrees sent by Mordechai and Esther—which is the text of *Megillat Esther*—that these days shall be observed forever.

On *Chanukah*, *Hallel* is recited every day, for the miracle occurred in ancient Israel. Because the *Purim* story unfolded in Persia, and not within the boundaries of ancient Israel, *Hallel* is not recited on *Purim*. The presence of God is undeniable in the story of *Purim*, yet, His Name is never mentioned in *Megillat Esther*.

Chanukah and *Purim* are surely among the most enjoyable of all the Jewish festivals. They renew the spirit and revive the soul. On a deeper level, they reaffirm the miracle of God's intervention in the evil plans of mankind. They sustain the weak in the face of great adversity and inspire every generation to fight for the right to religious freedom and Jewish nationhood.

LOOKING AHEAD! *In Chapter 9, we will review the numerous ceremonies, rituals, and traditions that are unique to the Jewish life cycle.*

Word Works

Jewish Marriage:
"No man without a wife, nor a woman without a husband, nor both of them without God."

9

The Jewish Life Cycle

HE TORAH WAS, is, and always will be the guidebook for Jewish living. In this chapter we will discuss the major life-cycle events of Jewish life, explaining the traditions and observances of Judaism and providing the traditional vocabulary within the context of everyday life.

9.1 A Guide for Living

For the Jew, the Torah is the blueprint for living. The religious laws and rules of daily conduct are to be found in both the Written and the Oral Laws. From morning to night, from birth to death, life is spelled out in the Torah.

In the morning upon awakening, the Jew thanks God

> . . . for restoring my soul

and before going to sleep at night, the Jew repeats

> . . . the Lord is our God, the Lord is One

Every waking moment is spent in service to God, for whatever the Jew does or is supposed to do is set down in the guidebook that is the Torah.

9.2 Faith in the One God

The existence of God is a basic tenet of Jewish life. It is the belief that God was, is, and always will be. When God summoned Moses to the site of the burning bush, He referred to Himself in just that way.

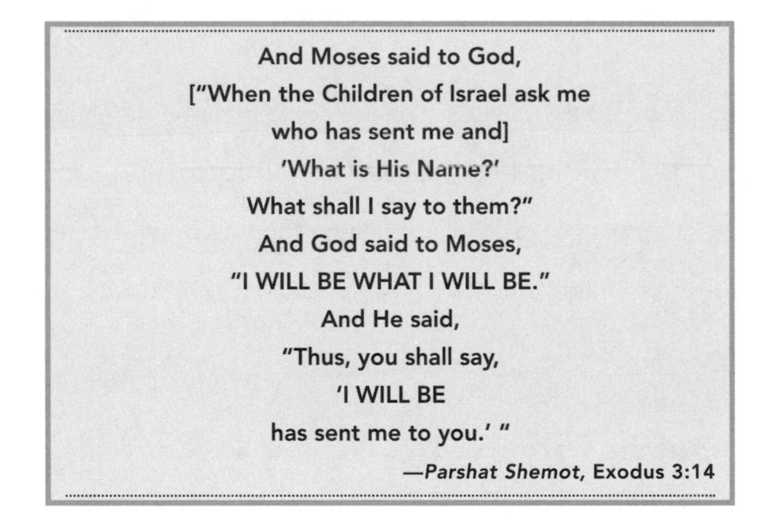

And Moses said to God,
["When the Children of Israel ask me
who has sent me and]
'What is His Name?'
What shall I say to them?"
And God said to Moses,
"I WILL BE WHAT I WILL BE."
And He said,
"Thus, you shall say,
'I WILL BE
has sent me to you.' "

—*Parshat Shemot,* Exodus 3:14

In Jewish tradition, monotheism, the belief in one indivisible God—and the subsequent transmission of that belief to future generations—is credited to the patriarch Abraham, with whom God made an eternal Covenant to bring the truth of the One God to all peoples.

Abraham, an ***Ivri,*** a Hebrew (derived from the word meaning *from the other side* of the Euphrates River), taught his son Isaac, who taught his son Jacob—later called Israel—who taught his twelve sons, the progenitors of the Twelve Tribes of Israel. Thus, the Name of God was spread to ***B'nai Yisrael,*** the Children of Israel or Israelites; and after the disappearance of the northern Ten Tribes of Israel, *B'nai Yisrael* were ultimately gathered into ***Shevet Yehudah,*** the Tribe of Judah; and from Judah, they became the Jewish people.

Abraham and his descendants evolved into a nation of multitudes as God had promised.

> **And I will make your seed like the dust of the earth;**
> **that if a man can count the dust of the earth,**
> **[so] shall your seed also be numbered.**
>
> **—*Parshat Lech Lecha,* Genesis 13:16**

> **And He brought him forth abroad and said:**
> **"Look now toward the heaven, and count the stars,**
> **if you are able to count them";**
> **and He said to him:**
> **"So shall your seed be."**
>
> **—*Parshat Lech Lecha,* Genesis 15:5**

Across generations, the Jewish people are linked by: (1) their faith in the One God; (2) the Hebrew language; (3) *Eretz Yisrael*—promised to them by God—and (4) their destiny to be His holy nation and His treasure.

> **Now . . . if you will, indeed,**
> **listen to My voice and keep My Covenant,**
> **then you shall be My own treasure**
> **among all the nations,**
> **for all the earth is Mine;**
> **and you shall be a kingdom of priests and a holy nation.**
>
> **—*Parshat Yitro,* Exodus 19:5–6**

The existence of God cannot be proven—nor can it be disproved. It is a matter of ***emunah,*** faith. It has been said that for those who have faith, there are no questions; and for those who have no faith, there can be no satisfactory answers.

The redemption of the Israelites from Egyptian bondage and the subsequent Revelation at Mount Sinai established the Children of Israel as God's chosen people. The question has often been asked: "chosen" for what? The designation of being "chosen" is not meant to suggest a superiority over other nations. Rather, it is an expression that confers on the Children of Israel the obligation to be better, an ethical duty to serve God and humankind. This exceptional status requires an exceptional level of commitment and responsibility. It is not that God has chosen *B'nai Yisrael* as the sole benefactor of His beneficence; rather, God has the exclusive right to Israel's service.

Throughout the liturgy, time and time again, we have found references to the "chosen people." When we begin to pray in the morning, we remember that God chose the Jewish people to receive His Torah. In *Birchot HaShachar* we find:

Blessed are You, Lord our God, King of the Universe,
Who has chosen us from all peoples
and given us Your Torah.

In the prayer *Ahavah Rabbah,* which is recited immediately before *Kriat Shema,* we find:

. . . Inspire us to understand, to hear, to learn and teach,
to observe, practice, and lovingly uphold
all the words of Your Torah. . . .
Blessed are You, Lord,
Who has graciously chosen Your people Israel.

During *Shacharit* on *Shabbat* morning, we are reminded that the Sabbath is not merely a day of rest, but a sanctified day that God gave only to the Jewish people.

. . . You did not give [the Sabbath day],
to the nations of the world . . .
to Israel, Your people, You have given it in love,
to the descendants of Jacob, whom You have chosen.

God chose to give the Jewish people the Day of Remembrance, *Rosh HaShanah,* and the Day of Atonement, *Yom Kippur.* So, too, with the *Shalosh Regalim.* In the recitation of the *Kiddush* for the Sabbath and all of the Pilgrimage Festivals, we find:

. . . Who has chosen us from all nations, . . .
and sanctified us with His commandments.
You . . . have lovingly given us . . .
holidays for gladness, festivals and seasons of joy.

God's redemption of the Israelites in Egypt ranged from the purely physical goal—ending the slavery—to the ultimate spiritual goal—making them His chosen people.

Just as God has chosen the Jewish people, so, too, have they chosen Him. Throughout history, Jews have chosen to die *al kiddush HaShem*, for the sanctification of His Name, rather than give up their love for Him and the observance of His precepts.

9.2.1 Returning to the Faith

For many years now, throughout the world and across denominational lines, more and more people have been seeking to reconnect with the faith of their ancestors. The return of Jews, young and old alike, to their religious roots and spiritual traditions has reached an all-time high, as they undertake the study of the Torah, Jewish history, Jewish law and customs, prayer, and numerous other topics, which are necessary to become conversant and comfortable with the observances of Judaism.

Called *ba'alei t'shuvah,* those who have repented and returned to the faith, they begin to learn about their Jewish identity, and slowly, with the guidance of supportive rabbis and the Jewish community at large, they make the commitment to live fully as Jews, according to the Torah. This is not an easy transition, nor is it accomplished in a fixed period of time. Deciding to become ***frum***, observant of Jewish law and tradition, is literally a life-changing event, requiring sincere devotion and patience.

As we discussed in Section 6.4, the laws of *t'shuvah* require that *ba'alei t'shuvah* complete several distinct actions:

- cessation of sin
- resolving not to sin in the future
- feeling genuine remorse for having sinned
- verbal confession of sin

More than a matter of repentance, the term *ba'alei t'shuvah* connotes *return,* for the root of the word *t'shuvah* is *shuvah,* return (see Section 6.4). Thus, a *ba'al t'shuvah* (*ba'alat t'shuvah* in the feminine) is someone who repents and returns to the faith. The opportunity to return is available to any Jew at any time of life. It applies equally to Jews who never observed Judaism's precepts and to those who observed and stopped, for whatever reason.

The commitment to repent and return to God involves a two-step program: studying Torah and living as a Jew. With learning comes understanding that it is not necessary to fathom the mysterious ways of God. His Torah is divine, and, thus, "because God commands it" is reason enough to be an observant Jew.

Judaism is a feeling that must be "caught," as much as it is a doctrine that must be taught and learned. It is a religion of deed more than creed. When the words of Torah are translated from ideas into actions, when the *mitzvot* blossom from intellectual ideals into positive achievements, when the customs and traditions are transformed from lovely concepts to hallowed acts, then God is being served.

Without a doubt, *ba'alei t'shuvah* have brought a new vigor and an energized spirit to Judaism. They have experienced the temptations of sin and have decided to abandon them, choosing, instead, to conduct themselves in accordance with the precepts of the Torah. They understand that the ethical and moral standard demanded of Jews by the Torah exceeds that required of other nations. So, their sincerity is born of a genuine love of God and His *mitzvot,* and they recognize that the Torah way of life nourishes their souls. The efforts of *ba'alei t'shuvah* should be supported, and their accomplishments in the face of numerous possible deterrents are to be lauded.

9.2.2 Choosing to Convert

When Abraham, and later his descendants, undertook the obligation to spread the message of monotheism to the world, their purpose was to convert the largely pagan society in their midst to this belief. Today, Judaism does not seek converts, but accepts those who come to the faith with a sincere desire.

According to Jewish law, there are only two ways to become a Jew: (1) birth, and (2) conversion. Children born of a Jewish mother are Jews; there is no such thing as *patrilineal* descent, that is, from the father, according to the Torah. Converts who seek to convert because of inner convictions rather than ulterior motives are welcomed fully into the Jewish fold, provided they fulfill specific religious requirements.

Jews born of a Jewish mother are Jews whether they observe the *mitzvot* or not. Converts, on the other hand, must earn the status of ***ger tzedek,*** righteous convert, by willingly accepting and meeting Judaism's standards. Satisfying the requirements for conversion is not a theoretical ideal, but an attainable goal.

Throughout Jewish history, there have been many illustrious converts to Judaism, the most notable being Ruth, the Mother of Royalty. Her decision to convert to the Jewish faith and her subsequent marriage to Boaz marked the beginning of the House of David, from which the Messiah will come to bring the ultimate redemption (see Section 7.16.2).

Two of the early giants of the pre-tannaitic era, Shemaiah and Avtalion, were righteous converts. Descendants of Sancherev, king of Assyria during the time of the prophet Isaiah, they both served on the *Sanhedrin.* Shemaiah and Avtalion are both quoted in the Mishnah.

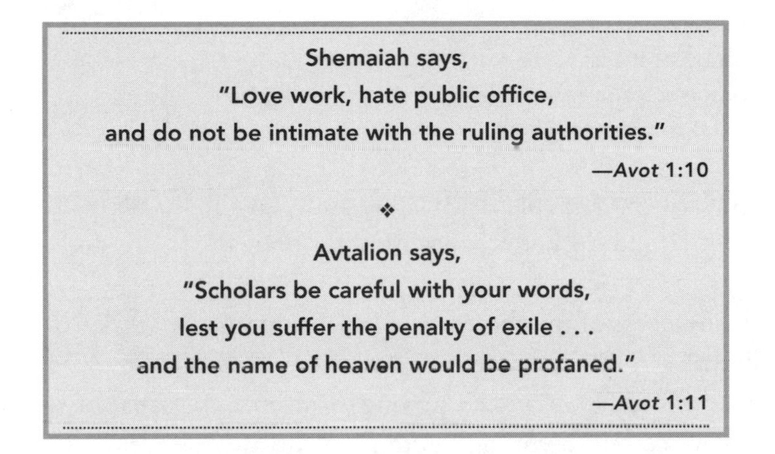

Shemaiah says,
"Love work, hate public office,
and do not be intimate with the ruling authorities."

—*Avot* 1:10

❖

Avtalion says,
"Scholars be careful with your words,
lest you suffer the penalty of exile . . .
and the name of heaven would be profaned."

—*Avot* 1:11

Another famous convert was Onkelos, the nephew of the emperor of the Roman Empire. In spite of his royal upbringing, Onkelos was drawn to the study of the Jewish religion. He traveled to *Eretz Yisrael,* where he studied Torah and became fully conversant with the Hebrew language and the laws and customs of the Jewish people. In time, he decided to become a convert.

A disciple of the *Tana'im* Rabbi Eliezer ben Hirkanus, Rabbi Yehoshuah ben Chananiah, and Rabbi Akiva ben Yosef, spiritual giants of the period, Onkelos lived as a pious Jew, becoming a great sage and scholar in his own right. His Aramaic translation of the Torah, known as ***Targum Onkelos,*** is remarkably faithful to the original Hebrew and is studied to this day.

Many other converts of lesser renown have also been accepted into the extended Jewish family, and today, the number of people seeking conversion to Judaism continues to increase.

Non-Jews, of course, are not commanded to observe the Torah. However, according to the Talmud, *Masechet Sanhedrin* 56a, the Seven Noahide Laws, upon which a civilized society must rely, are incumbent on all humankind. These laws constitute a universal faith, which finds its origin in the precepts imposed on Noah and his descendants—the whole human world—after the Flood. These laws continue to apply to all people.

There are six negative laws, that is, prohibitions, and one positive law.

1. Prohibition of idolatry
2. Prohibition of murder
3. Prohibition of theft
4. Prohibition of blasphemy
5. Prohibition of incest
6. Prohibition of eating the flesh of a living animal
7. Obligation to promote justice

The Noahide Laws are only the starting point for the Jewish people. Jews are expected to be better and do better, because their obligations are derived from God's Torah.

As family members of the chosen people, Jews accept the burden of the ***ol malchut shamayim,*** the yoke of the kingdom of heaven. Jews serve God by studying Torah, by observing the rituals and laws, and by striving to advance the cause of social justice. By bringing devotion, commitment, and enthusiasm to these endeavors, Jews fulfill the will of God and bring the knowledge of His sovereignty to the whole world. The purpose of Judaism is not to make the whole world Jewish, but to make the world recognize that God is the Sovereign of the World.

So, what should non-Jews who want to convert expect to encounter in their spiritual journeys? First and foremost, they should expect to be rebuffed. When would-be converts approach a rabbi about conversion, every attempt is made to dissuade them. According to the Talmud, an applicant is asked:

> **Why do you want to become a convert?**
> **Don't you know that the Children of Israel**
> **are afflicted, oppressed, downtrodden, harassed,**
> **and overcome with suffering . . .**
> **[that they are subject to punishment**
> **for disobeying the commandments of the Torah?]**
>
> —*Yevamot* 47a

If an applicant remains steadfast in the desire to convert and acknowledges an awareness of the burdens to be assumed as a Jew—that of *ol malchut shamayim*—then permission is granted to proceed with a regimen of study about the fundamental teachings and observances of Judaism.

By studying with a qualified rabbi, individually or in classes, and by gradually taking on the practices of Jewish life, would-be converts acquire a basic understanding of what it means to be a Jew and prepare themselves to appear before a ***Bet Din,*** a court of three men learned in the Torah, for the actual ritual of conversion.

Once the program of study and experience has been completed—and it can take six months to a year, or more—a *Bet Din* is assembled. The applicant will be asked questions about the observance of the Sabbath and festivals, Jewish history, and other basic tenets of Judaism. The questions are not meant to intimidate the applicant, only to assure the court that the convert understands the responsibilities that are inherent in becoming a Jew. The applicant must answer them to the satisfaction of the *Bet Din* and demonstrate sincerity as well.

After pledging to uphold the fundamental teachings of the faith and sincerely resolving to practice the rituals and traditions as a part of daily life as a Jew, the convert is accepted and proceeds to the actual ritual of conversion.

For men and women, immersion in a ritual pool, called a ***mikveh,*** is required; in addition, men require ritual circumcision (see Sections 9.5.2 and 9.10). If a man was already circumcised, it is still necessary to draw a symbolic drop of blood as a sign of the Covenant of Abraham.

In the case of minor children, circumcision and immersion with the intent of conversion for a boy and immersion for a girl must be performed in the presence and with the approval of the *Bet Din* (see Section 9.12). At maturity, these children must appear before the *Bet Din* and attest to their desire to live as Jews and their willingness to accept the *ol malchut shamayim.*

According to Jewish law, without circumcision and immersion, there can be no conversion. Sincerity and observance are not enough. After the proper performance of the rituals, all converts are given a Hebrew name, forever to be known as the son or daughter of Abraham our Father, who was the first Jew (see Section 9.9).

The *Bet Din* signs and issues a certificate of conversion to each convert, who must keep it should questions arise in the future about the status of the conversion.

Clearly, issues like marriage must be dealt with in the light of the convert's new status. Marriage between a Jew and a non-Jew is termed intermarriage and is forbidden. Marriage between a Jew and a person converted according to *halachah* is a marriage between two Jews and is permitted. However, because of the special status of the priesthood, a *Kohen* may not marry a convert.

Once the actual ritual of conversion is over, the spiritual journey of the *ger tzedek* parallels that of the *ba'al t'shuvah.* Steeping themselves in further Torah study, participating in communal activities, and being welcomed by the Jewish community help to further ease the transition. The Rambam once wrote a letter to a *ger tzedek:*

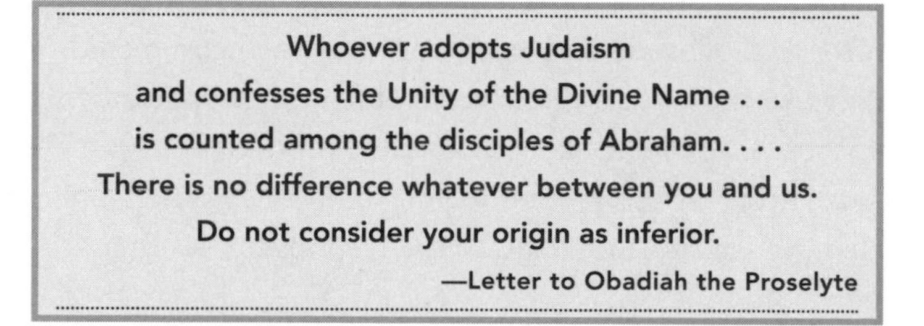

Whoever adopts Judaism
and confesses the Unity of the Divine Name . . .
is counted among the disciples of Abraham. . . .
There is no difference whatever between you and us.
Do not consider your origin as inferior.

—Letter to Obadiah the Proselyte

9.3 Preparing for Marriage

On the sixth day of Creation, God created Man, and He called him Adam, because he was formed from the ***adamah,*** the dust of the ground.

[And God] breathed into his nostrils
the breath of life,
and Adam became a living soul.

—*Parshat Bereshit,* Genesis 2:7

God placed Adam in the Garden of Eden and gave him dominion over all the creatures in the heavens and on the earth and in the seas. Then God said:

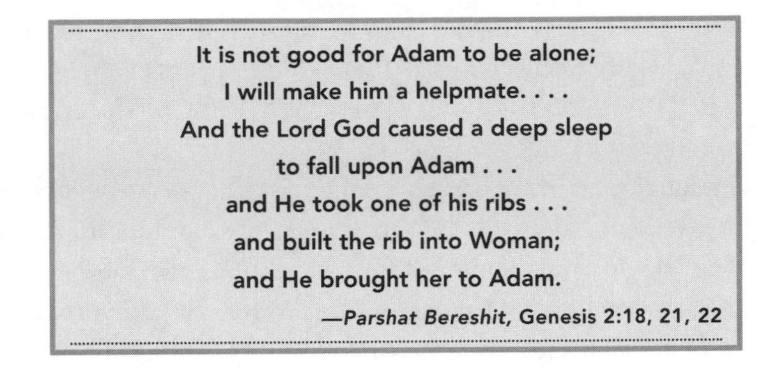

It is not good for Adam to be alone;
I will make him a helpmate. . . .
And the Lord God caused a deep sleep
to fall upon Adam . . .
and He took one of his ribs . . .
and built the rib into Woman;
and He brought her to Adam.

—*Parshat Bereshit,* Genesis 2:18, 21, 22

When Adam awoke, he said:

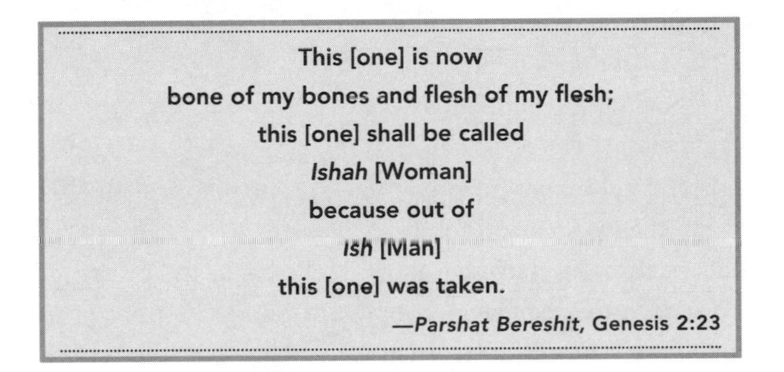

This [one] is now
bone of my bones and flesh of my flesh;
this [one] shall be called
Ishah [Woman]
because out of
Ish [Man]
this [one] was taken.

—*Parshat Bereshit,* Genesis 2:23

The Torah continues:

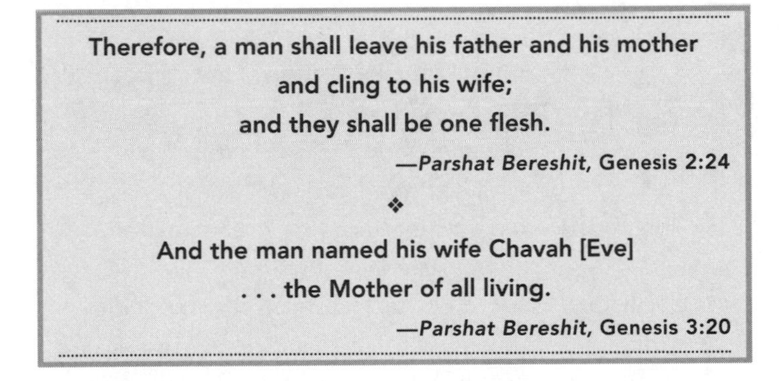

Therefore, a man shall leave his father and his mother
and cling to his wife;
and they shall be one flesh.

—*Parshat Bereshit,* Genesis 2:24

❖

And the man named his wife Chavah [Eve]
. . . the Mother of all living.

—*Parshat Bereshit,* Genesis 3:20

We gain insight into these names from the *Midrash, Pirke de Rabbi Eliezer* 12. Adam called himself ***Ish,*** from the Hebrew letters *alef, yud,* and *shin:* איש. He called his wife ***Ishah,*** formed by the three Hebrew letters *alef, shin,* and *hei:* אשה. The *yud,* י, from *Ish* in combination with the *hei,* ה, from *Ishah* spells the Name of God. If these two letters are removed, all that remains is *alef* and *shin,* which spell ***Aish,*** אֵשׁ, meaning fire. So, too, is the destiny of every Jewish couple. When God is a part of their lives, when *Ish* and *Ishah* are united, God's Name protects them. Without God's presence, only individual fires remain to destroy one another.

Throughout history, marriage has represented a socially acceptable opportunity to fulfill biological, psychological, emotional, economic, legal, and spiritual desires, which cannot be met in a single state. The need for procreation, companionship, love, economic benefit, legal protection, and above all, the promise of an ethical and sanctified union are all met in one divinely sanctioned and widely approved relationship: marriage. It is an ancient practice that continues to answer those needs. In the Talmud, it is called ***Kiddushin,*** a term that describes its most elevated status in Judaism, that of holiness and consecration.

9.3.1 A Marriage Made in Heaven

God, the first matchmaker, arranged and performed the first marriage in the world. According to the midrashic tradition of *Pirke de Rabbi Eliezer* 12, which was also cited above, we learn that God Himself adorned the bride and presented her to Adam. The angels stood around the marriage canopy, and God pronounced the blessings. The angels danced and played musical instruments, rejoicing with the bride and the groom.

The *Midrash* also relates the story of a woman who went to ask Rabbi Jose bar Halafta a question.

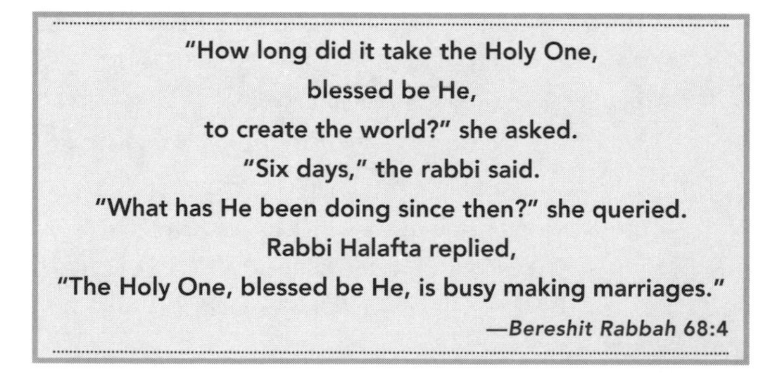
"How long did it take the Holy One,
blessed be He,
to create the world?" she asked.
"Six days," the rabbi said.
"What has He been doing since then?" she queried.
Rabbi Halafta replied,
"The Holy One, blessed be He, is busy making marriages."
—Bereshit Rabbah 68:4

In Jewish tradition, finding a suitable match is, indeed, the handiwork of God. According to the Talmud,

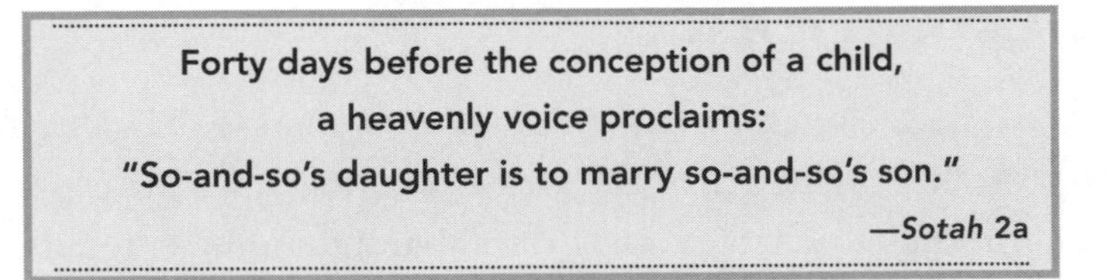
Forty days before the conception of a child,
a heavenly voice proclaims:
"So-and-so's daughter is to marry so-and-so's son."
—*Sotah 2a*

9.3.2 The Role of the *Shadchan*

To be sure, every young man or woman expects to find the ***bashert,*** the mate of destiny, the one intended by God to be the perfect spouse. In earlier times, Jews often entrusted the responsibility of making the perfect match to the marriage broker, the ***shadchan,*** who negotiated on behalf of the families and arranged the ***shidduch,*** the match, for a fee.

Matchmaking was a pious calling rather than a business. Its aim was to perpetuate the Jewish family, and the responsibility for this was often entrusted only to notable scholars and rabbis who were respected members of their communities.

The *shadchan* checked the ***yichus,*** the lineage of the family, before suggesting matches to prospective brides and grooms. It was an honorable profession and often aided in the fulfillment of the *mitzvah* of **hachnasat kallah,** dowering the impoverished bride.

By the twelfth century, as countless pogroms and persecution forced Jews to flee, the function of the *shadchan* became a matter of Jewish survival. The *shadchan* journeyed from ***shtetl*** to *shtetl,* sometimes risking danger in the little towns of Europe.

By the end of the sixteenth century, there was a shift in the attitude toward the *shadchan*. An object of derision, the *shadchan* was considered a miserly opportunist who misrepresented potential suitors. Consequently, the role of the *shadchan* underwent a change, as the profession, and those who practiced it, became the object of humorous and insulting jibes.

Once again today, however, numerous individuals and many Jewish organizations offer matchmaking services—some with computerized databases—to Jewish families. In many Jewish circles, it is considered a very acceptable way for young people to meet, and among the very pious, an arranged marriage is still very much in vogue. The choice of a mate is a critical decision, for marriage perpetuates the links of numerous generations and is tied to the fulfillment of many *mitzvot.*

9.4 The Engagement

According to the Mishnah, *Masechet Avot* 5:21, a man is obligated to take a wife when he reaches eighteen. While this is not the normative practice today, it nevertheless indicates that marriage was a desirable state to be entered into as early as practically possible.

In the time of the Talmud, Jewish engagement and marriage were two separate occasions. The betrothal, called ***Erusin,*** meaning *consecration,* often occurred up to a year before the wedding. This interval gave the bride's family time to prepare her dowry, and gave the groom's family—not the bride's—time to make the arrangements for the wedding.

The betrothal, which took place in the home of the bride, legally bound her to him, although she continued to live in her parents' home. The marriage, called ***Nisu'in,*** was the responsibility of the groom's family and took place in the home of the groom. Today, *Erusin* and *Nisu'in* both take place during the wedding ceremony itself (see Section 9.5.4).

Sometime in the Middle Ages, it became the custom to sign ***tena'im,*** a contract of terms, which set forth negotiations for the marriage. The signing of *tena'im* stipulates that the bride and the groom will wed each other at a future date. It is a custom for the mothers of the bride and groom to jointly smash a plate once the *tena'im* document has been signed. If the engagement were to be broken, the *tena'im* obligates the party who breaks it to pay a penalty to the other for the shame and embarrassment caused by the breakup.

In the last twenty years or so, it has become a prevailing practice in religious circles to hold a ***vort,*** literally, a *word,* as soon as possible after the couple announces their engagement. Attended by family and friends, the *vort* serves as a formal announcement of the intention of the families to wed their children to each other—but without the formality of signing *tena'im*. Someone is asked to say a ***d'var Torah,*** words of Torah, on behalf of the bride and groom and their families, perhaps attesting to their qualities, their *yichus,* and their commitment to create a Jewish home. It is a festive occasion for all.

Accordingly, most couples wait until moments before the actual wedding is to take place to sign the *tena'im*. In this case, the contract of terms is largely symbolic, and no penalties are enumerated in the text.

It is customary for the groom to give his bride a gift, usually an engagement ring. She, in turn, gives him a *talit,* required of married men during prayer, and purchases the *kittel,* the white robe he will put on under the ***chupah,*** the marriage canopy. They may also give each other watches. In some circles, it is also customary for the bride's father to give the groom a *Shas,* an acronym for the Talmud, an indication that he expects his son-in-law to be a ***ben Torah,*** a man who is not only observant of the *mitzvot* but a Torah scholar as well.

9.5 The Jewish Wedding

In the Prophets, the relationship between God and the Jewish people is described as that of a bride and groom.

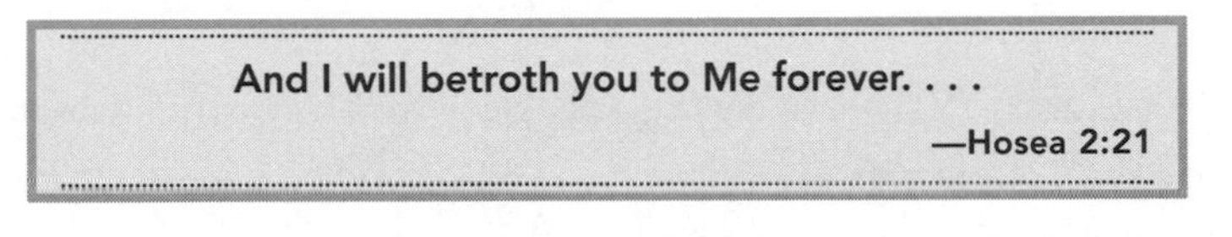

> **And I will betroth you to Me forever. . . .**
>
> **—Hosea 2:21**

So, too, in Jewish tradition, for marriage is a sanctification of life, a relationship intended to last a lifetime.

In Jewish law, it is also a legal contract, entered into willingly by the bride and groom, with no prior conditions set for the marriage. According to the Talmud, *Masechet Kiddushin* 2b, marriage requires the consent of the bride, so no woman can be married against her will. Marriage is a voluntary commitment made between two individuals, both of whom are seeking completion and fulfillment with the other.

The *Midrash* says it beautifully.

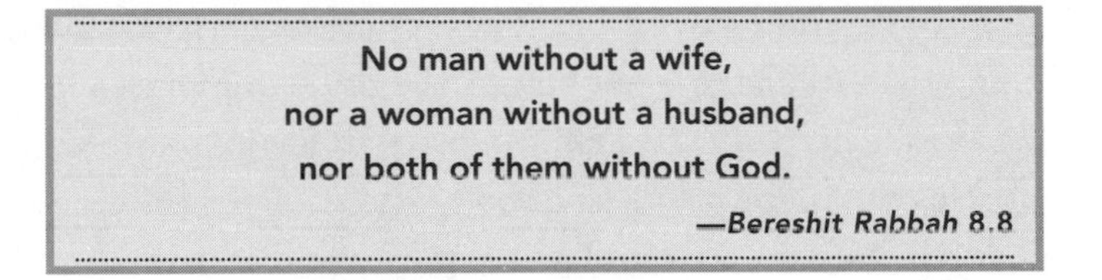

> **No man without a wife,**
> **nor a woman without a husband,**
> **nor both of them without God.**
>
> **—*Bereshit Rabbah* 8.8**

The following sections will provide an overview of the Jewish wedding. No plans should be made without discussing the occasion with the rabbi who will officiate at the ceremony. He will explain the religious laws that pertain to marriage and to the ceremony itself. No doubt the bride and groom—and their parents—will have numerous questions, so pre-wedding consultations are a very good idea.

9.5.1 A Canopy under the Heavens

The wedding ceremony takes place under a *chupah,* a canopy. This custom is derived from the Book of Ruth 3:9. We also learn that when Rebecca was brought into the tent of Sarah,

> **Isaac brought her into the tent . . .**
> **and he took Rebecca,**
> **and she became his wife; and he loved her.**
> **—*Parshat Chayei Sarah,* Genesis 24:67**

The *chupah* also suggests a state of privacy, necessary for the formalization of the union, and a symbol of the couple's future home.

Today Jewish weddings are held in any number of places, but a *chupah* is always required as part of the ceremony. Often made of velvet, adorned with flowers, and ornately embroidered with words taken from the marriage blessings, the canopy is held above the couple by supporting poles at the four corners. Male friends of the couple are often honored with holding the canopy. A *talit* may also be used as a *chupah.*

9.5.2 The Bride

There are several obligations and traditions associated with the bride's preparation for her wedding. They begin shortly before the wedding day arrives. A few days before the wedding, but not later than the night before, the bride immerses herself in the waters of the *mikveh,* as she prepares to begin her married life in a holy state (see Section 9.6). By observing this ritual, she purifies her body and soul and fulfills the will of God.

Attired in her white gown, a symbol of her purity, and adorned like the queen she is, every ***kallah,*** bride, is beautiful on her wedding day. No one may refuse her requests, and nothing is allowed to interfere with her happiness.

In some communities, on the Sabbath before the wedding, the bride's friends often will come to spend time with her. This custom, called ***Shabbat Kallah,*** the Bride's Sabbath, affords her a special opportunity to be with her friends.

On her wedding day, she recites the Confessional Prayer from the Day of Atonement. She fasts, taking neither food nor drink, until after the ceremony.

9.5.3 The Groom

On the Sabbath before the wedding, the groom is honored in the synagogue with an *aliyah*. This "calling up" of the groom is known as an ***Aufruf,*** and, according to the Talmud, *Masechet Sofrim* 19:12, may date back to the days of the *Bet HaMikdash,* when people gathered at the Grooms' Gate on the Sabbath to honor grooms who came there. After the Temple was destroyed, the sages decreed that grooms were to be honored in the synagogue.

It is also customary to prepare small bags of candies and nuts before the Sabbath and throw them at the groom after he has finished the closing blessings of his *aliyah*. This tradition may have evolved from the talmudic comment in *Masechet Berachot* 50b that toasted grains and nuts were to be thrown before the groom and bride, possibly as a symbol of good fortune.

In many communities, the *Aufruf* has become a major event of the pre-wedding celebration. Family and friends from both the bride and groom's sides are invited, and afterward a festive Sabbath meal is served. The bride herself does not attend, because it is customary for the couple not to see each other for a week before the wedding. Sometimes the *Aufruf* is held two weeks before the wedding, so that the bride may attend.

Like the bride, the ***chatan,*** groom, is a king on his wedding day. He, too, fasts, and at *Minchah,* he recites the Confessional Prayer from the Day of Atonement. He prepares his white *kittel* to wear under the *chupah,* a symbol of purity. He also removes his jewelry before the wedding ceremony, a sign of sorrow for the destruction of the Temple.

Just prior to the wedding ceremony, a special reception for the groom, the ***Kabbalat Panim,*** is held in a separate room where the male guests greet the *chatan* and rejoice with him. It is customary for the groom to deliver a talmudic discourse. The guests eat and drink (the groom is still fasting), and sing and dance with the groom until it is time for the ceremony to begin.

Surrounded by friends and relatives, the groom is escorted triumphantly to the bride who sits and awaits him. As the sound of joyous music reverberates in the air, he approaches her and lowers the bridal veil over her face, recalling the biblical Rebecca, who modestly covered her face as she beheld Isaac, her betrothed, from afar. The ***badekin,*** veiling of the bride, is one of the most beautiful customs of the wedding ceremony. It is appropriate at this time for those assembled to recite the blessing given to Rebecca by her mother and brother.

> **. . . May you be the mother of thousands of ten thousands.**
>
> **—*Parshat Chayei Sarah,* Genesis 24:60**

It is also traditional for the father of the bride to bless his daughter and the father of the groom to bless his son with the Priestly Blessing before the ceremony begins:

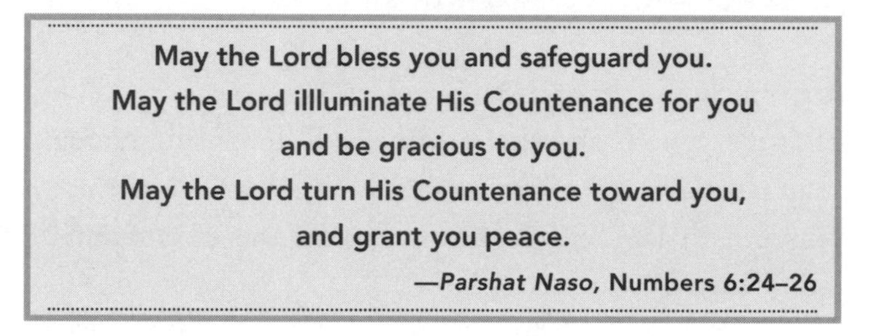

May the Lord bless you and safeguard you.
May the Lord illluminate His Countenance for you
and be gracious to you.
May the Lord turn His Countenance toward you,
and grant you peace.

—*Parshat Naso,* Numbers 6:24–26

9.5.4 The Ceremony

The traditions of the Jewish wedding can be likened to the events leading up to the Revelation on Mount Sinai. Rashi comments on *Parshat Yitro,* Exodus 19:17, that God went forth to meet the Children of Israel like a Bridegroom who goes forth to meet his Bride. As the ceremony is about to start, a hush falls over the assembled guests.

There are two parts to the ceremony: *Erusin* and *Nisu'in,* betrothal and marriage. The ***m'sader Kiddushin,*** the rabbi who *conducts the order of the sanctification,* officiates.

The wedding procession begins with the arrival of the rabbi and continues, as the groom's attendants proceed to the *chupah.* As we noted above (see Section 9.3), when God decreed that it is not good for Man to be alone, He created Woman from his rib:

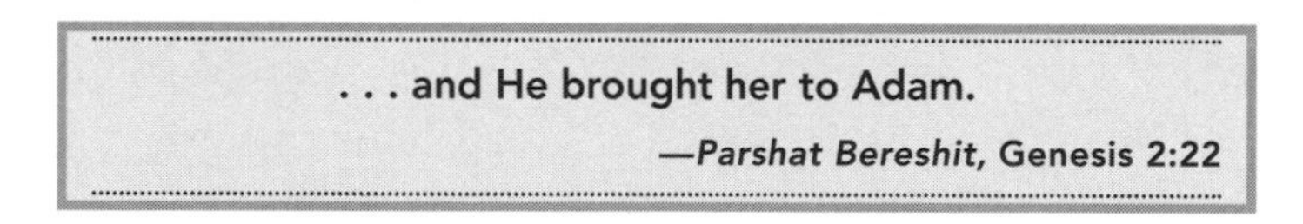

. . . and He brought her to Adam.

—*Parshat Bereshit,* Genesis 2:22

The Talmud comments on this verse in *Masechet Eruvin* 18b, teaching that God Himself made the wedding arrangements.

The groom, escorted by the ***unterfirers***, his parents (or another couple), is led to the *chupah.* As he passes, the assembled guests stand to honor him. As the groom approaches the *chupah*, the cantor greets him:

Baruch HaBa.

❖

Blessed is he who arrives.

The cantor then continues:

He Who is mighty above all,
He Who is blessed above all,
He Who is great above all,
May He bless the groom and the bride.

The groom, assisted by the *unterfirers*, puts on his *kittel* and waits for his bride.

Her attendants precede her, heightening the anticipation for the arrival of the queen. As she approaches, she is welcomed by the cantor:

B'rucha HaBa'ah.

❖

Blessed is she who arrives.

Beautifully gowned and adorned, her face covered by the veil, she approaches the *chupah,* escorted by the *unterfirers,* her parents (or other couple). Again, the guests rise to honor her as she passes.

The cantor continues:

He Who understands the speech
of the rose among the thorns,
the love of the bride,
who is the joy of beloved ones,
May He bless the groom and the bride.

She walks under the *chupah* and circles the groom, fulfilling the words of Jeremiah 31:21. According to various customs, the bride, followed by her mother and mother-in-law, circles the groom either seven times, recalling that God betrothed Himself to the Jewish people using seven different expressions (Hosea 2:21–22), or three times, based on the three biblical verses that include ". . . and when a man takes a wife" (*Parshat Ki Tetzei,* Deuteronomy 22:13; 24:1, 5). The bride stands to the groom's right, recalling the verse of the psalmist:

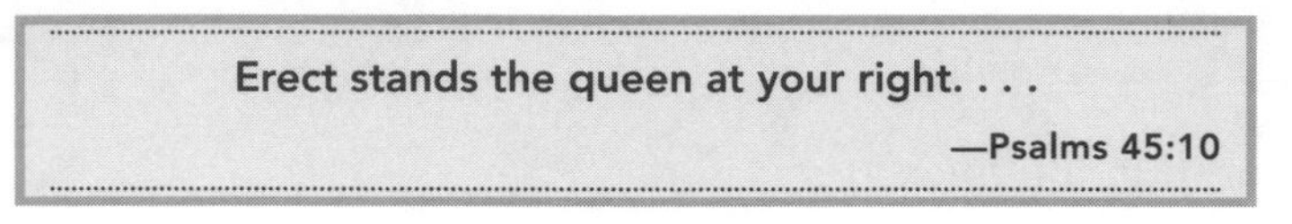

Erect stands the queen at your right. . . .

—Psalms 45:10

Erusin, the betrothal, begins with the *m'sader Kiddushin's* recitation of the two Blessings of Betrothal and by the drinking of wine from the same cup by the groom and bride.

The first blessing over the wine is customary for joyous occasions. The second, based on *Parshat Achrei Mot,* Leviticus 18:6–23, discusses forbidden marriages and relationships.

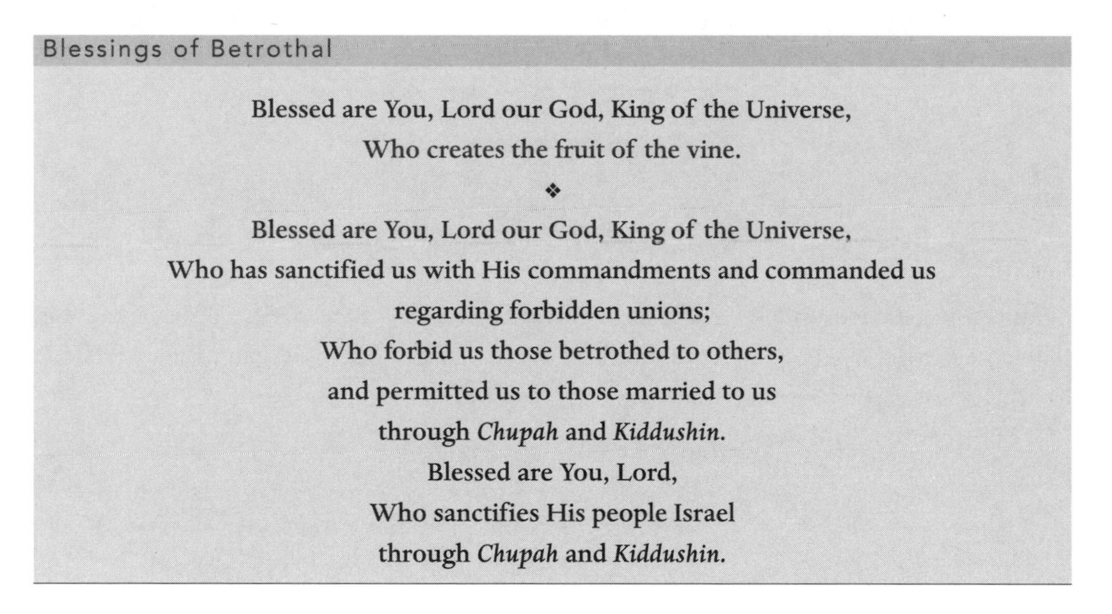

Blessings of Betrothal

Blessed are You, Lord our God, King of the Universe,
Who creates the fruit of the vine.

❖

Blessed are You, Lord our God, King of the Universe,
Who has sanctified us with His commandments and commanded us
regarding forbidden unions;
Who forbid us those betrothed to others,
and permitted us to those married to us
through *Chupah* and *Kiddushin.*
Blessed are You, Lord,
Who sanctifies His people Israel
through *Chupah* and *Kiddushin.*

The groom, and then the bride, sip from the cup of wine, a symbolic sharing of joy.

9.5.5 The Ring

The wedding ring is a universally accepted symbol of marriage. In talmudic times, a marriage could be effected if a man presented an eligible woman with an object of value in the presence of two ***eidim,*** witnesses. Since about the seventh century, a ring has been used as that object.

The wedding band must have a minimum value of one ***p'rutah,*** an ancient coin, equivalent today to one-sixth of a cent. It must not contain any stones, to preclude the possibility that the bride is entering into the marriage because of the value of the ring she will receive. The ring must be examined by two witnesses prior to the recitation of the Declaration of Betrothal to be sure it is halachically acceptable.

The groom must own the ring he gives his bride. Holding it in his hand, he recites the Declaration of Betrothal:

Declaration of Betrothal

Behold, you are consecrated unto me,
with this ring,
according to the laws of Moses and Israel.

He places the wedding ring on the index finger of the bride's right hand.

Only the words

Behold, you are consecrated unto me . . .

are mentioned in the Talmud, *Masechet Kiddushin* 5b, as the required formula for the Declaration of Betrothal. The words

. . . according to the laws of Moses and Israel.

were added later—"and Israel" indicates that the laws of *Erusin* are not only biblical in origin.

The phrase

with this ring

was added even later.

Once the ring has been given, the couple is betrothed, legally bound to one another. Their relationship can be dissolved only by divorce or death, but they are not yet married and are not permitted to live together as husband and wife. With the giving of the ring, *Erusin* is concluded.

9.5.6 The Marriage Contract

The second phase of the wedding ceremony, *Nisu'in,* begins with the reading of the ***ketubah,*** the marriage contract, which is written in Aramaic. The *ketubah,* which means *a written document,* sets forth in detail the husband's obligations to his wife, and provides for certain financial compensation to her should the marriage be dissolved by death or divorce. It is accepted by the groom prior to the wedding and signed by two religiously observant male witnesses, who must not be related to each other or to the bride or the groom. The format and content of the document and the terms of compensation are set by rabbinic law.

Some couples decide to have their *ketubah* handwritten by a *sofer,* a scribe. The beauty of the *ketubah* parchment is often enhanced by the artistic illumination of the text. It takes a few weeks to prepare an ornately decorated handwritten *ketubah,* so the couple should plan accordingly.

The *ketubah* is read aloud by the rabbi or other honored guest in the presence of all assembled. It is given to the groom, who, in turn, hands it to his bride for safekeeping. The *ketubah* is often framed after the wedding and displayed in the couple's home.

At the conclusion of the reading of the *ketubah,* a second cup of wine is poured, and the ceremony continues with the recitation of the Seven Benedictions, the ***Sheva Berachot.***

9.5.7 The Seven Benedictions

It is customary to honor friends and relatives with the recitation of the Seven Benedictions. In turn, each honoree is called to the *chupah.* He holds the cup of wine in his hand as he recites one of the seven blessings.

Recite the Seven Benedictions

(1)

Blessed are You, Lord our God, King of the Universe,
Who creates the fruit of the vine.

(2)

Blessed are You, Lord our God, King of the Universe,
Who has created everything for His honor.

(3)

Blessed are You, Lord our God, King of the Universe,
Who has formed Man.

(4)

Blessed are You, Lord our God, King of the Universe,
Who has formed Man in His own image . . .
and out of himself, an eternal [companion].
Blessed are You, Lord, Who has formed Man.

(5)

Bring intense joy and exultation to [Zion] the barren one,
when her children are gathered in. . . .
Blessed are You, Lord,
Who brings joy to Zion through her children.

(6)

Gladden the beloved companions as [those] in the Garden of Eden.
Blessed are You, Lord,
Who makes the groom rejoice with the bride.

(7)

Blessed are You, Lord our God, King of the Universe,
Who created joy and gladness, groom and bride,
mirth and cheerful song, pleasure and delight,
love and brotherhood, peace and companionship . . .
let there soon be heard in the cities of Judah
and in the streets of Jerusalem,
the sound of joy and the sound of gladness,
the voice of the groom and the voice of the bride. . . .
Blessed are You, Lord,
Who makes the groom rejoice with the bride.

When the seventh blessing has been recited, the groom and the bride both sip from the cup of wine. Their joy is shared by all, but it is to be briefly tempered.

9.5.8 To Remember the Holy Temple

As the ceremony concludes, the groom smashes a glass under his right foot, recognizing that even the joy of his wedding day cannot be complete until the Holy Temple is rebuilt.

At some ceremonies, the following verses are also recited:

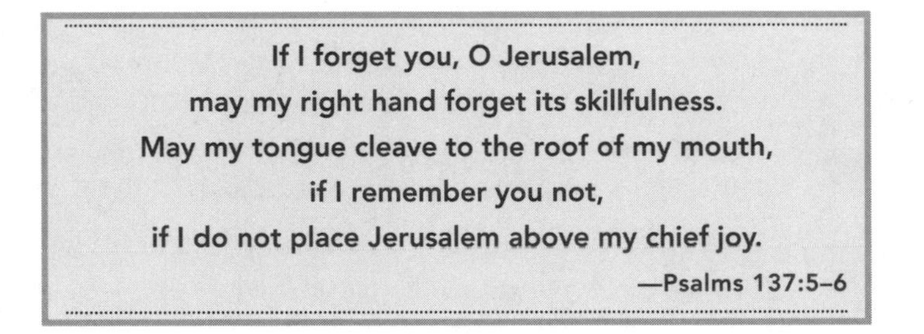

If I forget you, O Jerusalem,
may my right hand forget its skillfulness.
May my tongue cleave to the roof of my mouth,
if I remember you not,
if I do not place Jerusalem above my chief joy.

—Psalms 137:5–6

Jerusalem and the *Bet HaMikdash* are always uppermost in the Jewish consciousness. Even at a time of great joy, the Jew remembers Jewish suffering and tragedy. The sages teach that it is necessary to curb excessive merriment, so even in a place of joy, there should be trembling.

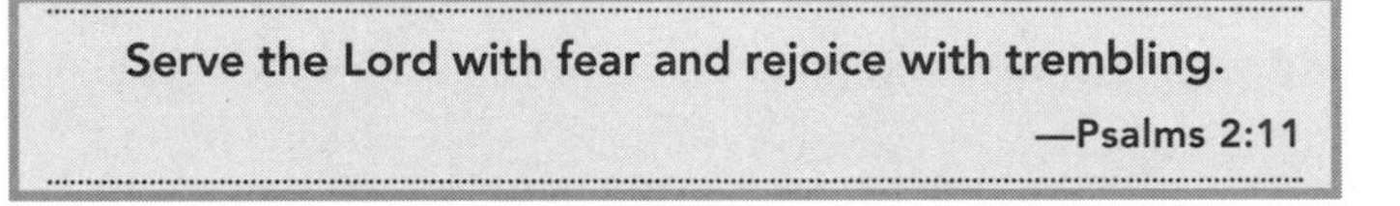

Serve the Lord with fear and rejoice with trembling.

—Psalms 2:11

9.5.9 To Rejoice with the Groom and Bride

After the ceremony, the bride and groom are ushered into a room for ***Yichud*** (privacy) where they are completely alone for the first time as husband and wife. They must stay alone for a brief time while two witnesses stand outside the door. They break their fast, partaking of food that has been prepared for them. This private act validates the marriage. After *Yichud*, they join their family and friends for a wedding feast. As they enter, a wish for *mazal tov* resounds throughout the room.

Everyone sings and dances for it is a Jew's obligation to rejoice with the groom and bride on their wedding day. As we noted in Section 9.3.1, the angels themselves danced and played musical instruments at the wedding of Adam and Eve. In the Talmud, the question is asked:

> **What words must we use when dancing before the bride?**
> **The School of Hillel said:**
> **"Say, 'O bride, beautiful and gracious.' "**
>
> **—*Ketubot* 17a**

From this we learn that we should dance with the bride, but what about rejoicing with the groom? The Talmud again provides an answer:

> **Anyone who benefits from the banquet of a bridegroom**
> **and does not make him rejoice**
> **violates the spirit of the five voices.**
>
> **—*Berachot* 6b**

What are the five voices? In Jeremiah 33:11, he prophesies that the desolate streets of Jerusalem and the cities of Judah would again be restored to joy and happiness. Once again, the voices—or the sounds—(1) of joy, (2) of gladness, (3) of the groom, (4) of the bride, and (5) of the people thanking God will be heard. According to Rashi, those who do not rejoice with the groom show no regard for any of the five sounds of rejoicing that God promised to grant Israel. Thus, we learn that we are obliged to rejoice with the groom, because by doing so, it is as if we studied the entire Torah.

The experience of celebrating at a traditional wedding cannot be expressed adequately in words. As the men dance around the groom, and the women around the bride, the pure joy becomes palpable as the excitement builds. You don't have to know the steps; just let the spirit move you along. When the bride and groom are lifted (in their chairs) in the air, the roar of approval swells with the music. The dancing is interrupted only to participate in the festive wedding dinner, and then it resumes, as exuberant as before. The wedding feast concludes with the recitation of the Grace after Meals and the *Sheva Berachot*. A guest, who is honored with leading the *Birkat HaMazon,* begins by pouring a cup of wine, which he holds in his hand. *Birkat HaMazon* is preceded by the responsive recitation of a tenth-century poem attributed to Dunash ben Labrat.

When the recitation of *Birkat HaMazon* is concluded, a second cup of wine is poured. The Seven Benedictions are recited, but the prayer over the wine is recited last rather than first. Thus, Blessings (2) to (7) of the ceremony become (1) to (6); and (1) of the ceremony becomes (7), at the end of the wedding feast. One person may recite all seven blessings, or they may be divided among other guests, each one holding the second cup as he recites the blessing. The final blessing is also recited by the one honored with *Birkat HaMazon*. At the conclusion of the seventh blessing, he drinks some of the wine from the first cup. Then he pours the two cups of wine together, mixing them, and one cup is given to the groom, the other to the bride. It is considered a ***kos berachah,*** a cup of blessing, and, therefore, it is desirable to sip from this wine.

The wedding is over, but the rejoicing continues. For seven days beginning with the wedding, the groom and bride are feted at the homes of family and friends. After each meal, *Birkat HaMazon* and the Seven Benedictions are recited, and this week-long period is referred to as the Seven Days of Feasting. At least one new guest, someone who did not attend the wedding, is invited to each meal during the week of *Sheva Berachot*.

9.6 The Concept of Family Purity

Procreation is one of the fundamental reasons for marriage. Within a Jewish context, it is a *mitzvah,* the first one proclaimed in the Torah.

> **Be fruitful and increase and fill the earth.**
>
> —*Parshat Bereshit,* Genesis 1:28

However, the sages are unanimous in the opinion that procreation is not the primary purpose of marriage. They have not lost sight that God created Eve to be a helpmate to Adam. In His wisdom, He made them companions who would love and cherish each other. The marital relationship is one of holiness, and this applies to the sexual relationship as well. Marriage includes a sexual relationship, but procreation is not meant to be the only purpose of the sexual union.

In Judaism, human sexuality is raised to a level of sanctity, above the mere satisfaction of the biological and psychological urges associated with it. The sexual union between a husband and wife is meant to fulfill those physical and emotional needs within a spiritual framework. In that context, it is never a shameful or sinful act, but rather a moral and pure expression of marital love.

This love finds its greatest fulfillment within the concept of family purity, called ***Taharat HaMishpachah.*** Based on the biblical verses, *Parshat Metzora,* Leviticus 15:19-28, Jewish couples are forbidden to engage in sexual intercourse from the time her menstrual period begins until seven days after the menstrual flow has ceased and she has immersed herself in the ritual bath, called the *mikveh.* This is, no doubt, the most neglected and misunderstood of the *mitzvot* of daily life.

You will recall that ritual immersion in a *mikveh* was required of the *Kohen Gadol* before the *Avodah* during *Musaf* in the *Bet HaMikdash* on *Yom Kippur* (see Section 6.28.1). It is also required of the convert (see Section 9.2.2). Immersion in a *mikveh* is not a matter of hygiene or cleanliness. Rather, it is a spiritual act of purification, in preparation for holiness. The laws of *Taharat HaMishpachah,* as set down in the Torah and expanded upon by the sages of the Talmud, are religious laws, and for that reason alone they are to be observed.

During the menstrual cycle (a minimum of twelve days), the Jewish couple remains separated, refraining from any physical contact, including touching, kissing, sharing food from the same plate or cup, even avoiding handing objects to one another. They do not engage in conversations which might arouse sexual thoughts, and for this reason, they do not sleep in the same bed, but rather have twin beds, in order that they might sleep separately during this time.

For twelve days, the wife is a ***niddah,*** in a state of ritual impurity. Admittedly, this complete physical separation is of great benefit to the physical well-being of the wife and to the emotional mood of the marriage. That they afford such benefit to the woman is an incidental good; it is not the purpose of the laws. By the observance of the laws of *Taharat HaMishpachah,* the couple renew their physical love each month with anticipation and in holiness.

After the menstrual flow has ceased (a minimum of five days), the wife washes herself and changes her bed linens and undergarments. She examines herself with a soft cloth in the evening of the fifth day and begins to count seven "clean days." She repeats the examination twice a day, morning and evening, for seven days to be certain that the menstrual flow has ceased entirely. If a stain should be found, she must wash again and begin to count the seven "clean days" again.

The laws of *mikveh* cannot be fulfilled in the ordinary bath at home. The water for immersion must be drawn from a reservoir of natural running water and must be present in the bath in required volumes set by the *halachah.* On the evening of the seventh clean day, the wife bathes thoroughly, taking special care to remove any impediments, including those on the skin or in the hair of the head or body. After dark, she goes to the *mikveh* and immerses herself. This immersion is called ***tevilah.***

Many Jewish communities maintain a *mikveh,* often in the synagogue or in a building adjacent to it. In larger cities, where many women use the *mikveh* each night, a special *mikveh* attendant is always present. In smaller communities, it is usually necessary to schedule an appointment with her. She is a pious woman, knowledgeable about the laws of immersion, and can help the women who come to the *mikveh* to prepare for immersion. She also observes the immersion to be sure that it is done properly.

Upon entering the *mikveh*, the *niddah* immerses herself completely under the water, leaning forward as if to feed a small child. She then rises, covers her head with a cloth, and recites the following blessing:

Recite the Blessing on Ritual Immersion

Baruch Atah, HaShem E-lo-kenu, Melech HaOlam,
asher kidshanu b'mitzvotav v'tzivanu
al hatevilah.

❖

Blessed are You, Lord our God, King of the Universe,
Who has sanctified us with His commandments and commanded us
concerning ritual immersion.

She then immerses again, rises, and recites the *Y'hi Ratzon* found at the end of *Shemoneh Esrei*. After a third immersion, she leaves the *mikveh* and gets dressed.

Ritual immersion has been observed under conditions of great hardship, even during persecution and war. To this day, the baths at Masada, the ancient Jewish fortress that overlooks the Dead Sea, bear silent testimony to the sacrifices Jewish women made to observe these spiritual laws.

Today, it is very convenient. Many *mikveh* buildings contain facilities for bathing prior to immersion as well as those necessary for setting and drying the hair, applying cosmetics, or performing other beauty rituals. There is usually a fee for the use of the *mikveh*. The fees are used to maintain the *mikveh* and to provide any linens or supplies a woman might require before or after immersion.

Ritual immersion may be performed any night, including the Sabbath and festivals, provided no laws of the Sabbath or festival are violated to do so. When immersion is scheduled to take place on the eve of *Yom Kippur* or *Tishah b'Av*, it is postponed until the next night.

The observance of *Taharat HaMishpachah* makes the wife as beloved as the bride throughout her married life. Ritual immersion purifies the body and the spirit as well, and when she returns home, sexual relations may be resumed.

The Torah requires the husband to provide his wife with food, clothing, and her conjugal rights. Observance of the laws of family purity raises the marital relationship to a higher plane, to one of sanctity, rather than one of physical gratification alone. There are also many laws, contained in the *Shulchan Aruch,* which specify exactly how and when intercourse may take place. The requirements for ritual immersion for the bride are similar to those for the married woman, with a few modifications.

9.7 The Jewish Home

The Jewish home has been the foundation of Jewish life since time immemorial. Based upon the premise that Jewish marriage and family life is a religious obligation, one that is inherently good, the Jewish home has always been the stronghold of the Jewish community. Without a solid grounding in the *mitzvot* associated with successfully establishing and maintaining a Jewish home, it will be all but impossible to foster the attitudes that future generations will need to sustain the Jewish way of life at all.

9.7.1 A Sign upon the Doorpost

It might be said that a Jewish home can be identified from the outside in. In the Bible, we find:

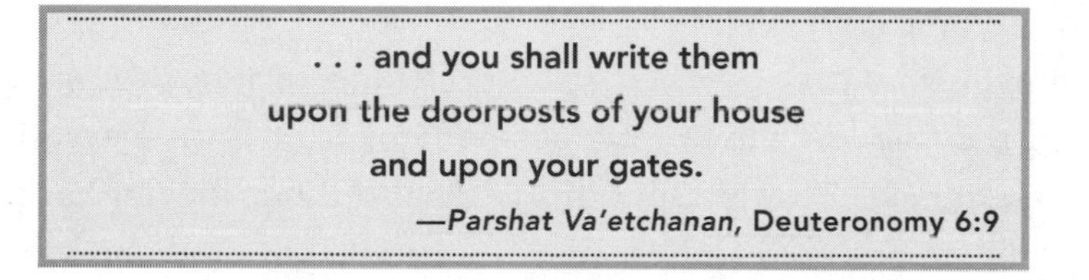

. . . and you shall write them
upon the doorposts of your house
and upon your gates.

—*Parshat Va'etchanan,* Deuteronomy 6:9

In fulfillment of this *mitzvah,* the doorpost, called ***mezuzah,*** on the outside of the Jewish home, and at the entryway into every room in the house (except the bathroom), is affixed with a small case, often decorative in design. Observing the *mitzvah* of *mezuzah* demonstrates our love of God and His Commandments.

The case contains a small parchment inscribed with the words of the *Shema* (see Section 3.7.4), the Jew's affirmation in the Unity of God, and with two biblical passages dealing with the love of God and His divine precepts. In common usage, the word *mezuzah* also means the small case and the parchment it contains. The cases are available in a variety of styles and price ranges.

These verses, taken from *Parshat Va'etchanan* and *Parshat Eikev,* Deuteronomy 6:4–9 and 11:13–21, are inscribed on the parchment, which is then rolled tightly and placed in the case. Only a qualified *sofer* may inscribe the parchment for a *mezuzah.* On the outer side of the rolled parchment, the name *Shaddai,* Almighty, appears. The three Hebrew letters of *Shaddai* also represent three Hebrew words meaning the "Guardian of the doors of Israel." The parchment is positioned in the case so that the name is visible through an opening near the top of the case. Some cases have the name inscribed on the outside. Others bear the Hebrew letter *shin,* the first letter of the Almighty's Name.

Facing into the room, the case is affixed at the bottom of the top third of the right doorpost, after the recitation of the blessing:

Recite the Blessing before Affixing a *Mezuzah*

Baruch Atah, HaShem E-lo-kenu, Melech HaOlam,
asher kidshanu b'mitzvotav v'tzivanu
likboa mezuzah.

❖

Blessed are You, Lord our God, King of the Universe,
Who has sanctified us with His commandments and commanded us
to affix a *mezuzah.*

The *mezuzah* should slant inward at the top, if the width of the doorpost permits. If not, it may be attached vertically with nails, screws, or glue.

When moving into your own home, it is preferable to attach the ***mezuzot*** immediately, although the *halachah* allows for a postponement of thirty days. If it is a rental property, it is permissible to wait up to thirty days, but not longer. Each room in the house (except the bathroom) requires its own *mezuzah,* but only one blessing is necessary at a given time. If a *mezuzah* is later replaced, the *berachah* must be recited again.

Mezuzot should be removed and checked by a *sofer* twice in seven years to be sure the parchment has not been damaged by humidity or dryness, for example. There is usually a fee for the inspection.

In general, when moving from a home, *mezuzot* should be removed, especially if there is the possibility that a non-Jew will move in. If it is a certainty that Jews will move in, it is proper to leave them, although it is not a requirement to do so.

The *mezuzah* provides Jews with a constant reminder of God's Unity, and of their obligations to live according to the precepts of the Torah. It is customary to touch the *mezuzah* with the fingertips, and then to kiss the fingers, when entering or leaving the house.

The *mezuzah*, which contains passages from the *Kriat Shema*, is a reminder of God's presence.

It is incorrect to consider the *mezuzah* an amulet that will provide protection from evil. Other uses of the *mezuzah*, such as in jewelry or as a dashboard ornament, have no basis in Jewish tradition.

A Witty Remark!

My friend's six-year-old son, a Hebrew Day School student, was being evaluated for placement in a reading group. A number of language skill tests were administered to assess his ability. One of the tests called for him to identify what was missing in a series of pictures. When a face was shown, he was supposed to reply that the eyes were missing; when a chair was shown, a leg was missing, and so forth.

The tester showed him a picture of a door. "What's missing here?" she asked, expecting him to say "doorknob." The little boy looked at the picture, and without a moment's hesitation, he replied, "The *mezuzah* is missing."

She marked him wrong, and when she discussed it later with his parents, they were very proud. They knew his answer was right.

9.7.2 The Concept of *Shalom Bayit*

Peace and harmony in the home, ***shalom bayit,*** is a cornerstone upon which the Jewish home is built. In the home, where it is often easiest to lose one's temper, the Jewish couple is enjoined to strive for peace. Nothing is more detrimental to people or more despised by God than strife.

The commitment to *shalom bayit* prepares the husband and the wife to conscientiously seek alternatives to anger and disagreement. Each partner seeks to be as sensitive to his or her own faults as to the shortcomings of the spouse.

Shalom bayit excludes making each other happy by promptly fulfilling personal desires outside of a Torah context. In all areas of life, including the sexual relationship, husbands and wives are commanded to seek fulfillment in accordance with the precepts of the Torah. Mutual respect for each other's needs, even the need to express anger or disappointment without vindictiveness, allows for the harmony necessary to sustain and nurture the Jewish couple and to make the Jewish marriage flourish.

The concept of *shalom bayit* applies to all relationships: between spouses, between parents and children, and among siblings. Respect among generations requires that grandparents and other relatives—including in-laws—be treated with honor, dignity, and courtesy.

9.7.3 The Jewish Husband

It is a biblical obligation of the Jew to marry. The Torah provides the basis for the Jewish view that marriage is a divinely ordained state in which husband and wife are equal partners. The Jewish people are instructed on the essence of the marital relationship:

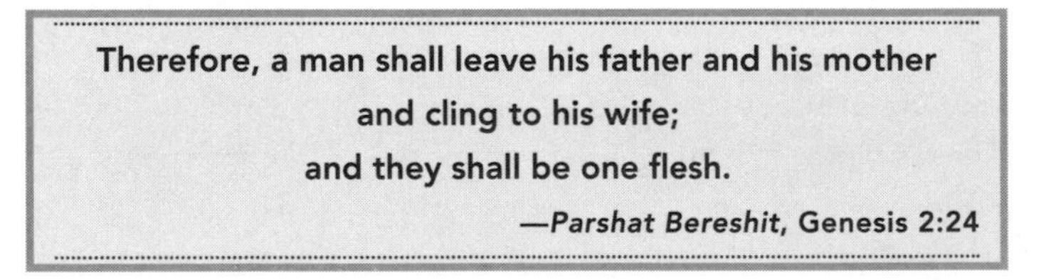
Therefore, a man shall leave his father and his mother
and cling to his wife;
and they shall be one flesh.
—*Parshat Bereshit*, Genesis 2:24

Many sages of the Talmud have discussed the proper attitude of a Jewish husband. For example,

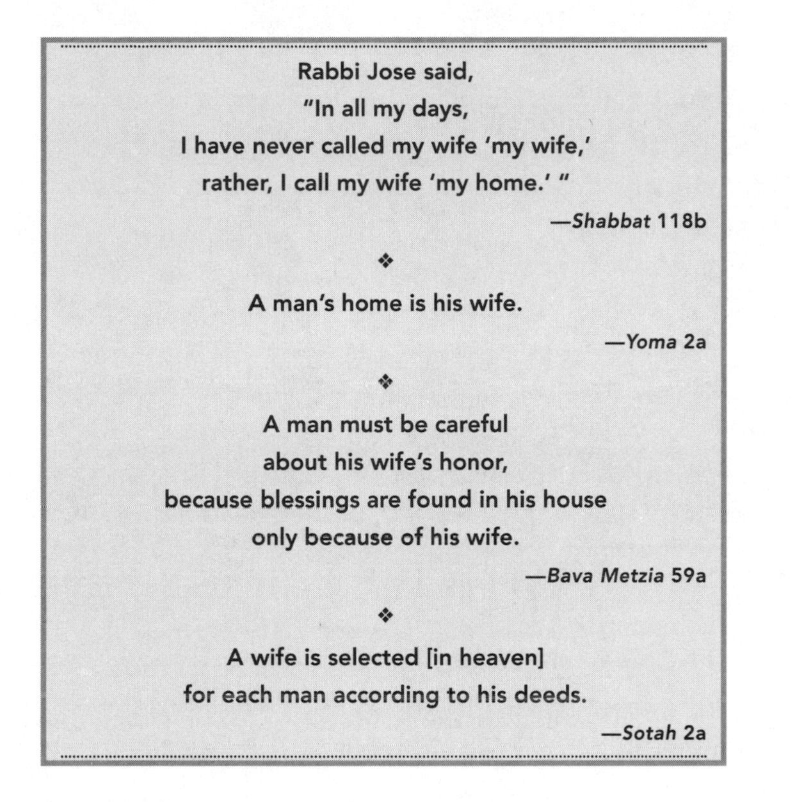

Rabbi Jose said,
"In all my days,
I have never called my wife 'my wife,'
rather, I call my wife 'my home.' "

—*Shabbat* 118b

❖

A man's home is his wife.

—*Yoma* 2a

❖

A man must be careful
about his wife's honor,
because blessings are found in his house
only because of his wife.

—*Bava Metzia* 59a

❖

A wife is selected [in heaven]
for each man according to his deeds.

—*Sotah* 2a

Others commented:

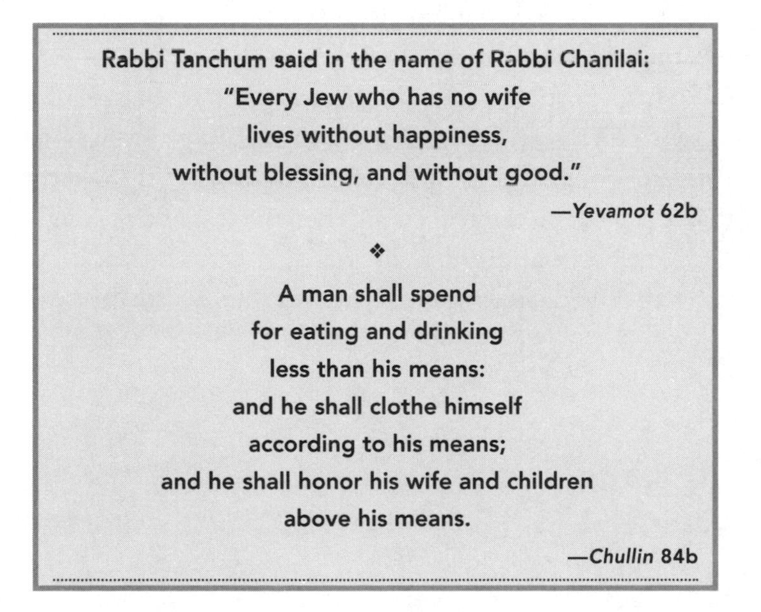

Rabbi Tanchum said in the name of Rabbi Chanilai:
"Every Jew who has no wife
lives without happiness,
without blessing, and without good."

—*Yevamot* 62b

❖

A man shall spend
for eating and drinking
less than his means:
and he shall clothe himself
according to his means;
and he shall honor his wife and children
above his means.

—*Chullin* 84b

and

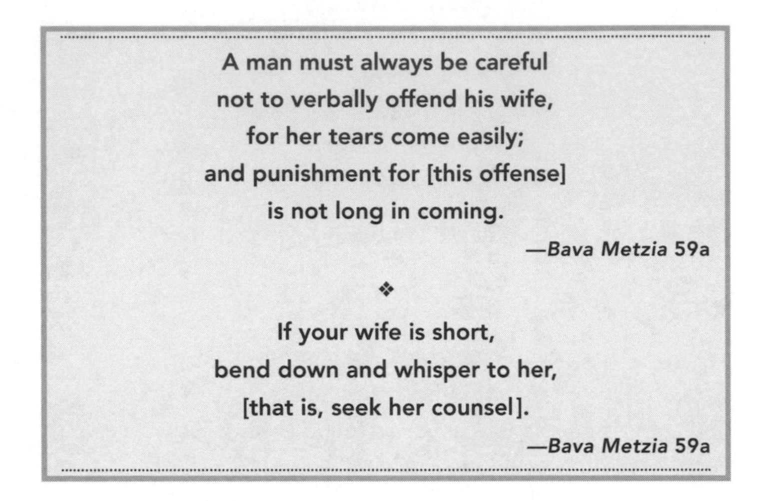
A man must always be careful
not to verbally offend his wife,
for her tears come easily;
and punishment for [this offense]
is not long in coming.

—*Bava Metzia* 59a

❖

If your wife is short,
bend down and whisper to her,
[that is, seek her counsel].

—*Bava Metzia* 59a

9.7.4 The Jewish Wife

There are three *mitzvot* that are the obligation of Jewish women, and more specifically, of the Jewish wife: (1) to kindle the Sabbath lights (see Section 5.2.1); (2) to observe the laws of *Taharat HaMishpachah* (see Section 9.6); and (3) to separate a portion of the dough in remembrance of the obligation to set aside a portion of the flour as a tithe for the benefit of the *Kohanim* in the *Bet HaMikdash.*

When preparing any bread product from one of the five grains—wheat, spelt, rye, barley, and oats—a small portion of the dough, equivalent to the size of an olive, is separated from the rest, a symbolic representation of the flour that was set aside for the *Kohanim.* This piece of dough, itself called *challah,* is placed in the oven and burned immediately, so that it will not be eaten in error. Then the rest of the dough is shaped into breads and baked. The burned portion is discarded.

A special *berachah* is recited when separating the *challah* from the rest of the dough.

Recite the *Berachah* when Separating the *Challah*

Baruch Atah, HaShem E-lo-kenu, Melech HaOlam,
asher kidshanu b'mitzvotav v'tzivanu
l'hafrish challah min ha'isah.

❖

Blessed are You, Lord our God, King of the Universe,
Who has sanctified us with His commandments and commanded us
to separate the *challah* from the dough.

The *challah* portion must be taken if the dough contains at least 3.69 pounds of flour, is kneaded with water, and is baked in an oven. If the dough contains less than 2.74 pounds of flour, it is not necessary to take *challah* at all. If the dough contains between 2.74 and 3.69 pounds of flour, or is kneaded with oil, eggs, or fruit juice, or if it is cooked or fried in a pot, the *challah* should be taken, but no *berachah* is recited.

Challah must be "taken" by kosher bakeries as well. Some *matzah* manufacturers actually print an assurance to the kosher consumer on their boxes: "The *challah* has been taken from every batch of dough."

There are several other laws of *challah* that pertain to the mixing of grains, preparing dough on *Yom Tov,* and requirements in the Land of Israel and in the Diaspora. In such instances, a qualified rabbi should be consulted.

Taking *challah* is an obligation of men as well, if they do the baking. However, in the home, women customarily perform this *mitzvah* themselves. The role of the Jewish wife is one of equal partnership with her husband. Their roles are complementary, for without a wife a man is considered incomplete. The Talmud comments on *Parshat Bereshit,* Genesis 5:2:

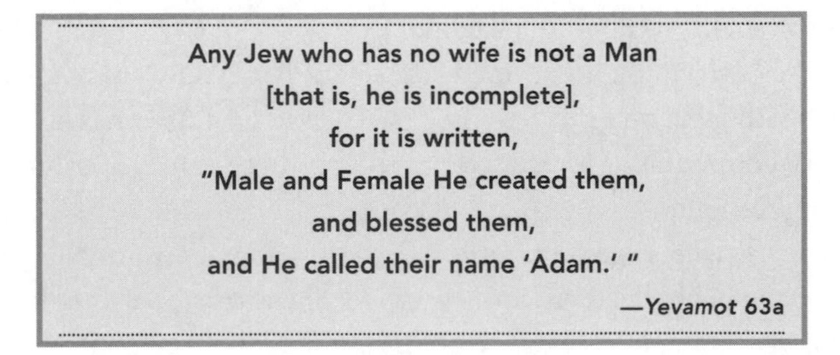

Any Jew who has no wife is not a Man
[that is, he is incomplete],
for it is written,
"Male and Female He created them,
and blessed them,
and He called their name 'Adam.' "

—*Yevamot 63a*

The **Kabbalah,** Judaism's body of mystical works, is comprised of several volumes, including the ***Zohar,*** which contains commentaries on the Bible. The following paraphrased excerpt interprets the previous verse in a mystical light. Man and Woman are, indeed, meant to be partners on earth in God's divine plan.

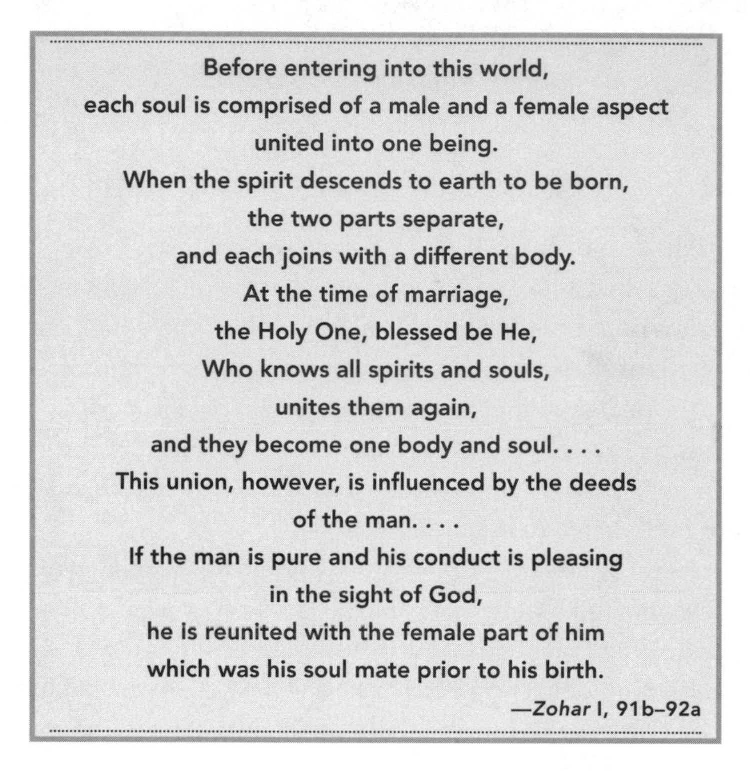

Before entering into this world,
each soul is comprised of a male and a female aspect
united into one being.
When the spirit descends to earth to be born,
the two parts separate,
and each joins with a different body.
At the time of marriage,
the Holy One, blessed be He,
Who knows all spirits and souls,
unites them again,
and they become one body and soul. . . .
This union, however, is influenced by the deeds
of the man. . . .
If the man is pure and his conduct is pleasing
in the sight of God,
he is reunited with the female part of him
which was his soul mate prior to his birth.

—*Zohar* I, 91b–92a

The traditional role of the Jewish wife is eloquently expressed in Proverbs 31:10–31. These twenty-two verses, which begin with *Aishet Chayil,* often translated as "A Woman of Valor," in praise of the Jewish wife, are an affirmation of the important contributions she makes to her home and family.

These verses, which form a Hebrew alphabetical acrostic, are recited by the husband at the Sabbath table on Friday evening (see Section 5.4.2). It has also become customary in many communities for the groom to sing these verses in tribute to his bride at their wedding reception.

She is an ideal wife: dignified, respected, industrious, responsible. She is kind to the poor and gentle in her dealings with everyone. She is trusted by her husband, and is praised by him and her children, who recognize her as the true source of their happiness.

Recite *Aishet Chayil*

A woman of achievement, who can find her?
She is worth far more than pearls.
Her husband trusts in her,
And he never lacks good fortune.
She brings him good and not harm,
All the days of her life. . . .
She rises while it is still night,
And gives food to her household. . . .
She girds herself with strength,
And invigorates her arms for work. . . .
She opens her palm to the poor,
and extends her hand to the needy. . . .
Her husband is distinguished
As he sits with the elders of the land. . . .
Strength and honor are her fashion,
She smiles confidently at the future.
She opens her mouth with wisdom,
And she teaches others to be kind.
She looks after the needs of her home,
She never eats the bread of idleness.
Her children rise and laud her,
And her husband acclaims her, saying:
"Many women are worthy of praise,
But you surpass all of them."
Charm is false and beauty is vain,
Only a God-fearing woman should be praised.
Give her the fruits of her hand,
And let her deeds praise her in the gates.

The Torah protects the rights of the Jewish wife.

> **Her food, her clothing, and her conjugal rights he shall not withhold.**
>
> —*Parshat Mishpatim*, Exodus 21:10

The sexual relationship is a woman's right, even when conception is no longer possible. Furthermore, a woman must be a willing participant in the sexual relationship, never forced to submit against her wishes.

Because the wife will be largely responsible for running the home and raising the children, the Talmud cautions the husband:

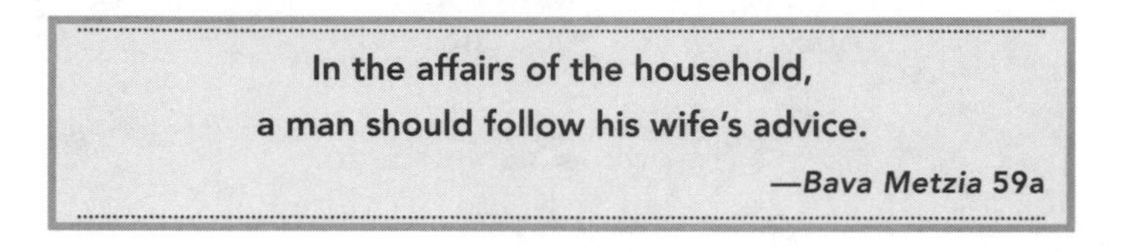

> **In the affairs of the household,**
> **a man should follow his wife's advice.**
>
> **—*Bava Metzia* 59a**

The wife also sets the moral tone of the home. According to a midrashic tale,

> **A pious man was married to a pious woman;**
> **but they were childless and so agreed to divorce. . . .**
> **The pious man married a wicked woman,**
> **and she made him wicked.**
> **The pious woman married a wicked man**
> **and she made him righteous.**
> **We can conclude that all depends on the wife.**
>
> **—*Bereshit Rabbah* 17:12**

According to the sages, a woman is more naturally attuned to spiritual matters. The Maharal of Prague, Rabbi Judah Lowe (1512–1609), explains that a woman's personality is innately more serene, a characteristic necessary for spiritual achievement. While caring for the conduct of the home and the children should not be her exclusive responsibility, on a day-to-day basis, she can either foster or hinder her family's spirituality. To be sure, her own aspirations, style, and unique skills are reflected in the accomplishment of her family's goals; but it is her Jewish identity and commitment to Torah values that will leave a lasting impression and assure the survival of future generations. It is an awesome responsibility and trust.

9.7.5 Keeping Kosher

Just as we are advised to eat a variety of foods to properly nourish the body, the Torah prescribes a nutritional program for the soul. In a Jewish home ***kashrut,*** the Jewish dietary laws, are observed. The word ***kasher,*** which has been adopted in the English vernacular as "kosher," means "ritually fit." The word is most often used to refer to the preparation and eating of food, although that is not its only application. For the moment, we will examine *kashrut* in terms of food and its preparation.

Why must Jews observe the laws of *kashrut* in the first place? Suffice it to say that the laws of *kashrut* impose a discipline upon the Jew. They require a commitment to the observance of these *mitzvot* based largely on faith in the belief that they represent divine precepts given by God to the Jewish people. We do not observe the laws of *kashrut* because it will make us healthier to do so. Rather, we submit ourselves to God's wisdom, willingly accepting His commandments without having to know the specific reasons for them.

The laws of *kashrut* are largely derived from *Parshat Shemini,* Leviticus 11:1–43, where we find a list of what may and may not be eaten. The very next verse, by its very proximity to the food laws, serves as a call to be holy and suggests a reason for the dietary laws.

> **For I am the Lord your God;**
> **therefore, sanctify yourselves, and be holy; for I am holy;**
> **nor shall you defile yourselves. . . .**
>
> **—*Parshat Shemini,* Leviticus 11:44**

Kashrut is not a measure of physical cleanliness, but of spiritual purity. To keep the laws of *kashrut* means to not defile oneself with that which is impure. Spiritual defilement is incompatible with holiness. The concept of *kashrut* applies to all aspects of Jewish life. We must resist the temptations that would defile us, by learning to distinguish between the pure and the impure, whether in terms of food, sexual conduct, or ethics. We are enjoined to:

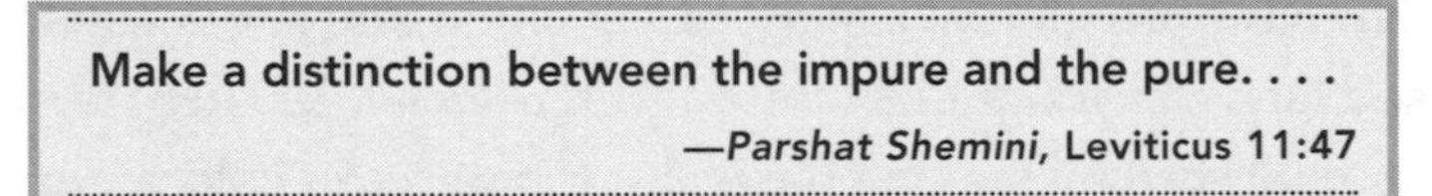

Make a distinction between the impure and the pure. . . .

—*Parshat Shemini,* Leviticus 11:47

Many rabbinic *mitzvot* are also connected with the sanctity of the table. Which foods are permitted? Which foods are prohibited? How must kosher food be cooked? What blessings are recited before and after eating (see Chapter 3)? How are dishes, pots, and other utensils sanctified before use? These questions and so many more cannot be answered fully within the scope of this book. We will touch briefly on these few here, but a qualified rabbi should be consulted on all questions of *kashrut*.

With regard to food, the most fundamental biblical and rabbinic precepts include the following six categories.

1. To be ritually fit, an animal must be a quadruped that *both* chews its cud and has a completely split hoof. If only one of these characteristics is present, the animal is not kosher.
2. To be ritually fit, fish must have *both* scales and fins. If only one of these characteristics is present, the species is not kosher. Shellfish and other seafood are not kosher.
3. Birds of prey and those that eat decaying flesh cannot be ritually fit and are not kosher.
4. Winged and creeping insects and other small creeping creatures cannot be ritually fit and are not kosher.
5. Ritually fit animals or birds that die naturally or are improperly slaughtered by the ***shochet,*** ritual slaughterer, are called ***nevelah*** and are not kosher.
6. A ritually fit animal or bird that is torn to death by other animals or birds is called a ***treifeh.*** This term also applies to those creatures that are inherently ritually unfit—that is, do not have the proper characteristics.

To be ritually fit for use, kosher animals and birds must be slaughtered according to the humane laws of ***shechitah,*** ritual slaughter. A Jew must be specially trained to be a *shochet.* He must be a God-fearing man, well-versed in the *halachot of shechitah,* and observant of the *mitzvot.* The role of *shochet* has always been one of great importance in the Jewish community. Fish require no special slaughtering. Removing kosher fish from the water is considered their *shechitah.*

When a kosher animal or bird is slaughtered, the blood is drained. After *shechitah,* the ***bodek,*** ritual inspector, examines them to determine if any organic diseases or injuries are present. If such conditions are found, then even that animal or bird is considered ***treif,*** ritually unfit.

In addition to the prohibition against eating blood, the Jew is also forbidden to eat certain veins and fats, which must be removed after *shechitah.* Then, further removal of the blood is accomplished by soaking the meat or poultry in cold water, salting it with kosher salt, and rinsing it according to the requirements of the *halachah.* Eggs must be inspected for blood spots before use.

One further precept of *kashrut* is fundamental to proper observance. Based upon biblical verses, the Jew is prohibited from eating meat products and milk products together, in any form.

> **You shall not seethe a kid in its mother's milk.**
>
> —*Parshat Mishpatim*, Exodus 23:19
>
> —*Parshat Ki Tissa*, Exodus 34:26
>
> —*Parshat Re'ei*, Deuteronomy 14:21

Why does this prohibition occur three times? (1) to forbid cooking of meat and milk together; (2) to forbid eating of meat and milk together; and (3) to forbid deriving any benefit or enjoyment from such a mixture—for example, savoring the aroma or feeding a pet.

Meat and milk may not be cooked together in the same pot or served together on the same plate. Therefore, the kosher home requires separate pots, dishes, and other utensils associated with the preparation of food, for dairy and for meat. Dairy and meat utensils should be of different patterns or styles, so that they are not inadvertently confused. Tablecloths, dish towels, dish racks, sink inserts, sponges, dish brushes, soap pads, and the like, must also be kept separate for meat and dairy.

New dishes, pots, flatware, and other glass and metal utensils used in the preparation and serving of food should be immersed in a special ***mikveh kelim***, utensil *mikveh*, if they were manufactured by non-Jews. This separate *mikveh* is usually in a room on the premises of the *mikveh* used by women for ritual immersion. Anyone can bring new items to the *mikveh kelim* and immerse them, usually by lowering them in an open basket so that the water touches them completely.

The following blessing is recited at the time of immersion.

Recite the Blessing before Immersing Utensils

Baruch Atah, HaShem E-lo-kenu, Melech HaOlam,
asher kidshanu b'mitzvotav v'tzivanu
al tevilat kelim.

❖

Blessed are You, Lord our God, King of the Universe,
Who has sanctified us with His commandments and commanded us
concerning the immersion of utensils.

It is customary to pay a fee to the *mikveh*. Additionally, in Jewish neighborhoods, especially where many of the customers are observant, houseware stores will have a *mikveh* on the premises. Customers may immerse their own utensils, or the store may offer the service to those who shop there at no additional cost.

In addition to the prohibition of eating meat and dairy products *together,* a period of separation is required *between* eating meat and dairy. After eating meat or poultry, Jews wait from three to six hours before eating any dairy, depending on custom. After eating dairy, it is *usually* sufficient to brush your teeth and rinse your mouth thoroughly before eating meat. Exception: Certain hard cheeses require a six-hour waiting period before meat can be eaten.

Foods that contain neither dairy nor meat ingredients are called ***pareve,*** neutral, and may be served with either meat or dairy meals. These include all raw fruits and vegetables, spices, sugar, salt, coffee, tea, nuts, and other products that are prepared without meat or milk products. Kosher fish and eggs are also *pareve,* but may lose their neutral designation if they are cooked with meat or dairy products. A qualified rabbi should be consulted, if necessary.

The laws of *kashrut* apply to all foods. For example: baked goods must not contain animal fat from a nonkosher animal, such as lard. All foods, to be considered kosher, ritually fit for the Jewish consumer, be they baked goods, cheeses, salad dressings, candies, potato chips, ice cream, margarine, processed foods, cereals, sauces, flavorings, spices, dried fruits, wines, condiments, and dozens of others, must be prepared under the supervision of ***mashgichim,*** men and women trained in the laws of *kashrut* who are responsible to the Jewish community for the supervision of food production. *Mashgichim* are supervised by rabbinic authorities, and need not be rabbis themselves. Dish detergents, soap pads, aluminum foil, plastic food bags and wrap, and other food-related products are also subject to ***hashgachah,*** supervision.

Many corporations, hotels, airlines, hospitals, and other vendors, who want to accommodate the religious needs of the kosher community, pay fees for *hashgachah,* to regulatory organizations established by the Jewish community to oversee the production and distribution of kosher products. These organizations, in turn, pay the ***mashgiach*** who does the actual supervision. All organizations imprint a distinctive symbol on the packages of products under their supervision. If a question arises about the trustworthiness of the service, a reliable rabbi should be consulted.

Kosher butchers must also be supervised by a reputable *mashgiach* or *hashgachah* service. The butcher must be skilled in the *halachot* regarding the internal fat, the arteries, tendons, and sciatic nerve, which must be removed before the animal can be prepared as kosher food.

Many communities have established a ***Va'ad HaKashrut,*** a *Kashrut* Council, whose responsibility it is to supervise the *mashgichim* and make them available to the kosher vendors in its jurisdiction. They oversee kosher supervision in local businesses, such as bakeries, pizza stores, ice cream and yogurt shops, candy and dried fruit vendors, take-out foods—both meat and dairy—and restaurants. Most often, this committee is comprised of local rabbis and laymen who are knowledgeable about the laws of *kashrut* and committed to the proper observance of these *mitzvot.*

Contrary to a popular misperception, kosher does not mean "blessed by" or "prayed over by" a rabbi. It is also erroneous to think of kosher in terms of cleanliness, *per se. Kashrut* transcends the concept of hygiene because it demands a spiritual cleanliness derived from adherence to the discipline the observance of *kashrut* demands. The term "kosher-style" is a meaningless expression—a product is or isn't kosher. It also tends to lend credibility to merchants doing business in the Jewish community by attaching a quasi-religious label to their wares, when in fact, no kosher status exists.

In addition, so-called "Jewish foods" are not inherently kosher. Things like wine, *challah, cholent, gefilte* fish, potato *kugel, blintzes, hamantashen,* honey cake, potato *latkes,* and other culinary delights are not kosher just because they are associated with Jewish traditions. They all must be prepared from kosher ingredients according to the laws of *kashrut.* A chicken is a ritually fit bird, but it cannot be eaten unless it has been slaughtered by a *shochet,* deveined, soaked, salted, and rinsed according to *halachah,* and cooked and served in kosher pots and dishes.

It is not difficult in today's world to maintain a kosher home. Literally thousands of ready-to-use kosher products are available in most cities of the world; but it is not sufficient for the Jew to maintain a kosher lifestyle at home and also to partake of the nonkosher world, which is so readily available. The double standard of kosher at home and *treif* outside the home is inappropriate and totally antithetical to the teachings of the Torah. The laws of *kashrut* provide an atmosphere of holiness, and to be a Jew requires the kind of discipline that *kashrut* implies. To do less is to observe less than God requires.

Kashrut must be part of an integrated lifestyle that includes the observance of the fundamental practices of Judaism: belief in the One God; sanctity of the Sabbath and festivals; commitment to holiness in the marital partnership; and ethical and moral conduct in all relationships.

Standards are established within every home in every sphere of activity: personal, professional, educational, social, and spiritual. It is the responsibility of the Jewish couple to study and observe the Torah's guidelines in order to set the standards for religious observance for the next generation. There is no greater responsibility than this.

Setting the feet of our children on the pathways of Torah is the best chance we have for preserving the Jewish people and contributing to the nurturing of society as a whole.

> **Train a child according to his way;**
> **even when he grows old,**
> **he will not turn away from it.**
> **—Proverbs 22:6**

9.8 The Birth of a Child

The First Commandment in the Torah is:

> **Be fruitful and multiply, and fill the earth, and subdue it.**
> **—*Parshat Bereshit,* Genesis 1:28**

For the Jew, the observance of this *mitzvah* is more than an obligation to populate the world. Rather, it is part of God's plan to assure that there will be Jews to fulfill the *mitzvot* of the Torah.

There are many biblical accounts of the significance of the birth of a child. Sarah, the wife of Abraham, laughed when she was told by an angel that she would bear a child, for she was ninety years old (*Parshat Vayera,* Genesis 18:10–12). She was told that God can do anything. When her son was born, Abraham named him Yitzchak, Isaac, which means *laughter.* Then Sarah said:

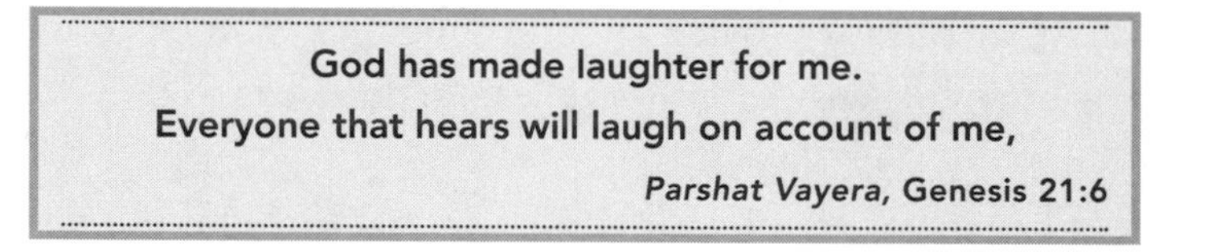
> **God has made laughter for me.**
> **Everyone that hears will laugh on account of me,**
> ***Parshat Vayera,* Genesis 21:6**

According to Rashi's interpretation, everyone who heard of the birth rejoiced with Sarah, for God had blessed her.

In the biblical account of Rachel, we find that her envy of her prolific sister, Leah, caused her untold pain. So great was her desire to have a child that she cried to her husband, Jacob, in grief and shame:

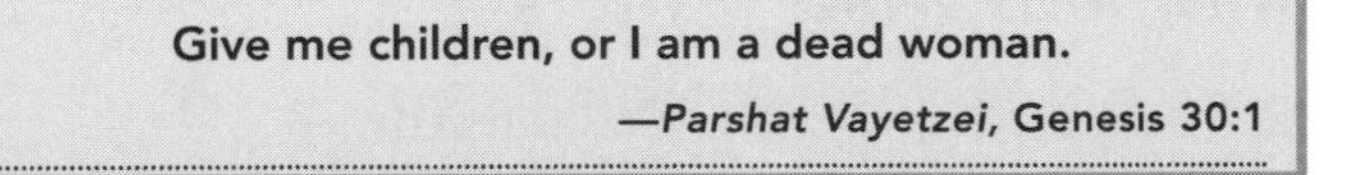
Give me children, or I am a dead woman.

—*Parshat Vayetzei,* **Genesis 30:1**

When her son, Joseph, was conceived and born, she said that God had taken away her rebuke, for she would no longer be childless (*Parshat Vayetzei,* Genesis 30:23).

On *Rosh HaShanah,* the *Haftarah* is from I Samuel 1:1–2:10, which relates the poignant story of the despairing Hannah, who wept and could not eat for she was childless. She went to pray, and Eli, the *Kohen Gadol,* spoke to her, saying that the God of Israel would grant her what she had asked of Him.

God answered her prayers, and when her son was born, she named him Shmuel, Samuel, meaning, *I asked the Lord for him.* When Samuel was weaned, she took him to the Temple. In gratitude for her child, she gave him over to Eli, for a life devoted to serving God.

> **I am the woman who stood here praying to the Lord.**
> **I prayed for this boy,**
> **and the Lord has granted me what I asked.**
> **So I lend him to the Lord;**
> **for all his days, he is loaned to the Lord.**
>
> **—I Samuel 1:26–28**

He grew up to be Samuel the Prophet.

Hannah's prayer, read on *Rosh HaShanah,* speaks of God's justice, and reminds the Jewish people that a child must be raised to a life of righteousness.

From the moment of birth, a Jewish child is welcomed into the family of Israel with rituals and celebrations. According to the Talmud, *Masechet Gittin* 57a, it was a custom in Betar, a city in ancient Israel, to plant a cedar tree when a boy was born and a pine tree when a girl was born. When they grew up and were to be married, the trees were cut down and used to build the *chupah.*

As we learn from the accounts of Sarah, Rachel, and Hannah, God is the third partner in the creation of a child. The parents certainly provide the physical attributes that constitute the body, but God provides the soul, the divine spark that gives the child life. Only in combination with Him can a Jewish couple bring forth a child.

9.9 Naming a Jewish Child

From the time a baby is named, the wish is uttered:

May the parents merit to raise their child
to Torah, chupah, and good deeds.

The significance of naming of a Jewish child is rooted in the Torah. As we know, the early chapters of Exodus deal with the enslavement of the Israelites by the Egyptians. It has been asked:

How did the Children of Israel
manage to maintain their identity and their standard of holiness
during the years of exile and slavery
in the face of the pervasive Egyptian influences that surrounded them?

In the midrashic literature, *Vayikra Rabbah* 32:5, the sages reply that the Israelites distinguished themselves from the Egyptians by:

- not changing their names
- not changing their language
- not gossiping among themselves
- not acting promiscuously

When a Jewish child is born, it is a time of great joy. It fulfills the desire for continuity, not only in the sense of carrying on the family name, but also in perpetuating the Hebrew or Yiddish names of ancestors. There are many customs associated with the naming of a Jewish child.

Biblical names have always been popular choices, but the most common tradition is to name a child after a departed relative. A name which recalls ancestors, especially those respected for the righteous conduct of their lives, is often selected. Ashkenazic Jews do not customarily name their children after living members of the family, although this is the tradition among Sephardic Jews. In some families, the mother of the child chooses the name for her first-born, and the father's choice is honored for the second-born child.

When a girl is born, it is the father's religious obligation to go to the synagogue on a Monday, a Thursday, or on the Sabbath, when the Torah is read—as soon after the birth as possible—to name her. Some Jews wait until the baby is at least three days old before giving her a name.

The father is honored with an *aliyah*. When his portion has been read, a special prayer, called a *Mi She'Berach,* meaning *He Who Blessed,* referring to God, is offered by the *ba'al korei* on behalf of the mother and the infant, and the child is named.

Recite on Naming a Daughter

May He Who blessed our forefathers,
Abraham, Isaac, and Jacob,
bless the woman who has given birth,
(mother's Hebrew name),
daughter of (mother's father's Hebrew name),
with her daughter
who has been born at an auspicious time;
and may her name be called in Israel
(baby's Hebrew name), the daughter of (father's Hebrew name).
May they merit to raise her
to Torah, the marriage canopy, and good deeds.

A toast of ***l'chayim,*** to life, often follows the services. It is also customary for the parents to invite family and friends for *Kiddush* in their home or in the synagogue on the Sabbath after the birth. Additional celebrations of the birth of a daughter are certainly appropriate, for it is always permissible to thank God for the good He brings into our lives. However, these celebrations should not mirror the trappings of ritual associated with the birth of a son.

When a boy is born, different customs are observed. On the Friday night immediately following the baby's birth, family and friends gather after the Sabbath meal to rejoice and celebrate. This gathering, called ***Shalom Zachor,*** is considered a *se'udat mitzvah* and is usually held at the home of the child. The *Shalom Zachor* honors the newborn boy and serves as a means of expressing gratitude to God for his safe birth. The *Shema* is recited if the child is present.

According to the Talmud, *Masechet Sanhedrin* 32b, in the time of the Roman Empire, when Jews were forbidden to circumcise their sons, a feast was held shortly after the child's birth, but before his circumcision, in an attempt to convince the Romans that no circumcision was to follow on the eighth day. In some communities, numerous candles were lit as well, to indicate where a celebration was being held. Lighting candles at the circumcision continues to be a popular custom.

Today, the tradition of *Shalom Zachor* continues. Good wishes for the recovery of the mother and the well-being of the child are offered by all, and light refreshments are served. The baby will not be named until the eighth day after birth, when he is entered into the Covenant of Abraham, the rite of circumcision, ***Brit Milah.***

In many families, the Jewish child is given a secular name as well. Often, parents try to choose a name that begins with the same sound as the Hebrew name, although there is no reason to do this. Not every Hebrew name has a specific English equivalent, but all Jewish children should have, know, and use their Hebrew names.

9.10 The Covenant of Circumcision

Circumcision is a religious obligation which must be performed on the eighth day after birth. It is the obligation of the father to circumcise his son, or to appoint a qualified ***mohel,*** ritual circumcisor, to perform the circumcision on his behalf. This rite is called *Brit Milah,* the Covenant of Circumcision, and is derived from God's commandment to Abram.

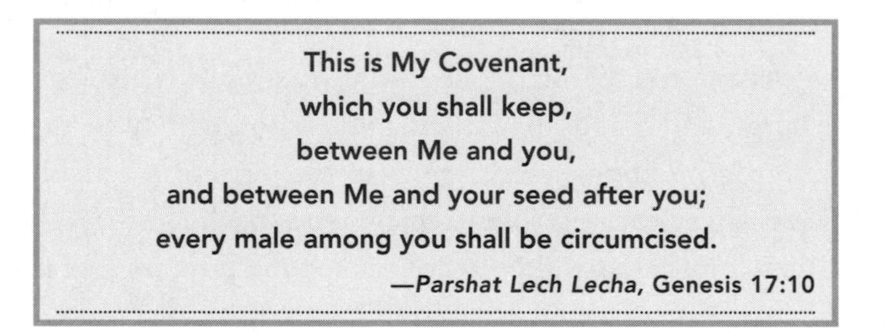
This is My Covenant,
which you shall keep,
between Me and you,
and between Me and your seed after you;
every male among you shall be circumcised.
—*Parshat Lech Lecha,* Genesis 17:10

Abram circumcised himself at the age of ninety-nine, and God changed his name to Abraham, father of multitudes.

The *Brit Milah* (often referred to simply as the ***brit*** or ***bris***) may be performed on any day—even on the Sabbath or *Yom Kippur*—if that is the eighth day after birth. Circumcision may be postponed if a doctor advises against it because of the fragile health of the child. Once the circumcision is postponed, however, it may not be held on the Sabbath or major festival day.

Brit Milah is always held in the daytime, preferably in the morning and in the presence of a *minyan,* if possible. It is customary to inform family and friends that the *Brit Milah* will take place at a specified time and place. Rabbi Moses Isserles (1530–1572), known as the Rema, explains in his commentary to the *Shulchan Aruch, Yoreh De'ah* 265:12, that a person who declines an invitation to participate in a *se'udat mitzvah* is subject to divine disfavor. Therefore, no formal invitations are extended.

9.10.1 The *Mohel*

Circumcision is a surgical procedure in which the foreskin is removed. If the child is born without a foreskin, or was circumcised prior to the eighth day, a symbolic drop of blood must be taken from the area where the circumcision would have been. *Ritual circumcision (or the symbolic alternative) may not be performed by a surgeon.* Only a qualified *mohel,* a man both learned in the *halachot* of circumcision and skilled in the surgical aspects of the rite, may circumcise the child. A *mohel* does not have to be an ordained rabbi, although often rabbis are also ***mohalim.***

The *mohel* undertakes very specialized training before he is qualified. He is a highly respected member of the Jewish community, but not every community has a *mohel.* Often, parents must arrange to bring a *mohel* from another city in order to fulfill the *mitzvah* of *Brit Milah.* The *mohel's* fee varies from community to community.

9.10.2 The *Sandek* and the *Kvater*

In addition to the baby, the *mohel,* and the child's father, who are the main participants in the ceremony, a grandfather or other close male friend or relative is honored as the ***sandek.*** It is the privilege of the *sandek* to hold the child during the circumcision.

The ***kvater*** brings the infant from his mother to the *sandek.* If a married or engaged couple has been chosen for this honor, the woman brings the child into the room, and the man takes the child from her and brings him to the *sandek.*

Someone is also designated to recite the blessings after the circumcision.

9.10.3 Elijah the Prophet

The invisible participant at every *Brit Milah* is Elijah the Prophet who is referred to by the prophet Malachi (3:1) as the *Angel of the Covenant.* A special chair, sometimes called the Chair of Elijah, is set aside for the prophet. In many communities, the chair was designed in two sections; one side was reserved for Elijah, who protects the child, and the *sandek* sat on the other side and held the baby for the *mohel*. The father of the baby or the *mohel* may designate any chair by saying:

> **This is the Chair of Elijah,**
> **the Angel of the Covenant, who is remembered for good.**

It is customary to leave the Chair of Elijah in position for three days after the circumcision, a period of time considered critical for the child's recovery.

9.10.4 Blessed Is He Who Arrives

When the baby is brought in, all those present stand (and remain standing throughout the circumcision) and greet his arrival with the words:

> *Baruch HaBa!*
> **Blessed is he who arrives!**

After the *sandek* is seated, the father places the child on the Chair of Elijah. An honored guest picks up the infant and holds him for a moment. The baby is then placed on the lap of the *sandek*, and the ceremony of circumcision proceeds. (The full Hebrew text and translation for the ritual of *Brit Milah* is available in most prayer books.)

The father announces:

> **Behold I am prepared and ready to perform**
> **the positive commandment**
> **that the Creator, blessed is He,**
> **has commanded me—**
> **to circumcise my son.**

The father appoints the *mohel* as his agent. The *mohel* recites:

> **Blessed are You, Lord our God, King of the Universe,**
> **Who has sanctified us with His commandments and commanded us**
> **concerning circumcision.**

As the circumcision is performed, the father responds:

Blessed are You, Lord our God, King of the Universe,
Who has sanctified us with His commandments and commanded us
to bring him into the Covenant of Abraham, our forefather.

When the circumcision is completed, all those present say:

Just as he has entered into the Covenant,
so may he enter
to Torah, the marriage canopy, and good deeds.

A cup of wine is poured and the designated honoree recites the blessing over it and drinks from it (other customs: the wine is given to the mother or the *sandek*). Additional prayers of praise and petition are then offered, and the name of the child is revealed. A little wine is then put in the mouth of the infant. Just as Abram became Abraham after his circumcision, so, too, is every Jewish boy named at his *Brit Milah*. The following prayer is recited after the name is announced:

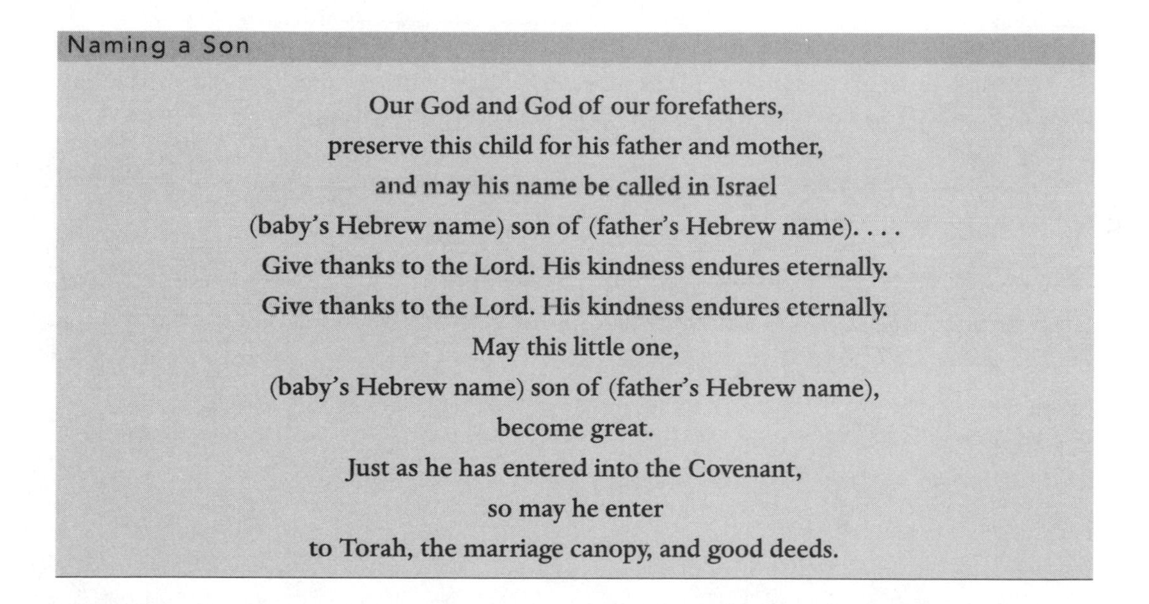

Naming a Son

Our God and God of our forefathers,
preserve this child for his father and mother,
and may his name be called in Israel
(baby's Hebrew name) son of (father's Hebrew name). . . .
Give thanks to the Lord. His kindness endures eternally.
Give thanks to the Lord. His kindness endures eternally.
May this little one,
(baby's Hebrew name) son of (father's Hebrew name),
become great.
Just as he has entered into the Covenant,
so may he enter
to Torah, the marriage canopy, and good deeds.

The *mohel* blesses the child, praying for his complete recovery, and the father recites a special *tefillah,* seeking God's blessing for his son. A *se'udat mitzvah* is then enjoyed by all. Special poems are recited, and during the Grace after Meals, additional prayers are read by honored friends and relatives, invoking God's blessing on the *sandek,* the *mohel,* the parents, and their son.

> **May the Merciful One**
> **bless the father and mother of the child,**
> **and may they merit to raise him,**
> **to educate him, and to make him wise . . .**
> **and may the Lord his God be with him.**

The *mohel* stays in touch with the family for a few days, should any problems arise before the circumcision has healed. For the baby, the rite of circumcision causes minimal pain. For the parents, it is a time-hallowed tradition.

Throughout Jewish history countless Jews have given their lives because they were forbidden to perform the *Brit Milah.* The rite of circumcision is the eternal sign of the Covenant between the Jew and God. It will be a sign between them forever.

9.11 The Redemption of the First-Born Son

For a first-born son, another rite of passage, the ***Pidyon HaBen,*** the Redemption of the First-Born Son, will take place when the baby is thirty-one days old. It is a hallowed tradition based on biblical commands. In the Torah, we find:

[The Lord said]
Sanctify unto Me all the first-born,
[that is] those that open the womb,
among the Children of Israel;
both of man and beast—it is Mine. . . .
[When a son will ask his father about sacrifices,
the father shall say]
And it came to pass,
when Pharaoh would not let us go,
that the Lord slew all the first-born in Egypt,
the first-born of man and of beast;
therefore I sacrifice to the Lord
all those [male animals] that open the womb;
but the first-born of my sons, I redeem.

—*Parshat Bo,* Exodus 13:1, 2, 14, 15

God also said to Moses:

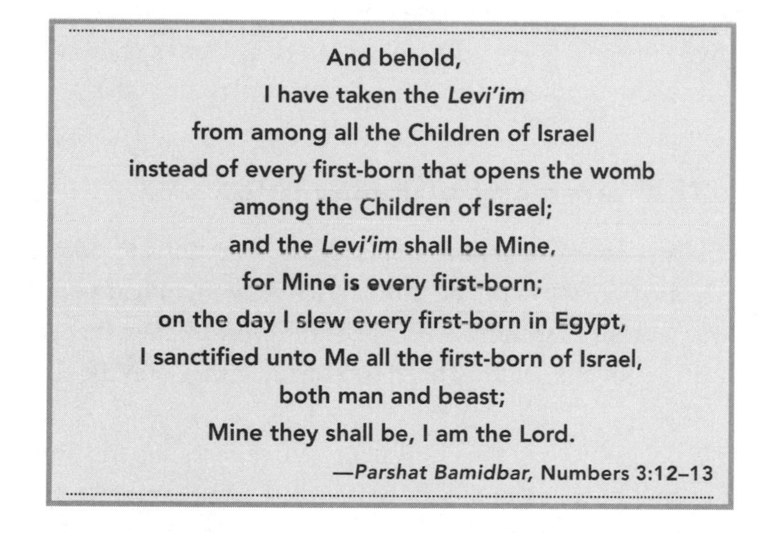

And behold,
I have taken the *Levi'im*
from among all the Children of Israel
instead of every first-born that opens the womb
among the Children of Israel;
and the *Levi'im* shall be Mine,
for Mine is every first-born;
on the day I slew every first-born in Egypt,
I sanctified unto Me all the first-born of Israel,
both man and beast;
Mine they shall be, I am the Lord.

—*Parshat Bamidbar,* Numbers 3:12–13

According to the *Midrash, Bamidbar Rabbah* 4:6, originally the rituals of sacrifice were performed by all first-born males, who were to serve as the Priests. They were brought to the High Priest to be trained in the service of the Lord (see Section 9.8). After the sin of the golden calf, they were stripped of this honor, and the tribe of Levi—

which includes the descendants of Aaron, who became the *Kohanim*—was appointed to assist the *Kohanim* in the sacrificial service, because they did not participate in the sin.

Thus, the *Levi'im,* the descendants of the tribe of Levi, assumed this function on behalf of all the tribes of Israel. In return for this, every first-born son of Israel was required to pay a *Kohen* the sum of five *shekalim,* an amount equivalent to the value of his service to the Priest. By this payment all first-borns were redeemed from service and their sanctity was transferred to the *Levi'im* who replaced them in the Temple.

> **And those that are to be redeemed—**
> **from a month old, you shall redeem them—**
> **according to your valuation, five *shekalim* of silver,**
> **after the *shekel* of the Sanctuary. . . .**
> **—*Parshat Korach,* Numbers 18:16**

Today, when a first-born son reaches the age of thirty-one days, he must be redeemed in the same way. By giving the redemption money (or goods equivalent to that amount) to the *Kohen,* the father is considered to have dedicated his son completely to the Lord's service. Payment is made in silver of local currency in an amount equivalent to the value of five *shekalim.* There is no obligation to redeem a child whose father is a *Kohen* or a *Levi,* or whose mother is the daughter of a *Kohen* or a *Levi.*

9.11.1 The Ceremony of Redemption

A *Kohen* officiates at the ceremony. He may ask questions to determine that the child is, in fact, the first-born son of the mother. If the woman had a son from a previous marriage, who was her first-born (who opens the womb), then that son would have been redeemed. If the child is the first-born son of the father only, he does not have to be redeemed.

The father is obliged to pay the equivalent of five *shekalim,* in silver coins, to the *Kohen.* Payment cannot be made in bills or by check. The *Kohen* may return the money to the father or give it to charity, but payment is never made with the stipulation that he must return it or give it to charity.

The child is dressed in special clothes for the occasion. The father presents his son to the *Kohen,* as he places the money before him. He states:

Begin the Ceremony of *Pidyon HaBen*

This is my first-born son,
the first-born of his mother's womb,
and the [child] the Holy One, blessed be He,
has commanded [me] to redeem.

The *Kohen* asks:

Which do your prefer:
your son or the five *shekalim*
you must give me in order to redeem him?

The father answers:

I want my first-born son,
and here is the money for redeeming him,
as I am obligated to give you.

As he holds the money, the father recites two blessings:

Blessed are You, Lord our God, King of the Universe,
Who has sanctified us with His commandments and commanded us
concerning the redemption of the first-born son.

❖

Blessed are You, Lord our God, King of the Universe,
Who has kept us alive, sustained us,
and brought us to this season.

The father gives the *Kohen* the money, and the *Kohen* takes a cup of wine, recites the blessing over it, and drinks it. Holding the money over the child's head, he exchanges the child for the silver, saying:

This is instead of that; this is exchange for that; . . .
May the child live and learn Torah,
and may the fear of heaven be upon him.
May it be Your will
that even as he has been redeemed,
may he enter to Torah, the marriage canopy, and good deeds.

He then places his hand on the child's head and blesses him that he may grow to be like Ephraim and Menasheh, the sons of Joseph. He continues with the Priestly Blessing (see Section 7.8.2), the *Birkat Kohanim:*

May the Lord bless you and safeguard you.
May the Lord illuminate His Countenance for you
and be gracious to you.
May the Lord turn His Countenance toward you,
and grant you peace.

The *Kohen* concludes the ceremony:

The Lord is your Guardian;
the Lord is the shadow on your right hand.
For length of days, and years of life and peace
shall they add to you.
The Lord will guard you from all evil;
He will guard your soul.

A *se'udat mitzvah* is served following the ceremony.

9.11.2 Special Circumstances

A child born after a miscarriage does not require redemption, if the miscarriage occurred after the third month of pregnancy. A baby delivered by cesarean section is not redeemed either. In all cases of doubt, a qualified rabbi should be consulted.

If the thirty-first day is a Sabbath or major holiday, the *Pidyon HaBen* is postponed until the day after the Sabbath or holiday. The *Pidyon HaBen* cannot simply be scheduled for a day when it would be convenient for people to attend.

The full Hebrew text and translation for the ritual of *Pidyon HaBen* is available in most prayer books.

9.12 Adoption

Adopting the children of biological parents who are unable or unwilling to care for them is a laudable act. In the Talmud, this deed of charity (in particular, raising an orphaned child) was praised by the sages.

> **One who raises another's child**
> **is considered to have given birth to that child.**
>
> —*Megillah* 13a
>
> —*Sanhedrin* 19b

The customary obligations and responsibilities of parents to natural children apply equally to adopted children. However, certain religious issues must be considered in the adoption process.

Is the child Jewish?

- If the adopted child's mother was Jewish, but the father was not, the child is Jewish.
- If the adopted child's father was Jewish, but the mother was not, the child is not Jewish, and requires conversion by a *Bet Din.*

Religious status of the adopted child is determined only according to the biological mother's religious identity.

If the child is Jewish . . .

- If the adopted child is a Jewish boy, and his father is a *Kohen* or *Levi,* the boy retains the religious designation of his natural father, regardless of the adoptive father's designation.
- If the adopted child is a Jewish boy, he requires ritual circumcision. If he was circumcised, but not by a *mohel,* the symbolic drawing of blood must be performed.
- If the adopted child is a Jewish boy, and he was the first-born of his mother, he requires a *Pidyon HaBen.*
- If the adopted child is a Jewish boy and the first-born of his mother, but she was the daughter of a *Kohen* or *Levi,* he does not require a *Pidyon HaBen.*

- Adopted children may be given Hebrew names as the son or daughter of the adoptive father. A girl should be named in the synagogue and a boy at the time of circumcision according to tradition.

If the child is not Jewish . . .

- An adopted boy requires circumcision (or the symbolic alternative) with the intention of conversion and immersion in a *mikveh.* Circumcision should be performed as soon as possible, immersion, when the child is mature enough to be immersed safely. The *Bet Din* recites the appropriate blessings on immersion on behalf of the child.
- An adopted girl requires immersion in a *mikveh,* as soon as she is mature enough to be immersed safely. The *Bet Din* recites the appropriate blessings on immersion on behalf of the child.
- All the laws of conversion that apply to an adult apply equally to a child, except that the child may be circumcised/immersed before undertaking the study of Torah. The adoptive parents, however, are obligated to train and educate the child to love God, observe the *mitzvot,* and perform deeds of charity and lovingkindness.

A special concern . . .

- Does the adopted child have any siblings who were also adopted? If so, are their whereabouts known? This would be a serious problem if the siblings grew up, met, and planned to marry, without knowing each other's identity.

Appropriate documents are drawn by the *Bet Din* or by the rabbi who arranged for the *Bet Din* to attest to the child's conversion according to *halachah.* A child is required to personally accept the *ol malchut shamayim* when he or she is old enough to understand the significance of the conversion and Jewish identity.

Civil court documents attesting to the legal adoption of a non-Jewish child by a Jewish couple do not convey any religious status on the child. Giving a Hebrew or Yiddish name in the synagogue does not automatically make the child a Jew. Circumcision/immersion are required.

Children owe the same love, respect, and devotion to their adoptive parents as they would to their natural ones, during their lives and after their deaths.

9.13 Raising a Jewish Child

The obligations incumbent on parents are awesome responsibilities. In addition to caring for a child's physical needs, they must provide emotional support, moral guidelines, and educational opportunities to prepare their child to live in the world. Both parents are entrusted with these duties.

> **Listen, my child,**
> **to the ethical instruction of your father,**
> **and do not forsake the teachings of your mother.**
> **—Proverbs 1:8**

9.13.1 Educating the Jewish Child

The education of the Jewish child is the obligation of both parents, but in most homes, it is the mother who is the first teacher. When the Torah was given at Mount Sinai (see Section 7.13), it was given first to the women of Israel, because they would transmit it to their children. In *Parshat Yitro,* Exodus 19:3, we find:

You shall say to the House of Jacob and tell the Children of Israel . . .

From Rashi, we learn that "House of Jacob" refers to the women and "Children of Israel" to the men. Thus, the Torah was given to both women and men—*but to the women first.*

According to the *Midrash,* when God was about to reveal the Torah, He asked the Jewish people to bring guarantors who would pledge that the Torah would be observed. Israel replied that the patriarchs would be their guarantors, but this was not acceptable to God.

> **Then the Jewish people declared,**
> **"Our children will be our guarantors."**
> **[and God replied]**
> **"For their sake, I will give you the Torah."**
> ***—Midrash Aseret HaDibrot***

According to the Talmud, *Masechet Niddah* 30b, every Jewish soul is taught the entire Torah in the womb. At the moment of birth, an angel taps the child on the lip, and all Torah knowledge is forgotten. However, the child remains disposed to reacquiring that knowledge throughout life.

Jews are required to study Torah all the days of their lives. It is the obligation of the father, specifically, and of the mother, as well, to begin teaching their child Torah as soon as the child can speak, because the study of Torah will lead the child to the observance of the *mitzvot*. Teaching the first verse of *Kriat Shema* or the *berachot* for various foods is a beginning of doing *mitzvot*. Songs and rhymes with Jewish themes prepare very young children to participate in Sabbath and festival observances at home. For older children, going to the synagogue with their parents sets an example and teaches them that being part of the Jewish community is as important as praying.

As soon as children are old enough, the parents must provide teachers for them.

9.13.2 Teaching and Learning Torah

Scholarship has long been a hallmark of Jewish tradition. Hillel, the first of the *Tana'im*, reminds us in the Mishnah that:

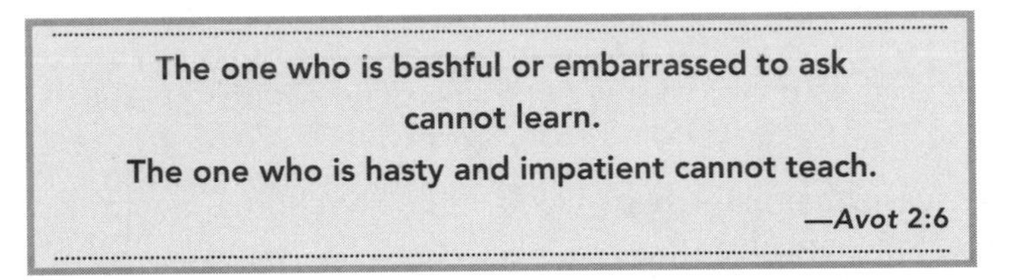
The one who is bashful or embarrassed to ask cannot learn.
The one who is hasty and impatient cannot teach.
—Avot 2:6

The role of the teacher has always been one of the most important in the Jewish community, and cities and towns were often renowned for the scholars who lived there.

In the bygone days of the ***cheder,*** the one-room school, parents brought their children to the ***melamed,*** the teacher, who encouraged even the youngest child to learn by putting a drop of honey on the pages of the *alef-bet*. The child was enticed to learn and to associate the acquisition of Torah knowledge with sweetness (Psalms 19:10–11).

In front of the fireplace that warmed the *cheder* room, the child asked and the *melamed* patiently taught, and, thus, the cycle continued: from generation to generation, learning and the sweetness of acquiring knowledge were indelibly connected in the child's mind.

With every drop of honey, a new generation was inspired to learn Torah.

The old Yiddish folk song *Oif'n Pripetchok* recalls the devoted, if often beleaguered, *melamed* huddled in front of the fireside with his young students. As they repeat again and again the names of the vowels and letters of the *alef-bet,* he reminds them that someday they will be older and understand how many tears are hidden deep inside every letter. The English translation of this haunting Yiddish classic barely does it justice.

Oif'n Pripetchok

Oif'n pripetchok brent a fierel,
un in shtub iz heis,
Un der rebbe lerent kleineh kinderlach,
dem alef-beis,
Un der rebbe lerent kleineh kinderlach,
dem alef-beis.
Zetje kinderlach, gedenktjeh ti'ereh,
Vos ir lerent daw,
Zogtjeh noch a mol un takeh noch amol,
Kometz, alef, aw,
Zogtjeh noch a mol un takeh noch amol,
Kometz, alef, aw.
Lerent kinder mit grois cheishek,
Azoy zog ich eich awn,
Ver es vet fun aich kenen ivreh,
Der bekumt a fon,
Ver es vet fun aich kenen ivreh,
Der bekumt a fon.
Ir vet kinder elter veren,
Vet ir alein farshtein,
Vi fil in di osiyos ligen treren,
Un vi fil gevein,
Vi fil in di osiyos ligen treren,
Un vi fil gevein.

—Old Yiddish Folk Song

By the Fireside

By the fireside, a small fire is burning,
and in the house, it is very warm;
and the rabbi teaches little children
the *alef-bet;*
and the rabbi teaches little children
the *alef-bet.*
Look, children, and remember well
what you learn here;
say it once more and yet another time,
kometz, alef, aw;
say it once more and yet another time,
kometz, alef, aw.
Learn, children, with great enthusiasm,
this is what I say to you;
whoever among you learns to read Hebrew
will receive a flag;
whoever among you learns to read Hebrew
will receive a flag.
You will grow older, children,
and you will understand yourselves,
how many tears lie in the letters
and how much weeping;
how many tears lie in the letters
and how much weeping.

Historically, both the rabbi and *chazan* were teachers. In many communities today, they continue to serve as teachers of Torah. Rabbinical seminaries and cantorial schools prepare the spiritual leaders of tomorrow, and several educational institutions in the United States and Israel continue to train men and women to be teachers of Torah.

Teachers should be learned in Torah and demonstrate high standards of conduct. Good character, appropriate dress, and a dignified and respectful manner are all desirable qualities for the men and women who will serve as role models for their students. Ideally, teachers should treat their students as if they were their own children.

They should be courteous and friendly to their students, and students must honor their teachers as they would honor their parents. The Rambam states that the reverence one must show a teacher is even greater than that due one's parents. Parents have given their children life and sustain them in this world. Teachers prepare them for the World to Come.

Today, Jewish education remains a priority in all segments of the Jewish community. Its purpose remains the same: (1) teaching the classical texts of Judaism, including the Bible, Mishnah, and Talmud, and making them relevant to the modern world; (2) instilling the moral values that are an integral part of Jewish tradition; (3) encouraging active participation in the daily rituals and observances that animate Jewish life; (4) fostering strong emotional and enduring ties with the Jewish people as a religious, cultural, and national entity on the world scene; and (5) imbuing a sense of pride, love, and commitment to the family and to its spiritual goals.

Education has always been valued among the Jewish people, who are often called ***Am HaSefer,*** People of the Book, meaning the Torah, of course. Although the surroundings have changed dramatically—computers and CD-ROMs have replaced the slate blackboards, and the roaring fireplace no longer provides heat and light, for example—the basic educational style remains the same in the ***yeshivah*** (plural, ***yeshivot***) schools of today. Whenever students gather to study Torah, ***chazarah,*** repetition and review, remains the enduring pattern.

Indeed, for many, teachers and students alike, the goal is to become a ***talmid chacham,*** a wise and learned individual, a scholar in Torah and all it represents. The singular devotion of the ***matmid,*** the diligent and persevering student, to the study of Talmud is exemplary, and attaining the status of a ***gaon,*** a rare genius, or even an ***iluy,*** a prodigy, is the ultimate achievement.

The very behavior of Jewish scholars must be above reproach. To be sure, wisdom and high ethical standards mark those who are called ***talmidei chachamim,*** the "nobility

Volumes of the Talmud go hand in hand with CDs and software in today's *yeshivah* world.

among the learned." So, too, deportment and demeanor distinguish them from other people: in the tone of their speech, in the way they dress, in the manner in which they conduct their affairs.

In the Mishnah, Shammai urges us:

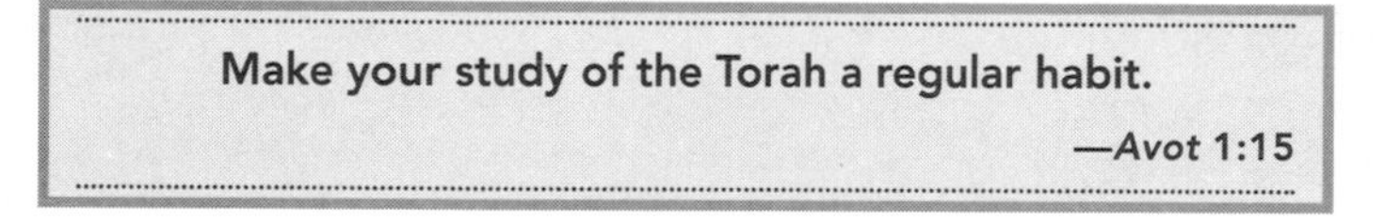

Make your study of the Torah a regular habit.

—*Avot* 1:15

and Hillel cautions us:

If you do not increase your knowledge, you decrease it.

—*Avot* 1:13

and, even more pointedly, he says:

> **Do not say,**
> **"When I have leisure I shall study,"**
> **for you may never have any leisure.**
> ***—Avot 2:5***

Thus, tradition continues to inspire and guide Jewish students.

Judaism reinforces the importance of Torah study, and the esteem in which it is held is reflected even in the respect shown to sacred books.

- No objects should be put on top of a sacred book.
- A sacred book must not be touched with dirty hands.
- A sacred book that has fallen on the floor must be picked up immediately and kissed.
- Sacred books that are damaged or torn and cannot be repaired—or even a page fragment that contains sacred words—must be buried in hallowed ground.
- A sacred book should not be left open, even for a short time.

Needless to say, the respect shown for sacred books is exceeded only by that shown for the *Sefer Torah* itself.

9.13.3 Secular Education

In today's world, Jewish students, boys and girls alike, have the opportunity to study Torah and acquire a meaningful secular education in the same school environment. Hebrew day schools, at both the elementary and high school levels, are preparing Jewish students for the real world by offering sacred and secular instruction within a Jewish framework. At the university level, as well, more and more Jewish students are enrolling in Jewish studies programs, along with their secular courses.

The sages understood that having a trade or profession was also an important goal. In the Mishnah, Rabban Gamliel teaches:

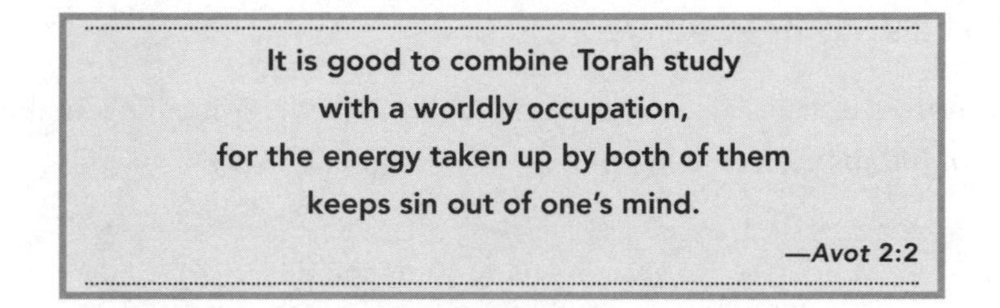

**It is good to combine Torah study
with a worldly occupation,
for the energy taken up by both of them
keeps sin out of one's mind.**

—*Avot* 2:2

In a similar vein, Rabbi Elazar ben Azariah teaches that:

**If there is no Torah, there is no worldly occupation;
if there is no worldly occupation, there is no Torah;
if there is no wisdom, there is no fear of God;
if there is no fear of God, there is no wisdom;
if there is no knowledge, there is no understanding;
if there is no understanding, there is no knowledge;
if there is no flour, there is no Torah;
if there is no Torah, there is no flour.**

—*Avot* 3:21

The interpretation of these verses is that the study of Torah, with its ethical laws regulating commerce, makes it possible to conduct business properly. Worldly occupations alone, without Torah as a guide, may lead to sin. If individuals cannot support themselves, then they will be unable to study Torah properly. If they do not learn the proper conduct in the Torah, they will not be able to provide sustenance (flour) for themselves and their families.

In the Talmud, Rabbi Yehudah says:

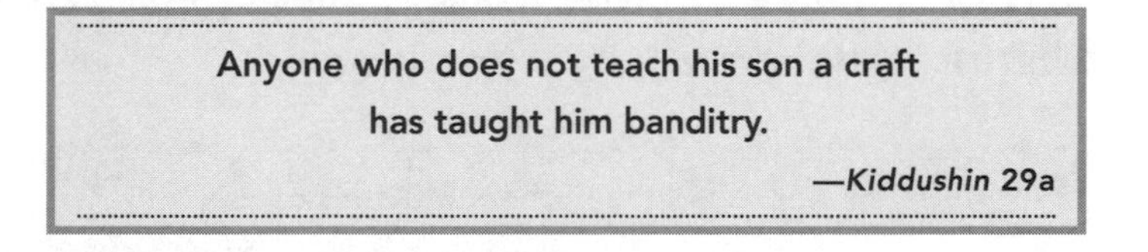

**Anyone who does not teach his son a craft
has taught him banditry.**

—*Kiddushin* 29a

Thus, parents are obligated to teach their children Torah and prepare them to earn a living as well. Both are equally important.

9.14 Rites of Passage

In their wisdom, the sages set down a timetable, as it were, for life's major events. In the Mishnah, Judah ben Tema says:

> **At five years begin to study the Bible.**
> **At ten, for the study of Mishnah.**
> **At thirteen, for the fulfillment of the *mitzvot*.**
> **At fifteen, for the study of Talmud.**
> **At eighteen, for marriage.**
> **At twenty, to pursue a livelihood. . . .**
> **—Avot 5:21**

Indeed, there are many occasions in Jewish tradition that mark personal milestones in the spiritual growth of the Jewish people. Circumcision, the first haircut, the first day of learning Torah, the acceptance of religious responsibility, the engagement, the wedding, the birth of a child—the cycle of Jewish life repeats itself over and over. We have already discussed some of these events. Let's take a look at the others.

9.14.1 The First Haircut

During the period of *Sefirat HaOmer,* many of the rituals of mourning, including not cutting one's hair, are observed (see Sections 4.6.2 and 7.4.16) in commemoration of the plague that killed twenty-four thousand students of Rabbi Akiva. On *LaG baOmer,* the eighteenth day in the *Omer* period, we observe a semi-holiday, because the plague stopped on that date.

The Torah prescribes how a man's hair should be cut and prohibits cutting off his sideburns, thereby making the area of the temples smooth.

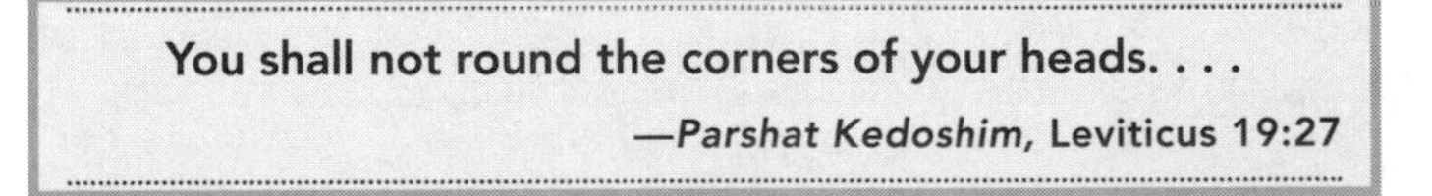
You shall not round the corners of your heads. . . .
—*Parshat Kedoshim,* Leviticus 19:27

Because it is permissible to cut the hair on the eighteenth day of *Iyar,* which is the thirty-third day in the *Omer,* it has long been a tradition to cut a boy's hair for the first time on the *Lag baOmer* closest to his third birthday. This first haircut is known as ***Upsherin*** and represents a milestone for the young child, who is now old enough to begin to study Torah. Often a Torah scholar is asked to take the first snip of the child's hair.

It is customary to give the little boy his first *kipah* and *talit katan* on the day of his *Upsherin,* so he can recite the *berachah* on *tzitzit* (see Sections 3.6.3 and 3.6.4). On the first day of school, his parents joyfully take him by the hand and lead him to the beginning of the study of Torah, the *alef-bet* (see Section 2.4.1).

9.14.2 Religious Responsibility

Jewish boys and girls become adults in terms of their religious obligations and rights when they reach the age of religious maturity. It is the task of parents and teachers to train the child in preparation for this sacred event. The ceremonies and celebrations attached to this rite of passage vary from family to family and community to community, but there is no magical transfer of Jewish identity inherent in these rituals.

As we discussed in Section 3.5.5, Judaism requires a quorum of ten men, a *minyan,* in order to conduct congregational worship services. A Jewish boy reaches religious maturity when he is thirteen years and one day old, according to his Hebrew date of birth. At that age, he is called a ***bar mitzvah,*** a son of the commandments, and he becomes fully responsible for his religious conduct. He is entitled to all the privileges and rights of his new role, but he is also obligated for all the responsibilities attendant to it.

On the day after his thirteenth birthday, the *bar mitzvah*—the term is used both for the celebrant and the occasion—the young man attends *Shacharit* services with his father, either in the synagogue or in his *yeshivah,* and puts on *tefillin* for the first time. This *mitzvah* is now one of his obligations, so this is truly a milestone.

His status as a *bar mitzvah* is also marked in the synagogue on the Sabbath when he is called to *Kriat HaTorah* for the first time. He usually receives the *aliyah* of *Maftir,* which includes the recitation of the prophetic reading, the *Haftarah,* associated with the Torah portion of the week. After the *bar mitzvah* has completed his *aliyah,* his father, who until now has been liable for punishment if his son's religious observance was deficient, is called to the *bimah* to recite the following prayer.

Blessed are You, Lord our God, King of the Universe,
Who has freed me from the punishment due this boy.

With this prayer the father conveys the responsibility for his son's observance of the *mitzvot* to him, and it is a time for gratitude and joy.

Depending on synagogue custom and on the boy's level of Jewish educational achievement, he may also chant all or part of the Sabbath services, read the entire Torah portion, and offer a *d'var Torah* based on biblical and talmudic study before the congregation.

Close relatives and friends of the family are usually chosen for all the Torah honors, including opening the Ark and lifting and dressing the Torah, because they want to share in the great joy this day represents.

Being called to the Torah marks this rite of passage publicly. His religious privileges and obligations are those of any adult Jewish male, not more, not less. How meaningful and inspirational this ritual can be if the young man is trained in the values and teachings of his heritage; then it can truly be a day of celebration for all of the House of Israel.

A *Bar Mitzvah* (we will capitalize the name of the ritual) may, in fact, be observed on any day that the Torah is read, including Monday, Thursday, *Rosh Chodesh, Purim*, and all eight days of *Chanukah*. Although the Torah is also read on the *Yamin Nora'im* and the *Shalosh Regalim*, a *Bar Mitzvah* is usually not scheduled for those days because of practical considerations.

After the services, the parents usually host a *Kiddush* for the entire congregation. It is also appropriate to have a *se'udat mitzvah*, either after the *Kiddush* or the next day. At the *se'udah*, the young man may deliver a Torah discourse, highlighting the religious significance of the day. He expresses his gratitude to his parents and teachers, whose love and dedication have prepared him to assume his religious duties. The practice of making extravagant parties detracts from the spiritual significance of the day. To celebrate with a nonkosher dinner is most inappropriate.

Family and friends should attend the *Bar Mitzvah* service and the celebration. To go only to the party sends the message that the religious service is not the important part of the event. Gifts should never be brought to the synagogue on the Sabbath.

More in tune with the sacred nature of the event is the more recent tradition of observing the *Bar Mitzvah* in Israel, often in sight of the *Kotel*, one of Judaism's holiest sites.

A Jewish girl reaches the age of ***bat mitzvah***, daughter of the commandments, at the age of twelve years and one day, according to her Hebrew birth date. On that day she assumes full accountability for her religious observance.

Within the context of traditional Judaism, there is no analogous ceremony to the *Bar Mitzvah* for young women. Congregational worship, including *Kriat HaTorah*, does not allow for the participation of women in the conduct of the service. However, it is fully in keeping with Jewish tradition for the day of *Bat Mitzvah* to be observed with celebration and thanksgiving.

It is appropriate for the *bat mitzvah* to deliver a *d'var Torah* during the festivities. Depending on the level of her Jewish education, she may discuss the Torah portion, explain the laws and customs of an upcoming festival, or comment on the requirements of a particular *mitzvah* she has studied. As long as the event does not compromise halachic considerations in the synagogue, it is in consonance with traditional Jewish practice.

Both the *bar mitzvah* boy and the *bat mitzvah* girl should be encouraged to continue their Jewish education and their participation in the synagogue. Religious maturity marks the beginning of their public commitment to a Torah way of life.

9.15 When a Marriage Fails

Jewish marriage is a sacred commitment based on mutual respect, love, companionship, physical attraction, and shared values and goals. It is the intention of every couple to live happily ever after, but sometimes the marriage fails.

Jewish couples are encouraged to attempt to reconcile their differences, to regain *shalom bayit,* the peace and harmony of their home. *Shalom bayit* is an ideal, a goal, that is, nevertheless, achievable with very hard work. There is no place for innuendo, half-truths, flaring tempers, or violence in the home. Peace must be actively pursued, because the easiest place to lose sight of peace is at home, with the ones who are closest to us. It is much easier to be polite and cordial to those outside our immediate family.

With the guidance of their rabbi and other professionals he may recommend, the couple should seek to resolve matters, one way or the other, within a Torah framework, but divorce should be considered only when there is no other option.

Judaism recognizes that sometimes it is necessary and proper to dissolve a marriage, and Jewish law provides a means for its legal dissolution. Just as the marriage was consecrated "according to the laws of Moses and Israel," so, too, must the divorce be conducted within the parameters of Jewish law.

The writ of divorce, called a ***get,*** must be prepared according to very strict halachic requirements. It can only be issued with the consent of a *Bet Din,* comprised of three pious rabbis, all well versed in the *halachot* of Jewish marriage and divorce, none of whom are related to either the husband or the wife, or to each other.

Only the husband may authorize the preparation of the writ of divorce, but both the husband and the wife must consent to its preparation. While each *get* is handwritten on parchment (or paper, which is preferable, to prevent any additions or forgeries) by an expert *sofer* specifically for each couple (in their presence, where practical), the legal formula essentially states that the *get* frees the woman from her husband and permits her to remarry.

The *get* is written in Hebrew in a precise twelve-line format. Many of the letters are written so that they extend from one line to the one above or below (for example, *lamed, chaf sofit,* and *nun sofit*), in order to preclude any insertions between the lines. The witnesses sign the *get* on two short lines below the last line of text.

The *get* includes: (1) the Hebrew names of the husband and wife (and any nicknames by which they are known), but not the family names; (2) the name of the city where it is written, including such specific information as the name of a river or other body of water that pinpoints the location more precisely; and (3) the Hebrew date on which it is written, including the day of the week, the month, and the year, as reckoned from Creation.

No grounds are stipulated. After the two witnesses sign the *get,* it is delivered by the husband, or his authorized representative, to the wife in the presence of the witnesses and the *Bet Din.*

It takes about two hours to complete the procedure, if both husband and wife are present. When she accepts the *get,* she is legally divorced according to Jewish law. The *get* is cut to indicate that it has been issued, and it remains on file with the *Bet Din.* Both the husband and wife are given a letter of release, ***p'tur,*** proof that they are divorced and free to remarry. If a *get* has been properly issued, the husband may remarry immediately. The wife must wait ninety-two days, in order to determine that she was not pregnant at the time of the divorce, and to assure the paternity of any children born after her remarriage.

A civil divorce without a *get* does not free the partners to remarry according to Jewish law. If a husband has already obtained his civil decree and refuses to authorize a *get,* he is still considered married according to Jewish law.

Some states now enforce the so-called *get* law, requiring a Jewish husband seeking a civil divorce to first grant a *get* to his wife. When a husband refuses to give his wife a *get,* she is called an ***agunah,*** an abandoned wife. This term also applies to a wife whose husband is missing—such as during war—and she cannot provide proof of his death. Such a woman is considered "chained." (A qualified rabbi should also be consulted in the case of a man whose wife has disappeared.)

The tragic situation of the *agunah* seeks remedy and resolution within Jewish law. Some rabbis have found halachic ways to release ***agunot*** without the issuance of a *get.* Regrettably, there is no consensus on their rulings.

The issuance of a *get* in no way negates the terms of a civil decree and has no bearing on custodial agreements about children or on financial and property settlements concluded by the parties.

The *halachot* of divorce are numerous and complex, and, accordingly, only those with extraordinary experience and expertise in this field should undertake the preparation of a *get*. The issue of divorce is not a matter taken lightly.

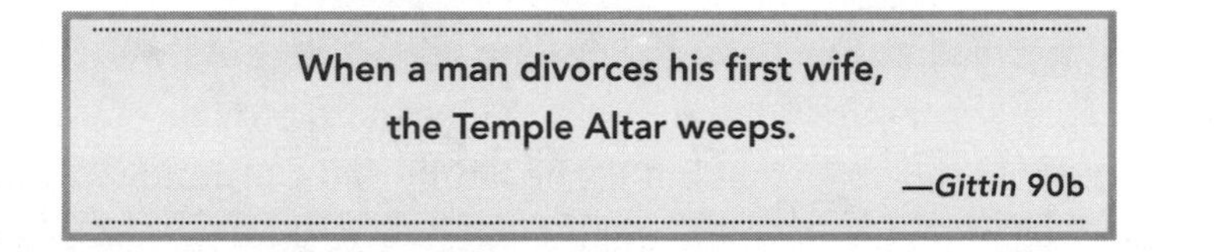

> **When a man divorces his first wife,**
> **the Temple Altar weeps.**
>
> **—*Gittin* 90b**

There are also many questions of Jewish law that deal with the issue of the wife who refuses to accept a *get*. In all matters of divorce, a highly qualified rabbi should be consulted.

9.16 When a Jew Dies

Death is considered a passageway between this temporal world and ***Olam HaBa,*** the World to Come. At the time of death, the soul that brought the body to life at birth is returned to God, Who gave it. The body is returned to the earth, but in the World to Come, the soul never dies. The Torah speaks to all when it says:

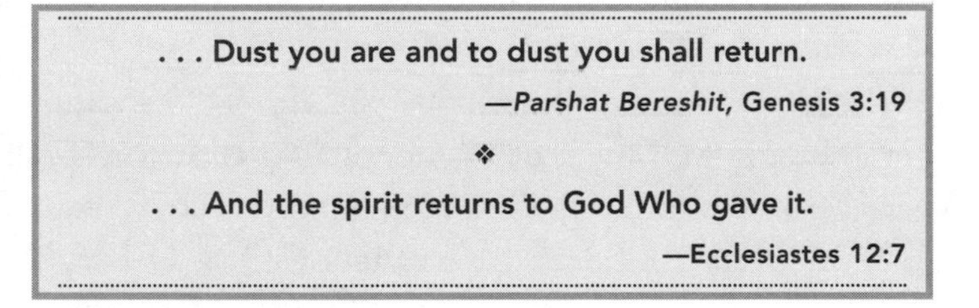

> **. . . Dust you are and to dust you shall return.**
>
> **—*Parshat Bereshit,* Genesis 3:19**
>
> ❖
>
> **. . . And the spirit returns to God Who gave it.**
>
> **—Ecclesiastes 12:7**

Everything the Jew does in this world is in preparation for *Olam HaBa*. Every *mitzvah* has its own reward, and sometimes the *mitzvah* that seems the least important, in fact, merits the greatest reward. Everybody will die—the most saintly and the most evil—and judgment will be rendered at the time of death.

Jews believe in the intrinsic goodness and mercy of God, and, therefore, they should face death without fear of eternal punishment. According to the Talmud, *Masechet Berachot* 17a, the righteous will dwell in *Olam HaBa,* where they will sit with crowns on their heads and delight in the radiance of the Divine Presence. In *Olam HaBa,* neither food, nor drink, nor procreation will be necessary. There will be no need to conduct business, and jealousy, hatred, and competition will be unknown. The World to Come is also referred to as ***Gan Eden,*** the Garden of Eden.

9.16.1 Dealing with Illness

Judaism offers many approaches for dealing with illness. As we will discuss, they are all interwoven in the fabric of religious life. All of them provide emotional and spiritual relief, not only to the ill person, but to the family and community as well.

Every day, except on the Sabbath and festivals, we recite the nineteen blessings of the *Shemoneh Esrei.* Blessing (8) asks God to mercifully restore the sick to health (see Section 3.7.5).

> **Heal us, Lord, and we will be healed;**
> **save us and we will be saved,**
> **for You are our praise.**
> **Grant complete recovery from all our ailments,**
> **for You are the faithful and compassionate God, King and Healer.**
> **Blessed are You, Lord,**
> **Who heals the sick among His people Israel.**

It is customary to insert the names of sick family members and friends that we wish to pray for in this *berachah.*

We also remember the sick during *Kriat HaTorah.* Immediately after an *aliyah,* a *Mi She'Berach* is offered for the well-being of the honoree. It is customary at that time to also recite a special *Mi She'Berach* for the sick in his family, if he so requests. Recited by the *ba'al korei* on behalf of the petitioner, it is a variation of the blessing for the honoree himself.

A *Mi She'Berach* for the Sick

May He Who blessed our forefathers,
Abraham, Isaac, and Jacob,
Moses and Aaron, David and Solomon,
may He heal the sick person,
(Hebrew name of patient)
son/daughter of
(Hebrew name of patient's mother).
May the Holy One, blessed be He,
mercifully and speedily restore him/her
to perfect health of the body and the spirit.

As we discussed in Section 9.9, a Jew is given a Hebrew name at birth (or upon adoption or conversion) and is always known thereafter as the son/daughter of the father. This is the only name that is used in all religious documents or in conversion or adoption records. However, at the time of illness, a Jew is referred to as the son/daughter of the mother.

There are other traditions associated with serious illness. An additional Hebrew or Yiddish name, usually one connoting long life or blessing, may be given to the sick person. For example, the following names may be added, to avert the severe decree (see Section 6.11.1).

For Males

NAME	MEANING
Chayim	life
Alter	old (Yiddish)
Raphael	God heals
Azriel	God is my help

For Females

NAME	MEANING
Chavah	life
Chayah	life
Berachah	blessing

Often, a call will go out in the community when someone is critically ill, and, in response, people undertake to recite the entire book of Psalms over and over, until the crisis passes. The text is usually divided up so that someone is always saying Psalms throughout the day.

Psalms 20, 27, 30, 41, and 102, among others, are specifically for healing and may be recited when someone is undergoing surgery or other serious treatments. They may be recited by others in behalf of the patient or personally by the individual who is ill. Sometimes particular Psalms are chosen because together the first letters spell out the patient's Hebrew name.

It is also customary to recite prayers of repentance and to donate to charity in the hope of a recovery, for repentance, prayer, and charity can cancel the decree of heaven. Some people even commission the writing of a *Sefer Torah,* an exceptional *mitzvah* that few have the opportunity to fulfill.

People often ask travelers to carry prayers written on small pieces of paper to Israel and insert them in the cracks of the *Kotel.* This tradition of offering prayers at the Western Wall dates back to antiquity, but modern technology—via the Internet—has made it possible to have prayers recited there without leaving home.

God is called the Healer of the Sick, and His miracles can bring about the recovery that is out of reach to mere humans. It is, therefore, always appropriate to wish a sick person ***refuah sh'leimah bi'm'heirah,*** a complete and speedy recovery, no matter how dire the circumstances appear. Sometimes ordinary human beings, including doctors and nurses, serve as agents of God in the healing process. The *mitzvah* of visiting the sick provides us with the opportunity to bring a brief respite from pain or to lift the patient's spirits, all of which can contribute to healing.

A WITTY REMARK!

A good number of years ago, my father was facing surgery on his throat. Always a man of great faith, he approached the day of the operation with confidence in his doctors and trust in God, the true Healer of the Sick.

The night before the surgery, his anesthesiologist came to his room. He seemed upset, and he said to my father, "Rabbi, I came here to tell you that I am afraid I can't be in the operating room with you tomorrow."

My father, with great sensitivity and insight, replied, "Well, you know I want you to be in the operating room, so would you like to tell me what is troubling you?"

"I am a doctor, but you are a rabbi, a holy man of God. How can I take your life in my hands?" he asked.

My father smiled. "I assure you, Doctor, you think I will be in your hands, but you are wrong. You were appointed by God to be in this place, but I most certainly will be in His hands. I am not afraid, and you shouldn't be either."

The doctor kissed my father's hand and thanked him. In the morning, they smiled at each other as the surgery got under way. Everything went beautifully.

Even using the expression "God bless you" when someone sneezes has biblical origins. According to the midrashic teachings of *Pirke de Rabbi Eliezer* 52, in the days of the patriarchs, there was no such thing as illness before death. Instead, a person would sneeze and the soul would depart.

Jacob prayed and asked God to grant people a short period of illness before death. Accordingly, it became customary to say "God bless you," and to wish others "good health" or "long life" when they sneeze.

9.16.2 The Rituals of Dying

There are many *halachot* and rituals associated with dying and death. These end-of-life traditions resonate with the same intent to perform acts of kindness and charity that mark the entire Jewish life cycle, and their purpose is to protect the dignity of the deceased and console the grieving.

According to the Talmud, *Masechet Shabbat* 32a, when death is thought to be near, it is proper to encourage the patient to recite the Confession on the Death Bed and to assist in making this final declaration of faith. For fear that this may frighten the patient and hasten death, which is prohibited, it is permissible to remind the Jew that the recitation of the Confession does not mean death will occur immediately thereafter. Rather, the Confession is an opportunity to acknowledge God's divine judgment, perhaps, for the last time. If a patient is too ill to speak, the Confession should be said with one's mind and heart, but if even this would be too emotionally taxing, a person should not be forced to confess, for in the Mishnah, we find the promise:

> **All Israel is guaranteed a portion in the World to Come.**
>
> —***Sanhedrin* 90:1**

The *Shulchan Aruch,* the Code of Jewish Law (*Yoreh De'ah* 338:2), provides the minimum text for the Confession.

Confession on the Death Bed

I acknowledge before You, Lord,
my God and God of my forefathers,
that my recovery and my death are in Your hands.
May it be Your will to send me a complete recovery;
but if I die, may my death be an atonement
for all the sins, iniquities, and transgressions
that I have [committed] before You.
May You grant my share in the Garden of Eden
and find me worthy for the World to Come
that is concealed for the righteous.

If possible, the *Viduy,* full confessional of *Yom Kippur,* may be recited as well. At the very end, those in the room should recite Psalms.

When a Jew dies, it becomes the duty of the community to assist in preparing the body of the deceased for burial. This ***chesed shel emet,*** act of true lovingkindness, is unlike other good deeds or favors, because it is a kindness that the recipient can never repay.

Upon hearing of a death, all Jews pronounce the blessing

Blessed is the true judge

referring, of course, to God. Among family members, seven close relatives are considered mourners: the mother and father; the spouse; sisters and brothers; and sons and daughters. Between the time of notification of death and burial, each of these individuals is called an ***onen,*** and specific restrictions apply to them in regard to the performance of certain *mitzvot.* A qualified rabbi should be consulted. After the funeral, each mourner is called an ***avel.*** Each of them is obligated to rend his or her garment upon hearing of the death (although this is often deferred until just before the funeral). They stand and recite the following blessing at that time:

Blessed are You, Lord our God, King of the Universe, the true judge.

Upon hearing of the death of a parent, a child rends the garment on the left side, over the heart. All other mourners rend the garment on the right side. The popular custom of wearing a black ribbon, which is cut by the undertaker, does not fulfill the requirements of ***k'riah,*** tearing one's clothes, as a sign of mourning. Rather, this practice makes a mockery of the rite which has been practiced by the Jewish people since biblical times (*Parshat Vayeshev,* Genesis 37:34). Rending the garment is an emphatic and authentic expression of Jewish grief, and it should not be diminished by insignificant gestures.

When a death occurs, the family of the deceased should call their rabbi, who will assist them in making the necessary arrangements. After the rabbi has been notified, the Jewish burial society and the Jewish funeral home should be contacted.

9.16.3 Reverence for the Dead

The underlying theme of all the rituals of death is that God's judgment is righteous. Even in the bleakest of hours of grief, a Jew believes in His infinite wisdom and benevolence, recognizing the limitations of human beings to fathom the mysteries of God. Faith, ***bitachon,*** in the immortality of the soul, and the belief that everything God does is for good, provide the support to accept His judgment and contribute to the consolation of the mourners. Everything is not given to humankind to understand, and the inability to always understand does not negate the commitment of faith.

In all aspects of ritual, the body of the deceased must be treated with reverence and honor. This is referred to as ***kavod hamet,*** honoring the dead. Except under unique circumstances, an autopsy is forbidden. This prohibition is based on the tradition of according the deepest respect to the deceased, a human being created in the image of

God. A qualified rabbi should be consulted if an autopsy is requested by medical or legal agencies.

Many Jewish communities have a ***Chevrah Kadisha,*** a Holy Society, whose members are responsible for the sacred duties of preparing the body before the funeral and for assisting the family in making preparations for burial. The Torah specifically requires interment.

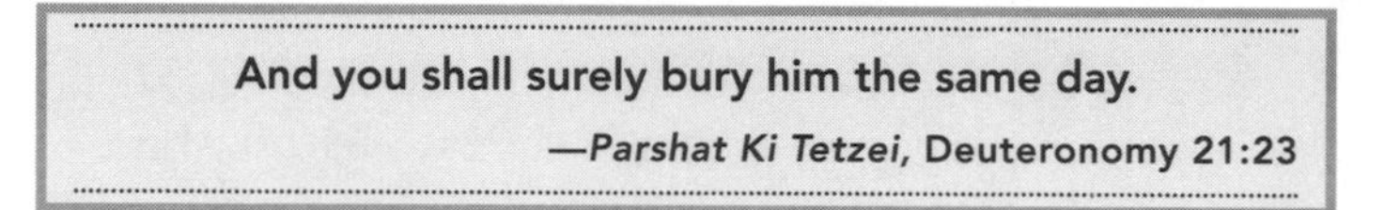

And you shall surely bury him the same day.

—Parshat Ki Tetzei, Deuteronomy 21:23

According to *halachah,* this means directly in the ground. Where local law and custom require the use of a coffin, it is permitted.

Often the *Chevrah Kadisha* owns land set aside for use as a cemetery. Synagogues and benevolent organizations often maintain their own cemeteries for the benefit of their members. Families may purchase burial plots from the synagogue or organization, the *Chevrah Kadisha,* or the cemetery itself.

Cremation is forbidden, even if it was the wish of the deceased, and embalming of the body is likewise prohibited.

The *Chevrah Kadisha* brings the body from the place of death to the funeral home where it will be ritually prepared for burial. A special room is equipped and set aside for this purpose in the funeral home, and for this reason alone, a Jewish funeral home should be used. There are two groups: the men's group prepares the body of a man; the women's group, that of a woman. This preparation is called ***taharah,*** ritual purification.

Those performing the *taharah* begin with the ritual washing of their own hands three times. They then recite the following prayer.

God of kindness and mercy,
Whose ways are merciful and truthful,
You have commanded us
to practice righteousness and truth with the dead
and engage in properly burying them,
as it is written, "And you shall surely bury him."
May it, therefore, be Your will, Lord, our God,
to give us fortitude and strength
to properly perform our undertaking of this holy task
of cleansing and washing the body,
and putting on the shroud and burying the deceased.
Keep us from any harm or fault
that we not fail in the work of our hands
and grant the fulfillment of the verse regarding us:
"He who observes the commandments shall never know any evil."
May our merit,
in the performance of this work of lovingkindness,
prolong our lives in happiness,
and may the mercy of God rest on us forever.

In accordance with ritual law, the body is washed, cleansed, and dressed in simple white ***tachrichin,*** burial shrouds made of linen. The procedures for purification must be carried out with meticulous care and consideration, always remembering the nobility of the life just past. The shrouds consist of several garments, which are sewn by hand without hems, seams, pockets, or knots.

For a deceased man, the *tzitzit* of one corner of his *talit* is tied in a knot, and the *talit* is spread in the bottom of the coffin. Jewish tradition discourages the use of ornate coffins, an indication that in death all are equal. The ***aron,*** casket, should be made of wood, and wooden pegs are preferable to build and close the coffin. No fancy linings or pillows are permitted in the interior, and the practice of sending floral arrangements or covering the casket with flowers is inappropriate. It is preferable to make a donation to a charity in memory of the deceased instead. (In Israel, the body is placed in the ground without a casket, returning the body directly to the earth from which it came.)

Once the *taharah* has been completed, the funeral can begin. From the time of death until the *taharah,* and from the *taharah* until the funeral, a ***shomer,*** or guardian, stays with the deceased as a sign of respect. It is customary for the *shomer* to recite ***Tehillim,*** Psalms, continuously until the funeral.

9.16.4 The Funeral

The Jewish funeral service is called ***halvayat hamet,*** accompanying the dead, or simply, ***levayah.*** A funeral should take place as soon as possible, even on the day of death if time permits; it should not, however, be held at night, when certain prayers are omitted (see below).

In any case, it should not be unnecessarily delayed, unless a Sabbath or festival intervenes, or to wait for mourners to arrive from a distance. If delaying the funeral will permit the arrival of the deceased's son, who must recite the Mourner's *Kaddish,* then waiting is permitted. The funeral should never be held in the sanctuary of the synagogue, unless the deceased was a revered Torah scholar.

In accordance with the traditions that require *kavod hamet,* the coffin should not be opened at any time after the *taharah* has been completed. It is not a Jewish practice to view the body—in fact, it is considered a sign of disrespect—nor is it appropriate for the mourners or those in attendance at the funeral to wear black clothing.

The service begins with the recitation of several Psalms. Most families ask their rabbi to then deliver a eulogy, usually a tribute to the memory of the deceased. It is certainly appropriate for a mourner, other members of the family, or friends of the deceased to speak as well.

When the funeral service in the chapel has ended, the mourners and others in attendance proceed to the cemetery for the burial. It is a *mitzvah* to *accompany* the funeral procession—this is the actual *mitzvah* of *halvayat hamet*—a distance of at least seven-and-a-half feet. At the cemetery, those carrying the casket are required to make seven stops as they approach the grave. During each stop, Psalm 91 is recited by the officiant until the verse

He will charge His angels for you, to protect you in all your ways.

In Hebrew, this verse contains seven words, and at each of the seven stops, an additional word is recited, until the last stop when the entire verse is said. The casket is then lowered into the grave, and the grave is filled and covered with a mound of earth. ***Tziduk HaDin,*** a prayer which marks the acceptance of God's judgment, is recited by the mourners.

The ***E-l Malei Rachamim,*** a request that God grant complete and perfect rest to the soul, is recited and is followed by the Burial *Kaddish,* if a quorum of ten men is present. It is not traditional Jewish practice to merely cover the grave with a grass-like cloth and allow the gravediggers to fill in the grave with a bulldozer after everyone has left. A Jew should be buried by other Jews. Those filling in the grave should not pass the shovel directly from one to the other, but should put it down and let the next person pick it up.

On the days when *Tachanun,* Prayers of Supplication, are not recited, *Tziduk HaDin* is not recited either, since it is considered similar to a eulogy. Both *Tziduk HaDin* and the Burial *Kaddish* are omitted if the burial, of necessity, takes place at night.

The first section of the Burial *Kaddish* is unique. It speaks of the Resurrection of the Dead and the restoration of worship of the One God.

Recite the Burial *Kaddish*

Mourners:
Magnified and sanctified be His great Name . . .
All:
Amen.
Mourners Continue:
. . . in the world which will be created anew,
where He will revive the dead and raise them up to eternal life,
rebuild the city of Jerusalem and establish His Temple . . .
and where the Holy One, blessed is He,
will reign in His sovereignty and glory, speedily,
and let us say, "Amen."
All:
Amen.

The remaining verses are the same as those found in the other *Kaddish* prayers. After the Burial *Kaddish,* those in attendance then form two parallel lines and recite the following verse of consolation as the mourners, now called ***avelim,*** pass between them.

May the Omnipresent One comfort you
among all those who mourn for Zion and Jerusalem.

It is customary for those in attendance to stop as they prepare to exit the cemetery and tear some grass from the earth and throw it behind them, saying:

He remembers that we are dust.

This is symbolic of the resurrection of the dead, who will rise from the earth, as it is written:

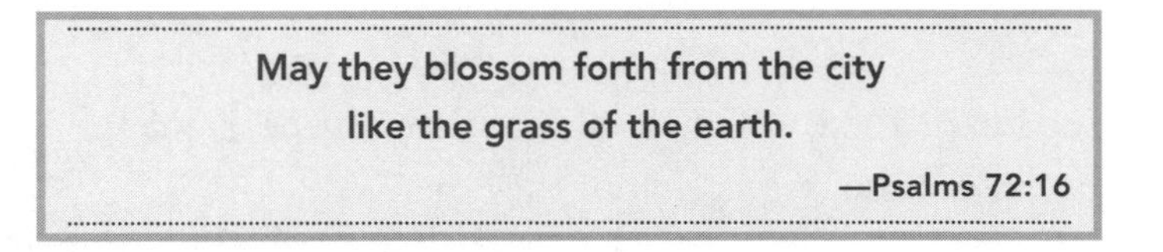

May they blossom forth from the city
like the grass of the earth.

—Psalms 72:16

Then, using a utensil to pour water (this is usually available at the cemetery or it may be prepared in advance at one's home and left outside the door), everyone is obligated to wash their hands (*Shulchan Aruch*, *Yoreh De'ah* 376, Paragraph 4), saying:

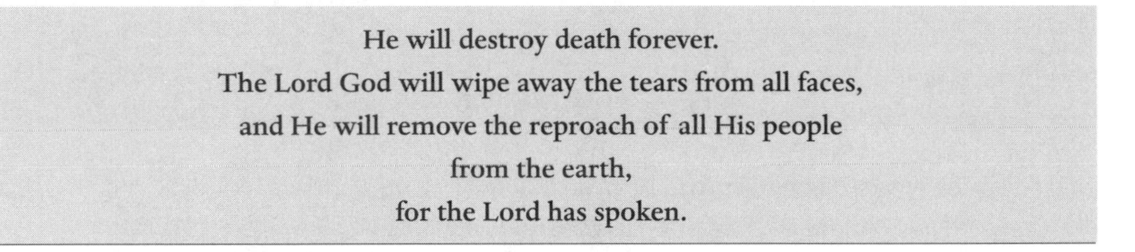

He will destroy death forever.
The Lord God will wipe away the tears from all faces,
and He will remove the reproach of all His people
from the earth,
for the Lord has spoken.

The utensil should not be handed from one person to the next, but should be put down and picked up again, in turn. The prevailing custom is to not dry one's hands after washing.

After the funeral, the mourners are once again obligated to observe all *mitzvot*. They return home and partake of the ***se'udat havra'ah,*** the meal of condolence, which is customarily prepared by friends and neighbors and brought to the mourners' home. It is traditional to serve hard-boiled eggs, lentils, and other round foods, their shape representing the cycle of life. The meal should not be a social event where neighbors and friends gather to chatter idly and eat. It is a solemn occasion, and it should be conducted with dignity.

Special Note: A *Kohen* is not permitted to come in contact with the dead, with the exception of those relatives of his immediate family for whom he would be obligated to mourn. For example, he should not

- enter the premises where a Jewish patient lies dying
- enter the premises where the deceased lies before or during the funeral
- approach within eight feet of any grave on the cemetery, even in a vehicle

There are many other restrictions that apply to the *Kohen,* and a qualified rabbi should be consulted.

9.16.5 The Period of Mourning

There are many rituals associated with the mourning period. In the Torah, we find:

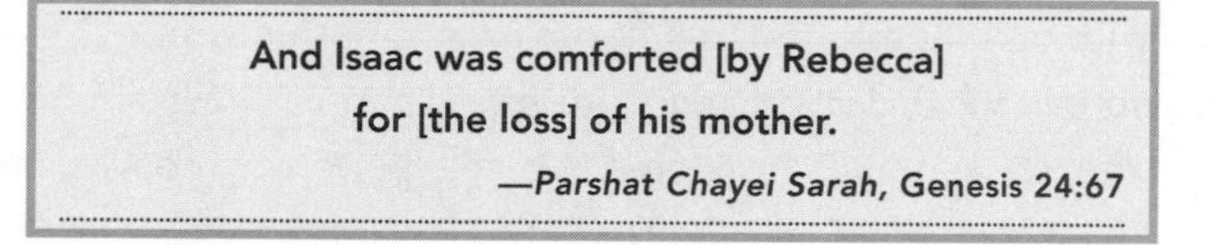

> **And Isaac was comforted [by Rebecca]**
> **for [the loss] of his mother.**
> —***Parshat Chayei Sarah,*** **Genesis 24:67**

and God Himself consoled Isaac after the death of his father Abraham, according to the Talmud, *Masechet Sotah* 14a.

When Jacob thought his son Joseph was dead, he

> **. . . rent his garments and put on sackcloth . . .**
> **and mourned . . . and his sons and daughters**
> **all arose to comfort him.**
> —***Parshat Vayeshev,*** **Genesis 37:34–35**

Years later, when Jacob died,

> **. . . Joseph fell upon his father's face and wept . . .**
> **and he mourned for his father seven days.**
> —***Parshat Vaychi,*** **Genesis 50:1, 10**

We also find:

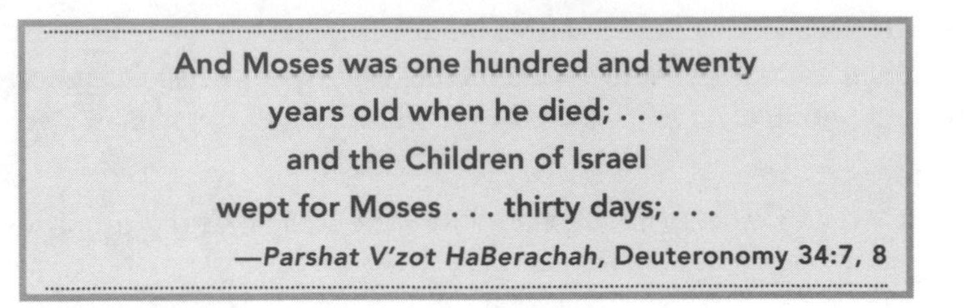

And Moses was one hundred and twenty years old when he died; . . . and the Children of Israel wept for Moses . . . thirty days; . . .

—*Parshat V'zot HaBerachah,* Deuteronomy 34:7, 8

Thus, we see that the various customs of mourning and consolation date back thousands of years.

According to the Talmud, *Masechet Mo'ed Katan* 27b, there are three stages to the period of mourning, each observed with somewhat less intensity. As a practical matter, we consider them to be five distinct phases: (1) the period of the *onen,* between notification of the death and the funeral, when the *onen* is both exempted from the performance of certain *mitzvot* and restricted from participating in certain activities; (2) the first three days after the funeral, considered to be the period of most intense grief for an *avel*; (3) the seven-day period of ***shivah*** (from the Hebrew for *seven*), which includes the first three days; (4) ***sh'loshim,*** the first thirty days after burial; and (5) ***yahrtzeit,*** the observance of the first-year anniversary after the death, according to the Hebrew calendar.

The seven-day period immediately following burial is called *shivah.* For seven days, including the day of burial, if it is concluded before sundown, the mourners are obligated to sit *shivah.* A memorial candle that will burn for the entire week is lit when *shivah* begins, a symbol of the departed soul.

Mourners are permitted to sit only on the floor or on low stools or benches during *shivah,* which is customarily observed in the home of the deceased. If that is not possible, mourners may sit separately in their own homes, designate one mourner's home as the *shivah* house, or return to their own homes at night and come back to the *shivah* house each morning.

The outer garment, which was torn upon notification of the death, is worn throughout the entire week. If it should be necessary to change the torn garment, the fresh garment must also be torn. Leather shoes are not worn during the period as an additional sign of mourning. Shaving, cutting the hair, and bathing for pleasure are prohibited, but one may wash parts of the body separately in cold water. Mourners refrain from marital relations during *shivah* as well. In the home, wherever mourners are present, all the mirrors are covered, so that the mourners will not see their own images.

During the *shivah,* relatives, who are not mourners, and friends come to offer consolation to the mourners on their loss. This *mitzvah* is called ***nichum avelim.*** Visitors should not come before the funeral, and according to one custom, not until after the third day of *shivah*, giving the mourners an opportunity to deal with their most profound sorrow in privacy. Visitors should not greet the mourners when they enter the *shivah* house, nor are they greeted by them.

It is appropriate to talk about the deceased during a condolence visit. Visitors must really let the mourners lead the way in terms of conversation, and should not prolong their visit in order to give others the opportunity to offer words of consolation as well. Many friends bring prepared food for the mourners so that they do not have to bother with such preparations themselves during the *shivah*. The first meal, in particular, should be prepared by others and brought to the *shivah* house for the mourners.

Throughout the *shivah* period mourners may not go to work and should refrain from all business matters by telephone or otherwise. They may not attend social events, or participate in activities that include music or other forms of entertainment. In many communities, daily worship services are held in the *shivah* house. Mourners do not sit *shivah* on the Sabbath, but *shivah* resumes after the Sabbath. They may not study Torah, even on the Sabbath, except for the *halachot* of mourning or the books of Job or Lamentations. There are special laws regarding the observance of *shivah* when a festival intervenes. A qualified rabbi should be consulted.

Visitors should not eat in the *shivah* house, nor take anything, including food, from the house of mourning, even if it is offered. At the conclusion of a condolence call, while the mourner is seated, the visitor expresses words of consolation, the same words offered at the cemetery after burial.

May the Omnipresent One comfort you
among all those who mourn for Zion and Jerusalem.

The fourth stage of mourning is the thirty-day period called *sh'loshim*, from the Hebrew for *thirty*. When the *shivah* period is over, mourners may return to work, but they continue to refrain from cutting their hair (and shaving) and attending festive occasions during the *sh'loshim*.

All mourners observe a minimal period of the *sh'loshim*, which includes the seven days of *shivah*, during which the Mourner's *Kaddish*, called *Kaddish Yatom*, is recited daily during services. The Mourner's *Kaddish* makes no reference at all to death or the sadness associated with the loss of a loved one.

Recite the Mourner's *Kaddish*

Mourners:

Magnified and sanctified be His great Name . . .

All:

Amen.

Mourners Continue:

. . . in the world which He has created according to His will;
may He establish His kingdom,
during your life and during your days, and during the life
of all the House of Israel, swiftly and soon,
and say "Amen."

All:

Amen.

All Continue:

Let His great Name be blessed forever and ever
and to all eternity—blessed . . .

Mourners Continue:

Blessed and glorified, exalted, extolled, and honored,
magnified and lauded be the Name of the Holy One,
blessed is He, . . .

All:

Blessed is He, . . .

The Mourner's *Kaddish* continues.

Mourners Continue:

. . . beyond all the blessings and hymns, praises and consolations
that are ever spoken in the world;
and say, "Amen."

All:

Amen.

Mourners Continue:

May they have abundant peace, lovingkindness,
mercy, long life, ample sustenance, and salvation
from their Father Who is in heaven,
and say "Amen."

All:

Amen.

The mourner then concludes the *Kaddish Yatom.*

Conclude the Recitation of the Mourner's *Kaddish*

Mourners Continue:
May there be great peace from heaven,
and life for us and for all Israel,
and say "Amen."
All:
Amen.
Mourners Continue:
He who makes peace in His celestial heights,
may He make peace for us and for all Israel;
and say "Amen."
All:
Amen.

The *sh'loshim* marks the end of the mourning period for all relatives except one's parents. A man may remarry after the passage of the *Shalosh Regalim,* in any sequence, but if he has young children who need to be cared for, he may remarry after the *sh'loshim.* A woman does not have to wait for the passage of the three Pilgrimage Festivals to remarry, but must wait at least three months. Only thirty days of mourning are required on the loss of a child or a sibling.

The fifth stage of mourning is the period of one year following death, when the soul of the deceased undergoes divine judgment. Mourners in the first eleven months after the death of a parent, must recite the Mourner's *Kaddish* during services.

According to the Mishnah, *Masechet Eduyot* 2:10, a sinner is punished for twelve months. However, in the *Shulchan Aruch, Yoreh De'ah* 376, Paragraph 4, the Rema states that a righteous person is judged for only eleven. By reciting the Mourner's *Kaddish* for eleven months, the mourner sanctifies the memory of his parent whose upright soul was not required to be judged for a full year.

Throughout the twelve-month period, mourners continue to refrain from attending weddings, *Bar Mitzvah* celebrations, and other festive events. They should not listen to music, attend the theater, or go to the movies. In all cases, a qualified rabbi should be consulted.

If there are no surviving children who are obligated to recite the Mourner's *Kaddish,* it is customary for other relatives to recite it or to engage the services of an observant Jew who will recite it in their place. Some *yeshivot* often arrange for the daily recitation of the Mourner's *Kaddish* in consideration of ***tzedakah,*** charity, donated to the school, inasmuch as they also conduct daily prayer services with a quorum.

Of course, each person's grief is measured not by the number of days required by Jewish law to mourn. It is simply that the *halachah* provides a framework so that the Jew does not mourn excessively and goes on with life.

Once the full year has passed, all restrictions are suspended for those mourning a parent. At the end of the first year and every year thereafter, all mourners observe the *yahrtzeit* (year's time) by reciting the Mourner's *Kaddish* on the anniversary of the Hebrew date of death.

A *yahrtzeit* may be observed for any relative, even someone other than one of the seven close relatives for whom mourning is required. Therefore, it is appropriate for grandchildren to observe the *yahrtzeit* of grandparents, for example, if no original mourners are still alive.

Some Jews observe the custom of fasting on the day of a *yahrtzeit,* especially of a parent. On the eve of the *yahrtzeit,* it is a custom for most Jews to light a *yahrtzeit* candle, which will burn for at least twenty-four hours, symbolizing the light of the soul which was extinguished. This custom finds expression in

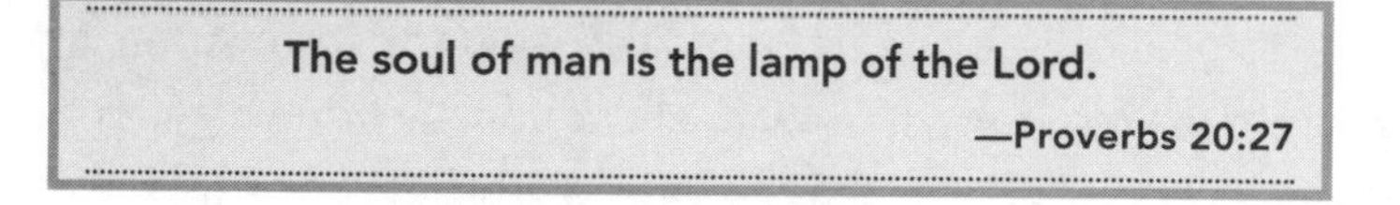

The soul of man is the lamp of the Lord.

—Proverbs 20:27

Organizations which have made arrangements to recite the Mourner's *Kaddish* during the first year customarily send the mourners a yearly notice shortly before the *yahrtzeit* will occur so that they can recite the Mourner's *Kaddish* themselves on that day.

9.16.6 Marking the Gravesite

It is a religious obligation to erect a monument, an upright stone ***matzevah,*** at the gravesite by the time of the first *yahrtzeit*. We find the earliest reference to this in the Torah.

> **And Jacob set up a pillar on her grave—**
> **the same pillar which is on Rachel's grave to this day.**
>
> **—*Parshat Vayishlach,* Genesis 35:20**

In the Talmud, *Masechet Horayot* 13b, we find a reference to "inscriptions on the graves," an indication that the practice of erecting monuments was well established by talmudic times.

Placing the monument at the head of the grave is a religious obligation and an act of respect for the dead. It marks the grave as a sacred resting place, one that must not be desecrated. Standing as a testament to the life of the deceased, it symbolizes that the dead will not be forgotten. Marking the grave with a brass plate that lies flush with the ground is not an equivalent observance.

The inscription on the monument should include the full Hebrew name of the deceased and the Hebrew date of death, so that prayers on behalf of the deceased may be recited at the gravesite in the future and the *yahrtzeit* can be observed on the correct date. It is also appropriate to include the name and date in English (or other familiar language) and expressions of praise and love.

The monument of a *Kohen* is often engraved with the symbol of two hands, fingers spread apart, as is customary for *Birkat Kohanim.* Other symbolic engravings include a flame or a candelabra, signifying the eternal spark of the soul; the Torah, especially for a revered sage; a sheaf of grain, symbolizing resurrection; a *shofar,* symbolizing the Messiah; and a broken branch, for someone who died young. In the Middle Ages, one's professional calling was often indicated on the tombstone: a pair of scissors for a tailor; a violin or harp for a musician; and a lion carrying a sword for a physician.

It is also customary to inscribe a Hebrew abbreviation at the bottom of the *matzevah*: ת״נ״צ״ב״ה, which stand for five Hebrew words meaning *May his/her soul be bound up in the bonds of eternal life.*

The prevailing custom is to not erect the monument until twelve months have passed. By then, the soul's period of judgment has passed; the intense grief has diminished; there is no obligation to say the Mourner's *Kaddish* on a daily basis; and there is a greater likelihood that the memory of the deceased will begin to fade. However, it is permissible and even laudatory to erect the *matzevah* as soon as possible, even during *shivah.*

Once the monument has been erected, it is a tradition, but not a requirement, to unveil the *matzevah* in the presence of family and friends. A special service of unveiling is then conducted, usually by a rabbi. It begins with the recitation of Psalm 1, and may be followed by *Aishet Chayil,* Proverbs 31:10–31, for a wife and mother, and other appropriate Psalms, such as 15 and 23. The rabbi usually offers a eulogy, recalling the highlights of the deceased's life. The memorial prayer for the soul of the departed, which was also offered at the funeral, is recited at the unveiling. It again requests that God grant complete and perfect rest to the soul. The unveiling service concludes with the recitation of the Mourner's *Kaddish,* if a *minyan* is present.

Before leaving the unveiling, it is customary for each person to place a small pebble on the top of the *matzevah.* One explanation for this suggests that this is done to assure *shalom bayit,* harmony in the family, as visitors see that the deceased is being remembered by others as well. It is also obligatory to wash one's hands before leaving the cemetery (see Section 9.16.4).

9.16.7 Visiting the Cemetery

According to talmudic sources, including *Masechet Sotah* 34b and *Masechet Ta'anit* 16a, it is an ancient custom to visit the graves of the departed to ask them to intercede on behalf of the living. It is appropriate to recite prayers at the gravesite, but it is not permissible to pray to the deceased. It is appropriate to leave a small stone on the *matzevah* after these visits as well.

Most often, visits to the cemetery are made on the *yahrtzeit,* on *Tishah b'Av,* during the month of *Elul,* and during the *Aseret Y'mei T'shuvah,* especially on the eve of *Rosh HaShanah* and *Yom Kippur.* Special prayers are recited at the gravesite on a *yahrtzeit,* before the *Yamim Nora'im,* and other specific occasions. All of these *tefillot* are poignant expressions of sorrow. They ask for God's mercy on the souls of the departed, so that their eternal rest will be in *Gan Eden,* where, according to the *Midrash, Bamidbar Rabbah* 13:2, God Himself will fete them, and fragrant breezes will perfume their heavenly abode.

While the wicked often seem to prosper in this world and the righteous seem to suffer, in the World to Come, the righteous souls will achieve their ultimate reward—attainment of the concept of God, which is impossible on earth. Before leaving the cemetery, it is obligatory to wash one's hands (see Section 9.16.4).

9.16.8 The Resurrection of the Dead

Resurrection of the Dead, ***Techi'at HaMetim,*** is a fundamental belief of Judaism. In the words of the Prophets, in the Talmud, and in the daily prayers, Jews reaffirm their belief in the immortality of the soul and the restoration of the body. For example,

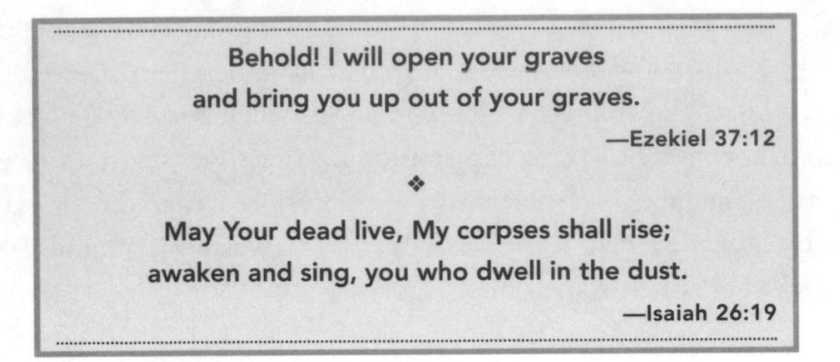
Behold! I will open your graves
and bring you up out of your graves.
—Ezekiel 37:12

❖

May Your dead live, My corpses shall rise;
awaken and sing, you who dwell in the dust.
—Isaiah 26:19

In *Birchot HaShachar,* every morning, Jews recite the following talmudic passage as an expression of thanksgiving for the restoration of the soul after sleep. Ultimately, it refers to the Resurrection of the Dead. In the Talmud, we find:

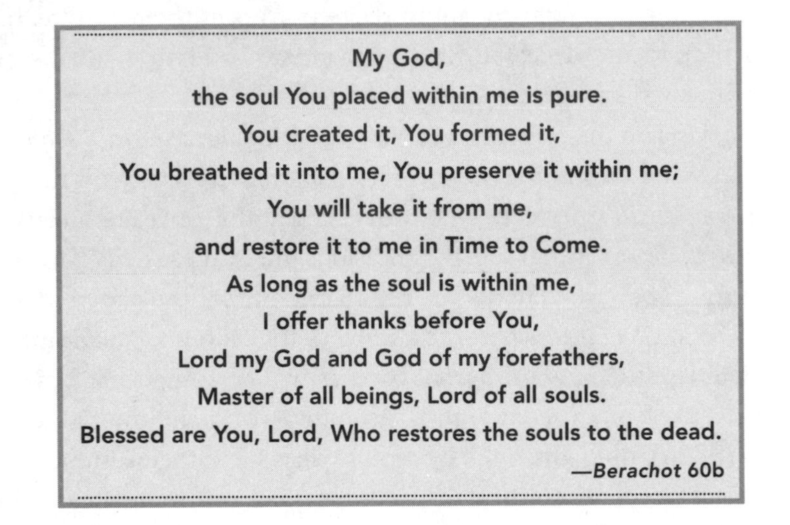
My God,
the soul You placed within me is pure.
You created it, You formed it,
You breathed it into me, You preserve it within me;
You will take it from me,
and restore it to me in Time to Come.
As long as the soul is within me,
I offer thanks before You,
Lord my God and God of my forefathers,
Master of all beings, Lord of all souls.
Blessed are You, Lord, Who restores the souls to the dead.
—*Berachot* 60b

Techi'at HaMetim is associated with the coming of the Messiah, the *Mashiach,* who will herald the restoration of the Holy Temple in Jerusalem. The *Mashiach* will descend from the House of King David, according to the promise of the prophet.

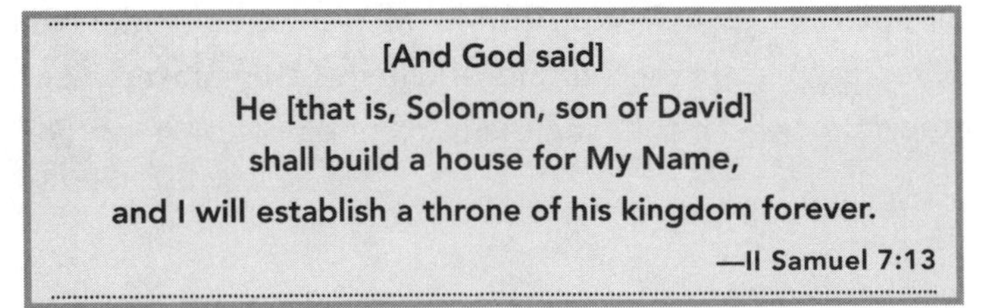
[And God said]
He [that is, Solomon, son of David]
shall build a house for My Name,
and I will establish a throne of his kingdom forever.
—II Samuel 7:13

Originally the title *Mashiach* was bestowed on the anointed of Israel—the priests and kings. When David received this promise, the title of *Mashiach* attained a special significance: the lineage of the House of David. The prophecy linked the anointed of Israel—that is, the one called *Mashiach*—with the eventual establishment of God's divine kingdom on earth.

According to the Mishnah, *Masechet Sotah* 9:15, the advent of the *Mashiach* will be preceded by a period of decadence, when scholarship will decline, observance of the precepts will be denied, insolence will dominate the household, and enemies will dwell within one's own walls.

According to the Rambam, *Mishneh Torah,* Book of Judges, Laws of Kings 12:2, the Coming of the Messiah will be foreshadowed by the arrival of the prophet Elijah, who will proclaim world peace. The messianic age will be a time of universal peace and prosperity, and the very essence of nature's forces will be altered.

> **. . . a wolf shall lie down with a lamb,**
> **and a leopard shall lie down with a kid. . . .**
>
> **—Isaiah 11:6–9**

Every generation has believed that the arrival of the Messiah was imminent. Some have been led to believe in false messiahs, the most notable, Shabbtai Tzvi, in the seventeenth century, who was arrested and exiled.

To this day, Jews continue to proclaim the words of the Rambam, in his Thirteen Articles of Faith:

> I believe with perfect faith
> in the Coming of the Messiah;
> and though he may tarry,
> in spite of this,
> I will await him until the day he comes.

LOOKING AHEAD! *In Chapter 10, we will examine a number of special words and phrases that are also part of the vocabulary of Jewish tradition.*

Word Works

The flag of the State of Israel is comprised of two blue stripes and a Star of David on a white background, reminiscent of the *talit.*

10

Special Words and Phrases

HIS CHAPTER PROVIDES additional words and phrases that are part of the Jewish experience. All of them offer a little more insight into the Jewish perspective and are reminders of the Jewish people's connection to their God, their homeland, their heritage.

10.1 With God in Mind

The Jewish people always include God in their plans. Ever mindful of the nearness of the Almighty, they keep Him in mind in every decision or promise they make, in every wish or hope they utter.

Several expressions leap to the tongue, a daily part of a vocabulary of Jewish tradition. They include:

Im Yirtzeh HaShem
If the Lord Wills It
and
B'Ezrat HaShem
With the Help of the Lord

These assertions express and reaffirm their abiding faith in God and the undeniable importance of His role in human destiny. At the same time, a Jew may say, "I will be there, with the help of God, . . ."

B'li Neder
Without a Vow

meaning "but I make no vow about it."

When Jews meet one another, they exchange greetings of peace. The first one says:

Shalom Aleichem
Peace unto You

and the other replies:

Aleichem Shalom
Unto You, Peace

When the first inquires of the other's well-being, the response is invariably prefaced by:

Baruch HaShem
Blessed is the Lord
(Thank God)

A lengthy tale of woe may follow, but it will also conclude with:

Baruch HaShem
Blessed is the Lord
(Thank God)

acknowledging that but for the benevolence of God, things would be worse.

Many Jews write the Hebrew letters *bet* and *hei* at the top of their correspondence, ב"ה, an abbreviation for *Baruch HaShem*. Others use the Hebrew abbreviation *bet, ayin, hei*, בע"ה, for *B'Ezrat HaShem*. Still others, write *bet, samech, daled*, בס"ד, which stand for three Aramaic words:

B'Siyata Dishmaya
With the Help of Heaven

Even when contemplating the possibility of bad news, a Jew exclaims:

Chas v'Shalom or ***Chas v'Chalilah***
God Forbid

In good times and bad, the Jew knows God is listening and can call upon Him at any time.

10.2 The Traveler's Prayer

When setting out on a trip of at least three miles, it is customary to recite ***Tefillat HaDerech***, the Traveler's Prayer. It is recited in the plural and asks for God's protection, not only for the Jewish traveler who recites it, but for all those who also make the trip.

In the Talmud, we find that Rabbi Yaakov says in the name of Rav Chisda:

> **Whoever sets out on a journey**
> **must recite the traveler's prayer.**
> —***Berachot* 29b**

The Talmud asks: What is the traveler's prayer? It answers:

Recite *Tefillat HaDerech*

May it be Your will, Lord our God,
(and God of our forefathers)
that You lead us toward peace,
place our footsteps toward peace,
and make us reach our desired destination
in life, gladness, and peace.
May You rescue us from the hands
of every foe . . . along the way,
and from all manner of punishment. . . .
May You send blessing in the works of our hands,
and grant us grace, kindness, and mercy
in Your eyes and in the eyes of all who see us.
May you hear the sound of our supplication,
because You are God Who hears prayer and supplication.
Blessed are You, Lord, Who hears prayer.

Tefillat HaDerech then continues with verses from *Parshat Vayetzei,* Genesis 32:2–3:

Continue to Recite *Tefillat HaDerech*

Recite Three Times:
Jacob went on his way and angels of God encountered him.
Jacob said when he saw them: "This is a Godly camp."
So, he named the place Machanayim
[two camps: Jacob's and that of the angels].

The Traveler's Prayer also includes the following verse from *Parshat Vaychi,* Genesis 49:18:

Continue to Recite *Tefillat HaDerech*

Recite Three Times:
For Your salvation I long, Lord.
I long, Lord, for Your Salvation.
Lord, for Your salvation I long.

Additional scriptural verses recalling God's protection of the Jewish people are also recited. There is a special version of the prayer for airplane flights as well.

It is customary to give those who are about to embark on a journey a small sum of money, in order to make each of them a ***sh'liach l'dvar mitzvah,*** an emissary charged with the performance of a *mitzvah.* By giving them the money and obligating them to deliver it to a charity when they reach their destination, they will be protected from any harm along the way.

In the Talmud, Rabbi Elazar says:

> **Those sent to perform a *mitzvah* are not harmed on their way to do a *mitzvah* nor on their return.**
>
> **—*Pesachim* 8b**

10.3 Avoiding Even a Hint of Impropriety

The concept of ***marit ayin,*** literally, *what the eye sees,* goes a long way to assure that a Jew avoids even the suspicion of improper conduct. For example, Jews should not go into a nonkosher establishment even to get change or use the telephone, lest someone else see them and think that they have gone there to eat nonkosher food.

10.4 With Every Good Wish

The Hebrew expression ***mazal tov*** is familiar to almost everyone. In fact, it has become part of the English vernacular. The word ***mazal*** has several meanings, including a star, a planet, or a sign of the zodiac, the so-called symbol of destiny or fortune. Accordingly, the wish for *mazal tov,* good fortune, became an expression of congratulations.

In the Talmud, Rav rejects astrology, the belief that planets and stars can influence the fate of human beings, when he states:

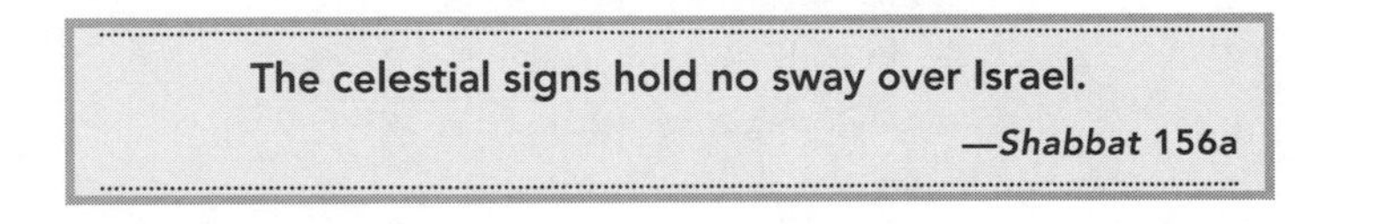
The celestial signs hold no sway over Israel.

—*Shabbat* 156a

Nevertheless, other sages acknowledged a link between an individual's destiny and the planets. For example, Rava says:

> **The length of a person's life,**
> **the number of his children,**
> **and the extent of his sustenance—**
> **none of these matters depends on his merit;**
> **rather [each] matter depends on *mazal.***
> ***—Mo'ed Katan* 28a**

Despite a diversity of opinions, it is clear from talmudic sources that the destiny of the Jewish people is not determined by the stars. Nevertheless, *mazal tov* remains a favorite, if misunderstood and misused, expression in Jewish life.

It is also a popular custom to toast a joyful occasion with *l'chayim,* to life. A variation on this is ***l'chayim tovim u'l'shalom,*** to a good life and to peace. Sometimes a wish for ***berachah v'hatzlachah,*** blessing and success, is offered.

10.5 Evil Eyes and Amulets

The term ***ayin hara,*** evil eye, suggests the sins of envy and greed. Someone who is stingy, resentful, or mean-spirited is said to have an *ayin hara.* Such people may pretend to be generous, but in truth, they are begrudging in nature. Those with the opposite personality are said to have an ***ayin tovah,*** a good eye.

In the Mishnah, we find:

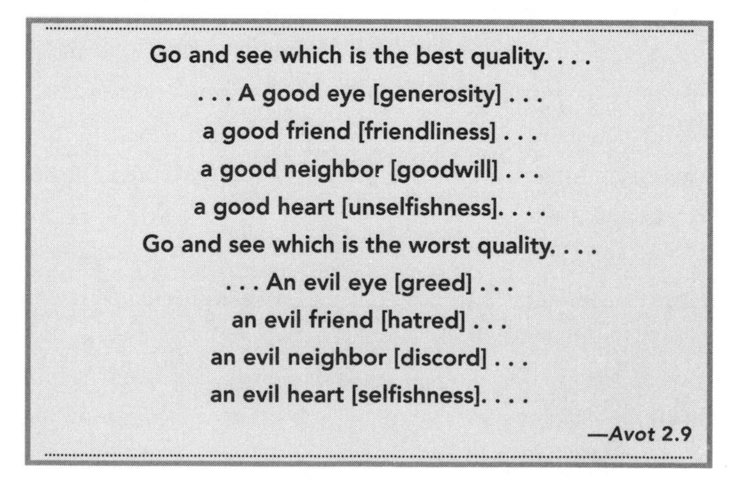

Go and see which is the best quality. . . .
. . . A good eye [generosity] . . .
a good friend [friendliness] . . .
a good neighbor [goodwill] . . .
a good heart [unselfishness]. . . .
Go and see which is the worst quality. . . .
. . . An evil eye [greed] . . .
an evil friend [hatred] . . .
an evil neighbor [discord] . . .
an evil heart [selfishness]. . . .
***—Avot* 2.9**

It became a popular notion that a person could cast an evil eye on others. In the Talmud, Rav comments on this:

> **Ninety-nine of a hundred die from an evil eye.**
>
> —*Bava Metzia* 107b

Because a jealous glance was thought to bring evil, the expression ***b'li ayin hara,*** without an evil eye, was uttered whenever a complimentary remark was said.

Some people even resorted to wearing amulets to ward off the *ayin hara.* Called ***k'miot,*** these amulets were thought to have curative powers and were intended to protect the wearer from evil spirits and illness.

Sometimes *k'miot* were inscribed with mystical writings and symbols. The amulets were formulated according to instructions in kabbalistic texts and often included the use of divine names. The mystical writings were inserted into artistically designed pendants of gold and silver, which were often adorned with angel-like forms. In addition, each pendant had the name *Shaddai,* Almighty, on the front.

The rabbinic authorities opposed the use of all *k'miot.* They taught that the study of Torah and the performance of *mitzvot* was the only prescription necessary against evil. Rabbi Judah the Pious wrote in the twelfth century:

> **Do not wear an amulet as a charm against evil,**
> **but put your implicit trust in God alone,**
> **for He will watch over you.**
>
> —*Book of the Pious,* Paragraphs 914 and 972

10.6 Bad Dreams

There is a tradition to perform a special ritual when one has had a bad dream. Based on the talmudic teaching in *Masechet Berachot* 55b, the dreamer asks three close friends to gather on the morning after to participate in ***HaTevat Chalom,*** Remedying a Dream. According to the Talmud, these three confidants assemble to encourage the dreamer to interpret the dream for the good.

The dreamer need not relate the exact details of the bad dream, but should keep it in mind as the ritual progresses. It is comprised of the dreamer's recitation of specific verses and of the responses of the three listeners. All of the verses are taken from *Tanach*.

The ritual begins as the three friends recite in unison:

Don't interpretations belong to God? Tell it to me please.

The recitation begins and is repeated seven times.

Dreamer:
I have seen a good dream.
Friends in Unison:
You have seen a good dream.
It is good and may it become good.
May the merciful One transform it to good.
May heaven decree upon it seven times
that it become good and always will be good.
It is good and may it become good.

Additional verses are recited responsively by the dreamer and the listeners. Some are said just once, others, three times. It is also suggested, but not required, that the dreamer fast and repent on the day of the ritual. If the dream is especially troubling, fasting is permitted even on the Sabbath or on a festival.

10.7 Respect for the Living and the Dead

It is appropriate to use expressions of respect when speaking of one's parents. The concept of ***kibud av va'em,*** honoring father and mother, is explicitly stated in the Fifth Commandment. One should never address a parent (or grandparent) by his or her first name. The same applies to one's in-laws. When speaking of one's parent, it is customary to say ***avi mori,*** my father, my teacher, or ***imi morati,*** my mother, my teacher.

When writing to another person, it is traditional to use the abbreviation *ayin, mem, vav, shin,* עמו"ש, which stands for ***ad me'ah v'esrim shanah,*** *to one hundred and twenty years*, after the individual's name. This wish for long life probably is derived from the fact that Moses lived to that age.

When writing to a Torah scholar, the acronym ***shlita,*** שליט"א, which means *may he live a long and good life,* is added after the name.

Even when speaking or writing about the deceased, it is necessary to show respect. The following six expressions are used after an individual's name.

Expressions of Respect for the Deceased

Hebrew	English For Men	Abbreviation
alov hashalom	May he rest in peace.	ע"ה
zichrono liverachah	May his memory be blessed.	ז"ל
	For Women	
aleha hashalom	May she rest in peace.	ע"ה
zichronah liverachah	May her memory be blessed.	ז"ל
	For the Righteous	
zecher tzaddik liverachah	May the memory of the righteous (man) be blessed.	זצ"ל
zecher tzidkanit liverachah	May the memory of the righteous (woman) be blessed.	זצ"ל

It is also customary to inscribe a Hebrew abbreviation at the bottom of the *matzevah*, "ת"נ"צ"ב"ה", which represents five Hebrew words meaning *May his/her soul be bound up in the bonds of eternal life* (see Section 9.16.6).

10.8 What's in a Name?

After the *Shemoneh Esrei,* but before the concluding verse

> May the words of my mouth
> and the meditation of my heart please You. . . .

(see Section 3.7.5), it is considered meritorious to recite a special ***pasuk,*** scriptural verse, that begins with the first letter of one's Hebrew name and ends with the last letter. In many *siddurim,* a list of appropriate verses are presented with different letter combinations. For those with biblical names, it is also proper to recite a *pasuk* that contains the name itself.

10.9 The Holocaust

The term "Holocaust," referred to in Hebrew as ***Shoah*** (which is defined as *cataclysm, darkness, abyss,* and *destruction,* among other terms), has almost become a catchall word for any catastrophic event; but its usage should be reserved for the dehumanization and brutal devastation of most of European Jewry between 1933 and 1945.

Before the Second World War, there were at least nine million Jews living in Europe. By the time the war ended, six million of them had been murdered. These deaths were not merely of individuals: Whole families were wiped out, and, thus, all their future generations were destroyed. The precise numbers of those martyred can never be counted. The figure of six million does not represent the countless unborn millions whose very existence was denied them.

Annual memorial gatherings are held on *Nisan* 27, designated as *Yom HaShoah,* Holocaust Remembrance Day. This date was chosen because it can never fall on the Sabbath. It is customary to light a *yahrtzeit* candle on the eve of *Nisan* 27 in memory of the Six Million.

As the number of survivors continues to dwindle every year, the opportunity for these witnesses to provide testimony of the atrocities they endured is slowly slipping away. Today, several museums and organizations help keep the memory of the Holocaust at the forefront of the world's conscience. They were established, for the most part, to perpetuate the memories of the Six Million and to advance public awareness and understanding of the Holocaust by educating Jews and non-Jews alike about the evils of intolerance. In addition to amassing huge numbers of archival documents and artifacts, these institutions are collecting oral histories from survivors to provide an eternal record of the inhumanity of mankind. They include:

Israel

- Yad Vashem
  The Holocaust Martyrs' and Heroes' Remembrance Authority
  P. O. B. 3477
  Jerusalem 91034
  Phone: 011-972-2-675-1611

United States

- The United States Holocaust Memorial Museum
  100 Raoul Wallenberg Place SW
  Washington, DC 20023-2150
  Phone: (202) 488-0400
- Simon Wiesenthal Center
  9750 West Pico Boulevard
  Los Angeles, CA 90035
  Phone: (310) 553-9036
- The Museum of Jewish Heritage
  A Living Memorial to the Holocaust
  18 First Place, Battery Park City
  New York, NY 10004-1484
  Phone: (212) 509-6130
- Survivors of the SHOAH Visual History Foundation
  P. O. Box 3168
  Los Angeles, CA 90078-3168
  Phone: (818) 777-4673

Numerous other Holocaust resources are available online as well.

10.10 Israel: Ancient Homeland, Modern State

The Land of Israel, *Eretz Yisrael,* has been and continues to be the focus of the spiritual yearning of the Jewish people. It is also Judaism's historical homeland.

From the days of King David more than three thousand years ago, ***Yerushalayim,*** Jerusalem, has been at the center of the Jewish experience. The love of Israel, and of Jerusalem, the ancient and modern capital city, in particular, is not a mere sentiment shared only by the very observant. Rather, Jerusalem is the heart and soul of Jewish existence for Jews of diverse cultural, religious, and geographic backgrounds.

When Jews pray, they face toward ***mizrach,*** the east, in the direction of Jerusalem. When they conclude the festive Passover *seder* or the solemn day of *Yom Kippur,* they proclaim, "Next year in Jerusalem." Under the marriage canopy, the groom breaks a glass, a remembrance of the destruction of the *Bet HaMikdash* in Jerusalem.

Out of the near-total destruction of European Jewry, *Medinat Yisrael,* the modern State of Israel, rose up to be a haven for Jews. The establishment of the Jewish state represented the fulfillment of the Zionist dream: the return to Zion of the Jewish people.

Modern Zionism's roots date back to the mid-nineteenth century. In 1840, in response to a charge of ritual murder against several members of the Jewish community in Damascus, Sir Moses Montefiore (1784–1885) led the first serious effort to settle the Holy Land. As the decade progressed, early Zionist leaders, like Rabbis Zvi Hirsch Kalischer (1795–1874) and Samuel Mohilever (1824–1898), urged resettlement on a religious basis.

In the 1880s, pogroms in Russia led to the organization of grassroots movements whose supporters went to Israel to settle. The first settlement was called Rishon l'Tzion (First in Zion). The settlers were ill-prepared to undertake the hard physical labor necessary for land reclamation in the desolate region. With the assistance of French philanthropist Baron Edmond de Rothschild (1845–1934), the development of Jewish agricultural settlements was put on a steady course.

In the infamous Dreyfus Affair, which began in 1894 in France, a Jewish officer, Captain Alfred Dreyfus (1859–1935), was accused of treason. He was tried and convicted twice, but was ultimately acquitted in 1906. This case propelled Theodor Herzl (1860–1904) to define the goal of political Zionism. At the first Zionist Congress (August 29–31, 1897) in Basel, Switzerland, the aim of the movement was declared: "Zionism strives to establish a homeland for the Jewish people in Palestine secured by public law."

Herzl's attempts to found a Jewish homeland created international controversy. A British proposal to establish a temporary homeland in Uganda was rejected. Political Zionism as an ideology found itself side-by-side with a more practical approach, as settlers colonized the land little by little.

Another stream of thought viewed Zionism as a cultural phenomenon and advocated that Jews in the Diaspora be encouraged to assist in creating the foundation for a national movement. Chaim Weizmann (1874–1952), one of the early proponents of cultural Zionism, intensified the political struggle, gaining the sympathy of the British government, which issued the Balfour Declaration on November 2, 1917. The Declaration stated:

His Majesty's Government view with favor
the establishment in Palestine of a national home for the Jewish people
and will use their best endeavors to facilitate the achievement of this object,
it being clearly understood that nothing
shall be done which may prejudice the civil and religious rights
of existing non-Jewish communities in Palestine
or the rights and political status enjoyed by Jews in any other country.

The Declaration was adopted by the League of Nations, and Britain was granted a mandate in Palestine in 1922.

New settlements were established, and by and large, religious and secular Jews alike joined to rebuild the Jewish homeland. In the early 1930s, in the wake of Nazi persecution, tens of thousands of Jews fled from Germany to settle in Palestine. In response to this influx of Jewish immigration, the Arabs rioted, rebelling against the British authority. In 1939, Britain replied to the unrest by issuing the White Paper, limiting Jewish immigration to no more than fifteen thousand Jews per year for five years, after which no Jews could be admitted without Arab consent. After the war, the remnant of the Jewish people clamored to enter Palestine, but the British government refused to ease the immigration policy.

The Zionist movement, which had continued its efforts in Palestine throughout the war, was joined by Jews throughout the world, pressuring for the establishment of a Jewish state. So-called "illegal" immigration was stepped up, and Jewish resistance to British policy gave way to acts of reprisal.

Because of the certain chaos that was to ensue, the British government decided to abandon the mandate and evacuate the region. The matter was turned over to the United Nations. On November 29, 1947, in a historic vote, the United Nations voted to partition the region into two separate but independent entities, a Jewish state and an Arab state.

This was unacceptable to the Arabs, who declared war on the new Jewish state. After the War of Independence, the establishment of the modern State of Israel was proclaimed on May 14, 1948, by the first prime minister, David Ben-Gurion. Chaim Weizmann, the great Zionist leader, became Israel's first president. United States President Harry S Truman was the first world leader to recognize the Jewish state.

On October 28, 1948, the Provisional Council of State proclaimed that the flag of the World Zionist Organization, reminiscent of the Jewish prayer shawl, was to be adopted as the flag of *Medinat Yisrael.* A published proclamation in the Official Gazette stated:

. . . The background is white,
and on it are two stripes of dark sky-blue . . .
across the whole length of the flag.
In the middle of the white background,
between the blue stripes and at equal distance from each stripe
is a Star of David
composed of six dark sky-blue stripes . . .
which form two equilateral triangles,
the bases of which are parallel to the two horizontal stripes.

The ***Magen David,*** Star of David (literally, Shield of David), is not historically a Jewish symbol. The six-pointed design has been found on artifacts, both Jewish and non-Jewish, that were in use during the period of the Second Temple, and has also been identified in mosaic pavements that date back to the Roman period. It was used as an ornamental symbol on a third-century synagogue in Capernaum, an ancient city on the Sea of Galilee in northern Israel, and was found on a Jewish tombstone in southern Italy that dates back to the same period.

Occasionally, the six-pointed star was used as a decoration on *k'miot,* and in the Middle Ages, it appeared on the Jewish communal flag of Prague and on synagogues in Germany. A fourteenth-century kabbalistic work, entitled *Magen David,* may be the first use of the phrase, perhaps linking the name of David and the House of David, from which the Messiah will descend, to the hexagram. By the seventeenth century, the Star of David was widely used as a messianic symbol. By the nineteenth century, it had become a familiar symbol of Jewish identity, uniting Jews throughout Europe, although it had no inherent religious significance. Subsequently, it became the symbol of the Zionist movement in 1897 and, ultimately, of Jewry as a whole.

In addition to the flag, the State of Israel is represented by an emblem, which incorporates symbols representing the past and the future of Israel. At the time of the destruction of the Second Temple, the seven-branch *menorah,* the golden candelabra of the *Bet HaMikdash,* was captured by the Romans. Its removal from Jerusalem was depicted on the Roman Arch of Titus.

The final design of the national emblem is comprised of three elements: (1) the seven-branched *menorah* shown on the Arch of Titus, now returned symbolically to Israel, marking the beginning of the end of the Diaspora; (2) olive branches, which surround the *menorah* and represent the Jewish people's love of and yearning for peace; and (3) the word ***Yisrael,*** Israel.

This emblem of sovereignty was proclaimed by the Provisional Council of State on February 10, 1949. It appears on official documents of the state, on the presidential flag, and on public buildings throughout the country.

The modern State of Israel is a parliamentary democracy. The head of state is the ***nasi,*** president, but presidential duties are largely ceremonial. The ***Knesset,*** Israel's Parliament, is a one-house body elected every four years in national elections. There are one hundred and twenty members of the *Knesset,* chosen from numerous political parties. After the election, the newly elected ***rosh memshelah,*** prime minister, is asked to form a government. Within forty-five days of the election, a coalition of parties must be achieved to provide the prime minister with a majority of at least sixty-one delegates in the *Knesset.* From among these delegates, the prime minister appoints the cabinet ministers. There must be at least eight and not more than eighteen ministers in the cabinet. The remaining delegates in the *Knesset* constitute the opposition.

Since the establishment of *Medinat Yisrael* in 1948, thousands of Jews have "gone on ***aliyah***" or "made *aliyah,*" phrases that mean they have "gone up" to settle in the Jewish homeland. From numerous countries and from every walk of life, they have chosen to make *aliyah* to be among their own people in their own land.

The majority (about 90 percent) of Israel's six million citizens, comprised of approximately 80 percent Jews and 20 percent Arabs, live in cities. The remaining population lives on settlements called ***kibbutzim*** or ***moshavim.***

The national anthem of the State of Israel was written by the Zionist poet Naphtali Herz Imber (1856–1909). The melody has been identified with a Sephardic hymn. Originally adopted as the hymn of the Zionist movement at its first Congress in Basel in 1897, it is called *HaTikvah,* The Hope.

HaTikvah
Kol od balevov p'nimah
nefesh yehudi homiyah,
u'l'fa'atei mizrach kadimah
ayin l'tziyon tzofiyah,
od lo avdah tikvatenu,
hatikvah sh'not alpayim,
li'h'yot am chafshi b'artzenu,
Eretz Tziyon v'Yerushalayim.

❖

The Hope
As long as deep in his heart
the Jewish soul yearns,
and toward the East
an eye is turned toward Zion,
our hope is not yet lost,
the hope of two thousand years,
to be a free people in our land,
the Land of Zion and Jerusalem.

10.11 Responsa Literature

After the sealing of the Talmud, questions arose in various Jewish communities with regard to specific areas of Jewish law and practice. The replies to these inquiries, which were always written down, became the basis of the Responsa Literature, ***Sh'elot u'T'shuvot,*** questions and answers. The respondents were recognized scholars whose opinions were accepted by all. This body of *halachah* evolved into a special category of rabbinic literature.

This approach to halachic inquiry continues to this day. A prominent and recognized scholar who is consulted on a regular basis is called a ***posek,*** an arbiter of the *halachah.* Every time a Jew approaches a scholar for a response to a halachic question, the rabbi's response is called a ***p'sak halachah,*** a final judgment of the law. The greatest of these scholars are referred to as ***Gedolim*** (from the Hebrew for *great*), ***Gadol,*** in the singular.

10.12 The *Chasidim*

Chasidim, Jews who follow the teachings of Rabbi Israel Ba'al Shem-Tov (1698–1760), known as the Master of the Good Name, are devoted to the belief that God is best served through joy. The term ***Chasid*** is derived from the word ***chesed,*** signifying piety, kindness, holiness, and goodness.

A great scholar, the Ba'al Shem-Tov (also referred to by the acronym Besht) rose from very humble beginnings to achieve the status of a legend. He settled in Medzyboz in the western Ukraine. His disciples revered him as a ***tzaddik,*** a saintly and righteous man, and honored him for his holiness, for his compassion, and for his wisdom. He taught that every *mitzvah* is to be performed with joy, enthusiasm, and inspiration, rather than by rote, in a mechanical and cold fashion.

The Ba'al Shem-Tov taught that Jews should make the practice of the precepts a celebration of life, enhancing the fulfillment of the *mitzvot* with singing and dancing. He emphasized that all Jews, regardless of their scholarly attainment, were equal before God.

The modern religious and social movement which evolved in the eighteenth century as a result of the influence of the charismatic Ba'al Shem-Tov is called ***Chasidut,*** Chasidism. *Chasidut* appealed to the emotions. It preached love for the untutored and the sinner out of a genuine humility that makes all Jews love all other Jews, in a sincere effort to bring them closer to God. There were ***Mitnagdim,*** opponents, who did not subscribe to the philosophy that Jews required a ***rebbe,*** a Chasidic master, to act as an intermediary before God. To the ***Mitnagid,*** the attainment of scholarship was considered more important than the fervor of the devotion *Chasidut* represented. By the nineteenth century, however, the *Chasidim* and *Mitnagdim* were largely reconciled, acknowledging their equal devotion to Jewish life.

Rabbi Dov Baer of Mezeritch (1704–1772) was a disciple of the Ba'al Shem Tov. Known as the *Maggid,* the Preacher, Rabbi Dov Baer was largely responsible for spreading the teachings of *Chasidut* after the Ba'al Shem Tov's death. As his successor, Rabbi Dov Baer moved the Chasidic court from Medzyboz to Mezeritch. What started as a local religious experience swelled to a spiritual phenomenon that swept through most of Eastern Europe.

Rabbi Shneur Zalman of Liadi (1745–1812) was a disciple of Rabbi Dov Baer. Renowned as the founder of a branch of *Chasidut* called Chabad, he preached that to serve God properly Jews required wisdom, insight, and knowledge, in combination with humility, joy, and singing. Today, the influence of Chabad, also known as Lubavitcher Chasidism, has spread worldwide.

Chasidut is famous for its stories, including those of Rabbi Nachman of Bratslav (1772–1810), a great-grandson of the Ba'al Shem-Tov. These parables, written in Yiddish, and available in English translation, have enriched Jewish culture and endeared *Chasidut* to thousands.

A Witty Remark!

There are innumerable Chasidic tales that tell of the wondrous acts of Chasidic masters; but it isn't necessary to go back to the nineteenth century for such a story. I honestly have no clear memory of the events, but I heard the following story many times from my mother.

When I was almost four years old, my father took me to a venerable Chasidic sage, a *tzaddik* renowned for his wisdom and miraculous deeds. This was not a social visit, nor a spiritual outing for a young boy and his father. No—my father brought me to the *Rebbe,* the Grand Rabbi, because he wanted to ask him to give me a blessing.

The *Rebbe's gabbai,* who served as his secretary, opened the door. My father began to explain why we had come, but the *gabbai* held up his hand, signaling him to stop. He handed my father a small piece of paper. "Before you can speak to the *Rebbe,*" he said solemnly, "you must write your request on a *k'vitel.*"

With a firm hand, my father wrote a note to the *Rebbe* in Yiddish, explaining why he needed to speak to him. He gave it to the *gabbai,* and after a short wait, we were ushered in to the holy man's private chamber. Sacred books lined the shelves, and an aura of sanctity lit up the sage's face. I felt a little afraid, and my father held my hand tightly.

"How can I help you?" asked the *Rebbe* softly.

"My son," replied my father, with a catch in his throat, "is almost four years old; but he does not speak. He has never said a single word. The doctor says that he doesn't speak because he has nothing to say. How can that be? Can you help him?"

The *Rebbe* looked at me with kind eyes, and without hesitation, he said, "When you leave here, you will meet a tall man with an ice cream cart. He will ring the bell. Your son will ask for ice cream, and you will buy it for him. From then on, he will speak."

My father thanked the *Rebbe,* who smiled at me, and we left quickly. Sure enough, there, at the end of the block, was the ice cream cart. The man rang the bell. I asked for chocolate. My father bought it gladly.

Miracle? Why not? Even if I spoke because I wanted the ice cream and understood that the only way I was going to get it was to ask, *how did the Rebbe know?* By the way, chocolate is still my favorite flavor.

After the Holocaust, many of the survivors were transplanted to several countries throughout the world where they reestablished their Chasidic enclaves. Today, there are many Chasidic dynasties, each headed by a *rebbe,* whose leadership is often passed on to his son and grandson in turn.

10.13 To Perfect the World

In the *Alenu* prayer (see section 3.12) we find the following words:

> **We hope in You, therefore, Lord our God,**
> **that we will soon behold Your majestic splendor, . . .**
> **when the world will be perfected under the reign of the Almighty. . . .**

The concept of perfecting the world is called ***tikkun olam.*** As expressed in *Alenu,* this will be achieved when all idolaters have been destroyed and the entire universe accepts the sovereignty of the One God.

In recent years, the call for *tikkun olam* has become a rallying cry for Jewish activism, stirring people to action on behalf of important social issues. Judaism emphatically supports the cause of social justice. It is part of the moral and ethical teachings of the Torah, which require Jews to care and show concern for all God's creatures, man and animal alike. Righteousness is expressed in many ways in Jewish life.

10.13.1 Righteousness and Lovingkindness

In the Mishnah, Simon the Righteous, one of the last members of the *Anshei Kenesset HaGedolah,* says:

> **The world depends on three principles:**
> **on Torah, on *avodah,* and on *g'milut chasadim.***
> **—*Avot* 1:2**

As we have discussed, Torah comprises the entire legal and moral code of Jewish life, the Written and the Oral Laws; *avodah* refers to the worship of God, through various sacrifices in the days of the *Mishkan* and the *Bet HaMikdash,* and today through prayer and the performance of *mitzvot*; and ***g'milut chasadim,*** encompasses acts of benevolence and lovingkindness.

G'milut chasadim obligates all Jews to recognize the shared responsibility they have for each other. In the Talmud, we find:

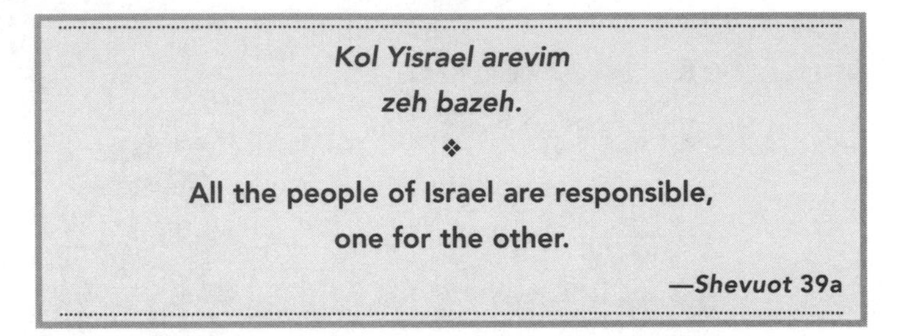

Kol Yisrael arevim
zeh bazeh.

❖

All the people of Israel are responsible,
one for the other.

—*Shevuot* 39a

Judaism obligates Jews to give ***tzedakah,*** charity, derived from the word ***tzedek,*** righteous. Giving *tzedakah,* however, involves more than a handout to the poor or a check to the charity drive. It is an obligation, based on biblical law, not a voluntary act determined by one's kindness or pity.

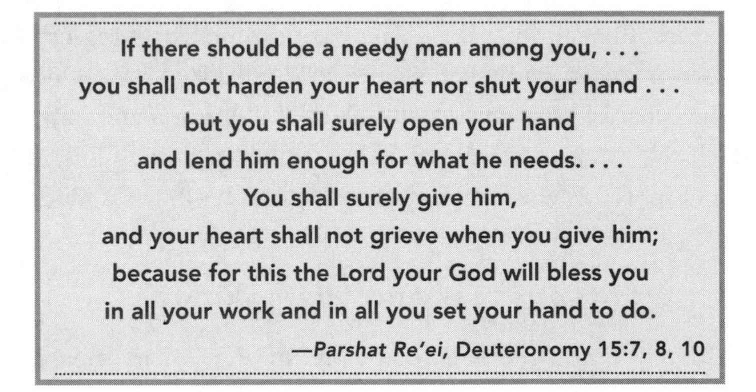

If there should be a needy man among you, . . .
you shall not harden your heart nor shut your hand . . .
but you shall surely open your hand
and lend him enough for what he needs. . . .
You shall surely give him,
and your heart shall not grieve when you give him;
because for this the Lord your God will bless you
in all your work and in all you set your hand to do.

—*Parshat Re'ei,* Deuteronomy 15:7, 8, 10

The familiar biblical story of Cain and Abel, perhaps, is proof enough that God expects man to be his brother's keeper. In the Jewish community, Jews have always taken care of their less fortunate brethren.

The psalmist reminds us that human beings are only the temporary guardians of whatever they may possess on earth.

> **The earth is the Lord's and the fullness thereof. . . .**
>
> **—Psalms 24:1**

We, therefore, thank God and revere Him as the Creator of the Universe, to Whom everything belongs. We acknowledge our responsibility to share the beneficence He bestows on us with those less fortunate.

Acts of *tzedakah* differ from *g'milut chasadim.*

- *Tzedakah* can be performed only with money, but acts of *chesed* can be performed with money or with personal service.
- *Tzedakah* can be performed only for the poor, while acts of *g'milut chasadim* may be performed for the rich as well.
- *Tzedakah* can only be performed for the living, while the greatest act of *g'milut chasadim* is the burial of the dead, referred to as the *chesed shel emet,* the true act of kindness, for it can never be repaid.

In the *Mishneh Torah*, the Rambam instructed the Jewish people to:

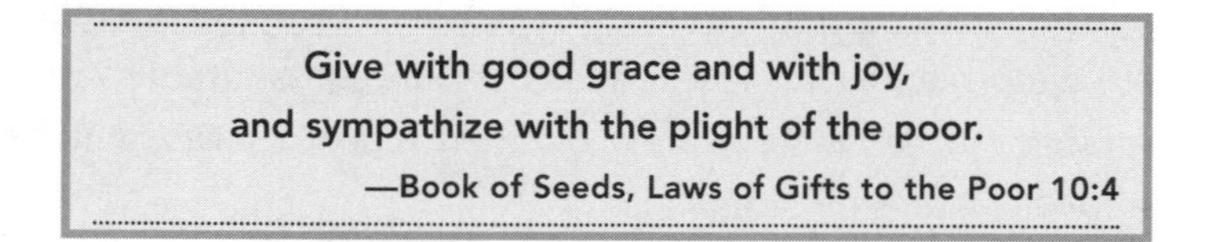

Give with good grace and with joy,
and sympathize with the plight of the poor.

—Book of Seeds, Laws of Gifts to the Poor 10:4

In Laws 7–14, he explains the proper way to perform the *mitzvah* of *tzedakah* in his Eight Steps of Charity. On the lowest step is the

1. Giver who gives unwillingly or begrudgingly;
   a step above this is the . . .
2. Giver who gives less than is necessary, but gives it cheerfully;
   a step above this is the . . .
3. Giver who gives directly to the poor, but, only after being asked;
   a step above this is the . . .
4. Giver who gives directly to the poor, but before being asked;
   a step above this is if the . . .
5. Giver is known to the recipient, but the recipient is not known to the giver;
   a step above this is if the . . .

6. Recipient is known to the giver, but the giver is not known to the recipient; a step above this is if the . . .
7. Giver and the recipient are unknown to each other; a step above this is . . .
8. Helping a person to help himself before he is in need, by giving him a substantial amount of money as a gift; by lending him money, becoming his business partner, or finding a job for him so that he does not need anyone's help. This is the highest form of *tzedakah*.

Charity is to be given according to one's means, and even those who receive charity are obligated to give something, if they can do so without jeopardizing their own sustenance. Ten percent of one's annual income should be allocated to charity each year.

In every season of Jewish life, the Jew is enjoined to give charity and perform acts of kindness—all the laws of tithing, including gifts to the *Kohanim* and *Lev'im* during the days of the *Bet HaMikdash;* the annual obligation in Temple times to contribute a half-*shekel* for communal sacrifices; the required donations for wheat money, *ma'ot chitim,* before Passover; sending gifts to the poor on *Purim*; the duty to leave the gleanings and the produce of the corners of one's fields and vineyards for the needy; the recitation of prayer that reminds us that charity will save us from the unfavorable verdict of heaven on the *Yamim Nora'im*—all these are really prescribed acts of charity, which foster a continuing concern for the needs of others.

10.13.2 Jewish Philanthropy

Jewish communities have supported and continue to support a large number of philanthropic institutions:

- ***kupah***
  communal fund for the poor
- ***tamchui***
  soup kitchen
- ***hachnasat orchim***
  guest house for travelers
- ***hachnasat kallah***
  fund to provide dowry and wedding expenses for needy brides
- ***g'milat chesed***
  fund to offer interest-free loans
- ***talmud Torah***
  school to provide a free education for poor children

- *bet y'tomim*
  home for orphans
- *moshav z'kenim*
  residence for the elderly
- *bikur cholim*
  volunteer organizations that visit and assist the sick (and their families) in hospitals, nursing homes, and at home

In some cases, the goals of these organizations have been modified to meet current needs. Other services include:

- *tomchei Shabbat*
  volunteer organizations that package and anonymously deliver donated foods to needy families before every Sabbath and festival
- *hatzalah*
  volunteer medical emergency squads

Numerous other organizations also provide funding for educational and social programs in Israel and elsewhere.

A Witty Remark!

Several years ago, my brother served on a *hatzalah* squad in New York, where he lived for many years. As a trained member of a medical emergency team, he was permitted to wear his beeper and respond to calls, even on the Sabbath or holidays.

On the first night of *Pesach,* as he sat with his family around the *seder* table, his beeper went off. Reacting immediately, he dashed from the house, his white *kittel* fluttering behind him. He raced to the home of an elderly woman whose family thought she was having a heart attack. Quickly assessing the situation, he and the other team members who met him there started to carry the hysterical woman into the ambulance.

"Am I dead? Am I dead?" she kept shrieking in Yiddish. "I must be dead! I must be dead!"

"No, no, you're going to be fine," my brother said, as he tried to reassure her and calm her down.

"Yes, yes, I am dead," she insisted. "I see them, I see the angels. They all have long beards and are wearing white robes."

From that time on, my brother never responded to an emergency call on *Pesach* or *Yom Kippur* without taking a moment to remove his *kittel* before hurrying out the door.

Jewish life provides ample opportunities to help and care for others. As the Rambam assures us in the *Mishneh Torah*:

> **No one has ever become impoverished by giving charity, and no evil or damage has ever resulted from charity; . . . whoever displays mercy to others will be granted mercy.**
>
> **—Book of Seeds, Laws of Gifts to the Poor 10:2**

10.13.3 Remembering the Animals

Kindness is to be extended to animals as well.

> **The righteous consider the needs of [their] beasts.**
>
> **—Proverbs 12:10**

One's animals must be fed first, as it is written:

> **And I will give grass in your fields for your cattle, and [then] you shall eat and be satisfied.**
>
> **—*Parshat Eikev,* Deuteronomy 11:15**

It is forbidden to cause pain to any living creature. Hunting is considered a cruel act that fulfills no purpose. On the other hand, the laws of *shechitah* are intended to provide food for human consumption in the most humane manner possible.

10.14 Above All, Peace

Three times a day, Jews pray for ***shalom,*** peace. In the morning, we ask God, "Grant peace." In the afternoon and evening, we recite, "Establish abundant peace for your people Israel forever."

When we greet the Sabbath angels, we bid them, "Bless me with peace, angels of peace." When we greet a friend, we say, *Shalom Aleichem,* "Peace unto you." Our friend replies, *Aleichem Shalom,* "Unto you, peace."

In our home, we strive for *shalom bayit.* After eating, in the *Birkat HaMazon*, we repeat, "He who makes peace . . . may He make peace upon us and all Israel." When we embark on a journey, we pray, "May it be Your will . . . that You lead us toward peace."

When we bless the new month, we ask God to ". . . grant us long life, a life of peace . . ." and to "renew it . . . for life and for peace. . . ." In the repetition of every *Shemoneh Esrei,* we hear the Priestly Blessing, "May God turn His Countenance toward you and grant you peace."

On Sabbath afternoons, when we study the Ethics of the Fathers, *Masechet Avot* of the Mishnah, we find that Rabbi Simon ben Gamliel says:

> **The world endures on three principles:**
> **on truth, on justice, and on peace. . . .**
>
> **—*Avot* 1:18**

and the psalmist says:

> **The Lord will give strength to His people;**
> **the Lord will bless His people with peace.**
>
> **—Psalms 29:11**

Above all, *shalom,* peace.

Word Works

A

B

C

D

E

F

G

H

I

K

L

M

N

U

V

Y

Z

Sum and Substance

C

D

E

F

I

J

K

L

M

N

R

S

T

U